FROM THE REALM OF A DYING SUN

FROM THE REALM OF A DYING SUN

Volume 1: *IV. SS-Panzerkorps* and the Battles for Warsaw, July–November 1944

DOUGLAS E. NASH SR.

CASEMATE
Pennsylvania & Yorkshire

First published in the United States of America and Great Britain in 2019.
Reprinted as a paperback in 2024 by
CASEMATE PUBLISHERS
1950 Lawrence Road, Havertown, PA 19083, USA
and
47 Church Street, Barnsley, S70 2AS, UK

Paperback Edition: ISBN 978-1-63624-487-7
Digital Edition: ISBN 978-1-61200-636-9

A CIP record for this book is available from the British Library

Maps by Thomas Houlihan and Phillip Schwartzberg

Printed and bound in the United Kingdom by CPI Group (UK) Ltd, Croydon, CR0 4YY

For a complete list of Casemate titles, please contact:

CASEMATE PUBLISHERS (US)
Telephone (610) 853-9131
Fax (610) 853-9146
Email: casemate@casematepublishers.com
www.casematepublishers.com

CASEMATE PUBLISHERS (UK)
Telephone (01226) 734350
Email: casemate@casemateuk.com
www.casemateuk.com

Contents

Dedication by Oberstleutnant d.R *Günther Lange* vii
Introduction ix
List of Maps xxiii
List of Figures xxv

1 Activation of *IV. SS-Pz.Korps* 1
2 Organization and Duties of the *Panzer* Corps Headquarters and Staff 13
3 Organization of Corps and Army Troops 43
4 The Leaders and Divisions 65
5 The Tank Battle of Praga, 28 July–6 August 1944 93
6 Operational Interlude: *Unternehmen Brückenschlag,* 8–13 August 1944 137
7 The First Defensive Battle of Warsaw, 18–30 August 1944 157
8 The Second Defensive Battle of Warsaw, Part I: 31 August–9 September 1944 207
9 The Second Defensive Battle of Warsaw, Part II: 10–22 September 1944 251
10 An Unexpected Lull in the Action, 23 September–9 October 1944 325
11 The Third Defensive Battle of Warsaw, 10–28 October 1944 353
12 The Battle of Modlin, 29 October–25 November 1944 439

Appendix A: Command and Staff 479
Appendix B: IV. SS-Pz.Korps *Battle and Campaign Participation Credits* 482
Appendix C: Selected Orders of Battle 484
Appendix D: German Army, Waffen-SS *and U.S. Army Rank Equivalents* 487
Appendix E: German Corps Staff Positions and U.S. Army Equivalents 489
Appendix F: Glossary 491
Endnotes 499
Bibliography 527
Index 533

The photo above depicts Lange in May 1944 while stationed in Lublin, Poland, wearing the rank of *SS-Standartenoberjunker* (officer aspirant) shortly before his promotion to *SS-Untersturmführer* (second lieutenant). His awards shown include the Iron Cross, 2nd Class, the General Assault Badge in Silver, and the Black Wound Badge.

As a former orderly officer of the *IV. SS-Panzerkorps,* which was composed of volunteers from 11 different European nations, I am pleased that the author is dedicated to understanding the military-historical context of this era. He has been very meticulous in his painstaking description of the details. I am particularly touched that Mr. Nash has committed himself to the study of our history and wish his book much success.

Günther Lange
Handeloh, Spring 2019

SS-Untersturmführer
Generalkommando
IV. SS-Panzerkorps
and
Oberstleutnant d.R.
der Bundeswehr
Panzer-Lehr-Brigade 9

Introduction

During World War II, the armed or *Waffen-SS* branch of the Third Reich's dreaded security service expanded from four regiments and 20,000 men in 1939 to 38 divisions by the end of the war, eventually growing to a force of over 900,000 men until Germany's defeat in May 1945. Not satisfied with allowing his nascent force to be commanded in combat by traditional corps or army headquarters of the *Wehrmacht*, Heinrich Himmler, chief of the SS, began to create his own SS corps and army headquarters, starting with the *SS-Panzerkorps* (soon renumbered as *II. SS-Panzerkorps*) in July 1942. As the number of *Waffen-SS* divisions increased, so did the number of corps headquarters, with 18 corps and two armies being planned or activated by the war's end.

The histories of the first three SS corps are well known—the actions of *I.*, *II.*, and *III. (Germanic) SS-Panzerkorps* and their subordinate divisions, including the *Leibstandarte SS Adolf Hitler*, *Das Reich*, *Hitlerjugend*, *Hohenstaufen*, *Frundsberg*, and *Nordland* divisions, have been thoroughly documented and publicized. In addition, their leadership rosters include some of the best-known (and most notorious) commanders and leaders of the *Waffen-SS*—Paul Hausser, Sepp Dietrich, Felix Steiner, Hermann Priess, Wilhelm Bittrich, "Panzer" Meyer, Jochen Peiper, Fritz Witt, *et al.* Their key roles in some of the war's greatest battles, including Kharkov, Kursk, Caen, Falaise, Arnhem, the Ardennes and Berlin, have been acknowledged and widely studied by students of the art of war and figure prominently in wargaming and battle simulations as well.

Overlooked in this pantheon is another SS corps that never fought in the west or in Berlin, but one that participated in many of the key battles fought on the Eastern Front during the last year of the war—the *IV. SS-Panzerkorps*. Committed to battle for the first time during the initial stages of the defense of Warsaw in late July 1944, the corps, consisting of both the *3.* and *5. SS-Panzer Divisions* (*Totenkopf* and *Wiking*, respectively) was born in battle and spent the last 10 months of the war in combat, figuring prominently in the battles of Warsaw, the attempted relief of

Budapest, Operation *Spring Awakening*, the defense of Vienna, and the withdrawal into Austria, where it finally surrendered to U.S. forces in May 1945.

Though perhaps not as glamorous as the other three aforementioned corps, Herbert Otto Gille's *IV SS-Panzerkorps* was renowned for its tenacity, high morale, and, above all, its lethality, whether conducting a hard-hitting counterattack or a stubborn defense in situations where its divisions were hopelessly outnumbered. Often embroiled in heated disputes with its immediate *Wehrmacht* higher headquarters over his seemingly cavalier conduct of operations, Gille's corps remained to the bitter end one of the Third Reich's most reliable and formidable field formations.

***

The corps, as a modern military concept, traces its origins to the middle of the 18th century, when European armies had expanded in size to a point where field armies, unwieldy formations consisting of dozens of regiments, had become too difficult to command by one man alone. With large standing armies becoming the norm, even after wars had ceased, the administration and control of large and usually geographically dispersed bodies of troops had to be distributed among subordinate commanders to ensure that armies could function efficiently and effectively. With the advent of mass citizen armies during the wars of the French Revolution and Napoleonic era, the corps, as a body of troops, had evolved to the point where it usually consisted of two or more infantry divisions, a cavalry element, supporting artillery regiments and so forth, as well as supporting logistics, engineer, and signal organizations—ranging in size between 10,000 and 50,000 men.

Miniature armies in themselves, the named or numbered corps of the early to mid-19th century could operate nearly independently of one another, yet were able to mass in time and space at the direction of their higher command—in the case of a corps, this usually meant a field army. With the advent of the telegraph, followed by the telephone and radio, the control of the corps was greatly enhanced, allowing the corps commander to lead and direct his subordinate divisions, brigades, and regiments in ways that Frederick the Great and Napoleon could only dream of.

Just as important a development as the corps was that of the corps staff. Evolving alongside the corps itself, the corps headquarters, by the end of the 19th century, had become a specialized staff that could not only exercise the will of its leader through his ability to command, but more importantly, could control the actions of its subordinate units to ensure that they conform to his will. Though generations of division commanders may decry the corps headquarters as being overly meddlesome and demanding, the advent of the modern corps made the armies of Europe and the United States, including those of the Confederacy during the American Civil War, more efficient in fighting battles, though not always effectively.

To increase the ability of the division, corps, and army-level staffs, European, American, and, during the late 19th century, Asian armies instituted general staff schools that sought to select and groom prospective officers, who would become, in effect, the brains of their armed forces general staffs. To increase the capability of staffs to assist commanders with leading and controlling their organizations, they became more specialized, organizing themselves into separate departments responsible for personnel, intelligence, operations, and logistics, as well as many other less important but still vital specialized areas such as military law or veterinary services. Introduction of the telegraph, landline telephones, and radio required the establishment of specialized organizations that existed solely for supporting the needs of the commander and his staff, such as signal battalions, military police companies, motor transport columns, and last but certainly not least, the corps headquarters' support battalion, which provides the administrative, logistical, and security support for the headquarters.

The Prussian Greater General Staff, as it was developed under the tutelage of Generals Carl von Clausewitz and Gerd von Scharnhorst, became the epitome of the modern general staff by the mid-19th century. Britain, France, America, and other countries were quick to adopt similar organizations, especially after the spectacularly successful 1870 Prussian campaign against France. It was under the guidance of such organizations that the modern wars of the 20th century were waged, whether commanding and controlling battles and engagement (tactics) by divisions and corps, wide-ranging operations carried out by armies designed to connect battles and engagements in time and space towards achieving a certain goal, or theater-level strategy, designed for an army group or several army groups to achieve the overall goals of a given conflict.

Staffs, in their basic organization, have changed little despite the advent of modern command, control, communications, computers, and intelligence-gathering (C^4I) technology, with today's division, corps, and army staffs remaining remarkably similar to those of 100 years ago. Surprisingly, there has been very little written about the role of staffs in wartime, with most of the historical treatment focusing on divisions, regiments, battalions, and companies. Leading personalities have also received their due, but most biographies, or autobiographies for that matter, choose to elaborate on battles lost and won, bold maneuvers or political intrigues between the generals, their political overlords, and their opposing numbers. The reader is challenged to find anything that covers the activities of the staffs concerned, where, working in obscurity and with limited time, they are responsible for translating the thoughts and intents of their great captains into orders and directives that guide the actual divisions, corps, or armies under their command and enable the battle, once joined, to be controlled in some manner to ensure that the leader's intent is achieved.

While the activities of American and British staffs of World War II are well documented and preserved, at least in their own formal command histories or chronologies, the staff histories of the German Army of that period—the *Wehrmacht*—have a checkered past. Not only did Germany lose the war, but unlike previous wars that Germany had won or lost, the institutions of the *Wehrmacht* did not survive the war—its *Generalstab* (General Staff), as well as the *Luftwaffe*, *Heer*, and *Kriegsmarine*, were disbanded, the *Waffen-SS* labeled a criminal organization, Germany split between the two Cold War-era factions, and a 10-year hiatus ensued that would last until 1955. That year, West Germany (quickly followed by East Germany) was finally allowed to establish its own federal armed forces, the *Bundeswehr*, which deliberately chose, on account of the stain of National Socialism, not to tie itself to the traditions of the past.

More importantly from a historian's viewpoint, many unit war diaries, operational records, and histories covering the period after 1943 were destroyed during the war, especially when RAF Bomber Command destroyed the troop barracks and facilities housing the German Army's military history department in Potsdam in February 1945. Though many records survived and were spirited away to the United States or Great Britain shortly after the war for analysis, the remainder was confiscated by the Soviet Union. While the United States National Archives and Records Administration (NARA) returned most of their records to the West German *Bundesarchiv* in the 1960s and 1970s after they had been copied on microfilm, the bulk of the records in the Soviet (now Russian) Army archives were kept under lock and key, with accessibility tightly controlled, until only recently.

The records of the Armed SS, or *Waffen-SS*, are a case in point. Though not technically part of the *Wehrmacht*, the *Waffen-SS* was organized in almost mirror fashion, including the staffs at all levels, though the staff of Heinrich Himmler's *SS-Führungshauptamt* (*SS-FHA*), or main SS leadership office, itself is another matter entirely and will not be covered in this work. Many *Waffen-SS* leaders had begun their careers as officers in the *Heer* (Army) and some had even completed general staff officer training. Many others came from the police (*Ordnungspolizei*), where they had similar training. So as the *Waffen-SS* began to expand in 1942 to include the creation of its own corps headquarters, it made sense to copy *Heer* organizational doctrine, down to the names and departments of each individual staff section. After all, the organizational doctrine was sound, was understood by most of the *Waffen-SS* key leaders, and would enable the future divisions and corps of the *Waffen-SS* to seamlessly integrate into field armies of the *Heer*.

Additionally, promising young SS officers were sent to the *Heer*'s general staff officer course beginning in early 1940, where they would receive the necessary specialty training to allow them to function as general staff officers in SS divisions, corps, and later armies. There were never enough of these men available to fill the demand though, since the *Waffen-SS* was expanding faster than they could be trained. In turn, the *Waffen-SS* resorted to requesting qualified *Heer* general staff officers be seconded or loaned to the *Waffen-SS* to fill this shortage, and based on the records of the 22 men who were given this assignment, most of them seemed to have been qualified for their positions and performed their duties admirably. In some cases, so great was the shortage of qualified general staff officers that several SS corps organized in 1944 or 1945 were predominately staffed by *Heer* personnel, who were not required to transfer to the *Waffen-SS* or even wear SS uniforms.

With the war's end approaching and defeat staring them in the face, the German Armed Forces High Command, or *Oberkommando der Wehrmacht* (*OKW*), directed in late April 1945 that before capitulating, units in the field were to destroy all of their records, by burning if possible. While many *Heer* units failed to comply with this directive, thankfully leaving their historical records for posterity, most *Waffen-SS* units, ranging from battalion to field army headquarters, obeyed their orders to the letter. Few operational records of the *Waffen-SS* thus survived the war, making any attempt to chronicle the history of *Waffen-SS* corps headquarters problematic. As previously mentioned, a large amount of *Heer* operational records did survive, and those of corps and field armies with attached SS units are most instructive, offering a glimpse into the inner workings and deliberations of the *Waffen-SS*, at least in regards to daily reports, situation reports, and message traffic. However, any prospective writer must first be aware of which *Heer* corps and field armies *Waffen-SS* divisions or corps were attached to throughout the war; a daunting task for the uninitiated.

The history of the *IV. SS-Panzerkorps* is a case in point. Committed to battle as an operational field headquarters in July 1944, its staff officers kept a daily record of its activities in its *Kriegstagebuch*, a combat journal that captured everything of interest that occurred until the corps' demise in May 1945. A *Kriegstagebuch*, otherwise known as the *KTB*, not only recorded the daily events, but in most cases separate versions were kept by each of the major staff elements. For example, the *I. Generalstabsoffizier* (First General Staff Officer, or *Ia*) maintained a *Ia Kriegstagebuch*. The Second and Third General Staff Officers usually maintained their own logistics and intelligence *KTB*s as well.

So depending on their particular staff sections responsibilities, whether operations (*Ia*), intelligence (*Ic*), or logistics (*Ib*), each respective *KTB* would have reports, message traffic, records of supply requisitions, personnel records etc. contained therein, including annexes or appendices as appropriate. This amounted to a voluminous amount of records that were updated daily. Each year, a division, corps, field army, or army group was required to bundle up their previous year's documents and send them to Potsdam for storage and safekeeping, to be used after Germany won the war to write the official histories. For the *Waffen-SS*, instead of Potsdam, by late 1944 these records were being sent to the *SS-Kriegsarchiv* located in a castle in Sasmuk, a small village in the Kolin district in the Protectorate of Bohemia and Moravia, nowadays a region of the Czech Republic. Most of these records were destroyed either deliberately on orders by its director, *SS-Obersturmbannführer* Albin

Scherhaufer, or during the fighting at the end of April 1945. Only a small number were saved and are presently archived in Prague.

The records of the *IV. SS-Panzerkorps* (*IV. SS-Pz.Korps*) were destroyed deliberately in May 1945, shortly before its surrender to the Americans, on the order of its commander, *SS-Obergruppenführer* (*Ogruf.*) *und Generalleutnant der Waffen-SS* Herbert Otto Gille. Thus, reconstructing what occurred during the corps' brief life proved to be a challenge in regards to its official documents, but fortunately there was an abundance of primary *Heer* sources, contemporary eyewitness accounts, postwar recollections, and publications produced by the various veterans organizations of divisions assigned to the corps. Of particular interest were the morning and evening situation reports that were submitted to the field army headquarters that commanded Gille's corps. In this case, all of the daily *Morgenmeldung*, *Vororientierung*, and *Tagesmeldung* (morning, mid-day, and daily reports) have been preserved in the files for the *2. Armee* and *9. Armee*, under which the *IV. SS-Pz.Korps* served from 27 July 1944 until 25 November 1944. These reports, submitted under Gille's direct supervision and in his name, contain a wealth of information about daily events, including accounts describing the outcome of combat operations. Another important record was the evening commander's commentary maintained by the army commanders, which usually included contributions by their chiefs of staff, found in each field army's *Führungsabteilung* war diary. These particular records shed light on the thoughts and plans of senior leaders, which are not usually reflected in the operational records.

Another useful source that has only become recently available is the archive of German documents captured by the Red Army at the end of the war. This enormous collection of documents is still being processed and slowly added to a website established by the Russian-German Project on Digitization of German Documents in the Archives of the Russian Federation. To date (2019), the consortium has added thousands of previously unseen captured German documents from nearly every command level of the *Wehrmacht*, ranging from the *OKW* to *Heeresgruppen* (army groups) level, then *Armeeoberkommando* (field armies), and as far down as division, regiment, and even battalion level. The author has sifted through this gigantic hoard of online documentation and was able to access a wealth of information that directly concerned the *IV. SS-Pz.Korps* as well as its higher headquarters and subordinate units. In fact, the need to incorporate this information into the manuscript led to delays in this book's publication, but it could not have gone to press without it.

A byproduct of years of research in the archives of the former Soviet Union is Colonel David M. Glantz's excellent *Atlas of the Lublin-Brest Operation and the Advance on Warsaw*. Working with cartographer Michael Avansini, Colonel Glantz used copies of contemporary maps produced by the First Belorussian Front found in the Russian archives as well as those used by the German *2.* and *9. Armeen* to produce a day-by-day visual account of the fighting that took place between 18 July and 30 September 1944. In addition to depicting the location of the *IV. SS-Pz.Korps* at any given point, it also names the Red Army and Polish Army units, ranging in size from army to regiment, as well as the direction of their advance. This proved to be an invaluable guide which allowed the author to identify which units were fighting opposite the Germans as the campaign progressed through the tank battle of Praga, the three battles of Warsaw, the Warsaw Uprising, and the siege of Modlin.

Though not included in the German Documents in Russia website, of particular usefulness were the monthly readiness accounts submitted by divisions under the corps' command to the German Army's Inspectorate of *Panzer* Troops, detailing personnel status, available tank numbers, serviceable artillery pieces, and, interestingly, the narrative account provided by each division commander describing his overall assessment of the combat worthiness of his division. In addition, there are a plethora of daily situation reports and other message traffic that circulated between the corps and the three field armies under which *IV. SS-Pz.Korps* served between July 1944 and May 1945. Another equally useful source are the daily armor strength reports that each corps was required to submit to its army headquarters, as well as the weekly personnel strength reports, in which every division operating under a corps or field army headquarters was required to submit a tally of their *Kampfstärke*, that is, the effective combat strength of each battalion measured in terms of available infantrymen, combat engineers, and reconnaissance troops—in short, the foot soldiers who did most of the fighting and dying, and whose numbers helped commanders understand the relative combat power of their organizations at a given point in time.

Another source that must be mentioned is the magisterial *Germany and the Second World War*, the official German government account of the war written by a consortium of historians under the supervision of the *Militärgeschichtliches Forschungsamt* (Research Institute for German History) in Potsdam. Edited by noted military historian Karl-Heinz Frieser, this is undoubtedly the most complete and comprehensive account of the war from the German perspective ever written. Volume VIII of the series, *The Eastern Front 1943–1944: The War in the East and on the Neighboring Fronts* (2017), was used as a reference for this book, which provides an illuminating overview of operations from the perspective of the *OKW* and *Heeresgruppen* (Army Groups). Accompanied by an excellent series of maps that clearly depict the unfolding operations, it should be mandatory reading for anyone attempting to understand the ebb and flow of the fighting during those two critical years.

While this is the first attempt to chronicle the history of *IV. SS-Pz.Korps*, three previously established SS *panzer* corps have already had their accounts entered into the historical record. Major General Michael F. Reynolds, a highly decorated officer of the British Army, has published two meticulously researched books about the *I.* and *II. SS-Pz.Korps*, titled respectively *Men of Steel: the Ardennes and Eastern Front* and *Sons of the Reich: II Panzer Corps–Normandy–Arnhem–Ardennes–Eastern Front*. He also authored the definitive history of the *I. SS-Pz.Korps'* experience in Normandy during the Allied invasion (*Steel Inferno: I. SS Panzer Corps in Normandy*) as well as another about Jochen Peiper, one of the *1. SS-Panzer Division*'s most notorious commanders (*The Devil's Adjutant: Jochen Peiper, Panzer Leader*). Told from the perspective of these two corps and their most prominent commanders, he provides extremely detailed and coherent accounts of their important contributions towards the German effort to hold the Allies at bay in Western Europe from D-Day until the failure of the Ardennes offensive, followed by a brief account of their commitment to battle in Hungary and Austria during the last two months of the war.

Wilhelm Tieke, a *Waffen-SS* veteran and noted historian in his own right, also wrote a very fine history of the *II. SS-Pz.Korps*, *In the Firestorm of the Last Years of the War: II. SS-Panzerkorps with the 9. and 10. SS-Divisions "Hohenstaufen" and "Frundsberg."* The English translation by J. J. Fedorowicz Publishing of a work that originally appeared in Germany, this account has the added advantage of having an insider's view of how the corps operated, augmented by personal accounts by many of his *Waffen-SS* acquaintances with whom he served during the war. Concerned that another famous SS corps, the *III. (Germanisch) Pz.Korps*, might be omitted by the historical record, Tieke also penned *The Tragedy of the Faithful: III. SS Panzer Korps*. Another excellent account of this corps has also recently been published, *III. Germanic SS Panzer-Korps: The History of Himmler's Favorite SS-Panzer-Korps, 1943–1945* (Volume 1) by Lennart Westberg, Petter Kjellander, and Geir Brenden (Helion, 2019). What these publications demonstrate is the continuing fascination by a significant number of military historians in this topic, and studies of other SS corps would help shed light on this late-war phenomenon.

The last-mentioned corps, established by and led for most of its two-year life by *SS-Obergruppenführer* Felix Steiner, was an attempt to incorporate all of the "Germanic" SS units consisting of northern European volunteers into an "international" *panzer* corps. Steiner, an advocate of physical fitness and storm trooper tactics, was a *Heer* veteran of World War I and instructor *par excellence* who is credited with having much to do with the early *Waffen-SS* reputation as being an elite body of troops. Although his corps fought for its entire existence on the Eastern Front, the *III. (germ.) SS-Pz.Korps'* most remarkable episode occurred during the Battle of Berlin, when Steiner famously refused to commit the corps (renamed "*Armee Abteilung Steiner*" or Army Detachment Steiner) to come to Hitler's assistance on 22 April 1945, when he knew it would lead only to the senseless slaughter of his men.

Steiner also wrote two books after the war describing his experiences as a regimental, division, corps, and army commander titled *Der Freiwilligen* (The Volunteers) and *Armee der Geächteten* (Army of Outlaws). Though neither dealt exclusively with his *III. (germ.) SS-Pz.Korps,* Steiner does describe its operations in great detail, though with a certain degree of embellishment to further the cause of *Waffen-SS* historical rehabilitation. Sadly, he makes little reference to Gille's *IV. SS-Pz.Korps*, though Steiner does highlight the complexities of commanding units consisting predominately of foreign volunteers.

Any objective account of *IV. SS-Pz.Korps* must include the following unit histories, without which this book would have not been written. The most detailed from the division perspective are Volumes Va and Vb of Wolfgang Vopersal's excellent *Soldaten Kämpfer Kameraden: March und Kämpfe der SS-Totenkopf-Division* (*Soldiers, Warriors, Comrades: the Campaigns and Battles of the SS Death's Head Division*), which of course focuses primarily on the *3. SS-Panzer-Division*'s operations between July 1944 and the end of the war. Vopersal, a veteran of the *Totenkopf* Division, gathered a tremendous amount of material, including interviews, wartime accounts, reports, and correspondence, giving the reader an excellent chronological perspective of how that division's operations figured prominently in the battles waged by Gille's corps from July 1944 until the end of the war. Sprinkled throughout are snippets of official message traffic between the corps and the *Totenkopf* Division that provide context for the engagements and battles that followed. Given that the corps' records are lacking, this fills in many of the gaps that the writer encountered.

Another source that provides a context from a regimental commander in the *Totenkopf* Division as well as division commander of the *Wiking* Division during this period is Karl Ullrich's *Like a Cliff in the Ocean: The History of the 3. SS-Panzer-Division "Totenkopf,"* the English translation of Munin-Verlag's earlier *Wie ein Fels im Meer*. Though not as detailed as Vopersal's work, Ullrich was present for many of the corps' conferences and orders group meetings with Gille, Hellmuth Becker (commander of the *Totenkopf* Division), and other commanders, providing a perspective in his book that Vopersal lacks, as well as Ullrich's own insights into what he saw unfolding before him. A number of useful appendices and maps complement the book, including copies of original orders that have been helpfully translated into English.

A far more ambitious work is Georg Maier's *Drama Between Budapest and Vienna: the Final Battles of the 6. Panzer-Armee in the East–1945*, another J. J. Fedorowicz translation of a well-known Munin Verlag book. Maier, who had been the operations officer of the *6. SS-Panzerarmee* (*6. SS-Pz.Armee*) during the last year of the war, describes in great detail the operations in and around Budapest between December 1944 and February 1945, focusing on the activities of *IV. SS-Pz.Korps*. With the arrival of Sepp Dietrich's SS tank army on the field in late February 1945, Maier covers the fateful *Frühlingserwachen* (*Spring Awakening*) offensive in Hungary, Germany's last and most desperate offensive.

From the army headquarters perspective, Maier is able to describe the actions of the several corps under Dietrich's command, as well as neighboring armies, which were fated to play a prominent role in the attack. Maier thankfully has reproduced numerous operations orders and examples of headquarters message traffic, as well as a plethora of contemporary operational and planning maps, which enable the reader or researcher to easily grasp what was actually taking place. His remarks and conclusions are backed up by endnotes and 130 appendices, allowing the reader, should they desire, to delve even deeper into the condition of the Germany Army in general and the *Waffen-SS* in particular during the last phase of the war in the East.

Though not as comprehensive as Vopersal's division history, Peter Strassner's *European Volunteers*, which appeared in 1968 as *Europäische Freiwillige: Die Geschichte der 5. SS-Panzerdivision Wiking*, covers the division's history from its inception in 1940 until the end. Relying primarily on participants' personal accounts, Strassner's coverage of the last year of the war from the perspective of the *Wiking* Division sheds some light on the machinations of *IV. SS-Pz.Korps*, since so many of the *Wiking*'s senior officers were appointed to prominent positions on the corps staff when the corps was committed to battle at the end of July 1944. Their point of view as corps staff officers helps explain why the division was ordered to carry out a number of desperate counterattacks at the gates of Warsaw and during the relief attempts of Budapest, at a time when the division itself had little time for reflection, only to carry out its orders. A number of appendices, including actual strength reports, provide a windfall for researchers seeking to understand the relative combat power of the division during this critical stage of the war.

Though more narrowly focused than Strassner's account, *Wiking Panzers: The German SS 5th Tank Regiment in the East in World War II*, the Stackpole Books translation of Ewald Klapdor's 1981 study, *Mit dem Panzerregiment 5 Wiking im Osten*, is a must for those trying to piece together the operations of *IV. SS-Pz. Korps*, especially those where tank battles prominently figured. Klapdor, a former tank battalion commander in the *Wiking* Division himself, weaves a highly detailed account of the operations of *SS-Panzer-Regiment 5*, augmented by dozens of personal accounts that are buttressed by numerous references from portions of the regiment's war diary, which somehow survived the war. His book allows the reader or researcher to gain insight into the effects that a year of prolonged combat had on a tight-knit organization as it struggled to overcome Soviet numerical superiority and its own dwindling capability. Reinforced with numerous maps and detailed appendices, Klapdor's work is a worthy companion to Strassner and a valuable historical document in its own right.

Of course, any accounts of and by *Waffen-SS* veterans must be balanced by books written by their comrades in the German Army. In this regard, there is certainly no shortage of eyewitness accounts by men who had either fought alongside *IV. SS-Pz. Korps* or had the corps assigned under them. One excellent account, written by an officer who served in a neighboring division, is *Die 1. Panzerdivision 1935–1945* by Rolf O. Stoves. Long recognized as one of the most complete and detailed divisional histories of the *Wehrmacht* ever written, Stoves devotes a considerable amount of the book towards the attempt to relieve Budapest, when *1. Pz.Div.* was attached to

Gille's corps. A very fair and balanced work, Stoves neither derides the *Waffen-SS* or Gille's leadership, nor does he write about the corps in glowing terms. It is, and remains, an excellent example of how to write a divisional history. In it, Stoves inadvertently debunks most of the complaints hurled against the performance of Gille and his corps by his army commander, *Generaloberst* Hermann Balck, stating the bald facts as they appeared to him from his perspective as a staff officer in *1. Pz.Div.*, considered one of the finest divisions of the German Army.

Not so rosy in his assessment of *IV. SS-Pz.Korps* was the aforementioned Hermann Balck, considered by many to be among the best tacticians produced by the German Army in World War II. In his autobiography, *Order in Chaos*, which originally appeared in 1981 shortly before his death, Balck provides an interesting overview of the situation in Hungary as he found it upon his transfer there from the Western Front in late December 1944, where he had commanded *Heeresgruppe G* (*H.Gr.* or Army Group G) in Alsace-Lorraine. Charged by Hitler himself with relieving Budapest, Balck was assigned a number of German and Hungarian formations, some of dubious worth, to carry out what to many would have seemed an impossible mission—carve a way through several Soviet field armies in the dead of winter, relieve an encircled city with over 800,000 trapped civilian residents, and reestablish a stable front line.

No Pollyanna, Balck saw the situation clearly and quickly came up with a plan to achieve his objectives. Not so clearly did he perceive the situation involving *IV. SS-Pz.Korps*, whose commander he considered incompetent and whose staff he felt were nothing short of criminally negligent. Balck, who found his army group commander, *Generaloberst* Wöhler, often in agreement, attempted to relieve Gille of his command and fire his staff, but to no avail. Nevertheless, *IV. SS-Pz.Korps*, with its hard-fighting *3.* and *5. SS-Panzer-Divisionen*, along with *1. Pz.Div.* and other divisions of the *Heer*, achieved most of their operational objectives and repeatedly defeated far larger Soviet formations and nearly relieved Budapest. Though he never misses an opportunity to condemn the performance of the *Waffen-SS*, Balck's account of how the fighting in general unfolded between December 1944 and May 1945 is extremely cogent and gives one an idea of what might have been accomplished had he been given the forces he thought necessary to carry out all of his tasks. It remains a must-read for anyone trying to understand what happened on Germany's southeast front during the last six months of the war.

Readers will note that this study was written almost exclusively from the perspective of the German Armed Forces using their own sources. Every attempt was made to draw upon contemporary Soviet and Polish sources, though English-language translations of their official records are not yet available. As a result, the author has had to rely on the biographical account by Marshal Konstantin Rokossovsky, commander of the First Belorussian Front, Igor Nebolsin's *Stalin's Favorite: The Combat History of the 2nd Guards Tank Army from Kursk to Berlin*, and the memoir by Colonel General Pavel I. Batov, commander of the 65th Army. The most useful of these sources written from the Soviet and Polish perspective is Norbert Bacyk's brief but detailed *Warsaw II: The Tank Battle of Praga July 1944 and the 4th SS Panzer Corps versus the First Belorussian Front*. Bacyk, a Polish military scholar, draws upon a wealth of contemporary Soviet and Polish official accounts, as well as German records of the fighting, covering the period from July–October 1944. Lastly, the author was able to secure the cooperation of several Russian military scholars, some of whom requested anonymity, who translated selected portions of the official records of the First Belorussian Front and the VIII Guards Tank Corps.

As a note to readers, extensive use of German military terminology is found throughout the text in italicized form. Where appropriate, English translations are provided alongside, while others may be found in the glossary. Many of these terms may already be familiar to those with experience studying the German Armed Forces, but for those new to this field of study, it will hopefully help to expand their military vocabulary. In many cases, German military terminology is a sort of shorthand developed over the centuries that expresses more complex terms that do not readily or smoothly translate into English. In some instances, the author has done his best to explain them in laymen's terms. Additionally, names of German units and their allies are italicized, as well as Russian terminology where appropriate. The official names of units fighting under the banner of the Union of Soviet Socialist Republics (U.S.S.R.) and its allies are not italicized, and when the title of a particular unit is unknown, the generic terms to describe them are "Soviet" or "Red Army" divisions, regiments, battalions, etc.

Volume I covers the formation of the corps, its leaders, staff organization, and brief histories of its two key units—the *Totenkopf* and *Wiking panzer* divisions—from the corps' inception in August 1943 until the end of the battles for Warsaw in November 1944. Volume II will focus on the period December 1944 to May 1945, during which *Operation Konrad I, II*, and *III* (the relief attempts of Budapest), the corps' defence of Stühlweissenburg, its role in *Unternehmen Frühlingserwachen* (Operation *Spring Awakening*), Germany's last large-scale offensive of the war, the retreat to Vienna, and the final events of the war took place.

Work on this manuscript took four years and could not have been completed without the advice and assistance of numerous individuals, military historians, and authors in their own right, living in the United States, Europe, and Australia. They generously provided documents, translations, maps, photographs, and clues that enabled this work to go forward. In the United States, in this list I would like to thank Tom Albright, Mike Constandy, David Glantz, Tom Houlihan, French MacLean, Edward Miller, Michael Miller, John Moore, George Nipe, Marc Rikmenspoel, Phillip Schwartzberg, Remy Spezzano, and the late Mark Yerger. In Europe, I would like to thank Christian Ankerstjern, Artyom Astafiev, Christoph Awender, Norbert Bacyk, Mirko Bayerl, Pedrag Blanusa, Martin Block, Geier Brendan,

Carol Byrne, Piet Duits, Edi Eberle, Ron Erlings, Andrew Found, Timm Haasler, Richard Hargreaves, Petter Kjellander, Klemen Kocjancic, Bert Kossen, Wolfgang Lange, Martin Månsson, Mike Melnyk, Roland Pfeiffer, Bram von Straalen, Norbert Számvéber, Charles Trang, Jan-Hendrik Vermeulen, Hans Weber, Lennart Westberg, Lars Westerlund, Ian Michael Wood, and David T. Zabecki. Last but certainly not least, I would also like to thank Jason Mark and Scott Revell in Australia for their advice and cooperation.

Another primary source has been a number of *Waffen-SS* veterans of the *Wiking* Division, who lived through many of the battles described in this book. They have helped me over a number of years, beginning in 1994 when I was working on my Master's thesis at the U.S. Army Command and General Staff College at Fort Leavenworth, Kansas. Most of these men, with the exception of Günther Lange, have since passed on. They most graciously provided me with a number of photographs, personal correspondence, books, maps, and other materials from their personal archives which I have mined repeatedly, beginning with my first book, *Hell's Gate: The Battle of the Cherkassy Pocket*. I would like to thank the late (*SS-Ostuf.*) Wolfgang Brandstetter, (*SS-Ostubaf.*) Fritz Darges, (*SS-Ostuf.*) Hans Fischer, (*SS-Ostuf.*) Fritz Hahl, (*SS-Hstuf.*) Theodor Eberhard Heder, (*SS-Hstuf.* and *Bundeswehr Oberst a.D.*) Willy Hein, (*SS-Hstuf.*) Günter Jahnke, (*SS-Ustuf.*) Karl Jauss, and last but not least, (*SS-Hstuf.*) Karl-Heinz Lichte.

Lastly, I would like to thank my wife and family for their patience and understanding during this process. Many weekend activities and travels were postponed or delayed while I worked on this book, but none of this would have been possible without their encouragement and support.

Douglas Nash
Washington, D.C., July 2019

List of Maps

1. The Eastern Front 10–22 July 1944 94
2. The *IV. SS-Pz.Korps* East of Warsaw 25–28 July 1944 99
3. The Soviet Advance 18–31 July 1944 106
4. The Tank Battle of Praga 1–4 August 1944 114
5. The Three Defensive Battles for Warsaw 5 August–28 October 1944 159
6. The First Battle of Warsaw 13–30 August 1944 161
7. The Second Battle of Warsaw 31 August–22 September 1944 211
8. The Third Battle of Warsaw 10–28 October 1944 361
9. The Battle of Modlin 29 October–25 November 1944 441

List of Figures

1. Diagram depicting organizational structure of the *IV. SS-Panzerkorps* Headquarters and Corps Troops, August 1944. This diagram depicts the inclusion of its heavy tank battalion, *SS-schwere-Panzerabteilung 104*, which was never activated. 3
2. Diagram depicting phase lines and troops movements envisioned for *Unternehmen Brückenschlag*, 8–13 August 1944. 140
3. German city map of Warsaw including outlying suburbs, *circa* August 1944. 208
4. Example diagram of a front-line troop shelter for the Vistula Defense Line, July 1944. 440
5. Diagram of the *IV. SS-Panzercorps* Cemetery in Modlin, dedicated 9 November 1944. (Courtesy of Günther Lange Archive) 454
6. Surrender leaflet dropped on *Wiking* Division troops, August 1944. (Courtesy of Günther Lange Archive) 462

CHAPTER 1

Activation of *IV. SS-Pz.Korps*

The process of what was to result in the creation of the fourth *panzer* corps of the *Waffen-SS* occurred in an ordinary, bureaucratic manner, without fuss or fanfare. The order directing the creation of *Generalkommando IV. SS-Panzerkorps* (General Command, IV SS *Panzer* Corps) was signed on 5 August 1943 at the *SS-FHA* office in Berlin by *SS-Obergruppenführer und General der Waffen-SS* Hans Jüttner, the chief of staff of the bureau that supervised the administration of the *Waffen-SS*.[1] Though virtually unknown outside of the higher SS leadership circle, Jüttner had worked tirelessly since 1939 to transform the *Waffen-SS* from a small internal police force of the Nazi Party into an organization that would rival *das deutsche Heer* (the German Army) in loyalty, professionalism, and lethality, if perhaps not in size.

Drawing his authority from a *Führerbefehl* issued under Hitler's name on 1 June 1943, Jüttner, with his chief Heinrich Himmler's full support, stipulated that the corps was to be activated in the area of Poitiers, France, where it would assume control of two new mechanized divisions of the *Waffen-SS* then undergoing activation themselves. Another reason for the creation of the new corps was to prevent these two divisions, *9. SS-Panzergrenadier Division "Hohenstaufen"* and *16. SS-Panzergrenadier-Division "Reichsführer SS"*, from being placed under the immediate supervision of the *Heer*, long considered by the senior SS leadership to be institutionally hostile to any expansion at its expense, since many senior officers of the *Heer* saw the SS as posing a challenge to its own status as the sole bearer of the nation's arms.

A corps headquarters, therefore, would serve as a protective administrative layer or buffer between these divisions and the next higher organization, in this case *H.Gr. D* (Army Group D) commanded by *Generalfeldmarschall* Gerd von Rundstedt, an officer of the old *Kaiserheer* (Imperial Army) who, like most of his peers, initially viewed the *Waffen-SS* with skepticism if not outright disdain. Once its formation was completed, Himmler envisioned that the corps would command more SS divisions in battle, just as *SS-Generaloberst* Paul Hausser's *SS-Panzerkorps* had been doing in the Soviet Union since February 1943.[2]

The activation order also named the corps' first commander—*SS-Obergruppenführer und General der Polizei und Waffen-SS* Alfred Wünnenberg. A former policeman and World War I veteran, Wünnenberg was an odd choice for the position of *panzer* corps commander, but had recent combat experience in the Soviet Union, where he had commanded the *SS-Polizei* (Police) *Division* for the past 18 months in the northern sector of the Eastern Front, including fighting outside of Leningrad and Rshev. Arriving in Berlin on 10 June 1943, he was available for future assignment, having just given over command of his division to *SS-Oberführer* Fritz Schmedes. Despite having no armor experience whatsoever, at least Wünnenberg would bring with him his good contacts with Heinrich Himmler, the head of the SS, as well as with Jüttner, both of whom would ease his transition from division to corps command.

To fill the key positions on his staff, Wünnenberg brought along officers who had served under him in the *SS-Polizei Division*. For example, on 5 August the former *2. Generalstabsoffizier*, or *Ib*, of his old division, *SS-Sturmbannführer* (*Stubaf.*) Hans Pruss, was assigned as the corps' *Quartiermeister* or chief logistics officer. He was accompanied by *Obersturmbannführer* (*Ostubaf.*) Karl Wagenknecht, who had commanded the division's supply and service organization, and would serve as the corps' transportation and traffic regulation officer.[3] Though both would be assigned with the corps only until the middle of October, they brought the necessary administrative and logistical skills that Wünnenberg needed in order to carry out his mission of establishing the corps as well as the two aforementioned *Waffen-SS* divisions.

Oberführer Nikolaus Heilmann, another officer hand-picked by Wünnenberg from the ranks of the *SS-Polizei Division*, was selected to become the corps *Chef des Stabes* (chief of staff). Though not trained as a general staff officer, Heilmann, a career officer from the prewar *Ordnungspolizei*, or *Orpo* (Order Police), had a reputation as a problem-solver and a tireless worker, both attributes that would stand him in good stead for the challenges to come.[4] Wünnenberg in the meantime had been named as the overall commander of the *Ordnungspolizei* on 31 August 1943, causing him to relinquish command of the corps at some point shortly thereafter.

The structure of the corps headquarters would adhere to that prescribed by the *Heer*, as specified in *Kriegsstärkenachweisung* (*K.St.N.*) *Nummer 15* (War Strength Inventory Directive Number 15), a document similar to the modern U.S. Army's tables of organization. This document was accompanied by the complementary *Kriegsausrüstungsnachweis*, or *K.A.N.*, which describes what types and amounts of equipment the corps headquarters was required to possess, down to the last typewriter and field telephone.The *K.St.N.* for a *Generalkommando* (*motorisiert*, or *mot.*) was designed to enable the headquarters of a *panzer* corps to command and control the operations of a variety of motorized, *Panzergrenadier* (mechanized infantry), or *Panzer* divisions (see Figure 1). It differed from its infantry corps counterpart only in the degree of motorization of the staff as well as by the addition of specialized

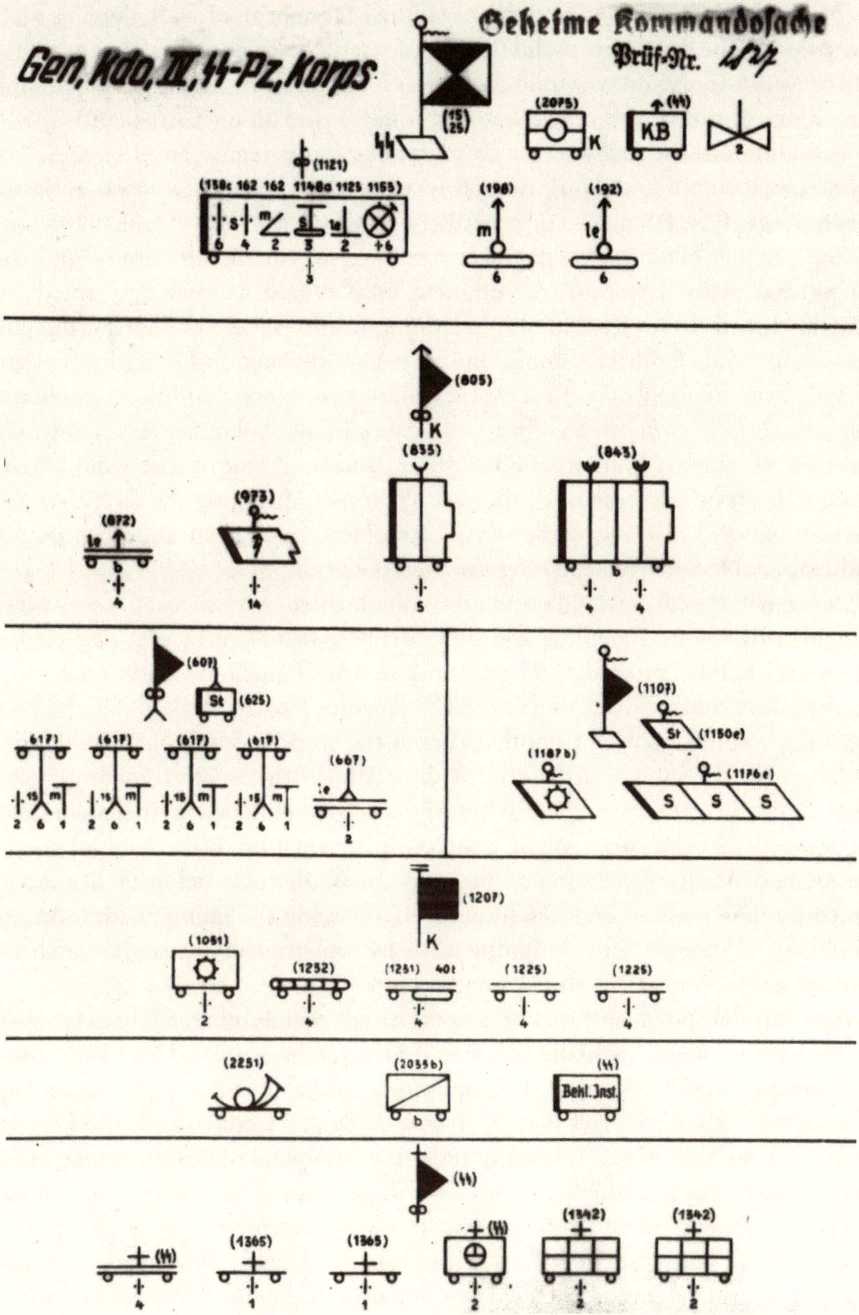

Figure 1. Diagram depicting organizational structure of the *IV. SS-Panzerkorps* Headquarters and Corps Troops, August 1944. This diagram depicts the inclusion of its heavy tank battalion, *SS-schwere-Panzerabteilung* 104, which was never activated

radio and communications equipment tailored for control of wide-ranging mobile formations.[5] The new SS corps did not have a veterinarian, since it was not authorized any *bespannte* (horse-drawn) units.[6] Nor was it authorized a chaplain, unlike similar formations of the *Heer*, a reflection of Himmler's disdain for Christianity.

In addition to the staff and the corps *Hauptquartier* (equivalent to a U.S. Army corps special troops battalion), the newly activated *IV. SS-Pz.Korps* was authorized a corps signal battalion, a corps artillery command, a heavy tank battalion, a rocket launcher battalion, an engineer battalion, an antiaircraft battery, and corps supply and medical troops.[7] All of these units would have to be formed from scratch, with their enlisted personnel coming from a variety of sources, including non-commissioned officer schools, replacement battalions, and levies from existing units throughout the *Waffen-SS* as well as convalescent hospitals. Officers would come from the *SS-Junkerschulen* (SS officer candidate schools), voluntary reassignments, or involuntary transfers from other SS corps or divisions. Some officers would even be taken in from other elements of the vast SS empire, including the *Sicherheitsdienst* (security service), *Totenkopfverbände* (Death's Head or concentration camp units), and inactive officers from the *Allgemeine-SS* (General SS).

In combat, the corps would ordinarily be augmented by a variety of *Heerestruppen*, or field army troops, including additional artillery battalions or brigades, engineer units, antiaircraft, antitank, and rear area security battalions. Additional supply, maintenance, and medical units, while frequently located throughout the corps' area of operations, were not normally under the corps' control, but would remain under the field army's or army group's direction. With the attachment of two or more *Panzer* or *Panzergrenadier* divisions, the corps would be considered complete, though at times the corps might also control normal infantry, light infantry, or mountain divisions, depending on the mission. While stationed in France though, the corps' duties would be more mundane, overseeing the training, administrative and logistical support, and equipping of its two subordinate divisions, which were themselves involved in the throes of activation.

As events transpired, only the corps signal battalion and antiaircraft battery actually began forming along with the corps staff and *Hauptquartier*. There were simply not enough vehicles, weapons, and equipment available to equip *IV. SS-Pz.Korps*, especially in light of the fact that *III. (germanisches*, or Germanic*) SS-Pz.Korps* was forming at the same time. This unit, under the command of *Gruppenführer* (*Gruf.*) Felix Steiner, had a far higher priority in the allocation of war material, since it was slated for assignment to the Eastern Front by December 1943. Consequently, Wünnenberg's corps had to take a back seat with regards to activating its corps troops units, though it was intended to equip them as soon as conditions permitted.

Thus, the corps operated for the next two-and-a-half months primarily as an administrative and logistics hub. On 3 October 1943, the list of the corps' subordinate divisions was changed when *10. SS-Pz.Gren.Div. "Karl der Grosse"* was assigned in place of the *16. SS-Pz.Gren.Div. Reichsführer SS*, which was to be activated on 6 October in Italy rather than in France. Shortly thereafter, the *10. SS-Pz.Gren.Div.* was redesignated as a *panzer* division and its named changed to *Frundsberg*, joining its sister division, *9. SS-Pz.Div. Hohenstaufen*, in the *IV. SS-Pz.Korps* order of battle. Thus, the corps staff was primarily employed in requisitioning supplies, arranging the assignment, equipping, transportation, and billeting for replacement personnel, and coordinating with the various SS and *Heer* depots, factories, and the *Reichsbahn* (German state railway) for the shipment of hundreds of vehicles, tanks, supplies, and other items needed to arm and equip the two armored divisions.

While the *IV. SS-Pz.Korps* was going through the growing pains common to nearly every new organization, developments on the Eastern Front set in motion a train of events that would temporarily result in a suspension of the corps' further progress. Earlier that year, Hitler had approved Himmler's request to activate two Latvian volunteer divisions and incorporate them into the *Waffen-SS*, which were to be grouped into a "Latvian Volunteer Corps" led by a new SS corps headquarters created for that purpose. This corps, designated the *VI. Waffen-Armeekorps der SS (Lettisches)*, was to begin forming on 8 October 1943 at Frankfurt an der Oder, while the corps troops would be organized at the Grafenwöhr *Truppenübungsplatz* (training and maneuver area) in Bavaria.[8] The entire organization was to be made combat-ready in the shortest possible time. But where would the necessary staff and corps troops needed to create this organization come from on such brief notice?

Jüttner and Himmler soon found a ready solution. Since *IV. SS-Pz.Korps*' administrative and logistics functions could temporarily be carried out by its higher Army command, *H.Gr. D*, until the end of December 1943 when *Gruf.* Hausser's *II. SS-Pz.Korps* could assume that responsibility after it returned from the Eastern Front, Jüttner decided to use Wünnenberg's personnel and its corps assets to form the new Latvian corps headquarters. Shortly upon receipt of the unexpected order, the staff, personnel, and equipment of what had formerly been *IV. SS-Pz.Korps* headquarters were quickly loaded onto trains and trucks and transported across France and through Germany, eventually reaching their temporary quarters at Grafenwöhr by mid-October 1943, where corps headquarters and corps troops were united for the first time. The corps commander would be *SS-Gruppenführer und Gen.Lt. der Pol.* Karl von Pfeffer-Wildenbruch, whose path would cross with that of the newly reactivated *IV. SS-Pz.Korps* a year later. After two months of formation, the *VI. Waffen-Armeekorps* was shipped to the northern sector of the Eastern Front, finally assuming command of its two subordinate Latvian divisions in January 1944 near Pleskau.

Nicolaus Heilmann, the corps chief of staff, remained as acting commander of what had remained behind in France, though *IV. SS-Pz.Korps* was now merely a shell. The monthly organizational structure diagram submitted to the *Generalstabes des Heeres* (Army General Staff), a means used by staff officers to monitor the readiness status of all combat units and headquarters under its purview, indicated that the corps was still in the "process of being activated" throughout the reporting period covering 15 October to 8 November 1943. After that date, due to the lack of available personnel to staff the corps, it was reported as being only "in the planning stages" and with the exception of a few remaining members of the staff who had stayed behind, it was a corps in name only.[9]

Wünnenberg's replacement as corps commander, as least on paper, was *Gruf.* Walter Krüger, who only recently had commanded the *2. SS-Pz.Div. Das Reich* on the Eastern Front. Taking over the corps on 24 December 1943, Krüger was merely a figurehead, with nothing to command. Most of the vacant positions on his staff had not been filled since the majority of its personnel had been transferred to Wünnenberg's *VI. SS-Korps* the previous October. *Gruppenführer* Krüger himself was finally transferred on 14 March 1944 to assume his new position as Inspector General of the Infantry Troops of the *Waffen-SS*, and *IV. SS-Pz.Korps* had once again practically ceased to exist for the time being. By 15 March 1944, only two men—an officer and non-commissioned officer—remained behind in Poitiers to serve as caretakers.[10]

While the original *IV. SS-Pz.Korps* was still undergoing its growing pains, Adolf Hitler, on Himmler's and Jüttner's urging, had ordered the establishment of another SS armored corps headquarters on 22 October 1943 that would control the other two remaining SS mechanized divisions then forming in France—the *17. SS-Pz. Gren.Div. "Götz von Berlichingen"* and *10. SS-Pz.Div. Frundsberg.*[11] This organization, *VII. SS-Pz.Korps*, was briefly referred to as the *Landesknecht Korps*, in honor of the namesakes of both divisions who had been prominent leaders of German *Landsknechts* (German mercenaries made famous for their devil-may-care attitude) who fought in many small wars during the late 15th and early 16th centuries. Jüttner directed that the corps be activated in the French town of Mörchingen (Morhange) near Metz in Alsace-Lorraine before it would be moved to a reserve position closer to the French coastline.[12] Here it would be positioned along with its two divisions to respond to any Allied landing attempt. Some of its corps troops, such as its signal battalion and mapping office, began forming as early as 8 January 1944.

After the activation order was published, little happened during the next several months until the end of December 1943, when its activation was finally elevated to a higher priority, signified by the appointment of *Gruf.* Matthias Kleinheisterkamp as its first commander.[13] At the time, Kleinheisterkamp, an experienced veteran of World War I and the *Reichswehr*, was serving as the commander of *6. SS-Geb.Div. Nord,* where he had proven himself a capable and well-liked commander. However, the corps' activation was delayed yet again in early January 1944, when he was ordered to serve as acting commander of the *III. (germ.) SS-Pz.Korps*, then fighting at Narva with Army Group North, until *Ogruf.* Felix Steiner, its actual commander, returned from detached duty. Here, Kleinheisterkamp gained two months of valuable experience leading a corps in battle that would stand him in good stead a year later in Pomerania and during the defense of the Oder Front.[14]

In March 1944, *Gruf.* Kleinheisterkamp handed command of *III. (germ.) SS-Pz. Korps* back to Steiner, and returned to Germany to attend a leader's course in Berlin. With its commander finally having returned from the Eastern Front, the activation of *VII. SS-Pz.Korps* resumed in earnest. Though even as late as 15 March 1944 the corps headquarters still had only a few officers and NCOs assigned, by the end of April, newly assigned officers, NCOs, and enlisted men began to stream by the hundreds into its assembly areas in and around Mörchingen. Equipment ranging from trucks to radios and machine guns soon also began to pour in from various SS and *Waffenamt* (the *Heer* ordnance department) depots throughout Germany.

Though Kleinheisterkamp had brought over a dozen veterans from his old division to serve as key staff officers in the new corps, there were not enough of them to fill all of the required positions, with 59 *Führer* (officers) needed for the corps headquarters alone, excluding corps troops. Anticipating this need, a number of SS officers from the *SS-Führerreserve* (a pool of "reserve" SS officers maintained by the *SS-FHA*) were assigned to fill out the remaining corps staff and corps troop officer positions beginning in the middle of April 1944. They came from nearly every corner of the SS Empire—from the *Waffen-SS*, the concentration camp system, SS reserve hospitals, the *Sicherheitsdienst*, and the various SS administrative organs, including lawyers and notary publics whose previous positions had become superfluous with the changing tides of war.

By 1 July 1944, 446 officers and men had arrived to fill the various positions within the *Hauptquartier*, and 140 more men slated to join the corps were attending *Unterführer* (non-commissioned officer, or NCO) training courses in Holland, leaving the corps *Hauptquartier* only 159 men short of its authorized strength of 789. In regards to manpower, the situation with the corps antiaircraft battery and signal battalion was encouragingly similar.[15] *SS-Panzergrenadier Ausbildung und Ersatz Bataillon 9* (*SS-Pz.Gren.A.u.E.Btl.*, or SS Armored Infantry Training and Replacement Battalion) in Stralsund was designated as the corps headquarters' home depot unit, from whence it would draw its replacements and where its men would report when on leave in Germany or attending schools in the homeland.

Once again, *Oberführer* Heilmann, who had served for two-and-a-half months as the chief of staff of the original *IV. SS-Pz.Korps* from 5 August until 19 October 1943, was named as the corps' chief of staff, but his arrival was delayed until 25 June. Heilmann had taken over temporary command of the *15. Waffen-Grenadier Division der SS (Lett. Nr.1)*, a division composed of Latvian volunteers, in February 1944 and could not leave until a replacement was found. Before that assignment, he had served as the chief of staff for the *VI. SS-Freiwilligen Korps* in Latvia for four months.[16] Combined with his previous assignment as chief of staff of the original *IV. SS-Pz.Korps*, Heilmann would have been well acquainted with the duties required of his new assignment. Before the *SS-FHA* could secure his transfer from the Eastern Front, the position was temporarily filled by *SS-Standartenführer* (*Staf.*) Peter Sommer, a *Generalstabs Oberst* (General Staff colonel) of the *Heer* who had been temporarily seconded to the *Waffen-SS* on 20 June 1943 and was later appointed as the *Chef des Stabes* of the *VI. SS-Freiwilligen Armeekorps*.[17]

With enough officers and men on hand to actually make the corps a reality (though with no divisions yet to command), Kleinheisterkamp formally assumed command of his corps in Mörchingen on 1 May 1944. The month of May went by without incident, and even the Allied landings in Normandy on 6 June failed to interrupt the corps' activation. Besides, Mörchingen was hundreds of kilometers away from the front lines and a near-peacetime atmosphere prevailed. The establishment of the corps staff and formation of the remaining corps troops continued as before until 30 June 1944, when, to the surprise of everyone, *VII. SS-Pz.Korps* was suddenly redesignated as *IV. SS-Pz.Korps* by the *SS-FHA*.[18] The staff was also informed that the corps would soon be committed to battle, but the order did not specify where.

Since it had begun formal activation on 1 May 1944, and had only partially reached its authorized strength and was still far short of qualified officers and non-commissioned officers, it was scarcely ready for such a mission. Still, Kleinheisterkamp expected that he, and the rest of his staff, would be assigned to the Western Front to assume command and control of the several SS divisions then employed under Army command in containing the Allied landings in Normandy. Instead, much to their surprise, the officers and men of the corps headquarters were ordered to begin movement to the Eastern Front by *Eiltransport* (express train) on 19 July to take control over the *5. SS-Pz.Div. Wiking* and *3. SS-Pz.Div. Totenkopf* fighting "somewhere" east of Warsaw.

The reason given for this decision for the move was the "unfavorable development of the situation in the East," an understatement to say the least given that the collapse of *H.Gr. Mitte* (Army Group Center) the previous month had rendered any coherent defense in the East nearly impossible.[19] Why the corps was renumbered from *VII.* to *IV. SS-Pz.Korps* was not stated. It would have made more sense to allow the corps to keep its original designation, rather than waste valuable time and energy changing the numerical designations of all of the corps units. Another *VII. SS-Pz.Korps* was never raised. Why the decision was made to move the corps to the East instead of keeping it in the West is also open to conjecture; perhaps the *OKW* (German Armed Forces High Command) thought that the *I.* and *II. SS-Pz.Korps* were sufficient additions to the *Heer* armies, corps, and divisions already arrayed against the Allies in Normandy. Perhaps the presence of three SS corps in such a small *Kampfraum* (area of operations) might have prompted the fear that the SS would want to create its own field army to control them, a concept that was still anathema to the *Wehrmacht* at the time.[20] Nevertheless, at the end of June 1944, the newly redesignated *IV. SS-Pz.Korps* was still classified as "undergoing formation" and not yet combat ready, since it still lacked the authorized number of troops and required amount of equipment and vehicles to fulfill its intended purpose. A rapid move to the Eastern Front, where such facilities and equipment were in short supply, would certainly delay the process.

The situation regarding the remaining corps troops, including the heavy tank battalion, corps artillery battalion, rocket launcher battalion, and medical battalion, was even worse. Most of these units would not even begin forming until late July or early August, while the heavy tank battalion would not be raised at all due to the shortage of *Panzer VI* Tiger tanks (a total of only three SS heavy tank battalions would be raised by the end of the war) and personnel to crew them. Suffering from shortages of men, equipment, vehicles, and weapons, these corps troop units would not join the rest of *IV. SS-Pz.Korps* until late August or early September 1944, by which time the battle at the gates of Warsaw was being fought in earnest.

In his first readiness evaluation of his *Hauptquartier*, *Gruf.* Kleinheisterkamp noted on 1 July 1944 that, "The elements of the corps headquarters are still in a stage of activation [but] after the delivery of its vehicles and certain items of equipment, [it] will be ready for action in eight days." This was to prove a bit optimistic, since the delivery of its equipment would be prolonged until nearly the end of the month. In regards to equipment, the corps' signal battalion was in no better shape than the corps headquarters. Its first commander, *Stubaf.* Karl Krüger, wrote on the same date as Kleinheisterkamp that:

> The general training situation of the battalion, with the exception of the *2. Feldfunk* [radio] *Kompanie* which is still in its second week of activation … is looking very positive. The battalion will be ready for action in six weeks upon the receipt of all of its vehicles. The morale of the troops is good. The battalion at this time is only 12 percent mobile and at this moment is suitable for only limited self-defense.[21]

The corps antiaircraft company, while it had been issued all nine of its 3.7cm self-propelled antiaircraft guns, had received no other vehicles at all and its gun crews still lacked training in using the *Flakvisier 37* (antiaircraft sighting device) and range calculators, but its commander, *SS-Obersturmführer* (*Ostuf.*, or First Lieutenant) Adolf Eberhard, believed that it, too, would be soon ready for action once it had received the rest of its vehicles and equipment.

Thus, the corps headquarters and corps troops were unanimous in claiming that they would be conditionally ready for battle by the end of July 1944. However, the corps' readiness suffered another blow on 19 July, when the *SS-FHA* ordered *Gruf.* Kleinheisterkamp to relinquish his post after less than three months in command. He was further informed that on 1 August 1944 he would take command of *XI. SS-Korps*, a new infantry corps then being raised from the wreckage of the German Army's *V. Armeekorps*, which had been all but destroyed in the Crimea two months before. No reason for the change in command was given, though Kleinheisterkamp's lack of experience in leading armored formations may have been a factor.

Gathering up five of the key staff officers he had brought with him from *Nord* and a few *Unterführer* and drivers, Kleinheisterkamp then departed for the Eastern Front once again to join his new command.[22] This sudden loss of so many key personnel, coupled with the shortage of vehicles and equipment, left the corps headquarters incapable of doing much of anything, let alone its primary task of controlling a corps. Nevertheless, the *Hauptquartier* and corps troops were ordered on the same day that Kleinheisterkamp received his new orders that they were to begin movement immediately to Poland, where the corps would assume command of both the *3.* and *5. SS-Panzer-Divisionen*. The corps *Chef des Stabes, Oberfüher* Nikolas Heilmann, who himself had only been back with the corps for less than a month, was charged with the supervision of the movement of the corps headquarters and corps troops to the battle zone.

In Kleinheisterkamp's place, the *SS-FHA* named *Gruf.* Herbert Otto Gille, commander of *5. SS-Pz.Div. Wiking,* as the new commander of *IV. SS-Pz.Korps*, effective from 20 July 1944.[23] However, Gille had no corps headquarters with which to exercise command, since his newly activated corps headquarters and corps troops had only just begun the weeklong process of travelling to eastern Poland in three separate trains from France through Germany. It was just as well, since Gille only had control of one division (*Wiking*) and was completely occupied leading that division in heavy defensive fighting between Bialystok and Brest-Litovsk. For its part, the *3. SS-Pz.Div. Totenkopf* was operating several hundred kilometers to the north near Grodno, where it had been beating back Soviet attacks along the Nieman River defensive line since 7 July. It had received no immediate orders to join *IV. SS-Pz. Korps* and was decisively engaged in the defense of the town of Sokolka, where it could not be spared.[24]

Now leaderless and without most of its key staff officers, the corps staff, now derisively known as a *Rumpfstab* (rump staff), and its headquarters battalion, along with the only corps troops assigned at the time, its signal battalion and antiaircraft battery, continued their journey to the unknown. Across war-torn France, Germany, and Poland they travelled in dingy *Reichsbahn* (state railway) passenger or cattle cars, at a slow pace that seemed even slower when they were shunted off to remote sidings in railyards along the way on account of other higher priority trains having the right-of-way. Except for occasional hot soup and bread provided by *Betreuungs-Einheiten* (troop health and welfare units) at stations along the way, the troops had nothing to eat but bland *Marschverpflegung* (travel rations) issued to them when they departed France. Confined to sweltering rail cars baking in the hot July sun when the trains were not moving, all the troops could do, officers and enlisted men alike, was nap when they could, drink whatever alcohol they had smuggled aboard, and play endless rounds of *Skat* (a popular German card game).

Oberfüher Heilmann, who had arrived in the lead train, could do little during this stage except keep track of where the various trains were and do his best to ensure that they all arrived where they were supposed to, which in their case was the enormous main railway yard in Warsaw. The first train arrived on 22 July, a fact that was duly reported to its newly designated higher headquarters, *Armee-Oberkommando 2* (*AOK 2*, or *2. Armee*). The remaining trains arrived on 23 and 24 July and were quickly unloaded without incident.[25] There were no other corps troops included in this movement—such as the field hospital or logistics units, which would begin arriving the following month. Once the corps staff, headquarters battalion, signal battalion, and antiaircraft battery were all assembled in march columns, they began their road movement the following day to the town of Rembertów, an eastern suburb of Praga on the eastern side of the Vistula River, where Heilmann and the rest of his men would await orders directing them where to go next.

Due to lack of key personnel, vehicles, and equipment, the corps' *Hauptquartier* was still incapable of fulfilling its mission. Meanwhile, their new corps commander was fighting 150 kilometers to the east, where he was leading the *Wiking* Division in heavy fighting north of the Bug River, where they had been subordinated to *General der Pionier* (*Gen.d.Pi.*) Otto Tiemann's *XXIII. Armeekorps* since 16 July. What lay ahead was anyone's guess. Unknown to them, however, one of the largest tank battles on the Eastern Front was about to begin and all the efforts of *IV. SS-Pz.Korps* would now be directed in slowing down the rapid Soviet advance aimed at Warsaw. It was during the following three months of nearly non-stop operations that the corps was to prove itself as a competently led and lethal organization. But before picking up the threads of the *IV. SS-Pz.Korps*' history during the battles for Warsaw and afterwards, an explanation of the composition of the corps, its key personnel and their duties, how it operated, and the history of the corps' two foremost divisions is in order.

CHAPTER 2

Organization and Duties of the *Panzer* Corps Headquarters and Staff

Herbert Otto Gille's *panzer* corps was not defined solely by two of the most famous *panzer* divisions of the *Waffen-SS* that initially made up its order of battle. While the wartime accomplishments of the *Wiking* and *Totenkopf* Divisions had become fodder for Nazi war correspondents between 1940 and 1945 and for military historians ever since, there was a great deal more to *IV. SS-Pz.Korps* than these two units. Gille's corps, like any other, was a complex organization composed of many parts, the ground combat divisions being only the most prominent. But without a guiding hand to control their activities, *panzer* divisions were mere blunt instruments.

As Helmuth Reinhardt noted in his detailed postwar study of German staff organizations of World War II, the most important function of a corps headquarters was to serve as the command authority controlling a number of divisions and other units within a field army, which itself normally consisted of two to four corps.[1] As such, the corps headquarters' primary purpose was threefold—the first being tactical and operational in nature, serving as the intermediary command layer between the division and the field army headquarters. This included the interpretation of orders originating from above and issuing its own set of orders to its subordinate units and ensuring that they were carried out.

The second mission, and just as important as the first, was the corps' role as a supply and administrative hub, responsible for estimating the requirements for food, fuel, ammunition, and other supplies for its subordinate units and requesting that these items be provided by the field army. The corps itself did not maintain its own supply depots for its divisions and the various attached *Heerestruppen*, but relied upon the field army and army group to funnel these supply goods directly to the corps' fighting formations, via a logistical process that nowadays is called "throughput," though the field army frequently maintained its own supply and ordnance depots within the corps' rear area, but not controlled by the corps.

Based on the corps' planning estimates, a variety of transportation means—including rail, truck, river, and airlift—were used to move supplies forward. In addition to determining logistics requirements, the corps was also responsible for the evacuation of damaged vehicles and equipment, its own local security, and even the harvest of local crops using troops or civilian labor. To assist the corps' *Quartiermeister* staff with their duties, detailed tables for calculating ammunition requirements, supply consumption rates, movement timetables, and a variety of other supply requirements could be found in several doctrinal publications that were excellent guides.

The corps' third role was to ensure that sufficient manpower was made available to replace losses by monitoring current casualty rates and forecasting what the needs would be for future operations so that sufficient *Marsch* (replacement or "march") battalions could be dispatched by the *Ersatzheer* (Home Replacement Army) through the army group or field army.[2] By fulfilling these last two roles—its supply administration and its personnel "strength management" roles—the corps headquarters could keep its subordinate divisions and corps troops up to authorized strength or at least as strong as possible; that is, maximizing combat power by providing supplies, replacement troops, vehicles, and weapons and by evacuating the wounded, while ensuring that deserving individuals were promoted, awarded, or even demoted. The successful performance of these myriad tasks was carried out primarily by a small number of staff officers and non-commissioned officers, who had the knowledge, skills, and abilities to carry them out. Their efforts were orchestrated and supervised by an even smaller number of qualified general staff officers, usually three or four to a corps at the most (and sometimes less).

Corps or field army commanders were not required to be general staff officers themselves, though there were several SS senior officers who did fill these leadership positions during the war who were. One of these men was *Ogruf.* Paul Hausser, who was a *Kriegsakademie*-trained general staff officer who had served on the *Kaiserheer*'s Great General Staff at the outbreak of World War I. *Gruppenführer* Gille himself was not a general staff officer, having served as an artillery officer during World War I and at one time acted as his battalion's *Adjutant* (operations officer). He *was* an experienced troop commander though, having led at the battery, battalion, regiment, and division level when he was finally selected to take over *IV. SS-Pz.Korps* in July 1944. In fact, he had already successfully led the *Wiking* Division for 14 months prior to being selected for corps command, an assignment that provided the kind of leadership experience that would stand him in good stead in his new position.

He was assisted in his daily duties by an aide-de-camp (ADC), usually a junior *Leutnant* or *SS-Untersturmführer* (*Ustuf.*), who was designated as *Ordonnanzoffizier* or *O5* (also described as his *Begleit* or escort officer), and an enlisted man to serve as his personal butler. In *Gruf.* Gille's case, his *O5* was *Ustuf.* Günther Lange, who had been selected for the position from *SS-Pz.Rgt. 5*, and *SS-Unterscharführer* (*Uscha.*) Balk. Both worked in tandem to see that the commander's everyday personal needs were met, that his transport was always at the ready to take him wherever he needed to go, and that he was provided with whatever tools he needed (binoculars, maps, telephone connection, etc.) to perform his duties. In addition, Gille had two dedicated drivers—one, *Uscha.* Pipp, who drove the corps commander's all-terrain vehicle, a Maybach *Geländewagen*, and the other, *Uscha.* Laschitzer, who drove Gille's Opel limousine.

When he served as corps commander of *IV. SS-Pz.Corps*, *Gruf.* Gille adhered to a set schedule as much as possible. In the morning, he would eat breakfast with his *O5*, who would brief him on any activities that had occurred during the evening while he was sleeping. Then Gille would be driven to the forward command posts of the divisions and corps troops to meet with their leaders and be briefed on their current situations in order to maintain situational awareness within his corps area. At noon, he would return to the corps command post to have lunch with his chief of staff, who would then update him on what had happened in his absence and whether any directives had been issued from the field army headquarters. Following lunch, which consisted of the same food being issued to his soldiers, Gille would visit units in the field before returning late in the afternoon for another briefing on that day's events. Finally, he would eat a late dinner with up to six commanders of corps units, ranging from leaders of battalions up to division level, before going to bed. The position of corps commander was a vital one that placed great demands on the health and stamina of the individual, but from all appearances and eyewitness testimony, it was a position in which Gille thrived.[3]

To assist the corps commander to lead the corps and to fulfill the corps' command and control as well as its administrative and logistical responsibilities, he was authorized a staff and headquarters consisting of 238 officers, officials, non-commissioned officers, and enlisted men. This included not only the individual staff sections, but the headquarters company that included, among others, a number of signalers, motorcycle dispatch riders, and a 15-man local security element. As were most German headquarters, it was a relatively lean organization. By comparison, a contemporary 1944 U.S. Army corps headquarters was authorized nearly twice as many men (397) and nearly three times the number of officers (103 vs. 40).[4]

The corps staff itself was composed of three main elements or functional groups which operated as the corps "brain": the *Führungsabteilung* (tactical group), the *Quartiermeister-abteilung* (supply and administrative group), and the *Adjutantur* (personnel group). The exact duties and responsibilities of each member of the staff was spelled out in detail in *Heeres-Dienstvorschrift* (Army Regulation) *H.Dv. g 92*, *Handbuch für den Generalstabsdienst im Kriege* (*Handbook for General Staff Service in Wartime*), the primary doctrinal publication governing German Army staffs at all levels, published by the *Oberkommando des Heeres* (*OKH*, or German Army High Command) on 1 August 1939.[5]

The other equally vital doctrinal work from the standpoint of the supply and administrative group in particular was *Heeres-Dienstvorschrift H.Dv. 90, Versorgungs des Feldheeres* (*Supply of the Field Army*), which described the duties to be carried out by logistical leaders at all levels. It also contained a wealth of reference tables, charts, and diagrams covering every conceivable aspect of wartime logistics for the division level and above, ranging from ammunition consumption rates to calculating road march vehicle intervals. The *Waffen-SS* followed the *Heer* doctrine virtually to the letter and wrote no unique doctrine of its own to govern how its ground combat unit staffs worked.

The *Waffen-SS* also used the same *K.St.N.* that the *Heer* used, so when it came to forming its corps (and later field army) staffs, they were identical in nearly every way, with certain exceptions, such as the aforementioned omission of the corps' chaplain position. According to *H.Dv. g 92*, which remained in effect throughout the war, the most important staff position in a corps *Hauptquartier* was the *Chef des Stabes* (chief of staff), who held overall responsibility for the supervision of the entire staff and reported directly to the corps *Kommandierender General* (*K.G.*, or commanding general).

The *Chef des Stabes* was an officer of the general staff or a graduate of the general staff course who directed and coordinated the work of all sections of the staff and was chief advisor to the commander. The 1942 *Armeekorps (motorisiert)* or *Panzerkorps* table of organization (which were identical) called for an *Oberstleutnant* (lieutenant colonel), or *SS-Obersturmbannführer* in the case of the *Waffen-SS*, to fill the chief of staff position, though the duty could be temporarily performed by an appropriately qualified *Major* or *SS-Sturmbannführer*.

Among his many duties, the chief of staff disseminated relevant tactical information to other key members of the staff in order for them to maintain situational awareness. He followed no set pattern of activity, as this was dependent upon the personality of the individual and his relationship with the commander and the rest of the staff. It was considered standard practice in the *Wehrmacht* as well as the *Waffen-SS* for the commander to select his own chief of staff, someone whom he felt comfortable operating with and could trust absolutely.

In larger staffs, such as a corps headquarters, regular briefings were customary but were usually attended only by key officers. Occasionally, the entire staff would be invited to attend, but this happened less frequently, yet again this was dependent upon the personality of the commander and his chief of staff. The chief of staff ensured that information was given out to the staff and subordinate units through a steady flow of *Befehle* (orders), *Bekanntmachung* (bulletins), *Meldungen* (reports), and other *Mitteilungen* (announcements) from higher headquarters. It was a demanding role where an individual's performance could spell the difference between the corps' success and failure. Hence, officers nominated to fill this key position were held to a very high standard of competence. The chief of staff could have a junior officer such as a *Leutnant* or *SS-Untersturmführer* (lieutenant) assigned to serve as his *Ordonnanzoffizier* or personal assistant, though this position was not authorized by the *K.St.N.*

Tactical Group

Next in importance to the chief of staff was the *Führungsabteilung* or tactical group, which performed the functions similar to those of the G-3 (operations) and G-2 (intelligence) staff sections of today's armies. The tactical group fought the current battle, planned for follow-on operations, and kept abreast of the enemy's order of battle and likely intentions. This was the largest of the corps headquarters' three functional groups and included several special staff officers as well as liaison officers. The tactical group was led by the *I. Generalstabsoffizier* (*Ia*, or First General Staff Officer).

Normally a field-grade general staff *Oberstleutnant* or *Major* or a general staff-qualified *SS-Obersturmbannführer* or *SS-Sturmbannführer*, the *Ia* was responsible for the conduct of operations, issuance of orders, messages, and reports, directing the task organization of major subordinate elements, and training and cooperation with other branches of the *Wehrmacht*. Should no qualified field-grade officers be available, in extenuating circumstances the position could be filled by a *Hauptmann* or *SS-Hauptsturmführer* undergoing preliminary general staff officer training or identified to be a potential general staff officer. One of the other prerequisites for the position was stamina, since the *Ia* usually worked 18–20 hours a day.

To assist him with his duties, the *Ia* was authorized an *Ordonnanzoffizier 1*, or *O1*, who acted as his deputy. This officer, usually a senior *Oberleutnant* or *SS-Obersturmführer* (first lieutenant), maintained the command's *Kriegstagebuch* (*KTB*, or war diary) under the supervision of the *Ia*, using the *Bestimmung für die Führung von Kriegstagebüchern* (*Regulations for the Conduct of War Diaries*) as his guide. The *O1* was normally an officer being considered for general staff training himself, based on his demonstrated proficiency or desire to become a general staff officer. He performed the duties of the *Ia* in his absence and was considered the *Ia*'s "eyes and ears" on the staff.

Another member of the *Ia* staff section was the *Id* or *Offizier für Verkehrsregelung* (March Supervision Officer), whose duties included the planning of tactical and administrative troop movement within the corps' area of operations in concert with his counterpart on the field army's staff. This included movement of the corps and its subunits by railroad, highway, air, or waterway. He was also responsible for the development of movement tables to regulate and control the pace of marching units to minimize traffic congestion, crucial when considering the movement of mechanized forces with thousands of motor vehicles. Usually, this positon was filled by a reserve *Oberstleutnant* or *SS-Obersturmbannführer* with the requisite experience in logistics, enabling him to double as a supply and transportation advisor to the *Ia*. Though often senior in rank to the *Ia*, the *Offizier für Verkehrsregelung* deferred to him as well as to the corps' chief of staff. He also could double as the *Stabsoffizier für Gasabwehr* or *Gabo* (corps gas defense officer).

The other element of the tactical group was the intelligence and counterespionage section, headed by the *3. Generalstabsoffizier* or *Ic*. This officer, usually a *Major* or *SS-Sturmbannführer*, was responsible for the procurement of intelligence information, determination of the enemy's situation and intentions, drafting orders for reconnaissance activities, communications camouflage (operational security), deception measures, and prisoner of war or civilian interrogation. Before the war this position was required to be filled by a qualified general staff officer, but by mid-1943 the shortage of these *Kriegsakademie*-educated graduates was so great that this requirement was relaxed and the *Ic* could be someone, such as a non-general staff corps reserve officer, who had gained his skills by on-the-job training in a similar or related position at the division level.[6] Both the *Ia* and *Ic* worked closely together to devise the best possible plan for approval by the corps commander and once the battle was joined, would monitor its progress and issue appropriate instructions from the commander or chief of staff via field telephone, radio, or messenger.

The *Ic* was authorized his own *Ordonnanzoffizier* as well, the *O3* (and occasionally an *O4*), who assisted him with the performance of his duties. Like the *O1*, the *O3* was also a young officer selected for his potential to become a general staff officer or who had demonstrated the ability to perform the job of *Ic*. The *Ic* might also handle his own trusted civilian agents or spies (*Vertrauensmann*, or *V-Mann*) to operate behind enemy lines, as well as maintain vigilance for any spies or agents that the enemy might be employing among the local civilian population. The corps' *Feldgendarmerie* (field police) platoon or field army *Geheime Feldpolizei* (secret field police) unit and local collaborators might also assist in this regard, along with any SS security or *Ordnungspolizei* (non-*Wehrmacht* order police) units operating in the area.

If need be, the *O1* and *O3* could work the "night shift" in the corps headquarters, enabling the tactical group to operate in battle continuously and giving the opportunity for the *Ia* and *Ic* to get some rest. Both the *Ia* and *Ic* were assisted by a number of commissioned specialists, translators, non-commissioned officers, staff corporals, and privates, for a total of 10 officers and nine enlisted men authorized for the *Führungsabteilung* by the *K.St.N.*[7] They would be supported by an additional team of signalers who would operate field telephones, radios, and teletype equipment for the tactical group. A number of mounted dispatch riders and messengers would also be at the tactical group's beck and call, ever ready to deliver messages or dispatches to higher or lower headquarters.

The tactical group also included a corps *Kartenstelle* (Map Section), consisting of one *Oberleutnant* or *SS-Obersturmführer* from the *Pionier* (engineer) branch, who was designated the *Ia Mess* or topographical officer, and three NCOs and 13 enlisted men. This section maintained a supply of relevant maps in various scales that were used by the *Ia*, *Ib*, and *Ic* for operational and planning purposes. Although this section could create maps from scratch using its own enlisted cartographers, printers, and photocopiers, it was dependent upon the field army mapping section for bulk map-printing services and resupply. This small but vital staff section ensured that hundreds of copies of maps were available and distributed throughout the corps in a timely manner, providing the tools that commanders and staffs needed to perform their duties.

In addition, the *Führungsabteilung* was augmented by several special staff officers, who advised the commander on the capabilities and employment of their respective units. Under this heading would be found the *Stabsoffizier der Pioniere* (corps engineer officer), the *Korps-Nachrichtenführer* (corps signal officer), and the

Stabsoffizier der Flakartillerie (corps antiaircraft officer). In the case of the corps signal and antiaircraft officers, they also served as the commanders of their respective corps troops battalions, in this case *SS-Nachrichten-Abteilung 104* and *SS-Flak-Kompanie 104*. In addition to their previously mentioned duties, these officers also handled the training and special supply problems of their own units, as well as that of any attached *Heerestruppen*. The *Nachrichtenführer* also supervised the establishment of the corps signal network, including landline communications, radio communications, and *Fernschreiber* (teletype) communications.[8]

Another officer who worked closely with the Tactical Group was the *Korps-Artilleriekommandeur* or *ARKO* (corps artillery commander). Although not considered a member of the corps' staff *per se*, this individual, who normally held *Generalmajor* or *SS-Brigadeführer* rank, commanded the corps' artillery headquarters and advised the corps commander on artillery matters, including the employment, capabilities, and organization of assigned or attached artillery and rocket projector units and the adjustment fire of available super-heavy artillery.[9]

The *ARKO* (a term that interchangeably denotes both the commander or the unit itself) was actually a separate organization, with its own unique *K.St.N.* Though it supported the corps staff's tactical group, it was not a part of it and could, should circumstances warrant it, be detached and assigned to another corps. In addition to the duties already mentioned, the *ARKO* was responsible for reorganizing and planning the artillery's *Schwerpunkt* (main point of effort) in cooperation with its supported corps, coordinated the fire of all artillery elements in the command, determined artillery observation missions, and laid down the framework for the communications network (both wireless and landline) of all the artillery under its supervision. The *ARKO* was normally co-located with the tactical group in order to ensure close cooperation but frequently maintained an observation post located close to the front lines.

Led by an experienced artillery officer, the *ARKO* was authorized a brigade-level staff of five officers, four NCOs, and 12 enlisted men, forming its own *Ia*, *Ib*, and *IIa/IIb* staff sections to carry out operational and logistical planning. To ensure its mobility, the *ARKO* was authorized by its own *K.A.N.* to have a total of six vehicles—two light staff cars, a 15-passenger omnibus, a medium cargo truck, and two motorcycles. The *ARKO* for *IV. SS-Pz.Korps*, which was created specifically to support it, was initially designated *SS-ARKO 104*, though by the war's end it had been redesignated *SS-ARKO 504*. Initially, *SS-ARKO 104* controlled several field army *schwere-Artillerie-Abteilungen* (*schw.Art.Abt.*, or heavy artillery battalions) and *Werfer Abteilungen* (rocket launcher battalions), but many other artillery units with varying capabilities and weapons were to be attached and detached from August 1944 until the end of the war.

Though German World War II artillery never approached the proficiency of the U.S. Army's field artillery branch, especially in regards to the ability to quickly mass fires across unit boundaries, it did allow the corps commander some options for the effective employment of artillery within that force's limited capabilities. Fortunately for *IV. SS-Pz.Korps*, all of its organic artillery regiments and battalions were motorized, enabling its *ARKO* to move them around more rapidly than horse-drawn units, which were much more common in the standard infantry corps of the era.[10]

Supply and Administrative Group

Just as the tactical group was responsible for all operations and intelligence matters, the *Quartiermeister-Abteilung* (supply and administrative group) and *Adjutantur* (personnel group) were tasked with all aspects of logistics, administration, and personnel matters. Both staff elements were generally co-located, with control being exercised by the *2. Generalstabsoffizier* or *Ib*, known more officially at the corps level as the *Quartiermeister.* This officer, who normally held the rank of *Oberstleutnant* or *SS-Obersturmbannführer*, was responsible for the overall supply situation of the corps, to include supervision of ongoing logistics operations as well as anticipating and planning for the logistics requirement of future operations. Within the supply and personnel group installation, he was also responsible for maintaining maps depicting the supply situation, special orders concerning the requisition of supplies, and for the operation of the corps' rear services. His responsibilities also included traffic regulation and supply route clearance in the corps rear area, and for these purposes he was given operational control of the corps' *Feldgendarmerie* platoon.

He, through his personal staff, was additionally responsible for the supply and administration of the corps troops and attached *Heerestruppen*, orders concerning all of the various sub-sections that concerned his staff, road construction, and passive air defense measures, such as camouflage and concealment of supply depots in the corps rear area. Finally, the *Ib* was responsible for the guarding, care, and evacuation of prisoners of war, collection of war booty such as civilian vehicles or captured enemy weapons, confiscated food supplies, and the collection and salvage of damaged materiel for repair or recycling.

Before the war, the *Ib* was required to be a qualified general staff officer. With the expansion of the *Wehrmacht* and *Waffen-SS*, the shortage of these men resulted in exceptions being made as early as 1940 to fill the necessary billets, providing that each individual, on a case-by-case basis, had either the equivalent civilian expertise or had gained sufficient experience through on-the-job-training at a lower level staff.[11] To assist him with his immediate duties, he was authorized an *Ordonnanzoffizier* or *O2*, typically an *Oberleutnant* or *SS-Obersturmführer*, generally a general staff officer aspirant, who acted as his personal staff secretary and escort officer. The *Ib* was also authorized a *Waffen- und Munitions Mitarbeiter* (specialist for ammunition, or *WaMun*), normally a *Hauptmann* or *SS-Hauptsturmführer*, a *Waffen- und Gerät Mitarbeiter* (specialist for weapons and weapons-related equipment or ordnance, or

WuG), five NCOs, and three enlisted men, for a total of 12 men in the *Quartiermeister* office, including the *Ib* himself.

The "number two" man on the corps' *Ib* staff was the *IVa*, or *Korpsintendant*. This individual functioned as the *Ib*'s deputy and was responsible for the direct supervision of the supply and administrative services that supported corps troops, including attached *Heerestruppen*. He was normally a non-general staff-qualified reserve officer, either a *Major* or *SS-Sturmbannführer*, who had civilian experience in the logistics arena. He was also responsible for the supply of the corps headquarters and corps troops with rations, the procurement of billeting areas for corps troops, arranging cash for payroll disbursement, issuing of replacement or seasonal clothing, and the stocking of individual troop items of equipment. His duties required that he work closely with the *Korps-Nachschubführer*, who commanded the corps' *Nachschubtruppe* (supply and transportation troops), a battalion-sized unit that consisted of two truck companies, a motor vehicle maintenance platoon, and a clothing repair and maintenance company, which directly supported the *Hauptquartier* and corps troops.

Inherent in his duties was the handling of supply requests from divisions and corps troops, overseeing the availability of supply and administrative personnel, monitoring the status of ration supplies within the corps, and the provision of animal feed, should mounted units come under the corps' control. Finally, the *Korpsintendant* was responsible for procuring and issuing sundry items (i.e., Post Exchange or NAAFI supplies, such as shaving soap, razor blades, toothpaste, etc.). The *Korpsintendant* would normally act as the corps' *Quartiermeister* in the *Ib*'s absence. He was assisted in his section's duties by two *Beamten* (civilian government officials holding officer rank), an NCO, and three enlisted men.

One way in which the *Waffen-SS* practice of describing staff member duty positions differed from that of the *Heer* was the former's awarding of officer ranks to those filling the positions normally staffed by civilian *Beamten* in the *Heer*. While their pre-war civilian qualifications for the positions might be the same, the senior SS leadership believed that all men serving in officer rank positions, regardless of the nature of their duties, must be SS officers first. Thus, civilian specialists desiring a career in the *Waffen-SS* must become officers and that entailed attending one of the *SS-Junkerschulen* like every other officer aspirant did. As such, these men, although performing the same civilian-type logistical and administrative functions as their *Heer* counterparts, also absorbed a degree of tactical-level training and experience that would stand them in good stead in the fighting to come.

Despite his position as the corps' senior supply officer, the *Ib* could not be knowledgeable about every aspect of logistics operations. But in addition to being assisted by the *O2* and *Korpsintendant*, he had a number of specialists working under him who were responsible for a myriad of different supply and administrative functions. For example, the *WuG* officer was responsible for overseeing the acquisition and repair of weapons and weapons-related equipment, to include artillery pieces, rocket launchers, antitank guns, and mortars. The *WaMun* officer was responsible for monitoring the status and anticipating the consumption of ammunition supplies in the corps' area of operations and submitting requests for additional shells, bombs, and bullets to the field army through the *Ib*'s office.

The *Quartiermeisterabteilung*, in addition to the usual logistics matters, also had five or six other *zugeteilte Fachbearbeiter* (assigned subject matter experts) responsible for related administrative departments that fell under the *Ib*'s supervision. These included the *IVb*, *IVc*, *IVd*, *IVe*, *V/TFK*, and *FPO* sections. The *IVb* or *Korpsartz* (corps surgeon) officer was responsible for medical matters, including the supervision of medical affairs in the corps, the care and evacuation of sick and wounded, employment of medical units, replacement of lost medical equipment or supplies, and provision of medical support to corps troops. The *IVb* was usually a surgeon or medical doctor of *Oberst* rank (*Oberstartz*) or an *SS-Oberführer*, in the case of an SS corps. He also supervised the activities of, but did not command, the corps' organic *Sanitätsabteilung*, or medical battalion. He was supported in his duties by an *Adjutant*, an *Apotheker* (apothecary, normally a civilian official), two NCOs from the medical field, and two enlisted men.

The *Korpsveterinär* or *IVc* (if assigned) was responsible for the care and evacuation of sick and injured horses, horse replacements, veterinary antiepidemic measures, and the supervision of processing of meat and meat products, as well as the employment of veterinary units. This officer usually held the rank of *Oberstabsveterinär*, equivalent to a major. The *IV. SS-Pz.Korps* did not have such an officer authorized by its *K.St.N.*, since none of its organic units were horse-drawn or mounted, so if an *Oberstabsveterinär* was assigned, he would have to be seconded by the *Heer*.

The *IVd* or *Heerespfarrer* (corps chaplain) was responsible for religious matters and the guidance of divisional chaplains as well as *Betreuungs* (spiritual welfare) work in hospitals operating in the corps' area. Since the SS considered itself above mere Christianity and in fact was rather paganist in its spiritual outlook (at least in the mind of Heinrich Himmler, who was partial to Norse mythology), no such chaplain was assigned. This flew in the face of the fact that a majority of SS men were nominally Christian or at the very least *Gottgläubig* (agnostic) and probably would have spiritually benefitted from having a chaplaincy, especially if they were seriously or mortally wounded and facing imminent death. In practice, this role was fulfilled by the *VI* staff officer or the *weltanschauliche Führung und Erziehungs Offizier*, or *WEF*, who worked for the *Adjutantur* (see below).

Since the SS did not have chaplains, the *IVd* designation was used for the *Korpszahnartz* (corps staff dentist) who was responsible for dental matters including the supervision of dental affairs in the corps, the care of dental patients, employment of dental units, replacement of lost dental equipment or supplies, and provision of dental support to corps troops. The *IVd* was usually a dentist of *SS-Sturmbannführer* rank.

The *V* staff officer or *Korpsingenier* (corps engineer), also known as the *Technischer Führer für das Kraftfahrwesen* (*TFK*, or technical leader for training transportation troops/corps motor vehicle maintenance officer), was not responsible for construction or *Pionierwesen* (the combat engineer function, which fell within the domain of the *Korpspionierführer*), but for replacement of motorized vehicles (including armor), vehicle maintenance, the training of motor maintenance personnel, and the employment of motor maintenance troops within the corps area of operations. He normally held the rank of *Oberst* or *SS-Oberführer* and was assisted by a uniformed civilian official, an NCO, and two enlisted men.

The last important element of the supply and administrative group was the *Feldpost* or field post office, led either by a civilian official with the equivalent rank of *Oberleutnant* (in the *Heer*) or an *SS-Obersturmführer*. Though technically not a subordinate element of the corps headquarters, being a separate entity with its own *K.St.N.*, in practice it was subordinated to the corps' supply and administrative group. In addition to handling the official and unofficial mail of the corps headquarters and corps troops, the field post officer advised the *Quartiermeister* concerning the employment of the field post office and provided advice on personnel matters. His additional duties included the supervision of the other field posts located in the corps area, the replacement of technical post office-related equipment, and the employment of any specialized equipment concerning the field post office.

The third staff element of the corps headquarters was the *Adjutantur* (personnel group), which was co-located with the *Quartiermeister*'s supply and administrative group. The *Adjutantur* was responsible for officer and enlisted personnel management, staff judge advocate and administrative law functions, and the supervision of the headquarters commandant. The *Adjutant*, known as the *IIa*, was overall responsible for the functioning of this staff element. Normally filled by a non-general staff *Oberstleutnant* or *SS-Obersturmbannführer*, this position was usually assigned to individuals especially trusted by the corps commander and chief of staff, since the *Adjutant* was personally responsible for officer assignments, promotions, replacements, and awards. He also supervised the *IIb*, *III*, and *VI* staff elements and headquarters commandant and was responsible for issuing staff orders and orders of the day. To carry out these duties, the *Adjutant* was assigned an additional officer (the *IIb*) and three *Beamte* (officials), three NCOs, and five enlisted men.

The *IIb* was responsible for enlisted personnel management, to include assignments, promotions, and decorations of enlisted men and non-commissioned officers, including requisitioning replacements for men killed in action or wounded so severely that they had to be evacuated to hospitals at the field army or the zone of the interior. Working closely with the *IIa*, he was usually a *Hauptmann* or *SS-Hauptsturmführer* and could fill in for the *IIa* if necessary. The corps' *III* or *Justizbeamter* (Staff Judge Advocate) was a civilian official equivalent in rank to an *Oberstleutnant* or *SS-Obersturmbannführer*. He advised the corps commander on all legal problems and issues connected with the exercise of judiciary power, including courts-martial. He also exercised review authority over judgements and sentences handed down by division judge advocates or other corps major subordinate commands.

A peculiar addition to the *Adjutantur* of SS units was the *Abteilung VI.* staff officer position, which was also called the *Weltanschauliche Führung- und Erziehungs Offizier* (*WEF*, or political guidance officer). This position, which became mandatory for all elements of the *Wehrmacht* on 1 February 1944 when they were given the formal title of *Nationalsozialistischer Führungsoffizier* or *NSFO* (for the *Waffen-SS*, the position had been required since 1937), was required to be filled by a committed Nazi in the rank of *Oberleutnant* or *Hauptmann* (or in the SS, by an *Obersturmführer* or *Hauptsturmführer*). In essence, this individual acted as the command's political officer, part cheerleader and part commissar. If officers or soldiers in certain cases were deemed to be lacking in loyalty to the regime or short of the necessary Nazi virtures, the *VI.* staff officer had the authority to have those individuals removed from their position of responsibility and recommend what sort of action be taken against them.

Gille's *IV. SS-Pz.Korps* had its own *VI.* staff officer, *SS-Hauptsturmführer* Dr. Franz Wehofsich, a 43-year-old Austrian with roots in the old Austro-Hungarian Empire. In addition to being an outgoing personality and enthusiastic Nazi (which Gille did not seem to hold against him), Dr. Wehofsich's ties to the ethnic German community in southeastern Europe made him particularly valuable, especially in light of the fact that a significant portion of Gille's command consisted of ethnic Germans (the so-called "*Volksdeutsche*") from Yugoslavia, Hungary, Rumania, and the U.S.S.R. As the corps' *VI. Stabsoffizier*, his ability to understand and motivate the corps' ethnic German contingent, especially when their homelands were being overrun by the Red Army, was a trait that Gille particularly valued, as recorded in the two efficiency reports that he wrote about Dr. Wehofsich. He was also responsible for establishing and supervising the maintenance of the corps' cemeteries as well as troop rest areas behind the front lines, echoing many of the tasks normally performed by military chaplains, which of course the *Waffen-SS* lacked.

The last part of the *Adjutantur* that the *IIa* was responsible for was the *Kommandant des Hauptquartiers* (*K.d.H.Qu.*), or headquarters commandant, whose duties will be described in greater detail in the following chapter. Though not considered a member of the corps staff, this officer, who according to the *K.St.N.* was required to be a *Hauptmann* or *SS-Hauptsturmführer*, was responsible for the internal administration of the headquarters *Unterstab* (the NCOs and junior enlisted men) and headquarters premises, rations, pay, and supervision of the corps staff's motor pool, and the guarding of the corps headquarters premises. He was directly supervised by the *Adjutant*, who was overall responsible for the day-to-day functioning of the corps' *Hauptquartier*.

Thus structured, a *panzer* corps headquarters would have been manned and equipped to conduct its three main functions—plans and operations, logistics, and personnel administration. In many respects, the corps staffs and headquarters of today's modern armies have not changed much in the past 75 years. Though different nomenclatures and titles are used to describe the various staff elements, their three basic functions have not changed at all. While they have become more complex and specialized, the corps headquarters of today would still be easily recognizable by *Ia* or *Ib* of the *IV. SS-Pz. Korps*. However, knowing how a 1944-era *panzer* corps was organized is not the same as knowing how it operated, or what sort of men were needed to function as its central "brain," let alone what their qualifications were. The following sections will examine these aspects of *IV. SS-Pz.Korps*, concluding with a brief description of the men who served in these key positions when the corps was first committed to battle in late July 1944.

Corps Operations

German headquarters staffs, like other modern armies of the period and all of those created since, relied heavily upon regulations and doctrine to guide their day-to-day operations. While the instructions contained within *H.Dv. g 92* clearly enumerated the duties of the individual staff members and staff functions to ensure commonality among divisions, corps, field armies, and army groups, the regulation did recognize that the commander and his chief of staff needed the leeway to run their headquarters as they saw fit. Generally, the corps' success relied to a great degree upon mutual trust, respect, and cooperation among its staff members in its day-to-day operations. This was one of the cornerstones of German tactical doctrine, as spelled out in *Heeresdienstvorschrift H.Dv. 300/1, Truppenführung*, and was one of the keys to their early wartime successes.

This level of harmony was increased if the commander, chief of staff, the *Ia*, *Ib*, and *Ic* had previously served alongside one another. In this manner, the corps commander would know the strengths and weaknesses of each of his key staff members, knowledge that made his duty as commander far less burdensome because it freed him from having to carry out mundane daily chores to concentrate instead on the more pressing concerns posed by any tactical situation he may have been confronted with at any particular moment. Conversely, a staff whose members had served with him before would already know their commander's idiosyncrasies, his manner of issuing orders, and most of all, how best to interpret his vision or intent for the conduct of operations—how he thought. This mutual understanding would speed up the process of analyzing a given mission and result in a more efficient and effective orders-issuing process for subordinate units, not to mention a greater chance for success.

In addition to the human dynamic inherent in a corps staff, how the headquarters facility itself was physically organized also played a role in how effectively the corps staff operated. Frequently overlooked, where and how the staff and its supporting elements were laid out, in particular the communications network, were an important determinant in its battlefield success. Unlike the massive and unwieldy headquarters staff installations of World War I, those of the successive generation had to be much smaller and more nimble, able to anticipate and react to dynamically changing battlefield situations, as well as to make the detection of their location by the enemy as difficult as possible.

This frequently required the physical separation of the *Hauptquartier* into two distinct entities—one composed of the tactical group and the other of the supply administrative and personnel groups—which might be located several or even several dozen kilometers apart from one another, depending on the situation. In such cases, the *Quartiermeister*, who generally exercised a wide degree of autonomy, would exercise control of the *Quartiermeisterabteilung* and *Adjutantur*, while the *Ia* would be responsible for the direct supervision of the *Führungsabteilung*. The supply administration and personnel staff elements would be located in the corps rear area, generally in a centrally located position or even near the corps rear boundary to facilitate communication with the field army's headquarters.[12]

The *Führungsabteilung* or tactical group's *Gefechtsstand* (command post) was smaller and more compact that the *Quartiermeisterabteilung*, and had to be mobile. It was usually located forward, often just across the rear area boundary of one of the corps' subordinate divisions, often, but not always, within the range of enemy artillery fire. This closeness to the front lines was necessary in order for the corps commander to observe and control the battle, particularly when the division in question was carrying out the corps' main effort—the *Schwerpunkt*—whether fighting defensively or offensively. The Germans believed that such intuitive understanding of the unfolding battle—often referred to as *Fingerspitzengefühl*—could only be developed in such a manner.

Often, the corps commander himself would move as far forward as a division's command post, leaving his *Chef des Stabes* or *Ia* temporarily in charge of directing the corps' operations at the tactical group's location. In such cases, the commander would move forward in his staff car, accompanied by his *Begleitoffizier*, a tracked or wheeled radio section enabling him to keep in touch with his tactical group as well as his main headquarters. This practice was a forerunner of the "jump command post" (CP) or corps "TOC" (tactical operations center) concepts practiced today by the U.S. Army as well as many NATO nations. A small element from the corps' *Begleit-Kompanie* would accompany him to provide local security. This was a prudent precaution, since several German corps commanders had already been killed in action during the past two years while visiting the front and the destruction of a corps forward command post by enemy armored or mobile forces was not unknown.[13]

At the very least, the death of a corps commander or destruction of his forward command post would have a disruptive effect on the corps' operations and often led to one of its divisions or the corps' logistics and personnel installation in the corps' rear area having to serve as a temporary corps command post until one could be reconstituted or a new corps commander appointed. This, too, happened more often than one would expect, particularly in the Soviet Union during the course of the many large-scale mobile operations that became commonplace during the summer and fall of 1943, when the Germans began their long, slow retreat to the Dnieper

River defensive line. On such occasions, Soviet mobile units would penetrate the front lines and roam in the Germans' *ruckwärtiges Gebiet* (rear area) until located and destroyed by a corps' reserve or its *Begleit Kompanie*.

The reported destruction of the entire headquarters installation of an unnamed corps during the first weeks of July 1944 by a Soviet deep attack led the commander of *Heeresgruppe* (*H.Gr.*) *Mitte*, *Generalfeldmarschall* (*G.F.M.*, or Field Marshal) Walter Model, to issue an order directing corps and divisions not to concentrate all of their command and logistics functions in one location. Rather, he directed that *Führungsabteilung* and the rest of the corps *Hauptquartier* be located no less than two kilometers apart from one another, with communications networks set up in such a way that should one command node be placed out of operation or destroyed, command and control could immediately be resumed at the alternate location. He further specified that this order applied not only to headquarters, but to artillery commands and other major subordinate units. This order naturally applied to the *IV. SS-Pz.Korps* as well.[14]

With regards to selection of the location of the "main" *Hauptquartier*, where the logistics administration and personnel staff elements were located, according to *Heeresdienstvorschrift H.Dv. g. 92*, it might occasionally have to be set up at a location chosen by its higher headquarters—e.g., the field army or *Armeeoberkommando* (*AOK*). The most decisive factor to consider when establishing a headquarters was that it had to have the potential for good communications—a good geographic location for radio communications and landline (wire) telephones, as well as road networks that allowed unrestricted movement of liaison vehicles in and out of the compound. Determining where to install telephone or radio networks, a task done in concert with the corps' signal battalion commander, took precedence over deciding where the staff would be quartered.[15]

While the use of existing buildings in towns or villages as facilities to house the corps staff was encouraged, obvious structures that would draw attention or easily recognizable locations on a map, such as a crossroads, were discouraged. Since the corps did not possess sufficient tentage to house both the headquarters and all of its personnel, the headquarters commandant, whose task was to set up the *Hauptquartier*, had to select buildings with care. While combining all of the staff elements into one facility made the functioning of the staff somewhat easier, it also made it more vulnerable to enemy direct or indirect attack.[16]

The regulation suggested instead that it was better to house each staff section in a separate building, if possible, and establish the living areas for the personnel in another area. Staffs were directed to erect air raid shelters for themselves (usually a bunker or nearby slit trench) as well as gas-proof rooms, should the installation be attacked by the enemy using poison gas. The *Adjutant* was to make his determination on the specific location of billets and headquarters locations, with the final approval being made by the chief of staff. The exact location of the corps headquarters was to be kept a secret from the enemy to ensure operational security. This was done by a variety of passive measures, including camouflage, radio, and land-line telephone discipline, and local security to prevent enemy agents from discovering its location.

The buildings containing the offices of the leadership (corps commander, chief of staff, and the tactical section), quartermaster, and personnel sections were to be denoted by the placement of command flags, signs, or directional arrows to make it easier for messengers and other visitors to find them. The regulation stressed the importance of controlling the movement of traffic through the vicinity, using one-way routing if possible. Parking of the myriad vehicles attached to the headquarters was another challenge the headquarters commandant had to face. To keep their number at a minimum to ensure that the headquarters did not attract the enemy's attention, all vehicles were to be parked several hundred meters away and camouflaged if possible. Additionally, a reporting station or waiting room for messengers had to be set up nearby, where couriers and other drivers would be readily available for service while at the same time be provided the rest and refreshment they needed between missions.[17]

Clustered nearby would be elements of the corps headquarters company, the signal battalion, the post office, field kitchen, the clothing repair and maintenance company, and other corps troops, such as the corps antiaircraft battery. Also located close by would be any field army units and installations, such as supply or ammunition depots, local security battalions, engineer units, and even prisoner of war collection points. The presence of all of these organizations would have to be registered by the corps staff, which was responsible for "real estate management" in its *Operationsgebiet* (area of operations) and to guarantee that every unit occupying ground within its corps footprint would be tied into the overall defense plan. Since there were few actual combat elements located in the corps' rear area beyond the fighting divisions' rear boundaries, most of the units located there would have to rely on their proximity to one another for local defense.

As for the routine within the headquarters, first and foremost, everything would have been governed by the tactical situation—depending on the severity of the fighting, each element of the staff would have focused on their individual duties and responsibilities. A certain order ruled over everything though, in that reports had to be received at a certain time each day from subordinate units, and reports had to be drafted and approved by the chief of staff for outgoing message traffic. A *Geschäftsordung*, or daily operating procedure, issued by the headquarters of the *9. Armee* on 10 April 1944, and still in effect when the *IV. SS-Pz.Korps* was subordinated to it, provides a good example of what the daily "battle rhythm" of a corps headquarters was like.[18]

Most important were the scheduled reports which were expected to be composed and sent periodically to the field army—such as the *Morgenmeldung* (morning report), *Mittags-* or *Zwischenmeldung* (mid-day and interim reports), and the *Tagesmedlung* (daily report).[19] From a historical standpoint, the *Tagesmeldung* was the most important, since it consisted of the summary of the day's activities and intentions for the following day. It would sometimes include the number of available armored fighting vehicles, a key indicator of the unit's combat strength.[20] The *Quartiermeister* would submit his own reports and supply requisitions separately to the field army's *Oberquartiermeister*. Often, the commander or chief of staff kept his own diary, wherein he recorded his innermost thoughts concerning what occurred on a particular day, which would have been included in the official record. Subordinate units were required to submit similar reports.

Interspersed throughout the day's events or battle rhythm would be scheduled or unscheduled conferences, situation briefs, or periodic updates. Occasionally, individual staff members might leave the command post in order to pay courtesy visits or make inspections of subordinate divisions or corps troops. Food and beverages would either be delivered to the command post in insulated containers or, if time permitted, the staff would walk to the field kitchen operated by the headquarters company. All in all, each day was filled from dawn to midnight with myriad activities that kept every member of the staff perpetually occupied, especially if the command post was displacing forward, in the case of an advance, or to the rear, in the event of a retreat.

On top of that, most staff members had to get by for weeks at a time on little sleep, perhaps four or five hours a day, and sometimes less.[21] The life of a general staff officer was best summed up by *General der Kavallerie* Siegfried Westphal, who after the war wrote:

> In wartime, the general staff officer's life was made up of work and ceaseless activity from early morning until late at night. He knew no such life of his own, as did his comrades at the front, who could at least occasionally relax during a rare rest period. For him there was no respite.[22]

Life on a corps staff was certainly not glamorous, and demanded the utmost of physical and mental effort. Few Knights' Crosses were awarded to staff officers for service on a staff. Maintaining and operating a military organization of more than 30,000 or 40,000 men was a serious business, and the strain on both officers and enlisted men could be enormous. Small wonder, then, that most officers and enlisted men, if given a choice, gladly chose to serve in a line or combat unit instead of on a division or corps staff.

Which begs the question—why would anyone want to serve as a staff officer in the first place? The work was hard, the hours long and usually thankless, with most of the credit for any successes assigned to the commanders (which is why most staff officers even today remain nameless). So the question remains: why did the *Waffen-SS* even need a general staff, if there was so little enthusiasm for one? The answer, of course, is that if it ever wished to expand and be taken seriously as a professional military organization by its rivals in the *Wehrmacht*, it had to.

The General Staff Officers of the *Waffen-SS*

Like any other military organization of its kind, it was ultimately not a corps headquarters' organizational structure, its doctrine, or equipment that gave it its military potential; it was the people who were assigned to fill the positions authorized by its table of organization who led and directed it. And not just ordinary soldiers, either, but soldiers—primarily officers—who had been specially trained to be members of the general staff.[23] In this regards, the *Waffen-SS* began World War II at a great disadvantage, in that it had very few such men, except for those who had attended the Wilhelmine-era *Kriegsakademie* prior to and during World War I. Most of these men were already occupying senior leadership positions in the SS, and therefore not available to perform these duties at the division and corps level, which were generally carried out by men in their late twenties to mid-thirties.

As a young service, the SS had no *Kriegsakademie* of its own, nor did it initially believe that it would even require a general staff or general staff officers to operate it. During the first decade of Himmler's elite guard's existence, the thought of having a formal general staff smacked of the kind of *Kaiser*-era elitism that the prewar SS and *Sturmabteilung* (SA) held in contempt, deeming such a reactionary institution to be against the tenets of National Socialism. And as an elite para-military organization dedicated to its mission of serving as the Nazi Party's Praetorian Guard, its founder, Heinrich Himmler, thought it did not need a general staff either, since most of the staff duties for their small force were of an administrative nature and could be easily performed by anyone who had served in the police, the concentration camp guard force, or the border guards, where the SS initially drew most of its young officers.

It was one of these World War I-era veterans, *SS-Brigadeführer* (*Brig.Fu.*, or Brigadier General) Hermann Cummerow, who recognized the looming problem and suggested to Himmler in the spring of 1938 that it would be advisable to think ahead and determine how many young officers then graduating from the *SS-Junkerschulen* (officer candidate schools) should be groomed for future general staff-level duties. Cummerow, the officer at the *SS-FHA* responsible for officer training and professional development, was a former *Oberst* in the *Reichsheer* and a qualified *Generalstabsoffizier* of the old *Kriegsakademie*, who knew the value of having rigorously trained officers on the staff of any respectable military organization.

Until 1936, Himmler did not believe that any would be necessary, because the armed units of the SS—the *Leibstandarte Adolf Hitler* and *SS-Verfügungstruppe*—consisted of only three independent regiments as well as four separate battalion-sized units, and were therefore not in need of a general staff since Hitler believed that no SS division-level field command led by a general officer would be created, should there be a war.[24] Hitler was not, at first, even convinced that the SS needed to serve in combat. However, when the first two SS divisions were raised after the end of the Polish campaign in October 1939 (the *SS-Verfügungs-Division*, which was later redesignated as *Das Reich,* and *SS-Division Totenkopf*), Himmler's thinking began to quickly evolve on the subject. Shortly afterwards, he approved a proposal in 1940 to create up to three general staff positions on each division's staff.[25]

However, any further progress on Cummerow's proposal required cooperation on the part of the *Heer*. During the fall of 1939, the *Heer* itself had insufficient numbers of qualified general staff officers for its own units (that year it required 730, more than double its peacetime number), and certainly was not willing to loan any to the SS, which it still viewed as a paramilitary organization. Hitler's thoughts are not known, but he most likely would have deferred to the *Heer*, at least in this instance. Finally, on 18 November 1939, the *Heer* relented. In an *Erlass* (decree) announced by the *OKH* on that date, it agreed to allow up to two SS officers to attend the school (out of a total of 60 students), but with the *Kriegsakademie* in Dresden having been closed "for the war" in September, SS attendance was rendered moot.[26] Fortuitously, it was reactivated in January 1940 after a four-month hiatus, but a new staff and faculty had to be recruited and assigned from scratch. New lesson materials had to be produced, instructors trained, and facilities rehabilitated, but the first wartime course began as scheduled before the end of January.[27]

Himmler did attempt to work out an arrangement before the war that would have had general staff officers from the *Heer* seconded to the SS on a temporary basis. He believed that they would help raise the professional standards of his organization so that its units would be able to participate in peacetime large-scale exercises and increase the *Verfügungstruppe*'s combat readiness. This secret memorandum, addressed to Hitler, was signed by Himmler on 18 May 1939 and proposed, among other things, that SS officers also be allowed to stand for the *Kriegsakademie* exams and to attend the peacetime general staff course. Nothing came of this, however, because the *Heer* at that point was less than enthusiastic about allowing SS officers to become enrolled in school, where vacancies were at a premium, and was short of trained staff officers for its own units.

With the *Kriegsakademie* back in operation by January 1940, it still took behind-the-scenes persuasion on the part of Cummerow, Hausser, and Jüttner to convince the *Heer* to actually make student seats available for up to two SS officers. However, they could only attend as *Gasthörer* (guest students) in the second *Generalstabslehrgang* (general staff course) conducted from April–June 1940. Neither officer, though they successfully completed the course, were allowed to join the *Heer*'s *Generalstabkorps*, which considered itself a closed community that did not welcome outsiders, especially any from an organization that was still considered to be primarily political in nature as well as a possible rival to the *Heer*. Even Himmler perpetrated an indignity upon the two graduates, whom he refused to allow adding the traditional term *in Generalstab* or i.G. after their ranks—the only title he allowed them to claim was that of *Führungsgehilfe*, or leader's assistants.

Another impediment to attending the *Kriegsakademie* was that potential applicants had to have completed six years of active duty service as officers, in addition to having demonstrated the potential to successfully complete the course. This applied to any general staff officer aspirant, whether he was in the *Heer* or not. This ruled out the majority of SS junior officers then serving, since most of them did not receive their officer patents until after 1934, when the first *Junkerschule* class graduated. In contrast, the *Heer*, which by comparison was a much larger organization, was a continuation of the *Reichsheer* and had an entire generation consisting of thousands of young officers who met the preliminary entrance requirements. Like the *Waffen-SS*, it also was in the process of expanding in size and needed additional general staff officers to fill its own newly activated divisions, corps, and field armies.

Despite the *Heer*'s less than welcoming attitude in regards to allowing more than two SS officers to attend the *Kriegsakademie*, as many as 200 young SS officers, especially those serving in the *Verfügungstruppe* or the *Leibstandarte Adolf Hitler* bodyguard regiment, as well as 100 from the *Ordnungspolizei* (Order Police), had already served as exchange officers in neighboring army units from 1936–39. The orders mandating that the *Heer* institute the exchange program originated from Hitler himself, who felt that this *Kommandierungen zum Heer* (secondment to the Army) was needed in order to foster greater cooperation and to upgrade the status of the SS in the eyes of the three branches of the *Wehrmacht*.

Here, young officers such as future *Ostubaf.* Paul Kausch, *Ostubaf.* Otto Weidinger, and *Staf.* Johannes Mühlenkamp performed duties as platoon or company commanders for several months. Mühlenkamp made such a positive impression within the army unit he was seconded to, *Kradschüzten-Bataillon 2* (2nd Motorcycle Battalion) of the *2. Pz.Div.*, that its commander attempted to induce him to switch over to the *Heer*. One well-known individual who later served in the *Wiking* Division as a regimental commander, Franz Hack, was one of these young officers seconded to the *Heer*, assigned to *Infanterie-Regiment 69* in Ingolstadt in mid-1938. After the war, he commented:

> I was assigned as a platoon leader in the *4.* [M.G. or Machine gun] *Kompanie* of the *IV. Bataillon* in Eichstätt. *Oberstleutnant* Philippi first introduced me as a *Leutnant* to the officer corps of the battalion … in the first weeks I was taken in hand by key leaders in the company to be taught the basics before they would allow me to lead without direct supervision, then in May I was allowed to take over the leadership of the battalion's NCO training course, followed by assignment to the regimental staff as an *Ordonnanzoffizier* during its live-fire exercises at the training area. The officer corps [of the regiment] treated me from beginning to end in a very friendly manner and displayed a great deal of comradeship. In many conversations, the subject of the situation concerning the relationship between the *Heer* and SS was freely discussed … the commander repeatedly mentioned to me that he was trying to arrange for my transfer [from the SS to the *Heer*] to serve as his regiment's training officer for heavy infantry weapons. In the autumn of that year, I rode with the others during the regiment's *Hubertusjagd* and even temporarily took command of the *4. (MG) Kompanie.*[28] In December 1938, this secondment came to an end, and I went back to the *SS-Verfügungstruppe*.

Hack went on during the war to put the skills he learned from his time with the Army to good use and ended the war as an *Obersturmbannführer* leading a *Panzergrenadier* regiment. In addition to fostering a greater sense of comradeship with the *Heer*, as related in Hack's account, *Brig.Fü.* Cummerow and other prominent SS leaders, such as *Ogruf.* Steiner, believed that this program also enhanced the professional skills of the SS junior leadership and saw it as a model to prepare SS officers for possible entry into the *Kriegsakademie*.

The wartime prerequisites for selecting of SS officers for general staff training at the *Kriegsakademie* were the same as those for the *Heer*. The officer had to have demonstrated meritorious service for at least half a year as front-line company, battalion, or battery commander, an unsullied character record, and an unconditional recommendation for general staff service by superior commanders.[29] As previously related, no SS officers were selected to attend the first wartime general staff course that graduated on 6 April 1940, but two were chosen for the second course, which they successfully completed on 14 June 1940. One of them, *Stubaf.* Willi Baumann, served as the *Ib* of *6. SS-Gebirgs-Division Nord* from December 1943 until April 1944, when he was assigned as the *Quartiermeister/Ib* of *VII. SS-Pz.Korps*. When that corps was renumbered as *IV. SS-Pz.Korps* in July 1944, he was taken along by *Ogruf.* Matthias Kleinheisterkamp in July 1944 to form the staff of the new *XI. SS-Armeekorps*.

Of the two SS officers who attended the third wartime course, now relocated from Dresden to Berlin, only one, *Hstuf.* Georg-Waldemar Rösch, graduated on 5 January 1941 with a *sehr gut* (excellent) evaluation, while the other officer failed. Four *Hauptsturmführer* graduated from the fourth *Generalstabslehrgang* on 15 March 1941. At the same time, five additional SS officers attended a sub-course specially set up at the *Kriegsakademie* to train supply officers; upon successful completion, all of them were subsequently assigned to serve as a corps or division *Quartiermeister* or *Ib*. Following the graduation of the fourth wartime course, the *Kriegsakadmie* temporarily shut down from April–December 1941 due to the personnel turmoil caused by the heavy losses of general staff officers during the first six months of the campaign against the Soviet Union, which resulted in the posting of the entire staff and faculty to the Eastern Front.

The school did not begin classes again until 2 March 1942, when the fifth wartime course commenced. Five SS officers attended this course, which graduated on 9 May 1942. Included in this number was *SS-Ostubaf.* Georg Meier, who later rose to become the *Ia* of *6. SS-Pz.Armee* during the February 1945 offensive in Hungary. Future leaders Manfred Schönfelder and Max Wünsche both graduated with honours from the sixth *Lehrgang* on 9 August 1942 along with four other SS officers. However, *Hstuf.* Wünsche would go on to command the panzer regiment of the *12. SS-Pz.Div. Hitlerjugend* and would not see general staff duty despite having the qualifications to serve in that capacity. The attraction of serving as a commander of troops still outweighed the potential benefits of serving as a member of the SS general staff.

While SS officers had proven themselves by this time as being just as qualified to be general staff officers as their equally talented *Heer* counterparts, the numbers being graduated fell far short of what was needed for both services. By the summer of 1942, eight *Waffen-SS* divisions were in the field or being activated, with more being contemplated, creating an immediate need for up to 24 qualified general staff officers—e.g., a *Ia*, *Ib*, and *Ic* for each division. The activation of an *SS-Panzerkorps* headquarters was also being contemplated, which would raise the demand even higher.[30] The various offices in the rapidly expanding *SS-FHA* also needed qualified general staff officers to manage its growing empire.

A plan was needed to manage the increasingly complex SS officer professional development program, so on 11 April 1942 *Ogruf.* Jüttner signed an order which laid out the wartime standards and requirements for *Waffen-SS* general staff officer candidates. Among other things, the order required that commanders provide by-name nominations of those officers they considered to have potential to serve as general staff officers. Still, it did little to increase the number of school vacancies available to SS officers at the *Kriegsakademie*, which frustratingly remained beyond Himmler's and Jüttner's control. While the few *Kriegsakademie*-trained SS officers were beginning to make their professional competence felt, most of the staff officer positions throughout the *Waffen-SS* were still filled with men who were only minimally qualified for their jobs, a factor that lessened the efficiency, and hence the combat effectiveness, of the SS units serving in the field.

Matters came to a head in the spring of 1943 when *Ogruf.* Hausser, by then in command of the *SS-Pz.Korps* and while the battle of Kharkov was still raging, wrote to Himmler on 15 March informing him that the system for acquiring general staff officers was totally inadequate and that the units in the field were suffering due to the lack of qualified incumbents and the incompetence of a few. Hausser wrote:

> Losses of *Waffen-SS* general staff officers and of the young officers who have been selected to be future staff officers, as well as the considerable shortages of qualified men to fill these positions, has led me to propose to you that young general staff officers of the *Heer*, who have a wish to do so, be temporarily taken into our ranks [as general staff officers] in exchange for some of our own officers, who desire to pursue a general staff career of their own, be seconded to army field commands where they would gain the necessary experience. The use of proven troop leaders in general staff positions without the fundamental education in general staff duties has not stood the test. In hindsight, the operation that we have recently concluded highlighted serious difficulties that showed that not all of our officers filling general staff positions had the necessary schooling.[31]

Hausser thought that this problem was so significant, and the need for general staff officers in his corps so urgent, that he proposed to Himmler that a discussion be initiated with *Generaloberst* Kurt Zeitzler, the chief of staff of the *OKH*, as soon as possible in order to "borrow" general staff officers from the *Heer*.

In order to temporarily address the acute shortage, Hausser was even willing to consider replacing his own general staff officers with Army ones "on temporary loan" until sufficient qualified SS staff officers became available. Although Himmler summarily dismissed Hausser's request, which only four years before had been suggested by Himmler himself, by the end of the year he was forced to relent and began to accept the secondment of Army general staff officers. By the war's end, 22 Army general staff officers had been assigned to fill *Waffen-SS* staff positions, ranging from service as the *Ia* at division level (such as *Major* Mitzlaff with the *8. SS-Kav.Div. Florian Geyer*), to service as chief of staff at a corps (*Gen.Maj.* Joachim Ziegler, *III. (germ.) Pz.Korps*), to chief of staff of a panzer army (*Gen.Maj.* Fritz Kraemer, *6. SS-Pz.Armee*). While some of these men retained their Army uniforms, a few transferred to the *Waffen-SS*, exchanging their traditional *Kragenspiegel* (collar insignia) for SS runes.

Becoming a general staff officer did not merely entail successful completion of the wartime *Kriegsakademie* course; there were also preliminary requirements that had to be completed. First, the officer had to have successfully served as an *Ordonnanzoffizier* on the staff of a regiment or higher, followed by successful command of a company-sized unit in the infantry, *panzer* troops, cavalry, combat engineers, or artillery. Having demonstrated his potential, he would then request to attend the general staff officer course. Once his request was approved, he would serve in various temporary staff positions in both field and staff for a period of up to two months to gain practical instruction and experience. During this probationary period, he might serve as a division *Ic* for two or three weeks, then move to a corps headquarters to serve as its *Ia* for the same amount of time. He would also, if circumstances permitted, temporarily command a battalion in the field before he would finally be released to attend the *Kriegsakademie*. All the while he would be evaluated by the responsible division or corps commander, who would determine whether he demonstrated his fitness to attend the general staff course.

The general staff officer course was gruelling, to say the least. The course, which normally lasted a year-and-a-half in peacetime, had to be condensed in order to accommodate the rapidly growing number of vacancies created as the *Wehrmacht* expanded after 1940. For the student, each day was packed with instruction periods, lectures, and practical exercises, including sand table exercises and tactical exercises without troops. After classes were complete for the day, students would participate in sports activities, cultural events, or sightseeing. If they were married, they were allowed to bring their family with them, and wives would be expected to participate in social activities. Family accommodation was not provided and students were expected to pay for their lodging.

The 12-week curriculum, in its final form, included general education, tactics (which received the greatest amount of students' time), military intelligence, logistics (including supply and transportation), working with other branches of the *Wehrmacht*, and ideological indoctrination. As a result of this training, the student was expected to have developed the ability to judge a situation quickly, accurately, and realistically, as well as the technique of issuing proper orders. The final portion of the course was set aside for their formal evaluation, which would result in the student receiving a "qualified/ready for assignment as a general staff officer" evaluation, a "not yet ready" evaluation, or a "not suitable for assignment" evaluation, which equated to a failing grade. Those deemed "not yet ready" would be returned to their units where they would be tutored in their weakest subjects before being re-evaluated at some point in the future to determine whether they had the knowledge to receive a "qualified" evaluation.

The course itself, once it was reinstated, initially required eight weeks to complete (in 1940), then six months, and finally standardized at four months during the last year of the war. Upon graduation, the newly minted general staff officer would most likely first be sent to a weapons school for a month of refresher training before being posted to the front to serve as *Ia* or *Ib* at the corps level. Then, having proven himself after two or three months in this position, he would be assigned as a division *Ia*, where the demand for qualified general staff officers was greatest. The total amount of time required to become a general staff officer, including practical instruction while seconded to a front-line unit, was generally 18 months.[32] A total of 17 general staff officer classes, including over 1,000 students, were conducted by the *Kriegsakademie* during the war, with the last one still in session when the war ended.

Obersturmbannführer Manfred Schönfelder, who served as the chief of staff of *IV. SS-Pz.Korps* from August 1944 until the end of the war, was an early graduate of the course, having completed it on 8 August 1942. After the war, he commented that:

> The course included a preliminary secondment to the *Heer* from January to May 1942. I was assigned to the *18. Pz.Div.* in the area of Suchinitschi. Within this timeframe, I was placed at the disposal of the division for practical instruction and experience in combat as leader of a tank company, a combat engineer company, and a heavy infantry howitzer battery. This was then followed by a 14-day period of service within the *Quartiermeister Abteilung* of a corps headquarters [*XXIV. Armeekorps*]. In my student section at the General Staff Course, I was the only one with wartime experience as the commander of a *Panzergrenadier* battalion and already had experience in battle with combined arms within the framework of a battalion-sized task force. On the occasion of a visit [to the *Kriegsakademie*] by the then-Chief of the General Staff General Halder near the end of the course, I was employed as a division commander for a planning exercise, a task I apparently carried out successfully. Based on my own experience, I can only describe the relations between officers of the *Waffen-SS* and those of the *Heer* as ranging from good to very good."[33]

His evaluation, signed by the commander of the *Kriegsakademie*, *Generalmajor* Kurt Weckmann, states that Schönfelder "promised to be an excellent general staff officer" and that he possessed an "unusually pronounced sense of what was possible" and an "outstanding tactical sensibility." This is a noteworthy statement, in that it contradicts the assertion made in January 1945 by *General der Panzertruppe* (*Gen.d.Pz.Tr.*) Balck that Gille's chief of staff was untrained and incompetent, during an incident which will be related in a following chapter.

Meanwhile, despite the war's changing fortunes, the size of the *Waffen-SS* general staff officer corps continued to grow, though the number of officers attending the

Kriegsakademie never kept pace with the corresponding growth of their organization. Four more officers of the *Waffen-SS* took part in in the first general staff course taught during 1943; one graduate obtained a *hervorragend qualifiziert* rating (outstanding qualification), while three others failed. A total of 13 graduated that year, with another 13 graduating by the end of July 1944. Each successive *Lehrgang* allocated more vacancies to the *Waffen-SS*, though never enough to satisfy the need. Over a dozen additional officers successfully graduated from the last two complete courses taught during the war, while at least a dozen others were still enrolled in the final two when the war ended, including *Hstuf.* Werner Westphal, who had briefly served as Gille's *1a* between August and November 1944.

Most of these men, if not captured when the *Kriegsakademie* (finally located at Lengries at the war's end) was overrun, were rolled into last-ditch organizations where they were put to use as staff officers, whether they had completed the course or not. Some of them, such as *SS-Stubaf.* Richard Pauly, who had been *IV. SS-Pz. Korps'* first *Ia*, found themselves posted to the hastily raised *38. SS-Grenadier Divison "Nibelungen,"* formed using 1,000 cadets from the *Junkerschule* at nearby Bad Tölz, 8,000 teenaged draftees from the 1928 year group, and several battalions of Hitler Youth. This division, like every other unit still fighting in Bavaria, was overwhelmed by the Allied offensive and forced to surrender near Trauenstein to the U.S. 101st Airborne Division on 8 May 1945.

Most of the *Kriegsakademie* records of the SS officers who attended the last two general staff officer courses were lost in the maelstrom of the war's last few months. According to the *Bundeswehr*, the postwar successor of the *Heer*, none of the SS officers who completed the general staff officer course are considered to have been general staff officers, even to this day. In the semi-official history of the German general staff officer corps, *der deutsche Generalstabsoffizier*, their names are not even mentioned. In all, approximately 100 SS officers attended or completed the *Kriegsakademie* course from June 1940 to May 1945. Failure or non-completion of the course did not leave a blemish on a man's service record; even if an SS officer failed his final examination, he would still have been used as a staff officer or a line officer once he returned to his former unit, in the hope that he could apply to retake his evaluation at some point in the future.[34]

Despite Himmler's attempts to put more SS officers into the general staff course, he was only partially successful; the supply never came close to meeting the demand. As of 1 August 1944 there were only 57 graduates serving in general staff officer billets, along with 22 others who had been seconded from the *Heer*. The number does not take into consideration how many may have been killed, captured, or incapacitated by that point.[35] Therefore, in August 1944 there were only 79 men serving in the *Waffen-SS* as general staff officers to fill the 190 authorized positions in the 38 SS divisions, 17 SS corps, and two SS field armies (*6. SS-Pz.Armee* and *11. Pz.Armee*) activated by the end of the war. The number of available qualified general staff officers amounted to a huge shortfall, even if one discounts the *Ic* positions, where the general staff officer qualification requirement had been dropped the year before.[36]

This change, decreed by the *Heer* (which was facing the same challenge) in mid-1943, lowered the numbers of qualified general staff officers that the *Waffen-SS* needed from 190 to 133, but it left it still 54 men short of what was required. By this point of the war, the standards had been relaxed so much that even the *Quartiermeister* or *Ib* position could be filled by a non-general staff officer, as long as he had demonstrated the potential in a lower-level assignment (such as serving as a division *Ib*) or had civilian-acquired skills that were equivalent.

This lowered the number of required general staff officers to a bare minimum—usually only one or two on an SS division staff (the *Ia* and *Ib*) and two or three on an SS corps staff (the *Chef des Stabes*, *Ia*, and *Ib*). As previously mentioned, the *Heer* was also suffering from a lack of qualified staff officers, but it gave its own needs a higher priority over that of the *Waffen-SS* until August 1944, when Himmler took over as head of the *Ersatzheer* (Replacement Army).[37] This finally allowed him to dictate *Heer* personnel policy and allocate more school vacancies to the *Waffen-SS*, but by then the war was already as good as lost.

During its short history, only four fully qualified general staff officers were ever assigned to *IV. SS-Pz.Korps*, with no more than two serving together at one time. While the norm for a contemporary *panzer* corps of the *Heer* usually had three or four simultaneously assigned, *Gruf.* Gille's corps had to make do with less since the number of available qualified general staff officers in the *Waffen-SS* was smaller. The first of its two chiefs of staff, 41-year-old *Oberführer* Heilmann, who served from 25 June to 5 August 1944, was not school-trained, having transferred from the prewar *Schutzpolizei* into the SS in May 1939. He departed the corps after only two weeks in combat, being reassigned to the *SS-FHA* on 5 August. His successor, *Ostubaf.* Schönfelder, was a graduate of the sixth general staff officer course, graduating on 15 August 1942. He served as the *Chef des Stabes* from 5 August 1944 to 8 May 1945, and was present throughout all of the corps' toughest battles and the retreat into Austria.

From July 1944 until May 1945, *IV. SS-Pz.Korps* was assigned six permanent or temporary *Erste Generalstabsoffizier* or *Ia*. The first was *Stubaf.* Richard Pauly, a general staff aspirant who served as the acting *Ia* of the corps from 15 July–5 August 1944 during the practical instruction phase of the training program. He had initially been appointed an infantry officer in the *Totenkopf* Division, where he served as a company commander and regimental adjutant on the Eastern Front from 1941–42. Following this duty, he was assigned as an instructor and student group leader at the *SS-Junkerschule* in Braunschweig, where he spent the next two years. Before his assignment to *IV. SS-Pz.Korps*, he had already fulfilled a month of his general staff officer probationary status in France from 15 June–15 July 1944 on the staff of *9. SS-Pz.Div. Hohenstaufen* and with the headquarters of *II. SS-Pz.Korps*. After successfully completing three more weeks at the corps level with *IV. SS-Pz.Korps*, he served as the acting *Ia* of *5. SS-Pz.Div. Wiking* from 5–22 August 1944. Having completed these prerequisites, he was sent home to Germany, where he attended the *15. Generalstabslehrgang* at Hirschberg from 20 September 1944 to 26 January 1945. Following successful completion of the course, Pauly later served as a general staff officer with *38. SS-Gren.Div. Niberlungen* in April 1945.

Hauptsturmführer Pauly's successor was *Hstuf.* Westphal, a veteran *Wiking* officer who, like Pauly, was a general staff officer aspirant assigned as acting corps *Ia* from 18 August–9 November 1944 to complete his preliminary period of practical instruction. He had already served as the *O1* of the *Wiking* Division for several months, and had commanded a *Panzergrenadier Kompanie* in the division for two months before being elevated to the corps headquarters. Before replacing Pauly, Westphal had been serving as the corps *O1* since 28 July and probably performed the *Ia*'s duties until being formally designated so on 18 August. Because he was kept on beyond the starting date for the same general staff officer course that Pauly was scheduled to attend, Westphal was instead enrolled in the 17th course, which did not begin until mid- to late January 1945. It is unknown whether he successfully graduated; the course was still in session at the end of war and any subsequent assignment would be mere conjecture.

Sturmbannführer Wilhelm "Willi" Klose was the corps' third *Ia*, and its first fully qualified general staff officer course graduate, having successfully completed the *14. Generalstabsoffizier Lehrgang* on 6 September 1944. A veteran of the *Wiking* Division, he had served in its *SS-Pz.Gren.Rgt. 9 Germania* on the Eastern Front for over a year until he was seriously wounded in October 1942. He then served as a tactics instructor at the *SS-Junkerschule* in Bad Tölz in January 1943 and at the *SS-Panzergrenadier* school in Prosetschnitz in March 1943 until he began general staff officer preliminary training in May 1944 on the staff of the army's *XXI. Armeekorps*. After completion of this phase, he was assigned as the corps *Ia* of *IV. SS-Pz.Korps* from 9 November 1944 to 16 January 1945 before he was finally reassigned to become the *Ia* of *Wiking* Division, where he served until the end of the war. Interestingly, he replaced *Major i.G.* Otto Klein, a general staff officer of the *Heer* who had been seconded as the *Ia* of *Wiking* on 5 August 1944, who himself had replaced *Ostubaf.* Schönfelder, who of course had moved up to become the corps chief of staff.

The corps' fourth *Ia*, *Stubaf.* Fritz Rentrop, like Klose, was a graduate of the same *Lehrgang* of the staff officer course and served as Klose's successor from 16 January 1945 until he was wounded and captured by the Soviets on 2 February while returning to the corps' *Gefechtstand* in Hungary (he succumbed to his wounds soon thereafter). The 27-year-old Rentrop, a recipient of the Knight's Cross awarded for valor on 13 October 1941 for commanding an antiaircraft battery of the *Das Reich* Division on the Eastern Front, had been an instructor at the *SS-Junkerschule* in Bad Tölz before being selected to attend the *Kriegsakademie*. Prior to attending the staff officer course, he had fulfilled his preliminary instructional period while serving on the staff of *XVII. Pz.Korps* from 10 April–2 May 1944.

Until a replacement for Rentrop could be assigned, *Hstuf.* Johann-Freidrich Velde served as acting corps *Ia* from 2 February–1 March 1945. Until that time, the highly decorated Velde had been serving as the corps *O1* since September 1944, and would have had the experience and situational awareness needed to effectively function in this highly demanding duty position. A Dane from the town of Aarup, he had already been identified as a potential general staff officer and was slated to fill the next available vacancy in the *16. Lehrgang*, but would now have to wait until a student seat opened up for the 17th wartime course, scheduled to begin in mid-April 1945. That opportunity, of course, never came, and Velde continued to serve as the corps *O1* until the end of the war after the assignment of Friedrich Rausch as *IV. SS-Pz.Korps*' last *Ia*.

The aforementioned *Stubaf.* Friedrich Rauch, a graduate of the *15. Lehrgang*, conducted from 20 September 1944 until 26 January 1945, took over his duties as corps *Ia* from acting *Ia* Johann Velde on 1 March 1945. Rauch, an artilleryman from Berlin, had served as a battery commander in the artillery regiment of *3. SS-Pz. Div. Totenkopf* before being chosen as an instructor and student group leader for the *SS-Junkerschule* in Bad Tölz. Rausch had earned the Iron Cross First and Second Classes, as well as the Infantry Assault and Black Wound Badges while serving on the Eastern Front with *Totenkopf*. Prior to attending the general staff officer course, Rauch had completed his preliminary practical instruction period as the *O1* of *II. SS-Pz.Korps* from 15 June–15 August 1944, while that corps fought against the Allied invasion in Normandy. His arrival coincided with the beginning of the Third Reich's last offensive on the Eastern Front, Operation *Frühlingserwachen (Spring Awakening)*, which began on 6 March 1945. He was Gille's last corps *Ia* and went into captivity along with the rest of the corps headquarters on 8 May 1945.

There were three other staff positions that in peacetime would normally have been filled by graduates of the *Kriegsakademie*—the *Quartiermeister/Ib*, the *Ic*, and the *Adjutant*. None of these positions in *IV. SS-Pz.Korps* were occupied by qualified general staff officers, there being too few to spare, so instead they were filled by officers whom the *SS-FHA* deemed to be *durch Leistung qualifiziert* (qualified based on their performance) in similar positions. Upon the departure of *Ogruf.* Kleinheisterkamp at the end of July 1944 to take command of the *XI. SS-Korps* along with his own hand-picked staff, all three of these now-vacant positions were filled in early August by officers who had been performing the same duties while assigned to the *Wiking* Division, and therefore already had Gille's trust. All three held their staff positions until the end of the war.

The corps *Quartiermeister/Ib* was *Ostubaf.* Hans Scharff, a native of Kassel-Harleshausen. After a 12-year career in the *Reichswehr*, where he served as both an infantryman and artilleryman, he joined the SS in July 1934. His career in the

Waffen-SS began when he was briefly assigned to the elite *Leibstandarte Adolf Hitler* regiment on 19 June 1940. He was transferred to the *Wiking* Division in August 1940, where he served as an infantry company commander before being assigned as the artillery regiment's supply officer, then as its adjutant, and finally as a battery commander before being chosen to serve as the division's *Ib* in January 1944. When Gille selected him in August 1944 to serve as *IV. SS-Pz.Korps' Ib*, he already had amassed a year-and-a-half of practical experience as a supply officer at the regimental and division level. At 41 years of age, he was too old to be eligible to attend the general staff officer course, but evidence indicates that he performed his duties as *Quartiermeister* efficiently, as evidenced by the awarding of the German Cross in Silver on 10 February 1945.

The corps *Ic* or staff intelligence officer was *Stubaf.* Dr. Herbert Jankuhn, a native of Angerburg in East Prussia and a well-known archeologist before the war. Born in 1905, Dr. Jankuhn began his active duty SS career in 1942, after rising to the honorary rank of *SS-Obersturmbannführer* in the *Allegemeine SS*, which he joined in 1936. Here, he served as a specialist in the *Presse und Kriegswirtschaft* (Press and Wartime Economic Administration) branch of the *SS-Ahnenerbe* office of the *SS-Hauptamt*, being responsible, among other things, for surveying the museums and cultural inheritance in the occupied areas of Eastern Europe.[38] Promoted to the active duty rank of *SS-Sturmbannführer* on 30 January 1944, Dr. Jankuhn was assigned to *Wiking* Division to be its *Ic* in March 1944 before being elevated to become *IV. SS-Pz.Korps Ic* in August of that year, due to his "excellent conduct," and as an officer who had proven himself in "conduct before the enemy."

Lastly, the corps' *Adjutant* or chief personnel officer was *Stubaf.* Karl-Willi Schulze, a veteran officer from Kiel who began his SS career in the *Germania* Regiment in December 1936. He rose through the ranks from platoon leader to company commander and then as its regimental adjutant, when it was incorporated into the *Wiking* Division in 1940. He was elevated to the position of division *Adjutant* in April 1944, so it was natural for him to become the *IV. SS-Pz.Korps' Adjutant.* As Gille's trusted advisor on personnel matters, Schulze would have had intimate knowledge of all of the corps' officers and their personal issues, and would have maintained good connections with the *SS-FHA* personnel office in Berlin. A proven officer and leader, by 1941 Schulze had earned both the Iron Cross, First and Second Classes as well as the German Cross in Gold for his actions during the breakout from the Cherkassy Pocket.

Thus composed, the staff of *IV. SS-Pz.Korps* was certainly adequately led, if not equipped. With the corps commander, in the person of *Gruf.* Gille, providing the guidance and dynamic leadership they needed, the staff would do their utmost to interpret his intent for the conduct of current and future operations while conforming as closely as possible to their superior field army's or army group's orders. Although a corps commander and his staff's ability to exercise creative

Truppenführung (mission-type leadership) was becoming ever more constrained by Hitler's increasingly restrictive meddling in tactical affairs by the summer of 1944, a corps could operate with a limited amount of independence and still attain most of its objectives, even with fewer troops or tanks to work with. The successful operations of *IV. SS-Pz.Korps* at the gates of Warsaw from August–November 1944 is a case in point, demonstrating what results could still be achieved if commanders were only left alone to fight their battles the way they saw fit. Of course, a *panzer* corps was not composed solely of a commander and his staff, nor of infantry or *panzer* divisions, no matter how talented or battle-proven they were. In order to function effectively, a corps still had to be supported by corps and army troops—the last ingredient of a successful corps—and *IV. SS-Pz.Korps* was fortunate in this regard.

CHAPTER 3

Organization of Corps and Army Troops

A corps is made up of far more than two or three armored or infantry divisions. While these constituted the corps' primary striking power, they were but one aspect of an organization that, with corps and army troops accounted for, could grow in size to as many as 50,000 or more men. Each corps commander and his *Korpsstab*, whether they commanded and controlled a *Panzerkorps*, an *Armeekorps,* or a *Gebirgskorps*, were supported by several affiliated organizations whose purpose was to provide communications, logistical, medical, and administrative services. The corps was also authorized organizations whose purpose was to either protect the corps headquarters installation itself, or to serve as a means to control other subordinate organizations of a similar function, such as the corps artillery command.

All of these units were known collectively as *Korpstruppen* (corps troops), with their commanders reporting directly to the corps commander. They remained with the corps wherever the corps was sent, and seldom if ever were attached to support other corps headquarters, unlike *Heerestruppen* (army troops), units that frequently rotated between corps, armies, and even army groups, such as heavy tank battalions, artillery brigades, and independent infantry formations. Without these corps and army troops, a corps headquarters would have limited capability to perform its command and control function over its subordinate units or mass its combat power, and would also be vulnerable to enemy ground and air action.

The *IV. SS-Pz.Korps* was no different. Within the *Waffen-SS*, these corps troops were considered to be *Sondertruppen des Reichsführung-SS* (Special Troops of the SS High Command). When they were formed between 1942 and 1943, they were considered part and parcel of the corps headquarters and headquarters troops organization, but in accordance with an order issued by Himmler's *SS-FHA* on 4 October 1944, these units, with a few exceptions, were renumbered and could be detached from the corps they had a habitual relationship with and be assigned anywhere the army or army group required.[1] The evidence shows, however, that in the case of *IV. SS-Pz.Korps,* most of these units remained with their original corps headquarters until the end of the war.

Initially, these units carried the numerical designation starting with 100 and ending with the corps number (e.g., *I SS-Pz.Korps* headquarters troops were designated with the number 101, or in the case of *IV. SS-Pz.Korps* it was the number 104), but after the order of October 1944 most were renumbered into the 500-series, designating them as the SS equivalent of *Heerestruppen* (Army Troops), subject to assignment within a field army as the need dictated.[2] Thus, in October 1944 all *IV. SS-Pz.Korps* troops that fell into this category were redesignated as *SS-Werfer Abteilung 504*, *SS-Sanitätsabteilung 504*, and so on, but as previously mentioned, this hardly seems to have affected their day-to-day relationships within the corps.[3] Regarding the units that remained with the corps as traditional "corps troops" (the signal battalion, supply and transportation battalion, antiaircraft company, field post office, security company, and maintenance platoon), they retained their previous numerical designation of 104.

The order establishing *IV. SS-Pz.Korps*, signed by *Ogruf.* Jüttner at the *SS-FHA* in Berlin on 5 August 1943, specified that the corps was to be composed of a corps staff and *Hauptquartier*, a corps artillery command, map section, military police platoon, war correspondent company, antiaircraft battery, escort company, signal battalion, heavy tank battalion, rocket launcher battalion, supply battalion, maintenance company, clothing repair company, and medical battalion.[4] One of these units, the heavy tank battalion, was never activated, though the corps was occasionally augmented by the temporary attachment of *Heerestruppen* not mentioned in the original order, such as *Schwere-Panzerabteilung* (Heavy Tank Battalion) *509*, which was equipped with 45 *Pz.Kfw. VI* Tiger II tanks. The corps did have, however, one Tiger company, *9. Kompanie* in the *3. SS-Totenkopf Division*'s *panzer* regiment, which at full strength was authorized 14 tanks.[5] This, of course, applied only when *Totenkopf* was actually operating within the corps' order of battle.

According to the August 1943 activation order, the corps headquarters, signal battalion, and antiaircraft battery, considered to be the nucleus of the corps, were authorized a combined total of 1,679 men.[6] With the addition of the yet-to-be-named *Sondertruppen des Reichsführung-SS* mentioned above, the corps with its various *Korpstruppen* was authorized a total strength of 4,348 men, without the addition of additional *Heerestruppen* or subordinate divisions.[7] With divisions included, *IV. SS-Pz.Korps* could theoretically have controlled between 30,000 and 60,000 troops at any given time.

The Corps Headquarters and Headquarters Battalion

Every German corps, whether a normal *Armeekorps, Panzerkorps,* or *Gebirgskorps* had a *Hauptquartier* (*H.Qu.*), or headquarters, (equivalent to a U.S. Army corps headquarters battalion) that was responsible for providing all the necessary life support that such a large organization requires for its day-to-day operations, including housing, feeding, guarding, and transporting the various staff elements, from the corps commander down to the lowliest messenger. Details such as upkeep of individual pay records, administration, dentistry, clothing issue and repair, chemical warfare defense, and all legal matters were handled by specific sections within the headquarters. The *H.Qu.* also had its own medical section designed to support the immediate medical needs of its personnel; a soldier with any illness or injury that could not be treated was evacuated to the corps' *Sanitätsabteilung* (medical battalion).

All of these requirements were addressed in the basic organizational document laid down for a *panzer* corps headquarters, *K.St.N. Nr. 15,* dated 1 March 1943, which the *Waffen-SS* was required to adhere to just as units of the *Heer* were. The organizational structure and personnel requirements were laid out for each staff element, in a tabulated format with an accompanying illustration that was easy to understand.[8] Using this as its foundational document, the officers and senior NCOs comprising the heart of the corps staff and headquarters battalion could determine what they required in order to fill all of the vacant manpower spaces with the appropriately qualified men. Having *Kriegsakademie*-trained general staff officers as members of the staff simplified this task enormously, but officers who had served at the regimental or division level would also know what to do.

With regards to the individual constituent elements of the corps' *Hauptquartier*, or headquarters battalion, the authorizations were spelled out in black and white. For example, security of the corps *Gefechtstand* (command post), where the corps commander, chief of staff, *Ia*, and *O1* were normally to be found, was provided by a small security platoon, consisting of 15 infantrymen led by a senior NCO. They could be augmented when necessary by the corps' 33-man *Feldgendarmerie* (military police) platoon, a unit whose primary function was traffic regulation and control. In addition, each staff element was expected to provide armed soldiers to serve in an *Alarm* (emergency) unit should the local threat dictate a higher level of readiness requiring foot soldiers.

All told, the *Hauptquartier*—excluding the signal battalion, the escort and antiaircraft companies, the *Kriegsberichter Kompanie* (war correspondent/ propaganda company), the field police platoon, and the map section (all of which were organized under their own unique *K.S.t.N.*) —was authorized 238 men, including 27 *SS-Führer* (officers), 11 *Beamte* or officials (though in the *Waffen-SS* these positions were filled by qualified reserve officers), 46 *Unterführer* (equivalent to NCOs), and 154 *Mannschaften,* or enlisted men.[9] The accompanying *K.A.N.* dictated exactly the make and model of vehicles, how many typewriters, field desks, telephones, lamps, electrical generators, and other odds and ends that were authorized for issue to each of the various staff elements to provide them with the basic necessities to perform their mission.

The duties of the staff officers responsible for each staff element was spelled out explicitly in a handbook published by the German Army. This document,

Heeresdienstvorschrift H.D.v. g 92, Handbuch für den Generalstabsdienst im Kriege, published in 1939 by *OKH*, served as the official reference for organizing corps staff and describing the functions of the various elements of the *Hauptquartier* and the corps troops. It was used by the *Waffen-SS* as well as by the *Heer*. For example, concerning administration within the *Hauptquartier* itself, *H.D.v. g 92* stated that in cases where disciplinary action concerning NCOs or enlisted men was deemed necessary, judgement was to be meted out when necessary by the *Kommandant des Hauptquartiers*, or headquarters commandant, who in his capacity as a commander of the headquarters battalion, reported directed to the *Korpsadjutant* or *IIa* (officer disciplinary actions were dealt with by the *Chef des Stabes* himself).[10]

Maintaining control of this menagerie was no simple task, as its commander would be responsible for feeding and billeting nearly 300 men at any given time, including the corps commander. The headquarters commandant had to deal with higher-ranking officers on the staff who were under his administrative supervision, but not in his chain of command. Friction, when it arose, such as disputes or arguments about individual soldiers in staff sections who had committed various infractions or squabbles about equitable allocation of materiel, would be settled by the *IIa* (*Korpsadjutant*) or the *Chef des Stabes* if the staff section head was superior in rank to the headquarters commandant or *IIa*. This required mature judgement and circumspection.

Maintaining awareness of where all of his men were at all times, and especially keeping an attentive eye on the needs of the corps commander, ensured that the headquarters commandant would get little sleep at night. All in all, it was a thankless job for the man responsible for the daily "housekeeping" of the corps headquarters, and he would have had to possess an unusual amount of judgment and maturity. The first *Kommandant des Hauptquartier* was *SS-Stubaf.* Hans Kasten, who served briefly in an acting capacity between late July and early August 1944. Kasten was a proven officer who had served with Gille since January 1941 when both were assigned to *SS-Artillerie-Regiment 5*, so he was a natural choice.

As with many other officers from the *Wiking* Division, Gille had Kasten temporarily moved from his previous position as *Kommando des Div. Hauptquartier* of the *Wiking* Division to the similar position at the corps, since he would have already been familiar with the position's duties and responsibilities. Kasten reverted to his previous position in the *Wiking* one week later after being succeeded by 33-year-old *SS-Hstuf.* Ferdinand Zachmann, who assumed the responsibility in August1944 when he arrived with the rest of the "rump" staff, with whom he had been serving as the *Kommandant* since 24 March 1944.[11] Zachmann had previously served in the *6. SS-Geb.Div. Nord,* having been transferred to the nascent *VII. SS-Pz.Korps* before it was redesignated two months later. Zachmann remained as the *Kommandant des Hauptquarters* until the end of the war. Though it was an obscure assignment for an SS officer, without the *Kommandant des Hauptquartier*'s unsung performance of duty, no corps headquarters would have functioned effectively for long.

Corps Map Reproduction Center

Military operations, especially during combat, require that a large number of maps in various scales and sizes be reproduced, in color if possible, and distributed to the units and staff elements engaged in planning and conducting the various activities required in wartime, such as conducting an attack, a deliberate defense, a river crossing, or a delaying action. Mobile operations, which are characterized by armored or mechanized forces operating over a large geographic area, especially rely upon maps, from the corps commander down to the lowest platoon leader in an infantry battalion. Staffs, whether at corps, division, regiment, or battalion level, are also particularly dependent on maps, especially when they are operating in an unfamiliar area. To address this need, each German division and corps headquarters was authorized its own *Kartenstelle* (map reproduction center).

The *IV. SS-Pz.Korps* was no different. Its map reproduction center, *SS-Panzerkorps-Kartenstelle 104*, was located within the corps *Hauptquartier* area, with its commander being subordinated to the *Ia* staff section, where he served under the title of *Ia Mess* (corps topographical surveying officer). According to its *K.St.N.*, the 20-man section, led by an engineer corps *SS-Hauptsturmführer*, consisted of mapmaking specialists, including several cartographers, photocopiers, book binders, and printers, as well as the equipment required to draft, produce, copy, and print hundreds of maps at a time.[12] Their products usually included 1:100,000 kilometer scale *Generalstabskarte* (general staff maps), 1:300,000 scale *Übersichtskarte von Mitteleuropa* (overview of Central Europe maps), and 1:25,000 scale *Meßtischblatt* or *Topographische Karte* (topographic maps).

Their equipment, carried aboard four specially configured trucks, had the capability to print in color and operate at night, using light sets powered by a trailer-mounted electric generator. When necessary, it could also overprint or reproduce copies of Soviet maps, though these were usually created using map scales unknown in Western Europe, such as 1:21,000, 1:42,000, and 1:84,000 sizes. Should it lack the time or capability to produce sufficient maps for itself and subordinate corps or field army troops, the *Kartenstelle* could request assistance from the field army's *Kartenstelle* or a larger map-making battalion at *Heeresgruppe* level. Like all of the other corps troops, the map section was armed, being provided with two pistols, one submachine gun, and 17 rifles for self-defense. For most of its existence, the corps mapping section was led by *SS-Ostuf.* Karl Tönnies.

Corps Signal Battalion

The most important of the *Korpstruppen* was its *Nachrichtenabteilung* (signal battalion), which was designed to enable the corps commander and staff to communicate with all of the corps' subordinate elements, as well as to maintain continuous contact with adjacent units and its superior field army command, using landline telephone, radio, and continuous wave devices such as the teletype or *Hellschreiber*. In order to do this across a front line between 50 and 100 kilometers wide and a corps depth of up to 100 kilometers, the signal battalion had to be very robust indeed. For without its modern means of communication, a *Panzerkorps* commander would have had no more ability to command and control his troops than General Robert E. Lee had at his disposal during the battle of Gettysburg nearly 100 years earlier.

SS-Pz.Korps Nachr.Abt. 104, the *IV. SS-Pz.Korps'* signal battalion, was established at the same time as *VII. SS-Pz.Korps* headquarters in January 1944, where it was first known as *SS-Pz.Korps Nachr.Abt. 107*. According to the various *K.St.N.*s of the sub-components comprising the battalion, it consisted of a staff and battalion headquarters company, cable-laying company, field radio company, field telephone operations and maintenance company, and supply company. It was a big battalion—the authorized personnel strength of *SS-Pz.Korps Nachr.Abt. 104* was 789 men, including 26 officers. It was also authorized 22 motorcycles, 39 sedans or staff cars, and 140 trucks of all types, several dozen of which were used to carry radio or field telephone sets.[13]

The rest of its vehicles were used to haul supplies and other items of equipment needed to operate in the field—tents, chairs, tables, lighting sets, generators, and so forth. Each company was also authorized its own field kitchen to feed their men. Besides vehicles and other equipment, the battalion was authorized 707 rifles, 53 pistols, 53 submachine guns, and 24 machine guns, a reflection of the fact that its men would be exposed to danger and be expected to defend themselves or even take part in local fighting as *Alarm* units. The battalion's first commander in early 1944 was *Stubaf.* Georg Janensch, followed by *Hstuf.* Martin Müller, who served in the position until he was replaced in January 1945 by *Stubaf.* Karl Krüger, who himself was finally replaced between February and March 1945 by *Stubaf.* Hubert Hüppe, who was moved up to the corps from his previous position as commander of *SS-Nachrichtenabteilung 5* of the *Wiking* Division.

The heart of the battalion lay in two of its companies—the *Korpsfernsprechbetriebskompanie*, or *Kps.Fsp.Betr.Kp.* (Corps field telephone operations and maintenance company), and *Panzerkorpsfunkkompanie*, or *Pz.Kps.Fu.Kp.* (field radio company). While it did have a dedicated field cable-laying company (*Feldfernkabelkompanie*, or *Ffk.Kp.*), it was the first two whose mission was to ensure that the corps commander and his staff were able to remain in constant contact with all the various organizations that fell under the commander's purview, as well as with the separate staff sections and departments of the corps headquarters itself.

Whenever a *Panzerkorps* was occupying a static defensive position and no friendly or enemy offensive action was contemplated or imminent, the corps and its subordinate elements normally used field telephones for communications. Reliable and easy to operate, this form of communication gave no electronic signature that could be detected, hence the commander's preference for its use in order to ensure operational security. Though enemy agents could and did tap the telephone lines, wire parties constantly patrolled along the lines to prevent infiltration. Another secure means of communication was the use of messengers, who would travel by whatever means available (aircraft, motorcycle, motor vehicle, etc.) to relay messages back and forth. Normal distribution through the *Feldpost* was used for non-urgent messages of a routine nature, though of course this was totally unsuitable for mobile situations.

During mobile operations, the field radio company became paramount, since the laying of field telephone cable was impractical and often nearly impossible to carry out due to rapid changes of position by the corps headquarters. Radio provided the means to allow the corps commander to communicate with his far-flung subordinate divisions, brigades, and corps troops engaged in combat. This technology, which had matured tremendously since first being introduced into battle during World War I, was one of the factors that made German *Panzer* formations so successful early in the war as well as aiding their temporary successes during the grinding defensive battles of 1943–45.

The corps radio company was equipped with sturdy and reliable state-of-the-art equipment, which was surprisingly advanced for that era. Normally, a *Pz.Kps.Nachr. Abt.* had the following equipment in its *Pz.Kps.Fu.Kp.*: two 15-watt *Sender-Empfänger* Type b (*W.S.E.b*) *Funkgerät* (*Fu.G.*, usually shortened to just *Fu.*, meaning "radio equipment") model 19 radios, each drawing 15 watts of power, with a frequency of 3–7.5 Megahertz (MHz). Its transmitting range, when using Continuous Wave (C.W.) mode, was 100 kilometers, while it had a range of 32 kilometers in Voice/A.M. mode. It was designed for local use within the corps headquarters area or by infantry units.[14]

The radio company was also equipped with six 80-Watt *Sender* Type a (*W.S.a*) model *Fu.* 12 radios with 80 watts of power, with a frequency from 1.12–3.0 MHz, and a range in C.W. mode of 200 kilometers, 72 in Voice/A.M. This was the primary means for communicating with subordinate divisions and corps troops.[15] The company had 10 *100 W.S.a.* model *Fu.* 11 radios with 100 watts of power and a frequency of 1.1–6.7 Mhz with a range in C.W. mode of 320 kilometers and 110 in Voice/A.M. These sets were the primary means for communicating with adjacent corps and higher headquarters, such as army or army group headquarters.[16] Finally, the company had two 20-Watt *Sender* Type c (*W.S.c*) model *Fu.* 6 radios with 20 watts of power, operating at a frequency between 27.2 and 33.3 MHz, with a range of 100 kilometers in C.W. mode and 32 in Voice/A.M. These last items were used for communicating with *Luftwaffe* aircraft by forward air controllers or *Luftwaffe* liaison officers attached to the corps staff.[17]

In addition, the *Pz.Korps* headquarters signal battalion was authorized 10 Enigma encryption/decryption devices, used to communicate primarily with division, adjacent, and higher headquarters.[18] The advantage of the Enigma system was that it enabled timely (the Germans of course thought that its code could never be broken) encryption and decryption of classified information. Usually, the *Führungsabteilung* (the *Ia* and *Ic* of the corps staff) in the corps *Gefechtstand* had one set each, the commander had his own personal set, and another one was allocated to the commander of the corps artillery. The logistics administration and personnel staff branches (*Quartiermeister/Ib* and *IIa*), located in the corps rear area, would also have one each, while the corps signal battalion had the remainder for its own use, with one or two spare sets ready in case.

Just as important as the transmitter equipment were the receiver sets, which in some cases were separate items connected to the transmitter by cables. While voice reception was more convenient for users, broadcasting on the A.M. band used more power, had shorter range, and of course was easier for the enemy to intercept. In contrast, when transmitting and receiving using the C.W. band, messages could be sent via *Feld-Hellschreiber* using far less power and at two to three times the range. The *Hellschreiber* (named after Dr. Rudolf Hell, the German scientist who invented it) was the German equivalent of the teletype, but it transmitted graphic images rather than individual numbers or characters, that a teletype would then convert back into text. Messages sent via *Hellschreiber* were also extremely difficult to intercept, unless the enemy had obtained a similar set in working order tuned to the proper settings.[19]

Once the message had been received, the operator would print out the message on a continuous strip of paper using a special printer. The message would then be cut and pasted onto the standard paper message tablet. Once completed, the *Hellschreiber* message would be delivered to its recipient in the headquarters like any other paper message. Even when reception was weak, the message would almost always come through, since it was an image and not a series of individual characters, susceptible to interruption or atmospheric phenomena. German radios could also send and receive in Morse code of course, but the *Hellschreiber* was preferred since knowledge of Morse was not necessary—the operator merely typed in the letters using a keyboard like any teletype system while the receiver had only to hold the strip of paper until the message was finished with printing.

The Corps Anti-Aircraft Company

SS-Fliegerabwehr-Kompanie 104, or *Fla.Kp. 104* (SS-Antiaircraft Company 104), was not actually established until April 1944, when the orders were issued for the activation of *VII. SS-Pz.Korps*. Its mission was the point protection of the corps headquarters installation, including co-located *Korpstruppen*, from both low- and medium-level air attacks. It consisted of three platoons, each equipped with three 8-ton *Sd.Kfz. 7/2* half-track-mounted 3.7cm *Flak* 36 or 37 antiaircraft guns, for a total of nine guns. With an authorized strength of 145 men, including three officers, 26 NCOs, and 116 enlisted men, as well as 16 *Hilfswilliger*, or *Hiwis* (prisoner of war volunteer helpers), the company boasted considerable firepower.[20] When operated by trained crews, the 3.7cm *Flak* could shoot down any fighter or medium bomber in the Allied inventory that got within its 6,583-meter maximum range using high-explosive ammunition.[21]

As of 1 July 1944, the battery still had not received any of its vehicles (except for the guns and half-tracks), so was unable to sustain itself without augmentation by corps transportation assets. Fortunately, by the time it arrived in Poland by the end of July it had been issued enough vehicles to ensure at least partial mobility. Several accounts mention that it had been upgraded from a battery to an *Abteilung* (battalion), with additional guns and personnel forming its second battery, which would have made it technically *Sondertruppen des Reichsführung-SS*. However, an order issued in March 1945 concerning these units does not reflect this.[22] The *Flak* Company's first commander was *Ostuf.* Adolf Eberhard.

The Corps Escort Company

The *IV. SS-Pz.Korps* was authorized a *Begleit* (escort) *Kompanie*, whose mission was to provide physical security for the entire corps headquarters and headquarters troops installation, protect it during movement, and form a limited capability for local offensive action. Based on the *Panzer* division escort company, which itself had been developed based on bitter experiences gained on the Eastern Front, the *Korps Begleit-Kompanie* (also referred to as the *Sicherungs*, or security, *Kompanie*) was a relatively robust organization with tremendous firepower for its size.

Organized into five platoons, the *Kompanie* fielded an infantry platoon with a heavy machine-gun squad, a mortar platoon with two 8cm medium mortars, an antitank gun platoon equipped with three towed 7.5cm *PaK* 40 antitank guns, an infantry howitzer platoon with two 7.5cm light infantry howitzers, and a motorcycle platoon.[23] Totaling 187 men, this highly mobile unit could rapidly respond to any low-level threat against the corps headquarters installation, and at a pinch could function as a reaction force to combat any enemy units that had penetrated into the corps rear area until larger forces could be mustered. Its commander has not yet been identified, though evidence suggests that he may have been *Ostuf.* Heinz Grashorn.

Corps Supply Troops

German corps and corps-sized units did not, as a rule, duplicate the same logistical elements found at the division or field army level. Instead, a corps' supply services—including fuel, food, ammunition, repair parts, and medical items—were only as large as necessary to provide logistical support to corps troops and *Heerestruppen* temporarily operating in the corps' rear area. German *Versorgungs*, or supply doctrine, generally dictated that all items of supply were to be transported from the field army directly to the fighting divisions using rail, highway, air, or waterborne means of delivery, bypassing the corps echelon in most cases (a method known in today's armies as "throughput"), except when the material was slated for delivery to the corps headquarters itself. The field army logistical services established supply depots in the corps area, but these were administered by the field army, not the corps. However, the corps' *Nachschubdienste* (supply services, equivalent to a U.S. Army supply and transportation battalion) still had to be robust enough to not only support the corps headquarters, but up to 4,000 or 5,000 additional corps and army headquarters troops attached at any given moment.

To sustain itself logistically, an *SS-Panzerkorps* in the aforementioned August 1943 establishing order was authorized two *kleine Kraftwagenkolonne* (light wheeled motor transport columns), each capable of carrying 30 tons of supplies, a *Maultier* ("mule") equipped half-tracked *grosse Kraftwagenkolonne* (heavy motor transport column) capable of carrying 60 tons of supplies, a *grosse Kraftwagenkolonne für Betriebstoff* (large fuel column) to carry up to 50 cubic meters (approximately 13,000 U.S. gallons) of gasoline, and a *Kraftfahrzeug-Instandsetzungszug* (motor vehicle maintenance platoon) designed to maintain and repair the various wheeled and tracked vehicles authorized for the corps headquarters and its subordinate corps troops. Each of these elements were organized according to their own separate *K.St.N.*[24]

Command of this 233-man battalion-sized organization was exercised by the corps' *Nachschubführer*, though its employment was dictated by the corps' *Quartiermeister*, who was responsible for forecasting and calculating requirements for all classes of supply needed by the corps headquarters and corps troops, as well as its subordinate combat divisions. When the corps headquarters went into action at the beginning of August 1944, *Ostubaf.* Christian Steinmetz, a veteran of the 6. *SS-Geb.Div. Nord*, was serving as *IV. SS-Pz.Korps' Korpsnachschubführer*, answering to *SS-Ostubaf.* Hans Scharff as the corps' *Quartiermeister*. Steinmetz had been a part of the original *VII. SS-Pz.Korps* staff under Kleinheisterkamp, but departed Gille's command on 20 August 1944 after serving as the *Korpsnachschubführer* in combat for only three weeks. He was replaced by *SS-Ostubaf.* Wilhelm Honsell.

Neither the various *K.St.N.* nor *K.A.N.* for the battalion specified the make and model of each vehicle that it required, only the size, cargo-carrying ability, and off-road capability. The number and type of wheeled and tracked vehicles employed by the corps' *Nachschubdienste* during the war varied considerably depending on factory output. Vehicles ranged from the popular two-wheel drive Opel 6700 Type S *Blitz*, capable of carrying up to 3 tons of cargo on paved roads, to the considerably larger and more powerful Büssing-NAG Type 500A four-wheel drive diesel that could operate cross-country with a 4.5-ton load. The tracked column was usually equipped with *Maultier* half-tracked cargo trucks, generally consisting of either an Opel *Blitz* or a Ford V3000 modified with a set of British-designed Carden-Lloyd tracks instead of the usual rear wheels. While their cargo-carrying capability was lessened by a third with this modification, they could at least negotiate muddy roads where conventional trucks would quickly bog down. Complementing the cargo trucks was a number of trailers of various types designed to carry either additional bulk items or liquids. As a *Panzerkorps* was not authorized any horse-drawn supply columns according to *K.St.N. 15*, should such units be assigned to the corps for special missions, a veterinarian would be temporarily transferred to the corps from the *Heer* or *Waffen-SS*.

From its inception, the corps headquarters and *Nachschubtruppen* were chronically short of wheeled and tracked vehicles. German industry, which had belatedly gone over to "total war" production only in the spring of 1943 after four years of trying to simultaneously meet the demand for both civilian and military manufactured goods, could never keep up with the demand for more vehicles to equip *Wehrmacht panzer* units and the newly activated *SS-Panzerkorps*, despite Himmler's and Jüttner's urgent demands for more.

Authorized a total of 259 motor vehicles of all types, including 92 motorcycles, the *IV. SS-Pz.Korps* headquarters and its supply units only had 76 vehicles actually on-hand at the beginning of July 1944, far below what it required. While many additional vehicles were received by the end of the month, deliveries of replacement vehicles never kept up with the number of those lost through accidents, enemy action, or mechanical breakdown, forcing the remaining trucks and *Maultiere* to carry even more of the load. At one point during the fighting east of Warsaw during August 1944, *IV. SS-Pz.Korps' Nachschubdienste* was temporarily augmented by *Transport-Brigade Speer*, an element of the *Nationalsozialistisches Kraftfahr Korps* (*N.S.K.K.*), or National Socialist Motor Corps, a paramilitary organization that was used to haul supplies within the corps' area of operations due to shortages of vehicles within its transportation company.[25]

As *Reichsminister* Albert Speer and the German armaments industry worked feverishly to meet the continuing demand for vehicles and equipment to offset the heavy loss of materiel during the summer and fall of 1944, economizing became the order of the day, impacting both *Waffen-SS* combat units and the *Heer*. To maintain mobility of Gille's corps while saving vehicle wear and tear whenever possible, an order was issued by the *SS-FHA* on 4 October 1944 that dictated changes in the *K.St.N.*s of the corps' *Nachschubeinheiten*.[26] In place of the two 30-ton light truck supply columns and the 60-ton *Maultier* column, the *IV. SS-Pz.Korps*—as well as the other three *SS-Panzerkorps*—were instructed to reconfigure its truck columns into a 90-ton and a 60-ton wheeled *Kraftfahrkompanien*. Though this represented more transport capability, the corps had to give up its fuel column entirely, a reflection that gasoline, due to the Allied strategic bombing campaign, had become such a critical item of supply that its distribution from that point onward would be strictly controlled at the field army level.

Corps Clothing Repair and Maintenance Company

In addition to the supply elements discussed above, the corps was also authorized an *SS-Bekleidung-Instandsetzungs-Kompanie* (Clothing repair and maintenance company). Although it was not officially part of the corps' *Nachschubdienste*, it was grouped along with them for administrative purposes, falling under the overall purview of the *Korpsnachschubführer*. This uniquely SS organization was established in December 1942 following testing on the Eastern Front in the summer of 1942 to provide a forward repair capability for clothing, headgear, and footwear. Acknowledging the weaknesses of the supply system employed by the *Heer*, as well as the distances involved and the increasing scarcity of raw materials, the clothing repair company allowed the corps to keep its men smartly outfitted with serviceable uniforms while lessening the strain on the supply system.[27]

While uniforms were continuously manufactured by the various *SS-Bekleidungswerke* (clothing factories) in Germany, repairing or overhauling clothing that had either been damaged or worn out provided the commander greater flexibility and speed in outfitting his troops. In order to fulfill its mission, the 109-man company was equipped with 14 sewing machines for clothing, seven heavy sewing machines used for shoe and saddle repair, and one machine designed specifically to attach the soles to shoes using wooden pegs. The company was also authorized two trailer-mounted electric generators used to power all of the unit's equipment and a multitude of clothing presses, irons, and ironing boards.[28] Initially commanded by an *SS-Hauptsturmführer*, Alfred Häusser, the unit was authorized 24 vehicles of various types to move its equipment as well as its store of clothing and repair materials. In recognition that the company might be pressed into duty occasionally as an *Alarmeinheit*, it was equipped with 91 rifles, nine pistols, and nine submachine pistols.

Due to the general reduction in force throughout the *Waffen-SS* logistics establishment during the late fall and early winter of 1944–45 that was carried out in order to free up more manpower for the *kämpfenden Truppe* (fighting troop formations), the company was downsized in November 1944 to a platoon-sized element and was correspondingly renamed *SS-Bekleidung-Instandsetzungs-Zug 104*.[29] Most of the men whose positions were eliminated were transferred to the *Wiking* and *Totenkopf* divisions, whilst the company command position was reduced in rank from a *SS-Hauptsturmführer* to *SS-Obersturmführer*, with *SS-Ostuf.* Aloys Thome, formerly of the *SS-Bekleidungswerk* at Dachau, serving as the platoon commander thereafter.

Corps Post Office

Every unit in the German armed forces of battalion size and higher was authorized a *Feldpostamt* (field post office), which served to send and receive official and personal mail from units in the field to their homes in Germany or the occupied countries.

In many cases, individual companies, batteries, or specialized units were authorized their own *Feldpostamt* as well. Each *Feldpostamt* was assigned its own unique five-digit *Feldpostnummer* (*F.P.Nr.*, or field post office number), which made for greater operational security, since senders of mail, packages, or official correspondence had only to write the soldiers' name and field post office number on the envelope or package. The *IV. SS-Pz.Korps* was no exception and followed the *K.St.N.* for a corps *Feldpostamt* (*motorisiert*, or *mot.*) of the *Heer.*[30]

SS-Feldpostamt 104 was rather small, being authorized only 18 men and four wheeled vehicles. Commanded by a reserve SS officer who had served in the German postal service before the war, the post office included mail sorters, censors, and other officials whose job was to receive, process and forward various kinds of correspondence, including packages from home or delivery of specialized materials being sent through the post office, such as batteries, film, and sound media from the SS war correspondent platoons (see below). Mail and other postal distribution for the corps' divisions and other subordinate units were forwarded directly to their field post offices, bypassing that of the corps. The *Feldpostamt* was entirely dependent upon the corps *Hauptquartier* for life support and protection, and worked closely with the *Adjutant* and *Kommandant des Hauptquartier*, including that organization's own mail clerks. Records indicate that *SS-Feldpostamt 104* was commanded by *SS-Ostuf.* Ludwig Viktor.

Corps War Correspondent Elements

In recognition of the immense positive propaganda value embodied by the three new SS armored corps being created during the summer of 1943, Himmler directed that each *SS-Panzerkorps* would receive its own *SS-Kriegsberichter Kompanie* (*KB-Kp.*, or war correspondent company). These units' mission were similar to that of the existing SS division *KB-Züge* (platoons) in that they were to publicize by word, print, and film the exploits and successes of the *Waffen-SS* on every front. Much of their material was featured in the in-house periodical of the SS, *Das Schwarze Korps*, but the rest was distributed throughout the various media organs of the Third Reich, such as the *Völkischer Beobachter*, *Berliner Illustrierte Zeitung*, and *die Deutsche Wochenschau.* This allowed the average German citizen, as well as the populations of occupied countries and opposing nations, to gain an appreciation (however exaggerated or falsified) of the power and might of National Socialism and how men of the SS were contributing to Germany's inevitable victory.

To perform its mission, the *SS-KB* company would have had a headquarters elements and two or more 68-man *Kriegsberichter Züge*, one for each of the SS divisions under its control (the *3.* and *5. KB-Züge*, for the *Totenkopf* and *Wiking* Divisions, respectively), but these would necessarily change should either of these divisions pass under the control of another corps headquarters. The *I.*, *II.*, and *III.*

(germ.) SS-Pz.Korps had already received their *SS-KB* companies, numbered 1, 2, and 3 respectively, and the new *IV. SS-Pz.Korps* would receive one as well. After all, its two divisions had already had their *SS-KB* platoons since 1941, and both were well-established and proven organizations.[31] Control of the *SS-KB Kompanie* would not be exercised by the corps headquarters, however, but by the *SS-Standarte "Kurt Eggers"* in Berlin, the headquarters of the SS propaganda department, led by *SS-Standartenführer* Günther D'Alquen.

According to the special SS *K.St.N.* dated 1 January 1943, each *SS-KB* platoon was composed of a platoon headquarters section, print media section, still photography and motion-picture section, audio recording section, support element, and motor pool consisting of 27 wheeled vehicles and motorcycles. The *SS-KB* platoons were highly mobile, enabling their *Kriegsberichter* to travel throughout the division and corps' area of operations, gather material, and return to its headquarters in order to draft, edit, and transmit its film, sound, photographic, and print media to higher SS headquarters once it had been approved by the division commander or his chief of staff. Later in the war, the *SS-KB* platoons were authorized to bypass their division headquarters entirely and submit their material directly to Berlin, a sign of how important their role had become to the overall strategy of Hitler's rapidly shrinking Third Reich.

Evidence indicates that the *IV. SS-Pz.Korps'* dedicated war correspondent company, the *4. SS-KB Kompanie*, had been activated by January 1944 and was stationed somewhere in Western Europe, but with only one platoon.[32] But without a corps headquarters to support since the corps itself was in a caretaker status, it had very little to report on. On 1 May 1944, D'Alquen issued an order that abolished all *SS-KB* companies, including *4. Kompanie*.[33] This occurred before the "new" *IV. SS-Pz.Korps* was activated in June 1944, so it can safely be said that by the time Gille took command in July, there was no longer an *SS-KB* company supporting the corps, only the aforementioned platoons operating with each division. Instead, each corps had a small war correspondent staff attached, with less than a dozen men. The *IV. SS-Pz.Korps' Kriegsberichter* staff consolidated the materials from the two *SS-KB* platoons working in the corps' two divisions and published the corps' troop newspaper, *Kämpfer des Führers* (*The Führer's Fighters*), which was distributed to each division in the corps with copies being sent as far down as each individual *Kompanie*.

The reason given for the decision to disband the *SS-KB* companies was that by doing so, 250 *SS-KB* troops and 80 vehicles would be freed up which would allow them to be used to form a special-purpose task force to form *Operaton Skorpion*, D'Alquen's brainchild that was envisioned to be used to wage psychological warfare against an anticipated Allied landing in France as well as against Soviet forces in the East.[34] Another reason for the deactivation of the companies was the ongoing expansion of the *SS-Kriegsberichter* organization from a battalion to a regiment between 1943 and 1944.[35] This regiment, named *SS-Standarte "Kurt Eggers"* after one of its members who was killed in action while fighting with the *Wiking* Division in 1943, continued to build up its structure until the end of the war, including the addition of *Kampfpropaganda* (psychological warfare) units. The original *SS-KB* platoons remained in the field though, still attached to their original divisions but now bearing their supported division's name instead of a number.

These *SS-KB* platoons remained under the operational control of the *"Kurt Eggers"* regiment headquarters in Berlin, though for practical reasons they had to coordinate their activities with their associated division's staff. Each platoon was authorized an *SS-Obersturmführer* as its commanding officer, but shortages in this grade led to lesser-ranking officers being appointed instead, as in the case of the *Wiking* Division, whose platoon leader was *Ustuf.* Kristian Zarp. The acting platoon leader of the *Totenkopf* Division's *SS-KB* platoon was *Standartenoberjunker* (officer cadet) Otto Dibowski. Both Zarp and Dibowski were veteran journalists by this point, and hardly needed any supervision by a company headquarters anyway, had one been established for *IV. SS-Pz.Korps.*[36]

During January 1945, *Kampfpropaganda-Zug Ungarn* (psychological warfare platoon Hungary) led by *Ustuf.* Erich Kernmayr, was attached to *IV. SS-Pz.Korps.* Kernmayr not only received his general direction from the *SS-KB* headquarters in Berlin, but also tactical direction from the *Ic* of the corps, *SS-Stubaf.* Jankuhn.[37] Incidentally, Kernmayr became a well-known author of German nationalist literature after the war under the pen name "Erich Kern", as well as a leading figure in neo-Nazi circles in West Germany. We will hear more about him later. Unfortunately, most of the photographic and written material produced by both *SS-KB* platoons and by Kernmayr's company seems to have been lost, having either been captured or destroyed at the war's end.

The Corps Artillery Command

Besides the *Panzer* divisions themselves, one of the most powerful tools the corps headquarters could bring to bear to influence the battle was its artillery, whether assigned to the corps as *Korpstruppen* or artillery battalions and brigades from the large number of *Heerestruppen* units spread throughout the front. Lacking any kind of organic fixed or rotary wing assets found in today's modern corps, this was one of the few combat assets the corps commander could employ as he saw fit. Corps artillery would be allocated in support of subordinate *Panzer* or infantry divisions based upon the corps' *Schwerpunkt*, where the commander wished to employ the greatest amount of firepower in order to achieve offensive or defensive success.[38]

As such, dozens of different *Heer* artillery units from the common pool of Army troops were temporarily attached to the *IV. SS-Pz.Korps* between August 1944 and May 1945, ranging anywhere in size from individual firing batteries to artillery brigades, employing everything ranging in caliber from 7.5cm infantry howitzers to 21cm heavy mortars. These units could be shifted across the corps' front, as the mission dictated, in order to provide continuous support to the divisions engaged in combat as well as to help the corps commander to "shape the battlefield." It could help him to achieve certain desirable effects at a given point in time, such as destroying an enemy tank concentration or any enemy headquarters that had been located via radio direction finding. Once their mission had been completed, the guns could be reassigned to support another corps or field army.

The complex planning required to coordinate supporting artillery fire could not be adequately handled by the corps staff alone, which by any measure was fully occupied in its normal duties; therefore, in order to provide that capability, a new specialized organizational structure called an *Artilleriekommandeur*, or *ARKO*, was instituted in the *Kaiserheer* during World War I and continued by the *Reichswehr* and its successor, the *Wehrmacht*. Though numbering only 22 men, including six officers, the *ARKO* was led by the corps' *Artillerieführer*, considered to be a brigade-level command position who reported directly to the corps commander, not the chief of staff.[39] Usually, this position was filled by an Army *Generalmajor* or an *SS-Brigadeführer*. Those selected to command an *ARKO* were naturally artillerymen themselves, often with both World War I and II experience.

The *ARKO* was responsible not only for coordinating and deconflicting artillery fire within the corps' *Kampfraum*, but also for the planning and supervision of the logistical support required by attached artillery units, including ammunition, fuel, and food. In this regard, it functioned similarly to a brigade headquarters supply staff section, with each subordinate element, no matter how temporary its assignment, passing on its resupply needs to the *ARKO*'s *Offizier für Versorgungsangelegenheiten* (supply officer).[40] The corps' *Nachschubdienst* itself did not normally provide these things, but rather the *ARKO* coordinated for the allocation of these items, especially artillery ammunition, with the next higher headquarters. This higher headquarters, normally an *Armeeoberkommando* (field army), would then supply the corps' artillery units directly from its own depots to the unit requesting resupply. *SS-ARKO 104* (later *504*) was commanded by the highly capable *Brigadeführer* (*Brig.Fhr.*) Kurt Brasack, about whom much will be said later.

The *IV. SS-Pz.Korps* was fortunate in that not only did it have its own dedicated *ARKO*, but was authorized its own corps-level rocket launcher and heavy artillery battalions as well. The first unit, *SS-Werfer Abteilung 104* (from October 1944 *504*), was not activated until the late summer of 1944, but its arrival at the front on 7 September came at a time when its heavy firepower was sorely needed.[41] Activated in August 1944 at the Kurmark Training Area, it consisted of a staff battery, four firing batteries—each equipped with six 15cm *Nebelwerfer 41* towed rocket launchers—and a supply and service battery.

The 75lb high-explosive projectile fired by the *Nebelwerfer* had a maximum effective range of 2,200 meters.[42] Although it could range as far as 6,900 meters, beyond its maximum effective range the odds of hitting anything were greatly diminished. Known by the Americans who encountered it as the "Screaming Meemie," the low-pitched moaning sound that attended its flight was more damaging to morale than the actual impact of the rocket itself. Still, as an area-suppressing weapon, especially when fired *en masse*, it could be extremely effective. The *Abteilung* was commanded until the war's end by *Hstuf.* Otto Krosta.

The corps was also authorized a heavy artillery battalion, *schwere SS-Artillerie-Abteilung 504*. Difficulties in procuring equipment and personnel meant that this battalion could not join the corps until the end of January 1945.The lack of a dedicated corps heavy artillery battalion was compensated for by the attachment of several *Heer* army headquarters artillery units between August and December 1944, including *Heeres-Artillerie-Regiment Stab 140*, *10. Batterie/Heeres-Artillerie-Abteilung 732*, and *Heeres-Artillerie-Abteilung 154* among many others.[43] Their firepower augmented that of the division's artillery regiments, though even with this addition, Soviet artillery usually outnumbered German artillery by an order of magnitude.

The *schw. SS-Art.Abt. 504*, which began forming in December 1944, consisted of three batteries, two equipped with six 15cm *schwere Feld-Haubitze* (heavy field howitzer) *18*, and a third equipped with three 21cm *Mörser 18* (actually a heavy howitzer, not a mortar), giving the battalion a total of 15 guns. The 15cm *s.FH 18*, introduced in 1935, had a maximum effective range of 13,377 meters and could fire high-explosive, armor-piercing, and smoke projectiles, each weighing about 95.7lb. The 21cm howitzer fired a 249lb high-explosive shell, which it could hurl to a distance of 16,733 meters. It could also fire a concrete-piercing round for use against fixed positions.[44] All three batteries were motorized. The *schw. SS-Art.Abt. 504*, which achieved combat-ready status on 15 January 1945, was initially commanded by *Stubaf.* Alfred Neuwirth.

To assess the effectiveness of the shells and rockets fired by both of these battalions, as well as by additional attached artillery *Heerestruppen*, the corps was authorized its own *Beobachtungs-Batterie* (observation battery). This company-sized unit, *SS-Beobachtungs-Batterie 104/504*, served as the *ARKO*'s eyes and ears, not only locating and spotting targets, but providing feedback to both the *ARKO* and firing batteries in the form of observed fire effects on various targets as well as recommending firing adjustments to improve accuracy. It normally would have been located close to the front lines, where it would be able to conduct its mission, a duty that often placed its troops at considerable risk from enemy fire.

To carry out its mission, its organizational structure included target range-finding, long-range observation, and meteorological observation sections, as well as sound and flash ranging platoons. Based on these observations, the battery could construct an enemy artillery order of battle, which summarized information about enemy capabilities and intentions that would be used when conducting staff estimates for future offensive or defensive operations. Should weather conditions and the tactical situation allow, the battery could even launch observation balloons to provide a deeper look into enemy territory, but as Soviet control of the air became a fact by the fall of 1944, these were used less often.

The corps observation battery had originally been established as *SS-Beob.Bttr. 104* to support the first incarnation of *IV. SS-Pz.Korps* in October 1943, but was reassigned to the *9. SS-Pz.Div. Hohenstaufen* when that division was preparing to be shipped to the Eastern Front in late March 1944.[45] In November of that year, when observation batteries were ordered to be removed from all *panzer* divisions, it was transferred to the SS Artillery School in Glau and in January 1945 to the school in Beneschau, where it was reorganized as a corps artillery observation battery and redesignated as *SS-Beob.Bttr. 504*. It was not ordered to join *IV. SS-Pz. Korps* until 6 February 1945, when the corps was enmeshed in the bitter fighting for Stuhlweissenburg.[46] In the interim, this critical function would be performed by a similar *Heer* unit, *Beobachtungs-Abteilung (t.mot.) 21*, which operated under the control of Gille's *ARKO* from August 1944 until the arrival of *SS-Beob.Bttr. 504* six months later.[47] The SS battery was commanded by *Hstuf.* Ernst Schandera, who assumed the leadership when it was first attached to the *9. SS-Pz.Div.*, until the war's end.

Corps Medical Troops

Each SS *panzer* or infantry corps was authorized an *SS-Sanitätsabteilung (mot.)*, a motorized corps-level medical battalion, consisting of a battalion staff, two *Feldlazarett* (field hospitals), two *Krankenkraftwagen-Zug* (ambulance platoons), a *Krankentransport-Kompanie* (casualty evacuation company), and a *kleine Kraftwagenkolonne* (light truck column).[48] The battalion was primarily intended to serve corps or army headquarters troops operating in the corps *Rückwärtige Gebiet* (rear area), to include attached units lacking their own medical treatment capability, though it could serve front-line units should their organic medical treatment units be overwhelmed with patients, which happened with increasing regularity the longer the war lasted. Generally, the battalion operated in the corps rear area, anywhere from 30–80 kilometers behind the front lines, depending on the situation.[49]

When the formation of *SS-Sanitätsabteilung 104* (later *504*) began in June 1944, there were simply not enough SS medical personnel available to fill out its ranks, particularly in regards to the second *Feldlazarett* and ambulance platoons. Having initiated a too-rapid expansion of the *Waffen-SS*, Himmler's training establishments could not produce enough trained and skilled personnel to satisfy the demand, especially in light of the heavy casualties his formations were already experiencing during the summer of 1944. Fortunately for Himmler, in the wake of the 20 July assassination attempt against Hitler and the implication and elimination of many of the *Ersatzheer*'s (Replacement Army) key leaders, Hitler appointed him its commander, a position which gave him a free hand in controlling the *Wehrmacht*'s personnel replacement policy, to include the allocation of replacements.

Consequently, Himmler was able to incorporate a number of fragmented *Heeres-Einheiten* into the *Waffen-SS* that had survived a series of calamities on the Eastern Front during the late spring and early summer of 1944, such as the destruction in the Crimea of nearly all of *17. Armee* except its headquarters and support troops that May, which had been successfully evacuated by sea. As a result, there were many rescued units without troops to lead, such as the headquarters of *V. Armeekorps,* which was incorporated into the *Waffen-SS* in July 1944 in its entirety as the new *Hauptquartier* of the *XI. SS-Korps.*[50] With the addition of SS uniforms and a few senior SS officers to lead and staff it, such as *Ogruf.* Kleinheisterkamp as its first (and only) commander, its incorporation into the *Waffen-SS* was complete.

Other examples of units that were incorporated into the *Waffen-SS* were some of the medical units of the ill-fated *73. Infanterie-Division*. The *73. Inf.Div.*, then under the *IV. SS-Pz.Korps*' order of battle, was virtually destroyed in battle east of Warsaw in September 1944, though most of its sub-units survived the debacle, including its supply and support units.[51] The division's infantry regiments had to be rebuilt nearly from scratch the following month and its *Sanitäts-Kompanie 173* was reorganized, having to give up half of its medical assets as part of an overall reorganization of medical units in the *Heer*. Both the former *Sanitäts-Kompanie 1./173* and *Kraft-Krankenwagen Zug 1./173* were accordingly incorporated into the battalion structure of *SS-Sanitätsabteilung 104/504* respectively as *SS-Pz.Korps San. Kp. 504 and SS-Pz.Korps Kr.Kw.Zug 504* on 25 October 1944.[52] Their members now found themselves trading in their *Wehrmacht* uniforms for those of the SS.

The *IV. SS-Pz.Korps* was chosen to receive these additional two *Heer* medical units because the *SS-FHA* had been able to activate only one field hospital, *SS-Feldlazarett 104/504*, instead of the two as stipulated in the order establishing the corps. The overall shortage of SS medical personnel by the summer of 1944 had resulted in a reduction of a *panzer* corps' medical treatment capability, a situation that could not be tolerated for long. Therefore Jüttner, exercising his authority via Himmler, as head of the *Ersatzheer* and the ultimate arbiter of *Wehrmacht* and SS personnel policy, concluded an agreement with the *Allgemeineheeresamt/Chef der Heeresrüstung* (Army General Office and its Ordnance Department) directing that these medical units from the old *73. Inf.Div.* be incorporated into the *Waffen-SS* by the end of October 1944. They were accordingly redesignated as SS units on 25 October 1944.[53] What the former *Heer* medical personnel thought about their involuntary transfer has not been recorded.

The corps' *SS-Feldlazarett* had a patient capacity of 200 beds, but casualties that required more than three to four weeks of recuperation were usually evacuated to a *Kriegslazarett* (base hospital) in the army or army group rear area as soon as possible. *SS-Feld.Laz. 104/504* could treat approximately 100 casualties a day during normal operations, especially when triage and initial treatment was performed by the *Sanitäts-Kompanie*, which was set up along the lines of a field dressing station. Casualty evacuation would be provided by the two motorized ambulance platoons. Should the number of casualties be more than the corps' combined *Feldlazarett* and *Sanitäts-Kompanie* could handle, *SS-San.Abt. 104/504* could be augmented by an additional *Feldlazarett* from the field army, especially whenever heavy fighting was taking place.

According to *K.St.N.* Nr. 1342 dated 1 January 1943, a *Feldlazarett*, whether located at the division or corps level, was staffed with two surgeons and four general practitioners. It fielded two surgical platoons, each consisting of two doctors and 26 *Sanitäter* (enlisted medical personnel). Equipped with seven vehicles, including an ambulance and an omnibus for patients, each platoon was highly mobile, giving it the ability to move throughout the corps or even division rear areas based on the need. Should the number of patients be more than they could realistically treat, the *Feldlazarett*, which most closely resembled a 1950s-era U.S. Army Mobile Army Surgical Hospital (or M.A.S.H.), would often be supplemented by surgeons from other units in the battalion or from neighboring *Sanitätsabteilung* in other corps or even front-line divisions.

A *Feldlazarett* could be set up and placed in operation in as little as three hours, or be taken down for transport in the same amount of time. It was primarily intended for the reception and temporary retention of casualties who needed urgent live-saving operations or resuscitation, followed by a few days of post-operative recovery before further evacuation to a *Kriegslazarett* in the army rear area or in Germany. Each *Feldlazarett* also had its own surgical team that was fully equipped to handle any type of casualty.[54] Comprising six doctors, four specialists, and 66 enlisted men, it was normally commanded by an *SS-Obersturmbannführer* of the SS medical branch. *SS-Feldlazarett 104/504* was initially commanded by *Ostubaf.* Dr. Peter Metzmacher, succeeded by the war's end by *Stubaf.* Wilhelm Giese.

The two 41-man ambulance platoons (one of which had been transferred from the *Heer*, as previously mentioned) provided immediate medical evacuation capability from the point of injury in the corps area to the corps' *Feldlazarett* or *Sanitäts-Kompanie*, where they would then administer emergency medical care to the casualty. Both platoons were authorized 15 *Kraftfahrwagen* (*K.f.w.*) Model 31 ambulances, each capable of carrying up to four litter patients or 10 sitting patients.[55] The *Krankentransport-Kompanie* was designed to transport patients from the corps rear area to army rear area hospitals by truck once their injuries or surgeries had stabilized to the point where they could be safely moved. It was also capable of setting up and manning a *Krankensammelstelle* (casualty collecting station) at a railhead, where wounded soldiers would be loaded onto specially configured rail cars for transport to a hospital in Germany.[56] The battalion's *SS-Sanitätskollone* (supply column) carried supplies and equipment for the battalion, to include fuel, food, extra tentage, and medical supplies, as well as an *SS-Hygienezug* (preventive medicine platoon).[57]

The *IV. SS-Pz.Korps' Sanitäts-Abteilung* was commanded by an *SS-Oberführer*, in this case by *Oberführer* Dr. Bruno Rothardt, who doubled as the corps' *IVb*, or chief medical staff officer. The battalion's *Stab einer Heeressanitätsabteilung* (equivalent to a U.S. Army medical battalion headquarters and headquarters company) consisted of 73 personnel, including 16 female nurses from the *Deutsches Rotes Kreuz*, or *DRK* (German Red Cross).[58] The company's mission was to support the field hospital, medical company, and ambulance platoons with surgeons and specialists, logistical support to include the provision of specialized medical supplies and equipment, an apothecary, and ophthalmologist, as well as administrative services, including a paymaster. In all, the *Sanitäts-Abteilung* could have had as many as 336 medical and support personnel assigned or attached at any given time. Judging by all indicators, *SS-San.Abt.104/504* was well-trained and equipped, fully capable of carrying out its mission of providing adequate medical support to the corps headquarters and corps troops once it was augmented by the aforementioned field hospital and ambulance platoon from the *73. Inf.Div.*

With all of these corps troops, army troops, and sub-units combined, *IV. SS-Pz. Korps* was authorized, according to the various *K.St.N.*, a grand total of 4,348 men, including the corps *Hauptquartier*. Despite the immediacy of the situation, personnel and equipment transfers to flesh out these units arrived slowly. From the date of its renewed activation in mid-April 1944 (originally as *VII. SS-Pz.Korps*), records indicate that even as late as 20 September 1944, the corps still only had 2,198 men actually assigned, roughly 50 percent of its authorized strength. Though the corps did receive an influx of 10,000 excess *Luftwaffe* personnel by the end of September, most of these went to *Wiking* and *Totenkopf* to make up for the enormous losses both divisions suffered during the bitter fighting outside of Warsaw in August and September 1944.

Nevertheless, whether or not staffed and manned to its full wartime requirement, *IV. SS-Pz.Korps* tried to carry out to the best of its ability the mission of commanding and controlling not only its two subordinated SS divisions, but many other divisions of the *Heer*. It would also lead dozens of separate *Heer* artillery, engineer, assault gun, and antitank battalions, medical units, supply and transportation units, security units, and even a Hungarian division as well as a heavy tank battalion between its introduction to combat at the end of July 1944 and the end of the war—too many to list here.[59] In this regard, Gille's corps was remarkably similar to the corps of the *Heer*, and were it not for its SS designation, would have been nearly indistinguishable from them, in performance as well as in appearance.

CHAPTER 4

The Leaders and Divisions

Though he has been mentioned earlier, no study of the *IV. SS-Pz.Korps* would be complete without a brief synopsis of the career of the man who served as its commander during its entire battle history, *Gruppenführer* (promoted to *Obergruppenführer* in November 1944) Herbert Otto Gille. Nor would this study be complete without a brief history of the two divisions that constituted the corps' initial order of battle when it first engaged in combat at the end of July 1944, as well as descriptions of their leaders. The names of these men were to be inextricably linked with the titles of their commands; once they were confirmed by early October 1944, the line-up remain unchanged until the end of the war—a remarkable occurrence, especially when other division and *Armeekorps* commanders seemed to change as the war reached its horrifying end with a dizzying rapidity that confounds scholars and historians even to this day.

Herbert Otto Gille was born on 8 March 1897 in the small village of Gandersheim, nestled in a valley in the Harz Mountains of northern Germany. His father managed a factory, but Gille felt the call of military service instead of that of a humdrum middle-class life in manufacturing. On Easter Sunday, 11 April 1909, Gille entered the *Kadettenkorps* (corps of cadets) at the military academy in Bensburg-am-Rhein at the age of 12, a not unusual practice at that time. After completing his preliminary course of instruction in the spring of 1914, at the age of 17 he was accepted as a cadet at the prestigious corps of cadets at Gross-Lichterfelde in Berlin, which was the source of the bulk of the *Kaiserheer*'s regular army officers. This was a marked elevation of Gille's social status, bringing him a step closer towards becoming a member of the German military aristocracy.[1]

The outbreak of World War I saw Gille's time as a cadet quickly come to an end. He was posted on 1 September as a subaltern to *II. Bataillon*, *Badische-Feldartillerie-Regiment 30* in Rastatt, where he remained until the beginning of November 1914 undergoing additional training designed to make him a fully qualified artillery officer. His training complete, he was assigned to *Reserve-Artillerie-Regiment 55* of the *75. Reserve-Infanterie-Division*, which was then in the process of mobilization. Sent to the Eastern Front in early February 1915, the division fought against the Russians until December 1917, when it was transferred to the Western Front. Here, Gille took part in the ill-fated Ludendorff offensive that began in March 1918 and ended the war fighting against the Americans in the Meuse-Argonne region.[2]

During this period, Gille served first as a battery lieutenant leading a gun section, next as a forward observer, then as a battery commander in a variety of combat conditions in both the east and west, including fighting on some of the battlefields that he would revisit during the next war, such as Kowel in Galicia. The war's end found him serving as an *Oberleutnant* commanding a battery with his old unit, *Badische-Feld-Art.Rgt. 30*, on the Western Front. Awarded both classes of the Iron Cross for valor, as well as the Austrian War Service Cross 3rd Class for service in the east and both classes of the Brunswick Service Cross, Gille had proven himself both as a leader and as a soldier. However, Germany's defeat not only marked the end of the Second German Empire and the Kaiser's reign, but also seemed to spell the end of Gille's dream of pursuing a military career.

Like many other German officers and men serving in the wake of demobilization as required by the Versailles Treaty, Gille found himself without a military future and had no choice but to resign from the Army in April 1919. He had accumulated 10 years of service, including his time as a cadet, but his military talents were no longer needed in a nation reeling from the harsh provisions of the Versailles Treaty that required Germany to reduce its Army to a mere 100,000 men. Unlike many of his contemporaries, Gille did not join the *Freikorps* to fight against the communist movement, nor did he attempt to restart his military career in the new *Reichswehr*. Instead, he enrolled in a local college that year to study agriculture, a career field where he was to be employed as an estate manager for the next 10 years. In 1929, Gille abandoned this career and started another in the automobile manufacturing industry, working at a factory in Brunswick until 1931, when he struck out on his own to form his own automobile-related business which he ran until 1934.[3]

Gille had steadfastly avoided politics, and up to 1931 had only enrolled in one veteran's group, the *Stahlhelm*, where he was a member from 1922–26. His political neutrality changed on 1 May 1931, when the joined the Nazi Party (the *Nationalsozialistische Deutsche Arbeiter Partei*, or *N.S.D.A.P.*). Five months later he enlisted in the part-time *Allgemeine-SS* (the General SS), where the value of his leadership talents and combat experience were quickly recognized. Thereafter he rose rapidly in the ranks, finally reattaining his earlier wartime rank of *Leutnant* (*SS-Untersturmführer*) on 20 April 1933 while serving as a company commander with the *49. SS-Standarte* (Regiment) located in Braunschweig. He was not fully vested in the organization until 10 October 1932, when he was formally given the SS membership number (*SS-Nr.*) 39854.[4]

No longer satisfied with serving as a part-time officer, Gille formally joined the full-time *SS-Verfügungstruppe* on 29 May 1934.[5] Posted to the *IV. Bataillon* of

SS-Standarte 1 (later renamed *"Deutschland"*), then stationed in Ellwangen in the state of Baden-Württemberg, Gille first served as the battalion's political readiness officer, then the following year as commander of its *11. Kompanie*. Now with a secure military career that afforded a steady income with opportunities for advancement, Gille chose to wed, marrying Sophie Mennecke of Stemmen near Hannover on 3 January 1935, to whom he had proposed in 1927. Six years younger than the 38-year-old Gille, they remained married until Gille's death; they had one daughter, born in October 1935, but since Gille failed to file an "Aryan" family background check dating back to 1750, the *SS-Rasse und Siedlungs Hauptamt* (*RuSHA*, Race and Settlement Office) would not recognize her birth as legitimate.[6]

As the pre-war *Verfügungstruppe* expanded at a rapid pace between 1936 and 1939, experienced officers were at a premium, and since the new *SS-Junkerschulen* (officer's candidate schools) were only beginning to fill the need for junior officers, men such as Herbert Gille soon found themselves being promoted rapidly and assigned to positions of increasing responsibility. Promotions to *SS-Obersturmführer* and *SS-Hauptsturmführer* closely followed one another in 1935, and he was elevated to *SS-Sturmbannführer* in 1937. During this period, he attended several Army schools, such as the infantry commander's course at Döberitz, the motor transportation staff officer course, and the gas warfare defense school which would have broadened his knowledge of modern warfare.[7]

After having demonstrated his competence as an infantry company commander, he then served from 1936–39 as *Bataillonsführer* (acting battalion commander) of *II./ SS-Regiment Germania* in Arolsen, after which he was officially named commander of the same battalion. According to a contemporary source, his performance while leading the battalion was apparently unremarkable; one of his former platoon leaders, future *Staf.* Hans Lingner, stated in captivity that he and his fellow junior officers did not think much of Gille as a leader and that they thought he was a bit of a *Dickkopf* (a particularly stubborn man), though decent.[8]

He finally resumed his earlier profession of artilleryman on 12 June 1939 when he was assigned as commander of *I. Bataillon, SS-Artillerie-Regiment 1*, which later became the artillery regiment of the *SS-Verfügungs-Division* before being renamed *SS-Division Reich*. Four months later, the 42-year-old Gille was promoted to *SS-Obersturmbannführer* and led his battalion through the Polish campaign and 1940 campaign in Western Europe. Subsequent awards of both classes of the Iron Cross (known as *Spangen*, or "clasps") soon followed in recognition of his leadership and bravery in Poland.

After the successful conclusion of the French campaign, Himmler decided to create another SS division which would be given the honorary title of *Wiking* (Viking). This division, the fourth in a body of troops which would be renamed the *Waffen-SS* on 19 July 1940, was formed on 1 December 1940 in the Munich area, using both native Germans and a smattering of volunteers from the Nordic countries.[9] It was to consist of *SS-Regiment Germania* (transferred from the *Reich* division) and the newly activated *Nordland* and *Westland* infantry regiments, as well as an artillery regiment and other division services. The new division's commander, *Ogruf.* Felix Steiner, who had commanded the pre-war *Germania* Regiment, personally selected Gille to serve as the artillery regiment's first commander. Promoted to *SS-Standartenführer* on 30 January 1941, Gille would exercise command over four artillery battalions—three with 10.5cm howitzers, with the fourth equipped with 15cm howitzers.

Gille led his regiment into the Soviet Union on 22 June 1941, where it, along with the rest of the *Wiking* Division, experienced heavy combat in the Ukraine throughout that long, hot summer as Hitler's armies plunged deep into the hinterlands of Stalin's empire. Attached to *H.Gr. Süd* (Army Group South), the *Wiking* fought at Tarnopol in late June and by August had crossed the Dnieper River at Dnepropetrovsk. The division continued to take part in the advance until it and the rest of *H.Gr. Süd* were halted at Rostov in November before finally being driven back to the Mius River during the course of the Soviet winter counteroffensive.[10] Gille demonstrated consistently good leadership and ensured that his artillerymen maintained a high level of proficiency, despite the challenges imposed by a campaign conducted at the end of a long supply line that forced batteries to ration the number of shells they fired each day. Decorated with the *Deutsches Kreuz in Gold* (*DKiG*, or German Cross in Gold) on 28 February 1942 in recognition for his consistent leadership and bravery before the enemy, he was one of Steiner's few regimental commanders who survived into the spring.

Given temporary command of the *Westland* regiment in July 1942, Gille led a mixed *Heer* and *Waffen-SS* motorized battlegroup into the Caucasus, testimony to his mental agility and innate grasp of how the combat arms complemented one another. He was no mere artilleryman—he was at home whether commanding panzers, infantry, or artillery units. On 9 November 1942, shortly before the encirclement of the Sixth Army at Stalingrad, he was promoted to *SS-Brigadeführer*—his first general officer rank—soon after being awarded the *Ritterkreuz* (Knight's Cross) on 8 October for his leadership of the artillery regiment.

When the German forces in the Caucasus were forced to retreat all the way back to Rostov in the wake of the Stalingrad debacle, *Wiking* served as the *H.Gr. A* (Army Group A) rearguard, successfully covering the withdrawal as pursuing Soviet forces launched repeated attacks. During this phase of the campaign, *Brig.Fhr.* Gille demonstrated the kind of leadership in crisis situations that was to become his hallmark. Resuming command of his artillery regiment once the division began its withdrawal, he was able to extricate his men along with most of their guns and bring them to safety, all the while providing artillery support to the rest of the division.

When *Ogruf.* Steiner was selected to take charge of the newly activated *III. SS (germ.) Pz.Korps* in the spring of 1943, *Brig.Fhr.* Gille was chosen to succeed him as commander of the *Wiking* Division, which was formally confirmed during a ceremony conducted on 1 May 1943 while the division was in its rest area preparing for the summer offensive. Although not committed during the battle of Kursk, the *Wiking* Division was engaged in heavy defensive fighting near Kharkov and along the Mius River throughout the summer.[11] Gille, though not considered a brilliant tactician, nevertheless provided solid, unflappable leadership during a number of crisis situations during the retreat to the Dnieper River and succeeded in leading his division to safety and into its new defensive positions on the west bank. In recognition of his leadership during this difficult phase of the campaign, Gille was awarded the *Eichenlaub* (Oak Leaves) to his *Ritterkreuz* on 1 November 1943, followed a week later by his promotion to *SS-Gruppenführer*, the equivalent of a major general.

By November 1943, he had proven his mettle as a division commander and, moreover, had earned the respect and affection of his troops, who nicknamed him "Papa Gille" for his sincere interest in their well-being and morale. As a token of affection and respect, his troops presented him with a distinctively gnarled wooden walking stick, nicknamed a *Wolschowstock* by the *Landser* (German slang for ordinary infantryman) that he carried for the remainder of the war. Finally, 34 years after entering the military academy at Bensburg-am-Rhein, he had attained the pinnacle of his career and had fulfilled his fondest dream—that of commanding a division in combat. All of his proven leadership qualities and the abilities of his division staff and subordinate commanders would soon be needed when the Red Army launched its winter offensive between November 1943 and January 1944.

Gille was assisted in leading his division by his *1a*, *Stubaf.* Manfred Schönfelder, who had been serving in that capacity since 26 October 1942. A graduate of the *Kriegsakademie*'s sixth general staff *Lehrgang* (the same one attended by *Stubaf.* Max Wünsche, one of Himmler's favorites), Schönfelder was widely respected within the division, where he had been serving in one capacity or another since its inception in December 1940.[12] Like his commander, he was also known for his calmness in moments of crisis at the front. Schönfelder and Gille made a good pair, a partnership that would endure from the time of Gille's assumption of division command until long after the war was over. Conclusive testimony to their good working relationship was demonstrated by Gille bringing Schönfelder with him from the *Wiking* Division to become his new corps chief of staff in August 1944.

With Schönfelder to run his headquarters and take care of the planning details, Gille was free to practice the type of leadership that he knew best—leading from the front. Based on the evidence, that is all he ever wanted to do. Throughout his service in the *Waffen-SS*, Gille had styled himself a "*Nur-Soldat*"—that he was merely a soldier and not interested in politics or any of the ideology of National Socialism, especially the mystical origins of the SS that Himmler was so fond of. Rather, like many others were to claim after the war, Gille felt that he had voluntarily joined the SS to serve his nation, and in the words of one scholar, felt that he had been "neither exploited nor victimized by [his] leaders." Accordingly, Gille had made his decision based on patriotism, and not on compulsion.[13] The danger in this attitude lies in the tendency to treat orders as something that must be obeyed to the letter, regardless of the cost, almost as if orders from above were sacred and should be viewed as such. This attitude would have consequences during the defense of the Dnieper River line.

There is historical evidence to back up Gille's claim of being politically aloof. During the fall of 1941, Gille's headquarters was visited by *Ostubaf.* Ernst Fick, the *Wiking* Division's *VI* staff officer who served as its "ideological observer." A lecture he gave to then-*Oberführer* Gille and his staff on Nazi and SS philosophy evidently did not go down well, particularly when the attendees noticed that Fick was wearing a brown shirt under his uniform jacket instead of the regulation field gray one. Remonstrating with Fick in front of several witnesses, Gille growled to him that "Wearing the brown shirt [i.e., Nazi garb] is not permitted in this aristocratic artillery regiment [no doubt hearkening back to his time as a cadet in Berlin]. I'll put a clean-out squad in your room!" Fick later reported Gille's "disrespectful" attitude to *Ogruf.* Karl Wolf at Himmler's headquarters in Berlin, but Felix Steiner, then division commander, intervened to prevent any reprisals against Gille for his political unorthodoxy and evident dislike of Fick, a belief that Steiner apparently shared.[14] Shortly thereafter, Fick was transferred out of the division and assigned to the training center at Sennheim, where he remained for the next three years.

But Gille's indifference to Nazi ideology must have clashed at some point with his "only a soldier" blind-adherence-to-orders attitude. One thing, however, is beyond dispute: his inexplicably lackluster performance during the Foxtail Island debacle of 10 October 1943. He had been ordered by his higher headquarters to clear out a small Soviet bridgehead on an island—named Foxtail Island due to its shape—near Kanev on the Dnieper. After four days of attacks by two *Heer* divisions had failed, Gille ordered one of his regiments—*SS-Pz.Gren.Rgt. 10 Westland*—to retake it *unter Alle umstände* (at all costs). Repeated attempts by the regiment's two battalions, both badly understrength, to eject the stubborn Red Army troops failed. By this point, individual rifle companies were down to eight to 10 men each and most of the regiment's companies were being led by *Unterführer*. Uncharacteristically, Gille failed to visit the front line to ascertain the actual situation, something that he had always done up to this point.[15]

According to survivors, attempts by the regimental commander, *Ostubaf.* August Dieckmann, one of the division's most distinguished soldiers, to convince Gille in person of the pointlessness of the assault fell on deaf ears. Returning to his headquarters empty-handed, Dieckmann rounded up a last-ditch force of clerks, radiomen, and other headquarters troops and led the final counterattack himself. After hand-to-hand fighting, he and his troops finally dislodged the Soviet defenders and forced them to retreat back across the Dnieper. Dieckmann, however, was killed in action at the head of his men just as the position was finally carried. Only 30 combat troops from his regiment were left standing. His death shocked the entire division, which had come to view Dieckmann as one of its most indestructible and well-liked commanders. While Gille's division had indeed accomplished its mission as ordered, the cost in lives had been exorbitantly high; additional or more imaginative courses of action to achieve the same result appeared not to have been explored, leaving embittered veterans after the war to wonder what Gille was thinking.[16] Less than two months later, the island was abandoned to the Soviets without a fight.

Fortunately for the men under his command, the available evidence shows that by January 1944 he had adopted a much more realistic view of things. Regardless of the merits of Gille as a tactician and his unyielding tendency to obey orders to the letter, two events occurred between January and April 1944 that cemented him in the *Waffen-SS* pantheon of heroes. The first was the encirclement of two German corps from 25 January–17 February 1944 near Korsun in what became later known as the battle of the Cherkassy Pocket; the second was the defense of an encircled German garrison town in Galicia from 18 March–5 April 1944 known as the siege of Kowel. During both, Gille was spotlighted at his finest—as a steadfast commander who never lost his composure even in the most hopeless of circumstances and as a leader who was able to inspire his men to perform great deeds of valor and selflessness.

When his division along with five others was encircled at Korsun, Gille led his division during a complex series of rearguard movements that were designed to place *Gruppe Stemmermann* into the proper position at Shanderovka when *H.Gr. Süd* commander *Generalfeldmarschall* (*G.F.M.*) Erich von Manstein finally ordered the breakout on the night of 16 February 1944. While carrying out his instructions to the letter, Gille's troops endured constant and unrelenting Soviet pressure but managed to take all of the division's objectives, all the while attacking "to the rear" as the pocket slowly wandered westwards. A skillfully led armored battlegroup from the division serving as the encircled force's only mobile reserve was able to thwart multiple Soviet attempts to break up the "wandering pocket" and prevent Soviet tanks from punching through the thinly held German lines and wreaking havoc among the sorely pressed supply troops and columns of wounded.

Gille was seemingly everywhere, constantly assessing the situation at the front lines while boosting morale with his boundless reserves of optimism. It was his optimism that is credited, by *Wiking* veterans at least, with fortifying the resolve of the commander of the pocket, *General der Artillerie* Wilhelm Stemmermann, his chief of staff *Oberst* Heinz Gaedke (about whom we will hear much later), as well as the other division commanders with the spirit of resistance at a time when the situation appeared hopeless and Soviet captivity seemed inevitable. Gille quashed any talk of surrender, and in the words of several eyewitnesses projected an infectious sense of optimism.[17] During the breakout itself, when his division and others were blocked from reaching the relief force holding Lysyanka by the Gniloy Tikich, a rapidly flowing stream, Gille coolly organized a human chain across the river that enabled hundreds of men, if not thousands, to escape. For this and other deeds of leadership during the battle of the Cherkassy Pocket, he was recognized by the award of the *Schwerter* (Swords) to his *Ritterkreuz*, which was presented to him by Hitler himself on 18 February 1944.

Perhaps the greatest test of Gille's leadership occurred during the seige of Kowel, which took place from 18 March 1944, when that garrison was encircled by Soviet troops, until its relief by a combined *Heer-Waffen SS* task force on 5 April. During this 19-day siege, the Kowel garrison, which numbered less than 5,000 men, withstood repeated attacks by several Soviet infantry divisions that compelled the defenders to pull back into a steadily shrinking perimeter. Initially, Kowel was supposed to be the location where the *Wiking* Division would undergo reconstitution after its breakout from the Cherkassy Pocket while it defended a vulnerable portion of the front. To arrange billeting for his division and to conduct a leaders' reconnaissance, Gille was flown in the city aboard a Fiesler 156 *Storch* (Stork) on 15 March, but soon found himself ordered to replace as fortress commander the incompetent *Obergruppenführer* (*Ogruf.*) Erich von dem Bach, who had in the meantime contracted a mysterious illness that all but paralyzed him.[18]

At first, upon assessing the seemingly hopeless situation, on 16 March Gille recommended to his higher headquarters, *4. Pz.Armee*, that the garrison be allowed to retreat to the west before it was completely encircled and link up with a relief force spearheaded by a battlegroup from the *Wiking* Division attacking from the opposite direction on 17 March. Shortly thereafter, he received a radio message from *G.F.M.* von Manstein himself, informing Gille that he was duty bound to obey the orders of the *Führer* and to hold Kowel until relieved. The city was subsequently completely encircled by Soviet forces on 18 March and the railroad line linking it to the west was cut. Once reconciled to his situation, Gille quickly re-energized the demoralized defenders, had several Army officers summarily executed for cowardice, and instilled in his men the "spirit of resistance" needed to hold out until the relief force could fight its way through. Skillful employment of the encircled Germans' few remaining heavy weapons kept Soviet tanks at bay, while a hastily organized airlift dropped enough ammunition and medical supplies to provide the bare minimum needed to enable Gille's troops to keep fighting.

Assisted by his *O1* from *Wiking*, *Hstuf.* Westphal, Gille practiced his daily habit of visiting every unit that he could, including *Reichsbahn* (state railway) personnel, policemen, *Landesschützen* (home guardsmen), and SS cavalrymen trapped in the city. His optimism, readily apparent during the battle of the Cherkassy Pocket only a month before, radiated throughout the siege, which at times, even to him, seemed on the verge of a Soviet victory. Outside the pocket, a mixed battlegroup composed of elements of the *Wiking* Division, the *131. Inf.Div.*, and the *4.* and *5. Panzer Divisionen* ground their way forward through successive Soviet defensive belts, all the while battling horrendous late winter weather conditions, which witnessed snow one day and rain the next. In a race against the clock, German tank crews and infantrymen battled against equally determined Red Army troops, who were struggling to eliminate the encircled garrison before additional German reinforcements could be brought up to tip the balance in the defenders' favor.

Finally, just as it seemed that the *Kessel* (cauldron) was on the verge of collapse, a tank company led by *Ostuf.* Karl Nicolussi-Leck from *SS-Pz.Rgt. 5* fought its way through the Soviet outer defensive ring and forced its way into the pocket on 30 March, and not a moment too soon. Now reinforced, Gille's troops, with Nicolussi-Leck's eight *Pz. V* Panthers, were able to thwart a renewed Soviet thrust in the nick of time. *Ostuf.* Nicolussi-Leck and his men's appearance bolstered the defenders' combat power and morale enough to allow Gille's troops to hold out for five more days, until the garrison was finally relieved by a *Kampfgruppe* from the *4. Pz.Div.* on 5 April.

Reunited with the men of his division, Gille continued the defense of Kowel until the end of April, when he was relieved of his title of fortress commander and allowed to take his exhausted division out of the line and bring it to the Heidelager SS training area near Debiča in Poland for reconstitution, a process that would take the next two months. In recognition of his impressive leadership achievement, Hitler personally awarded Gille the *Brillanten* (Diamonds) to the Knight's Cross with Oakleaves and Swords, one of only two *Waffen-SS* soldiers to receive the award, the only other being Sepp Dietrich. Gille had now earned the reputation of being one of the few German generals who had successfully led troops during two seemingly hopeless encirclements, a standing that would come back to haunt him nine months later.

Between the beginning of May 1944 and mid-July, Gille supervised the reconstitution of the *Wiking* Division at the training area in Poland. In addition to receiving thousands of new replacements to fill the ranks thinned during the Cherkassy breakout and the relief of Kowel, the division also had to receive a completely new issue of equipment in nearly every category. The only exception was the *panzer* regiment headquarters, plus one Panther battalion (*II./SS-Pz.Rgt. 5*) and one *Panzergrenadier* battalion (*III.(gep.)/SS-Pz.Gren.Rgt. 9 Germania*), neither of which had been present at Cherkassy and were therefore relatively intact. However, these units were quickly formed into *Kampfgruppe* (*KGr.*) *Mühlenkamp* and were transferred back to the front near Kowel on 9 June 1944 to serve as the *H.Gr. Nordukrain* (Army Group Northern Ukraine) mobile reserve. Here it would remain until 14 July, when *KGr. Mühlenkamp* was commanded to rejoin the rest of the division, hastily ordered out of its rest area to a forward position near Bialystok. Left behind at Heidelager were the division's antiaircraft, reconnaissance, and antitank battalions and one *Panzergrenadier* battalion, all of which were being rebuilt from scratch and were hardly ready for combat.

As the Soviet summer offensive, Operation *Bagration*, surged into eastern Poland, the *Wiking* Division soon found itself committed to action between Bialystok and Brest-Litovsk in a series of running battles and counterattacks. Gille's men, along with a number of other German and Hungarian units, gradually rebuilt a cohesive front line, at the cost of having to give up ground including the aforementioned cities. From 18–27 July, the *Wiking* Division operated under the close supervision of the *2. Armee* commander, *Generaloberst* (*Gen.Oberst*) Walter Weiss, who issued detailed orders directing its daily actions. While the bulk of the division directly confronted the main body of the Soviet armored forces south of Bialystok, an armored battlegroup was placed under the temporary control of the *7. Inf.Div.* during the fighting in order to reinforce the *Heer* troops during a critical phase of the battle revolving around their breakout from encirclement at Brest-Litovsk.

Despite having to parry numerous Soviet thrusts, the *Wiking* Division managed to fulfill all of its assignments while suffering relatively light casualties, though Soviet penetrations on its northern and southern flanks finally forced Weiss to order *Gruf.* Gille to withdraw his division beginning on 27 July. While the Soviet's First Belorussian Front had been thwarted in its attempt to seize a bridgehead over the Narev River, a far more dangerous situation was developing to the south of the *Wiking* Division and *2. Armee*, where the First Belorussian Front had smashed through *4. Pz.Armee* between Brest-Litovsk and Kowel on 18 July and was rapidly advancing on Warsaw from the southeast. Holding the Soviets along the Bug River line no longer made any operational sense and the commander of *H.Gr. Mitte* (Army Group Center), *G.F.M.* Model, made the decision to shift the *Wiking* Division to the west to head off the spearheads of the onrushing Soviet 2nd Tank Army before they trapped the bulk of Model's army group east of the Vistula and Narew Rivers. To get into position, Gille would have to direct his division to perform an about-face and shift towards the west, beginning on 27 July.

It was during this chaotic situation when *Gruf.* Gille learned that he was to assume direct command of the new *IV. SS-Pz.Korps* that same day. Though he had been informed of his selection as corps commander two weeks before, he had not expected to take charge so early. As outlined Chapter 1, the actual corps headquarters was still *en route* from France, which left Gille with few of the communications systems he needed to exercise adequate command and control of a corps, forcing him to improvise using what was available from his old division. For several days, the *Wiking* Division's *Hauptquartier* had to function in a dual capacity—as both a division and a corps headquarters.

Thanks to the hard work and efficiency of *Ostubaf.* Schönfelder, serving as the acting corps *Chef des Stabes*, and the rest of his division staff, Gille was able to temporarily carry out his dual role, but he must have breathed a sigh of relief when he finally linked up with the corps' actual chief of staff, *Oberführer* Heilmann, on 28 July. Thus, when he did formally assume command of the corps, *Gruf.* Gille was as aware of the actual tactical situation as anyone could be and had a solid staff to support him. Fortunately for Gille, he had two of the most experienced SS *panzer* divisions in existence under his command, both of which would be under *IV. SS-Pz. Korps'* direction for most of the remaining months of the war.

As vital as *Gruf.* Gille's leadership was, the *IV. SS-Pz.Korps* was more than a single man, no matter how talented or dedicated he happened to be. Just as its commander and staff functioned as the brain and central nervous system of the corps, and the corps troops as its arteries supplying the body with sustenance, the corps' maneuver elements—its ground combat divisions—served as the bone and muscle. While the corps headquarters performs the planning for battle and provides guidance once the battle is joined, it is the fighting divisions that strike the enemy and spill his blood. They also suffer the lion's share of casualties and, through the application of combat power using fire and maneuver, accomplish the corps' mission, whether it be attacking or defending. So it was with *IV. SS-Pz.Korps* from July 1944 until May 1945.

Throughout this 10-month period, many different divisions from the *Waffen-SS* and *Wehrmacht*, as well as the Royal Hungarian Army, operated for shorter or longer periods as a part of Gille's corps, including the *9. SS-Pz.Div.*, *1.*, *3.*, *6.*, *19.*, and *25. Panzer-Divisionen*, the *Hermann Göring Fallschirm-Panzerdivision* (*Fs.Pz.Div. Hermann Göring*), the *35.*, *73.*, *96.*, *356.*, and *711. Infanterie-Divisionen*, the *542. Volks-Grenadier Division*, the *2nd Hungarian Panzer Division*, the *25th Hungarian Infantry Division*, and the *1st Hungarian Cavalry Division*. In addition to these divisions, a number of separate brigades and regiments served as part of the corps at one time or another, including two Hungarian SS infantry regiments, which will be described later in detail in the second volume. But the two divisions that were most closely associated with the *IV. SS-Pz.Korps*, and were under its command for most of its existence, were two of the most well-known divisions of the *Waffen-SS*—the *3. SS-Pz.Div. Totenkopf* and the *5. SS-Pz.Div. Wiking* (hereafter referred to as the *Totenkopf* and *Wiking* Divisions for the sake of brevity).

By the summer of 1944, both divisions had gained an enormous amount of combat experience, having participated in the war in the East since its inception on 22 June 1941. Both had acquired a reputation for steadfastness and lethality that was rivalled by few other *panzer* divisions in the *Wehrmacht*. Indeed, they formed the backbone of Gille's corps and took part in all of its major battles. Just as the *1.* and *12. SS-Panzer Divisionen* are forever associated with *I. SS-Pz.Korps*, and *9.* and *10. SS-Panzer Divisionen* with *II. SS-Pz.Korps*, so it was with the *3.* and *5. SS-Panzer Divisionen* and *IV. SS-Pz.Korps*. Their performance in battle until the war's bitter end left an indelible mark on the corps' history, more than any of the other divisions that served under Gille's command. It is fitting, therefore, to provide a brief history of both organizations, an introduction of their leaders, and a brief outline of their material condition when they joined *IV. SS-Pz.Korps* at the end of July 1944.

Before delving further into that subject, a description of their organizational structure and weapons is in order. Both divisions had been redesignated as *panzer* divisions the previous year, having previously been organized as *Panzergrenadier* (mechanized infantry) divisions the year before that.[19] By the summer of 1944, both divisions, just like the remaining *panzer* divisions of the *Heer* and *Waffen-SS*, were either in the process of or had completed conversion to the new "*Panzer-Division Type 1944*" structure, with two major exceptions. Essentially, this new framework stripped down and simplified both the command and administration of a *panzer* division, standardized weapons and equipment, and achieved economies in nearly every aspect of its various *K.St.N.*s and *K.A.N.*s, including personnel. Conversion was to have been completed by 1 September 1944.[20]

These changes resulted in a *panzer* division that consisted of a *panzer* regiment with two tank battalions, two *Panzergrenadier* regiments of two battalions each, an artillery regiment with four battalions, and combat engineer (*Pionier*), armored reconnaissance, antitank, signal, and antiaircraft battalions, as well as the usual division services. On paper, this gave the standard *Heer panzer* division a total strength of 13,725 men, 136 tanks and tank destroyers (*Panzerjäger*), 42 artillery pieces (excluding infantry howitzers), and eight 8.8cm antiaircraft guns.[21] The numbers varied between divisions, of course, depending upon whether the division was engaged in combat, was transitioning from the older structure to the new one, and the ability of the German industrial base to produce the needed weapons and equipment to replace what had been lost in combat.

Due to a variety of factors, SS *panzer* divisions, even after transitioning to the new *Panzer-Division 44* structure, remained slightly more robust, primarily in two major areas. Each *Panzergrenadier* regiment had three mechanized infantry battalions instead of two as in *Heer panzer* divisions, and the first three SS *panzer* divisions (*1.*, *2.*, and *3. SS-Pz.Div.*) each had their own *Schwere-Panzerabteilung* (heavy tank company) equipped with the formidable *Panzerkampfwagen VI* Tiger tank as an organic component of their *panzer* regiments. This happy situation lasted until the fall of 1943, when *1.* and *2. SS-Pz.Div.* had to give up their Tigers in order for the *Waffen-SS* to begin formation of independent heavy tank battalions. Due to Hitler's personal intervention, *3. SS-Pz.Div. Totenkopf* was allowed to keep its Tiger company in its *panzer* regiment (*9. Kp./SS-Pz.Div. 3*) until the end of the war.[22]

Even with the transfer of their Tiger companies, SS *panzer* divisions by the summer of 1944 had an authorized end strength of 17,809 men (including Russian *Hiwi*), 180 tanks (both *Pz. IV* and *Pz. V* Panthers), and 33 *Panzerjäger IV*s. Due to production shortfalls in the manufacture and issue of *Pz. IV*s, some divisions, such as the *Wiking*, were authorized as many as 22 turretless *Sturmgeschütz III* assault guns in lieu of a company's-worth of tanks. Increasingly effective Allied bombing of German industrial centers and transportation networks was slowly beginning to impact the delivery of armored vehicles to front-line units; this trend would continue until the end of the war. Despite the fact that tank production increased during the fall of 1944, armored vehicles were being lost faster than they could be produced, and this impacted the *Waffen-SS* just as much as it did *Heer panzer* units.

On paper, at least, the divisions being assigned to *IV. SS-Pz.Korps* were powerful formations in their own right, equipped with the latest weapons then being produced, and adequately manned and equipped. The corps would not face the same challenge that *II. SS-Pz.Korps* had three months before, when its commander, *Ogruf.* Paul Hausser, had to direct two recently activated SS *panzer* divisions, the *9.* and *10. SS-Pz.Div*, in a complex and risky relief operation of the *1. Panzerarmee* at Kamenets-Podolsk in April. Though successful, both divisions suffered heavy losses in men and materiel in their combat debut, having to learn their lessons the hard way against a tough and determined enemy. Luckily for Gille, the divisions inherited by *IV. SS-Pz.Korps* would not have to undergo the same growing pains.

The first division to join the corps was the *Wiking* Division, which provided not only the new corps commander, but most of its primary staff officers as well. Though much of its history has already been outlined in the description of Herbert Gille's wartime career above, a few words are in order about this veteran division. Redesignated as a *panzer* division on 22 October 1943, it had barely begun the process when it was encircled during the battle of the Cherkassy Pocket three months later. Though it lost all of its equipment, vehicles, and many of its leaders in the course of the breakout from 17–18 February 1944, the 8,278 unwounded survivors were not given the respite they had long hoped for; instead, they were quartered in Lublin, a city in the *Generalgouvernement* (the Nazi-administered remnant of what once had been Poland), where they would begin the reconstitution process designed to bring the division back to full strength by early summer. Even this rest period was interrupted, on 15 March, when the division was ordered to form a regimental-sized battlegroup, *Kampfgruppe Richter*, to join the relief force then being assembled for the rescue attempt of the Kowel garrison, which was in immediate danger of being encircled. The survivors of the depleted division were soon joined by the new *panzer* regiment headquarters and its Panther battalion during the latter stages of the relief attempt.

From 5 April until the end on 8 May 1944, they continued improving defensive positions around Kowel, while it began its long-delayed reconstitution. This period of relative calm was disturbed several times when elements of the division were called upon to repel Soviet attacks, with the largest operations being *Unternehmen Ilse*, a multi-division operation led by *LVI. Pz.Korps* designed to encircle and throw back Soviet troops across the Turiya River south of Kowel. The successful accomplishment of this attack allowed the rail line into Kowel to be reopened and created a shorter, more defensible front line. On 8 May, the division was ordered to move from Kowel to the Lublin area, where it continued the initial stages of the rebuilding process. During this brief pause in combat operations, hundreds of members of the division were finally allowed to take leave, using their two-week furloughs to visit family members back home, see children that had been born in their absence, or to get married.

The division was transferred to the Heidelager training camp in Debiča near Cracow on 16 June 1944, where it began conducting collective training at the company, battalion, and regimental level, all the while receiving thousands of replacements, new weapons, equipment, and armored fighting vehicles. The only element of the division that did not partake in this process was *Kampfgruppe Mühlenkamp*, which had remained behind in the Kowel area as the *H.Gr. Mitte* mobile reserve. By 1 July, the division had reached a total personnel strength of 14,921 men, nearly double its strength after the breakout from Cherkassy, but still short by 2,888 men compared to its authorized number. The status of its armored fighting vehicles was slowly improving, with 123 tanks and assault guns available out of the 180 authorized, and the overall number of artillery pieces was reported to be at 90 percent of its required strength.

The division, which was reunited with *Kampfgruppe Mühlenkamp* on 14 July, was quickly drawn into the heavy fighting in eastern Poland in the *Kampfraum* Bialystok–Brest Litovsk from 17–27 July. Here, the division was seen as one of the few nearly full-strength divisions available to the *OKH* that could stop or slow down the next phase of Operation *Bagration*, which had already virtually annihilated *H.Gr. Mitte* between 22 June and the first week of July. This phase, codenamed the Lublin-Brest offensive by the Red Army, aimed at the Bug River crossings west of Brest Litovsk, with the objective being nothing less than the city of Warsaw itself and the strategically important crossings along the Vistula and Narew Rivers, the historic gateway to Berlin.

Only by the decisive action of the *Wiking* Division, along with other units of *Generaloberst* Walter Weiss' *2. Armee*, such as the *4. Pz.Div.*, were the Soviet spearheads, consisting primarily of the 65th and 28th Armies from the First Belorussian Front, finally brought to a halt or destroyed, though not without cost. But the road to Warsaw and the Vistula, at least from the eastern approaches, had been successfully blocked. During these two weeks, the *Wiking* Division suffered 764 casualties, though it had maintained unit integrity and its fighting spirit remained intact. Indeed, the division actually ended the month of July stronger than it had been when it started, since 3,654 replacements had been received throughout the month, allowing its end strength to be reported on 1 August at 18,004 men, 194 more than it was authorized.[23]

This positive number, however, was offset by the fact that the division was still lacking 1,037 *Führer* and *Unterführer*, forcing it to elevate more junior men into these leadership positions without the necessary experience to perform the duties which they entailed. Despite the heavy fighting of the past two weeks that had placed excessive demands on its armored vehicle fleet, the *Wiking* still boasted 110 tanks and assault guns, though only 65 were fully ready for action at the time of the report.[24] In addition, the division possessed 52 serviceable artillery pieces, 18 heavy 8.8cm antiaircraft guns, and 27 *PaK* 40 7.5cm antitank guns. These numbers would change dramatically during the following month as combat took its toll. On 1 August, the division still lacked its reconnaissance battalion, *SS-Pz.Aufkl.Abt. 5*, and *III.Btl./SS-Pz.Gren.Rgt. 10 Westland*, which were still undergoing reconstitution at the Heidelager training area and would not rejoin the division until September. Its newly refitted anti-tank battalion, *SS-Pz.Jg.Abt. 5*, with its 21 operational *Jg.Pz. IV/70*, had been temporarily loaned to *9. Armee*, where it was further attached to the *73. Inf.Div.* to bolster its defensive capability and would not rejoin the division until 21 August.[25]

Obergruppenführer Gille's elevation to corps commander on 28 July did not immediately impact the leadership situation of the division, because he still had to continue officially serving as its commander until 8 August. Such "dual-hatted" command situations were rare, and usually not a good thing, especially when both the corps and division were engaged in heavy fighting. Consequently, Gille appointed *Staf.* Johannes Mühlenkamp as *Divisions-Führer* (acting division commander) on 8 August. Doing so defied the wishes of Himmler, who wanted to appoint *Staf.* Dr. Eduard Deisenhofer instead. Gille held firm, letting it be known that Deisenhofer, who had recently commanded *SS-Pz.Gren.Rgt. 21* of the *10. SS-Pz.Div. Frundsberg* in Normandy, was not experienced enough to command an armored division. Though considered a junior officer for such a demanding position, especially when compared to Deisenhofer, who was senior in rank, Mühlenkamp successfully led the division until his departure on 23 October 1944, when he was replaced by *Oberführer* Karl Ullrich, a more senior officer brought over from *Totenkopf* for that purpose. Ullrich, a competent and well-liked officer, would then lead the *Wiking* Division until the end of the war.

Since *Ogruf.* Kleinheisterkamp had taken nearly all of the corps' primary staff officers (the *Ia*, *Ib*, *Ic*, *Adjutant*, and *IIb*) with him when he departed at the beginning of July to take command of *XI. SS-Korps*, a remedy had to be quickly found to fill these key positions. Characteristically, Gille acted quickly to fill the void with men whom he knew and could trust—men from his old *Wiking* Division. Upon Gille's assumption of command of *IV. SS-Pz.Korps* on 28 July, *Ostubaf.* Schönfelder initially remained as Mühlenkamp's division *Ia* until 5 August, when he was formally appointed as Gille's chief of staff upon the departure of Nikolaus Heilmann. Schönfelder was temporarily replaced as *Wiking*'s acting *Ia* by *SS-Stubaf.* Richard Pauly, who was completing his mandatory period of practical training prior to attending the 15th General Staff Officer course at the *Kriegsakademie*. On 22 August, having fulfilled the requirement to serve as both a corps and division *Ia*, Pauly departed, to be replaced by *Major i.G.* Otto Kleine, a *Generalstabsoffizier* from the *Heer*, who had been seconded to the *Waffen-SS* but retained his Army uniform.

As previously related, *Ostuf.* Hans Scharff, who had been the *Ib* for the *Wiking* Division, was selected by Gille to be the corps' new *Ib*. Scharff in turn was replaced by *Hstuf.* Dr. Heinz Fischer, another longtime veteran of the *Wiking*. The division's *Ic*, *Stubaf.* Herbert Jankuhn, moved up to the corps staff as its new *Ic* along with Scharff, and was replaced on the division staff by *Hstuf.* Georg Glanert. Finally, *Stubaf.* Karl-Willy Schulze was elevated to the corps staff to become its new *IIa* (*Adjutant*) and was replaced by *Hstuf.* Fritz Zimmermann, making the transfer of authority complete. All of the *Wiking*'s new primary staff officers were either long-serving veterans of the division who had been the deputies for the men just transferred to the corps' staff, or, like Kleine, were a *Kriegsakademie* graduate with a great deal of combat experience under their belt. In any case, the *Wiking* under its new commander and staff would function just as professionally as it had with its old ones. It would need all of their talents in order to survive the ordeal that was about to begin.

The other division constituting the corps' two maneuver elements was one of the most controversial, even notorious, divisions of the *Waffen-SS*. It was also undeniably one of its hardest-fighting ones—the *3. SS-Panzerdivision Totenkopf.* After three years of combat in the East, the *Totenkopf* Division had acquired one of the most fearsome reputations of any division in the German armed forces, but it did not begin that way. Raised from a variety of units and troops from the concentration camp *Totenkopf* (Death's Head) guard regiments, the *SS-Verfügungstruppe*, and even the *Allgemeine-SS*, the division, originally simply titled *SS-Totenkopf-Division*, formally came into being as an infantry division on 16 October 1939 in Dachau.[26]

Led by its first commander, former head of the SS concentration camp system *Gruf.* Theodor Eicke, the division had already earned a reputation even before the French campaign of 1940 as heir apparent to the spirit of the ancient *Landesknechts* and post-World War I *Freikorps*—typified by a swaggering *braggadocio*, fanatical dedication to National Socialism, lack of respect for anyone not part of their division, and blind obedience. Eicke personally infused his new division with his personal ethos, but in addition to being a Nazi fanatic, he was also a very able administrator who used his close contacts with Himmler to obtain the weapons and equipment to outfit his division, although at first it had to make do with a large quantity of captured materiel. He also made certain that his men were well fed and provided with all of the necessities of a soldier's life—cigarettes, alcohol, and other comfort items.[27]

Lacking the solid professional cadre of former *Heer* officers enjoyed by the *SS-Verfügungsdivision* and even the *Leibstandarte Adolf Hitler*, the men of the *Totenkopf* at first reveled in the division's lack of professionalism, gloried in its beer-hall origins, and adored their division commander, who was foremost in his advocacy of brutality. However, this attitude was insufficient when facing a modern opponent, a lesson the division soon learned to its regret during the French campaign. Haphazardly motorized, the division was rushed from its reserve position near Kassel to join the drive through Belgium on 17 May 1940 as part of the *XV. Armeekorps.* After arriving in Dinant, Eicke's troops were placed into the line of battle on 19 May between Le Cateau and Cambrai, where they soon encountered French troops, who administered the *Totenkopf*s first real taste of battle the following day.[28]

During the days that followed, the *Totenkopf* performed well during the battle of Arras, where it helped stop the armored counterattack launched by the British on 21 May after initial jitteriness was overcome. The attempt to force a crossing of the La Bassee Canal the next day against British forces did not go as well. The division suffered a number of casualties and was forced to wait until 24 May to try again. This failed too, with over 168 casualties resulting from the fiasco, which might explain the mood of the division when British forces finally began to withdraw on 27 May. Here, the division experienced the blackest day in its short history that left an indelible mark on its record forever.

While attempting that day to overcome a hard-fighting rear guard of the Second Royal Norfolk Regiment at Le Paradis, *I. Btl./SS-Totenkopf Infanterie-Regiment 1* (*I. Btl./Totenkopf Inf.Rgt. 1*) was repeatedly beaten back with heavy losses. The fighting only ended when the British ran out of ammunition. Waving the white flag of surrender, the 100 survivors expected to be treated as prisoners of war. Enraged by the heavy losses his regiment had suffered that day, the company commander on the scene, *Hstuf.* Fritz Knöchlein, had them lined up against the wall of the farmhouse the British had been defending and shot down with machine-gun fire. Knöchlein's men walked among the bodies, shooting or bayonetting anyone showing signs of life.[29] Two survivors escaped to warn others. When word of the atrocity reached the *Totenkopf* Division's corps commander, *Gen.Lt.* Erich Hoepner, he ordered an investigation and wanted to charge Eicke with the crime, but nothing ever came of it. It was to be one of the first, but certainly not the last, of the atrocities committed by this division.[30]

It was here, during the battle of France, where the *Totenkopf* Division earned the reputation that it would carry into battle in the Soviet Union the following year—that, in the words of it most famous historian, it had displayed a "reckless bravado that hardened into suicidal zeal and ferocity when seared by the intense heat of combat."[31] Partly as a result of the influence of Eicke's fanaticism, its thoroughgoing military training, and political indoctrination, the men of his division soon became known for a "reckless contempt for death and a vehement hatred for the enemy" rivalled by few other units in the *Waffen-SS*.[32] More than any other, the *Totenkopf* embodied the legendary "SS spirit" that would follow it wherever it went afterwards. While it could lead to criminal excesses with civilians and prisoners of war, this same spirit would also sustain it during the brutal and exhausting combat that it would experience in the East. The French campaign was a mere preview of what was to come—in 10 days of combat, the division had suffered 1,140 casualties, a high number for such a short period of time (at least by the standards of 1940) that drew the unwanted attention of even Heinrich Himmler.

After a year carrying out tedious garrison duty along the French coast, where it underwent reorganization along the lines of an Army motorized infantry division and incorporated replacements for its men who had fallen in France and Belgium, the *Totenkopf* was once again alerted for movement to the East on 30 April 1941. Assigned to *4. Panzergruppe* of *H.Gr. Nord* (Army Group North), the division was part of the motorized spearhead targeting the capture of Leningrad, a move that involved heavy fighting in pursuit of retreating Soviet units through Lithuania and Latvia. Finally forced to a halt on 24 September after steadily advancing for nearly three months, the division began constructing defensive positions near the town of Lushno along the Pola River.

They soon attracted the attention of the resurgent Red Army. Beating off numerous determined Soviet counterattacks which threatened at times to overwhelm Eicke's men with human wave attacks, his men held firm, though suffering horrendous casualties. By the evening of 26 September, *II. Btl./SS-Totenkopf Inf.Rgt. 1* was down to 150 men (out of an authorized strength of over 850), but it not only held its position, but retook Lushno during a night counterattack.[33] By this point, the invasion of the U.S.S.R. had cut a deep swath in the ranks of the division—constant, unremitting combat from 22 June–29 September had cost Eicke 6,610 casualties out of 17,265 men that the division had started with, and only 2,500 replacements had arrived during the same period.[34] Most of the casualties had been sustained in the division's three infantry regiments, but the antitank battalion had also suffered heavy losses as it sought to combat Soviet tanks with their inadequate 3.7cm antitank guns.

Shortly afterwards, the division, along with a number of Army units of *II. Armeekorps*, was encircled in the Valdai hills southwest of Leningrad in what was to become known as *der Kessel von Demjansk* (the Demyansk Pocket). Here, the *Totenkopf* Division and elements of five divisions of the *Heer*—nearly 100,000 men under the command of *General der Infanterie* (*Gen.d.Inf.*) Walter von Brockdorff-Ahlefeldt—were encircled from 8 February–22 April 1942. During this three-month siege, the Germans, enduring horrendous winter conditions, fought off numerous offensives by the Red Army's Southwest Front, which did everything in its power to eradicate its trapped opponent. German losses mounted, reaching approximately half of the force that was initially encircled, despite over 30,000 replacements being flown in to buttress von Brockdorff-Ahlefeldt's dwindling ranks.

Soviet losses were astronomical, with nearly a quarter of a million men of General Pavel Kurochkin's Southwest Front killed, wounded, or captured. Reduced to hard cinder, the remnant of the *Totenkopf*, led by a fanatically determined Theodor Eicke, proved to be the soul of resistance, but even the legendary SS-spirit could not hold off the Red Army forever unaided. Without the dedicated airlift of the *Luftwaffe*, which flew in thousands of tons of ammunition, food, and other supplies—and flew out thousands of wounded—the Demyansk Pocket would have eventually succumbed. Eventually, a relief force spearhead from outside of the pocket by *Gen.*

Lt. Seydlitz-Kurzbach shook hands with a *Kampfgruppe* from the *Totenkopf* attacking from the inside, finally raising the siege on 22 April after a week-long battle to link up with the garrison.

While victorious, the German forces inside Demyansk got no reprieve whatsoever, except that now the wounded could be evacuated by ground instead of by air and sufficient supplies were finally flowing into their positions. But instead of relief, the Demyansk position had only been reincorporated into the new main line of battle, or *Hauptkampflinie* (*HKL*), so the units who had been dug in there since November 1941 would have to remain there a while longer. This applied to the *Totenkopf* as well, which by this point was a division in name only. During the fighting that began in January 1942 and the subsequent siege that finally ended on 22 April, the division had suffered 6,674 killed, wounded, and missing in action—well over half of Eicke's remaining men. At the end of the Soviet offensive against the Demyansk Pocket, the *Totenkopf* could only count 9,669 men still on their feet at the end of March 1942, and this was after absorbing hundreds of replacements since the encirclement began. Few of the remaining men had been with the division during the French campaign, and the loss of junior and middle-grade leaders was particularly hard felt. Though it had fought well, the division had been practically destroyed as an effective fighting force and would need an extensive period of rehabilitation and reconstitution if it were ever to regain its original pre-invasion strength.

Fortunately for Eicke and his remaining men, the division was chosen on 6 March 1942 to be re-established in the West as a motorized infantry division.[35] This led to no improvement to their immediate situation, as the *Totenkopf* had to continue holding its portion of the front line in Demyansk throughout the spring and summer. During the last two weeks of July, it was involved in several major defensive actions near Demyansk, where it suffered over 2,000 casualties while repulsing two major Soviet offensives.[36] After this battle, *SS-Inf.Rgt. 9 Thule* was so weakened that it was disbanded, though its regimental staff and one battalion would be retained to form the nucleus of the newly organized *Schnelles-* (mobile) *Regiment Thule* with the additional of a *Kradschützen* (motorcycle infantry) battalion.[37] The division would retain two of its infantry regiments, now renamed *Panzergrenader-Regimenter*, and would be brought back up to strength by the addition of the men from the disbanded *Thule* regiment. This seemingly radical step had to be carried out after the heavy fighting that summer, when the combined *Kampfstärke* (actual number of men in direct combat positions) of the two remaining regiments had shrunk to only 959 men by 28 August.[38]

Other elements of the division were incrementally relieved at the front during the summer of 1942 and transported back to Germany, where they would join other elements, including two newly raised infantry battalions and a new artillery *Abteilung* then being formed at the Sennelager training area. Finally, the remaining portion of the division was ordered to begin shipment to France on 16 October 1942, but would leave behind the graves of nearly 5,000 of its men who had fallen in and around Demyansk since the previous November.

Joining the new elements of the division that had just been activated at Sennelager, it was formally renamed *SS-Panzergrenadier Division Totenkopf* on 9 November 1942, at the same time as were its two sister divisions, the *Leibstandarte SS Adolf Hitler* and the *Das Reich*. It would also gain a tank battalion and a corresponding increase in the number of other armored vehicles, including *Sturmgeschütze* (assault guns) and *Schützenpanzerwagen* (*SPW*, armored personnel carriers) for one battalion, as well as additional artillery, engineers, and other technical and logistical assets needed to supply and maintain a mechanized unit of over 18,000 men.

During this four-month reconstitution process, most of which took place near the city of Bordeaux, the division would be completely rebuilt and would absorb thousands of new replacements, including 6,000 young men involuntarily transferred directly from the *Reichsarbeitsdienst* (National Labor Service), and thousands of new vehicles. This unexpected largesse on the part of the *Heeresrüstungsamt* (the German Army's ordnance branch), which had begrudgingly armed and equipped the original *Totenkopf* Division, did not happen by accident. Under Eicke's fanatical leadership, the division had earned Hitler's admiration and respect, especially after its determined stand at Demyansk. In recognition of this achievement, Hitler rewarded it, as well as its two sister divisions, with the weapons and additional personnel that Himmler had been requesting for the past two years.[39] With this step, which also included authorization to form four new divisions, the *Waffen-SS* began its meteoric rise as an unofficial fourth arm of the German armed forces, a development the *Wehrmacht* would view with increasing alarm.

Eicke made good use of the limited time he had to rebuild his division. With nearly three-quarters of its men being conscripts or men from other SS organizations with no combat experience, Eicke and his veteran regimental, battalion, and company commanders worked hard to instill in them the same SS spirit that had motivated the division when it was first formed in 1940. Few of the new men had voluntarily joined the division, as it had already developed a reputation as one that got results but suffered high casualties. On account of this, Eicke and his subordinate commanders faced a dual challenge of motivating them while at the same time re-forming and training the division. Significantly, on 15 November 1942 the division was authorized a *Pz.Kfw. VI* Tiger heavy tank company, which was to be equipped with nine Tigers and 10 *Panzer III* support tanks. Challenged by the short period of time in which to complete the reconstitution of his division, by all accounts Eicke succeeded and when the call came for the division—now part of the newly activated *SS-Panzerkorps* under *Ogruf.* Paul Hausser—to deploy to the Soviet Union on 1 February 1943, it was ready for battle.

Obergruppenführer Hausser's corps had been hastily transferred to the Eastern Front in the wake of the Stalingrad disaster, which had led to the near-collapse of the German southern front. The overall shortage of enough armor and infantry units to stop a follow-on Soviet offensive that began on 2 February meant that additional mechanized forces were needed immediately, but there were few German reserves available on the Eastern Front. This Soviet offensive, codenamed Operation *Star*, was led by the Voronezh Front under General Filipp Golikov and was spearhead by four Soviet tanks corps led by Lieutenant General Popov. Another supporting attack was simultaneously launched from the south by General Nikolai Vatutin's Southwest Front. Together, both offensives were aimed at nothing less than cutting off and destroying *G.F.M.* von Manstein's *H.Gr. Süd* and driving the Germans completely from the Donets Basin and the Ukraine.

Arriving at the beginning of February 1943, the first two units of the corps, the *Leibstandarte* and *Das Reich* Divisions, immediately commenced combat operations aimed at slowing down the lead elements of Popov's armored group, but were ordered to abandon the key city of Kharkov by 16 February. *Obergruppenführer* Hausser had made a controversial decision the day before to withdraw from the city, disobeying a direct order from Hitler that it be defended to the last man. The *SS Panzerkorps* commander believed that no advantage could be gained by sacrificing his corps to hold a city that no longer offered any tactical advantage. This was especially so because he knew that his corps would soon be needed for any German counteroffensive; he was later proven to be correct. Both of his divisions then carried out a skillful delaying action as they withdrew from the city, buying time until 19 February while *G.F.M.* von Manstein developed his own plan for a counteroffensive.

Delays in rail movement meant that the advance party of the 21,156-man *Totenkopf* Division would not begin arriving near Poltava until 18 February, the last of the three divisions in *Ogruf.* Hausser's corps to arrive. The sudden transfer to the Eastern Front marked the last time that the division would serve in the West; thereafter, it would fight exclusively against the Soviet Union until the end of the war. The division's performance in the third battle of Kharkov was noteworthy for its adherence to orders as well as its cold-blooded effectiveness. Even the loss of its division commander on 26 February, when *Gruf.* Eicke's Fiesler Fi-156 liaison aircraft was shot down while he was visiting one of his forward units, did nothing to stem its combat efficiency.

Thanks to *Ogruf.* Hausser's decision on 15 February to evacuate Kharkov in violation of Hitler's stand-fast order to "fight to the last round," he was able to marshal his three SS divisions and strike back at the Soviet forces, encircling and destroying the bulk of them, while retaking most of Kharkov by 14 March. The personnel losses in Hausser's corps had been very heavy, totaling nearly 12,000 officers and enlisted men, of which 2,880 had been killed in action. Because it was a relative latecomer to the battle, the *Totenkopf* suffered fewer casualties than the *Leibstandarte* and *Das Reich*, losing "only" 2,709 killed, wounded, and missing in action during four weeks of battle.[40] Most of the division's losses were in the infantry units, which suffered disproportionately, especially in its officer and NCO ranks.

With the German front line in the Ukraine restored, the *Totenkopf*, now under the command of *Brig.Fhr.* Hermann Priess, was able to dedicate the next several months towards rebuilding and replacing the losses suffering during the Kharkov counteroffensive. During this period of relative calm, which was to last from early April until the end of June, the division allowed many of its troops to have home leave, the first that many were able to take in over a year. In addition, the division became a *panzer* division in all but name when it was directed to expand its *Panzer Abteilung* to eight tank companies, including the aforementioned Tiger company, which was later renumbered as the regiment's *9. Kompanie* when another tank company was later added. The *Panzergrenadier* regiments were renamed and the *SS-Schnelle-Regiment Thule* was disbanded, being broken up and divided between *SS-Panzeraufklärungs-Abteilung Totenkopf* and *SS-Kradschützen-Bataillon Totenkopf*. The former *SS-Pz.Gren.Rgt. 1 Totenkopf* later inherited its name, becoming officially known as *SS-Pz.Gren.Rgt. Thule* on 1 August 1943, but was later renamed yet again on 12 March 1944 as *SS-Pz.Gren.Rgt. 5 Totenkopf*. The division's second *Panzergrenadier* regiment was renamed *SS-Pz.Gren.Rgt. Theodor Eicke* on 2 March 1943, later renumbered as *SS-Pz.Gren.Rgt. 6 Theodor Eicke* on 22 October 1943 in honor of its fallen division commander.

On the eve of the Kursk offensive, *Unternehmen Zitadelle* (Operation *Citadel*), the *Totenkopf* Division had nearly 20,000 men assigned, with 92 operational tanks, including 10 Tigers, out of the 125 tanks assigned.[41] During the period of calm before the offensive began on 5 July, the division underwent an intensive training program that focused on assault troop tactics, clearing minefields, and combating antitank defenses. The 1,400 new replacements who arrived during this period were incorporated into the various sub-elements of the division. Under the tutelage of experienced *Unterführer*, these men quickly became acclimatized to the conditions prevailing on the Eastern Front, not only to the environmental ones, but to the combat methods of the Red Army as well. Many of the new replacements were draftees, the first of many, while a few others were involuntary transfers from the *Luftwaffe*, which no longer needed so many superfluous personnel. Some of the new men were even transfers from SS concentration camp guard units, who had been replaced by less-able men who were either overage or suffered from debilitating combat injuries that rendered them unfit for front-line service.[42]

Unlike is sister divisions, the *Leibstandarte* and *Das Reich*, the *Totenkopf* had suffered far fewer casualties during the battles around Kharkov and also did not have to transfer several thousand men after the battle was over to form a new division, such as the *Leibstandarte* had when it was ordered to provide the cadre for the new *SS-Hitlerjungend* (Hitler Youth) Division to be formed in France that summer. With its company, battalion, and regimental leadership core mainly intact, including such notable commanders as *Staf.* Helmuth Becker, Georg Bochmann, and Erwin Meierdress, the loss of *Gruf.* Eicke made barely an impression on the division's combat effectiveness. If anything, the lingering spirit of Eicke continued to animate the division as it entered into the most tumultuous phase of its history, where it was to fight in some of the largest offensive and defensive battles ever witnessed on the Eastern Front. Aggressive on the attack, or defending like "a cliff in the sea" when all other units gave way before the Soviet flood, the *Totenkopf* Division was to continue adding to its dread and terrible reputation until the end of the war.

Although the Kursk offensive eventually failed, the *Totenkopf* advanced farther than any other division in Hausser's *II. SS-Pz.Korps*. Its infantrymen and tank crews fought to exhaustion at the epic tank battle at Prokhorovka on 12 July 1943, and throughout the course of the Kursk offensive destroyed or knocked out several hundred Soviet tanks. This achievement came at a high cost—after a week of heavy fighting, the division had suffered several thousand casualties and only half of its tanks were still operational. Even though the offensive was officially cancelled by Hitler on 13 July following the Allied landings in Sicily, there was to be no rest period for the division. Taking advantage of the pause that followed the cancellation of the German attack, the Soviet Steppe and Briansk Fronts launched a counteroffensive of their own, forcing the Germans back to their starting lines by the end of the month, threatening to completely tear open their enemy's entire front line between Kharkov and Orel. July 1943 proved to be another costly month of combat, with the division losing 2,026 men, including 317 killed in action.[43] It was but a foretaste of what was to come.

Now thrown on the defensive, the *Totenkopf* was committed along the Mius River defensive line, and joined by the *Das Reich* and *Wiking* Divisions, along with several German Army *panzer* divisions, was able to buy time as the bulk of *H.Gr. Süd* withdrew to the Dnieper River line between August and September. The dawn of its role as an Eastern Front fire brigade had begun, roughly coinciding with the division being officially designated as a *panzer* division on 22 October. This official recognition of its *de facto* status as a *panzer* division that it had held since June 1943 came with no time to catch its breath. The newly renamed *3. SS-Pz.Div. Totenkopf* would be in constant contact with the enemy for the next eight months, being shuttled about to destroy enemy penetrations and temporarily restore the front line in dozens of threatened locations. It fought at Stalino in August to repel Soviet breakthroughs, and after successfully withdrawing across the Dnieper at Kremenchug, it was transferred from *4. Pz.Armee* to *8. Armee* in September, with whom it immediately went into action.

Here, the division fought along the lower Dnieper at Krivoi-Rog and then with *1. Pz.Armee* south of Cherkassy between November 1943 and February 1944. After further withdrawals between March and April 1944 while being reassigned once again to the *8. Armee*, the *Totenkopf*, though now considerably weakened, eventually found itself near Kishinev in Rumania in May, after it had participated in two highly successful defensive actions fighting alongside *Pz.Gren.Div. "Grossdeutschland"* at Iași

(Jassy) and Targul Frumos between 9 April and 8 May. Taking advantage of a two-month pause in the fighting, the division underwent a brief period of reconstitution designed to restore it to its former high state of readiness, while acting as the reserve for *LXVII. Armeekorps*.

To this end, it absorbed 6,951 replacements during the month of May alone and as many as 500 wheeled vehicles to make good its losses of the past year of hard campaigning. The division also received 24 new *Pz. IV* and 10 *Pz. VI* tanks, to make up for the temporary loss of the entire *I. Abt./SS-Pz.Rgt. 3*, which had been transferred to France in September 1943 to be re-equipped with new *Pz. V* Panthers.[44] By mid-June 1944, the division had been rebuilt a certain extent to conform to the organizational structure of the new *"Panzer Division 1944"* standard, with 16,903 men assigned (out of 18,191 authorized) and 56 operational tanks and assault guns (out of 70 assigned). Though powerful, this was still a far cry from its strength on the eve of the Kursk offensive. Still, it was a potent force by 1944 standards and was rated as being "Conditionally ready for limited offensive assignments" by its division commander, *Brig.Fhr.* Priess. Despite the fact that it was still training the 7,275 replacements it had received since arriving in Rumania, morale was still rated as "good" and leadership as "confident."[45] And despite the loss of many officers and NCOs since Kursk, enough veteran leaders had survived to ensure that Eicke's legacy of audacity in the attack and tenacity in the defense would continue. To the men of the *Totenkopf*, the term "SS spirit" still meant something.

On the eve of the transfer of the division to the *IV. SS-Pz.Korps* at the end of July 1944, the division was shipped on 7 July from Rumania to the central area of *H.Gr. Mitte*, where it was scheduled to go into action near Brest-Litovsk to block a Soviet attack that had begun to unfold southeast of Kowel. Instead, it was diverted farther north to the Grodno area, where most of its units finally arrived on 17 July after enduring numerous interruptions in its rail movement timetable. The cause of this hasty transfer was the Soviet 1944 summer offensive, Operation *Bagration*, which aimed at nothing less than the complete annihilation of *H.Gr. Mitte*. Initiated on 22 June, the Soviets succeeded beyond their most optimistic predictions, destroying the bulk of the army group through a series of encirclement battles and blasting a 400 kilometer-wide hole in the front. *Heeresgruppe Nord* was nearly cut off and only by extreme efforts was it able to maintain continuity with the retreating remnants of its neighbor to the south. Even Hitler was shocked; during a staff meeting on 31 August, he stated, "Such a crisis as great as this, even in this year when we've already had a few, is beyond my imagination."[46] A total of 28 divisions were destroyed or shattered, and over 100,000 German soldiers marched into Soviet captivity, which many would not survive.

To retrieve the situation, the *OKH* directed a number of units, to include the *Wiking* and *Totenkopf* Divisions, to slow down and then halt the Soviet offensive and its various offshoots, while the front was cobbled back together with the addition of new units being brought from the homeland and remnants of the shattered *9. Armee. Generalfeldmarschall* Model, who had developed a reputation as a genius of defensive improvisation, was brought in as the commander of *H.Gr. Mitte* on 28 June to replace the hapless *G.F.M.* Ernst Busch, and was beginning to make progress until the First Belorussian Front opened a massive offensive of its own on 13 July focused in the area between Bialystok and Brest-Litovsk. As mentioned above, the *Totenkopf* Division was shipped by rail via *Eiltransport* to the area near Grodno beginning on 7 July, and after nearly a week in transit from Rumania was committed to battle as soon as its tanks were unloaded from the railcars.

For the next two weeks, it fought a series of running battles that temporarily stopped the Soviet offensive, but another one launched from the Kowel area towards the west on 18 July was even more dangerous, threatening to punch through German defenses and liberate Warsaw. Since it had for the moment successfully contained the Soviets' advance along the Niemen River near Sokolka while the front was being patched together there again, the *Totenkopf* was then ordered on 24 July to move immediately by road and rail to the Siedlce area 80 kilometers east of Warsaw, where it would join Gille's corps beginning 27 July. Here, after a 200-kilometer drive, the division's wheeled elements would unite at Siedlce with its tracked elements, which had departed the Grodno area by train.

Upon arrival at the railyards in Warsaw, the division's tanks, assault guns, and half-tracks then had to carry out an 80-kilometer road movement to reach Siedlce. The *I. Abt./SS-Pz.Rgt. 3*, fresh from Grafenwöhr where it had just finished training with its new Panthers, also arrived at the same time. The long road march from Warsaw to Siedlce soon led to the mechanical breakdown of many of the new Panthers because there had not been sufficient time to properly break them in, always a problem with factory-fresh tanks. Finally, most of the division was completely assembled in the same place at the same time by 28 July.

When it joined *IV. SS-Pz.Korps* at the end of July 1944, the *3. SS-Pz.Div. Totenkopf* was still in relatively good shape, despite the exertions of the past two weeks at Grodno. It counted 17,809 men present for duty, 52 operational tanks and assault guns (with 87 more in short-term repair, mainly due to the wear and tear on account of the road march from the railroad yard in Warsaw), 25 heavy antitank guns, and 42 pieces of artillery ready for action. Many of the armored vehicles would be repaired during the next several days when the maintenance platoons caught up with their units. Most worrying was the lack of serviceable trucks, which earned the division a low readiness evaluation of being only 52 percent mobile. Nevertheless, the division commander, *Oberführer* Helmut Becker, who took over command from *Brig.Fhr.* Priess on 12 July, rated the division as being fully capable of conducting defensive operations and limited offensive operations.

Oberführer Becker, born on 12 August 1902 in Alt-Ruppin, Prussia, was a 12-year *Reichswehr* veteran who joined the SS on 27 February 1933 as an enlisted man.

Upon his discharge from the *Heer*, he was evaluated by his commander as "physically strong, mentally sharp and in body and soul a soldier."[47] That would remain an accurate description of his career as a leader in the *Waffen-SS* during the war. After only a year in the *Allgemeine-SS*, he had transferred to the *SS-Verfügungstruppe*, being promoted to *SS-Untersturmführer* and appointed *Adjutant* of *SS-Standarte 74*. On 1 July 1935, he made the fateful move of transferring to the *SS-Totenkopf-Verband "Oberbayern,"* which provided the guard detachments for the Dachau *Konzentrationslager* (concentration camp). Shortly thereafter, he was promoted and appointed company commander of *2. Kompanie* of its *I. Bataillon*. For the next two years, as one of "Papa" Eicke's most trusted subordinates, he was closely involved in the day-to-day operations of the camp at Dachau. On 1 July 1937, when Eicke became obsessed with establishing a regular infantry regiment, *Hstuf.* Becker was appointed acting battalion commander of *I. Btl./Totenkopf-Sturmbann 1 Oberbayern* and promoted to *SS-Sturmbannführer* on 9 November 1937. Two years later, he was given command of *I. Btl./Totenkopf Inf.Rgt. 1*, which he successfully led during the 1940 Western Europe campaign. By 9 November 1940, he was promoted to *SS-Obersturmbannführer*.

In June 1941, Becker led his battalion into the Soviet Union, commanding it through some of the most intensive fighting it had ever experienced, including Demyansk. An *SS-Standartenführer* since January 1942, he was appointed to command *SS-Totenkopf Inf.Rgt. 3* on 15 March 1942 and brought its survivors back to France in August 1942, when his regiment converted to a *Panzergrenadier* regiment. When the *Totenkopf* Division was redeployed to the Eastern Front in February 1943 to take part in the Kharkov counteroffensive, he continued serving as its regimental commander after it was renamed *SS-Pz.Gren.Rgt. 6 Theodor Eicke*.

Now an *Obersturmbannführer*, Becker was awarded the Knight's Cross on 7 September 1943 for the leadership and personal bravery he displayed during the fierce summer battles in the Ukraine, after earning the German Cross in Gold the previous September. He briefly served as the *Führer* (acting commander) of the *16. SS-Pz.Gren.Div.* in Italy from 13 March–15 July 1944, when he was promoted to *SS-Brigadeführer*. Finally, Becker was officially appointed as *Kommandeur* of the *Totenkopf* Division on the same date as his promotion, relieving Hermann Priess, who was transferred to command the *I. SS-Pz.Korps SS-Leibstandarte Adolf Hitler* in Normandy. With Becker, the division had a commander who knew what his troops were capable of and possessed the leadership skills to get the most out of them. Though not known for his brilliance, Becker performed his duties as division commander professionally and capably. He would lead the *Totenkopf* until the war's end and would accompany its survivors into Soviet captivity.

Thus, though bloodied, Becker's division was in better shape than most *panzer* divisions then fighting on the Eastern Front. Within its ranks were still an impressive proportion of experienced leaders who still carried within their hearts the memory of

Eicke's fanatical dedication to the SS ideal and his iron will. Though an intangible, this memory would help hold the division together during the hard times ahead. Becker was assisted by an excellent division staff, headed by his *Ia*, *Ostubaf.* Erich Eberhardt, his *Ib*, *Sturmbannführer* Dr. Martin Weidlich, and his Ic, *Kriegsakademie Lehrgang Nr. 9* graduate *Ostuf.* Roland Willer.

Both of his *Panzergrenadier* regiments were also led by hardened veterans. As of 1 August 1944, the division's *SS-Pz.Gren.Rgt. 5 Totenkopf* was commanded by *Ostubaf.* Ernst Häussler and its *SS-Pz.Gren.Rgt. 6 Theodor Eicke* by *Staf.* Karl Ullrich, who would shortly take command of the *Wiking* Division. The division's *panzer* regiment, *SS-Pz.Rgt. 3*, was led by the extremely capable *Ostubaf.* Anton Laackmann. Lastly, the division's artillery regiment was commanded by *Ostubaf.* Josef Swientek, who had once served under *Brig.Fhr.* Kurt Brasack's tutelage. Commanders of the division's combat engineer, antiaircraft, antitank, and reconnaissance battalions were equally decorated and battle-proven. One thing that these men had in common was that all of them had been awarded the Knight's Cross by July 1944, a sure sign that during the fighting to come, they would do their utmost to carry out their assignments while ensuring "Papa" Eicke's legacy.

So when Herbert Otto Gille assumed direct command of *IV. SS-Pz.Korps* on 28 July 1944, in conformance to the order issued by his army group commander, it is safe to say that he now had command of two of the finest divisions in the *Waffen-SS*, if not in the whole *Wehrmacht*. Bloodied somewhat by combat during July after benefitting from a two-month rest and reconstitution period, both divisions, though no longer as powerful as they had been a year before, still represented a considerable amount of mechanized combat power that Gille would soon exploit to its fullest to prevent the Red Army from crossing the Vistula and seizing the prize of Warsaw. During this summer of decision, which witnessed the retreat of the armies of the Third Reich on all fronts, the *IV. SS-Pz.Korps* and its veteran leaders and formations would do their utmost to challenge and even roll back the Soviet advance.

CHAPTER 5

The Tank Battle of Praga 28 July–6 August 1944

"Gruppenführer Gille must assume command over the *3. SS-Pz.Div. 'T'* and *5. SS-Pz.Div. 'W'* by this evening. Report when this has been carried out completely. The corps will remain under *Gruppe von Roman* for the time being." With this order from the commander of *2. Armee*, *Generaloberst* (*Gen.Oberst*) Walter Weiss, issued at 8 p.m. on 28 July 1944, *Gruf.* Gille was charged with carrying out *IV. SS-Pz.Korps'* first combat mission since its reactivation the previous March.[1]

The mission was a demanding one. Although Gille's *Hauptquartier* lacked its own organic signal battalion and most of its corps troops, which were at that time still in transit or being formed, he still had to disengage his forces from the front between Kleszczele and Czeremcha, shift to the west, stoutly defend the Siedlce area, and clear up the local tactical situation, all the while still defending the town of Kaluszyn with a strong battlegroup. Gille was also instructed in no uncertain terms that he was to establish physical contact with the left flank of the recently arrived *Fs.Pz.Div. Hermann Göring*, located somewhere to the west, and hold the line. But what line? And with what troops? It was a distinctively unsettling situation, mere days before one of the largest tank battles of World War II—the battle of Praga.

Gille had been thrust into an unenviable situation, one that had been developing since 18 July 1944 when the third phase began of Operation *Bagration*, the Red Army's grand offensive to throw the Germans and their allies out of Belarus. This smaller offensive, code-named the Brest-Siedlce operation, involved units comprising the left or southern wing of the First Belorussian Front (equivalent to an army group), commanded by Marshal Konstantin Rokossovsky. Rokossovsky's mission was to penetrate as far as the Vistula River, destroy any German forces in their path, and seize bridgeheads in preparation for future operations aimed at the heart of Germany (see Map 1). Half of his Front, consisting of the 70th, 47th, 8th Guards, and 69th Armies, and the 2nd Tank Army, would be dedicated to this effort. His Front also contained the independent 1st Polish Army, the XI Tank Corps, and II and VII Guards Cavalry Corps that would be operating in support. All told, his army group had approximately 410,000 men and 1,600 tanks. His Front's left wing

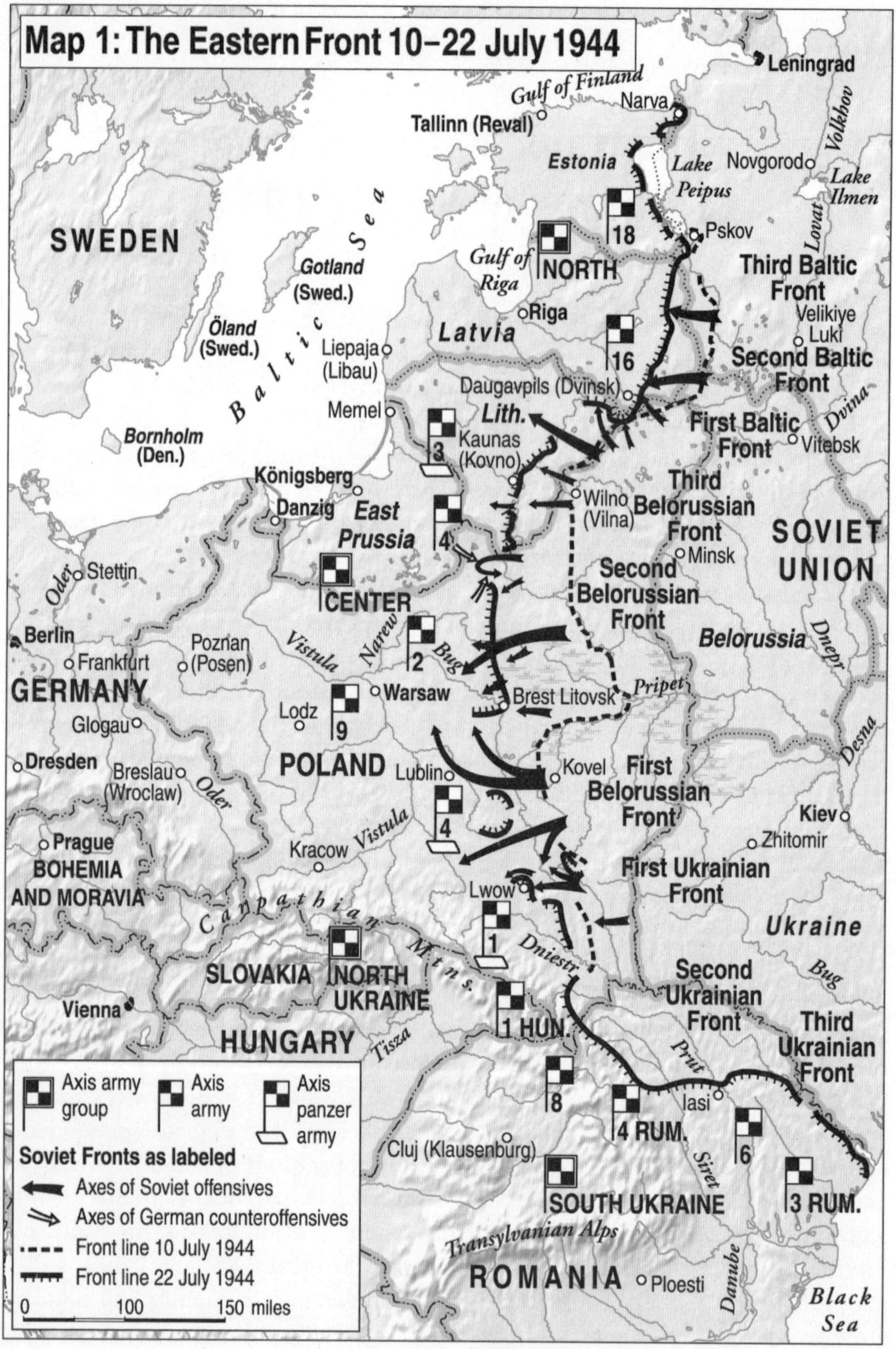

Map 1: The Eastern Front 10–22 July 1944

would be used to attack in a northwesterly direction from the region of Kowel and seize the cities of Brest-Litovsk and Siedlce on their way towards intended Vistula crossing sites north and south of Warsaw.[2]

Gille had already become acquainted with First Belorussian Front since the beginning of Marshal Rokossovsky's offensive, when as commander of the *Wiking* Division he had fought against its 65th and 28th Armies southeast of Bialystok in the Kamieniec-Litevski and Kleszczele area. Acting as one of *2. Armee*'s "fire brigades," Gille's division, in conjunction with *4. Pz.Div.*, had successfully helped to partially restore a coherent front line after carrying out a series of slashing counterattacks that cut off and destroyed major elements of the IV Guards Cavalry Corps between 22 and 25 July. Though the *Wiking* Division and its immediate higher headquarters, *XXIII. Armeekorps,* had been forced to gradually give up ground, the Germans and their Hungarian partners had been able to construct a more defensible front line while allowing the corps' hard-pressed infantry divisions to withdraw in good order. This was not to last. While the northern or left flank of *2. Armee* had managed to avoid a catastrophe, the situation on its right flank had become dire.

Here, the army's *XX. Armeekorps* and the garrison of the fortress city of Brest-Litovsk were threatened with imminent encirclement on 21 July, when a pincer movement was launched by Rokossovsky's 28th, 61st, and 70th Armies. Against such an overwhelming force, which saw the defenders outnumbered by 10 to one, the only logical course of action was to order a withdrawal no later than 22 July in order to save as many men and as much of their equipment as possible. But Hitler, now acting more and more frequently as the self-styled "*Feldherr*" (great captain) of the Eastern Front, forbade such a practical move. Efforts by the commander of *H.Gr. Mitte*, *G.F.M.* Model, to dissuade Hitler initially proved fruitless. The garrison, woefully unprepared to withstand a siege of any duration, dug in the best it could, using the ancient Austro-Hungarian citadel in the city's center as the core of its defense.

By 25 July, Soviet spearheads from the 47th Army had nearly reached Siedlce, 115 kilometers northwest of Brest-Litovsk, an event that threatened the survival of the entire right wing of *Gen.Oberst* Weiss' army, including the *XXIII.*, *XX.*, and *VIII. Armeekorps,* and of course the *Wiking* Division. Model had been badgering Hitler relentlessly for several days, arguing that in this fluid situation, holding Brest-Litovsk no longer made any tactical or operational sense. Model's inarguable logic finally began to bear fruit; an exasperated Hitler gave in and authorized an evacuation of the city on 27 July.[3]

The defenders of Fortress Brest-Litovsk, consisting of *Generalleutnant* (*Gen.Lt.*) Felzmann's *Korps-Abteilung* (Corps Detachment) *E* and the *203. Sicherungs Division* (*Sich.Div.*, or Security Division), finally managed to break out on the night of 27–28 July, after Soviet troops had penetrated its perimeter at several points, making any further defense impossible. Fortunately, two-thirds of the garrison (approximately

12,000 men) managed to fight their way west towards a relief force spearheaded by a *Kampfgruppe* from the *Wiking*. However, the relieved defenders had to abandon most of their heavy weapons and equipment in the process, while they were forced to fight off multiple Soviet attempts to split up and destroy the retreating columns piecemeal.[4] The survivors were moved to an assembly area behind the front at Losice, where they would need a week to reorganize and be partially re-equipped before they could be recommitted to battle. In the meantime, their presence was sorely missed, due to the increasing shortage of German infantry to hold any front line, even should one be constructed.

To make matters worse, *2. Armee*'s neighbor to the south, *4. Pz.Armee*, the northernmost element of acting commander *Gen.Oberst* Josef Harpe's *H.Gr. Nordukrain* (Army Group North Ukraine), was also being crushed by Rokossovsky's left-most armies, Colonel General (Col.Gen.) Vassily I. Chuikov's 8th Guards Army and Lieutenant General (Lt.Gen.) of Tank Forces Semyon I. Bogdanov's 2nd Tank Army. The two German corps defending the area, *VIII. Armeekorps* and *LVI. Pz.Korps*, were hopelessly outnumbered and lacked any armor of their own except for three assault gun brigades with a total of less than 100 armored fighting vehicles.

After initially attempting to make a stand, the two corps barely managed to withdraw their divisions across the Bug River, suffering heavy losses of men and materiel in the process. The battered *VIII. Armeekorps* was even pushed so far to the northwest that *Gen.Oberst* Weiss had to incorporate it into his own army's order of battle, though it proved but a scant addition to his overall combat power. Lublin fell to Lt.Gen. Bogdanov's tank army on 25 July, enabling Stalin to declare it the capital of the new "independent democratic Poland," a puppet state designed to forestall the installation of any Polish government that leaned toward the Western Allies.[5]

The two Soviet armies involved, however, made no effort to encircle and destroy these two German corps, being content instead to bypass and leave them for follow-on units to deal with.[6] For the 8th Guards and 2nd Tank Armies had only one goal in mind—get to the Vistula as quickly as possible and establish bridgeheads before the Germans could react and block them.

This follow-on operation was designed to set the stage for the next offensive phase, aimed at the complete destruction of Hitler's Eastern Front and the capture of Berlin. Once they had penetrated the German defenses, there was nothing in their rear area to stop the Soviet advance had they chosen to keep moving. Continuing its headlong advance, forward elements of acting commander Major General (Maj.Gen.) A. I. Radzievsky's 2nd Tank Army (Bogdanov had been wounded during the fighting around Lublin) reached the Vistula at Puławy by midnight on 25 July, less than 100 kilometers south of Warsaw. Here Maj.Gen. Radzievsky and his three tanks corps (3rd, 8th, and 16th) waited a day for the infantry of Col.Gen. Chuikov's 8th Guards Army to catch up, but on 27 July, Radzievsky did what Model had anticipated and feared the most—he ordered his army to execute a right turn, a daring move that swerved his tank corps to the north and sent them barreling directly towards Praga, the suburb of Warsaw lying on the eastern bank of the Vistula with its four bridges spanning the river. There was nothing to stop 2nd Tank Army except for the newly arrived *73. Inf. Div.*, recently rebuilt after being withdrawn from the Crimea the previous May.

By the third week of July, the German situation in the East was becoming seemingly hopeless. To the south, in *H.Gr. Nordukrain*'s area of operations, Army General Ivan Konev's First Ukrainian Front, which had launched the L'vov-Peremyshl' operation on 13 July, threatened to destroy the rest of *4. Pz.Armee* and push the Germans as far back as the Carpathian foothills, liberate L'vov, and advance as far as Peremyshl', where he had planned to bridge the San River. Employing similarly overwhelming force ratios against *H.Gr. Nordukrain*'s left flank units, Konev's spearheads had reached the San by 31 July before they were eventually stopped by a series of sequential German counterattacks carried out by three *panzer* corps. In the *H.Gr. Nord* area of operations, the situation by the end of July seemed equally desperate, with Soviet forces attempting to cut it off from *H.Gr. Mitte* by an attack through northern Poland towards the Baltic coast in the Memel region.

This was the overall situation that *Gruf.* Gille faced as he prepared to officially take over the reins of *IV. SS-Pz.Korps*. The news from every front, in fact, was bad. The Allies in Normandy were on the brink of breaking through German defenses at Avranches. Rome had been liberated and Finland was looking for a face-saving way to break its alliance with Germany. Though the overall situation must have weighed on Gille's mind, he had no time for such considerations. He styled himself, after all, as a *Nur-Soldat* who lived only to serve and obey. His corps now had an important mission to carry out, and to do this he had to respond that evening to the demand from *2. Armee* headquarters, which had directed him to exercise control of his new command before midnight on 28 July. But what troops did he have under his command, other than his own beloved *Wiking* Division? After all, in order to fulfill its mission, a corps by definition had to consist of more than one division as well as a corps staff.

Meanwhile, the actual corps staff (designated as the *Rumpfstab*, or "rump" staff) of *IV. SS-Pz.Korps*, still minus most of its key staff officers, after detraining in Warsaw had begun to arrive in the town Rembertów, an eastern suburb of Praga, on 25 July along with elements of its corps troops. Due to lack of key personnel, vehicles, and equipment, the corps' *Hauptquartier* was still incapable of fulfilling its mission. This included the corps' field hospital and portions of its supply column, which were still undergoing activation in Germany. The headquarters battalion did not even have direct contact with *Gruf.* Gille, who was located nearly 115 kilometers to the east with the *Wiking*. On the day the corps staff arrived in Rembertów, the *Wiking* Division was involved in heavy fighting north of the Bug River between Czeremcha and Kleszczele, where it had been subordinated to *Gen.d.Pi.* Otto

Tiemann's *XXIII. A.K.* since 18 July. To find *Gruf.* Gille and his forward command post, *Oberführer* Heilmann had to send liaison officers out ahead to query the various *Feldkommandanturen* (local area commanders) and *Verkehrsregulung* (traffic regulation) checkpoints as to the corps' whereabouts.

Realizing that neither Gille, with his improvised corps staff, nor the *Rumpfstab* under Heilmann would be able to exercise their intended role until they were combined and fully operational, *Gen.Oberst* Weiss removed Gille's "corps" from *XXIII. A.K.* on 27 July and placed both it and the *Wiking* temporarily under the control of *XX. Armeekorps,* led by *General der Artillerie* (*Gen.d.Art*) Rudolf Freiherr von Roman. Roman's corps had few intact units of its own, except the *102. Inf. Div.*, which had been shattered while withdrawing from the area north of Brest-Litovsk, after fruitlessly tried to maintain physical contact with the encircled garrison.

Korps Roman, as it was briefly known, would temporarily control Gille's "corps" consisting of the *Wiking* Division and the newly arrived lead elements of the *Totenkopf* Division. From the evening of 27–29 July, Gille's corps and his units would be under *Korps Roman*'s direction and all official message traffic to *2. Armee* would be temporarily routed through Roman's still-intact corps signal battalion.[7] This change in assignments was accompanied by the movement of Gille's makeshift corps headquarters and *Wiking* Division to a new area to the west, along with *Korps Roman*, which was under renewed pressure from pursuing Soviet forces that had been freed up as a result of the fall of Brest-Litovsk on 28 July (see Map 2).

The tactical situation east of Warsaw at the end of July was changing so quickly, and had become so desperate, that Gille had once before been ordered by *Gen.Oberst* Weiss to take over control of the corps, whether he had a corps staff or not, by 27 July.[8] This Gille was still unable to do, since he simply lacked the means to do so, and told Weiss as much. Consequently, his corps continued its subordination to *Korps Roman* until his new corps signal battalion, *SS-Nachr.Abt. 104*, could catch up with Gille's forward command post. By that point, the *Totenkopf* and other units of the *Heer*, including the elite assault battalion of *2. Armee*, *Sturmbataillon AOK 2*, had been ordered to report to Gille and were still in the process of making their way to his area of operations to link up with their new higher command. The situation north of Siedlce was chaotic, but order slowly began to exert itself as the Germans started to reconstruct their defensive line.

The extremely fluid tactical situation, which saw Soviet tank armies threatening Warsaw itself, left Gille little time to wait for the arrival of his new corps headquarters. Urged on by *Gen.Oberst* Weiss, Gille began to form a temporary *ad-hoc* corps staff on 27 July using the division headquarters of *Wiking* until Heilmann and the rest of the actual corps staff and headquarters battalion could arrive. Gille would also have to continue serving in a dual capacity as commander of *Wiking* and *IV. SS-Pz.Korps* until a successor for *Wiking* could be appointed, a situation that was temporarily remedied when Gille appointed *Staf.* Mühlenkamp as acting "tactical

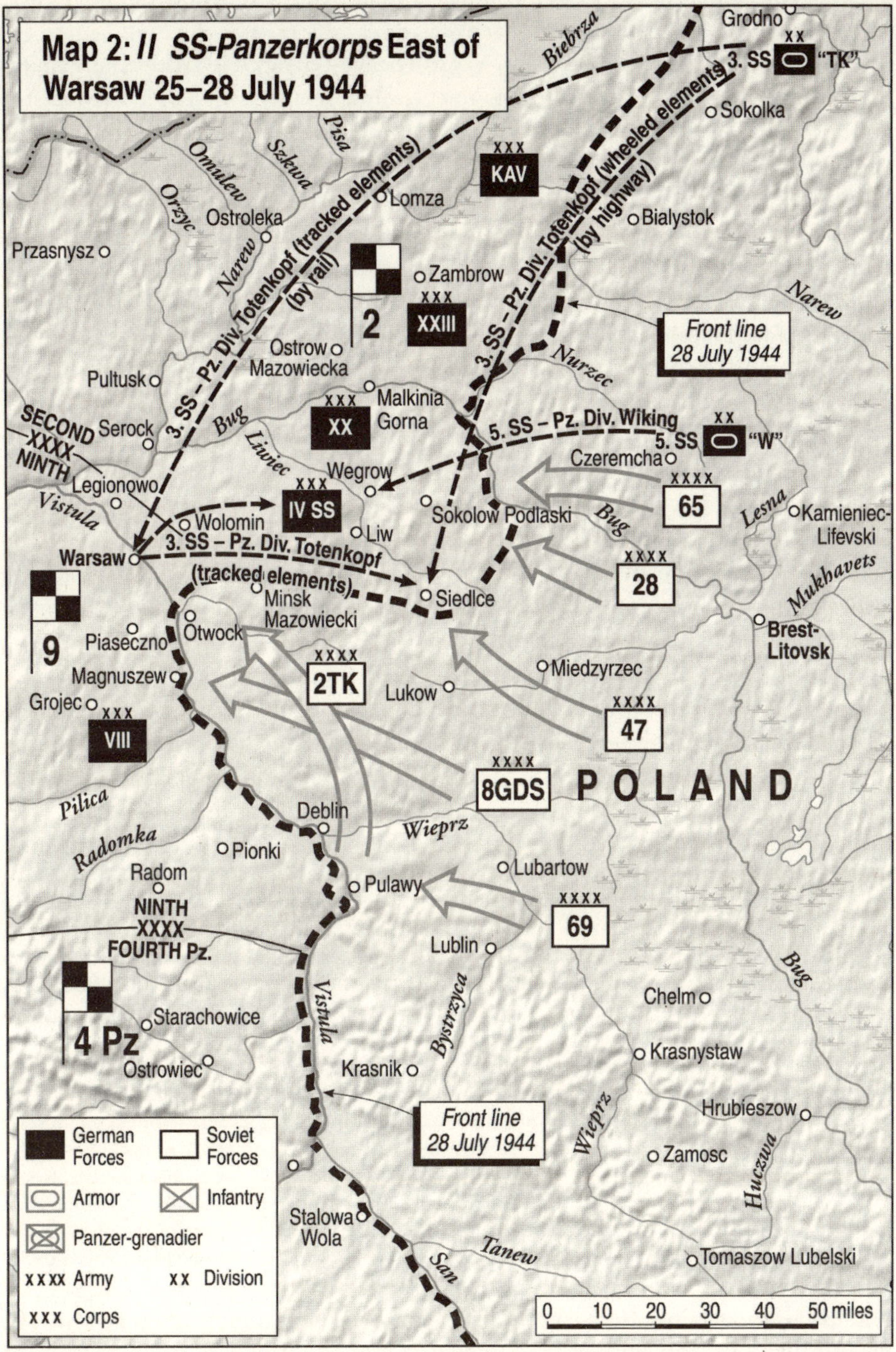
Map 2: II SS-Panzerkorps East of Warsaw 25–28 July 1944
3. SS – Pz. Div. Totenkopf (tracked elements) (by rail)
3. SS – Pz. Div. Totenkopf (wheeled elements) (by highway)
3. SS – Pz. Div. Totenkopf (tracked elements)
5. SS – Pz. Div. Wiking
3. SS "TK"
5. SS "W"
KAV
2
XXIII
XX
IV SS
9
VIII
4 Pz
2TK
65
28
47
8GDS
69
Front line 28 July 1944
Front line 28 July 1944
SECOND
XXXX
NINTH
NINTH
XXXX
FOURTH Pz.
POLAND
Grodno
Sokolka
Bialystok
Lomza
Ostroleka
Przasnysz
Zambrow
Ostrow Mazowiecka
Pultusk
Serock
Malkinia Gorna
Czeremcha
Wegrow
Legionowo
Wolomin
Liw
Sokolow Podlaski
Kamieniec-Lifevski
Warsaw
Siedlce
Minsk Mazowiecki
Otwock
Piaseczno
Brest-Litovsk
Magnuszew
Miedzyrzec
Lukow
Grojec
Deblin
Pionki
Radom
Pulawy
Lubartow
Lublin
Starachowice
Ostrowiec
Krasnik
Chelm
Krasnystaw
Hrubieszow
Zamosc
Stalowa Wola
Tomaszow Lubelski
Biebrza
Pisa
Szkwa
Omulew
Orzyc
Narew
Narew
Nurzec
Bug
Liwiec
Vistula
Bug
Lesna
Mukhavets
Pilica
Radomka
Wieprz
Vistula
Bystrzyca
Bug
Wieprz
Huczwa
Tanew
San
German Forces
Soviet Forces
Armor
Infantry
Panzer-grenadier
xxxx Army
xx Division
xxx Corps
0 10 20 30 40 50 miles

commander" on 29 July, a position similar to that held by the modern U.S. Army's division deputy commander for maneuver.

Despite the fact that their division was still heavily engaged in battle, the *Wiking*'s division staff now had to perform two roles simultaneously—that of a division staff and a corps staff—a stressful situation that it would have to endure for the next several days until the actual corps staff and its equipment would arrive and assume its mission. Part of the division staff consisting of the more senior staff officers would thus have to assume the functions of a corps staff, while the other part, with more junior officers, had to continue serving as the division's staff, thrusting junior officers into positions of responsibility that they had not anticipated. This battlefield necessity placed great demands upon all of the division's staff officers and its associated signal battalion, *SS-Nachr.Abt. 5*, which was never intended or equipped to exercise command and control over a corps.

Nevertheless, Gille was ordered to report on the evening of 28 July to *2. Armee* that he had indeed assumed actual physical command of the corps and its subordinate units. By that point, many of these units had already begun to arrange themselves under his banner, including the bulk of the *Totenkopf* that had arrived and had already taken up defensive positions in and around Siedlce.[9] The first and most immediate task was to establish contact with the *Totenkopf* so that Gille could coordinate with Helmuth Becker, its new commander, and issue him his orders for upcoming operations. Gille had not yet been able to raise its headquarters by radio, but that same day *Ostubaf.* Schönfelder, now acting as Gille's temporary corps *Ia*, was finally able to contact the *Totenkopf* Division using a still-working field telephone line that the Red Army had not yet severed, and was able to pass on orders instructing the division where to link up with *Wiking* and to issue its first mission orders.[10] After the war, Schönfelder recalled the situation vividly in a letter to Peter Strassner:

> Our initial worry concerned our future partner, the *Totenkopf Panzer* Division, and the swift establishment of contact with it. We knew nothing of its situation, other than what was contained in our orders. It could not have been rosy, since the Russian [*sic*] breakthrough must have caught them in the middle of assembly or unloading. Radio communication was not available. All that remained, therefore, was to conduct an armed reconnaissance towards Siedlce. A happy situation—or could one better call it coincidence?—had changed all of this. Namely, that the enemy had not destroyed all of the permanent field communications in an east–west direction, so that they could be of use to him. Perhaps they were all destroyed except the single line which the signals men now succeeded in finding against hope. In any case, it was like a gift from heaven when suddenly we could hear on the other end of the line the voice of *Totenkopf*'s commander, *Generalmajor der Waffen-SS* Becker [note: at this time Becker was still an *SS-Oberführer*]. The discussion at this vital moment enabled the first communication to be made from a distance as well as the first joint action in the sense of the order. It was the moment of birth for IV (SS) *Panzerkorps*. Soon afterwards the two divisions linked up.[11]

Because Gille badly needed a corps staff to carry out the planning and supervision of his two divisions, and since he could not rely on *Korps Roman* to do so beyond the evening of 29 July, when he was expected to begin operating independently, Gille continued improvising one by taking assets "out of the hide" of the *Wiking* Division. Gille had known since at least 20 July that *Ogruf.* Kleinheisterkamp was taking several key officers from the corps staff with him before he departed to take command of *XI. SS-Korps*, leaving him with no choice but to do the same thing, but with a twist—he was engaged at the time in shifting his corps to the west while fighting a major holding action to shore up the right flank of *2. Armee*. So Gille had to move quickly.

Meanwhile, on 28 July, the actual corps headquarters and corps troops, including the signal battalion and antiaircraft battery, had departed Warsaw and were struggling along roads packed with refugees and retreating units as they attempted to reach the front, but at the day's end were still 80 kilometers west of Gille, whose temporary headquarters was now situated near Łozy. At this point, the initial stage of what was to become the great tank battle of Praga was beginning to unfold, though Gille and his staff were as yet unaware of what was developing to the southwest. By midnight on the following day, 29 July, *IV. SS-Pz.Korps* formally became an independent command, operating directly under the control of *2. Armee* after three days of being supervised by *Korps Roman*.[12] On that same day, *G.F.M.* Model flew out to see Gille, arriving at the latter's temporary command post at Rogów, approximately four kilometers east of Sokólow, at 2:40 p.m. so he could congratulate him on his elevation to corps command and to brief him on the overall situation, including the danger posed by Radzievsky's 2nd Tank Army, as well as what he expected Gille's corps to accomplish during the critical days to come.[13]

During his hour-long visit, Model informed Gille that the *IV. SS-Pz.Korps* must assume actual tactical command that day of both the *Wiking* and *Totenkopf* Divisions as soon as possible. While the *Wiking* was intact and firmly under Gille's control, the *Totenkopf* was still strung out between Grodno and Siedlce. Nevertheless, *IV. SS-Pz.Korps* was assigned a very complex mission, but one befitting its military potential, which was to conduct a mobile defense in the vicinity of Siedlce and attack, and repeatedly cut off and destroy, the enemy's spearhead units attempting to penetrate into the town. Doing this, Model explained, would create the breathing space that Gille's new corps needed to get everything behind the front lines back in proper working order, including all war materials and armored vehicles, and to give the various corps and *Heerestruppen* time to get into position and begin providing the necessary support. Model instructed Gille that he should not seek to match the enemy on even terms, but rather use overwhelming force at key points to restore the front lines.

The actual corps staff and corps units under *Obf.* Heilmann's supervision finally linked up with Gille that same day (29 July), when Heilmann and the *Rumpfstab* arrived in Rogów. Miraculously, Heilmann and his column had traversed the same stretch of the Siedlce–Warsaw highway mere hours before it was severed by the vanguard of the III Tank Corps. In Rogów, Heilmann, Gille, and Schönfelder met for the first time. The corps staff and signal battalion would still need several days to orient themselves to the new situation and establish its signal networks, including landline and radio networks. This would be their first real-world "test." For his part, Schönfelder still believed that he was going to be appointed as the *Ia* of *IV. SS-Pz.Korps* since he had been serving in that capacity already for three days. However, Heilmann told Schönfelder that he would officially remain as the *Ia* of *Wiking* for the time being, since *Stubaf.* Richard Pauly, a general staff officer aspirant, who had been serving satisfactorily as the corps' acting *Ia* since 15 July as part of his general staff development training program, would continue to serve in that capacity until he had satisfied the time requirement two weeks later.[14]

Much to his surprise, Heilmann was told by his new corps commander to move the headquarters and corps troops the following day, 30 July, to the town of Liw. At the current pace of operations, Rogów would soon be in the front lines, an untenable location to position a corps headquarters. Instead of exercising command and control of corps operations, Heilmann and the staff would now have to partially retrace the route they had just traveled and set up at a new location some 30 kilometers further west of Rogów, where they would reestablish the corps headquarters and corps support area all over again. The advantage of this move, besides avoiding being embroiled in front-line fighting, was that for the first time, the actual *IV. SS-Pz.Korps* "rump staff" headquarters would finally link up with its commander and integrate with its new primary staff officers, with whom their fates would be intertwined until the end of the war.[15] The corps headquarters would be able to remain in Liw for only a few days, however, while it and the neighboring *XXXIX Pz.Korps* fought the tank battle of Praga.

Once they had arrived in Liw, the officers whom *Gruf.* Gille had appointed as his temporary corps staff were now permanently installed in their new positions, while their positions in the *Wiking*'s division staff were quickly filled by their deputies who were just as rapidly confirmed in their new positions. *Oberführer* Heilmann would continue to serve as Gille's chief of staff for two more weeks until he was finally replaced by *Ostubaf.* Schönfelder on 12 August. In addition to the other officers *Gruf.* Gille chose to fill the corps' key staff positions that have already been mentioned, many of the other vacant positions would also be filled by fellow *Wikinger*, such as the corps *O1* (deputy *Ia*), which would be filled by general staff aspirant *Hstuf.* Werner Westphal, who had been acting in that capacity since 27 July. Upon their departure for the corps staff, their former positions did not go empty for long, being immediately filled by other more junior officers already hand-picked by *Gruf.* Gille.

While a unified headquarters with one corps staff under *Gruf.* Gille had finally been achieved, the *Hauptquartier* and corps troops were still short of the required numbers of personnel and equipment, which impacted their ability to carry out all of their functions. Some, such as the corps' *SS-Nebelwerfer Abteilung 104*, were still in the process of formation in Germany and would not arrive until the beginning of September; others would not arrive until October or even later. In the meantime, *H.Gr. Mitte* would attach suitable units of the *Heer* as substitutes until their *Waffen-SS* counterparts could arrive. Because of all of this *hin und her* (slang for back and forth), the staff was in a considerable state of turmoil by the time it linked up with Gille's acting staff in Liw. Nevertheless, no time could be wasted; despite the difficulties inherent in its hasty transfer to Poland, the shake-up of key personnel, and shortage of equipment, the corps' staff, headquarters personnel, and corps troops went to work in earnest.

In regards to its two divisions, each was faced with two completely different challenges. For the regiments of the *Wiking* Division, they would have to disengage from the enemy near Czeremcha, conduct an 80-kilometer withdrawal over the Bug River, and make their way westwards as rapidly as possible past Siedlce, while leaving a *Kampfgruppe* behind temporarily in support of *XXIII A.K.* Since it had been conducting a mobile defense since being committed to battle on 18 July, losses in men and tanks had been relatively light; but the wear and tear involved in conducting so many attacks in so many directions at once had begun to tell on tank and other armored vehicle readiness rates. Spare parts were hard to come by, fuel was scarce, and many tanks, uncharacteristically *Panzer IVs*, were falling by the wayside for purely mechanical reasons.[16]

Despite its orders to withdraw, the *Wiking* Division's units were widely scattered, making command and control a challenge, a situation that placed a strain on its already overtaxed signal battalion. Were it not for the experience of its leaders such as Hans Dorr, Fritz Ehrath, Johannes Mühlenkamp, and Hans Bünning, backed up by the firm hand of Gille who relied upon mission-type orders to express his intent, the division might easily have disintegrated in the face of relentless mechanized Soviet attacks. As the *Wiking* Division rapidly reassembled in its new area of operations near Wegrow between 27 and 30 July, it was still a powerful force—at midnight on 29 July, it still had seven operational *Panzer IVs*, 32 operational Panthers, and seven operational *Sturmgeschütze*, out of the 108 tanks and assault guns still on its establishment.[17] It would put the three-day breathing space at Wegrow to good use, using it as an opportunity to clean and service its weapons, repair its broken-down or damaged vehicles, replenish its stocks of munitions, and restore a sense of order to its regiments and battalions, many of which had been fighting independently for the past 10 days.

Like its sister division, the *Totenkopf* had also been on the move, but it had to overcome the additional challenge of having to move 14 trains' worth of men and armored vehicles hundreds of kilometers by rail to Warsaw, where they would unload and then drive the rest of the way to reach *Gruf.* Gille's corps. Hundreds of the division's motor vehicles carrying the bulk of Ullrich's *SS-Pz.Gren.Rgt. 6 Eicke* (referred to hereafter as the *Eicke* Regiment) would convoy by road to the town of Sokolow, where they would then move tactically to the Siedlce area. Here, the regiment would occupy defensive positions in and around the town while its men waited for the arrival of the armor. Upon arrival, its regiments and battalions would have to go into action immediately after unloading, often in a piecemeal fashion, without having sufficient time to familiarize themselves with their new area of operations or to even conduct a rudimentary reconnaissance.

On 29 July, much of the division was still on the march as it struggled to reach its new staging area north of Siedlce (by 28 July, only four of its 14 trains had arrived). In the vicinity of Mordy, a small town roughly 30 kilometers northeast of Siedlce, elements of Meierdress's *I. Abt./SS-Pz.Rgt. 3*, which had begun to arrive as early as 24 July, were placed under the temporary control of *Gruppe von Roman*, where 23 of its available tanks were sent into action to attack an enemy grouping there. Thirty-six more of the division's tanks and assault guns were still in transit, while 40 others were inoperable due to mechanical problems, many stemming from the forced march that the armor had to make to reach its new area of operation from the railyard in Warsaw. Twenty-five of the *I. Abteilung*'s brand-new Panthers were included in this amount that had fallen out for maintenance reasons, having not had sufficient time for their crews to properly break them in before subjecting them to the strain of combat.

Each battalion of *Eicke*, the first complete regiment to arrive by wheeled vehicle, was given separate missions. The *I. Btl./Eicke* would be fighting north of Opole Stare (8 kilometers west of Siedlce) facing east, *II. Btl./Eicke* would also be fighting west of Siedlce but oriented to the south, and *III. Btl./Eicke* would actually be defending within Siedlce itself alongside several infantry battalions from the *Heer*, whose men were attempting to cut off and destroy a Soviet penetration on the city's eastern edge. Other elements of the division were employed along the main highway leading from Siedlce to Warsaw as far as Stanisławów, but had to constantly fight to keep it clear of enemy reconnaissance probes, ominous signs of previously unidentified Soviet forces approaching from the south. A company from the division's reconnaissance battalion, *Stubaf.* Arzelino "Lino" Masarie's *SS-Pz.Auf.Abt. 3*, had managed to effect a tenuous link-up with an armored patrol from the *9. Armee*'s newly arriving *Fs.Pz. Div. Hermann Göring*, located on *Totenkopf*'s far western flank near Kałuszyn, at 1:10 p.m. on 28 July, a thinly reinforced connection that was cut later that evening by the Soviet advance.[18]

Meanwhile, the bulk of the division's other mechanized infantry regiment, *SS-Pz.Gren.Rgt. 5 Totenkopf* (referred to hereafter as the *Totenkopf* Regiment), was still fighting far to the north in its previous area of operations, minus its *III. Bataillon* which had arrived at the outskirts of Siedlce on 28 July. Here, southwest of Grodno, most of the regiment was still supporting *Gruppe Weidling*, a unit that was composed of the remnants of the *XLI. Pz.Korps*, whose divisions had been shattered during Operation *Bagration* and were badly understrength. On account of this, the regiment would not be able to disengage and join the rest of the division for several more days, leaving the division with only one full-strength

Panzergrenadier regiment to carry out its mission of defending Siedlce. To compensate for the shortage of infantry, three *Landeschutz* (home guard) battalions and one battalion from *Gren.Rgt. 170* of the *73. Inf.Div.* were attached to the division as substitutes for its missing regiment. Some of the division's support units, primarily maintenance and supply columns, were still in Rumania, having been left there when the division had been shipped to Grodno two weeks earlier. The lack of their services was being sorely felt, as tanks lay idle without fuel and other vehicles were stranded due to lack of replacement parts.

Oberführer Becker had established his command post northwest of Siedlce but was still without most of his headquarters establishment, particularly the signal battalion, which was still in transit, like many other of the smaller elements of the division. Improvising a temporary staff on the spot using spare officers from his regiments until his actual staff could arrive, Becker did the best he could in an incredibly fluid situation to maintain control of his division, which was becoming increasingly embroiled in the fighting for Siedlce. On the evening of 29 July, *Gen. Oberst* Weiss, in his last report to *H.Gr. Mitte* before going to bed, wrote that the day was marked by heavy fighting for that city, where the Soviets had employed a series of battalion-sized, tank-supported infantry attacks in their attempt to seize this key centre. He remarked that most of the recently arrived elements of the *Totenkopf* Division were decisively engaged in Siedlce's defense, making it all the more important for all of the *Wiking* Division to get into its new position at Wegrow as quickly as possible in order to prevent an armor-led breakthrough from occurring north of the city, where *XXIII. Armeekorps* was fighting to hold the line.

The controversial decision to move the *Totenkopf* Division from Grodno to Siedlce and the *Wiking* from Czeremcha to Wegrow was made by *G.F.M.* Model himself. Alarmed by the rapid advance of 2nd Tank Army, whose lead elements reached the Vistula River near Puławy on 25 July, Model began rapidly assembling forces to counter Radzievsky's next move, which he instinctively felt would be a bold advance towards Warsaw along the river's eastern bank. Should the 2nd Tank Army seize Praga, site of four key bridges spanning the Vistula, Lt.Gen. Radzievsky would have been able to do one of two things—either cross the river and liberate Warsaw, an action that would sever the key Siedlce–Warsaw highway, or, an even more dangerous move, to keep pushing on after capturing Praga and take the key towns of Modlin, Zegrze, and Serock, all of which stood astride bridges over the Vistula, Narew, and the confluence of the Narew–Bug Rivers, respectively (see Map 3).

The loss of these towns would have immediately led to the entrapment of the bulk of *2. Armee* as well as the severing of the key supply lines to *9. Armee*. This would quickly lead to a catastrophe every bit as bad as the defeat of *H.Gr. Mitte* during the opening phase of Operation *Bagration*; only this time, nothing would stand between the Red Army and the Baltic Sea, because nearly everything still left in Germany that could be transferred to the Eastern Front had already been sent.

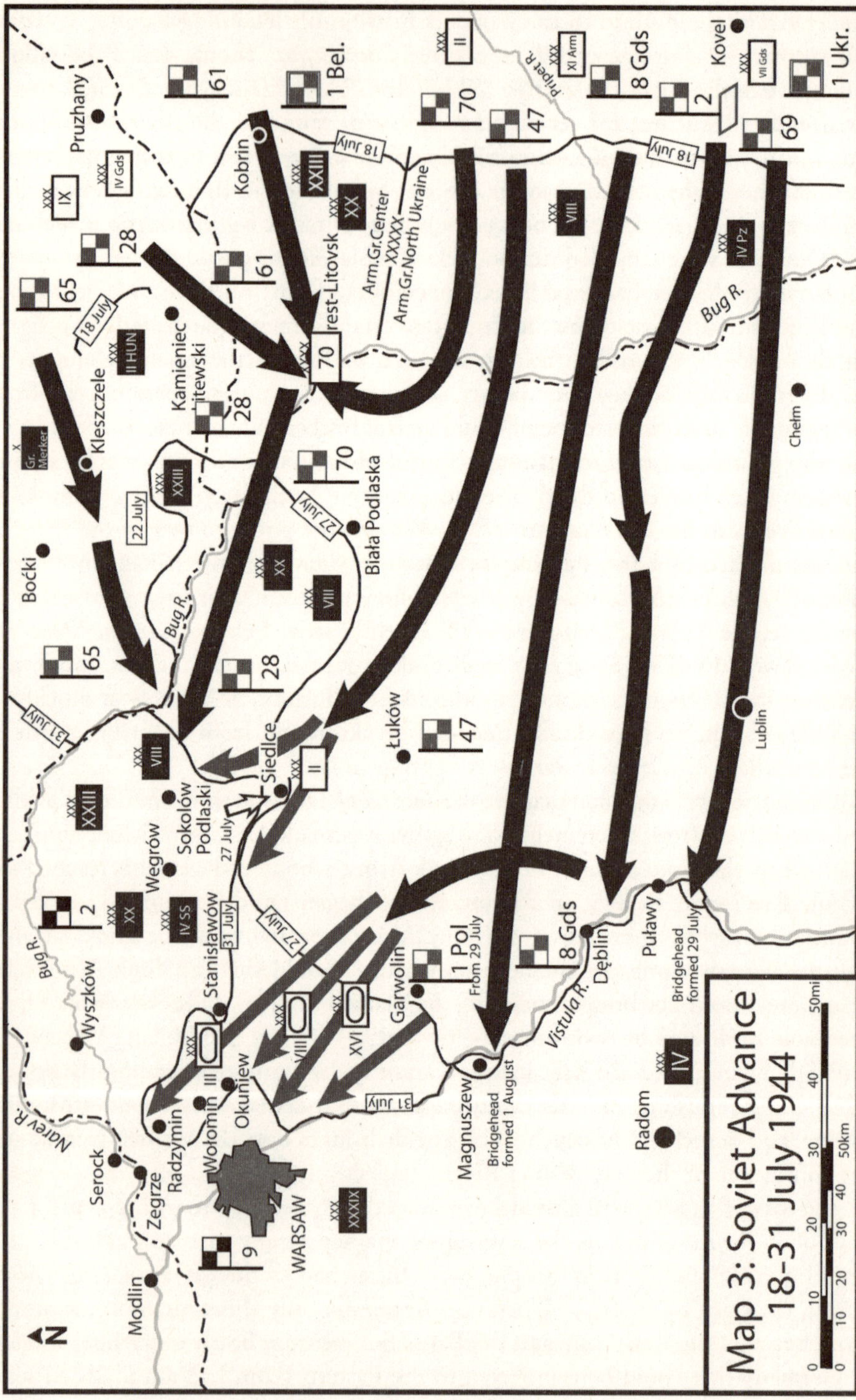

Map 3: Soviet Advance
18-31 July 1944
Pruzhany
Kobrin
Kovel
Pripet R.
1 Bel.
1 Ukr.
8 Gds
Arm.Gr.Center
Arm.Gr.North Ukraine
rest-Litovsk
Kamieniec Litewski
Kleszczele
Bocki
Biała Podlaska
Bug R.
Chełm
Siedlce
Łuków
Lublin
Sokolów Podlaski
Wegrów
Stanisławów
Garwolin
Dęblin
Puławy
Vistula R.
Magnuszew
Bridgehead formed 1 August
Bridgehead formed 29 July
1 Pol
From 29 July
Radom
Okuniew
Wołomin
Radzymin
Wyszków
Serock
Zegrze
Narev R.
WARSAW
Modlin
18 July
22 July
27 July
31 July
II HUN
Gr. Merker
IV Gds
IV SS
VII Gds
XI Arm
IV Pz

Complicating the situation was the fact that the inner flanks of both the *2. Armee* and *9. Armee* had not been able to link together east of Warsaw, nor was the right flank of *9. Armee* along the Vistula tied in with that of the *4. Pz.Armee* to its south. *Heeresgruppe Mitte* was in a very precarious situation indeed, with its left, right, and even interior flanks literally hanging in the air. Consequently, *G.F.M.* Model issued the following orders on 26 July to the two armies defending the approaches to Warsaw: *9. Armee* was to build up a defense line along the Vistula and tie in with the *4. Pz.Armee* between Pulawy and Warsaw, while *2. Armee* was to take responsibility for the southern front between Siedlce and Biała Podlaska.[19]

The first task was to hold Siedlce at all cost, a necessary decision in light of the fact that it had become the "corner post" or pivot point of *2. Armee*'s entire front line. Model's decision to defend, made on 25 July, had taken the *Totenkopf* away from *4. Armee* control beginning that same day and started its movement all the way down from Grodno. It was a logical choice, since it was the only *panzer* division north of Warsaw that could possibly be freed up at that point in time and sent there. The *Wiking* was still decisively engaged between Kleszczele and Czeremcha and could not be spared, as was the *4. Pz.Div.*, lest the front collapse. In any case, the bulk of *Gruf.* Gille's *Wiking* Division was still 60 kilometers away from Siedlce on the date that Model decided to hold it. Observing the shape of the German front line from the vantage point of Siedlce, one would have seen that the line ran north as far as łomża on the Narew River, where it linked up with *4. Armee*. A few kilometers southeast of Siedlce, the front line made a 90-degree turn to the west, stretching halfway to Warsaw, ending in thin air near the town of Stanisławów, which was practically undefended, save for a weak security screen erected by the reconnaissance battalion of the *Fs.Pz. Div. Hermann Göring*.

The fighting for Siedlce, which started on 25 July and raged until it was finally abandoned on the morning of 31 July, was exceptionally fierce and became the primary focus of Gille's command until the tank battle for Praga began. The home guard and security battalions and one grenadier battalion defending there would not have been able to hold the city without the timely arrival of the *Totenkopf* Division.[20] Attacked for nearly an entire week by the divisions of the Red Army's XI Tank Corps, II Guards Cavalry Corps, and three infantry divisions from the 47th Army, the *Totenkopf*, reinforced by the security troops and the battalion from the *73. Inf.Div.*, held firm. *SS-Kriegsberichter* Gösta Borg left a very vivid description of the opening stages of the battle:

> Things are nervous during the afternoon. To the east, the dust clouds rise, yellow-brown clouds mushroom in the air and on the ground. The Soviet frontline infantry is active … Fighting rages at several points. In one district, an attack is underway. The Corps' staff knows the defensive plans, reconnaissance pilots deliver their photos, the roads on the enemy's side are filled with convoys, every wooded area is bristling with tanks, infantry and heavy formations. Artillery is

> heaved from the road, barrel by barrel and a flood of all types of vehicles loaded down with shells, shells and more shells. During the evening, a counterattack is launched to lighten the pressure on an important position. Prisoners are taken from a new enemy division; defectors report the number of divisions [to be] double the number that had been assumed. The road from Bialystok is filled with artillery, Guards [units] and T-34s, many Joseph Stalin [tanks] and Stalin's Organs [rocket launchers] … Our own troops are wide awake, digging and improving, belting ammunition, priming hand grenades, stacking shells and Panzerfausts, improving camouflage, reading mail from home.[21]

Despite the fact that it had to defend a front line over 38 kilometers long, with an average of just 78 fighting men per kilometer of front, the *Totenkopf* Division was able to ward off every attack and inflict crushing losses on its opponents.[22] On 29 July alone, the day it was ordered to begin planning its withdrawal from Siedlce, *Obf.* Becker's division knocked out 24 Soviet tanks in and around the city.[23]

The division's own losses had not been insignificant, and the absence of the *Totenkopf* Regiment had been particularly felt, as its foot soldiers were urgently needed to hold the line and secure the town of Siedlce itself. But more importantly, the *Totenkopf* Division's defense of Siedlce had not been in vain, for the division had prevented any further Soviet penetrations into that area which would have sundered the entire defense line just erected by *2. Armee* during the past week. It also bought the time *G.F.M.* Model needed to marshal his formations for the upcoming counterattack.

The fighting for Siedlce was unusually bitter, often devolving into hand-to-hand combat, and the Soviet troops attacked with an enthusiasm not seen since the early days of the war. One eyewitness, *Uscha.* Fritz G. of *III.Btl./ Totenkopf*, later recalled the intensity of this period:

> One of the Soviet prisoners was interrogated right there on the spot by Lochner, our ethnic German comrade who spoke perfect Russian. As his questioning continued, the prisoner pulled a red flag out of his field jacket and informed us that he and his fellow Russian troops had been told to raise the flag on the top of the highest building in the city. Well, we would make sure that didn't happen.[24]

Though the *Totenkopf* Division would not initially play a direct role in the tank battle of Praga, at least during the first phase of the operation, its bitter defense of the town had created the necessary conditions that would allow Model's counteroffensive to succeed. After withdrawing from Siedlce during the early morning of 31 July, Becker's troops established new defensive positions several kilometers north and west of the town that over the next week frustrated Soviet attempts to rescue the overextended 2nd Tank Army at Praga.

In contrast, the *Wiking* Division saw little fighting, since it was engaged between 27 and 30 July with its withdrawal from the *2. Armee*'s front near Czeremcha and occupying its temporary assembly area near Wegrow, five kilometers northeast of *IV. SS-Pz.Korps*' command post at Liw. Here, it would conduct a three-day recuperation and reorganization period, where it would prepare for its upcoming mission. Long columns of its vehicles, some stranded for lack of fuel or mechanical breakdowns, were strung out along the 80-kilometer route that stretched between Wegrow and Czeremcha. Armored vehicles had to drive the entire distance, since the rail system in that area was no longer available, a necessity which caused excessive wear on vehicles' drive trains and tracked components as they conducted their 11-hour movement. Still, most of the division was in place by evening on 29 July, when the detached *Kampfgruppe* from *Germania* and its attached assault gun company, *4. Kp./SS-Pz. Rgt. 5*, began returning after their week-long support of *XXIII A.K.*

The only large element still operating near the front lines was *I. Abt./Pz.Rgt. 5*, which was tasked with providing security at the Bug River crossings south of Siemiatycze for the withdrawing *292. Inf.Div.* By midnight on 29 July, it had completed its own river crossing, including bringing all of its damaged or inoperable tanks to safety, and brought the *Wiking* Division together for the first time in several weeks.[25] The fighting during the last several days had been fierce indeed; a running total by *2. Armee* reckoned that the two divisions of *IV. SS-Pz.Korps* had destroyed 61 Soviet tanks and assault guns between 27 and 31 July, as well as 34 artillery pieces and antitank guns of various types.[26] While this appears to be an impressive achievement of arms by itself, when measured against the huge numbers of tanks and guns available to the First Belorussian Front, it was a mere drop in the ocean.

Despite its temporary successes, *IV. SS-Pz.Corps* could not afford to rest on its laurels, for on 29 July the German situation was still very precarious and growing even more so. Soviet forward units had seemingly penetrated everywhere, even far behind the front line. Though none of these were large units—battalion-sized or greater—and did not pose a direct threat except to rear area units, they were a worrying indicator of the Red Army's intentions. To the west, there were no German forces lying between Stanisławów and Praga save the thin security line erected between the *Hermann Göring* and *Totenkopf* Divisions, which were all that tied *Gen.d.Pz.Tr.* Nikolaus von Vornmann's *9. Armee*'s left flank to Weiss' *2. Armee*'s right flank. This had come about because the *Totenkopf* Division had been ordered to begin extending its positions farther to the west and form a new defense line before giving up Siedlce on 31 July. The *Wiking* Division would soon be inserted between the *Totenkopf* and *Fs.Pz.Div. Hermann Göring*, occupying a defense line beginning from a point east of Kałuszyn that stretched northwest as far as Stanisławów, a distance of approximately 16 kilometers.

The *Wiking* had been issued orders to redeploy from its assembly area near Wegrow to Stanisławów on the night of 29–30 July. Here it had been preparing for Model's next move, the counterstroke designed to entrap and destroy the 2nd Tank Army. When a *Wiking* battalion-sized *Kampfgruppe* reconnoitering the Kałuszyn area ahead of the division discovered that Soviet advance units had already arrived ahead of them and occupied the town, the battalion had to launch an immediate attack to throw them out. Similarly, the *Wiking* Division quickly learned that some Soviet reconnaissance units had also occupied Stanisławów before its lead elements arrived here, once again forcing the *Wiking*'s vanguard to immediately attack and clear this town before it could be occupied.

Perhaps the enemy was nearer than anyone thought, especially when the division had to fight for its designated assembly areas where no enemy presence had been previously reported or expected. However, before he could launch his attack, Model would first have to gather enough combat power in the form of *panzer* divisions to match or exceed the Red Army's superiority in numbers. On 29 July, that still seemed an optimistic goal. There were simply not enough of these divisions available, and it appeared that unless Model could concentrate what he did have as quickly as possible, both *2.* and *9. Armee* would be defeated and Warsaw lost. Before he could take his next step, Model had to see that *9. Armee* was shored up long enough to hold out for two or three more days, giving enough time for him to marshal his forces.

The *9. Armee*, under *Gen.d.Pz.Tr.* von Vormann, was being rapidly reconstituted after having been virtually destroyed during Operation *Bagration*, but it had nothing at the time to plug the gap developing south and east of Praga except *73. Inf.Div.*—one battalion of which was already committed to defending Siedlce—and the advance party of the aforementioned *Fs.Pz.Div. Hermann Göring*. Both of these divisions would be placed under the control of *XXXIX. Pz.Korps*, commanded by *Gen.Lt.* Dietrich von Saucken. The army's defensive front ran from Praga in a southerly direction along both sides of the Vistula, ending at Puławy, where its right flank unit, the *VIII. Armeekorps,* tied in with *LVI. Pz.Korps* of *H.Gr. Nordukrain* a few kilometers south of the town. The *VIII. Armeekorps* headquarters had been hurriedly rushed across the Vistula on 31 July from its old positions near Sokolow, leaving its two divisions behind to be taken over by *XX. Armeekorps.* Puławy was quickly occupied by the Red Army, whose 69th Army, commanded by Lieutenant General Vladimir Y. Kolpakchi, was strengthening its small bridgehead at that location, an ominous portent of what would later become a future focus of *9. Armee*'s defensive effort.

To carry out his new assignment, *Gen.d.Pz.Tr.* von Vormann only had two skeletal corps under this command—the *XXXIX. Pz.Korps* and *VIII. A.K.* It was all he had been given to defend a river defense line over 100 kilometers long. The *VIII. A.K.* was laughably weak, for on 29 July it had but one full division (*174. Reserve-Division*) composed of conscripts then undergoing training and the remnants of the *26. Inf. Div.*, which had been nearly destroyed in mid-July while fighting west of Kowel and was being reconstituted at a nearby training area. To bolster *VIII. A.K.*'s order of battle, the veteran but decimated *17. Inf.Div.*, recently escaped from encirclement itself, was hurriedly sent to its aid. Clearly, if *9. Armee* was to play a part in defending Praga and carrying out Model's plan for a counteroffensive, it would have to be significantly reinforced.

To this end, Model alerted two additional *panzer* divisions assigned to *H.Gr. Mitte* for possible commitment—the *4. Pz.Div.*, then operating north of Kleszczele as part of

Kavallerie-Korps Harteneck, and *19. Pz.Div.*, which he ordered to redeploy from its area of operations between Bialystok and Grodno, where it had been fighting since 21 July. While *4. Pz.Div.* was nearly at full strength, the *19. Pz.Div.* had only recently arrived from the Netherlands, where it had undergone a nearly complete reconstitution in the Breda area and was still arriving piecemeal.[27] It would be assigned to *9. Armee*'s *XXXIX. Pz.Korps*, while the *4. Pz.Div.* would initially operate directly under the control of *2. Armee*. Due to the conditions at the front, the departure of *4. Pz.Div.* was delayed by a day and it was still forced to leave behind one of its mechanized infantry regiments, leaving it with only half of its *Panzergrenadiers* for the upcoming battle.

As Lt.Gen. Radzievsky's 2nd Tank Army surged northward between 27 and 29 July, the crisis intensified. To the Soviets, it must have seemed as if their tank spearheads were pushing into a vacuum. The *73. Inf.Div.* had been ordered to move south on 26 July to establish blocking positions south of Praga in order to prevent a breakthrough, and barely managed to establish a thin screening position between the towns of Garwolin and Demblin straddling the main highway. But before it could get its defenses set, onrushing spearheads from the XVI Tank and VIII Guards Tank Corps blasted through the division's thinly manned positions, scattering its troops and forcing the rest back to Praga. Caught unprepared by the Soviet attack, the division's two-and-a-half infantry regiments suffered heavy casualties and barely escaped encirclement on 29 July by the XVI Tank Corps.

This near-disaster was worsened by the capture of its division commander, *Gen. Lt.* Fritz von Franek, who had been visiting the command post of *Inf.Rgt. 70* at the time the main Soviet attack began. Attempts by the division to rally, now under the temporary command of its *Ia*, *Oberstleutnant* (*Oberstlt.*) Otto Becker, and mount local counterattacks were crushed by the onrushing columns of Soviet tanks, which bypassed the Wilga position and raced towards the bridges at Praga. Only the timely arrival of forward elements of the *Fs.Pz.Div. Hermann Göring* and *19. Pz.Div.*, as well as *SS-Kampfgruppe Kröner*, which carried out a series of counterattacks, prevented the Soviets from taking Praga and the Vistula bridges.

After being intercepted by field police, who prevented them from fleeing all the way to Praga, the panic-stricken troops from the *73. Inf.Div.* were quickly reformed and sent back into the line at Otwock, where they would perform more steadily. A temporary commander, *Oberst* Kurt Hähling, was assigned on 30 July until a permanent one was appointed. To bolster the division's antitank capability, the newly reconstituted antitank battalion of the *Wiking* Division, *Stubaf.* Herbert Oeck's *SS-Pz. Jg.Abt. 5*, was attached to the *73. Inf.Div.* on 29 July, where it remained for nearly a month. Equipped with 21 *Panzerjäger IV/70* tank destroyers, it would render good service until it rejoined the *Wiking* Division later in August.[28] The battalion had not finished its training and was still lacking personnel, vehicles, and equipment, but the situation was so dire that it was ordered to move to the Warsaw front from the SS Heidelager training area anyway.

To the Germans' astonishment, however, Lt.Gen. Radzievsky's tanks brushed the battlegroup from *Fs.Pz.Div. Hermann Göring* aside and bypassed Praga entirely, continuing its push north with its III Tank Corps in the lead. On 29 July, the corps took Mińsk Mazowiecki and continued moving. It now became clear that the Soviets were not interested in liberating Warsaw at all, but were after bigger game. They had, at long last, made their move to seize the more important strategic objective—the bridges at Modlin, Serock, and Zegrze. To reach these objectives, Lt.Gen. Radzievsky's corps commanders cast caution to the wind and drove their troops to the north far more quickly than anyone anticipated. Having found little or no resistance to impede them, the tank and assault gun regiments of Maj.Gen. Vedeneev's III Tank Corps pushed forward with little regard to their flanks, while XVI and VIII Guards Tank Corps, moving slightly behind III Tank Corps, attempted to widen the penetration.

By 30 July, the key towns of Okuniev, Wolomin, and Radzymin had fallen to III Tank Corps, which by this point had carved a salient projecting deep into the rear of *2. Armee*. The tenuous screening line between the *Wiking* and *Hermann Göring* Divisions was severed near Okuniew, as Radzievsky's tanks shouldered aside the latter's feeble attempt to seal the breach. Secure in the belief that the Germans were finished and that they had nothing more to throw at them, Radzievsky and his corps commanders evidently felt confident that their gambit would succeed and that the infantry of the following 8th Guards and 47th Armies would fill in the gap and mop up what was left behind them. This was the opportunity that Model had been waiting for as he sprung his trap.

In the annals of World War II generalship, Walter Model has been described as being a defensively oriented tactician, belittled as the "*Führer*'s Fireman," who could retrieve any seemingly lost defensive situation, but was out of his element when conducting offensive operations. However, a closer examination of his performance as a commander at the operational level reveals a stroke of genius, and nowhere was this so clearly demonstrated than during the battle of Praga. His force of personality and military reputation often overawed Hitler, and he used this influence to achieve concessions from *der Führer* that eluded other less-forceful field marshals. His brashness with Hitler enabled him to save his troops by giving up territory in order to deal powerful counterblows against an advancing enemy. But posterity has not been kind to him. Military historians have relegated him to the second rank of German commanders, portraying him as a mere Nazi fanatic, who stood behind more august personages such as von Manstein, Rommel, von Runstedt, and Balck.

But Model's performance at Praga demonstrated that given the latitude to make his own decisions, and the troops to carry out his intentions, he had the skills that would have made him a rival to even the great von Manstein. Embodying a strong sense of what Rommel called *Fingerspitzengefühl*, a uniquely German term often described as meaning an instinctive feel for how a battle would unfold and what measures to take to ensure its successful consummation, Model's conduct of the battle was nothing less than brilliant. In the days that were to follow, he faced what was initially an impossibly bleak military situation and, within the span of 96 hours, was able to deal such a setback to the Red Army at the gates of Warsaw that it had to suspend its offensive for nearly two weeks, buying the time needed to rebuild a cohesive front line north and south of the Polish capital. His conduct during this battle merits a long-overdue complete reassessment of his performance as a leader.

When considering the advance of the 2nd Tank Army, Model realized that it was obvious that Lt.Gen. Radzievsky had overextended himself. Though the Soviet commander's army still counted between 560 and 680 operational tanks and self-propelled guns in its order of battle out of the 800 that it had started with 12 days earlier, its supply lines now stretched all the way from Okuniew to Puławy.[29] The 2nd Tank Army's men were also getting tired, having been on the move continuously since 18 July. Fuel and ammunition were running short, but Radzievsky, with Marshal Rokossovsky's blessing, continued to press forward to the bridges over the Narew and Vistula north of Warsaw, slicing ever deeper into German-held territory. At its zenith, the salient carved by Vedeneev's III Tank Corps between Okuniew and Radzymin was over 50 kilometers long but a mere 20 kilometers wide, an inviting target for a pincer attack (see Map 4).

Generalfeldmarschall Model had been waiting for just this opportunity since the Soviet attack began to unfold on 27 July, and immediately started moving his troops into position, in close coordination with army commanders *Gen.Oberst* Weiss and *Gen.d.Pz.Tr.* von Vormann, to carry out his counteroffensive. Orders had gone out to the corps and divisions between 27 and 29 July that would conduct the attack, including the aforementioned order to the *Wiking* Division instructing it to withdraw from the Czeremcha defense position on 27 July and begin assembling behind the front lines at Wegrow that same day. Seen in this context, the reason for the rapid movement by the *Wiking* Division across the Bug from 27–29 July and the hurried activation of *IV. SS-Pz.Corps* on 28 July becomes abundantly clear, though it is evident from reading contemporary accounts by veterans of the *Wiking* or *Totenkopf* Divisions that they had no idea of what was really happening. It is unclear whether even *Gruf.* Gille knew. Certainly, the situation was changing daily and it is possible that the only person who had an accurate understanding of what was taking place was Model himself.

In essence, Model intended to launch a counterstroke that would first cut off and destroy Radzievsky's lead tank corps (the III), followed by the sequential destruction of Maj. Gen. Alexei F. Popov's VIII Guards Tank Corps, and finally Maj.Gen. Ivan V. Dubovoi's XVI Tank Corps. The attacking units would consist of the *Wiking* Division, striking from the east, the *4. Pz.Div.* from the northeast, *Fs.Pz.Div. Hermann Göring* from the west, and two separate *Kampfgruppen* from the *19. Pz.Div.*, attacking from

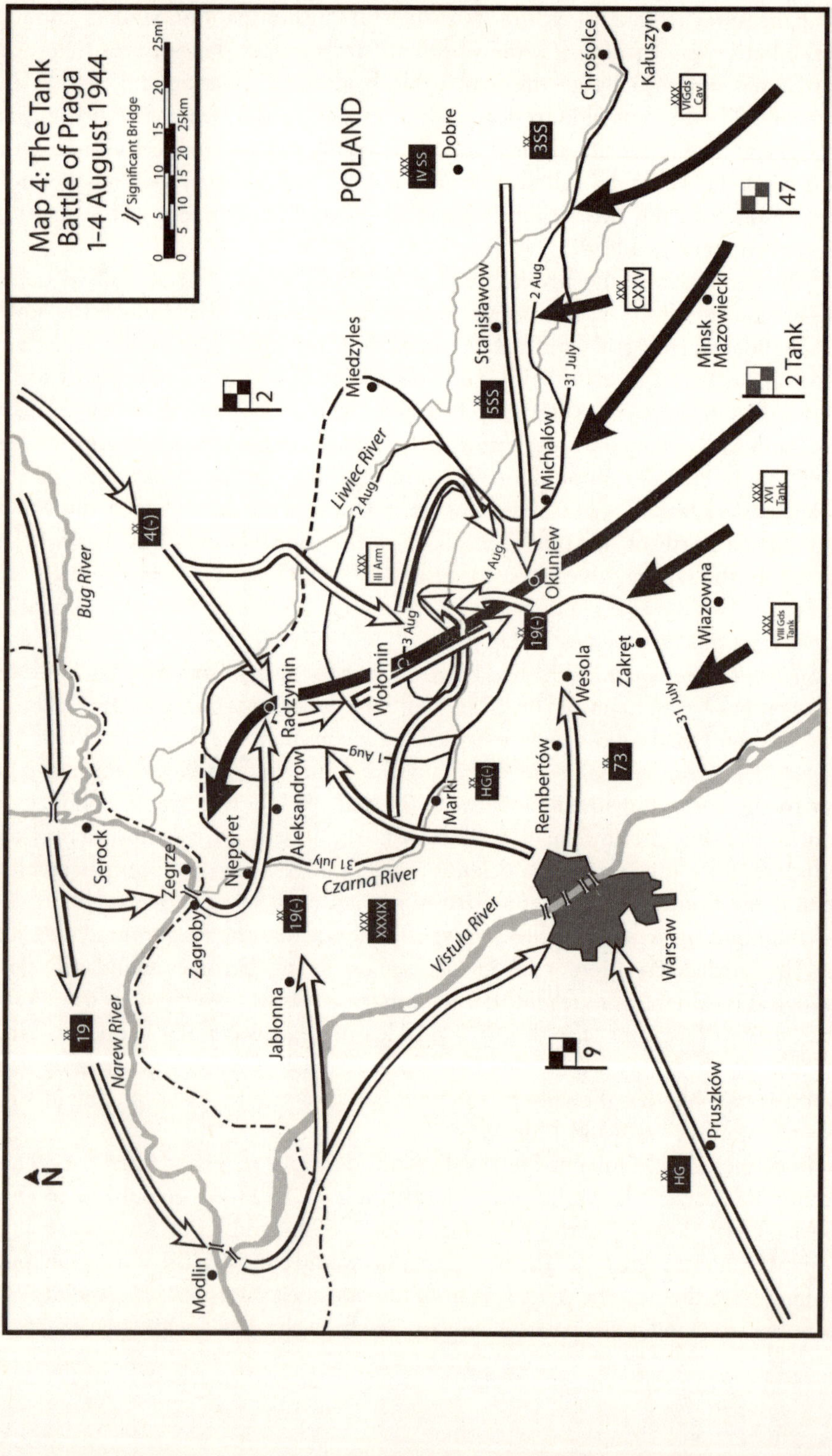
Map 4: The Tank
Battle of Praga
1-4 August 1944
Significant Bridge
0 5 10 15 20 25mi
0 5 10 15 20 25km
POLAND
Chrośolce
Kałuszyn
VIGds Cav
Dobre
IV SS
3SS
47
Stanisławow
2 Aug
CXXV
Minsk Mazowiecki
31 July
2 Tank
Miedzyles
5SS
Michalów
2
Liwiec River
2 Aug
XVI Tank
4(-)
III Arm
4 Aug
Okuniew
Wiazowna
VIII Gds Tank
Bug River
3 Aug
19(-)
Zakręt
Wołomin
Radzymin
Wesola
31 July
1 Aug
Rembertów
73
Aleksandrow
HG(-)
Marki
Serock
Nieporet
31 July
Zegrze
Czarna River
19(-)
XXXIX
Vistula River
Zagroby
Warsaw
Jablonna
19
9
Narew River
Pruszków
HG
Modlin

the northwest and southwest, sandwiching the *Hermann Göring* between them. While the *4. Pz.* and *Hermann Göring* Divisions would stop and then push back III Tank Corps from Radzymin, the *Wiking* Division and the bulk of *19. Pz.Div.* would both attack towards each other, with the goal of linking up at Okuniew, thus completing the encirclement. Model hoped to bag the entire III Tank Corps, and this he nearly did. As it was, it was developing into a major defeat for 2nd Tank Army.

It was not going to be easy though. First, the divisions named above all had to be in position by 31 July in order to attack the following morning. The III Tank Corps had not been idle either, and its spearheads were a mere 2 kilometers away from the vital Narew Bridge at Zegrze before they were stopped by newly arrived units of the *19. Pz.Div.* All four of the German divisions earmarked to conduct the operation had to move to the battle area and position themselves before they could begin their attacks. The supply lines of two of the divisions, the *19. Pz.Div.* and *Fs.Pz.Div. Hermann Göring*, ran through Warsaw and crossed the Vistula River at Praga, which Model's troops had barely managed to hold on to. The *4. Pz.Div.* was encountering difficulties withdrawing from *Korps Harteneck* and would not arrive on the battlefield until late in the afternoon on 1 August, but it did arrive at a most critical juncture. Fortunately for Model, until 1 August his army group had enjoyed a period of hot and dry weather, which aided mobility, though the sandy soil unique to the region raised enormous dust clouds on the roads whenever units used them. However, when it began to rain on the evening of 1 August after the first day of the battle, the unpaved country roads turned into ribbons of mud, slowing any attempt by both sides to move forces back and forth quickly or to resupply them.

In addition to these difficulties the Germans were experiencing, Lt.Gen. Radzievsky's army still held a numerical advantage in tanks and assault guns on 31 July. In comparison to the approximately 300 tanks he still had operational, the total number of serviceable tanks and assault guns available to Model were 223 and 54, respectively. However, nearly half of them had not yet arrived when the counteroffensive began the following day, though many joined the fight hours or even days later. This still gave 2nd Tank Army a nearly two-to-one advantage in numbers.[30] On the night of 31 July, the *Wiking* reported that it had only 33 tanks and assault guns ready for battle, with the *Totenkopf* reporting having 41 more, including one Tiger tank, though Becker's division would not be directly involved in the operation against the III Tank Corps. The *19. Pz.Div.*, with 70 operational tanks and assault guns, was the strongest force. Part of *Fs.Pz.Div. Hermann Göring*, which had a total of 63 armoured vehicles, was still fighting alongside the *73. Inf.Div.* south of Praga, where it was helping to keep the XVI Tank Corps at bay and keep the bridges over the Vistula at Praga open for German reinforcements. In all, Model would be able to commit 166 tanks and assault guns when the attack began the following day, with 78 more arriving two days later with the addition of *4. Pz.Div.*

Fortunately for Model, Radzievsky's tank army had not managed to bring up most of its supporting artillery, which was still strung out along runs leading to the south. Thus, 2nd Tank Army would be inadvertently deprived of one of the Red Army's most potent weapons at a time when it needed it the most, especially once it was inevitably forced to switch over to the defensive phase of its operation. Likewise, the 2nd Tank Army lacked sufficient infantry forces to protect its flanks when passing through towns or forests, when tanks are most vulnerable. While his army did include several mechanized infantry brigades (the 28th, 57th, and 15th Motorized Rifle Brigades), they had sustained heavy losses during the past 12 days of fighting and had dropped off many of their battalions along the way since leaving Puławy to hold defensive positions at key points along the flanks, such as at Okuniew. Colonel General Chuikov's 8th Guards Army was occupied with attempts to bridge the Vistula at Magnuszew to the south and Lt.Gen. Nikolai Gusev's 47th Army was still fighting in the Siedlce area several dozen kilometers to the east, and neither would be able to provide immediate assistance. Radzievsky's army was nearly alone.

For its role in Model's overall plan, *Gruf.* Gille's *IV. SS-Pz.Korps* would employ the *Wiking* Division as its main effort, pushing out of Stanisławów towards Okuniew. It had already begun a reconnaissance in force on 31 July, sending out its forward elements west, north, and south, but had found surprisingly little sign of the enemy except for two T-34s and 13 trucks that were destroyed. A further nine trucks and one T-34 were captured in Michałow, a village 12 kilometers to the west of Stanisławów. Holding the junction between both SS divisions stood the *Wiking* Division's *SS-Pz.Pio.Btl. 5*, under *SS-Ostubaf.* Fritz Braune, whose combat engineers erected a defense centered on the village of Grebkow. They would be sorely tried over the next several days, as they held off numerous attacks aimed at severing the connection between Gille's divisions.

Meanwhile, the *Totenkopf* Division held its defensive line on *Wiking*'s left flank, but after extricating the last of its forces from Siedlce earlier that morning, the division commander noted surprisingly little activity during the day by the opposing II Guards Cavalry Corps, with the exception of minor reconnaissance forays that were easily driven off.[31] The remainder of *2. Armee*, including *XXIII.* and *XX. Armeekorps*, as well as *Kav.Korps Harteneck*, were ordered to slowly displace from their previous front-line positions to a new one several dozen kilometers to the rear, while clearing up numerous minor breakthroughs that had occurred over the past several days. The *Totenkopf* Division would support these efforts with an armored battlegroup from *SS-Pz.Rgt. 3*, while still maintaining its long east–west defensive positions on *Wiking*'s flank oriented to the south.

The first phase of the attack began the next day, 1 August, at 4 a.m. when the *Wiking* Division's lead element, consisting of *III. Btl./Germania*, two companies from *II. Abt./SS-Pz.Rgt. 5*, and one self-propelled gun battery from *SS-Pz.Art.Rgt.*

5 crossed the line of departure west of Michałów and advanced towards Okuniew. At the same time, other elements of the division pushed out reconnaissance towards the southwest and northwest, seeking any further sign of approaching Soviet forces, particularly indications of the VIII Guards Tank Corps.[32] At roughly the same time, *19. Pz.Div.*, operating under *Gen.Lt.* von Saucken's *XXXIX. Pz.Korps* for this operation, began its own attack from the opposite direction, passing through the thin screen line maintained by the *Hermann Göring*.

For a variety of reasons, *4. Pz.Div.* had not been able to join the attack on time on 1 August, chiefly because of the distance it had to travel and the fighting between *19. Pz.Div.* and the forward elements of III Tank Corps at Zegrze that slowed the movement of traffic over the Bug River bridge. When it did arrive, it would bring with it 39 of its own tanks, as well as an attached tank company from *12. Pz.Div.* and 29 operational Tigers from *schwere-Pz.Abt. 507*. On account of having to leave one of its mechanized infantry regiments behind, *4. Pz.Div.* would be augmented by a regimental-sized *Kampfgruppe* from *Gen.d.Art.* Maximilian Felzmann's now-rested *Korps-Abt. E*, known as *Gruppe Felzmann*.

The *Hermann Göring* Division was also engaged north of the bulk of *19. Pz.Div.*, directing its attack towards the left flank of III Tank Corps west of Wołomin, where it soon found itself in heavy fighting. After numerous inquiries as to its whereabouts, the *Wiking* Division's armored battlegroup finally linked up with *19. Pz.Div.* at 7:15 p.m. on 1 August several kilometers north of Okuniew after encountering negligible opposition, though it did report being mistakenly fired upon by German artillery. *Standartenführer* Mühlenkamp, acting as *Wiking*'s tactical commander, reported that the town itself was held by Soviet forces in "great strength," including tank units. He made no attempt to attack the town, but prepared instead to fight off the Soviet relief attempts from the south that would inevitably follow the next day.[33]

Some of the tank battles took place at very close range. One of the soldiers whose tank participated in the advance to Okuniew that day was *Uscha.* Henk Kistemaker of *6. Kp./SS-Pz.Rgt. 5*, who served as a Panther *Richtschütze* (gunner) for his tank commander, *Ustuf.* Alfred Grossrock. He left a vivid account of the fighting that day in his biography written after the war. Of the engagement that day between his company and tanks from III Tank Corps, he wrote:

> Before us lay open terrain. We were the lead tank as the spearhead broke through the forest. Suddenly, there was a terrific crash as we were hit … the other Panthers pivoted to the right and left and began returning fire. On the other side of the clearing in front of us stood four Soviet tanks (Shermans and T-34) with their flanks exposed to us. They apparently expected us to approach from the other direction. The tanks' cannon made a hellish noise as the Russian shells flew through the woods in all directions. As suddenly as the scrap began, it was just as quickly over. Three Russian tanks had been shot up, but the fourth was hidden in the smoke and dust. We had been hit on the right side and our track was damaged, so we could no longer maneuver. So we now had to wait for the maintenance troop to arrive to help us repair it … Around us, the forest had become deathly still after all the shooting. I found it rather unsettling.[34]

None of the *Wiking*'s tanks were destroyed that day, though some had fallen out on account of mechanical failure or light damage, such as *Uscha.* Kistmaker's.

Things had not been quiet on the corps' eastern or left flank either. Earlier that day, the *Totenkopf* Division reported an increase in artillery fire and infantry probing attacks from the south, a clear sign that Lt.Gen. Nikolai Gusev's 47th Army was beginning to react to 2nd Tank Army's looming predicament. On a positive note, it was reported on this day that the two last trains carrying the rest of *Totenkopf*'s troops, chiefly from *SS-Pz.Gren.Rgt. 5 Totenkopf*, had finally arrived at the railroad yard in Sokolów, making the division complete once more. They could not have arrived at a more opportune time, as *Obf.* Becker needed every available man to hold his lengthening front line.

All message traffic that day between the *Wiking* Division's forward command post and the corps headquarters in Liw was relayed via radio, though the distances involved were almost at the maximum range of the equipment. Fortunately, *SS-Nachr. Abt. 104* was finally in place and was able to provide *Gruf.* Gille the rapid means of communication the situation required. However, radio contact with Mühlenkamp's lead units was patchy, possibly due to atmospheric and topographical interference, leading to a certain amount of impatience on the part of *2. Armee* headquarters as well as with *H.Gr. Mitte*, as revealed in a number of telephone conversations inquiring as to *Wiking*'s whereabouts.[35] Communications with the *Totenkopf* Division were still chiefly being carried out using landline telephone, more reliable but also more susceptible to interception by wiretapping. Owing to the continuing lack of replacement parts for the *Wiking*'s tank regiment that was adversely affecting readiness rates, *Stubaf.* Scharff, *IV. SS-Pz.Korps' Quartiermeister*, sent out a *Fernschreiber* message directly to the newly appointed General Inspector of *Panzer* Troops, *Gen. Lt.* Wolfgang Thomale, at 11:50 a.m. that day, urgently requesting that the *Luftwaffe* airlift the repair parts and components that had been previously requested.[36]

A minor controversy occurred earlier that day when *Fs.Pz.Div. Hermann Göring*'s commander, *Gen.Maj.* Wilhelm Schmalz, reported to *2. Armee* that one of its units had penetrated as far as Michałów, a town in *Wiking*'s sector, only to find it devoid of German troops. This prompted *Gen.Oberst* Weiss to call Gille directly at 6:20 p.m., inquiring whether this was true or not. Gille stated that this was incorrect and that his units had been occupying the town since the previous day. How any element of Schmalz's division could have cut across the corridor north of Okuniew without the notice of either the *Wiking* or *19. Pz.* Divisions (or the Red Army, for that matter) was a mystery. However, word of this false report had percolated up the chain of command to *Gen.Lt.* Hans Krebs, *H.Gr. Mitte*'s chief of staff, who informed Model that perhaps something was not in order at Gille's headquarters in regards to the efficiency of his general staff. Model, rising to Gille's defense, replied that everything was going fine, that Michałów was occupied by Gille's troops, and that any rumor to the contrary was an outright lie.[37] Model would not be the first general who would defend Gille against such unfair accusations, but he was certainly the most influential.

That evening, *H.Gr. Mitte* took stock of the day's accomplishments and setbacks. The most important action, the severing of the lifeline of III Tank Corps, had been carried out with relative ease. The efforts by *XXXIX. Pz.Korps* to bring the Soviet advance to a halt in the Radzymin and Wolomin areas had begun to bear fruit. The withdrawal from the eastern-facing front of Weiss' *2. Armee* had gone surprisingly well, with the Red Army mounting only a hesitant pursuit. The southern front of *2. Armee*, held by the *Totenkopf* and *Wiking* Divisions, had also stood firm. The next day, 2 August, would give an indication of what Lt.Gen. Radzievsky's next move would be, whether to keep attacking or withdraw, but in either case, the effort to constrict and then destroy the trapped III Tank Corps would continue. Aided by the belated arrival of *4. Pz.Div.*, that phase of the operation would begin in earnest the following day, 2 August. The greatest concern was that the Soviets would react by counterattacking the southern flanks of the *Wiking* and *19. Pz.* Divisions, both of which were holding the "neck of the bag" enclosing the trapped Red Army units, as well as the *Totenkopf* Division along its long, exposed front.

Two other events, which would both prove extremely worrisome and would influence the battle of Praga, also occurred that day. The first, and most dangerous, was the beginning of the Warsaw Uprising. Timed to take advantage of the rapid approach of the Soviet armor, the Polish Home Army, the *Armia Krajowa* or *A.K.*, rose up and attacked German troops throughout the city, threatening to cut off German forces operating on the eastern bank of the Vistula. The other event that day was the establishment of a strong bridgehead on the western bank of the Vistula at Magnuszew by Chuikov's 8th Guards Army. This bridgehead, 60 kilometers southeast of Warsaw, was also a dangerous development, since there were few German forces located in the area to contain it, except for the recently arrived *VIII. Armeekorps* headquarters with the *174. Res.Div.* and *17. Inf.Div.*[38] Anticipating such an emergency, Model had already developed a plan to detach some of the *panzer* divisions currently encircling 2nd Tank Army and send them back across the Vistula as soon as possible to prevent another massive Soviet breakthrough, should that occur.

The *2. Armee*'s orders for the following day went out via *Fernschreiber* at 8:50 p.m. on 1 August to the units involved, which primarily concerned *IV. SS-Pz.Korps*, *4. Pz.Div.*, and *Gruppe Felzmann* (*Korps-Abt. E*). *Gruf.* Gille's corps was ordered to continue attacking and solidify its rather tenuous connection with *9. Armee*'s hard-fighting *19. Pz.Div.* He was urged to prepare the defense of his southern front using both the *Wiking* and *Totenkopf* Divisions and to maintain a solid connection with the neighboring *XX. Armeekorps* on his left, or eastern, flank at Wierzbno, held by the *5. Jäger-Div. Gruppe Felzmann* was instructed to ensure that a strong battlegroup, already on the move from its assembly area near Dybów, conducted a link-up with the oncoming *4. Pz.Div.* as early as possible the following morning, before daylight preferably. Then Felzmann's *Kampfgruppe*, under *4. Pz.Div.*'s command, would conduct a reconnaissance in force towards Radzymin, locate the forward elements of *19. Pz.Div.* and renew the attack on Radzymin with *4. Pz.Div.* Once this had been completed, *4. Pz.Div.* would then connect to *IV. SS-Pz.Korp*'s right flank unit, the *Wiking* Division, and form an encircling ring around III Tank Corps.

The rest of *2. Armee* was instructed to complete its withdrawal to its new defensive positions, codenamed the "Blue Line," and hold.[39] *Gruf.* Gille's evening report to *2. Armee* stated the following:

> In the early morning hours the armored group of the *5. SS-Pz.Div. W* [*Wiking*] attacked further to the west, northwest and north from the assembly area that it had occupied the previous day. The armored group stormed forward via Michałów towards Okuniew and completed the link up with the assault group of the *9. Armee* approaching from the west north of Okuniew at 7:15 p.m. Okuniew is still strongly occupied by the enemy, including armor. At the security line along the corps' southern front, the enemy began conducting his first attacks with artillery and tank support, with his main effort directed towards Ladzyn, near Laziska and northwest of Kaluszyn. *3. SS-Pz.Div. T* [*Totenkopf*] has been pulled out of its previous positions [in Siedlce] and is on the move towards its new area of operations.

This bland military language conceals the drama that characterized the events of *IV. SS-Pz.Korps*' day, which included not only an armored attack towards the west by one division that cut off a Soviet tank corps, but a separate action focused towards the south by another division that defended a drawn-out front line extending over 38 kilometers between the *Wiking* Division's left flank at Stanisłowów and the area northwest of Siedlce.

It was against this thin defensive line held by 2,950 infantrymen of the *Totenkopf* Division—with, as we have seen, a density of only 78 men per kilometer—that the Red Army's 47th Army and II Guards Cavalry Corps would soon hurl its forces, as it sought to relieve the pressure on the encircled III Tank Corps. With little time to construct a fortified front line that would have included barbed wire, mine fields, and other obstacles, the men of the *Totenkopf* would have to wage a mobile defense, seeking out and attacking Soviet forces before they could locate and pin down their forward units with artillery fire. Outnumbered by at least four-to-one, the Germans' mobility and ability to strike rapidly and withdraw would prove to be one of the few advantages they enjoyed over their relentlessly approaching opponent.

In a field telephone conversation between *Gruf.* Gille and *2. Armee*'s *Gen.Oberst* Weiss at 6:20 p.m., Gille urgently requested that the *Luftwaffe* provide close air support to strike the long columns of Soviet vehicles that could be seen approaching along the main road leading to Warsaw south of Kałuszyn, as well as to destroy a Soviet observation balloon observed near the town.[40] It is unknown whether the strike was carried out, but it was an ominous portent for the next day. *Oberführer* Becker's division would make increasing demands for *Luftwaffe* support, only to see most of it go to the suppression of the Warsaw Uprising and the battle raging to the north between Radzymin and Wolomin. As the *Wiking* and *Totenkopf* Divisions began to extend their front lines further to the west, the corps' communications networks were becoming more extended, making it increasingly difficult to remain in constant contact with the forward units. To better control the battle, Gille's forward command post would displace that evening from Liw to Nowo Dobre, a distance of 21 kilometers and only ten kilometers away from the *Wiking* Division's new headquarters at Stanisłowów.

After being in Liw for less than three days, it was time for the corps' *Hauptquartier* to pack everything up and move again and be ready to operate early the next morning, which meant that the corps' *Gefechtstand*, a portion of the *Begleitkompanie*, and the *Führungsabteilung* would have had to load their bags and equipment aboard a few of the *Hauptquartier*'s vehicles and travel under escort to their new location under battlefield conditions, not knowing whether they might encounter T-34s at any point along the way. The signal personnel would reel in their communications wire, radio antennas would have to be lowered and stowed, and telephones packed and put away, only to be hurriedly placed back into operation as soon as the convoy arrived at Nowo Dobre, an event that was duly reported to *2. Armee* at 9:30 a.m. *Gruppenführer* Gille himself may have departed for the battlefield earlier than that, to take up his position at the *Wiking* Division's forward headquarters, where he would once again rub shoulders with acting commander *Staf.* Mühlenkamp, who was fighting the actual battle.

The night of 1–2 August passed relatively quietly, with little activity by the Soviet forces reported. The *Totenkopf* Division's units holding the corps' southern flank were able to withdraw several kilometers northwest to a more defensible position, while its right flank kept extending to the west, relieving a *Panzergrenadier* battalion from the *Westland* Regiment of the *Wiking* in the process. The *Wiking*'s armored *Kampfgruppe*, led by acting *panzer* regiment commander *Ostubaf.* Fritz Darges, had linked up with *19. Pz.Div.* in Okuniew and reported that it had not observed any activity at all and had passed the evening undisturbed. This relative quiet was not to last; at daylight, *IV. SS-Pz.Korps* reported a series of strong attacks by Soviet forces south of the defensive line stretching from Stanisławów through Mlenzin and terminating at the village of Grebkow. All of them were driven off, but observers could see that reinforcements were massing in the distance out of effective artillery range. On *2. Armee*'s eastern-facing flank, Soviet forces appear to have awoken from their slumber, launching a series of strong attacks with powerful artillery support against units of the *XX.* and *XXIII. Armeekorps,* as well as *Kav.Korps Hartineck*, though these were eventually driven off with some difficulty.

The focus of Model's counteroffensive that day was the effort of von Saucken's *XXXIX. Pz.Korps*—the *19. Pz.*, *Hermann Göring*, and *4. Pz.Divisions*—to constrict and then destroy the now-encircled III Tank Corps. While one *Kampfgruppe* from

19. Pz.Div. maintained the entrapment of Maj.Gen. Vedeneev's corps along with the *Wiking* Division at Okuniew, the remainder of von Saucken's corps attacked Red Army forces at Zegrze, Wołomin, and Radzymin. During the day, the assault group of *19. Pz.Div.*, personally led by its division commander, *Gen.Maj.* Hans Källner, seized the northwestern part of Radzymin, while *Gen.Maj.* Schmalz's *Fs.Pz. Div. Hermann Göring* attacked towards Wołomin. The bright spot of the day was the timely arrival of *4. Pz.Div.*, which along with its attached *Gruppe Felzmann* and *schw.Pz.Abt. 507* attacked the eastern outskirts of Radzymin as well as the town of Dobczyn, which had to be taken before it could advance to Wołomin. The *IV. SS-Pz. Korps* also received the order to begin extending its right flank to the north, where it was to link up with the left flank of the approaching *4. Pz.Div.* This maneuver, carried out by the *Germania* Regiment, would complete the ring around III Tank Corps, but would also mean that Gille's corps would have to extend its right flank over a dozen kilometers to the north.

The attack by *4. Pz.Div.* began that day at 1 p.m., when the division's spearhead, a *Kampfgruppe* centered around *II. Abt./Pz.Rgt. 35*, encountered and destroyed three Soviet tanks protecting the bridge at Dybów over the Rzadza River two kilometers northeast of Radzymin. The bridge had been previously reported as being destroyed, so the division commander, *Gen.Maj.* Clemens Betzel, taking advantage of the situation ordered the *Kampfgruppe* to cross as quickly as possible and set up a blocking position 500 meters beyond the bridge. Betzel was accompanied in his command vehicle by Model himself, who had flown in to visit the division only an hour before. Appraising the opportunity this windfall offered, Model countermanded Betzel's order and told him instead to push the entire division across and link up with *19. Pz.Div.* southwest of Radzymin before nightfall. Finding the town only lightly defended, Betzel's tanks knocked out seven T-34s at 5:45 p.m. and continued their advance to the southwest until they stopped at nightfall.[41] In this case, Model can be credited with a significant tactical success, for had he not been on the scene to personally urge the *4. Pz.Div.* onwards at this particular point in the battle, the bulk of the III Tank Corps may well have escaped.

The tank battle of Praga would eventually involve nearly 600 tanks, evenly split between both combatants. Unlike the battle of Kursk the previous year, this one would not involve hundreds of tanks fighting one another at the same time. Rather, it consisted of dozens of separate battalion versus battalion encounters, often fought at ranges of less than 500 meters, where each side jockeyed to make the best tactical use of the rolling farmland and small wooded areas that dotted the landscape. Unlike the open fields of the Ukraine, the area east of Warsaw had been densely settled for hundreds of years and was highly developed in comparison. Frequently, tanks fought each other in small towns and villages, playing an armored game of cat-and-mouse where victory depended upon who fired first. In these encounters, the best-trained crew usually won, though in many instances success depended on using the maximum range of a tank's cannon to best advantage. Close cooperation with *Panzergrenadiers* was essential, especially in regards to neutralizing the threat posed by antitank guns, which often knocked out more tanks than other tanks did. This kind of tank warfare persisted between Radzymin and Okuniew for nearly four days, as the Soviet spearheads first attempted to fight their way to Zegrze, then just as determinedly to battle their way back.

The units of III Tank Corps, realizing that the noose was rapidly being drawn around them, resisted fiercely, bitterly contesting every foot of ground. However, they were simply outmatched by the onrush of German armor, a situation that they had not experienced since Kursk the year before. The *Luftwaffe* flew hundreds of sorties in support of the attack that day, a welcome sight not seen by German troops in weeks. Tank-busting Ju-87 *Stukas* equipped with 3.7cm antitank guns slung under their wings claimed dozens of kills, while other ground-attack aircraft strafed and bombed Soviet supply columns. By the end of the day, the 51st Tank Brigade had been decimated and forced to withdraw from Radzymin to the south, while the 103rd Tank Brigade had been pushed back to the eastern outskirts of Wołomin. The *Hermann Göring* Division's attack towards Wołomin from the west did not fare quite as well, as the 50th Tank and 57th Motorized Rifle Brigades managed to hold their defensive line and inflict telling losses on their German assailants.

Attempts by the neighboring XVI Tank Corps to attack the *XXXIX. Pz.Korps* on its right flank were stymied by the *73. Inf.Div.*, whose men had recovered from their disastrous experience of the previous week and warded off every attempt by the Soviet tank corps to break through its position, aided by the attached tank destroyers from *Stubaf.* Oeck's *SS-Pz.Jäg.Abt. 5* of the *Wiking* Division and *Grenadier Brigade 1131*. However, later in the day, the situation appeared to be developing in favor of the 2nd Tank Army's attempts to rescue its beleaguered III Tank Corps, as its easternmost corps, the VIII Guards Tank Corps, began to push back. Its troops and tanks immediately exerted pressure on the *Wiking*, then holding the bag closed at Okuniew.

Throughout the day, VIII Guards Tank Corps, II Guards Cavalry Corps, and two divisions of the CXXIX Rifle Corps applied increasing pressure on *IV. SS-Pz. Korps*' south-facing defensive line between Wierzbno and Okuniew, launching numerous tank and tank-supported infantry attacks against the *Wiking* and *Totenkopf* Divisions. While both divisions successfully repulsed all of these attempts, the heavy fighting was beginning to take its toll on the three mechanized infantry regiments defending that portion of the corps' front—the *SS-Pz.Gren.Rgts Westland*, *Totenkopf*, and *Eicke*—all of which, including attached *Pionier* and *Panzerjäger* battalions, were beginning to suffer increasing numbers of casualties.

The only regiment not tied down in heavy defensive fighting at the beginning of the day was *SS-Pz.Gren.Rgt. 9 Germania*, whose armored half-track-equipped

III. Btl./Germania was supporting the armored *Kampfgruppe* being led by *Staf.* Mühlenkamp and *Ostubaf.* Darges on the corps' far western flank. This situation was not to last. A verbal order was issued by Model early that afternoon requiring Mühlenkamp to redeploy the bulk of the *Germania* Regiment in order to construct a north–south defensive line designed to seal off any attempt by III Tank Corps to break out. This action would force the *Wiking* Division to bend its front line 90 degrees to the north, pivoting at the town of Michałów.

Throughout the day, the corps' and division's artillery battalions had been firing non-stop, consistently engaging and dispersing Soviet units as they attempted to concentrate and initiate attacks. Later that day, the corps' acting *Ia*, *SS-Stubaf.* Pauly, sent the following radio message at 2:45 p.m. to the *Ia* at *2. Armee* headquarters, providing the corps situation update:

> We are suffering heavy losses from strong enemy artillery and mortar fire. Part of the *19. Pz.Div.* appears to have pulled back to the west from Okuniew, without attempting to notify us. They have withdrawn from the bridge at grid line 96. The situation in Okuniew is now uncertain. Our reconnaissance (battalion) needs to leave Stanisławów so we are having *Totenkopf* move over and assume responsibly for it. The roads are bad, delaying our forward movement. A relief in place [in Stanisławów] under these conditions won't be possible until early in the evening. *Totenkopf* must take over the flank protection of the [*Wiking*] division before it can continue its assault towards Radzymin. We request to be allowed to pull in our left flank all the way to Stanisławów, in order to free up forces for this mission.[42]

As the conversation continued, the *2. Armee Ia*, *Oberst. i.G.* Ernst-August Lassen, informed Pauly that the situation had changed and that while *IV. SS-Pz.Korps* was to continue its attempt to link up with *4. Pz.Div.* south of Radzymin, it would leave it up to that division to carry out the assault on the city, not the *Wiking*. Pauly was told to focus instead on maintaining the connection with the forces attacking from the direction of Warsaw (i.e., *19. Pz.Div.*) and find out whether Okuniew was still occupied, but its most important mission was now to extend its defensive line beyond Michałów, which was the shoulder of the penetration towards Okuniew.

The implication of this situation was that if Michałów could not be held, then the encirclement of III Tank Corps could not be maintained for long. Pauly retorted that *Gruf.* Gille did not want to extend his forces beyond that point but Lassen told him that he had to, since he did not know what would happen next if Gille did not carry out this order. Lassen stated that the situation concerning the *19. Pz.Div.* was very fluid, but that the SS corps needed to quickly form a strong reserve so it could attack either to the north or south, depending how the battle unfolded. *Oberst* Lassen said that the road to Radzymin should be clear soon, so the *Wiking* Division should not have to fight to get there, implying that the *4. Pz.Div.* would reach them soon anyway. Nevertheless, Gille's corps would have to extend a thin security line to the north regardless of whether its commander wanted to or not. The conversation ended when Pauly asked Lassen whether he could, at the very least, ask *19. Pz.Div.* to make a good faith attempt to maintain the linkage with the *Wiking* Division and not to withdraw from Okuniew without telling anyone first. But Lassen did not respond.

Throughout the day and into the evening, the III Tank Corps was pummeled as the combined attacks by the *19.* and *4. Pz.Div.* began to gather momentum. Pressure against *IV. SS-Pz.Korps*' southern flank continued to increase as well, but the troops from the *Wiking* and *Totenkopf* Divisions held despite the increasing ferocity of the attacks. Two additional orders were received later in the afternoon, reminding Gille that his corps must under all circumstances maintain the connection with *19. Pz.Div.*, but at some point in the day the link was broken, either by the unannounced withdrawal mentioned by Pauly or by a Soviet attack. It was duly reported by Gille at 6:40 p.m., stating "attempts to link up with *AOK 9* [*9. Armee*] south of Okuniew cannot be carried out on account of insufficient forces."[43]

This message set off alarms at both *2. Armee* and *H.Gr. Mitte*. That evening, an orders update was issued by *H.Gr.Mitte*, in which Model instructed both *9.* and *2. Armee* commanders, Generals von Vormann and Weiss respectively, to keep maintaining the pressure on the encircled III Tank Corps. Model singled out the *Wiking* Division and stated that it must attack north of Okuniew and reestablish the connection with *9. Armee* that had been broken earlier that day. Model further stated that maintaining the link between the two armies was important because it would deny the ability of 2nd Tank Army to reinforce its III Tank Corps as well as prevent the corps from escaping.[44] This, of course, reinforces the statement made earlier by the *2. Armee Ia* that the *Wiking* Division was not to be overly concerned with attacking towards Radzymin.

Significantly, Model directed that *4. Pz.Div.* be immediately subordinated to *9. Armee*'s *XXXIX. Pz.Korps* and that *IV. SS-Pz.Korps* should be prepared to follow suit and accept the attachment to *9. Armee* in the immediate future as soon as it finished its attack. This made a great deal of tactical sense, because *2. Armee* was more focused on holding its crumbling eastern flank rather than on the operation unfolding on its westernmost flank, which it considered a distraction from the more serious threat it faced. Consolidating all of the *panzer* corps carrying out the counteroffensive under one army headquarters would greatly simplify command and control, especially for an operation as complex as the one then underway. The second day of the counteroffensive ended similarly as the first one had, with a large number of Soviet tanks destroyed and the perimeter held by III Tank Corps being increasingly reduced, but with increasing pressure being exerted by Popov's VIII Guards Tank Corps and Gusev's 47th Army against *IV. SS-Pz.Korps*' southern front.

A worrying development that evening was the aforementioned severing or break of the connection between *9.* and *2. Armee*, an event that opened the possibility that the III Tank Corps might escape the tightening noose after all. A factor complicating the overall operation was the necessity of detaching a battlegroup from *19. Pz.Div.* and sending it back across the Vistula the next day to assist *VIII. Armeekorps* in its battle to contain the Magnuszew bridgehead established the previous day by Col. Gen. Chuikov's 8th Guards Army. To compensate for the loss of this *Kampfgruppe*, *Fs.Pz.Div. Hermann Göring* would have to rearrange its forces and assume the role previously performed by *19. Pz.Div.*, which would diminish that division's ability to continue pressing its attack towards Wołomin. One thing that *IV. SS* and *XXXIX. Panzerkorps* would not have to contend with was the ongoing uprising in Warsaw—that mission had been assigned to a special command led by a combined SS-Police headquarters commanded by *Ogruf.* Erich von dem Bach.

Though the uprising had no direct impact on the tank battle of Praga, it did influence the movement of front-line troops, supplies, and vehicles passing through the city along its main east–west avenue extending beyond the highway bridge at Praga. There had been numerous reports of convoys from the *Totenkopf*, *Hermann Göring* and *19. Panzer* Divisions being fired upon by the Polish Home Army, with many German troops being killed and wounded as they frequently had to fight their way through. Additionally, several army and *Waffen-SS* supply depots had been captured by the insurgents, which provided them with a source of weapons, ammunition, equipment, clothing, and even armored vehicles that they sorely needed.

On account of the Warsaw Uprising, the German response dictated that SS replacement troops intended for the *Wiking* and *Totenkopf* Divisions had been incorporated into some of the many polyglot SS *Kampfgruppen* that had been formed to quell the uprising, including the infamous *Dirlewanger* and *Kaminski* Brigades, Azerbaijani units, and assorted *SS-Polizei* units. The *Hermann Göring* Division's antiaircraft regiment was employed in a direct fire role as well at a time when its presence east of Praga might have had a material influence on the outcome of the battle. Generally though, the Warsaw Uprising had little impact on the fighting east of the Vistula during August, though by September, when the First Belorussian Front and 1st Polish Army began a series of attempts to come to its aid, various elements of *9. Armee* and even the *IV. SS-Pz.Korps* would be drawn into the fighting for the suburb of Zoliborz, Mokotów, and the Praga bridges.

The night of 2–3 August passed without further incident. In its morning report, submitted to *2. Armee* before dawn, *IV. SS-Pz.Korps* stated that the evening passed uneventfully. Except for artillery fire and patrol activity, the remaining corps of *2. Armee* reported very little, with the exception of *XXIII. Armeekorps*, which had to respond overnight to an attempt by the 65th Army to penetrate its positions northeast of Sokólow with a rifle division. This attack was pinched off and destroyed early that morning by a counterattack launched by the *541. Gren.Div.*, which quietened things down considerably, at least for that morning. The bulk of the action that day, as with the previous day, was on the *2. Armee*'s far western flank, where the tank battle of Praga was reaching its climax.

Here, on 3 August, the decisive phase of the battle was about to play out. As dawn broke, the *4.* and *19.* and the *Hermann Göring Panzer* Divisions intensified their attacks, squeezing the remnants of III Tank Corps into a 10-kilometer wide pocket between Wołomin and Okuniew. *Stuka* dive bombers roamed the sky, pouncing on the few remaining Soviet tanks that could be spotted from the air. Company and battalion-sized tank battles raged throughout this small area, and the sounds of the battle could even be heard in central Warsaw, nearly 20 kilometers away. Throughout the day, the *Wiking* held the line facing the southwest corner of the pocket, beating back repeated company and battalion-level attempts by the entrapped Soviet troops to escape, while it simultaneously warded off numerous attempts by the increasingly active VIII Guards Tank Corps and XXIX Rifle Corps of the 47th Army to come to their assistance from the south. The situation also heated up on *2. Armee*'s eastern front, as each of the corps engaged there reported numerous attacks possibly timed to coincide with the effort to relieve pressure on the encircled III Tank Corps.

By early evening, the situation in the *IV. SS-Pz.Korps* sector had become clearer, as it was evident that Maj.Gen. Popov's VIII Guards Tank Corps and Lt.Gen. Gusev's 47th Army were coordinating their efforts to relieve the increasingly desperate III Tank Corps. The *Wiking* and *Totenkopf* Divisions reported that in the afternoon and early evening hours, Red Army units in regimental strength had made numerous penetrations of the corps' defensive line that were thrown back only with great difficulty. Artillery and multiple rocket-launcher fire had intensified in the Stanisławów and Michałów areas, as had tank attacks in company strength. In short, *IV. SS-Pz.Korps* was beginning to experience the full might of the First Belorussian Front's response, as Marshal Rokossovsky sought to relieve the pressure on Radzievsky's army. But the most discouraging news of all that day was the *Wiking* armored *Kampfgruppe*'s inability to reestablish contact with Schmalz's *Fs.Pz.Div. Hermann Göring* of the *9. Armee*.

In his evening report, *Gruf.* Gille described how *Staf.* Mühlenkamp's battlegroup had attempted to push through newly established Soviet defenses north of Okuniew. It had managed to fight its way through to link up with Schmalz's forward outpost, but before Mühlenkamp was able to consolidate his own defenses, his troops, including *II. Abt./SS-Pz.Rgt. 5*, were counterattacked by a strong Soviet force that forced the *Wiking*'s battlegroup to pull back. Gathering every available unit, *Staf.* Mühlenkamp tried once again late in the afternoon with another attack, but the Soviet reaction was so fierce he was forced to pull his troops back to a more defensible line.[45] No action by *Fs.Pz.Div. Hermann Göring* to come to the *Wiking*'s assistance was reported, though the *Luftwaffe panzer* division's forward-most unit did send a false report to *XXXIX. Pz.Korps* that it had linked up with the *Wiking* Division at Okuniew that evening at 10:15 p.m. There is no evidence to support this assertion, since by that time, Mühlenkamp's tanks and infantry had pulled back at least a kilometer.[46] The end result of this action was that the escape route of the III Tank Corps was now open, if only by a gap two kilometers wide, and the fact that any Soviet unit escaping through this gap would be subject to German artillery fire was small consolation, especially during the night when observation was limited.

That evening, *IV. SS-Pz.Korps* submitted its first status report since the battle began three days earlier. The *Wiking* reported having nine *Pz. IV*s, 27 Panthers, and five *Sturmgeschütz* as being combat-ready, with the *Totenkopf* having eight, eight, and 23, respectively, for a corps total of 80 medium tanks and assault guns ready for battle. In addition, inside of Warsaw two *Pz. VI* Tigers were reported as still being fully operational, despite the fact that one other tank had been severely damaged and another destroyed when insurgents attacked them while parked on the side of the road awaiting movement in Warsaw.[47] An equal number of tanks and assault guns were in short-term repair, which meant that they could be restored to full mission-capable status as soon as the requested parts arrive. Providentially, that evening Gille's *Quartiermeister*, *Stubaf.* Scharff, was notified by *2. Armee*'s *Oberquartiermeister* (*O.Qu.*) that the requested repair parts had been delivered via rail on the orders of the Inspector of Armored Troops and were available in the town of Sochaczew, 30 kilometers west of Warsaw, waiting to be picked up.[48] Once in the hands of the *panzer* regiment's maintenance company, the readiness rates of the corps tanks would markedly improve when these needed repairs were made.

The same, however, was not true of the corps' infantry regiments. Between 29 July and 3 August, the *Wiking* had suffered a net loss of 299 men either killed or wounded, while the *Totenkopf* Division had lost 573. This does not count the shortages in manpower both divisions reported before the battle even started. Anticipating the looming shortage, *IV. SS-Pz.Korps* had reported its manpower requirements to *2. Armee* the previous day, which then dutifully passed them on to *H.Gr. Mitte*. The report stated that the *Wiking* requested 280 replacements, while the *Totenkopf* asked for 2,428 in order to be restored to full personnel strength.

How soon they would arrive could not be determined; many of these replacements had been diverted to fill up the SS units then engaged in quelling the resistance in Warsaw.[49] At any rate, neither *H.Gr. Mitte* nor *2. Armee* had the authority to handle *Waffen-SS* replacement requirements, which could only be dealt with by going directly to the *SS-Personalamt* in Berlin, as was the standard procedure. The replacement problem would be a recurring issue for Gille's corps, and for the *Waffen-SS* in general, especially considering Himmler's bid to expand the *Waffen-SS* during the summer of 1944 was coming into direct conflict with the need to replace the casualties his forces were beginning to suffer on both the Eastern and Western Fronts.

During the heavy fighting throughout the day, both *Wiking* and *Totenkopf* Divisions had expended a considerable amount of ammunition, particularly that fired by the artillery, which was being used to help the thinly spread infantry hold their ground. At 9:45 that evening, *SS-Stubaf.* Pauly called the *2. Armee O.Qu.* and informed him that although the armored *Kampfgruppe* of the *Wiking* had been able to reach the eastern outskirts of Okuniew, it had used up much of its ammunition and requested *2. Armee*'s assistance. What was needed, Pauly told him, was for *2. Armee* to arrange to have it brought as far forward as possible and deposited in the area north of Stanisławów, where it could be then distributed. Half an hour later, the *2. Armee O.Qu.* informed the *2. Armee*'s *Ia*, *Oberst* Lassen, that Gille had been allocated transport capacity for 400 tons of supplies, and that he should use these assets and get it himself from the corps' dedicated supply dump at Sokołów. In retrospect, this was an unrealistic and uncooperative attitude on the part of the *O.Qu.*, since the ammo dump was now nearly 100 kilometers east of Gille's current position and, *per* the prevailing doctrine, it was the field army's responsibility to support the corps.

That evening, Model's report of the day for *H.Gr. Mitte*, issued at 00:45 a.m. on 4 August and delivered to the *OKH* in Berlin, summarizing the counteroffensive that was now three days old, stated:

> East of Warsaw a concentrated attack by four panzer divisions has nearly succeeded in closing in on the encircled enemy forces east of Wołomin after extraordinarily hard fighting. Breakout attempts by the enemy to the south or southeast are anticipated. The numerically superior enemy has been offering especially tough resistance. During the fighting today, 76 enemy tanks were destroyed.[50]

The efforts of *2. Armee* and Gille's corps were also recognized. In his statement, Model said, "Today the enemy carried out numerous tank-supported attacks against the lengthy front line of the *IV. SS-Pz.Korps*, but it was able to hold despite having to deal with local breakthroughs in the vicinity of Ludwinów. Fighting to eliminate the enemy's penetration is still under way."

Orders for the following day's operations were issued by *H.Gr. Mitte* at 11:50 p.m. on 3 August. These directed that *2.* and *9. Armee* would continue the counteroffensive, since they had completed the first phase, the destruction of the bulk of the III Tank Corps at Wołomin. The next phase would focus on the destruction of the VIII Guards Tank Corps in the area south of Okuniew, while ensuring that the remnants of III Tank Corps did not escape. Once that had been completed, then the third and final phase—the elimination of the XVI Tank Corps south of Praga—would be carried out, if time and forces available permitted. Specifically, the order issued that evening directed that beginning at 8 a.m. on 4 August, *9. Armee* would attack from the area of Zakret via Zorawka towards the ultimate objective of Halinow, while *Gruppe Gille* (*IV. SS-Pz.Korps*) would attack towards *9. Armee*'s lead element (the *Hermann Göring* Division) with a tightly concentrated armored spearhead towards Halinow via Michałów and Dluga Kościelna.

Once both units linked up at Halinow, *H.Gr. Mitte* expected to have bagged the bulk of VIII Guards Tank Corps. Though *4. Pz.Div.*, now operating under the banner of *Gen.Lt.* von Saucken's *XXXIX. Pz.Korps*, would continue its attack, the rest of *19. Pz.Div.* would begin its move across the Vistula, joining the main body of the division as it prepared to counterattack and destroy the Magnuszew bridgehead to the south, leaving the counteroffensive short of one panzer division for the attack the next day. The plan marked a significant change of mission for the *Wiking* Division, which had not yet been involved in much tank-on-tank fighting. It had instead focused up to this point on holding the pocket at Okuniew closed in cooperation with *9. Armee* while it defended against Soviet attempts to break through and rescue III Tank Corps. Throughout the past two days, the front line had crept closer to Gille's corps headquarters in Nowo Dobre, bringing it within range of Soviet heavy artillery. In order to get his headquarters to a safer location, Gille decided to move his command post to Kąty-Borucza that evening, a movement of approximately 10 kilometers. Though a necessary move, it carried with it the risk that his field telephone and radio communications might be affected, a chance that Gille decided to take.

The *Wiking* Division would now have to carry out a quick reorientation to the southwest and modify its task organization to include more of its tanks. Both battalions of *Ostubaf.* Darges's *SS-Pz.Rgt. 5* had been widely dispersed between Stanisławów and Okuniew and the regiment would need to regroup before the attack could begin the following morning. It would be a busy night for *SS-Pz.Rgt. 5* as it sought to pull the individual tank companies out of their current battle positions and move them during the hours of darkness to take up their attack positions before dawn the next day. The mechanics had been working feverishly all evening to install the newly arrived replacement parts, and the results began to show. That evening, *IV. SS-Pz.Korps* reported the following tanks ready for battle: *Totenkopf* had seven *Pz. IV*, 24 *Pz. V* Panthers, three *Pz. VI* Tigers, and 23 *Sturmgeschütze*, for a total of 57; while *Wiking* reported 10 *Pz. IV*, 27 *Pz. V* Panthers, and eight *Sturmgeschütze*, for a total of 45;. In total, over 100 tanks and assault guns were now available to Gille, still a potent force by contemporary standards and 20 more than were available the day before.[51]

The last day of the counteroffensive did not begin on a positive note, at least not for *IV. SS-Pz.Korps*. Its field telephone lines to *2. Armee* were severed at 5:15 a.m., most likely by an artillery barrage that killed three soldiers, including *SS-Grenadier* Helmut Lep of the corps' *SS-Begleit Kompanie 104*. Whatever the circumstance, the corps had temporarily lost its communication capability and was unable to contact *2. Armee* headquarters to submit its morning report. After over an hour attempting to contact it by radio, *Gen.Oberst* Weiss finally succeeded in contacting Gille at 6:29 p.m., who informed his army commander that the attack that he was supposed to launch earlier that morning could not be carried out. Weiss radioed back less than half an hour later, demanding that *Gruf.* Gille launch the attack immediately regardless of his situation, but then radio contact was apparently lost again. *Gen.*

Oberst Weiss, faced with a quandary, informed *H.Gr. Mitte* headquarters of the problem. Model himself came on the line an hour later and ordered the *2. Armee* commander to send an officer to Gille's headquarters to ensure that the order was carried out. One of Weiss' staff officers, *Maj.* Wedekind, was duly sent out to locate Gille and inform him personally of the need to attack immediately.[52] One possible reason for the disruption besides artillery fire was Gille's aforementioned decision to move his *Hauptquartier* the night before to a new location, which would have affected communications for a brief period. Regardless, the loss of communications was not intentional but it did occur at a critical time.

While accusations flew back and forth between *2. Armee* and *H.Gr. Mitte* about *IV. SS-Pz.Korps*' alleged unwillingness to attack, and while allegations of its commander's dereliction of duty were aired by the *H.Gr. Mitte* chief of staff, *Gen. Lt.* Krebs, Gille's troops had been fighting hard since early that morning. Though the *Wiking* had established a firm connection on its right flank with the *4. Pz.Div.* near the town of Krubki, it reported a great deal of enemy movement to its front, describing long columns of enemy movement from north to south, most likely signifying the escape of the few remaining elements of III Tank Corps fleeing from Wołomin.[53] At the same time, Mühlenkamp's newly regrouped armor *Kampfgruppe* was attacked in its assembly area near Michałów by strong tank-supported attacks from the east, south, and west. This most likely signified that the VIII Guards Tank Corps had finally begun its relief attack, though a day too late to do anything but save the remnants of III Tank Corps. Nevertheless, Mühlenkamp's troops had to fight for their lives to prevent being steamrollered by this unexpected attack. By late morning they had cut off and eliminated the Soviet penetration, though their own attack had been set back by six hours or more.

Along the rest of the corps' front line, particularly that defended by the *Totenkopf* Division, the Soviets launched numerous battalion-sized attacks composed of infantry supported by tanks and artillery. These, however, were warded off, with the exception of one near Polkow Kopratyny that could only be sealed off with great effort.[54] The *Totenkopf*'s *SS-Pz.Rgt. 3*, acting as the division's own "fire brigade," was continuously employed throughout its wide division defensive sector, repeatedly carrying out counterattacks to seal off breaches like these or to destroy Soviet units that had broken through. The steady toll of killed and wounded in both divisions continued mounting, forcing ever-greater demands upon those remaining. By nightfall, it had become apparent that Mühlenkamp's attack towards Halinow as part of the overall plan to encircle the VIII Guards Tank Corps was going nowhere. The pressure on the German forces defending Michałów and Stanisławów had become so great that Gille feared that the *Wiking*, or at least a part of it, might be cut off. The *IV. SS-Pz. Korps* was not the only corps having difficulties that day, either.

Though *4. Pz.Div.* was enjoying continuing success in eliminating remnants of III Tank Corps trapped in the Wołomin pocket, the situation along the Vistula defensive line, particularly at Magnuszew, had become so serious that Model decided to move the entire *Fs.Pz.Div. Hermann Göring* there as soon as it could. The division itself had been alerted late in the previous evening that it might be transferred, so it had already anticipated the order that was finally issued at midday on 4 August. Its units began moving over the Vistula and around Warsaw beginning that afternoon. The responsibility for conducting *9. Armee*'s part in the attack towards Halinow would now fall upon the *73. Inf.Div.*, a unit hardly in the position to offer a credible defense against a nearly full-strength tank corps, much less an attack against one, though it had been temporarily reinforced by *Gren.Brig. 1131* and a small tank–infantry *Kampfgruppe* from the *Hermann Göring* Division that had remained behind. Nevertheless, only one battalion from *73. Inf.Div.*, *II.Btl./Grenadier-Regiment 170*, was to be sent to assist Gille, though how it was to cross the gap at Okuniew was not explained.

There were now only two *panzer* divisions remaining that were able to continue the attack against VIII Guards Tank Corps, and one, the *Wiking*, was already tied down in heavy defensive fighting. The *4. Pz.Div.*, capitalizing on its momentum after taking Wołomin, continued pushing south until it was only a kilometer north of Okuniew, killing and capturing hundreds of Soviet troops as it advanced. When its leading tank battalion from *Pz.Rgt. 35* ran into a well-organized *Pakfront* consisting of dozens of concealed antitank guns, 11 of its tanks were knocked out in short order, forcing the lead battalion to fall back. Newly arriving Soviet tank units, assessed to be from the VIII Guards Tank Corps, were also spotted in the vicinity, a worrisome development that made Betzel, the commander of *4. Pz.Div.*, halt and reassess the situation. Though his division was able to maintain its connection with the *Wiking* Division on its left flank and established a solid connection with the *73. Inf.Div.* on its right, further efforts to push through or around Okuniew proved fruitless. By this time, the steam clearly had run out of the German counteroffensive, but not before it had collapsed the Soviet pocket at Wołomin. As a side benefit, the German front line between Stanisłowów and Praga had been straightened out.

That evening, a new set of orders from *H.Gr. Mitte* via *2. Armee* were issued at 10:35 p.m. that began with a declarative statement, which admitted that, "During the fighting on 4 August 1944, the entire front line of *2. Armee* has scored a significant defensive victory." The *9. Armee*'s commander issued a similar proclamation in his *Tagesbefehl* the same day:

> The bulk of the 3rd Russian Tank Corps in the area of Wołomin has been crushed by the concentrated attack of the *XXXIX. Panzer-Korps*. The looming fall of Warsaw, as broadcast by Moscow Radio to practically the entire world, has been thwarted. The uprising in the Polish capital has thereby lost its purpose. After several long weeks, once again we have achieved a great success! This feat has been achieved by the true and loyal brotherhood in arms of the *10. Flak-Brigade*, the *4.* and *19. Panzer Divisions*, the *Fallschirmjäger-Panzer-Division* [sic] "*Herman Göring,*" the *73. Inf.Div.* and the *Grenadier-Brigade 1131* under the combined command of *Gen. Lt.* von Saucken. I am proud of you all! We will continue holding Warsaw and the Vistula![55]

Word of the success soon filtered down to the lowest echelons of Gille's corps. Within the *I. Abt./SS-Pz.Rgt. 5*, whose two companies (*3.* and *4.*) had been split up into separate elements and parceled out to the division's *Panzergrenadier* battalions since 31 July, it was reported that, "The morale of the troops is once again on the rise thanks to the news of the unfolding success that has changed our situation for the better."[56]

Despite the celebratory atmosphere, a great deal of fighting remained. That same day, Weiss tasked Gille's corps with a modified mission that directed it to hold on to its current position along the southern front of *2. Armee* by resorting to mobile defense tactics that would take advantage of its superior mobility. It was also instructed to continue its destruction of enemy forces in the Okuniew area and use its defensive success gained so far as a springboard to achieve even greater success. No mention was made of the misunderstanding that took place that morning, as Weiss and Model had probably been told about what had actually happened when the *Wiking* Division was attacked and Gille temporarily lost communications. Such is the fog of war.

Of greater import, as far as *IV. SS-Pz.Korps* was concerned, was the notification that in two days it would be reassigned to *9. Armee*, beginning on 6 August. This information was relayed to *Oberführer* Heilmann at 11:55 a.m. by Krebs at *H.Gr. Mitte* headquarters. This change of higher headquarters would simplify Model's command and control challenge by placing the responsibility for defending the southern approaches to Warsaw to one field army, rather than two. It would also free up Weiss's *2. Armee* to focus exclusively on defending the eastern approaches to Warsaw along the 100-kilometer line running in the south from Kałuszyn to the town of Małkinia on the Bug River in the north. Another development that day was *Staf.* Mühlenkamp's receipt of a notification through formal SS channels in Berlin that his selection as the acting commander of the *Wiking* had been formally approved. Krebs, apparently unimpressed when informed by Mühlenkamp of the news, responded that he should get in touch right away with his corps commander and let him know, since it was an SS matter, not a *Wehrmacht* one.[57]

Another administrative development was that collecting points had been established in the *H.Gr.Mitte* area for members of the *IV. SS-Korps* who were returning to their battalions from furlough or the hospital, as well as those men who had been separated from their units due to the heavy fighting of the past five weeks. *Totenkopf*'s *Sammelstelle* (collecting point) was set up in Modlin, the *Wiking*'s in Ostrow, and corps troops' was to be in Grodzisk. All of these towns were on the eastern bank of the Vistula and were areas that would become the scene of heavy fighting in the near future.[58] This was good news to the divisions, who were experiencing manpower shortages after the heavy fighting of the past week; an infusion of some of its sorely missed junior leaders and specialist personnel was badly needed.

By 5 August, *H.Gr. Mitte*'s focus had shifted to the Magnuszew bridgehead to the south of Warsaw and the equally serious situation developing in East Prussia to its north. While the uprising in Warsaw was troubling, its suppression was seen largely as the responsivity of the SS and Police, with the *Wehrmacht* largely in a supporting role. As long as it did not influence the fighting on the east bank of the Vistula between Praga and Razymin, *H.Gr. Mitte* did not appear to be overly concerned, since it could easily crush the uprising if it chose to do so. Still, Model must have breathed a sigh of relief when the 2nd Tank Army was not diverted to the relief of the Polish Home Army on 27 July. He must have understood, as Marshal Rokossovsky did, that greater operational opportunities could be had by resisting the temptation of an easy victory over a decisive one.

For his part, Rokossovsky was puzzled regarding the timing of the Warsaw Uprising himself. After the war, he wrote:

> It was so sudden that we were quite at a loss and at first we thought the Germans might have spread the rumor … Frankly speaking, the timing of the uprising was just about the worst possible in the circumstances. It was as though its leaders had deliberately chosen a time that would ensure defeat.[59]

When the Warsaw Uprising began, Marshal Rokossovsky's lead tank columns were over 30 kilometers away on the opposite side of the Vistula and could do very little at that point to lend any assistance to the Polish Home Army even if they had wished to do so. Two weeks later, Rokossovsky was vexed when a report written by the commander of the insurgents in Warsaw, General Tadeusz Komorowski (codenamed "Bór"), was broadcast by the BBC, in which Bór claimed that his forces were closely coordinating with the First Belorussian Front. Nothing could have been further from the truth, as Rokossovsky knew. This incident only increased the feeling of mistrust that already existed between the U.S.S.R. and the Polish exile government in London.

As it ground its way through the city, block by block, the German response, after recovering from the initial surprise, slowly and inexorably crushed the uprising during the next two months with overwhelming force, often with great cruelty against the insurgents and the civilian population alike. It was not until the uprising was coming to an end when it began to affect the battles east of Warsaw, when the Soviets finally allowed the 1st Polish Army to make an attempt to seize bridges over the Vistula to relieve the insurgents. However, by then the Vistula bridges at Praga would be blown up and Warsaw itself would lose its importance to both Nazi Germany and the Soviet Union, with the 1st Polish Army's sacrifice having been in vain.

Thus, the tank battle of Praga ended almost without fanfare. But the results were clear: III Tank Corps had been destroyed as a cohesive unit and had lost most of its tanks. The threat to the bridges over the Vistula had been eliminated, and *2.* and *9. Armee* no longer had to contend with the danger of being cut off from their lines of communication at Praga, Serock, or Zegrze. Though a large percentage of the Red

Army's troops had managed to escape the trap on foot, it would take several weeks for III Tank Corps to be reconstituted with new tanks, equipment, and above all, more manpower. The VIII Guards Tank Corps had suffered significantly as well, as its tank and mechanized infantry brigades had to fight to keep the escape route open for its sister corps and to keep carrying out continuous counterattacks to keep the German forces, in particular the divisions of the *IV. SS-Pz.Korps*, off balance. With its armor so reduced in strength, Lt.Gen. Radzievsky's 2nd Tank Army was no longer capable of conducting operations and was consequently withdrawn from the front lines and moved back to a rest area where its corps could be reconstituted.[60]

How many tanks were destroyed? No official Soviet number was ever released. German sources claim that most of the tanks of III Tank Corps were destroyed between 31 July and 6 August, and that *XXXIX. Pz.* and *IV. SS-Pz.Korps* had killed 3,000 of its men and captured an additional 6,000. The *4. Pz.Div.* alone claimed to have knocked out 111 Soviet tanks and assault guns, along with 45 antitank guns.[61] The *9. Armee* claimed that its divisions, including the *73. Infanterie-Division*, the *Hermann Göring* and *19. Panzer* Divisions, had knocked out 192 more, but these figures probably include some from the VIII Guards and XVI Tank Corps.[62] German losses had not been negligible, either. At the end of the counteroffensive, the *4.* and *19. Panzer* Divisions, *Fs.Pz.Div. Hermann Göring* and the two divisions of the *IV. SS-Pz.Korps* still reported 220 tanks and assault guns operational on 6 August, compared to the 318 they had on 31 July.[63] However, since they now owned the battlefield, they could recover and put back into service those tanks that could be repaired, while Soviet tanks left behind would be destroyed by special demolition teams.

Daily compiled reports indicate that from 18 July–4 August, 2nd Tank Army had been reduced in strength to only 263 fighting vehicles, including assault guns and self-propelled guns.[64] Lt.Gen. Radzievsky, in his own 2nd Tank Army after-action report written on 8 August, stated that III Tank Corps had only 56 tanks and assault guns of all types still on hand, VIII Guards Tank Corps had 125, and XVI Tank Corps had 166 available. The report does not state whether these were considered operational and may have included those undergoing repair or new ones issued from ordnance depots.[65] Thus, on 8 August, the 2nd Tank Army, after three days in a rest area, had only 347 tanks remaining out of the approximately 810 that its three tank corps had started the offensive with nearly three weeks earlier. Before it was pulled out for reconstitution, the III Tank Corps handed over all of its serviceable vehicles to the VIII Guards Tank Corps.[66]

When 2nd Tank Army was pulled out of the line with the exception of its VIII Guards Tank Corps, which remained behind, the only force available to cover the 80-kilometer front line running from the Vistula to Wegrow was Lt.Gen. Gusev's 47th Army with its three rifle corps and one tank regiment, with the II Guards Cavalry Corps in general support as the First Belorussian Front reserve.[67] While Gusev's army had suffered a significant number of casualties, estimated by one source as nearing 20 percent of its total strength (a loss approaching 14,000 men), it was still able to exert pressure on the German defenders from the *XXXIX. Panzer* and *IV. SS-Pz. Korps* and pound them daily with artillery.[68] Nevertheless, for about a week, a brief period of relative calm returned to the battlefield, at least east of Warsaw. Inside the city itself and around the Magnuszew bridgehead, savage fighting continued unabated until early October. But for the *Wiking* and *Totenkopf* Divisions, they would barely have enough time to prepare for the next phase of the campaign—a series of land battles that would later become officially known as the first, second and third battles of Warsaw in which they, and their corps headquarters, would play a prominent role. In the process, both would be so thoroughly decimated that by the end of November 1944, both divisions would emerge barely recognizable.

CHAPTER 6

Operational Interlude: *Unternehmen Brückenschlag* 8–13 August 1944

Generalfeldmarschall Model's audacious plan to strike the 2nd Tank Army at its most vulnerable point between 1 and 4 August had partially succeeded, though it did not achieve the decisive victory that he had hoped for. Despite his intentions to encircle and eliminate all of General Radzievsky's army, *G.F.M.* Model had to be satisfied with the destruction of one tank corps and the administering of a severe mauling to another. But more importantly, in terms of effects, his counteroffensive had accomplished two things—it succeeded in protecting the bridges over the Vistula, Bug, and Narew Rivers, thereby vouchsafing the lines of communications for *2.* and *9. Armee*, and had bought time for his armies to construct new defensive lines to withstand the inevitable next round of Soviet offensive operations. Another benefit from Model's standpoint was that action east of the Vistula had quietened down noticeably. *H.Gr. Mitte*'s war diary states that on the evening of 5 August, "The enemy forces opposite *9. Armee* … are strikingly idle."[1]

In recognition of the successful outcome of the operation, a *Wehrmacht* Communique was broadcast at 2:15 a.m. on 5 August that saluted the accomplishments of *XXXIX. Pz.Korps* during the battle, stating:

> By the destruction of a strong Soviet armored unit that had broken through, troops from the *4.* and *19. Pz.Div.*, as well as the *Fallschirm Pz.Div. 'H.G.'* under the leadership of *Gen.Lt.* von Saucken particularly distinguished themselves by their offensive spirit and cool-headed risk-taking, especially the troops of the *73. Inf.Div.* who displayed a firm and determined defense.

The broadcast also mentioned that von Saucken's corps had destroyed or captured 222 Soviet tanks and assault guns, 45 cannon or field pieces, 39 antitank guns, and a large amount of infantry weapons and other vehicles. Unaccountably, Gille's corps received no mention at all, though it had contributed just as substantially to the success of the operation, including the *Totenkopf* Division's successful defense of the corps' left flank and the contribution to the dismembering of the III Tank Corps by the *Wiking* Division.

From an operational standpoint, a brief pause had indeed settled in over the gently rolling fields, tiny villages, and wooded hills east of Warsaw. Model now could devote his attention to his other two primary concerns. The first and most dangerous lay on his army group's left flank, where the Red Army had severed the connection with the neighboring *H.Gr. Nord* and had pushed through Lithuania to the Baltic Sea near Riga, cutting off that army group from Model's and from Germany proper. The other was the Soviets' ever-expanding Magnuszew and Puławy bridgeheads over the Vistula south of Warsaw, which had proved to be too strong for the available forces of *VIII. Armeekorps* to eradicate. Both of these threats had to be dealt with immediately, but in order to gather the combat power necessary to carry out the counteroffensives that this would entail, Model would have to take a corps and several divisions away from *2.* and *9. Armee*, both of which had earned a breathing spell after the successes at Praga and Radzymin.

To strengthen *3. Pz.Armee*, which would carry out an operational-level pincer attack in conjunction with a *panzer*-led attack from the opposite direction by *H.Gr. Nord* (*Unternehmen Doppelkopf*, an operation named after a German card game), the ever-resourceful field marshal would need von Saucken's corps and two panzer divisions (the *4.* and *12. Pz.Div.*) plus another (the *5. Pz.Div.*). To bolster the forces from *9. Armee*'s right wing earmarked to eliminate the Magnuszew bridgehead, he had already identified the *19. Pz.Div.* and *Fs.Pz.Div. Hermann Göring* as reinforcements for *VIII. Armeekorps*, as related in the previous chapter, and had already prodded *Gen.d.Pz.Tr.* von Vormann to get their advance elements moving in that direction even before the fighting at Praga was over. This move would leave *Gruf.* Gille's *IV. SS-Pz.Korps* as the only armored reserve left east of the Vistula to counter the ever-growing list of Soviet units that had been identified moving into position.

The necessary castling maneuver envisioned by Model to concentrate the forces to launch these attacks, however, would have to be carried out in stages. A precipitous departure of so many armored units from the front would not only be noticed, but would weaken the remaining formations at a time when they could least afford it, since First Belorussian Front would undoubtedly resume its offensive once it recovered from its shock following the defeat of 2nd Tank Army. A shortening of the front would therefore have to be carried out, particularly concerning *2. Armee*, which held the longest and most easterly portion of *H.Gr. Mitte*'s front line. Thus, the concept for *Unternehmen Brückenschlag* (Operation *Bridge Building*) was born. In fact, Model already had this idea in mind when he had decided on 4 August to temporarily place *IV. SS-Pz.Korps* under the tactical control of *Gen.Lt.* von Saucken's *XXXIX. Pz.Korps*, thus creating *Panzergruppe von Saucken* (*Pz.Gr. von Saucken*), in a warning order issued to all units concerned on the evening of 5 August.[2]

Model's intent was encapsulated in the order issued by von Vormann's *9. Armee*, which would assume overall responsibility for the execution of the operation. The order stated that both *panzer* corps would be placed under one ad-hoc headquarters (*Gen.Lt.* von Saucken's) that would guarantee unity of command during this difficult maneuver by creating what in essence amounted to an army-sized organization, *Pz.Gr. von Saucken*, however temporarily.[3] *Generaloberst* Weiss's *2. Armee* would support by adhering to the same timeline as *Gen.d.Pz.Tr.* von Vormann's, withdrawing to its own designated phase lines on the *9. Armee* left flank. In addition to directing the attachment of Gille's corps, the *9. Armee* order also specified that both *Gruf.* Gille and *Gen.Lt.* von Saucken's corps would transition to the defense no later than 3 p.m. on 5 August. The order also directed *Gen.Lt.* von Saucken to move his corps headquarters to Radzymin by the evening of 6 August, a location where he would be able to exercise more effective radio communications with *Gruf.* Gille since it was 15 kilometers closer than his old headquarters northeast of Radzymin at Malopole.[4]

The rationale for the decision to create *Pz.Gr. von Saucken* was simple—the commander of *9. Armee* had his hands full planning his army's counterattack against the Magnuszew and Puławy bridgeheads and was also supporting the military response to the Warsaw Uprising, which was being carried out by the *Höhere SS-und Polizei Führer* (*HSSPF*, or Higher SS and Police Commander), *Ogruf.* von dem Bach. *Generalleutnant* von Saucken, a veteran *panzer* commander, was more than capable of directing the action of two *panzer* corps, and had a level of experience that *Gruf.* Gille did not yet possess. Key to the success of *Brückenschlag* was the withdrawal and repositioning of *IV. SS-Pz.Korps* to a shorter, more defensible line east of Radzymin. Here, along a line that ran roughly parallel with the Warsaw–Bialystok railroad, that ran in a northeasterly direction from Warsaw, *Gruf.* Gille's troops would take up new defensive positions 5–10 kilometers to its west.

In essence, this withdrawal meant that *Pz.Gr. von Saucken* would have to carry out a counterclockwise pivoting movement from the south to the east, with its fulcrum centered on the town of Stanisławów, the scene of heavy fighting during the past week. The bulk of *Gen.Oberst* Weiss's *2. Armee*, with its three infantry corps (*XX.*, *XXIII.*, and *Kav.Korps Harteneck*), would also be displacing to the west to a shorter line in concert with the withdrawal of Gille's corps. As a side benefit, this move would also free up additional forces that could be used as local reserves or sent elsewhere. Thus, *Brückenschlag* would be a complex movement that would have to be closely monitored by commanders on the ground to ensure that neither *2.* nor *9. Armee* lost contact with one another along their inner flanks and that all units concerned adhered to the timetable.

The detailed order for *Unternehmen Brückenschlag* was issued by *9. Armee* at 9 p.m. on 7 August. It laid out the tasks to be accomplished by both *Pz.Gr. von Saucken* and *2. Armee* during the operation, listed the four color-coded phase lines to be used as control measures, and the boundaries between both armies on the ground during each phase (see Figure 2). It was initially planned to commence on the evening of 10–11 August, but the order acknowledged that events might require that this date be moved up due to enemy interference. The final phase line, codenamed "Green," was to be reached by midnight on 12 August; at that point, units were to turn about, dig in, and hold their positions.

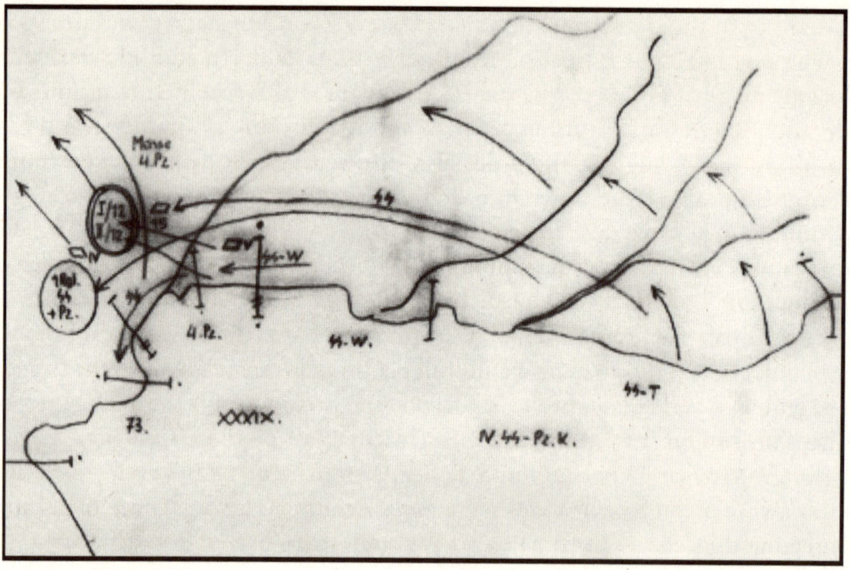

Figure 2. Diagram depicting phase lines and troops movements envisioned for *Unternehmen Brückenschlag*, 8–13 August 1944

During this withdrawal, which would involve over a dozen German divisions, the *4. Pz.Div.*, which was sandwiched between *73. Inf. Div.* to the west and the *Wiking* Division to the east, would be pulled out in stages in order to begin its rail movement to *3. Pz.Armee* for its role in *Doppelkopf*, to be followed by *XXXIX. Pz.Korps* headquarters and *Gen.Lt.* von Saucken himself by 10 August. At that point, *Gruf.* Gille and his corps headquarters would operate directly under *9. Armee* and would assume responsibility for the entire Modlin–Radzymin–Serock defensive sector, nestled between the triangle formed by the confluence of the Vistula, Bug, and Narew Rivers.

The division that would be most affected by *Brückenschlag* was the *Totenkopf*, which would have the farthest to move. To carry out its part of the withdrawal, it would have to displace from its 5 August positions facing south between Stanisławów in the west and Mokobody in the east to a new north–south line between Tłuszcz and Jadow, generally oriented along the Warsaw–Bialystok rail line, a road distance of nearly 60 kilometers for the battalion from *Pz.Gren.Rgt. Eicke* located on the division's leftmost flank. Upon arrival, it would relieve the elements of the withdrawing *4. Pz.Div.* and take up that division's defensive sector, while the *Wiking* Division would simultaneously displace to the north as the corps' front line swung to face east.

Thus, when the movement was complete, the *Totenkopf* Division would have inserted itself between the *Wiking* Division and *73. Inf.Div.* To ensure the continuity of the linkage between the *IV. SS-Pz.Korps* and its neighbor *XX. Armeekorps* of *2. Armee* during this "castling" maneuver, *II. Btl./Jäger Regiment* (*Jäg.Rgt.*) *75* of the *5. Jäger Division* (*Jäg.Div.*) would be temporarily attached to the *Totenkopf* Division. Fortunately, *Oberführer* Becker's division would not have to move the entire distance in one jump; because of the various phase lines inherent in the plan, the *Totenkopf* Division would be given several days to do this, as long as the original timetable held.

Unstated but implied in the operations order was that all divisions and corps involved in the withdrawal, including those from *2. Armee*, would have to relocate all of their supply dumps, field hospitals, repair facilities, and other rear area support elements of their respective *Heerestruppen* further to the rear before the front-line units pulled out. *Brückenschlag* would place a significant burden on units that were already short of fuel and wheeled transport, so the logistical planning would have to be very thorough to avoid any gaps in coverage, especially when it involved refueling *panzers* and other motor vehicles. Anything that the quartermasters could not take with them would have to be destroyed to prevent it from falling intact into the hands of the Red Army. To add to the sense of urgency, the field army and corps *Quartiermeister* staffs would only have one day to draft and issue their own orders to accomplish this.

When the order to begin planning for *Unternehmen Brückenschlag* was issued to the corps, most of the units that would take part had been involved in heavy fighting since 28 July, and had had little time to rest and maintain their equipment. The destruction of III Tank Corps and the crippling of the VIII Guards Tank Corps from 1–4 August had appreciably slowed down the First Belorussian Front's offensive, but it had by no means brought it to an end. Though things might have seemed quiet on the eastern side of the Vistula from the perspective of the *9. Armee* headquarters, for the units involved, the fighting was still intense.

This included the two divisions of the *IV. SS-Pz.Korps*, the *Wiking* and *Totenkopf*, which still found themselves subjected to numerous probing attacks and artillery barrages from the 47th Army, bolstered by the few remaining tanks of the VIII Guards Tank Corps. These attacks, though most were successfully smashed or driven off, took their daily toll in killed and wounded, particularly regarding infantry and combat engineers who bore the brunt of the fighting. Though they inflicted a much higher number of casualties on Soviet troops than they suffered, this kind of positional warfare would quickly sap the strength of these *panzer* divisions unless they were pulled out and allowed time to rest and service their equipment.

On 7 August, the day the withdrawal order was issued, *IV. SS-Pz.Korps* took stock of its units. While its *Panzergrenadier* regiments were beginning to show the strain, the improving readiness rate of the corps' armored fighting vehicles (AFV) was an encouraging sign. The *Totenkopf* Division, which had finally managed to bring up its maintenance echelon, was the strongest, with eight *Pz. IV*, 32 *Pz. V* Panthers, four *Pz. VI* Tigers, 24 StuG, and 19 towed antitank guns, for a total of

68 operational AFV. *Wiking* was not far behind, with 16 *Pz. IV*, 31 *Pz. V* Panthers, and nine StuG operational, for a total of 56, though it was handicapped by the continuing detachment of its *SS-Pz.Jg.Abt. 5* with 18 operational *Jagdpanzer IV* to *Oberst* Hähling's *73. Inf.Div.*[5] Roughly the same number of vehicles in each division were either in short or long-term repair (60 and 48, respectively). Much would be expected of these vehicles and their crews during *Unternehmen Brückenschlag*, since they would have to support the withdrawal of the infantry formations as they leapt back to the next phase line. The armor would perforce conduct a mobile defense, a tactic that would look to seek, strike, and delay any Soviet force attempting to pursue the withdrawing infantry too closely.[6]

As it turned out, events elsewhere were moving faster than the planners had initially anticipated. Despite the fact that *Pz.Gr. von Saucken* had reported on the morning of 8 August that there had been no combat activity in its defensive sector during the past evening worth mentioning, *H.Gr. Mitte* ordered *Brückenschlag* to begin that night, beginning at 9:30 p.m., two days earlier than expected. Units had to give up their old positions and arrive in their temporary positions along Phase Line Brown by dawn, and be ready to defend them on the morning of 9 August. Accordingly, units of the *2. Armee* on the left and troops of *Pz.Gr. von Saucken*, including *IV. SS-Pz.Corps*, on the right began to move out shortly after sundown, spurring into motion (from west to east) the *73. Inf.Div.* (which had the shortest distance to travel), the *1131. Grenadier Brigade (Gren.Brig.)*, the remaining elements of *4. Pz.Div.* (roughly half of the division), and *IV. SS-Pz.Korps*.

The weather remained dry and clear, a good omen for the beginning of a complex and dangerous operation. Unit commanders were ordered not to disclose the impending operation to their men until the last moment, lest the Soviets get wind of it. Despite this precaution, Lt.Gen. Gusev's 47th Army seemed to have sensed that something big was in the air, evidence that the operation had possibly been compromised before it had even begun. Whether German plans had been revealed by ULTRA intercepts is not certain; what is certain is that Marshal Rokossovsky ordered his sole remaining reserve, the now-rested 70th Army commanded by Col.Gen. Vasily Popov, to begin moving into position to the right of Gusev's 47th Army by 7 August. Here, inserted between the 47th and 28th Armies, it would soon make its presence felt.[7]

German suspicions were confirmed when the two divisions of *Gruf.* Gille's corps began to feel increasing enemy pressure immediately after they began moving out from their old positions during the early morning of 8 August to their new ones along Phase Line Brown, an imaginary line drawn several kilometers to the west. To their surprise, Gille's troops were closely followed by Soviet tank-supported reconnaissance forces in company strength that sought out any weak spots and opportunities to disrupt the German timetable. Though not a sign of a renewed Soviet offensive, some of the more aggressive probes, amply supported by artillery, penetrated the thin screen of troops of both the *Wiking* and *Totenkopf* Divisions covering the withdrawal. All of these attempts were driven off after brief counterattacks that temporarily restored the situation. An observation post manned by the *73. Inf.Div.* located atop Hill 500 near Zakręt was lost to a Soviet attack, but a counterattack was able to recover the lost ground.[8]

To relieve the pressure on the withdrawing troops and to deceive the Soviets as to German intentions, a 2-kilometer deep spoiling attack was launched at 1:30 p.m. on 9 August by *4. Pz.Div.* This successful operation, carried out by *II. Abt./Pz.Rgt. 35* against Soviet forces in an assembly area near Okuniew, was led by the division commander, *Gen.Maj.* Betzel, himself. The Red Army troops, evidently from the VIII Guards Tank Corps and 3rd Guards Cavalry Division, were caught completely by surprise by the German attack, which had been preceded by a short but sharp artillery barrage. The Soviet units suffered a significant number of casualties in the ensuing panic before their commanders reasserted control.[9] During the one-sided tank battle that ensued, 23 T-34s were destroyed against the loss of only three German tanks. In addition to scattering the enemy and pushing through the western outskirts of Okuniew, *4. Pz.Div.* was also able to destroy the railroad bridge over the Dluga River. Its mission accomplished, Betzel began to withdraw his troops that afternoon in preparation for the division's rail movement to the north, where it would play an important role in the upcoming *Unternehmen Doppelkopf* while operating under *3. Pz.Armee*.

Once the troops of *2. Armee* and *Pz.Gr. von Saucken* reached their designated intermediate positions along Phase Line Brown, they prepared to defend against another inevitable probing attack. Instead of remaining where they were for the next 24–48 hours as they expected, they received the order that same day to withdraw that very evening to their next positions along Phase Line Red, and again be prepared to defend the new front line by the next morning. Here, instead of staying along Phase Line Brown, *Pz.Gr.von Saucken*, including *Gruf.* Gille's corps, would hold for the next two days. Despite unrelenting Soviet probes, *IV. SS-Pz.Korps* was still able to arrive at its new phase line in good order and its divisions were in position by dawn on 9 August.

The only worrying development that day was an attempt by a Soviet tank unit supported by infantry to penetrate the *Wiking* Division's positions in the forest southwest of Stanisławów. Before the riflemen from LXXVII Rifle Corps could fortify their positions and emplace sufficient antitank defenses, they encountered a counterattack spearheaded by two tank-supported *Kampfgruppen* from the *Wiking* Division and were forced back. On the the *IV. SS-Pz.Korps*' left flank, the *Totenkopf* Division endured numerous battalion-sized attempts by the Soviets to breach their line but succeeded in warding off all of them, including three local penetrations, while still retaining a solid connection with the neighboring *5. Jäg.Div.*[10] Still, the continuous fighting, particularly supported by the seemingly endless amounts of Soviet artillery, continued to exact a daily toll of men and equipment.

On the evening of 9 August, *Gen.d.Pz.Tr.* von Vormann radioed *Gruf.* Gille that his corps would take over from *XXXIX. Pz.Korps* the next day by noon. That night, Gille's corps improved its defenses and prepared for the next round of troop withdrawals. His exhausted men dug hasty fighting positions, knowing that regardless of whether the Soviets attacked or merely sent out scouting parties, anything they did would be preceded by artillery fire, the greatest killer on the battlefield. *Panzer* units used the few hours of rest available to them to refuel and rearm their vehicles, repairing what battle damage they could. At 8:00 a.m. on 10 August, Gille sent a message to von Vormann via *Hellschreiber* that he had assumed command of his new sector from *Gen.Lt.* von Saucken. Once again, Gille would be operating directly under the control of a field army, with no intermediate headquarters between. With the battle hand off between *IV. SS-Pz.Korps* complete, von Saucken was now free to redeploy with the rest of his corps headquarters to its new *Kampfraum* in East Prussia, where it would once again play a prominent role in yet another desperate counterstroke.

Though the withdrawals to Phase Line Red by the *Wiking* and *Totenkopf* Divisions were carried out on the night of 9 August without incident, by mid-morning on 10 August, a Soviet force of unknown size had once more managed to penetrate German defenses in Stanisławów held by *Wiking* Division, forcing it to commit its division reserve in a counterattack to throw them out again. This area was the most critical defensive sector of Gille's entire front line and had to be held at all costs. A deep penetration at Stanisławów at this point would pose a great danger to the rest of *IV. SS-Pz.Korps*, since it was the hinge of the entire "door" that was swinging back to the Warsaw–Bialystok railroad line.

Should Gen.Lt. Gusev's forces break through and penetrate as far as the bridges at Modlin and Zegrze, Gille's corps would once again be faced with entrapment. Therefore, the bulk of the *Wiking* Division's remaining mobile forces were located there and would be heavily engaged that day. In addition to having to worry about his new defensive sector and seeing *Unternehmen Brückenschlag* through to its conclusion, Gille would also have to assume control that same day over *Oberst* Hähling's *73. Inf.Div.*, *Oberst* Wilhelm Söth's *Gren.Brig. 1131*, and the few remaining elements of *4. Pz.Div.* that had not yet pulled back to their railhead in Modlin.

As the day lengthened, 10 August was marked by increasingly heavy fighting, since it had by this point become clearly evident that 47th Army knew that a large-scale German displacement was underway. Lieutenant General Gusev's divisions were becoming increasingly aggressive, launching no fewer than 15 tank-supported battalion-sized attacks against the *Wiking* and *Totenkopf* Divisions as they sought to disrupt, disperse, and defeat *Brückenschlag*. On the corps' left flank west at Wegrow, the newly arrived troops of 70th Army were now beginning to launch their own attacks against the redoubtable *5. Jäg.Div.* None of these attempts to break through succeeded, though at several points they forced the SS and attached *Jäger* to withdraw several kilometers beyond the original contours of Phase Line Red. The *IV. SS-Pz. Korps* reported that its troops had inflicted heavy losses in men and materiel on the pursuing Soviet troops, including four tanks and 15 antitank guns, but that must have been small consolation.

During the course of the day, Gille's headquarters was displaced from its previous location at Novo Dobre to a new one at the Jaktory Manor, six kilometers northeast of Radzymin, taking over the same location used by *Pz.Gr. von Saucken* until that morning. The *Wiking* established its new division command post at the Kobiel Manor 10 kilometers northwest of Stanisławów, while the *Totenkopf* established its headquarters in the village of Rowne, 15 kilometers northeast of Stanisławów. These new locations, however temporary, would permit effective command and control for the next two days. The *Hauptquartier* of *SS-Gruf* Gille's corps, after its abrupt introduction to battle on 28 July, was now far more experienced than it had been when it began, having been displaced no fewer than four times in the past two weeks. For its two divisions, moving their headquarters to new locations while engaged in combat operations was nothing new.

Fighting throughout the day on 11 August was just as intense, made more challenging since the last *Kampfgruppe* from *4. Pz.Div.* was finally withdrawn from the front, leaving Gille three divisions and one brigade to defend his sector with. The most dangerous situation arose that day on the *Totenkopf*s front, when a regimental-sized attack, led by a Soviet tank battalion, managed to penetrate its front line at Solki after a lengthy artillery barrage. This dangerous situation forced the division commander to commit his armored reserve from *SS-Pz.Rgt. 3* to stop it before it could penetrate into the division's rear support area. The enemy had not been idle in front of the *Wiking* Division, whose troops had to ward off several large-scale armor-led reconnaissance forays aimed once again at seeking weak points in the German line around Stanisławów. Regardless of the situation at the front lines, the jump to the final line, Phase Line Green, was scheduled to happen that evening.

Throughout the night of 11 August, beginning at 9:00 p.m., the *Totenkopf* and *Wiking* Divisions managed to disentangle themselves from their enemy and slip away to their new defensive line, where they would establish what was intended to be a more permanent main line of defense east of the Warsaw–Bialystok railroad, running roughly along the line Rembertów–Wołomin–Tłuszcz. As they withdrew, every bridge they crossed was blown up after the last unit had passed over it and any installations that might benefit the enemy were destroyed as well, including electrical power plants, water purification systems, and railroad yards, in accordance with standing *9. Armee Auflockerung, Räumung, Lähmung und Zerstörung*, or *ARLZ, Massnahmen*, the so-called "scorched earth" orders.[11] Soviet units closely followed behind Gille's troops, and at one point between 5:00 and 6:00 a.m. on 12 August, troops from the *Wiking* Division barely managed to get into their new positions before forces of the Red Army did, an event that forced the battalion from the *Westland* Regiment to immediately turn about and counterattack.

Facing similar challenges, the three infantry corps of *Gen.Oberst* Weiss's *2. Armee* on *IV. SS-Pz.Korps'* left flank had also managed to disengage and withdraw on schedule, resulting in a far more coherent, cohesive, and defensible front line. With its last rearward movement, the *Totenkopf* Division, in leapfrog fashion, was inserted between the *Wiking* Division and the *73. Inf.Div.*, occupying the defensive sector formerly held by *4. Pz.Div.* two days before. Upon arrival in its new sector, *Obf.* Becker's division was ordered to temporarily incorporate *Oberst* Söth's *Gren. Brig. 1131* into its order of battle as its right-flank unit, while *II. Btl./Jäg.Rgt. 75* of the *5. Jäg.Div.* was released to return to its parent division at the same time, after being attached to the *Totenkopf* Division for the past five days.

Most of the units from *Gruf.* Gille's corps, except some of its rear guard elements, had arrived at Phase Line Green by 7:05 a.m., which was duly reported in his morning report to *9. Armee* headquarters. In turn, this information was passed up the chain of command to *H.Gr. Mitte*, whose attention was now focused on three other operations—the suppression of the Warsaw Uprising, destroying the Magnuszew and Puławy bridgeheads, and the impending attack by *3. Pz.Armee* into Lithuania from East Prussia. While Gille's corps had been engaged in *Unternehmen Brückenschlag* since 8 August, *Bau-Pionier Bataillon 421* (*Bau Pio.Btl.*, or construction engineer battalion), reinforced by pressed Polish civilian labor, had been employed building new front-line positions, anti-tank ditches, bunkers, and minefields. Though it was too small an effort to fortify the corps' entire new front line, what little that this battalion did accomplish was appreciated by the troops, after being on the move for most of the past week.

Throughout the day on 12 August, the front line was anything but quiet. The most worrisome fighting was in the *Totenkopf* Division's new sector, where a deep enemy penetration near Hill 123 north of Dworzec during the early morning forced that division to once again launch an armor-supported counterattack to retake it, an action that nearly lasted the entire day until the height was finally recaptured at sundown. Heavy artillery fire of nearly every caliber was reported by the *Wiking* Division upon their new positions in the town of Tłuszcz, as was heavy fighter-bomber activity by the Red Air Force along the German main supply route between Tluszcz and Jadow, a highway that figured prominently in *IV. SS-Pz. Korps'* logistics plan. While *Unternehmen Brückenschlag* had shortened the main defense line for *2.* and *9. Armee*, freed up troops, and in general resulted in a more defensible situation east of the Vistula and Narew Rivers, by no means had the fighting died down. Despite the withdrawal of the 2nd Tank Army from the First Belorussian Front's order of battle, Marshal Rokossovsky had no intention of granting *H.Gr. Mitte* any breathing space.

With his troops now occupying their new positions along their front line, Gille had time to take stock of his situation. By this point in the campaign, his two divisions (three, counting the addition of the *73. Inf.Div.*) had been in near-constant contact with the enemy for over two weeks. In addition to the stark human cost of this fighting, which resulted in figures recounting the number of dead, wounded, and missing, the losses in weapons and other materiel had been heavy as well. Though the *Wiking* and *Totenkopf* Divisions would not report their monthly status for two more weeks, there are existing reports from 13 August that present the status of their available combat power in terms of available front-line troops (infantry and combat engineers) and operational armored fighting vehicles.

For instance, on that date the *Wiking* had only 1,597 combat troops in the line, with an average *Kampfstärke* (front-line strength) of 266 men in each battalion, less than half of what each battalion normally fielded, about 546 men (this amount did not count support or administrative troops). However, two of its battalions (*III. Btl./SS-Pz.Gren.Rgt. 10 Westland* and *SS-Pz.Aufkl.Abt. 5*) were still in training elsewhere and not yet available for commitment. The *Totenkopf* Division was in somewhat better shape, having 2,591 men and all six of its *Panzergrenadier* battalions, as well as its combat engineer and armored reconnaissance battalions, with an average strength of 370 men.

The *73. Inf.Div.* added 2,521 additional front-line troops (which included *Gren.Brig. 1131*), giving Gille a total of 6,709 combat troops to occupy his new 45-kilometer main defense line. This new *Hauptkampflinie*, or *HKL*, ran along a jagged arc stretching southwest to northeast from the town of Grzybowa, located 10 kilometers east of Praga, to the town of Sulejów, 11 kilometers northeast of the tactically important town of Tłuszcz.[12] A quick computation shows that this resulted in a troop density of approximately 150 men to defend each kilometer of front, far less than what the situation required.[13] Of course, some of these soldiers would have been held back by their commanders to serve as a local reserve, so the ultimate troops density was probably even less.

Besides the shortage of combat troops, another concern involving the *Wiking* Division was its lack of motor transport, which was chronic even before it was committed to battle in July. In order to make up the shortage of trucks needed to move the division's grenadier battalions, many were taken from its logistics units, which in turn left them short of the needed transport to haul food, fuel, and ammunition. As a substitute, an *NSKK* truck column from *Einsatzstab Speer* was loaned to the division, a highly unusual action, since the drivers and mechanics of this unit were more properly paramilitary personnel, not soldiers. This attachment would last for most of August and into September before they were finally replaced. But during the first battle of Warsaw, they would keep the *Wiking* Division provided with the supplies needed to fight a high-intensity battle.[14]

The situation concerning armor was more encouraging. The *Totenkopf*'s *SS-Pz. Rgt. 3* counted 27 *Pz. IV*, 30 *Pz. V* Panthers, four *Pz. VI* Tigers and 31 assault guns operational, with 53 of all types in various stages of repair. The *Wiking* was slightly weaker, with 16 *Pz. IV*, 21 *Pz. V* Panthers and 12 assault guns available, plus 54 in repair. Attached to the *73. Inf.Div.*, *SS-Pz.Jag.Abt. 5 "Wiking"* reported 18 *Pz.Jag. IV* still operational, with three in repair. All told, Gille could count on 159 AFVs as being battle-ready and an additional 110 in short- and long-term repair, an impressively high readiness rate at that period of the war.[15] His corps also fielded 56 operational antitank guns, and every one of them would soon be put to good use. But due to the dwindling strength of their infantry battalions, the *panzers* would have to step into the breach and bear an increasingly heavy share of the fighting, which in turn would see fewer vehicles available each day due to wear and tear while the number of tanks available to Soviet forces continued to grow.

With regard to artillery, Gille's corps was still lacking what it was authorized and *SS-Brig.Fhr.* Kurt Brassack, the commander of *SS-ARKO 104*, would have to do the best he could with the corps' available assets. While Gille's three divisions still boasted nearly full-strength artillery regiments, with a total of 149 guns of all calibers, none of his corps' authorized SS artillery or rocket artillery battalions had as yet materialized. The shortfall was partially made up by the attachment of several artillery units from the *Heer*, including an observation battery from *Einsatz-Bttr./Beob.Abt. 1*, a single heavy artillery battalion, *schw.Art.Abt. 152 (mot.)*, equipped with 15cm howitzers, and a *Nebelwerfer* battalion (the *IV.*) from *Stellungs-Werfer Regiment 102*, equipped with the 15cm *Werfer* model 41, which would serve until *SS-Werfer Abteilung 104* arrived in early September.[16]

Though there were several additional artillery units within *9. Armee*, they all had general support missions and were thinly spread throughout the army's sector, with most of them focused on the effort to eliminate the Magnuszew and Puławy bridgeheads. By comparison, the Soviet 47th and 70th Armies opposing Gille's corps had four times as many guns and could call on more from the First Belorussian Front's general reserve if necessary. Aside from the aforementioned construction battalion, *IV. SS-Pz.Korps* received no additional assets from the *Heer*, and the attached infantry that it did have, two replacement companies originally destined for *Major* Friedrich-Karl Ritter's *Inf.Btl. z.b.V. 560* (a *Bewährungs*, or criminal rehabilitation unit, that had been nearly wiped out a week earlier), were taken away from *73. Inf. Div.* on 13 August and reassigned to *Inf.Btl.z.b.V. 550* (another *Bewährungs* unit) of the *VIII. Armeekorps.*[17] After two weeks undergoing *Auffrischung* (reconstitution), Ritter's *Inf.Btl.z.b.V. 560* would once again be sent back to the front lines, having incorporated several hundred new *Bewährungstruppen* into its ranks. With *Wehrmacht* discipline beginning to fray around the edges, by the summer of 1944 there was no shortage of such men, who were deemed expendable by the high command until they had "redeemed" themselves.

Much more worrisome besides the lack of ground troops was the critical shortage of all types of ammunition, especially the kind needed by the artillery regiments' 10.5cm and 15cm batteries. Destruction of ammunition stockpiles in Bialystok, Siedlce, and Brest-Litovsk the previous month, plus increasingly effective attacks against highway and rail traffic chokepoints by the Red Air Force and the heavy fighting that had occurred during the past four weeks, had all combined to leave units in the field with an insufficient amount of high-explosive shells to break up Soviet attacks and conduct counter-battery fire. The need to reroute traffic around Warsaw due to the uprising also complicated transport and delivery. The situation had grown so bad that on 10 August, the *9. Armee* commander was forced to issue an order declaring under which circumstances artillery could be utilized in order to conserve ammunition. In its preface he stated, "The situation concerning the supply of ammunition has now become one in which commanders must determine whether or not its expenditure is necessary to solve certain tactical situations."[18]

Among the restrictions the order listed, the use of shelling during quiet periods on the front lines was absolutely forbidden. Unit commanders were to avoid using their stockpiles to solve purely local problems, but could do so on their own authority if dire circumstances required it. Divisions were to build up a reserve of ammunition that could only be used in tactical emergencies with the division or corps commander's permission. The net effect of this order was that at the company or battalion level, commanders had to request permission to fire from division or corps headquarters. It most likely did not have a positive effect on the troops' morale either, because the infantry had come to depend on their own support weapons—including artillery, infantry howitzers, rocket launchers, and mortars—to break up the increasingly assertive and numerous Soviet ground assaults. This, of course, would also make it harder to defend their positions or launch successful counterattacks.

A good example of how this order impacted the ability of the front-line troops to hold their position was the situation graphically described by 21-year-old *Ostuf.* Fritz Hahl, who was serving as the commander of *6. Kompanie, II. Btl./SS-Pz.Gren.Rgt. 10 Westland*, which had occupied a portion of the front line southeast of Tłuszcz:

> Between 20 July and 13 August 1944, my company had shrunken from 143 to 30 men after 24 days of unbroken combat. We were holding an improvised front line defensive position. Before me, about 400 meters away, I could see about 30 Soviet T-34s occupying an assembly area in a swale, preparing to attack. The forward observer from the artillery battery located behind our positions was with me, and I asked him to call for supporting fire. The battery fired three rounds at the target to get its range and then I asked for the battery to fire everything they had. Then the battery commander responded through the forward observer that he had no more ammunition to spare. As a result, the tanks attacked and chased us out of our position, since we had no antitank weapons of our own. During this disaster I was wounded for the sixth time.[19]

Hahl's complaint was neither unusual nor isolated. But by mid-August 1944, German industry and the railroad network's ability to provide the troops with the tools they needed to fight the war was becoming increasingly strained by the Western Allies' incessant bombing campaign against the Third Reich's centers of production and the mind-boggling losses in nearly every category of weapon incurred during the long, disastrous summer of 1944.

Another directive that was issued by *Gen.d.Pz.Tr.* von Vormann's headquarters two days later was the one that directed Gille to immediately establish a *Korps-Sturm-Bataillon* (corps assault battalion) and a *Div.Sturm-Abt.* (division assault battalion) in each of his three divisions. Using their own assets, primarily their organic *Kampfschule* (combat school), as a basis, each division was directed to create a reserve force of at least two companies under a skeleton battalion staff, with an attached *Pionier Kompanie* supported by an assault gun battery. At his level, Gille was to form a corps reserve consisting of a grenadier battalion, a combat engineer company, and an entire assault gun battalion. Should assault gun formations not be available, divisions and the corps were instructed to form some sort of mobile antitank force using towed antitank guns. When not in combat, the order stated, the *Kampfschulen* were to conduct normal periods of instruction.[20]

The order began with the exhortation, "An imperative prerequisite for the successful conduct of the defense is a mobile assault force kept in reserve for the commander's use." This restating of one of the most obvious tenants of leadership might have insulted Gille's intelligence or at least chafed his sensibilities. Having fought for three years on the Eastern Front by this point, he and his division commanders certainly would have already worked out this tactical prescription for success themselves.

Needless to say, Gille's corps had no *Sturmgeschütz-Bataillon* to call its own, nor did any of his divisions. The *Wiking* Division had a single *Sturmgeschütz Kompanie* (the *4. Kp.*) that was part of its *panzer* regiment, while the *Totenkopf* Division still had its (though no longer authorized) *Sturmgeschütz-Abteilung*. The *73. Inf.Div.* still had 21 of the powerful *Jagdpanzer Pz.IV/70* from the *Wiking* Division attached, so at least each division had the foundation to build such a reserve force. What was lacking was the SS divisions' *Kampfschulen*, which were normally part of their *Feld-Ersatz* (field replacement) battalions. Both of these battalions were located far to the rear and had no replacement troops anyway to form such a reserve force, for they had already sent everything they had to the fighting front and were waiting for more replacements to flesh out their companies.

There is no evidence in the record to indicate whether *Gruf.* Gille complied with this order at the time it was issued; he and his commanders would have already formed such a reserve as a matter of routine anyway, whether they had a *Kampfschule* or not. Normally, a division commander would have formed his reserve using a single infantry battalion, but the standard practice for SS *panzer* divisions was to form a reserve assault force from its organic *Pz. V* Panther battalion and SPW-mounted *Panzergrenadier* battalion; division commanders would not need to be told to do this. Should this force be committed, the reserve of last resort would either be the division's combat engineer battalion or its *Divisions-Begleit Kompanie*. The corps had its own escort company too, of course, but the normal practice was to withhold a regiment or battalion from one of its divisions to serve this function. It remains unknown which force Gille retained as his corps reserve during this stressful period, since the available records are incomplete.[21]

With regard to the *Feld-Ersatz* battalions of both the *Totenkopf* and *Wiking* Divisions with their organic division combat schools, neither could serve at that moment in the manner which *Gen.d.Pz.Tr.* von Vormann intended. They were located at the SS training areas in Freystadt (in West Prussia) and Frankfurt an der Oder respectively, nearly two days' train ride from Warsaw. While both would eventually be moved forward to the Modlin area (*SS-Feld-Ers.Btl. 5* on 8 September and *SS-Feld-Ers.Btl. 3* by the end of October), neither played a role during the first battle of Warsaw. Gille apparently solved the problem to his army commander's satisfaction using the troops that he had to hand, since there is no further mention of the issue in the existing records. Another possible reason for the issue of the order is that some event may have occurred during the course of *Brückenschlag* where neither *IV. SS-Pz.Korps* nor its two SS divisions had a viable reserve to respond to a critical situation that arose during the operation; though had it happened, this would have been noted in the *9. Armee* daily situation report to *H.Gr. Mitte*, an event that its chief of staff, no admirer of the *Waffen-SS*, would have highlighted.

In addition to operational and organizational changes that took place from 5–12 August, a number of changes in key personnel positions occurred as well. On 8 August, *Staf.* Mühlenkamp was formally appointed *Divisions-Führer* (Acting Division Commander) of the *Wiking* Division during a small ceremony presided over by Gille at the former's command post. He had already been acting in that capacity for four days, having been notified on 4 August by the SS personnel office in Berlin that Gille's request to have Mühlenkamp fill that position, and not *Staf.* Dr. Eduard Deisenhofer, had been approved. This development had no impact on the division, since it had been known that Mühlenkamp was destined to lead the division anyway, though to his credit he had performed well as its commander throughout the heavy fighting during the battle of Praga and *Unternehmen Brückenschlag*. While his tenure as acting commander would be brief, during those nearly three months he would lead the *Wiking* Division through the first two battles of Warsaw and most of the third before he was recalled to Germany and replaced by *Staf.* Ullrich from the *Totenkopf* Division.

Standartenführer Mühlenkamp's elevation to *Divisions-Führer* consequently led to another leadership vacancy—that of his old regiment, *SS-Pz.Rgt. 5*. Though *Ostubaf.* Fritz Darges had been acting as temporary regimental commander since 5 August after Mühlenkamp was provisionally tasked with leading the division, Darges was unofficially appointed *Regiments-Führer* on 8 August, followed by official confirmation as the regiment's *Kommandeur* on 15 August. This, in turn, led to yet another necessary change in command, as Darges's promotion required that someone be chosen to serve as acting commander of his former battalion, *II. Abt./SS-Pz. Rgt. 5*. To fill Darges's position, *Hstuf.* Hans Flügel, who had previously served as Mühlenkamp's *Adjutant*, was appointed as his successor. Both Darges and Flügel were experienced veterans, and the new command arrangements would prove to have little impact on the tank regiment's performance, which remained high despite the heavy requirements being placed upon it.

Of more importance was the expected departure of Gille's chief of staff, *Oberführer* Heilmann, on 12 August, who was reassigned to the *SS-FHA* in Berlin before being appointed commander of the *28. SS-Waffen-Gren.Div.* in January 1945. *Obf.* Heilmann, who was originally scheduled to depart on 5 August, was kept on at Gille's insistence until *Brückenschlag* had been successfully concluded. He was immediately replaced by *Ostubaf.* Schönfelder, *Ia* of the *Wiking* Division, on the day he departed. Schönfelder himself was replaced as the *Wiking* Division's *Ia* on 5 August by *Stubaf.* Pauly, who had been serving as the corps' *Ia* as part of his *Kriegsakademie* preparatory training. He would remain as the *Ia* of the *Wiking* Division until 22 August, when he was sent to Germany to attend the 15th *Generalstabsoffizier* course, to be replaced by *Major i.G.* Otto Kleine, a general staff officer seconded from the *Heer*. Pauly's position as acting corps *Ia* was taken over by *Hstuf.* Westphal, also a *Generalstabsoffizier* candidate who had been acting as Gille's *O1* since 28 July. In turn, Westphal's *O1* billet at the corps headquarters was assumed by *Hstuf.* Heinrich Fockenbreck, another staff officer candidate.

Obersturmbannführer Schönfelder, who had acted as the chief of the extemporaneous corps staff for several days before Heilmann and the *Rumpfstab* finally linked up with Gille, was more than capable of filling the position, and, unlike Heilmann, he was a graduate of the general staff course taught at the *Kriegsakademie*. He was also not as irascible as Heilmann reportedly was and got along well with his superiors and subordinates, diplomacy being an important trait in a chief of staff. Schönfelder, who had essentially served as Gille's right-hand man for the past two years, had the advantage of automatically having his commander's full trust and confidence. They would continue their successful relationship for the next 10 months and after the war as well, ending only with Gille's death in 1966.

Regarding the *Totenkopf* Division, no major personnel changes at the regimental level and above took place. The temporary attachments of the battalion from *5. Jäg. Div.* and later the entire *Gren.Brig. 1131* during the first battle of Warsaw was the only change to its order of battle reflected in the historical record. The division, like its sister division the *Wiking*, had been experiencing a steady drain of its rank and file since being committed to battle in the Siedlce area during July. The necessity of having to defend such a wide frontage with so few troops meant that the Soviets could achieve overwhelming mass at any point they chose, a fact that could not be overcome by the sheer heroism of the *Totenkopf*'s and *Wiking*'s troops alone. Particularly hard felt was the loss of experienced NCOs and junior officers, who were difficult to replace but whose presence and infusion of "SS spirit" was responsible for achieving near-miraculous success on the battlefield against overwhelming odds.

All too often, their bravery and dedication to their troops led to their deaths or serious wounding, leaving a gap in the ranks that could not immediately be filled. One example of such a loss was the death of the commander of the *Totenkopf* Division's reconnaissance battalion, *SS-Aufkl.Abt. 3*, *Stubaf.* Arzelino "Lino" Masarié, who died on 9 August at the field hospital in Radzymin of wounds he received the previous day during the beginning of *Unternehmen Brückenschlag*. An awardee of the Knight's Cross and German Cross in Gold, Masarié was a popular and highly respected officer who had led his battalion with both skill and élan. A battle-hardened veteran and member of the SS since 1933, he would be difficult to replace.

As previously mentioned, during this period the *IV. SS-Pz.Korps* had its first division of the *Heer* placed under its command, the *73. Inf.Div.* In theory, it was a significant augmentation to the corps' infantry strength, though at times it would seem to be more of a handicap than a benefit. Nevertheless, its fate would be tied to that of Gille's corps for the next four months. Its history began as a first-class, front-line division that initially performed well. Formed on 26 August 1939 as part of the second mobilization *Welle* (wave), it consisted of three infantry regiments of three battalions each, a four-battalion artillery regiment, and other supporting arms. The 17,000-man strong division took part in the invasions of Poland, the Low Countries, France, and Greece before invading the Soviet Union from its jump-off point at Iaşi (Jassy), Romania, on 22 June 1941.

It fought in the southern sector of the Eastern Front from 1941–43, taking part in actions at Nikolaev, Cherson, Sevastopol, and the Kuban bridgehead among others. It was withdrawn from the fighting near Melitopol in mid-1943 after suffering heavy losses. Moved to the Crimea in early 1943, the few remaining fighting elements of the division surrendered to the Red Army in Sevastopol in May 1944, though approximately 3,500 men, primarily staff and combat support units (known collectively as the *Divisions-Rahmen*, or framework), were evacuated by the *Kriegsmarine* (German Navy) to Odessa before the surrender of the remaining German forces in the Crimea.

The division was hastily re-formed beginning on 16 June 1944 in Serbia, using *Urlauber* battalions (levies formed from men returning from leave) from other units stationed in the Balkans, and was then transferred to eastern Hungary shortly thereafter as a theater reserve. Only partially re-equipped and with little time to build unit cohesion and confidence, it was assigned in late July to *H.Gr. Mitte*'s *9. Armee*, where it was positioned astride the southeast approaches to Warsaw from 26–30 July. Here, while defending along the line Wilga–Garwolin–Latowicz, it suffered heavy casualties and barely escaped encirclement on 29 July by the XVI Tank Corps of the Soviet 2nd Tank Army, a near-disaster that also resulted in the capture of its commander, *Gen.Lt.* Fritz von Franek. Only the timely arrival of

Fs.Pz.Div. Hermann Göring and *19. Pz.Div.*, which carried out a series of successful counterattacks, prevented the Soviets from taking Praga and the Vistula bridges connecting Praga to Warsaw.

From 30 July–10 September, the division was placed temporarily under the command of *Oberst* Kurt Hähling, who led it while the division was hurriedly rebuilt a second time during the first week of August in the rear area of the *9. Armee*. A large number of the 743 replacements it received on 1 August came from various disciplinary and rehabilitation units, a sign that did not auger well for the division's future. By 4 August, it was placed back in the line, where it occupied a relatively quiet sector of the Vistula Front and continued the rebuilding process. During this period, for the first time it was placed under the command of *IV. SS-Pz.Korps* east of Warsaw, tasked with defending the southern approaches to the Praga bridgehead.

Though it reported 2,521 combat troops fit for duty in its six infantry battalions and combat engineer battalion on 13 August, its uneven performance was to prove to be a significant source of concern to Gille and *9. Armee*, as will be seen. In addition to providing much-needed manpower, the division also fielded 15 of the excellent 7.5cm *Panzerabwehrkanone* (*PaK*) 40 antitank guns, as well as the 21 self-propelled tank destroyers on loan from the *Wiking* Division. Seemingly as an afterthought, a platoon from *Panzer-Zerstörer* (tank destroyer) *Bataillon 475*, equipped with 20 launch tubes of then-new 8.8cm *Panzerschreck* crew-served bazookas, was attached to the division as well, though their unprotected crews, mere foot soldiers, were no substitute for armored vehicles. Still, if used properly, these highly effective close-range weapons could help the *73. Inf.Div.* redress its deficiencies, especially when faced by Soviet tank forces.

But the most momentous personnel change did not involve anyone assigned to the *IV. SS-Pz.Korps*, or even *9. Armee* for that matter. Due to the deteriorating situation on the Normandy Front, which had just witnessed the collapse of *H.Gr. B* in the wake of the Falaise Pocket disaster, Hitler had lost faith in the commander of *Oberbefehlshaber* (*OB*) *West*, *G.F.M.* Günther Kluge, whom he not only suspected of lacking the courage and ruthlessness the situation dictated, but believed that he might also have been involved in the July 20 assassination plot. As a result, Hitler sacked Kluge on 17 August (he committed suicide or was executed two days later) and sent the only man at that time who still had the *Führer*'s full trust and confidence—Walter Model.

Under his steady hand, *H.Gr. Mitte* had been led back from the brink of collapse, its front made whole, and had dealt a sharp setback to the plans of STAVKA (the Supreme High Command of the Soviet Union) by his successful counterattack against the 2nd Tank Army during the battle of Praga. Not only would his operational and tactical acumen be sorely missed, but so would his courage and readiness to confront and even overrule Hitler's commands. His replacement was the capable *Generaloberst* Georg-Hans Reinhardt, who had previously commanded the

3. Pz.Armee. While Reinhardt would prove to be a good army group commander considering the limitations he was operating under, when issued nonsensical orders emanating from Berlin, he rarely challenged them, unlike Model, who was known to fly to Berlin to argue his case. But Model was the exception, not the rule. Still, Reinhardt's calm demeanor and thoughtful deliberation would stand *H.Gr. Mitte* in good stead during the months to come.

Gruppenführer Gille took advantage of the relative calm that then pertained (at the corps headquarters, at least) to issue his first official proclamation to his new corps on 12 August. In his special corps order of the day, he stated:

> The Führer has charged me with the command of the *SS-Panzerkorps* effective 20 July 1944.[22] With pride, full faith and belief in the power and victory of our arms I have taken over this position of great responsibility. Only with difficulty do I leave my old, faithful *Wiking* Division. Deserving of my special thanks are all officers, non-commissioned officers and men who in untiring fulfilment of duty and readiness for action, in the heaviest fighting and in the most difficult situations, have always stood brave and true to our flag and done their duty. The order of the *Reichsführer-SS* fills me with particular joy since it states that *5. SS-Pz.Div. Wiking* will remain as the cadre division of *IV. SS-Pz.Korps* and thus we will remain together in the future."

The order then officially named *Staf.* Mühlenkamp as the acting commander of the *Wiking* Division, with Gille asking that the division show the same degree of loyalty and devotion to duty to him as they had their old commander. He also reserved a few words for the *Totenkopf* Division, which had fought alongside the *Wiking* Division during July and August of the previous year along the Donets front. Waxing eloquent, Gille went on to say:

> In addition, [the corps] has been allocated *3. SS-Pz.Div. Totenkopf.* I salute … the men of this division and I am particularly pleased that this veteran, battle-tested, experienced Eastern Front Division has been united with the *Wiking* Division in an *SS-Panzerkorps*. I am certain that *3. SS-Pz.Div. Totenkopf* under its new commander, *SS-Oberführer* Becker will strike with the same courage and reliability as it always has in the past … The *IV. SS-Pz.Korps* … must become in a short time a symbol of terror for the enemy. We wish not only to be iron hard and fanatical in defense, but also a sharp weapon in attack which stands ready to strike hard and quickly at any time. I expect, therefore, of every SS-man in the coming decisive times full and relentless action so as to earn the Führer's praise. Long live the Führer![23]

Less than a week later, the 40,000 men of *IV. SS-Pz.Korps* would be given an opportunity live up to the high expectations that their commander had just placed upon them, when they would fight the corps' first set-piece battle against overwhelming odds.

CHAPTER 7

The First Defensive Battle of Warsaw 18–30 August 1944

While *IV. SS-Pz.Korps* and the neighboring *2. Armee* settled into their new positions and consolidated their defenses following completion of Operation *Brückenschlag*, Marshal Rokossovsky's First Belorussian Front had not been idle either. In addition to closely shadowing the withdrawing German troops all along the front, Soviet forces had also been preparing to resume their general offensive aimed at the Bug, Narew, and Vistula River crossings (labeled the "neuralgic point on the Eastern Front" by a prominent German historian) and separating *2.* and *9. Armee* from one another.[1]

While his 2nd Tank Army had been decisively defeated and one of its corps destroyed, the Front commander saw this as only a temporary setback, the result of a single losing gamble in a long game he was winning.[2] After all, tanks and guns could be replaced, though it was becoming evident that the Soviet Union's once-inexhaustible pool of manpower was reaching the end of its potential. To make up for the shortfall in infantry, Lt.Gen. Zygmunt Berling's 57,000-man 1st Polish Army with four infantry divisions, an entirely Soviet construction not affiliated with the Polish government-in-exile, was shifted north to the Warsaw–Praga area to fight alongside General Gusev's 47th Army around Praga. This infusion of fresh troops, coupled with the reintroduction of the 70th Army to the battle, would give the next phase of Rokossovsky's plan a substantial boost in combat power.

Rokossovsky clearly intended to continue his offensive where the previous attempt launched by Lt.Gen. Radzievsky's tank army had failed. In addition to the arrival of the 1st Polish Army, First Belorussian Front had during the past week been able to stockpile additional supplies, bring up more artillery, and construct more roads and artillery firing positions. Temporary airfields would be scraped out of the ground closer to the front lines, which would allow the Red Air Force to operate more effectively and responsively than it had during the past month. The goal, though, remained the same: in the center, using the 1st Polish and 47th and 70th Armies, punch through the Narew–Bug–Vistula triangle, delineated by the cities of Modlin, Zegrze, and Serock, cross those rivers with overwhelming force, split *H.Gr. Mitte* in two, and establish well-defended bridgeheads that would set the necessary conditions for the next phase of the war—either the drive on Berlin or a drive to the Baltic via East Prussia.

Simultaneously, Rokossovsky's forces on his left wing would continue to defend and if possible expand the Magnuszew and Puławy bridgeheads with the 8th Guards and 69th Armies and do what they could to support the Warsaw Uprising, now in its second week. The right or northern wing of his Front, consisting of the 28th, 65th, and 48th Armies, would continue their frontal attacks against *Gen.Oberst* Weiss' *2. Armee* to push it west across the Bug and then the Narew Rivers if Rokossovsky's troops in the center could not eliminate the Germans entirely. In addition to the 15 infantry divisions that would be available for the offensive aimed at *IV. SS-Pz.Korps* arrayed in the 1st Polish, 47th, and 70th Armies, the First Belorussian Front would also commit seven independent artillery regiments and one artillery penetration division to the attack. Enough tanks had been repaired or brought up to re-equip the VIII Guards Tank Corps from the 2nd Tank Army's departing III Tank Corps, which would provide a respectable amount of armor (approximately 165 tanks and assault guns) to support the attack.[3] This was enough to give the Soviet forces an overall superiority of seven-to-one in infantry, two-to-one in armor, and four-to-one in artillery, which against any ordinary army would have signified an overwhelming advantage.[4]

In turn, *H.Gr. Mitte*'s mission was just the opposite: *Generaloberst* Reinhardt would simultaneously have to defend on his left flank (*2. Armee* and *IV. SS-Pz.Korps*), crush the Warsaw Uprising in the center (the SS, Police, and Army forces marshalled under *Gruppe von dem Bach*), and eliminate the Soviet bridgeheads across the Vistula on his right wing with *VIII. Armeekorps*. To carry out this high-stakes mission, Reinhardt had insufficient forces to hold his existing frontage, much less carry out any large-scale counterattacks, but over the next three months during the first, second, and third defensive battles of Warsaw (see Map 5) his troops would do just that. To the German soldier in the front line, the so-called *Frontschwein* ("front line pig," the German equivalent of the American G.I.'s "dogface"), the only notable difference between fighting delaying actions against pursuing Soviet forces and defending against a general offensive was the amount of artillery fired at him; in any case, the troops of *H.Gr. Mitte* would have little rest for the next several weeks.

The exact date when the first defensive battle of Warsaw began is still open to conjecture. Some Soviet historians claim 20 August as the date their new offensive started, when Berling's 1st Polish Army was moved into position to the south of Praga, while others suggest that it began on 10 August and ended five days later. However, the historical evidence shows that this "offensive" merely consisted of the 47th and 70th Armies' aggressive shadowing of German forces as they withdrew to their new front-line positions, as previously described, during the course of *Unternehmen Brückenschlag*. Though much ground was gained by the Red Army, Reinhardt had counted on giving it up anyway as part of the consolidation and shortening of the *2.* and *9. Armee* front lines. While the front was still considered too long to build

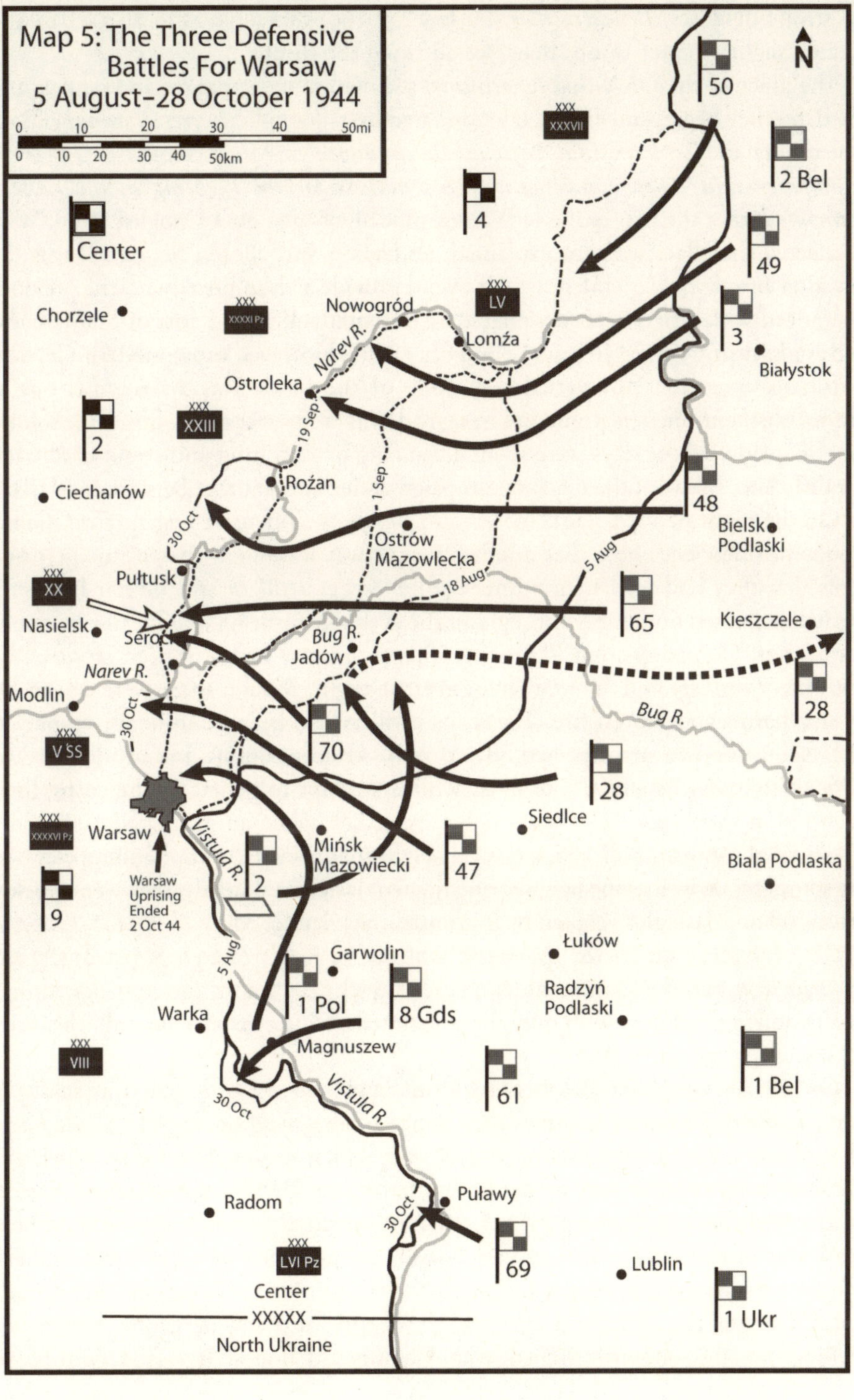
Map 5: The Three Defensive Battles For Warsaw 5 August–28 October 1944
0 10 20 30 40 50mi
0 10 20 30 40 50km
N
50
XXXVII
2 Bel
4
49
Center
LV
3
Chorzele
XXXXI Pz
Nowogród
Lomża
Białystok
Narev R.
Ostroleka
19 Sep
2
XXIII
Rożan
1 Sep
48
Ciechanów
30 Oct
Ostrów Mazowlecka
Bielsk Podlaski
5 Aug
XX
Pułtusk
18 Aug
65
Nasielsk
Serock
Kieszczele
Bug R.
Jadów
Narev R.
Modlin
28
Bug R.
30 Oct
70
V SS
28
Siedlce
XXXXVI Pz
Warsaw
Vistula R.
Mińsk Mazowiecki
47
Biala Podlaska
2
9
Warsaw Uprising Ended 2 Oct 44
5 Aug
Garwolin
Łuków
1 Pol
8 Gds
Radzyń Podlaski
Warka
Magnuszew
VIII
61
1 Bel
30 Oct
Vistula R.
Puławy
Radom
30 Oct
69
LVI Pz
Lublin
Center
XXXXX
North Ukraine
1 Ukr

up strong defenses, *Brückenschlag* did free up troops to serve as local reserves and created slightly better troops densities all along the front.

The office of the *OKH* that determined the names of campaigns and battles, and the dates they began and ended, later declared in its periodic *Heeresverordnungs Blatt* concerning the *Schlacht und Gefechtsbezeichnungen für die Kämpfe im Ostfeldzug* (*Campaign and Battle Participation Designations for the Fighting in the Eastern Campaign*) that the first battle of Warsaw officially began on 13 August 1944. Why it selected that date was not explained. Perhaps it was chosen because it was the day after *Brückenschlag* ended, which would provide a clean break with the previous operation, which had been designated "Counterattack in the area of Stanisławów and Radzymin from 28 July to 12 August 1944." However, most modern German historians agree that the actual beginning of the battle was 18 August, but as previously mentioned, it would not have made any difference to the front-line soldier on either side, whose days were spent advancing or retreating and could hardly tell the difference between the day one campaign ended and another began (see Map 6).

On the night of 17 August, mere hours before the offensive began, *Gruf.* Gille's troops instinctively knew that another assault was imminent, based on the usual signs that they had seen many times before. Soviet artillery and mortar harassing fire had increased noticeably throughout the evening, ensuring that his troops would get no rest. Company-sized Red Army infantry patrols had also been reported by both the *Totenkopf* and *Wiking* Divisions that night, though these were driven off by small-arms and mortar fire. The corps' artillery had been occasionally employed to break up known or suspected Soviet troops concentrations, but at night it was difficult to assess its effect. The most serious attempt to penetrate the corps' lines occurred in the *Wiking* Division's defensive sector, when an estimated 100 Soviet troops tried to storm Hill 105, a critical height that provided commanding views to the southeast, as well as the neighboring town of Jasienica. Luckily, they were quickly driven off and Jasienica retaken by a counterattack launched by *II. Btl./SS-Pz.Gren. Rgt. 9 Germania*, supported by several tanks of *7. Kp/SS-Pz.Rgt. 5*, personally led by their new battalion commander, *Hstuf.* Flügel.[5] By 5 a.m. the next day, things finally quietened down, with only the occasional shelling being reported. This brief calm was not to last.

On 18 August, First Belorussian Front launched its anticipated attack at 9 a.m., focused primarily on the inner flanks of the neighboring *IV. SS-Pz.Korps* of *9. Armee* and *XX. Armeekorps* of *2. Armee*, which meant that the two German divisions holding that part of the line of battle, the *HKL*—the *Wiking* Division on the *9. Armee* left flank and the *5. Jäg.Div.* on the *2. Armee* right—would bear the brunt of the attack. The ground assault was preceded by a powerful artillery and rocket barrage that reached *Trommelfeuer* (drumfire) proportions that ranged up and down the lines and even struck deeply into the divisions' rear areas, seeking out and targeting logistical and command nodes. It was, according to

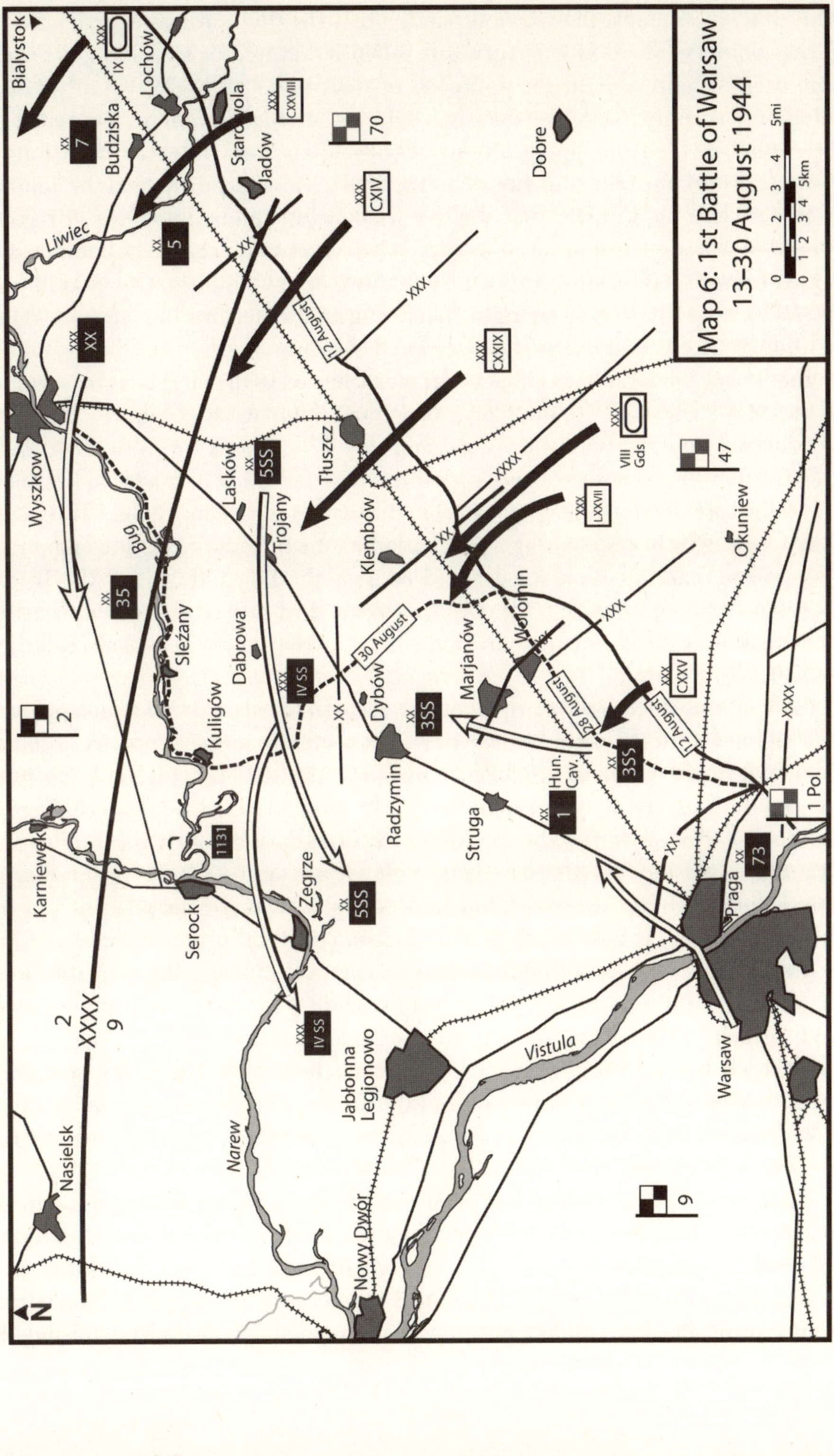
Map 6: 1st Battle of Warsaw
13–30 August 1944
0 1 2 3 4 5mi
0 1 2 3 4 5km
Bialystok
Lochów
Budziska
Stardavola
Jadów
Dobre
Liwiec
Wyszkow
Bug
Lasków
Tłuszcz
Trojany
Klembów
Okuniew
Wołomin
Marjanów
Slężany
Dabrowa
Dybów
Kuligów
Radzymin
Struga
Karniewek
Serock
Zegrze
Praga
Warsaw
Vistula
Jabłonna Legjonowo
Narew
Nasielsk
Nowy Dwór
12 August
30 August
28 August
12 August
IX
CXXVIII
CXIV
CXXIX
VIII Gds
LXXVII
CXXV
70
47
2
9
1 Pol
7
5
XX
5SS
35
IV SS
3SS
Hun. Cav.
1
1131
73
XXXX
2
9
N

some *Wiking* veterans, the heaviest barrage that the division had experienced up to that point, while *Totenkopf* survivors called it "unprecedented."[6] Smoke shells were fired to help conceal the approach of troops and tanks. Waves of infantry battalions, accompanied by tanks in company strength (eight to 10 vehicles), then assaulted the front-line positions of both *Wiking* and *Totenkopf* Divisions at multiple points after the four-hour barrage lifted. Most surprising was the amount of Soviet close air support that was reported, with hundreds of Red Air Force ground-attack aircraft employed in successive waves that accurately bombed and strafed front-line positions. This was something new. Curiously, *Oberst* Hähling's *73. Inf.Div.* on the corps' far right flank, dug in a defensive line around Praga, was not attacked at all except for occasional shelling.

The *Wiking* Division found itself under attack by no less than five infantry divisions of the XCVI and CXIV Rifle Corps of Popov's 70th Army, while the *Totenkopf* Division was attacked by five divisions from the 47th Army's LXXVII and CXXIX Rifle Corps in the first wave alone, with three more following in the second echelon. The *Totenkopf* Division also lay squarely in the path of the reconstituted VIII Guards Tank Corps, which was awaiting a penetration by the infantry before it could punch through and make a beeline for the bridges along the Bug and Narew. The *Wiking* Division's neighbor on its left, the *XX. Armeekorps'* hard-pressed *5. Jäg.Div.*, faced no fewer than four Soviet infantry divisions of the 28th Army's III Guards Rifle and CXXVIII Rifle Corps.

Each of the three Soviet armies listed also deployed their own independent tank regiments for the offensive, which would primarily support infantry assaults.[7] Unknown to the German intelligence network, the VIII Guards Tank Corps of the 2nd Tank Army, with approximately 143 serviceable tanks as of 18 August, had been shifted to the sector straddling the boundary between the *Wiking* and *Totenkopf* Divisions on the left flank of *9. Armee*, and had not redeployed to Kowel along with the rest of the 2nd Tank Army as the Germans believed.[8] As the attack developed, it became clear that the primary focal point of Rokossovsky's attack was this inter-army boundary, with the main blow falling on the inner flanks of the *Wiking* and *5. Jäger* Divisions. Here was where the commander of the First Belorussian Front sought the tactical penetration to gain his long-desired operational breakthrough. At that moment, the 1st Polish Army remained uncommitted along the Vistula south of the *73. Inf.Div.* behind the Soviet 176th Rifle Division from the LXXVII Rifle Corps, where they were awaiting the call to move forward when the conditions allowed.

Though the German defenders were not surprised by the attack, the ferocity and the intensity of the artillery preparation that blasted their field fortifications, destroyed minefields, and buried men in their foxholes and bunkers delayed their initial response. Strafing runs by Ilyushin IL-2 *Sturmovik* ground-attack aircraft on German front-line and artillery positions kept the men's heads down, while bombs ripped up communications wires and cratered movement routes behind the front lines. The lack of most of the the *Wiking* Division's organic antiaircraft battalion, *SS-Flak-Abt. 5*, with two of its three batteries posted in Warsaw to defend the Vistula bridges, was sorely felt, as only medium (3.7cm) and light (2cm) *Flak* from the remaining battery were available to engage the armored *Sturmoviks*, the Red Air Force's legendary "flying tank."

Covered by such effective preparatory fire, the Soviet troops and tanks surged forward, following routes through the woods and swales that they had reconnoitered during the past week. The SS troops and *Jäger*, quickly recovering from their initial shock, rushed from their shelters and manned their machine guns and fighting positions. They soon began to exact a fearsome toll on the onrushing attackers, but in many cases, the thinly spread German front-line troops were quickly overwhelmed. The *Totenkopf* Division, sandwiched as it were between the *Wiking* Division and the *73. Inf.Div.*, held the corps' widest divisional frontage, stretching over 30 kilometers from Zielona to Klembów. While *Obf.* Becker's troops were feeling pressure all along the line, the main Soviet effort was being directed against the division's left flank at Grabie Stare, where it linked up with the *Germania* Regiment on the *Wiking* Division's right flank. Some of the Soviet troops that tried to break through there were cut off by a *Totenkopf* counterattack and eliminated, while the rest were gradually forced back. In the division's account, the fighting seesawed back and forth all afternoon, but by nightfall it had been able to re-establish a continuous front line. Though it had been forced to yield some ground, the *Totenkopf* Division had managed to avoid any major Soviet penetrations.[9]

Fortunately for the *Totenkopf* Division, it still possessed a powerful armored reserve in its *panzer* regiment, which at that moment included four operational *Pz. VI* Tigers. The regiment's tanks were distributed piecemeal, company by company, close behind the infantry battalions, which could count on the support of a company's or platoon's worth of tanks or assault guns. Still, the fighting was particularly harrowing. Some indication of what the average soldier experienced was captured in a letter home by *SS-Oscha.* Steiger of *1. Kp./SS-Pz.Rgt. 3.* He wrote shortly after the battle that:

> [T]he enemy artillery drums unceasingly. Attack after attack of the Russians roll against our already weakened defense line. The overwhelming power of the enemy is inconceivable. The gaps in the front line grow larger and larger, often resulting in one Grenadier defending every 100–200 meters of ground. We are once again the fire department [of the division] and rush from one attack to another, from restoring the front at one place then onwards to another, then withdraw a few kilometers, then strike back in a counterattack in order to relieve the pressure on neighboring units. We are holding with only a few panzers against the storming masses of the Russians. Enemy tanks, appearing as numerous as flies, break through here and there and destroy baggage trains while some drive even further into our rear area. We are then thrown once again into pursuit, shoot them up and in the process lose one or two of our own tanks. When we return to the front line, we realize to our surprise that our old positions are now completely occupied by the Russians. And so it goes on, without interruption. The loss of [our] men and tanks is great.[10]

Still, the *Totenkopf* Division achieved a noteworthy defensive success that day and managed to maintain the integrity of its front line, at least on the first day of the Soviet offensive. The division commander's biggest worry that day was that if the attack continued at its current pace, he might lose contact entirely on his left flank with the *Wiking* Division.

As tense as the situation was on the *Totenkopf* Division's left flank, in the neighboring *Wiking* Division's sector things were much, much worse. Here, *Staf.* Mühlenkamp's troops were attacked along its entire 15-kilometer-wide front by four rifle divisions (76th Guards and the 260th, 165th, and 160th Rifle Divisions), which sought to break through and pivot in a northerly direction towards Klembów on the division's right and Tłuszcz on the left. Not only did they seek to drive the *Wiking* and neighboring *5. Jäg.Div.* apart, thus separating *IV. SS-Pz.Korps* from *XX. Armeekorps,* but also intended to split the *Wiking* apart from the *Totenkopf* Division. In effect, this would mean the encirclement of the *Wiking* Division should the Soviet attack succeed. For the troops of Mühlenkamp's division, the fighting here would be extraordinarily bitter and costly.

While the experiences of German troops fighting on the Normandy Front has been more than adequately captured during the past 75 years, little has been written with regards to what their brethren saw and felt on the Eastern Front during the late summer of 1944. While troops on both fronts experienced bombing, shelling, and air attacks as a matter of course, nothing could compare to the sheer overwhelming amount of artillery fire, massed tanks, and infantry attacks directed against the soldiers of *H.Gr. Mitte* in late August 1944. The open countryside east of Warsaw, unlike Normandy's enclosed fields, hedgerows, and sunken lanes, presented few natural obstacles to the attacker, while the defending troops of *9.* and *2. Armee* had little time to prepare fixed defenses and were short of everything they needed to construct antitank ditches, minefields, and barriers to Soviet movement.

Isolation was another factor. With so few troops to hold so broad a front, the hard-pressed infantry commanders of the *Wiking* and *Totenkopf* Divisions found themselves having to widely space their troops to cover the ground to their front. A single rifle squad of six to 10 men would have to defend over 100 meters of undulating, partially wooded terrain, which meant sections of three to four men, would have to hold 50 meters to their right and left, both day and night. Often they would be unable to see the foxholes of their closest neighbors. If they were lucky, they had time to dig connecting trenches; if not, they would feel even more isolated. If they were even luckier, the commander would have been able to form a squad-sized reserve to respond to any emergencies if he had enough men. But since rifle companies had shrunk from their full strength of 180 men to only 50 or 60 combat troops, this practice was becoming a luxury.

Should they be fortunate enough to have survived the initial artillery barrage, the *Landser* would immediately have to be on their feet awaiting the certain approach of the advancing enemy infantry as soon as the fire lifted. They would listen for the sound of tank engines and the squeal of tracks, which at least would let them know from which direction to expect the attack. If they had good visibility, they could shoot at the enemy with rifles, machine pistols, and machine guns when they were still 200–300 meters away and engage them with mortar or artillery fire if it was available. If not, they would have to wait until they could see the brown-clad *Iwan* (German slang for Soviet soldiers) emerge from the woods or smoke screen with their naked eyes, which would be the signal to begin firing with every weapon they had, throwing hand grenades as fast as they could pull the porcelain balls of the friction igniters. If equipped with MG-42 machine guns, German squads could exact a fearsome toll among the attackers, who rightly feared its rapid rate of fire, making a sound that had already earned it the Soviet sobriquet of "Hitler's buzz saw."

If they survived the initial assault, the infantry would await orders to stay put or pull back to the next defense line, where they would begin all over again. All too often, the thin grey line would be overwhelmed when its men ran out of ammunition and failed to withdraw in time. Often the fighting was close-in, hand-to-hand, where entrenching tools and knives decided the issue. Frequently, platoons would be reduced to five or six men in a matter of minutes, and companies reduced to platoons. There would be no respite until the Soviet attack was stopped or one was killed or wounded. Benumbed and weary, the German enlisted men kept fighting, urged on by their few surviving NCOs and officers.

There really were no other options; surrender for an SS man at this stage of the war meant almost certain death or, at best, a long period of mistreatment and privation in a Soviet gulag if captured. What still held them together at this point of the war was their high morale, ideological commitment, and superior training, but most of all, their loyalty to one another. The German soldier who came of age during the long, hot summer of 1944 was the last to have undergone the full *Wehrmacht* or *Waffen-SS* training regimen at the hands of experienced and dedicated veterans. The replacements who followed them were rarely able to perform at the same level of excellence, and suffered accordingly.

Under the tremendous assault that followed, the front lines of the *Totenkopf* and *Wiking* Divisions on 18 August bent but did not break. The primary recipient of the First Belorussian Front's attention that day was the *Wiking* Division, which soon found itself having to fight for its life, while the *Totenkopf*'s situation was only slightly less imperiled. After the initial barrage lifted, the Soviet attackers quickly broke through the *Wiking*'s *HKL* in several places early that afternoon, advancing through the town of Jadwinin on the right in the *Germania* Regiment's sector and through Sulejów on its left, defended by the *Westland* Regiment. The tank-supported Soviet battalion that broke through the *Germania* Regiment's defenses managed to gain a foothold with two companies in the southern outskirts of Tłuszcz in its railroad station, while another managed to force its way past Sulejów, seeking the boundary between *Wiking* and *5. Jäg.Div.*

One Soviet infantry battalion shouldered its way past *II. Btl./Westland* on the division's far-left flank at Sulejów and continued pushing to the northwest. Fifteen minutes later, a portion of this battalion, most likely from the 160th Rifle Division, arrived rather unexpectedly on the doorstep of the tactical command post of *Hstuf.* Walter Schmidt's *II. Btl./Westland* located at Wymysły. Before anyone in the battalion's *Gefechtstand* knew what was happening, three *Pz. IV* of *Ostuf.* Kurt Schumacher's *3. Kompanie* stationed there swung into action. Without the benefit of infantry support, Schumacher's tanks machined-gunned and ran over the Red Army troops with their tracks, driving the survivors back long enough for Schmidt to move his command post to a safer location. The remaining seven tanks of Schumacher's company had already been parceled out behind the two battalions of the *Westland* Regiment in direct support and were just as busy.

Meanwhile, four assault guns of *4. Kompanie*, led by its commander, *Ostuf.* Heinz Lüthgarth, launched a counterattack at Wólka Sulejowska that drove the attackers back and gained time for the infantry to withdraw before they were overrun. During a series of close-range melees that ensued northwest of Sulejów that afternoon, *I. Abteilung*'s two companies, personally led by its battalion commander, *Hstuf.* Rudolf Säumenicht, destroyed 17 Soviet tanks, including four of the new T-34/85s, and 10 antitank guns, though Lüthgarth was seriously wounded when his *Sturmgeschütz* was knocked out by a T-34. Evacuated to the division field hospital near Modlin, where he later succumbed to his wounds, Lüthgarth was temporarily replaced as commander of *4. Kompanie* by *Ustuf.* Harwik. A new *Westland* defense line was established 2 kilometers northwest by nightfall, but Sulejów was lost.

On the *Wiking*'s right flank, things were just as bad. After enduring several hours of artillery barrages followed by a smoke screen, two key terrain features south and east of Tłuszcz, Hills 107 and 99, were quickly taken from two companies from *II. Btl./Germania* (the *7.* and *8.*). The survivors were forced to fall back to the rail line west of the town, which was quickly taken by an overwhelming enemy force. The battalion's two other companies, (the *5.* and *6.*) were nearly overrun southwest of Tłuszcz near Jasienica by Soviet tanks and infantry that had broken through Jadwinin before a counterattack launched by *Hstuf.* Flügel's *II. Abt./SS-Pz.Rgt. 5*, supported by a *Schützenpanzerwagen* company from *III. Btl./Germania*, drove them off after destroying 12 Soviet tanks.[11]

In the *6. Kompanie* of the *Germania* Regiment alone, 30 men were killed or wounded, bringing the total number of casualties suffered by that company from 14–18 August to 50; an additional eight men were listed as missing in action. The neighboring *5. Kompanie* lost 51 men during the same period.[12] These losses were suffered within a battalion that had reported only 200 front-line troops present for duty on 17 August, so nearly half of its men had been killed or wounded in the space

Command and Staff 1943–1945

SS-Ogruf. und Generalleutnant der Waffen-SS und Polizei Alfred Wünnenberg, first corps commander from August–October 1943. (Author's collection)

SS-Ogruf. und Generalleutnant der Waffen-SS Matthias Kleinheisterkamp, second corps commander from May–17 July 1944. (Author's collection)

SS-Ogruf. und Generalleutnant der Waffen-SS Herbert Otto Gille, third and final commander from 27 July 1944–8 May 1945. (Courtesy of Günther Lange Archive)

O5 (Aide de Camp) SS-Ostuf. Günther Lange (center) with *SS-Gruf.* Gille (left) and Adjutant *SS-Stubaf.* Karl-Willy Schulze. (Courtesy of Günther Lange Archive)

SS-Brigadeführer Kurt Brasack, Commander *SS-ARKO 104/504*, July 1944–March 1945. (Courtesy of Chris Juskey)

SS-Oberführer Nikolaus Heilmann, first Chief of Staff from August 1943–12 August 1944. (Author's collection)

SS-Ostubaf. Manfred Schönfelder, second chief of staff from 12 August 1944–8 May 1945. (*SS-Kriegsberichter* Alfons Jarolim)

SS-Stubaf. Richard Pauly, first corps *Ia* (*1.Gen. Stabs Offz.*) from 15 July–5 August 1944. (Courtesy of Günther Lange Archive)

SS-Stubaf. Wilhelm Klose, third corps *Ia* from 3 November 1944–16 January 1945. (Courtesy of the late Mark Yerger)

SS-Hstuf. Hans Velde, acting corps *Ia* from 2 February–1 March 1945. (Courtesy of John Moore)

SS-Gruf. Gille upon arrival at the airfield in Lublin in May 1944 along with (from left to right) *SS-Ostubaf.* Schönfelder, division *Ia; SS-Stubaf.* Hans Scharff, division *Ib* (*Quartiermeister*); Gille's ADC, *SS-Hstuf.* Hermann Kaufmann; and *SS-Stubaf.* Karl-Willy Schulze, Gille's *IIa* (division adjutant). (Courtesy of the late Willy Hein's archive)

SS-Obergruppenführer Gille in Modlin with *SS-Stubaf.* Herbert Jankuhn, his *Ic* from 27 July 1944–April 1945. (Courtesy of Günther Lange Archive)

SS-Hstuf. Martin Müller, the first *Korps-Nachrichten-Führer* (corps signal officer). (Courtesy of John Moore)

SS-Ostubaf. Wilhelm Honsell, *Korps-Nachschubführer* (corps supply unit commander). (Courtesy of John Moore)

SS-Stubaf. Otto Brandt, *Korp-Ingenieur/TFK* (maintenance and motor transport). (Courtesy of John Moore)

SS-Hstuf. Herbert Hüppe, third corps signal officer. (Courtesy of John Moore)

Heer Commanders

SS-Gruf. Herbert Gille with *Generalfeldmarschall* Walter Model, 28 July 1944, at Gille's headquarters in Rogów. On the right stands *SS-Hstuf.* Werner Westphal, acting corps *Ia* at the time. (Bundesarchiv Bild 146-1991-023-11A)

Gen.Oberst Hans Reinhardt, commander of *Heeresgruppe Mitte* from 16 August 1944. (Author's Collection)

General der Panzertruppe Nikolaus von Vormann, commander of *9. Armee* until 21 September 1944. (Author's Collection)

General der Panzertruppe Smilo Freiherr von Lüttwitz, commander of *9. Armee* from 21 September 1944. (U. S. Army Signal Corps)

Generalmajor Hans Källner, commander of *19. Pz.Div.* (Author's collection)

Generalmajor Wilhelm Schmalz, commander of *Fs.Pz.Div.* Hermann Göring. (Courtesy of George Petersen)

Oberst Wilhelm Söth, commander of *Gren. Brig. 1131.* (Courtesy of U. S. National Archives and Records Administration)

Oberst Franz Schlieper, commander of *73. Inf. Div.* Shown here as a *Generalmajor*. (Author's collection)

Major Alfred Nähring, *Pz.Gren.Rgt. 73, 19. Pz.Div.* (Author's collection)

Generalleutnant Dietrich von Saucken, commander, *XXXIX. Panzer-Korps* (center), confers with *Gruppenführer* Gille (left) and his chief of staff, *Obersturmbannführer* Manfred Schönfelder (right) during the opening stages of the tank battle at Praga, 31 July 1944. (Courtesy of Günther Lange Archive).

SS Totenkopf Division

Speaking with *SS-Gruf.* Gille at Modlin on 9 November 1944 (from left to right) *SS-Staf.* Karl Ullrich, commander of *Wiking* Division; *Oberführer* Becker, commander of *Totenkopf* Division; and Gille's *O1, SS-Hstuf.* Hans Velde standing in the background. (Courtesy of Günther Lange Archive)

Oberführer Becker departs the memorial ceremony at Modlin, 9 November 1944. From left to right are (in the foreground with his back to the camera) *SS-Stubaf.* Manfred Schönfelder, chief of staff, *IV. SS-Pz.Korps*; Major Otto Kleine, *Ia* of the *Wiking* Division; *SS-Stubaf.* Herbert Jankuhn, *Ic, IV SS-Pz.Korps;* and *SS-Oberführer* Becker. On the rights stands *SS-Ustuf.* Günther Lange, Gille's ADC. (Courtesy of Günther Lange Archive)

Gen.d.Pz.Tr. Smilo von Lüttwitz meeting with *SS-Ostuf.* Paul Steinecke (2nd from right) and *SS-Hstuf.* Heinz Müller (3rd from right), Commander of *III. Btl./Regiment Eicke* in the field on 2 October 1944 during his first commander's visit. (Photo by Paul Steinecke, courtesy of John Moore)

As part of his normal duties, *Gruppenführer* Gille made it a point to visit every division command post at least once a day. In this photograph, taken in early August 1944, Gille is speaking to the commander of the *Totenkopf* Division, *Oberführer* Helmut Becker (center). Behind Becker stands two of his key officers, *Obersturmbannführer* Josef Swientek, his artillery regiment commander, and *Obersturmbannführer* Erich Eberhardt, his *Ia.* On the right, with map board slung over his shoulder, is *Untersturmführer* Günther Lange, Gille's new *Begleitoffizier.* (Courtesy of Günther Lange Archive).

A Panther from *I. Abt./SS-Pz.Rgt. 3* seen from a window in the town of Wegrow as it drives through on its way to Siedlce, 28 July 1944. (Photo by Ernst Baumann, courtesy of Herr Rudolf Baumann-Schicht)

Herbert Gille (left) confers with *Standartenführer* Eduard Deisenhofer (center) and Johannes Mühlenkamp (right), acting commander of the *Wiking* Division, late July 1944. Deisenhofer had been tentatively selected by the SS Main Leadership Department to command the division, but after interviewing him, Gille decided to keep Mühlenkamp instead. Deisenhofer returned to the Western Front to take command of the *17. SS-Pz.Gren.Div.* at the end of August. (Courtesy of Günther Lange Archive)

Kriegsberichter (war correspondent) Gösta Borg, a Swedish SS volunteer who was "embedded" with the *Totenkopf* Division during the battle for Radzymin. His eyewitness account provided eloquent testimony of the ferocity of the fighting that took place east of Warsaw during August and September 1944. (Photo courtesy of Geir Brendan and Lennart Westberg).

SS Wiking Division

Wiking Division Commanders' Conference, 17 July 1944. From left to right are *SS-Stubaf.* Paul Kümmel, *SS-Staf.* Johannes Mühlenkamp, Gille (seated at the table), *SS-Hstuf.* Alois Reicher, *SS-Ostubaf.* Hans Dorr, *SS-Stubaf.* Günther Sitter, and an unknown artillery officer. (Photo by Ernst Baumann, from Günther Lange Archive)

SS-Gruppenführer Gille with *SS-Unstuf.* Günther Lange (middle) and *SS-Stubaf.* Hans Dorr, Kowel, May 1944. (Courtesy of Günther Lange Archive)

SS-Staf. Karl Ullrich, commander of *Wiking* Division after 9 October 1944. (Courtesy of Günther Lange Archive)

During the early stages of the battle of Praga on 28 July 1944, *SS-Gruf.* Gille visits the headquarters of *III. Btl. (gep.)/Germania*. From left to right, *SS-Hstuf.* Hans Murr, *SS-Ostuf.* Wilhelm Warnke (behind Murr), *SS-Stubaf.* Paul Kümmel, and Gille's Begleitoffizier at the time, *SS-Ustuf.* Joachim Barthel. (Photo by Ernst Baumann, courtesy of Herr Baumann-Schicht)

Gen.d.Pz.Tr. Smilo von Lüttwitz greets *SS-Ostubaf.* Fritz Darges, commander of *SS-Pz.Rgt. 5*, in November 1944 near Modlin. (Courtesy of John Moore)

StuG IV from 4. *Kompanie/SS-Pz.Rgt. 5*, late July 1944. (Courtesy of Geir Brendan)

Infantry squad from *II. Btl./Westland* Regiment, late July 1944. (Courtesy of Geir Brendan)

Panther from *II Abteilung/SS-Pz.Rgt. 5* passing through a town near Siedlce, 28 July 1944. (Photo by Ernst Baumann, courtesy of Herr Rudolf Baumann-Schicht)

Nemesis: Marshal Konstantin K. Rokossovsky, commander of First Belorussian Front. (Ministry of Defense of the Russian Federation, www.Mil.ru)

of a few days.[13] While some replacements had arrived, many of them immediately became casualties themselves before they had time to become acclimatized to front-line conditions during a relatively quiet period, where they would have gained the necessary experience needed to survive beyond their first day in combat. At this rate, there would be few infantrymen left in another week; and the battle was only beginning.

Under such enormous pressure, *Gruf.* Gille's old division was forced back step by step, but by the close of the day, despite some of the most fierce and unrelenting attacks it had ever experienced, the division still maintained a tenuous hold on its right with the *Totenkopf* Division at Grabie Stare. But by late afternoon, the *Wiking* Division has fallen back 5 kilometers to a new defense line west of the railroad running along the Rzonza River from Klembów to Wólka Kozłowska and ending at Mokra Wieś. Here, it attempted to maintain the connection with its left-hand neighbor, the *5. Jäg.Div.* of *XX. Armeekorps,* which had faced similar enemy pressure throughout the day.

The *5. Jäg.Div.*, whose new commander, *Gen.Lt.* Friedrich Sixt, had only assumed his position the previous day, was hit hard on its right flank, where the Soviets intended to push through the division boundary and separate it from the *Wiking* Division. Quickly realizing the seriousness of the situation, *Gen.Lt.* Sixt ordered the movement of the division's *Aufklärungs-Abteilung* from the left flank to its right, where it counterattacked into the exposed flanks of the Soviet leading column near Szewnica, smashing it and scattering the survivors. The injection of the *XX. Armeekorps'* reserve force, *Gren.Rgt. 62* of the *7. Inf.Div.*, vouchsafed the connection between it and the *IV. SS-Pz.Korps*, at least for the rest of the afternoon.[14]

Counterattacks by the *Wiking* and *5. Jäger* Divisions late that afternoon only brought temporary relief. Shortly after nightfall, at 6:05 p.m., the *IV. SS-Pz.Korps* reported that a large Soviet combined infantry and armor force of at least regimental size had punched through the edge of the *Wiking* Division's left flank, crossed the railroad tracks north of Sulejów, and pushed as far as Sitne in the *Westland* Regiment's rear area, where the Soviet spearhead even came into direct contact with some of the division's artillery in their firing positions before it was brought to a halt. Most worrying was that this force, after being repulsed, had not retreated but instead occupied the large forested area that lay east of Mokra Wieś and north of Wólka Sulejowska.[15] Gille correctly assessed the dire threat that this attack posed to his corps' survival and must have known that on only the first day of the Soviet offensive, he was already facing a critical situation and that it would be difficult, if not impossible, to hold his present positions.

Without being told to do so by *9. Armee* headquarters, Gille ordered the *Wiking* Division to immediately carry out a counterattack and destroy the Soviet units that had broken through before they could consolidate; for once they had been reinforced, it was common knowledge that the Red Army would be difficult to dislodge and there would be very little to prevent them from driving even deeper into the division's rear area the following day. The *Totenkopf* Division was instructed to hold on to its front line and eliminate any breakthroughs, which it was able to do, thanks in part to its effective use of its armor. Efforts that evening by the *Wiking*'s armored *Kampfgruppe* to destroy the large force occupying the forest east of Mokra Wieś were unsuccessful.

Most worrying to Gille was the situation along the boundary between both SS divisions, where the Soviets had continued exerting pressure between Grabie Stare and Jasienica. Several company-sized units from the *Germania* Regiment had been cut off during the day and were still holding out, "with the strength of desperation," after being bypassed earlier. An unknown number of enemy troops were lurking somewhere in the rear area, and had apparently gone to ground to await the morning. In his report that evening to *9. Armee*, Gille described the enemy pressure as "overwhelming."[16] He reported that though his corps had killed a number of Soviet troops and destroyed 28 tanks and assault guns, his own losses, particularly those suffered by the infantry, had been enormous. Isolated one-on-one tank battles had raged all day, with the two companies of *I. Abt./SS-Pz.Rgt. 5* destroying 16 alone.[17] But it was not enough.

For his part, *Gen.d.Pz.Tr.* von Vormann at *9. Armee* headquarters quickly grasped the seriousness of the situation confronting both *IV. SS-Panzer* and the neighboring *XX. Armeekorps,* but aside from ordering the usual immediate counterattack to restore the front line, there was little he could offer besides encouragement. He had few assets that could be moved about to reinforce Gille, since everything was needed elsewhere on his army's front, where the situation at Magnuszew was even more dire, despite the intervention of the *19.* and *Hermann Göring Panzer* Divisions. Once again, Gille would have to make do with what he had. *Heeresgruppe Mitte* essentially echoed what *9. Armee*'s commander had said, ordering Gille, working in conjunction with the *XX. Armeekorps,* to counterattack, immediately seal off the penetration, and restore the old front line. Von Vormann was to report to *H.Gr. Mitte* as soon as this order had been successfully carried out. If it could not be done that evening, *H.Gr. Mitte* wanted the attack to be launched the following morning. In either case, it was a tall order for units that were already at the breaking point.

In his nightly war diary summary, von Vormann realized that there was little possibility of retaking the old front line, given the overwhelming power demonstrated that day by Marshal Rokossovsky's forces. Instead of telling Gille to re-establish the old *HKL* as *H.Gr. Mitte* wanted him to do—a task which would have been nearly impossible anyway—he followed up with a more realistic order to Gille instructing him to do everything in his power to stop further breakthroughs while simultaneously preventing any of his own units from being encircled and destroyed piecemeal. These orders included the need to eliminate as soon as possible the large mechanized force (most likely from the VIII Guards Tank Corps) that had gone to ground in the forest east of Mokra Wieś. At the most, Gille was told to try to restore the old front line as much as possible, but that he should use his own discretion in determining how far that should be.[18]

Most affected by the evolving situation was the *Wiking* Division, which had to pull back to the northwest side of the railroad. Most of the units made it that far, but some had difficulty doing so. Some units were cut off during the unavoidable confusion that night. The battalion headquarters tank section, with its three tanks, and *7. Kompanie* of *II. Abt./SS-Pz.Rgt. 5* under the command of *Hstuf.* Flügel, with perhaps a dozen tanks in all, spent a harrowing night in search of the new front lines while under strong enemy pressure. Pulling out from its positions north of Tłuszcz at 7 p.m., Flügel's and the other tanks fell in with a group of advancing Soviet tanks, most likely from the VIII Guards Tank Corps, and escaped undetected.

He and his men believed they had successfully escaped until the lead Panther commanded by *Ustuf.* Alfred Grossrock was hit by an antitank gun while driving under the railroad underpass east of Wólka Kozłowska. Their route blocked by Grossrock's burning tank, Flügel, whose own Panther was now carrying the severely burned Grossrock and his surviving crewmembers, turned to the west to attempt a breakout in the direction of the *Totenkopf* Division's front lines. The promised artillery support needed to effect the maneuver failed to arrive, because the guns had been forced to displace to the rear in fear of being overrun and had not yet set up in their new firing positions.

This second breakout attempt failed when the leading tank, commanded by Flügel's battalion *Adjutant*, *Ustuf.* Otto Schicker, drove into a deep bomb crater and became immobilized. Schicker was severely injured when his hand became entangled in the turret ring during the accident. Flügel felt he had no other escape option remaining except fording the Cienka River, a risky move, particularly in the dark. Blowing up Schicker's immobilized tank, Flügel's headquarters section tanks and *7. Kompanie* then moved several hundred meters to the safety of some woods near the river, where they halted for several hours while a foot reconnaissance for a suitable fording site was carried out.

To his disappointment, the most suitable location was overlooked by a Soviet bivouac site on the opposite bank, where voices could clearly be heard in the darkness. Rapidly formulating a plan of attack, Flügel ordered his headquarters' two 2cm quadruple *Flak* cannon, mounted on half-tracks, to fire into the enemy camp at 2 a.m. while his nine remaining tanks made their crossing attempt. The plan worked. Taking advantage of the element of surprise, all of the tanks safely crossed, following by the *Flak* wagons. Bypassing the encamped Soviet unit, which was now in a state of turmoil, Flügel was shocked when the lead tank, commanded by *Unterscharführer* Förster, was blown into the air after travelling only 300 meters beyond the fording site. It had hit an antitank mine. Förster, whose legs had been blown off, was beyond saving. As he lay there with his legs in shreds, he told *Ostuf.* Flügel to go on without him, saying, "It's all over. I'm checking out!"[19]

Now with only eight tanks remaining, it was beginning to grow light. The *7. Kompanie* then took the lead, searching for another route to safety. Again, the lead tank was suddenly blown up by demolition charges placed by Soviet infantrymen, who had been watching the Germans approach and prepared an ambush. Detouring around the now-flaming tank, Flügel and the other six tank commanders maneuvered through a lightly wooded area several kilometers north of Wólka Kozłowska. All seven tanks were now crowded with wounded and the bodies of the dead. Finally, after driving towards the sound of fighting, the little column spotted the new German front line positions of the *Germania* Regiment. Relieved, Flügel raised an aerial recognition panel and his tank and the others were allowed to pass through. Two hours later, he went out on another mission, since he still had three other companies under his command that needed his leadership.[20]

Neither Gille nor his divisions would get any rest that night; instead of halting operations like they usually did, the divisions of the 47th, 70th, and 28th Armies and the VIII Guards Tank Corps continued their attack throughout the night. This came as somewhat of a surprise to the Germans, who had become accustomed to the Red Army's aversion to large-scale operations at night, and who had adjusted their own daily cycle of operations accordingly. That attitude would now have to change, but this meant that the troops of the *9.* and *2. Armee* would not be able to get enough sleep or to properly maintain their weapons, forcing them to conduct operations on the verge of physical and mental exhaustion, with a corresponding loss of efficiency that would work to the Red Army's advantage.

Throughout the night, the men of the *Wiking* and *Totenkopf* Divisions were forced to endure unrelenting attacks and artillery fire; no one knew whether the tank they saw in the dark or a body of troops marching by was friend or foe. Signal flares occasionally soared overhead, casting their ghostly red, green, or white lights, while Soviet night bombers dropped their payloads randomly throughout the Germans' rear area. German antiaircraft fire lit up the firmament with their tracers, while the occasional Soviet bomber was hit and plummeted to the ground in flames, briefly lighting the sky like a comet. The only bright spot that evening was events on Gille's far right flank, where the *73. Inf.Div.* reported that an attempt by a battalion-sized enemy force to penetrate its sector on its right was pinned down in the open by heavy defensive fire and could neither advance nor withdraw, easy targets for the division's artillerymen, which flayed them mercilessly with high-explosive shells.[21]

The Soviet offensive continued the next day without any discernable pause. The sun rose on 19 August over the shell-cratered battlefield between Grabie Stare and Jadow, casting its rays over the smoke- and dust-shrouded landscape. The weary troops of *IV. SS-Pz.Korps* and *XX. Armeekorps,* after a night of uninterrupted combat, faced unrelenting pressure throughout the day that only increased as the sun rose higher, bringing with it high temperatures and humidity. The men of the *Totenkopf* and *Wiking* Divisions did their best to seal off the breaches in their front line and destroy those units that had broken through, but their efforts on 19 August were in vain. The Soviet mechanized force that had occupied the forest east of Mokra Wieś continued its attack at sunrise, pushing even further into the boundary between *9.* and *2. Armee*. By that evening, German attempts to stop and seal off penetrations had become futile, and the connection between the two armies was severed.

In the *Totenkopf* Division sector, tank-supported attacks in regimental strength, launched by the 143rd, 132nd, and 260th Rifle Divisions, continued with undiminished ferocity, achieving several minor breakthroughs between Grabie Stare and Klembów that were sealed off by tank-led counterattacks. Soviet heavy artillery, accompanied by a barrage from Katyusha (little Kate) 12.2cm multiple rockets launchers, the so-called "Stalin's Organ," began at 10 a.m., signifying that a new attack was imminent. Salvo after salvo pummeled the division's positions near Grabie Stare, enveloping the defenders in clouds of dust. The unit holding this particular sector, *III. Btl./Pz.Gren.Rgt. Eicke*, had to endure the barrage for over an hour and was actually relieved to hear the shouts of the advancing Soviet troops, who roared their battle cry "urrah, urrah!" as they charged the German positions.

Now at last they could strike back at their enemy, instead of huddling at the bottom of a trench, powerless to do anything about it. Several T-34s and one of the new Joseph Stalin (JS) II tanks rattled along closely behind the mass of infantry. Supported by several antitank guns of *SS-Pz.Jag.Abt. 3* and the division's artillery regiment, the battalion, commanded by *Stubaf.* Adolf Pittschellis, slaughtered the advancing enemy, leaving the slope below Hill 104 strewn with the bodies of dead and wounded infantrymen and the smoking wrecks of seven tanks. Another Soviet attack was immediately launched after the first one failed and Pittschellis' men were soon thrown off the hill, but he rallied them and with the support of the division's assault gun battalion retook it later that day.[22]

Most worrisome was a deep penetration achieved along the boundary between *Obf.* Becker's division and the *Wiking* Division, which progressed as far as the town of Krusze before the Soviet troops halted and dug in. Blasting through the thin defenses of *I. Btl./Eicke* south of Klembów, the spearhead units of the 260th Rifle Division, supported by an unknown number of tanks from the 62nd Heavy Guards Tank Regiment, rushed towards its objective, the town of Krusze, 10 kilometers northeast of the former town. Should they succeed in taking it, it would place a substantial force behind both SS divisions, a move that would completely unhinge Gille's corps' defenses and precipitate a general withdrawal, lest both divisions become entrapped. The commander of the *Totenkopf* Division, immediately sensing the danger, ordered a division-level counterattack consisting of seven *Pz. V* Panthers from the tank regiment's *1. Kp./I. Abteilung* and the four operational Tigers from *9. Kompanie* commanded by *Ustuf.* Helmut Neff.[23]

By the time the counterattack had begun, the Soviets had already erected a *Pakfront* (antitank gun screen) along the northern edge of the forest several hundred meters southeast of Krusze. Hidden within the forest were also several of the heavy JS-II tanks with their powerful 12.2cm cannon, capable of destroying even the mighty Tigers. The first attempt to eject the Soviets from the forest ended in dismal failure; one Panther was shot up by a JS-II at a range of 1,000 meters and destroyed, with another one badly damaged. Two Tigers were also immobilized and one destroyed. The survivors beat a hasty retreat, leaving it to the recovery crews to retrieve the damaged tanks after dark.

Shortly afterwards, another attempt was made to dislodge the enemy from the forest, but with more success. The remaining Tiger knocked out one JS-II at long range and immobilized two others, while *1. Kompanie*'s remaining Panthers penetrated the forest and proceeded to shoot up the antitank guns. One tank, commanded by *Ostuf.* Erich Schramm, knocked over trees and barreled down a narrow lane that ran through the forest, crushing Soviet infantrymen under his tracks and machine-gunning those who were brave enough to attempt a stand. Tracers arced through the treetops as a frantic, point-blank melee ensued when Schramm was joined by the other tanks from his company. Finally, the surviving Soviet troops, accompanied by their remaining tanks, fled out of the woods towards the east, with six Panthers in close pursuit. That brought them little reprieve, because at about the same time, a supporting counterattack from the opposite direction, led by *Ostsuf.* Karl-Heinz Lichte's *5. Kp./SS-Pz.Rgt. 5* of the *Wiking* Division, approached from the direction of Kozły and finished the job that Schramm had begun, with Lichte destroying five Soviet tanks on his own.

Over 100 Soviet dead were counted after the action, and the danger of a breakthrough between the inner flanks of the *Totenkopf* and *Wiking* Divisions averted for the time being. However, Schramm's company was ordered to remain in the woods and defend against any further attempts to seize Krusze. This order filled his men with apprehension, because they had no supporting infantry to protect them during darkness and Soviet troops were still everywhere. One of Schramm's tank commanders, *Oscha.* Steiger, later remembered:

> Although we had completed our mission by late afternoon, every attempt to contact battalion headquarters by radio failed. The military situation was completely unknown. It was clear to us that darkness would soon fall and that the Russians would come at us from all sides. And there we sat in our six tanks completely alone in the middle of the forest.[24]

The *Wiking* Division's reserve force soon found its hands full retaking Kozły, which had been seized by Soviet troops earlier that day at the same time Lichte was moving into position to begin his attack towards Krusze. Now united with the spearhead of *SS-Pz.Rgt. 3*, Lichte's company, along with a supporting infantry company from *Hstuf.* Heinz Mürr's *III. (gep.)Btl./Germania*, turned around and assaulted Kozły at 5:50 p.m., retaking it and wiping out the remaining Soviet units in the town. Another tank battle broke out shortly afterwards in the same area, when Lichte's company, joined by *Ostuf.* Karl Nicolussi-Leck's *8. Kompanie* of *II. Abt./SS-Pz.Rgt. 5*, encountered another Soviet tank battalion attempting to advance between Kozły and Wólka Kozłowska. In the ensuing engagement, *5.* and *8. Kompanie*, joined by tanks from the *Totenkopf* Division, knocked out 13 M-4 Sherman tanks and T-34s.[25] At the same time a kilometer further east, *Ostuf.* Kurt Schumacher and his *3. Kompanie, I. Abt./SS-Pz.Rgt. 5* fought a duel with more Soviet tanks, which seemed to be everywhere.

In the *Totenkopf*'s defensive sector that day, the line had held despite many occasions when breakthroughs had been narrowly averted. In the *Wiking* Division's sector, the situation had not developed nearly as favorably. Although the division had successfully maintained contact with the *Totenkopf* on its far right flank, an important achievement by itself, its line was pierced in the center at noon when a large Soviet force supported by 12 tanks attacked to the north out of Tłuszcz towards Wólka Kozłowska. The town's defenders, *II. Btl./Westland*, were forced to abandon their positions and pull back despite the concentrated supporting fire of the division's artillery regiment. Facing tanks that rolled over their individual fighting positions, the men of *Hstuf.* Schmidt's battalion had no choice but to withdraw or face annihilation.[26]

Once again it was demonstrated that while artillery fire could scatter and disperse an attacking force or support an attack, it could not take and hold ground—only infantry could do that. Schmidt's battalion, reinforced by the *panzer* regiment's assault gun company, made an attempt to retake the town later that afternoon, but *Ustuf.* Harwik, the acting commander of the *4. Kompanie*, was killed in action while leading the attack and two *Sturmgeschütze* were lost when the assault bogged down in heavy defensive fire. The town was given up for lost. The best that the *Westland* Regiment could do, since the division did not have enough tanks and assault guns to back them up everywhere, was to maintain its cohesion as it fell back while making its best effort to keep in contact with its left and right flanks.

The situation on the *Wiking* Division's far left flank along the corps boundary had only gotten worse since the previous evening. The powerful mechanized force that had ensconced itself in the forest east of Mokra Wieś continued its attack at first light, crossing the railroad embankment east of the town and pivoting towards the northwest, making a beeline towards its objective, the town of Trojany that lay only 30 kilometers away. Should they achieve their desired goal, the *Wiking* Division would be entirely cut off and the connection between *9.* and *2. Armee* completely sundered. Another equally strong enemy force that followed in the wake of the leading element attacked north towards Sitne, which marked the limit of the neighboring *5. Jäger Division*'s right flank.

This newly introduced Soviet tank force, which was preliminarily identified as belonging to the IX Tank Corps, was especially concerning, as there were now two tank corps (the VIII Guards Tank and IX Tank) involved in this offensive, an indicator that the First Belorussian Front was seeking an operational objective and not aimed merely at pushing back the German line. That evening, *Gen.d.Pz.Tr.* von Vormann correctly surmised that their goal was the Bug River line and the entrapment of the elements of *9.* and *2. Armee* that were positioned south of it.[27]

Nearing the close of 19 August, Gille was confronted with a difficult challenge. Facing no fewer than 12 Soviet rifle divisions, at least one tank corps and probably another, supported by a tremendous amount of artillery and tactical air support, the divisions of his corps, particularly the *Wiking* Division, were being slowly overwhelmed. Several small-scale breakthroughs had already occurred and though most of them had been sealed off, two of the most dangerous ones—east of Wólka Kozłowska and between Mokra Wieś and Sitne—had not. Units that had attempted to stand their ground, particularly within that division's *Westland* and *Germania* Regiments, were being ground to pieces and at the current rate would be soon be reduced to remnants.

Later that afternoon, Gille urgently requested reinforcements, preferably SS units, but the one SS battalion previously earmarked for him, *SS-Gren.Btl. 500*, was attached to the *292. Inf.Div.* within *2. Armee* and could not be released due to the tactical situation.[28] He had already committed everything his divisions and the corps had, with the exception of the *73. Inf.Div.*, which could not be moved from its position along the Vistula, where it faced off against a Soviet rifle division as well as the northernmost division of the 1st Polish Army. Both *Pionier* battalions from the two SS divisions had already been inserted into the front lines to serve as infantry and even their *Divisions-Begleit* companies had been employed as mobile reserves combatting enemy units that had broken through. The best he could do with the forces available to him was to trade space for time, using his still-powerful *panzer* units as a *Feuerwehr* (fire brigade) to prevent his infantry from being wiped out and to slow down the Soviet spearheads as much as possible. Another development that must have weighed on his mind was that the enemy had approached to within 15 kilometers of his corps' forward command post, a warning sign that it would have to relocate to another position soon.

Events on the corps' left flank took their course. The *Wiking* Division's attempt early that afternoon to cut off the enemy force that had broken through between Mokra Wieś and Sitne failed when the attacking force proved too weak for the task; Mokra Wieś fell to Soviet tanks and a counterattack by a grenadier battalion from the *Wiking* Division supported by several assault guns was driven away by Soviet defensive fire. A 10-kilometer-wide gap now yawned between *IV. SS-Panzer* and the *XX. Armeekorps.* The best that *Staf.* Mühlenkamp's division could do by that point was to attempt to slow down the Soviet columns with artillery fire as they pushed past the village of Mościska, since there were no *Wiking* Division tanks or infantry close enough to respond. A Soviet infantry force, led by seven SU-76 assault guns, quickly took possession of the town, which was situated at the southern end of a road network that led north to the Bug River.[29]

GenLt. Sixt's *5. Jag.Div.*, faced with the unrelenting attack by the 28th Army, had begun withdrawing north to the Bug along with the rest of *Gen.d.Art.* von Roman's *XX. Armeekorps,* part of a movement ordered by the *2. Armee* commander, who wanted to prevent his army's own right flank from being trapped south of the river. Von Roman was unable to secure permission to cross over with his forces, however, which was to Gille's advantage since he had no forces yet in position to stop any attempt by the Soviets to attack along the river if they chose to do so. But as a result of the successful Soviet penetration, the *5. Jäg.Div.*'s commander had given up trying to reconnect on his right with the *Wiking* Division, but focused instead on refusing his right flank to the enemy, whose tanks were pushing towards the operationally important town of Wyszków, where two bridges spanned the Bug. This explains why the *5. Jag.Div.* made no attempt to retake Mościska—it was clear that the fighting had moved on and Generals von Roman and Sixt had enough problems of their own to worry about. Thus, Gille could count on little support from his fellow corps commander—*IV. SS-Pz.Korps* would be fighting on its own for the next several days.

In his report that evening to *9. Armee*, Gille informed his army commander that with his left flank in the process of being enveloped, he had no choice but to order the *Wiking* Division to begin withdrawing to a new defensive line facing due east instead of southeast. While his two SS divisions had reported destroying 23 tanks and assault guns that day, this achievement had done very little to slow the momentum of the Soviet offensive, which remained focused on separating the *9. Armee* from the *2. Armee*. The *Wiking* Division's new line, which had swung back nearly 90 degrees counterclockwise from its previous 17 August position, would now be traced from Zabrodzie in the north through Krusze and terminating at Klembów in the south, where its right flank would tie in with the existing left flank of the *Totenkopf* Division, whose own defensive sector would remain relatively unchanged.[30] Thus oriented, the *Wiking* Division would be poised to block any attempt the following day by the Soviets to take Trojany and foil their advance to the Vistula, Bug, and Narew—at least in concept.

At Zabrodzie on the Bug River, the *Wiking* Division was to make contact with *Sicherungstruppen* (rear area security troops) of the *2. Armee*, so at least a sort of connection with that army could be maintained. The rest of the corps—meaning the *Totenkopf* Division and *73. Inf.Div.*—were ordered to continue defending their current front line. Whether Gille's divisions would have enough remaining power to handle their new assignment was an open question. As early as 2:50 p.m. that day, *Gen.d.Pz.Tr.* von Vormann had already informed the *H.Gr. Mitte* commander that,

"The combat strength of the battalions have now decreased to the point where the continuation of the defensive battle is no longer sustainable." After considering the problem, he decided that the only possible solution was to shrink the defensive sectors of both the *Totenkopf* and *Wiking* Divisions, and bring in another division to be inserted between them and the *73. Inf.Div.*, which would defend the new sector thus created.[31]

The only division available at that moment was the *Königlich 1. Ungarische Kavallerie-Division* (*1. ung.Kav.Div.* or Royal 1st Hungarian Cavalry Division), a Hungarian unit, which was already in the process of moving by rail from its rest area at Płońsk northwest of Warsaw to join the *VIII. Armeekorps* at the Magnuszew Front, where it was intended to become that corps' reserve force since it was still understrength. Rather than have the division's trains unload at its original destination west of the Vistula, they were redirected to the railyard at Jablonna-Legjonowo across the river east of Modlin. Here, its troops, horses, and other materiel would unload and commence their 26-kilometer road movement south to the division's new assigned defensive sector between Wołomin and Praga.

This decision was not without its risks, von Vormann knew, because it was common knowledge that Hungarian units were not equal in terms of fighting power compared to similar-sized German units, even though this particular division, commanded by *Gen.Maj.* Mihály Ibrányi, had a reputation of being one of the best in the Hungarian Army.[32] Shortages of modern equipment and weapons, as well as experienced leaders, meant that it might well be unsuited for facing a large-scale Soviet offensive. This perception dictated that it be employed in the sector where it was least likely to be attacked, which at that time meant the southeast portion of the evolving *IV. SS-Pz.Korps* front line.

The division had also recently undergone a month-long reconstitution process, having suffered heavy casualties and loss of vehicles and equipment southeast of Bialystok during the previous month while attached to *Kav. Korps Hartinek*. Having thus made his decision, von Vormann's orders went out to both the *1. ung.Kav.Div.* and *IV. SS-Pz.Korps*, directing the leading element of Ibrányi's division to begin moving into their new positions the next morning. Gille would have to be satisfied with this reinforcement, since there was nothing else in the offing and the division's front-line strength of 1,500 men with more to follow would certainly be a welcome addition to his thinly spread corps.

That night, the various sub-elements of the *Wiking* Division struggled to get into their new positions along the new line sketched out for them on the map. Most of the companies and battalions moved by foot, since there was only one motorized battalion left in the division—*III. (gep.) Btl./Germania*. Dozens of men whose platoons or forward outposts that been bypassed by the Soviets were able to find their way back to their old units, taking advantage of the darkness to slip through enemy lines. The few remaining front-line trenches were abandoned as the survivors of the *Germania* and *Westland* Regiments and *SS-Pio.Btl. 5* pulled out, while their artillery regiment fired thousands of rounds to cover their withdrawal using ammunition that had been stockpiled over the past two weeks, thanks to von Vormann's farsighted order issued during Operation *Brückenschlag*. Gille reported the following morning that the Soviets pressed the withdrawal closely throughout the entire night, and in several instances German troops had to mount immediate counterattacks to throw them out of their newly designated positions because the enemy had arrived before they did.[33]

At dawn on 20 August, the leading Soviet elements initiated a hasty attack against the *Westland* Regiment's positions at Zabrodzie, even before all of its companies had been able to take up their new positions. Only the day before, a breakthrough had been narrowly averted at the same location, where *I. Abt./SS-Pz.Rgt. 5*'s maintenance company had been stationed, when the commander of the company, *Ostuf.* Paul Senghas, quickly assembled a scratch force of 58 men supported by two *Pz. IV* tanks under repair. Led by Senghas, the tiny battlegroup drove off a larger battalion-sized formation of Soviet cavalry attempting to cross the railroad line and knocked out three Lend-Lease M-4 Shermans. Despite repeated artillery-supported attempts by this enemy battalion to break through to the Bug, Senghas' *Alarm-Kompanie*, composed of mechanics, clerks, and other headquarters personnel, were able to keep the Soviets at bay until the arrival of troops of the *Westland* Regiment early the following morning. At that point, Senghas was able to withdraw his company, taking with him all of the battalion's vehicles under repair, after suffering only six casualties.[34]

The *Totenkopf* Division was not spared Rokossovsky's attention, finding itself throughout the day having to ward off no less than six tank-supported regiment-sized attacks by mid-afternoon. Most of these, including a large-scale attempt at Klembów, were driven off, except for one dangerous penetration made in the town of Grabe Stare, which compelled *Obf.* Becker to commit his division reserve in a counterattack whose outcome was still in doubt by nightfall. *SS-Sturmmann* Erich Lemkuhl, a *Pz. VI* Tiger crewman of *9. Kp./SS-Pz.Rgt. 3*, later recalled the fighting:

> The company carries out several counterattacks in the area …we suffer some Tiger losses. [Our] loader Boxleitner is killed by friendly fire. The Russians [*sic*: Soviets] constantly attack us with artillery fire. Sleep is hard to come by, and life is to a degree unbearable."[35]

Another tank-led attack had penetrated beyond Krusze along the new boundary between the *Totenkopf* and *Wiking* Divisions, forcing *Staf.* Mühlenkamp to employ *Ostubaf.* Darges's *panzer* regiment in a counterattack of his own. During the day, Gille was forced to move his corps headquarters further to the rear at the Wieliszew railway station, 5 miles southwest of Zegrze, as was Mühlenkamp, whose old one at Dabrówka was now practically on the front line.

Throughout the day, the entire front line between Zielonka in the south and Lochow in the north was subject to continuous air attack, forcing the troops from

IV. SS-Pz.Korps and *XX. Armeekorps* to contend with wave after wave of *Sturmovik* raids, strafing and bombing the retreating columns as they struggled to reach their new positions. While several Red Air Force aircraft were shot down that day, it made no impact on their attacks whatsoever. After making its presence briefly known during the tank battle of Praga two weeks before, where its *Stukas*, *Messerschmidts,* and *Focke-Wulfs* ruled the skies, the *Luftwaffe* was now nowhere in evidence. The *Wiking* Division was now fully experiencing the negative effects of the lack of its *Flak* battalion, still tied down defending critical sites in Warsaw under the control of *Gruppe von dem Bach*. Soviet artillery continued to play up and down the line, inflicting more casualties than any other weapon. To make the situation even more intolerable, temperatures rose that day to the mid-80s (29 degrees Celsius) and high humidity prevailed. This, coupled with the dust and smoke lingering on the battlefield, meant that troops of both sides quickly became filthy, a situation that new troops had to learn to get used to. Veterans already knew that dirt and unwashed clothing were part and parcel of any battle fought on the Eastern Front during the summer.

Shortly after the *Wiking* Division had become "set" in its new defensive line stretching from Zabrodzie to Krusze, it was subjected to numerous attacks by fresh waves of Soviet forces beginning as early as 4 a.m. on 20 August. Its line was thin indeed, with both *Panzergrenadier* regiments having been reduced to less than half strength during the past three days of fighting, forcing the *panzer* regiment to fill in the gaps without the benefit of any infantry escort. The most affected unit was the *Westland* Regiment, whose two understrength battalions had been combined into one to maintain any measureable amount of combat power. The bulk of the regiment was concentrated in a hedgehog position centered on the town of Kochwolo-Lasków, where it endured numerous attacks that day.[36] It was only able to maintain a fragile link with the unit on its left flank, a *Sicherungs-Bataillon* from *XX. Armeekorps*. Away to the *Wiking* Division's far left, a mere 10 kilometers away, ran the Bug, a reminder that both corps would soon have their backs against the river unless preventive action was taken. Both corps increased the security surrounding the bridges at the various Bug crossing sites, but the lack of any tanks to block Soviet attempts to seize the bridges made successful defense unlikely. Consequently, all of the bridges over the Bug, several hundred meters wide at this point, were wired for demolition as a precaution should all else fail.

The corps and divisional artillery battalions were engaged continuously throughout the day, firing numerous missions in support of the *Totenkopf* and *Wiking* Divisions, breaking up assembly areas or stalling Soviet attacks, but Gille, Mühlenkamp, and Becker knew that this would only delay, not stop, the enemy's advance. The biggest defensive action fought in the *Wiking* Division's sector that day took place northwest of Wólka-Kozłowska on its right flank, where *Ostuf.* Schumacher's *3. Kompanie* of *I. Abt./SS-Pz.Rgt. 5*, fighting alongside the *Germania* Regiment, repelled several attempts by a much larger enemy force to break through at Fabianów. Initially confronted by an hour-long air attack that began at 12:30 p.m., Schumacher's company soon discovered that the attackers, most likely from the 165th Rifle Division supported by elements of the VIII Guards Tank Corps, decided at 7 p.m. to bypass them after suffering heavy losses all afternoon and move directly on the town of Trojany instead.

This attack had progressed to within 500 meters of the regimental headquarters of *SS-Pz.Rgt. 5* on the eastern edge of Trojany, when *Ostubaf.* Fritz Darges positioned a force of six tanks, including his own headquarters tank section and the regimental reconnaissance tank platoon, astride the road leading into town. As a number of soldiers from the *Germania* Regiment whose positions had been overrun fled past his tanks in panic, Darges and his six tanks awaited the inevitable onslaught. Close by, the regiment's *5. Kompanie*, accompanied by the *II. Abteilung* commander, went into position south of Trojany. Shortly afterwards, the Soviets, employing a smoke screen, initiated their attack, spearheaded by five T-34/85 tanks. In the short but sharp tank battle that ensued, three Soviet tanks were knocked out and their infantry driven to ground, long enough for the rest of the battalion from the *Germania* Regiment to withdraw in good order.

That night, the tank regiment withdrew its headquarters back to Karpin, a safer location 10 kilometers to the northwest. During that day, the regiment had destroyed 20 Soviet tanks, but this successful action, as it had on previous days, barely slowed the enemy's advance.[37] In all, on 20 August Gille's corps destroyed 25 Soviet tanks, including three of the big JS-IIs, 16 Shermans, five T-34s, and one assault gun.[38] The fact that most of them were destroyed in the *Wiking* Division's sector indicated that its destruction was still Marshal Rokossovsky's primary focus. With the *Wiking* removed from the battle, the way to the Bug, Narew, and Vistula River crossings would be wide open to the 70th Army, which had become the main effort at this point in the battle, supported by VIII Guards Tank Corps. Rokossovsky's plan required an operational-level breakthrough, and he meant to have it; it was here, along the southern bank of the Bug, where he saw his greatest opportunity.

Throughout the day, as the fighting intensified, Gille constantly badgered von Vormann's headquarters for reinforcements and intervention by the *Luftwaffe*. His greatest worry was his left flank, as well as his connection to the *XX. Armeekorps* (and *2. Armee*), which he said was "hanging in the air" north of Zabrodzie, where the *Westland* Regiment of the *Wiking* maintained a rather tenuous connection with the neighboring corps. By this point, the gap between the *Wiking* Division and the *5. Jag.Div.* had grown so wide that Gille informed von Vormann late that afternoon that he no longer had any forces that he could employ to close it and asked instead for *2. Armee* to commit its own reserves to do so.

In an exchange between *Gen.Oberst* Reinhardt of *H.Gr. Mitte* and von Vormann at 8:05 p.m., Reinhardt told his subordinate commander that he was on his own but that he had granted permission for *Gen.Oberst* Weiss of *2. Armee* to pull back all three of his corps (the *XX.*, *XXIII.*, and *I. Kav. Korps*) behind the Bug, including the *5. Jäg.Div.* from *XX. Armeekorps.*[39] While this provided some relief for Weiss, von Vormann realized that he would not benefit much from this decision, because he could no longer expect help from that quarter and would still have to defend south of the river with the attendant risk that *IV. SS-Pz.Korps* might become trapped.

With this in mind, Gille was directed by telephone 10 minutes later by von Vormann to defend a new front line that ran from Słopsk in the north (which rested on the southern bank of the Bug) to Krusze, and from there to Praga, a distance of over 50 kilometers. The two divisions that were the subject of most of the 47th and 70th Armies' attention (the *Totenkopf* and *Wiking*) were now seriously understrength, especially in regards to infantry, which was nearing breaking point. Should that occur, Gille realized, there would be nothing to stop the Soviets from driving to the Vistula unless he got help. He called von Vormann back three hours later, after his staff had studied the problem, and told his army commander that he doubted that he could hold this proposed line either, since he simply lacked the forces to man it. The front-line infantry combat strength of the *Totenkopf* Division had sunken by 20 August to only 1,297 men, while that of the *Wiking* Division had declined to just 497.[40]

By this point, Gille told him, he had committed all of his reserves and could not take anything away from the *73. Inf.Div.* without *9. Armee* permission, a fact which von Vormann was aware of. But he was not finished with Gille. In addition to instructing him to withdraw his left flank back to the new defense line described above, von Vormann also told the *IV. SS-Pz.Korps* commander that he was to begin planning a more permanent "bridgehead position" south of Serock at the confluence of the Bug and Narew Rivers, where his corps was to cover the exposed right flank of *2. Armee*, which was to withdraw to a new defense line east of the Narew beginning the following day. This would, over time, rebound to Gille's benefit. The area in the rear of his corps where the river converged resembled a funnel, with Serock at the bottom. The further to the west that Gille's corps withdrew, the smaller the funnel became, with a correspondingly shorter front line, thus allowing his divisions to build up a greater troop density with increased combat power per kilometer. This would take several weeks before the benefit would be realized, however.

Additional help was on the way, though. During the early hours, the *1. ung.Kav. Div.* began to be inserted between the *73. Inf.Div.* and the *Totenkopf* Division, a move that would free up *Gren.Brig. 1131*, which had been temporarily attached to the latter division a week earlier. Believing that the Hungarians would not perform well in a crisis situation if they was shifted to the left flank, the new grenadier brigade, which had performed solidly so far, was shifted late that afternoon from the right of the corps front to its left-most boundary between Zabrodzie and Słopsk.

One of the first elements to arrive was the brigade's tank destroyer company, *Pz.Jag. Kp. 1131*, which helped a platoon from the *Westland* Regiment beat back a Soviet attack towards Zabrodzie originating from the woods at Mostówka, 3 kilometers northeast of the *HKL*.

In addition to being given permission to employ *Gren.Brig. 1131*, von Vormann also advised Gille to comb through his SS divisions' *Trosseinheiten* (trains elements) for excess personnel to use as replacements for their depleted *Panzergrenadier* regiments, a proposal that Gille and his two SS division commanders had historically resisted. The *Waffen-SS* in general had also abjured absorbing Army replacements into its ranks, since these men were deemed to lack the requisite ideological indoctrination or SS spirit that typified their organization. When Gille protested, von Vormann informed his SS commander that it was a standard practice of the *Heer* divisions to do so and then reminded him that it was the only way he was going to get any replacements for his losses because no new SS forces would be available for the foreseeable future—those would have to come from the SS, since he had no administrative control over Heinrich Himmler's replacement apparatus.[41]

Besides the transfer of *Gren.Brig. 1131* to the left flank, von Vormann directed the *73. Inf.Div.* to release *SS-Pz.Jag.Abt. 5* with its 19 operational *Jagdpanzer IV* to its parent division the next day, where the battalion's tank-destroying capability was badly needed. The *Wiking* Division had suffered the total loss of 21 tanks since the battle started (including 17 Panthers), and the addition of these tank destroyers would double the number of available armored fighting vehicles. By this point in the battle, the *Wiking* Division's *panzer* regiment only had a total of 15 tanks and assault guns still considered battle-worthy, though there were over 50 in short- or long-term repair.[42] With these organizational changes, primarily the addition of the tank destroyers and the grenadier brigade, Gille hoped that the *Wiking* Division would be able to gain some breathing space.

Gren.Brig. 1131 was a relatively new unit, formed on 27 July 1944 in *Wehrkreis III* as a "Valkyrie" unit, as an emergency unit created by the *Ersatzheer* to fight on the Eastern Front in the wake of the collapse of *H.Gr. Mitte* earlier that month. In reality little more than a reinforced regiment, it consisted of two grenadier battalions of four companies each (*I. Btl.* and *II. Btl.*), an artillery battalion equipped with two batteries of 10.5cm howitzers and a battery of 15cm howitzers, a motorized anti-tank company with 12 self-propelled 7.5cm guns, and a combat engineer company. Formed primarily with new recruits led by a veteran cadre, the brigade, with an initial strength of 1,823 men, had a *Kampfstärke* of 797 men when it was attached to *IV. SS-Pz.Korps* on 17 August. Four days later, on the eve of its commitment on the corps' left flank, it still had a combat strength of 766 men, which represented more combat troops than all of the *Wiking* Division's battalions combined.[43] Led by its dynamic and capable commander, *Oberst* Wilhelm Söth, the brigade would enter the fray at a critical time.

In its morning submission at 5:47 a.m. on 21 August to *9. Armee*, sent by headquarters staff duty sergeant *Uscha.* Richer, *IV. SS-Pz.Korps*—now fully operational at its new location in Wieliszew—reported that in the *Totenkopf* Division's sector, enemy artillery fire had disrupted the displacement of *Gren.Brig. 1131*. Up to that point, three companies of the brigade had already moved out and been replaced by similar units from the *1. ung.Kav.Div.*, but would have to proceed more cautiously. In the *Wiking* Division's sector, continuing enemy pressure all along its front line was reported. The corps commander intended to begin construction of a new intermediary position behind the current front line along the general course between Klembów and Trojany, and from thence to Słopsk, which would be occupied by *Gren.Brig. 1131* as soon as it arrived. At the moment, the bulk of the *Wiking* Division was conducting an active defense, withdrawing where necessary but launching surprise armor counterattacks to keep the every-advancing enemy at bay while the infantry displaced to new positions. The report closed by stating that the corps' entire sector was at that moment under very strong artillery fire.[44]

As the Hungarian units were fed into the line company by company throughout that day, *Gren.Brig. 1131* arrived in its new sector incrementally, having to traverse the entire corps front line from south to north along roads clogged with withdrawing *Trossteile* (supply trains). Over 100 Soviet air attacks were reported that day, which also delayed the movement, but by nightfall most of *Oberst* Söth's brigade was in position to the left of the *Wiking* Division. It had proverbially arrived in the nick of time, helping to halt a regimental-sized breakthrough at the corps' far left flank near Słopsk that took place while the *Westland* Regiment was withdrawing to its new defensive position. By nightfall, this Soviet attack had been beaten back; von Vormann mistakenly stated in his journal that evening that he felt that their offensive had nearly run its course.[45] Though this area was seen by both sides as the main focus of the fighting on 21 August, the Soviet offensive had not stopped elsewhere.

In the corps center, the *Totenkopf* Division warded off several tank-supported battalion-sized infantry assaults on its left flank at Klembów, while the Soviet CXIV Rifle Corps managed to achieve a temporary breakthrough of the *Wiking* Division's new front line at Trojany. Here, a rifle battalion and a few tanks managed to penetrate several kilometers to the west of the town, forcing Mühlenkamp to commit his division reserve to contain it and force the Red Army troops into a wooded area on the town's edge, where they were hammered with artillery. To reinforce this section of the *Wiking* Division's crumbling front line, Gille ordered that *I. Btl./ Eicke*, along with a tank company from *SS-Pz.Rgt. 3*, be temporarily attached to Mühlenkamp's division west of Trojany, where it was able to shore up German defenses.[46] Here, the fighting was extraordinarily bitter, with the Soviets repeatedly demonstrating their willingness to take very heavy losses to achieve their objectives. One eyewitness to the fighting near Trojany was *Uscha.* Flesch of

III. Btl./Eicke, who wrote shortly afterwards about an infantry action his company fought at Dobczyn that same day:

> The attacking Russians were pinned down by our defensive fire about 150 meters in front of us. When they finally realized that they could not advance, they pulled back into the woods near Point 18, though a lot of their wounded were left behind on the field. Half an hour later, the Red Army soldiers stormed forward again out from the woods and came at our positions with renewed vigor. This attack too was brought to a complete halt just in front of us by our fire.[47]

The *Wiking* and *Totenkopf* Divisions both conducted counterattacks throughout the night. On the corps' right flank, no attack worth mentioning was launched against the newly arrived Hungarians; the front opposite the *73. Inf.Div.* was quiet as well. On the left flank, most of the *2. Armee* had managed to successfully get across the Bug, though the 28th, 65th, and 48th Armies pursued *Gen.Oberst* Weiss's troops closely in hopes of securing their own bridgehead before the German defenses could be consolidated.

Inside the city of Warsaw itself, the German response to the uprising was in full swing; though this no longer influenced the fighting across the Vistula to any serious degree. Supplies and reinforcements could now travel freely across the main avenues crisscrossing the northern part of the city and over the Vistula bridges, due to the efforts of *Gruppe von dem Bach* to brutally force the Polish Home Army back into the central core of the city, where fighting had intensified. Also on 21 August, the evacuation of the entire civilian population from Praga was begun in order to convert the Warsaw suburb into a defensive bastion and avert unnecessary civilian casualties. The continuing diversion of the *Wiking* Division's *flak* battalion towards the defense of the Vistula bridges and the ad hoc *Panzergruppe* from the *Totenkopf* Division was being felt however, because these precious assets were being denied these divisions at their greatest hour of need. The large supply depots maintained by the *Waffen-SS* inside the city had been plundered by the Polish insurgents, which meant that spare uniforms, boots, and other items of equipment would not be readily available to replace what was being worn out in the fighting and would have to be shipped directly from Germany instead, further extending the delay.

That evening in his daily summary to *H.Gr. Mitte*, von Vormann expressed his hope that the ongoing defensive battles would soon turn into a battlefield success. Despite several close calls, Gille's corps had prevented any major breakthroughs and the neighboring *2. Armee* had been able to successfully get across the Bug without any serious losses, thus guaranteeing the security of *9. Armee*'s left flank. While German losses had been high, Soviet casualties had been far greater during the past four days of fighting. Additionally, the Soviet's Magnuszew bridgehead had been successfully contained though not destroyed by the *VIII. Armeekorps* and *XLVI. Pz.Korps*, whose *Fs.Pz.Div. Hermann Göring* and *19. Panzer* Division launched furious counterattacks that almost drove the troops from General Chuikov's 8th

Guards Army into the Vistula. It also appeared that the Warsaw Uprising was not going to succeed, thanks to unrelenting pressure being placed on General Bór's ragtag forces by *Gruppe von dem Bach*.

Aware that Gille's corps was nearing its breaking point, von Vormann authorized the transfer of yet another infantry unit, *Grenadier Regiment 1145*—also known as *Grenadier-Regiment Ostpreussen 4*—to temporarily support the *Wiking* Division by taking over a portion of the front line, which would allow the *Germania* Regiment to be pulled out of the line for a few days so it could absorb replacements. This transfer would not occur until 26 August at the earliest, however. *Grenadier Regiment 1145* was the last reserve that the *9. Armee* commander had, and even this regiment had to be taken from the forces manning the outer encircling ring around Warsaw that had sealed off the uprising. By this point, the *9. Armee* commander's biggest worry was his army's high casualty rate and its inability to fill the gaps in the ranks of its combat divisions due to the *Ersatzheer*'s slow delivery of replacement personnel. Since being recommitted to battle at the end of July, *9. Armee* had suffered 17,000 casualties in all categories and had received only 700 individual replacements from the *Ersatzheer* in return. At this rate, von Vormann informed *H.Gr. Mitte*, he would soon be unable to hold unless his army was substantially reinforced.[48]

Tuesday, 22 August 1944 dawned with an unexpected lull in the fighting, with *IV. SS-Pz.Korps* reporting no ground combat overnight worth mentioning, with the exception of the ever-active Red Air Force, which had yet to see a decrease in the number of missions being flown.[49] This brief pause was not to last. Throughout the afternoon, Gille reported an increasing number of tank-supported battalion-sized attacks along his front between Klembów and Słopsk, provoking responses from both the *Wiking* and the *Totenkopf* Divisions. Most of these attacks were driven off, with the exception of those launched against Małopole and Dabrówka, which fell for the first time to the 152nd Rifle Division after heavy fighting.

By late afternoon, these towns were temporarily retaken by counterattacking German forces, while division and corps artillery dispersed two Soviet regiment-sized assembly areas east and southeast of Klembów. Another attack to the north from Trojany, which had finally been taken by Soviet forces after the *Germania* Regiment withdrew, attempted to hit the *Westland* Regiment and *Gren.Brig. 1131* from behind before finally being stopped by artillery fire. Overall, the withdrawal to the new defense line on 22 August proceeded on schedule. That evening, the now-consolidated *Westland* Regiment withdrew from its positions at Słopsk, having been replaced, temporarily at least, by *Oberst* Söth's *Gren.Brig. 1131*. After four days of heavy fighting, the *Westland* Regiment's *Kampfstärke* had sunk to a mere 150 men, roughly 10 percent of its authorized front-line strength.[50]

That evening, in recognition of his corps' performance during the fighting from 18–21 August, Gille singled out the *Totenkopf* Division for special praise for having destroyed 51 Soviet tanks and shooting down four aircraft during that four-day period. He wrote:

> Under the most extreme of circumstances the Division, which had to use all of its available strength, including using clerks and truck drivers, was able to smash all of the enemy's attacks, often by carrying out bitterly-fought counterattacks. This great defensive victory is directly attributable to the service of its magnificent leadership, their hard-nosed energy, and the actions of *SS-Oberführer* Becker. [He] could always be found at each crisis point during the battle, where his unshakeable calm, power of personality and personal bravery served as a shining example for his men.[51]

Gille went on to personally congratulate six infantrymen of the *Totenkopf* Division for earning the 3rd Grade of the *Nahkampfspange* (infantry close combat award) in Gold for having participated in over 50 days of close combat, including hand-to-hand fighting, during the past two months. This award was rarely given, as few soldiers lived long enough to receive it.

Though 23 August began with yet another attack against *IV. SS-Pz.Korps'* far left flank at Słopsk, attacks elsewhere had considerably diminished. The *9. Armee*'s staff noticed that afternoon that the Soviet offensive was beginning to show signs of running out of steam, including their efforts to break out of the Magnusziew and Puławy bridgeheads, though the Warsaw Uprising showed no immediate signs of ending.[52] During the past four days of undiminished fighting, Rokossovsky's First Belorussian Front had made impressive gains but still had not achieved the operational breakthrough that he had sought. Furthermore, his troops were becoming exhausted and were on the verge of outrunning their supply lines.

While Rokossovsky's forces had pushed Weiss's *2. Armee* back over the Bug by 22 August and had liberated sizeable swaths of Polish countryside, his armies, corps, and divisions had suffered at least twice as many casualties as the Germans had, based on prisoner of war interrogations. The losses in armored vehicles had been high, with *9. Armee* counting 249 Red Army tanks destroyed in its area of operations alone during the past four days. However, the 47th, 70th, and 28th Armies and the VIII Guards Tank Corps could take comfort in the serious losses that they had inflicted upon the two SS divisions of Gille's corps.[53] For the next day, there would be an operational pause across most of the First Belorussian Front, as its units rearmed and replenished their supplies, reorganized their scattered battalions, and got some rest.

If the Soviet offensive was running out of steam on 23 August, the men of the *Wiking* Division would not have noticed. German intelligence detected that a portion of the 28th Army had been shifted several kilometers to the south to assist the depleted 70th Army, including three newly identified divisions attacking *Staf.* Mühlenkamp's division alone.[54] Fighting raged undiminished all day along the line between the division's new right flank at Woła and left flank along the Bug at Słopsk. Once again, battalion-sized attacks of 200–400 men were beaten back by a combination of German corps and division artillery, along with the support of individual tanks from *SS-Pz.Rgt. 5* that often determined the outcome of the numerous company-size engagements that took place that day.

Most of the Soviet attempts at penetrating the main defense line in the division's center were cut off and wiped out, including the destruction of five of their tanks. Yet despite the supreme efforts of the troops to hold their ground, it was becoming obvious to both Mühlenkamp and Gille that the *Germania* Regiment, even after some of its battalions had been given a two-day rest period, would not be able to defend the area between Małopole and Dabrówka much longer. It had grown too weak, though its front-line strength was still nearly twice that of its sister regiment. After changing hands several times, both towns were finally given up late in the afternoon and the *Wiking* Division's front line pulled back several kilometers to the west.[55]

That evening, throughout most of *9. Armee*'s defensive sector, including the areas held by *VIII. Armeekorps* and the *IV. SS-Panzerkorps*, no fighting worth mentioning was reported. For once, Gille's troops finally received a respite, while the divisions of the *XLVI. Pz.Korps*, the southernmost unit in *9. Armee*'s sector, experienced the bulk of the Red Army's attention, as did the units of *Gruppe von dem Bach*, which were battling the Warsaw Uprising with increased ferocity. As the morning of 24 August turned into early afternoon, the *Wiking* Division reported that the only combat activity occurring that day worth mentioning was an attempt by two Soviet infantry companies to punch through south of Slopsk, but the defending troops of *Gren.Brig. 1131* killed many of them and drove the remainder back to their starting point. Everywhere else on Gille's front was comparatively quiet; even the *Totenkopf* Division was able to gain a measure of breathing space from the constant pounding it had received. The Hungarian cavalry division had yet to be tested and the *73. Inf. Div.* reported all quiet as well.

Gille's headquarters ordered the *Wiking* Division on 24 August to withdraw the *II. Abt./SS-Pz.Rgt. 5* from the front lines to rest, repair as many of its tanks as it could, and prepare for its upcoming mission as the corps reserve. By this point, it only had 10 operational *Pz. V* Panthers available; during the next two days, six more would be made operational, though two dozen others were idled for additional repairs or lack of sufficient spare parts.[56] The tank regiment's *I. Abteilung*, with just seven available *Pz. IV* and four *StuG IV*, was kept in the front line to bolster the infantry and supported the abovementioned successful defensive action by *Gren.Brig. 1131* between Słopsk and Dabrówka with their guns. The return of *1.* and *2. Kompanie* of *SS-Pz.Jag.Abt. 5* gave the division a badly needed boost to its overall armored fighting vehicles numbers; nearly half of the division's total consisted of *Jagdpz.IV/70* tank destroyers. That evening, things had quietened down so much that Mühlenkamp himself visited *6. Kp./SS-Pz. Rgt. 5* at 6 p.m. in its assembly area to award the Knight's Cross to *SS-Ustuf.* Grossrock for his previous acts of valor.[57] Grossrock, still suffering from the burns he received five days earlier, soon recovered sufficiently to return to action.

That day, von Vormann complemented the performance of the *IV. SS-Pz.Korps* in a message that was sent out to Gille and his troops. Issued at 9:35 a.m., the commander of the *9. Armee* proclaimed:

> To all members of the *IV. SS-Pz.Korps*! During the hard fighting you have just endured, you have prevented the enemy from achieving his hoped-for breakthrough to Warsaw. Since 10 August 1944 under the leadership of *Gruppenführer* Gille, you have stood in battle against 1–2 field armies and part of a tank army. Grudgingly, and after having to endure heavy and bloody losses, the brave men of the *SS-Pz.Korps* have managed to push back against overwhelming Soviet masses. The main burden of the fighting has been borne by the *SS-Pz.Div. Wiking*, which at times had to fight against as many as seven divisions and parts of a tank army arrayed against it and despite these attacks, still managed to launch counterattacks of its own. Parts of the *SS-Pz.Div. Totenkopf* and grenadier regiments of the *Heer*, who also had to repel overwhelming enemy attacks directed against their own positions, were able to bring some badly needed relief to their comrades. The 111 enemy tanks that have been destroyed by the corps since 10 August offer mute testimony to the heroism displayed by numerous tank crews, antitank gun crews, *Flak* crews and the many unnamed Grenadiers, who with their *Panzerschreck* and *Panzerfaust* tore huge gaps in the ranks of the enemy's tank forces … it is with a deep sense of gratitude that I honor the memory all of those who have fallen, whose sacrifices will ensure for us the final victory. To the wounded I extend my best wishes for their speedy recovery. For your inexhaustible, brave actions during these times of great stress, in which the fighting troops and homeland are closely united in a single defensive front against the masses of our enemies, you have my special recognition. May you continue to rise to the occasion that this great war demands of us! Long live the Führer![58]

The following day, 25 August, began auspiciously, with no significant Soviet activity taking place at all during the previous evening and the early morning hours across the entire front held by the *9. Armee*, which was eerily quiet. The troops of Rokossovsky's First Belorussian Front were putting this brief operational pause to good use, since they were just as exhausted as their opponents. Supplies were brought up during this lull in the action, primarily the food, fuel, and ammunition needed for the next push. The Red Army's troops were also busily recovering and repairing battle-damaged tanks, and rearming and refueling those that were still operational, just as the Germans were doing. By the morning of 25 August, the Soviets had been able to array 152 operational tanks and assault guns against Gille's corps along the front line shared by the 70th and 47th Armies and the VIII Guards Tank Corps of the 2nd Tank Army, giving them a nearly two-to-one superiority in tanks. Of those still serviceable, the VIII Guards Tank Corps had 89, including 10 JS-IIs, 30 T-34s, and 33 lend-lease M4A2 Shermans.[59]

Meanwhile, far to the south in Rumania, the great Soviet offensive to clear the Germans and their allies from southeast Europe and the Balkans was just getting underway, with the *6.* and *8. Armee* of *H.Gr. Südukrain* (Army Group South Ukraine) receiving the lion's share of the Red Army's attention. This campaign would ultimately result in the near destruction of both armies by the end of the month when their erstwhile allies, the Rumanians and Bulgarians, went over to the Soviet side in an act of betrayal that would have widespread implications for Germany's remaining allies and leave the southern approaches to Hungary unprotected. Had they but known it, this was a foreshadowing of where the men of the *IV. SS-Pz.Korps* would soon be fighting four months hence; yet they had enough of a fight on their hands at the moment to keep their minds occupied. The Soviet offensive seemed to have paused momentarily, so the German defenders put the time to good use in fortifying their defensive positions as best they could and reorganizing as much as the situation permitted. It was the last rest they would get for five more days.

Shortly after noon on 25 August, the Soviets initiated an barrage lasting several hours that pounded the entire main defense line of Gille's corps, from Słospk in the north to the sector along the Vistula River in the south held by the *73. Inf. Div.* Most of the attention of the Soviet gunners was directed at *Gren.Brig. 1131*, which reported drumfire artillery barrages impacting upon its positions. The Red Air Force was so effective at suppressing German artillery that *IV. SS-Pz.Korps* told *9. Armee* in its midday report that its firing batteries had been completely shut down and were unable to fire any missions in support of the infantry on account of the constant and effective low-level attacks by Soviet aircraft.[60] The Germans now realized that the relative calm of the past 24 hours had been spent by their opponents in bringing forward all of the heavy artillery that had been left behind during the advance of the past week, including all the ammunition they needed to blast apart the German defensive positions. Evidently, Marshal Rokossovsky had decided to toss aside any pretense of tactical finesse and to attain his goal of gaining mastery over the Bug–Narew–Vistula triangle by simply crushing Gille's corps with overwhelming brute force.

This time Rokossovsky's forces not only continued pounding away at the positions held by the *Wiking* Division between Klembów and Słopsk, but for the first time mounted an attack against those held by the *73. Inf.Div.* and *1. ung.Kav.Div.* Up to this point, both of these divisions had been seemingly ignored by the Soviets, but on this day they began to receive unwanted attention, in the form of a battalion-sized attack northeast of Rembertów that managed to penetrate the boundary between the divisions. This attack, carried out by the 78th Rifle Division of the CXXV Rifle Corps, caused a great deal of consternation at *9. Armee* headquarters, which was relieved to hear that by nightfall the breakthrough had been cut off and most of the attacking battalion wiped out, with 150 bodies being counted before it got too dark. Another battalion-sized attack against the center of the *73. Inf.Div.* sector at Zakret was also warded off.

More serious was a large-scale attack west of Grabie Stare in the defensive sector held by the *Totenkopf* Division, which had been able to enjoy two days of relative quiet. This assault, carried out in a westerly direction by a regiment of the 328th Rifle Division, managed to penetrate 10 kilometers and nearly reached the large town of Zagościniec by 1 p.m. At that point, three armored *Kampfgruppen* from the *Totenkopf* Division attacked the base of the penetration and cut it off, wiping out the enemy force, which included eight T-34s and five assault guns. Another attack carried out at roughly the same time attempted to outflank the position at Klembów held by the *Germania* Regiment by moving along the bank of the Rzondza River north of Dobczyn, at the juncture of both the *Totenkopf* and *Wiking* Divisions' main defense lines. This attack too was cut off by another *Totenkopf* counterattack, which pushed forward so far that the defense line was temporarily moved further east.

In the *Wiking* Division's sector, a large infantry force, spearheaded by a battalion of tanks from the VIII Guards Tank Corps, broke through the division's defenses west of Małopole along a wide front. Everything the *Wiking* Division could gather together, including its division reserve, *II. Abt./SS-Pz.Rgt. 5*, was thrown into a counterattack launched from the north from the Kolakow area. This quickly developed into the largest tank battle the *Wiking* Division had fought in nearly a month. Despite the loss of 26 tanks in one battle alone on the open fields east of Guzowatka, the Soviet commander on the scene, most likely from the CXIV Rifle Corps or VIII Guards Tank Corps, continued feeding more infantry and tank units into the fight. By nightfall, the situation was still uncertain but it appeared that the *Wiking* Division would survive the night. Another body of enemy troops had forced its way through and had occupied a large wooded area west of Dabrówka by nightfall, but the division lacked the infantry to do anything about it and could only shell them with artillery fire.

Slightly to the north, *I. Bataillon* from *Gren.Brig. 1131* clung stubbornly to Hills 103 and 106, which possessed commanding views of the area, despite numerous Soviet attempts to dislodge *Oberst* Söth's men. Attempts to bypass the hill via the open ground to the north were stopped by the few remaining tanks from *3. Kp./SS-Pz.Rgt. 5*, which carried out numerous counterattacks that forced Red Army troops to keep a respectful distance. These hills had become the focus of the breakthrough attempt because they connected the German defenses between the rest of Söth's brigade's positions at Słopsk with the *Germania* Regiment fighting west of Małopole, as well as with the troops from *2. Armee* on the northern bank of the Bug. By retaining possession of these hills as well as Słopsk, his brigade had not only managed to hold its ground, but was also able to remain in visual contact with the neighboring *5. Jäg.Div.*

However, his troops could not prevent a Soviet force of undetermined size from squeezing past his defenses at Słopsk at 7 p.m. and advancing as far to the west as the eastern outskirts of the village of Dręszew, where they went to ground for the evening, having bypassed Hill 103. Söth's brigade had performed well in its first pitched battle, but had already begun to experience the debilitating effects of having to fight around the clock. Due to the dangerous Soviet penetration that had taken place to its south, in the area west of Malopole, the brigade was now positioned too far to the east in front of the rest of the corps, a development that exposed its right flank to an attack that could cut it off from the rest of Gille's troops and pin it against the Bug. As a precautionary measure, Gille ordered *Gren.Brig.1131* to fall back to an alternate position several kilometers to the rear at Ślężany that evening. Here, along a series of low hills, the brigade dug in to defend this 10-kilometer-wide stretch of ground, which included the military bridge over the Bug at Ślężany. This bridge, along with the 70-ton bridge over the Narew west of Dabrowa, were the only physical links between the inner flanks of both *9.* and *2. Armee*, and the only ones capable of bearing the weight of *panzers*. As a precaution, both had already been rigged for demolition to prevent them from falling into enemy hands.

Despite being pounded throughout the day by some of the heaviest artillery concentrations yet experienced, unprecedented attacks by the Red Air Force, and seemingly unstoppable waves of infantry and tanks, Gille's *IV. SS-Pz.Korps* had held almost everywhere, giving ground only when necessary. Nearly every breakthrough had been cut off and eliminated, with the exception of the worrisome one in the *Gren.Brig. 1131* sector and the larger one west of Małopole. Forty Soviet tanks and assault guns had been destroyed, a one-day record for *IV. SS-Pz.Korps*. Even the *73. Inf.Div.* and the Hungarian division had performed reasonably well.

But there was one inescapable fact that Gille and his army commander, von Vormann, had to face—that the *Wiking* Division had lost so many troops and tanks over the past eight days that it was doubtful whether it could hold out much longer. Had not *Gren.Brig. 1131* been marched over from the right flank and hastily shoved into the line, the division would surely have collapsed. Its destruction had clearly been one of Rokossovky's priorities, and he was very close to attaining his goal. While Mühlenkamp's' division had weathered the storm, his last grenadier regiment, the *Germania*, was at the end of its rope and needed to be completely pulled out of the line, like its sister regiment, the *Westland*, had already been. *Grenadier Regiment 1145* would not arrive until the following day; until then, the *Wiking* Division would have to do the best it could, which meant that in the meantime, its rapidly shrinking *panzer* regiment would have to carry most of the burden.

The previous evening, alarmed at the rapid deterioration of the situation on his army group's left flank, von Vormann decided to order the immediate transfer to Gille of the *19. Pz.Div.* from the *XLVI. Pz.Korps*, where it had been attempting to eliminate the Magnuszew bridgehead. The division had spent most of 25 August disengaging from its battle positions and moving via rail and highway through Warsaw to its new assembly area on the eastern side of the Vistula, but would not be available for commitment until 26 August at the earliest. Von Vormann specifically intended to commit the *19. Pz.Div.* as a complete unit to shore up the left wing of *IV. SS-Pz.Korps*' front line in the Małopole area, where a full-scale breakthrough had been barely prevented on 25 August by the exhausted *Wiking* Division; but as events showed, its units were fed into the battle as soon as they arrived. The *9.*

Armee commander had taken a calculated risk in moving the *19. Pz.Div.*, because doing so would relieve the considerable pressure being placed on the Soviet units defending the Magnuszew bridgehead.

Whether it could ride to the aid of Gille's corps to stop the Soviet offensive before it was too late, then return in time to resume its previous attack on the bridgehead, was an open question. But it was a risk that von Vormann had to take, because if Gille's troops were defeated and Rokossovsky's armies reached the confluence of the three rivers northeast of Warsaw, the consequences were too dire for him to contemplate. At the very least, the addition of *19. Pz.Div.* to the *IV.SS-Pz.Korps'* lineup would give it a fighting chance.

Although it had been involved in numerous engagements since returning to the Eastern Front the previous month, the *19. Pz.Div.* still retained a high degree of lethality. In addition to the 2,059 front-line troops in its two *Panzergrenadier* regiments, its *Panzer-Aufklärungs Abteilung*, and *Pionier Bataillon*, the division still counted 50 operational *panzers* and eight antitank guns. Commanded by veteran *Gen.Maj.* Hans Källner, it had fought very well during the battle of Praga and the several attempts to wipe out the Magnuszew bridgehead. Its first units began moving at 4 p.m. on 25 August; once the division had arrived, it would be placed under the operational control of the *IV. SS-Pz.Korps* no later than the afternoon of the following day. Subunits of the division, such as the aforementioned *Panzergrenadier* regiments, would be fed into the battle as soon as they arrived, while it would take nearly two days for the division headquarters to displace.

But Gille's troops still had to survive 26 August, a hot and humid day that witnessed no cessation of Soviet attacks but rather their intensification. Gille's morning report stated as much, especially in the Małopole area, where fighting would reach its climax later that day.[61] Again, the day dawned with powerful Soviet artillery concentrations being placed on key German positions, immediately followed by two intensive strafing and bombing attacks by the Red Air Force, making it very difficult for his divisions to move along the roads crisscrossing the area. The *Totenkopf* Division found itself under attack again between Grabie Stare and Woła, as the CXXIX and XCVI Rifle Corps, supported by a brigade from the VIII Guards Tank Corps, launched numerous battalion-sized assaults focused primarily on the boundary between the *Totenkopf* and *Wiking* Divisions. With great difficulty, *Obf.* Becker's troops were able to repel most of these attacks, some of which required tank-led counterattacks, but a penetration at Dobczyn in the center of the line could not be "ironed out," forcing the battalion from the *Eicke* Regiment holding that position to pull back several kilometers. Besides preventing a breakthrough, his division was still able to maintain a tenuous contact with the *Wiking* Division's decimated *Germania* Regiment on its left flank. His division also destroyed 10 Soviet tanks that day, though he was forced to bend his left flank back so that it faced to the northeast.[62]

In the *Wiking* Division's sector, attacks continued throughout the day on 26 August, with the 48th and 76th Guard Rifle Divisions pushing ever deeper. Backed up by a tank brigade from the VIII Guards Tank Corps, the attackers managed to advance across the open farmland between Małopole and Kolakow by 5:55 p.m., with one battalion managing to get as far as the forest at Cisie before they halted and dug in. The *Germania* Regiment, now only a remnant with 224 front-line troops left in its three battalions, had to give way, pulling back to the south to prevent encirclement. The timely arrival that afternoon of the bulk of two mechanized infantry regiments from the *19. Pz.Div.—Pz.Gren.Rgt. 73* and *74*—with the aid of *II. Abt./SS-Pz.Rgt. 5*, enabled Gille to order an immediate counterattack that blunted the Soviet drive and destroyed five tanks by nightfall. But the most dangerous development that day was the unexpected advance by elements of the CXIV Rifle Corps, most likely by the 20th Rifle Division supported by at least a tank company, which managed to reach the Bug River by Kuligów late that afternoon.[63] With this move, the left flank of the *Wiking* Division, which consisted of *Gren.Brig. 1131* and *I. Abt./SS-Pz.Rgt. 5*, was cut off from the rest of the division, with the 25-ton capacity bridge over the Bug at Ślężany as their only way out.

The stage was set for one of the largest loss of tanks in one battle that *SS-Pz.Rgt. 5* had ever experienced. With Soviet troops now positioned along the Bug between *Gren. Brig. 1131* and the rest of the *Wiking* Division, von Vormann declared that Ślężany was now a "bridgehead" that had to be held in order to retain contact between his army and Weiss's *2. Armee*. The threatened far right flank of *2. Armee* now lay over 15 kilometers west of the *5. Jäg.Div.* right flank at Jackowo. To prevent an enemy crossing of the Bug in the rear of that division, which would have been disastrous, *XX. Armeekorps,* to which *5. Jäg.Div.* still belonged, rushed various *Alarm-* and *Trosseinheiten* to take up hasty defensive positions along the northern bank of the Bug to keep an eye on the Red Army troops and ensure they did not attempt a river crossing.[64]

Though Soviet troops had seized Kuligów, they could not continue their drive west with such a strong tank-supported German force still operating in their rear area. The Red Army commander on the scene therefore decided to attack the Ślężany bridgehead with a tank and infantry force via the approach that led through the neighboring town of Czarnów, while the rest of his force (an infantry regiment with an attached tank company) waited in Kuligów. As Soviet tanks approached Ślężany from the west, their artillery pounded the town and surrounding areas. A lucky hit on the bridge set off the demolition charge, causing most of the central portion of the bridge to collapse into the water. There was no other bridge or fording location within the bridgehead, which left *Oberst* Söth and the commander of *I. Abt./SS-Pz. Rgt. 5, Haupsturmfüherer* Säumenicht, few options. Fortunately, defensive fire from *Gren.Brig. 1131* and the *panzers* drove the attackers back to village of Czarnów 2 kilometers west of Ślężany, where the Soviet troops dug in and quickly established a *Pakfront* (integrated anti-tank gun defense) supported by four M-4 Shermans.[65]

The *Wiking*'s headquarters, notified by radio of the situation, then contacted Gille at corps headquarters. He then urged the battalion commander on the scene to take offensive action, but with no way to cross the Bug at Ślężany, *Hstuf.* Säumenicht had two choices: blow up his tanks and order his crewmen to cross the Bug atop the ruined bridge, or strike out to the west with his battalion and fight his way through Czarnów and Kuligów to the new *Wiking* Division defensive line being erected east of Serock, a distance of perhaps 15–20 kilometers, where the 70-ton bridge was still intact across the Narew west of Dabrowo. He chose the latter course of action.[66]

Säumenicht still had eight operational *Pz. IV* and four *Sturmgeschütze.* He initiated his attack without any artillery preparation at 1:30 p.m., thinking that perhaps he stood a fighting chance of getting through. He was wrong. During the approach to Czarnów, two of the *StuG IV*s from his *4. Kompanie,* which were positioned on the right, became bogged down in the swamp less than 500 meters from the town. With no recovery vehicles available, the crews abandoned them and blew them up. The attack by the rest of the battalion fared just as poorly. The terrain along the avenue of approach was deemed "totally unsuitable for *panzers,*" with no cover whatsoever. The Soviet *Pakfront* erected on the eastern edge of the town started placing accurate fire upon Säumenicht's tanks as soon as they got within range. To make matters worse, they had been joined by five JS-IIs later that morning, which added to the already formidable Soviet defensive firepower.[67]

The lead tank in the attacking wedge, commanded by the battalion chief himself, came under withering small-arms and antitank-gun fire as it negotiated the boggy ground. At 2 p.m., Säumenicht was shot in the head by a sniper, killing him instantly. Command of the nine remaining tanks and assault guns from the battalion devolved to *Ostuf.* Senghas, acting commander of *3. Kompanie,* who ordered an immediate retreat to Ślężany. Upon their return to their jump-off positions, he and his remaining men discovered that repairs had not been made to the damaged bridge, rendering any attempt to save his vehicles moot. After covering the withdrawal of the rest of Söth's brigade over the river, Senghas ordered the destruction of the remaining tanks after they had shot off all of their 7.5cm shells. Once they had removed each vehicle's machine guns and small arms ammunition to take with them, the remaining crewmen of *I. Abt./SS-Pz.Rgt. 5* blew them up with explosive charges. They then made their way across the shattered bridge on foot, where they joined the other *Wiking* Division survivors on the other side at Jackowo. Senghas was the last man to cross to safety, after ensuring there was no one left in the town. The remnant of the bridge was then destroyed. For the next several days at least, the battalion would cease to exist as an operational entity.[68]

The *Wiking* Division's commander ordered an investigation into Senghas's conduct during the incident, since the loss of one of his division's two tank battalions was a serious matter. Senghas was ordered to personally report to *Staf.* Mühlenkamp to explain in detail what had occurred. Fortunately, his actions were defended by the senior commander on the scene, Söth, commander of *Gren.Brig. 1131*. In his report about the incident, he wrote:

> The withdrawal movement was magnificently supported by the tank battalion of *SS-Hstuf.* Säumenicht. The coordination with the battalion could be characterized as exemplary on the preceding days as well. In my opinion, the tanks crews did not want to leave the hard-pressed grenadiers until every last one of them had crossed and then, after the last round had been fired, blew up the vehicles to prevent them from falling into the hands of the enemy. A withdrawal towards [my] *1. Bataillon* might have possibly saved the tanks, but strong pressure by a superior enemy would have caused heavy casualties to the infantry. Therefore I absolve the tanks crews, whom I had come to know as unflappable warriors, of any question of guilt.[69]

No charges were brought against Senghas, as the evidence proved beyond a doubt that both he and his battalion commander had done everything that could have been expected, and in fact had done far more than what was deemed possible in the face of overwhelming odds. The two remaining operational tanks and a single assault gun of the battalion, all located at the new headquarters at Serock, were reinforced by three Panthers from *II. Abteilung* and were hurried north through the town and over the bridge at Popovo to secure the northern bank of the Bug and assist the various emergency units from *XX. Armeekorps.*[70] Here, for a few days at least, they would prevent the Soviets from effecting a crossing until a more solid front could be established.

In *Hstuf.* Rudolf Säumenicht, the battalion had lost a leader whom they respected and admired. Wearing the Knight's Cross he had earned while commanding a company in the *Totenkopf* Division's tank regiment, he had led his men from the front and never shied away from a difficult assignment. According to one survivor of this engagement, "he was a leader the likes of which we'll never see again." Everyone in the battalion was affected by his death; as a measure of the esteem in which his men held him, his body was brought back across the river, where he received a burial with full military honors on 28 August at the division cemetery rapidly being established in the old citadel in the fortress at Modlin. Temporary command of what was left of the battalion, which amounted to three patched-up tanks from *3. Kompanie* and seven assault guns from *4. Kompanie*, devolved to *Ostuf.* Schumacher, whose task now was to gather the remaining crews and see to it that the vehicles still under repair in the regiment's workshop at Serock were placed back into operation as soon as possible.[71] It would mark the first time in over a week that the men had had any opportunity to rest. Meanwhile, back at the SS training area at Łódź (Litzmannstadt), the battalion's remaining *1.* and *2. Kompanie*, still awaiting delivery of their promised vehicles, were placed on alert for possible commitment.

That evening, *Gen.d.Pz.Tr.* von Vormann, taking stock of his situation, realized that any further attempts to restore and hold the line Woła–Małopole–Dabrówka–Słopsk were doomed to fail. Consequently, he requested and received permission from *H.Gr.*

Mitte headquarters to pull *IV. SS-Pz.Korps* behind the Rzadza River, the last major natural obstacle between Rokossovsky's forces and the Narew River.[72] This withdrawal would primarily impact the *Totenkopf* Division, which would have to abandon Woła, Grabie Stare, and Klembów, towns that its troops had stoutly defended for nearly a week. Now *Obf.* Becker's troops would have to withdraw under enemy pressure to unprepared defensive positions, which would require *SS-Pz.Rgt. 3* to keep the enemy at bay to buy time for the infantry to march 10 kilometers to the west that evening. Although the situation in the center of Gille's corps was serious, the situation along the Bug west of Słopsk concerned von Vormann far more, especially given the loss of Säumenicht and the bulk of his tank battalion and the continuing concentration of Soviet forces between that town and Kuligów. Should the 20th or 160th Rifle Divisions establish bridgeheads across the Bug at that location, the situation would become most unfavorable indeed.

The attack that afternoon by the two *Panzergrenadier* regiments of the *19. Pz.Div.* had made good headway, but without their division headquarters to direct them (they had been temporarily attached to the *Wiking* Division until it arrived) as well as the lack of the division's *Panzer* regiment which was still enroute, the main effort to cut off and destroy the Soviet units holding Kuligów would have to wait until the following day. Fortunately, little pressure had been brought against Gille's right flank, where the *73. Inf.Div.* and *1. ung.Kav.Div.* had remained relatively unmolested, except for an attack against the Hungarian division by an infantry battalion supported by a tank platoon that was easily warded off, with the division's antitank battalion claiming the destruction of two KV-1 tanks.[73]

Another of the *9. Armee* commander's concerns was the slow delivery of ammunition; having to fight three major battles simultaneously (in Warsaw, east of Warsaw, and at Magnuszew) had put an incredible demand on munitions of all types. That evening, he asked *Generaloberst* Reinhardt at *H.Gr. Mitte* to expedite deliveries to ensure that his troops got everything they needed. In the meantime, they would have to fight it out as best they could. Reinhardt had his own concerns about the developing situation and gave Weiss permission to pull his *2. Armee*, von Vormann's northern neighbor, behind the Narew River, should the Bug defense line prove untenable. It had already been penetrated in several places, but Weiss was worried most about his far right flank at Jackowo along the Bug. Should the divisions of the CXIV Rifle Corps manage to cross the river at that point or at Kuligów, it would greatly complicate any plans to withdraw to the Narew. Fortunately, the Soviets would not attempt to cross the Bug until 2 September, which gave the defenders nearly a week to improve and sharpen their defenses.

As predicted, 27 August would be a critical day. Gille reported at 7 a.m. that although the displacement of the *Totenkopf* Division the previous evening to its new positions along the Rzadza had gone according to plan, Becker's troops had been pursued very closely as they abandoned their old positions.[74] The division's

Panzer regiment had been forced to intervene in numerous instances and fight without infantry support. The corps commander's greatest worry that morning was three battalion-sized attacks launched against both flanks of the Hungarian cavalry division, near its left flank at Lipiny east of Wołomin, along the boundary between it and the *Totenkopf* Division, and against the town of Ossów, where its right flank linked up with the *73. Inf.Div.*[75] The Soviet CXXV Rifle Corps of 47th Army was clearly seeking a weak point in the German line; although it had forced the *Totenkopf* Division to pull back, that division had proved to be an exceedingly tough nut to crack. Perhaps the Hungarians would be easier. But despite Gille's fears, the Hungarians reportedly fought well that day. Not only did their headquarters state that they had managed to ward off two Soviet attacks, they also claimed to have cut off and destroyed the other battalion with the assistance of the *Totenkopf* Division.

The situation in the center of *IV. SS-Pz.Korps* remained tense. The renewed counterattack towards Kuligów by *Pz.Gren.Rgt. 73* and *74*, supported by *SS-Pz.Rgt. 5*, made little headway in the face of continuing Soviet attacks against their right flank, which forced them to face to the east and fight them off. Red Army troops from the XCVI Rifle Corps had closed up along the Rzadza River between Los and Dybów during the evening and were already seeking a crossing site, but found the *Totenkopf* Division waiting for them. A large concentration of Soviet armor was reported east of the village of Zawady by *Totenkopf* troops holding Mokre Stare, where a bridge over the Rzadza had once stood, but there were no German forces available to counterattack. Instead, the decision was made to disperse this enemy grouping with artillery fire, since no other forces were available, including the *Luftwaffe*'s ground attack fleet. On his far left flank along the Bug, Gille reported that his corps no longer had any firm contact with the neighboring *2. Armee*.[76] This was understandable, given that *2. Armee*'s southernmost division, the *5. Jag.Div.*, was in the process of preparing to withdraw to the Narew.

A favorable development that day was the noticeable lessening of the Red Air Force's activity. Rather than being subjected to intensive air attacks as they had been for the past week, the Germans were content instead to watch Soviet aircraft carrying out reconnaissance activity. Artillery fire had also slackened, but in this case, it was an ominous sign that meant that the 47th, 70th, and 28th Armies and the VIII Guards Tank Corps were moving up their artillery regiments and brigades closer to the ever-advancing front line of troops. That evening, in his last report of the day to *H.Gr. Mitte*, von Vormann described his greatest concern with regard to the *IV. SS-Pz.Korps* as being the continued Soviet buildup northeast of Radzymin, which Gille's troops had been unable to prevent. The most dangerous enemy course of action, in his opinion, was a thrust from this region northwest towards Serock that would split Gille's corps into two pieces, followed by a crossing of the Narew at that location that would compromise the right flank of the *Ostpreussenschutzstellung*

(East Prussian Defensive Position) and the defensive works being erected by the *9. Armee* along the confluence of the Bug and Narew Rivers.[77]

That night, the weekly tallying of the strength of his army's constituent elements was carried out by his operations section. The information derived from this exercise would provide von Vormann with an indication of the capabilities of his force, which in turn would guide his staff's development of future operations and contingency plans. Each corps headquarters, of course, would carry out a similar process. All three corps reported their statistics, which focused primarily on available infantry and armor strength. On paper, *Oberst* Hähling's *73. Inf.Div.* was the strongest, with 2,248 men and 46 medium and heavy antitank guns (but no armor). The next largest was the *Totenkopf* Division, with 2,017 men (including 500 men from its recently arrived *Feld-Ersatz-Bataillon*), 70 operational tanks and assault guns (including six *Pz. VI* Tigers), and 15 antitank guns.[78]

In third place was what Gille considered his least-reliable division, the *1. ung. Kav.Div.*, with 1,500 men in its six infantry battalions, 14 antitank guns, and four assault guns attached from the *Totenkopf* Division. Another regiment was on the way to join it, but would not arrive until the end of the month. The still-arriving *19. Pz.Div.*, whose tank regiment, *Pz.Rgt. 27*, had been directed to remain with the forces attempting to destroy the Magnuszew bridgehead, fielded 1,353 men, with 706 more still fighting at Magnuszew but scheduled to rejoin the division as soon as they could be relieved. In last place was the *Wiking* Division, with a *Kampfstärke* of only 650 men, 31 operational tanks, tank destroyers, and assault guns, and 11 antitank guns. However, to this number was added the front-line strength of 207 men from Söth's much-reduced *Gren.Brig. 1131* and 186 men from the just-arriving *Gren.Rgt. 1145* (also known as *Gren.Rgt. 4 "Ostpreussen"*), giving the *Wiking* Division a total of 1,043 men.[79] This number was deceptive, in that the *Westland* Regiment had not yet returned to the front lines, having spent the past several days reconsolidating and incorporating replacements into its shattered ranks at an assembly area near Zegrze (on that date, its fighting strength had increased to 293 men). It would soon be placed back into the line, as would the newly arriving *SS-Pz.Aufkl.Abt. 5* fresh from the training area at Debiča (less one company without vehicles), but in the meantime the *Wiking* Division would have to make the best of its situation.

All told, Gille's corps fielded 8,161 front-line troops, 105 operational armored fighting vehicles, and 71 antitank guns. While this might have sounded impressive on paper, in reality this force was far too weak to defend a front line that stretched nearly 50 kilometers from the Vistula at Praga to the Bug at Kuligów. His divisions faced the bulk of two Soviet field armies (the 47th and 70th), part of another (the 28th), and significant portions of the 2nd Tank Army (all of the VIII Guards Tank Corps) and part of the IX Tank Corps, amounting to at least 21 rifle divisions organized into seven rifle corps.[80] While all of these units had suffered casualties approaching 50 percent during the past month, including men lost during the battle of Praga, the portion of Rokossovsky's First Belorussian Front arrayed against Gille's corps still outnumbered it by a factor of three-to-one. This did not include the overwhelming amount of artillery and rocket batteries, which enjoyed a nearly 10-to-one advantage over that of the Germans, or tanks and assault guns, which still numbered at least 200. The 1st Polish Army had remained mostly quiescent during this time, a period of inactivity that would soon come to an end to the Germans' discomfort during the next phase of the Soviet offensive.

Astonishingly, the night of 27–28 August passed without any combat worth mentioning, not only in Gille's corps, but throughout the entire *9. Armee* front.[81] With the exception of the ongoing fighting in the Polish capital, which showed no signs of lessening, even Soviet artillery fire had slackened to the point where the night watch officer at the army headquarters operational section could write the next morning that the night passed quietly. Of course, for the average *Landser* or *Frontovnik* on the front lines, life was anything but quiet, with rifle, mortar, and machine-gun fire serving as constant background music, but with the exception of infantry patrols and troop repositioning, it was almost peaceful.

Most of the activity that day mirrored that of the previous evening, with the exception of the area east of Lipiny on the *Totenkopf* Division's front, where several Soviet tanks with mounted infantry attempted to attack forward outposts on the right flank of the division, but were driven off with little difficulty by Becker's troops, who reported destroying one tank. It was revealed during the day that the report submitted by the Hungarian division the previous evening had been incorrect; the Hungarians, in fact, had not conducted successful counterattacks as stated, but rather the Soviet penetrations had been "ironed out" entirely by a counterattack launched by three assault guns of the *Sturmgeschütz Abteilung* from the neighboring *Totenkopf* Division.[82] Such misreporting did not increase the Germans' confidence in their erstwhile ally, a trust that had never been great in the first place. When *9. Armee* headquarters suggested to Gille that he should allow the Hungarian division to increase the width of its division sector to enable the *Totenkopf* Division to free up some of its own forces, Gille stated in strong terms that this proposal was unworkable, as the Hungarians, if pushed hard, would quickly collapse and jeopardize the flanks of its neighboring divisions. These misgivings would only increase as the campaign continued.

Tuesday, 29 August was a hot and sultry day, partly cloudy with isolated downpours. The morning began much more violently that the previous day's, with the action unfolding at 2:30 a.m. Gille's headquarters reported to *9. Armee* at 6:55 a.m. that, "The enemy has attacked in unknown strength on both sides of Dybów [on the west bank of the Rzadza River in the Totenkopf's sector] and carried out two breakthroughs of the main defense line; countermeasures are now in progress."[83] This massive infantry assault was preceded by powerful artillery preparatory fires than ranged up and down the river line from the southeast near Dybów to the northwest at Ruda, a span of nearly 25 kilometers, striking both the *Totenkopf* and *Wiking* Division defensive sectors. In hard and difficult fighting, characterized by varying degrees of success, Soviet units managed to force their way through the defensive position at Dybów, which changed hands several times, and pushed back the left wing of the *Totenkopf* division, held by the *Eicke* Regiment, several kilometers.[84]

At the Ruda defensive sector, held by *Pz.Gren.Rgt. 73* of the *19. Pz.Div.* and a small *Kampfgruppe* from the *Germania* Regiment, Soviet troops from the 1st and 413th Rifle Divisions of the CXIV Rifle Corps crossed the river in broad daylight and assaulted the defense line with overwhelming force, driving the German defenders out of the town before they were finally halted a kilometer past its western outskirts. The attackers quickly secured a crossing over the river at Mokre and began fording tanks across, which immediately resumed their advance while still trailing water and pushed as far forward as the large forest southwest of the town. Soviet airpower once again reasserted itself, with Il-2 *Sturmovik* and Yak ground-attack aircraft hindering German attempts to launch counterattacks. The Rzadza defensive line had only held them back for two days.

The *Wiking* Division launched a large-scale counterattack at 3 p.m. using *Pz.Gren. Rgt. 73* and *74* and the *Germania* Regiment, supported by 20 tanks from *SS-Pz. Rgt. 5*, and forced the Soviet troops back about a kilometer with the aid of a strong artillery barrage. Continuing the previously planned attack to the north towards Kuligów was forgotten; the breakthrough at Dybów was far more dangerous. While the *Totenkopf* Division held grimly to the area between Dybów and Zjawisko north of Radzymin, Mühlenkamp's attack continued moving forward, rapidly driving eastwards through the town of Benjaminów before they finally halted outside the of the town of Los on the western bank of the Rzadza. An attempt by Soviet armored forces to encircle a portion of the *Totenkopf* Division's position at Kraszew along the Rzadza was driven off later that afternoon by determined tank and artillery fire. Five Soviet tanks were destroyed that day by the *Totenkopf*'s *panzer* regiment.[85]

By this point, in the center of the corps' line, no solid German front existed anymore. Rather, in his evening report to *9. Armee*, Gille reported that the front line between Radzymin and Ruda now consisted of a series of thinly spread strongpoints organized in a "security line" whose main strength lay in supporting artillery and armored forces to launch counterattacks. Both sides had fought each other to a standstill, for a few hours anyway. The Soviets had managed by the end of the day to push a substantial amount of forces across the Rzadza, a move that anyone could see would render the further defense of Radzymin pointless. To continue holding it made it extremely vulnerable to encirclement, no matter how well the *Totenkopf* Division fought. One unusual highlight of the day was a claim that the Soviets had dropped 40–50 paratroopers in the woods east of Załubice, which was duly reported, but the *Wiking* Division had no men available to determine their purpose, since every able-bodied soldier was holding the main defense line.[86]

Wednesday, 30 August was recorded as the last day of the first defensive battle of Warsaw. Though the rest of *9. Armee*'s front was reported as quiet throughout the night of 29–30 August, the *Totenkopf* Division was forced to endure unrelenting attacks along its entire division front. Though none of these succeeded, on the division's left flank several Soviet tanks managed to break through northeast of Aleksandrów, 5 kilometers due west of Radzymin, but all were knocked out before they could enter the latter town. This development sent shock waves throughout the division, and fears of encirclement grew. One member of the *Totenkopf* Division who was present at the scene of the fighting at Radzymin from 28–30 August was *Oscha.* Martin Steiger, a platoon leader in *1. Kp./SS-Pz.Rgt. 3*. After the war he recalled:

> During the same night [28 August] we moved out to secure the wooded area near the fork in the road from Radzymin to Wola. The next day Russian tanks attacked us. All of them were knocked out by us at 200 meters away. Then, Commander Meierdress [*I. Abteilung*] called us back to Radzymin to take over securing the rear for two days. But another tank alert came from the front. Russian tanks were preparing for an attack from Guzowatka. We advanced … without having seen any enemy tanks. Instead, we were welcomed by strong defensive fire, during which our comrade Hans Baumeister was killed in the loader's hatch by a shell fragment … For two days we secured the exit of the city of Radzymin. Then came an urgent alert from the neighboring *Wiking* Division on our left. The enemy had broken through in its sector.[87]

As mentioned in Steiger's account, on *IV. SS-Pz.Korps*' left flank, the *Wiking* Division had to give up the town of Borki, which fell to the 76th Guards Rifle Division during the night.[88] During the past 12 hours, *Pz.Gren.Rgt. 73* of the *19. Pz.Div.* had shuffled over to the left flank of the *Wiking* Division to take over the sector next to *Gren.Brig. 1131*, which still defended adjacent to the Bug west of Kuligów. Nothing worth reporting occurred overnight in the *73. Inf.Div.* and Hungarian cavalry division's sector between Wołomin and the Vistula.

As the day lengthened, it became apparent that the Soviets were focusing their main effort against Radzymin, which fell that afternoon when the *Totenkopf* Division was ordered to abandon the town and withdraw several kilometers to the west. Although Becker's division claimed the destruction of four tanks during this battle—an indication of its ferocity—holding on to the town at the risk of losing a major portion of the *Totenkopf* no longer made any tactical sense. In his report to *9. Armee* that evening, Gille lauded the performance of "the brave SS-Grenadiers and tank crewmen" who prevented a massive Soviet breakthrough. But even the vaunted *Totenkopf* Division was showing signs of weakening, particularly in the strength of its infantry battalions, which had been fighting without pause for nearly four weeks. The armored *Kampfgruppe* from the *Wiking* Division was forced back to Benjaminów, from whence its successful counterattack had been launched the previous day, but still managed to destroy 20 Soviet tanks before they withdrew.

Unfortunately, before the *19. Pz.Div.* headquarters could be established, take back control of its regiments from the *Wiking* Division, and assume responsibility for defending the corps' left flank, events at the Magnusziew bridgehead appeared to be spinning out of control, with a Soviet breakout imminent. Finding himself now in the very situation he had sought to avoid, von Vormann had no choice but to order the division to cease its movement, turn around, and return as quickly as possible to its old positions on the west side of the Vistula.[89] This affected most of the artillery regiment and combat engineer battalion, as well as *Pz.Gren.Rgt. 74*. The division's tank regiment, *Pz.Rgt. 27*, was still at Magnusziew, having never left. Only *Pz.Gren.Rgt. 73* would stay and continue supporting the *Wiking* Division. This division would rejoin *IV. SS-Pz.Korps* the following month, but the diversion of *19. Pz.Div.* at this point in the battle was a major setback for both von Vormann and Gille, though at least the crisis in Gille's corps seemed to have been averted for the time being. The remaining regiment from the *19. Pz.Div.* soon found itself engaged with the enemy before even getting established in its new positions, for that same day it had to fight off a battalion-sized attack emanating from Borki, which had fallen to the Red Army the previous evening. If the Soviet offensive was winding down, no one in *Pz.Gren.Rgt. 73* had seen any signs of it.

For the attack that day, no less than 15 infantry battalion and 70 tanks were employed to take Radzymin, with a tremendous amount of artillery firing in support.[90] However, it was becoming apparent that both sides were nearing exhaustion. Rokossovsky's forces had suffered enormous losses in both men and tanks, but they had held the initiative throughout and had created the preconditions for continuing their offensive. A deep wedge had been driven in *IV. SS-Pz.Korps*' left flank between Radzymin and the Bug River, but during this first defensive battle of Warsaw, Gille's line, though it had bent, had not collapsed. His right flank, held by the *1. ung. Kav.Div.* and the *73. Inf.Div.*, had barely been challenged at all. Most worrying to both Gille and von Vormann was the continuing erosion of infantry strength and the growing shortage of ammunition, particularly for the 10.5cm howitzer and the *Nebelwerfer* multiple rocket launcher. Almost all ammunition stocks had been exhausted, and a fuel shortage, vital for mechanized forces, had begun to raise its ugly head.[91]

The shortage of infantrymen, who were needed to hold the line, would be partially alleviated after 31 August by the return of *Gren.Btl. z.b.V. 560*, the probationary unit commanded by *Maj.* Ritter, which had just enjoyed a two-week period of rest and reconstitution after being nearly wiped out during the battle of Praga. Another unit that had been ordered to join Gille's corps to make up for the decline of infantry strength was the attachment of *Festungs* (Fortress)*-Infanterie-Battalion (Fest.Inf.Btl.) 1405*, while *Gren.Rgt. 1145* had also arrived in its entirety. All three of these units were placed under the command of the *Wiking* Division, which had suffered the greatest number of casualties during the past two weeks. This attachment of troops from the *Heer* created for the first time a situation where most of the ground troops serving in the *Wiking* Division were not members of the *Waffen-SS*.[92]

At the end of the month, Gille ordered his division commanders to submit their regular status report, which would provide him with far more detailed knowledge about the combat capabilities of his divisions as well as each commander's assessment. They would then be forwarded to the Inspectorate of Armored Troops in Berlin, where they would be used as a guide for determining future requirements for personnel replacements, as well as the amount of armored vehicles, soft-skinned vehicles, and crew-served weapons that would have to be produced by Germany's hard-pressed industrial base. The reports for his SS armored divisions still exist, and they provide insight into the impact that the campaign had upon the *3.* and *5. SS-Panzer* Divisions from 1 August.

The *Wiking*'s report, signed 1 September, states that as of 31 August it still had 14,528 men on the rolls, though this included recruits training with its *SS-Feld-Ers.Btl. 5* and *III. Btl./Westland*, which was undergoing final stages of training at the Debiča training area. The division had also suffered 1,807 casualties in all categories since 1 August, including 316 killed in action and 180 missing in action. It only had four operational *Pz. IV* tanks, 19 *Pz. V* Panthers and four *Sturmgeschütze IV*. An additional 18 tanks and assault guns were in short-term repair. Just as importantly, the number of operational *Schützenpanzerwagen* armored personnel carriers had declined to 187 (out of 346 authorized), while it fielded roughly 50 percent of its authorized number of trucks. A bright spot in the report was that the division still possessed 26 antitank guns and 49 artillery pieces, though barely enough prime movers to tow them all.[93]

In the commander's portion of the report, *Staf.* Mühlenkamp's assessment of this division was far from sanguine. This was the portion that usually drew the most attention, giving the corps commander a better understanding of the status of the division because it was based on his subordinate commander's personal insight and experience. In his first paragraph, he wrote:

> The personnel situation since the most recent situation report of 15 August 1944 has considerably worsened. The reason why is because of the constant counterattacks that the division has undertaken. As a result, both *Panzergrenadier* regiments need to be completely reconstituted. Especially bad is the heavy losses suffered by junior officers and NCOs. Losses of unit commanders have been particularly hard felt. These personnel losses cannot be made good by *SS-Feldausbildungs-Bataillon 5*.
>
> The division lacks sufficient weapons and equipment. The high loss rate of weapons can be traced to the effect of daily hours-long artillery drumfire. When the division underwent reconstitution in June 1944, not all of its weapons and equipment were delivered, especially concerning motor vehicles.
>
> The division's tanks were overcommitted to compensate for the declining strength of the *Panzergrenadier* regiments. Days-long battle with strong enemy tank formations brought further losses. The division's *Panzerkampfwagen* 'Panther,' some of which were delivered in December 1943, have accumulated an average of 2,500 kilometers. There are numerous tank crews without tanks. A new issue of tanks to replace our losses is urgently required. I also want to reiterate, that

> the division still has two full-strength tank companies worth of personnel [in its *I. Batallion*] available. During the reconstitution of the division in June 1944, an insufficient number of tanks were delivered to reequip them.
>
> Two heavy batteries of *SS-Flak Abt. 5* are still employed in Warsaw supporting *SS-Kampfgruppe von dem Bach*. In consideration of the constant air attacks the division is experiencing, the return of these batteries to the division is urgently requested.
>
> In our division baggage trains, the only transport we have at hand is a single *NSKK* truck column from *Einsatzstab Speer*. Our own division baggage train is not available [note: its own *Tross* vehicles were being used to provide mobility to its *Panzergrenadier* battalions].
>
> In conclusion, the division is not suitable for offensive operations. For the defense, only *SS-Pz.Art.Rgt. 5*, *SS-Pz.Rgt. 5*, and *Pz.Jag.Abt. 5* are still capable. The [recently arrived] *SS-Pz. Aufkl.Abt. 5* is fully combat-ready, with the exception of its *1. Kompanie*, which has not been issued its equipment.[94]

Unfortunately for Mühlenkamp and the men of his division, there would be no break from the fighting, giving the *Wikinger* precious few opportunities to recover from their ordeal. Instead, they would have to continue doing what they could with the forces and weapons on hand until the end of September, when large numbers of replacements would finally arrive.

The situation with the *Totenkopf* Division was similar, though not as dire as with the *Wiking* Division. Though it had fewer men assigned as of 1 September 1944 (13,868), it had far more operational armored vehicles than the *Wiking* Division fielded. It had suffered far heavier casualties than the *Wiking* though, with 4,443 men lost, including 549 killed in action. The bulk of these casualties were incurred during the heavy fighting for Siedlce at the beginning of the month, as well as during the last five days when the Soviets began their drive to retake Radzymin. The fact that it possessed all six of its infantry battalions as well as its entire armored reconnaissance battalion meant that these rather high personnel losses were evenly apportioned throughout the division. In addition, it still had 64 operational tanks and assault guns, twice as many as the *Wiking*, including six *Pz. VI* Tigers, with an additional 46 tanks in short-term repair. It had only 40 armored half-tracks, far less than the *Wiking* Division, but boasted 42 antitank guns and 53 artillery pieces as well as its entire *Flak* battalion.[95]

The division commander's assessment was short and succinct, unlike Mühlenkamp's. Becker wrote that he rated his division as being suitable for defensive missions, while able to carry out limited offensive missions. He rated the training of his troops as good, but bemoaned that no replacements had arrived since the beginning of the month. Morale was also assessed as being good, with troops displaying a positive attitude, despite the heavy fighting they had been experiencing. With regard to personnel, he noted the shortage of infantrymen, just as Mühlenkamp had. In conclusion, he stated that his areas of greatest concern were the "very great" shortage of veteran junior officers and the fact that wounded troops, after recuperating, were seldom sent back to the front to rejoin their division.[96]

By way of comparison, the *19. Pz.Div.* had 14,030 men present for duty, out of 14,976 authorized. It had suffered 3,131 casualties in all categories, but in contrast to the *Waffen-SS panzer* divisions, which got hardly any, it had received 2,513 replacements during the same period. As a result, its *Panzergrenadier* regiments were maintained at a 75 percent strength or better. This can be traced to the *Heer*'s long-standing and well-established replacement and training system, as opposed to that of the *Waffen-SS*, which was experiencing growing pains as it expanded to twice the size it had been the year before, activating one new division after another. The *19. Pz.Div.* also had 84 operational tanks and assault guns, with 52 in short-term repair. In his commander's assessment, *Gen.Maj.* Källner rated his division as fully capable to perform any kind of mission, with a *Kampfwert* (combat value) level of I, the highest attainable.[97] Part of this can be traced to the division having been employed strictly as a mobile assault unit, not tied down in positional warfare like both of Gille's SS divisions had been. It had been a welcome, though brief, addition to the *IV. SS-Pz.Korps* order of battle.

Von Vormann had his personnel staff draw up a list of the total number of casualties suffered within his army during August, including all nine of his divisions (excluding the *1. ung.Kav.Div.*) and one separate grenadier brigade, but not *Gruppe von dem Bach*, which was considered an SS entity and not subject to von Vormann's immediate jurisdiction. All told, *9. Armee* had suffered the loss of 19,856 men from all causes (killed, wounded, missing in action, and other causes) and had received only 3,871 replacements, leaving it with a shortfall of 15,985 men. The *IV. SS-Pz. Korps* (not including *19. Pz.Div.*) had lost a total of 6,471 men, a figure that also counted casualties suffered by attached units, including *Gren.Brig. 1131*, *Gren.Rgt. 1145*, *Gren.Btl.z.b.V. 560*, and *Fest.Inf.Btl. 1405*.[98] The only replacements worth mentioning that had gone to Gille's two SS divisions had been the arrival of the *Totenkopf* Division's *Feld-Ersatz Bataillon* and most of the *Aufklärungs-Abteilung* for the *Wiking* Division, plus an additional medical company of the division's field hospital, hardly considered combat troops. The *Wiking* Division's *Flak* battalion was still serving with *Gruppe von dem Bach*, a source of considerable friction between Gille and von Vormann.

Throughout this period, while the Germans had experienced heavy casualties, the First Belorussian Front had suffered far more. In the after-action report for August 1944, Rokossovsky's command admitted to the loss of 23,483 men killed, another 76,130 wounded, and 2,975 men missing in action, plus 11,812 men lost due to other causes, for a total loss of 114,000 men—nearly 25 per cent of his authorized strength and three times the number of casualties suffered by the Germans (including *2. Armee*).[99] His Front had also lost an estimated 90 per cent of its original armor strength of 1,553 tanks and assault guns on its establishment since 17 July, roughly 1,397 vehicles in all, though many of these were undoubtedly recovered and repaired.[100]

Of the units of the First Belorussian Front that had been directly engaged in battle against Gille's corps, primarily the 47th and 70th Armies and the VIII Guards Tank Corps, they had lost a total of 5,518 killed, 17,379 wounded, and 447 missing, with 1,506 men lost due to other causes, in sum 24,950 men, roughly four times the losses suffered by the troops under Gille's command.[101] These losses, though high, could be replaced, and what was more, there was sufficient fuel and ammunition being produced and shipped to the front lines by factories and refineries safely located in the Soviet Union that did not have to worry about the threat of a strategic bombing campaign. More than sufficient food, clothing, and trucks were being provided by the United States through its Lend-Lease program. It would only take a matter of days for the Red Army to prepare for the continuation of the offensive.

Thus, the Germans' first defensive of battle of Warsaw drew to an end but not to a conclusion. Its ending date of 30 August was a rather arbitrary determination, based on the fall of Radzymin more than anything else. True, once the Soviets had overcome the Rzadza defense line and taken Radzymin, an operational pause commenced, but for Rokossovsky's troops, their offensive would recommence once they had consolidated their forces on the ground they had just gained, reorganized their units, and brought up their artillery. To the left of *9. Armee*, the neighboring *2. Armee* was conducting an orderly fighting withdrawal to the Narew River, which would not only guarantee its flanks, but the left flank of *IV. SS-Pz.Korps* as well, which had been a concern to von Vormann and Gille ever since the middle of August.

Once again, to the ordinary German infantryman, tank crewman, combat engineer, or artilleryman, it was a distinction without a difference. The Red Army kept pushing forward, its artillery kept pounding their positions, and the Red Air Force maintained its unrelenting attacks on German front-line and logistics installations. Patrols still went out at night, tanks were repaired whenever possible, mines were laid, and men tried to sleep when they could. When the second defensive battle of Warsaw commenced the following day, none of the men of Gille's *IV. SS-Pz.Korps* would have noticed that they had moved from one phase of the campaign to the next. As bad as the first battle had been, the next would be far worse, compounded by the threat of disaster that always seemed to be hovering nearby. During this phase, Gille's leadership and his corps staff would reach their full maturity, as the battle slowly shifted from one of movement to static warfare reminiscent of World War I.

CHAPTER 8

The Second Defensive Battle of Warsaw Part I: 31 August–9 September 1944

On 31 August 1944, *Gen.d.Pz.Tr.* Nikolaus von Vormann could express some small satisfaction with how well his *9. Armee* had performed during the past month. Not only had his understrength forces managed to deny the First Belorussian Front the operational breakthrough that they had sought, but his troops had also dealt the 2nd Tank Army a major defeat during the battle of Praga. While the men in his three subordinate corps (the *IV. SS* and *XLVI Pz.Korps* and the *VIII. Armeekorps*) had been nearly forced back to the Vistula defense line in the north and had been unable to eliminate the Magnuszew and Puławy bridgeheads in the south, they had made the Soviets pay dearly for their gains.

True, the Warsaw Uprising had come at an inopportune time, but by the end of August, the Polish Home Army had been forced into a tight perimeter in the city's center and the suburbs of Zoliborz, Sielce, and Mokotow by *Gruppe von dem Bach* and no longer posed any appreciable threat to the movement of German forces through the city. Block by block and house by house, the city was slowly being retaken, as the Poles, beginning to show signs of desperation, anxiously awaited the arrival of the Red Army, which they believed would save them from annihilation (see Figure 3 for map of the city). However, the elimination of the valiant ragtag army that attempted to free Poland's ancient capital city was now only a matter of time. The most promising development from the Germans' perspective was the growing realization that Marshal Rokossovsky had no plans to lend any concrete assistance to the Poles, though his forces were not very far away. The situation in the *9. Armee* defensive sector could have been a lot worse.

The same could not be said about his neighbors to the north or south. On his left flank, *Gen.Oberst* Weiss's *2. Armee* was in the midst of a fighting withdrawal to the Narew River. Bereft of any *panzer* divisions to call his own, Weiss's three corps were doing the best they could with their horse-drawn infantry divisions to maintain a cohesive front line while under attack by no fewer than seven Soviet field armies. While he had been able to maintain a rather tenuous connection with *Gen.d.Pz.Tr.* von Vormann's army along the Bug River, that link was under constant threat of

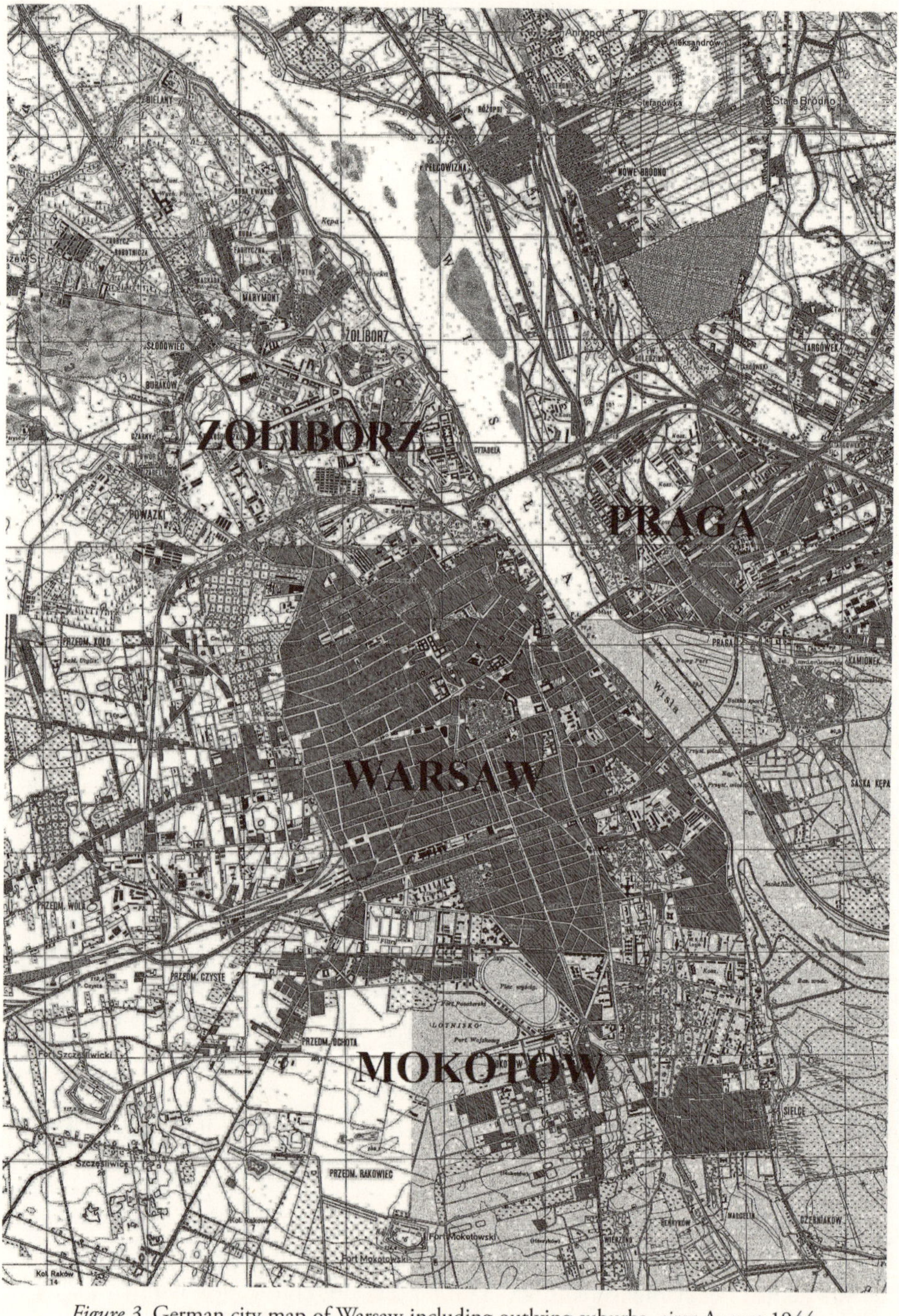

Figure 3. German city map of Warsaw including outlying suburbs, *circa* August 1944

separation and the introduction of the IX Tank Corps along the boundary between the two armies on 29 August did not bode well. Weiss had no substantial armored reserves of his own, except for a few *Sturmgeschütz* battalions. His army would soon be receiving a great deal of unwanted attention during the first week of September.

On von Vormann's right, the *LVI. Pz.Korps* of the neighboring *4. Pz.Armee* was poised along the boundary between *H.Gr. Mitte* and *H.Gr. Nordukrain*, sharing jointly, as it were, the mission of eliminating the slowly expanding Puławy bridgehead held by the 69th Army along the Vistula. Efforts to eliminate this bridgehead had come to naught, though a series of spirited counterattacks launched by the forces of *VIII. Armeekorps* and *LVI. Pz.Korps* during the second half of the month had kept it hemmed in against the river. As problematic as the Puławy bridgehead was, it paled in comparison to the other challenges that *4. Pz.Armee*'s commander, *Gen.d.Pz.Tr.* Hermann Balck, faced in his center and right flank, where he had to contend with General Ivan Konev's First Ukrainian Front, with up to seven armies poised to cross the upper Vistula at Sandomierz, liberate Cracow, and push deep into the eastern Carpathians before *H.Gr. Nordukrain* could stop him.

Far to the south, the collapse of *Gen.Oberst* Johannes Friessner's *H.Gr. Südukrain* due to the defection of Germany's Rumanian and Bulgarian allies was a brutal shock to the *OKW*, which could only helplessly look on while all of the *6. Armee* and a significant portion of *8. Armee* were annihilated by Marshal Rodion Malinovksy's Second Ukrainian Front. Bucharest surrendered to Marshal Fedor I. Tolbukhin's Third Ukrainian Front on 1 September, and the Rumanian government promptly switched sides, with its armies bringing their arms to bear against their former allies. Eighteen divisions went into the bag, making this one of the most costly reversals suffered by the Germans during World War II, after Stalingrad and Operation *Bagration*. This defeat not only initiated the campaign to liberate the Balkans, but exposed the far right flank of *Gen.Oberst* Josef Harpe's *H.Gr. Nordukrain*. Only due to the decisive actions by Harpe, *Gen.Oberst* Gotthard Heinrici's *1. Pz.Armee*, and a motley collection of alarm units, remnants of *8. Armee*, and Hungarian forces was it possible to establish a new defense line along the southern Carpathians and the eastern border of Hungary by the end of September, though this respite was only a temporary one.

On *H.Gr. Mitte*'s left flank, *General der Infanterie* Friedrich Hossbach had managed to stand firm with his *4. Armee* along the *Ostpreussen Schutz-Stellung* (East Prussia protective position), while *Gen.Oberst* Gerhard Raus, commander of the army group's left-most unit, the *3. Pz.Armee*, had managed to pull off the near-impossible task of successfully linking up with *H.Gr. Nord* in Lithuania on 21 August, when Raus's seemingly inadequate forces fought their way through to the Gulf of Riga, where they met with the spearhead of *16. Armee* near Jalgava in Lithuania. Naval gunfire support in the form of the German cruiser *Prinz Eugen* and other *Kriegsmarine* warships operating offshore provided the attacking *panzer* divisions with overwhelming artillery firepower, a heretofore unaccustomed experience that caught both antagonists by surprise. So while the situation everywhere, including the Western Front, was bleak, at least at the end of August 1944 German forces in the central and northern sectors of the Eastern Front saw a ray of hope.

As far as the Red Army was concerned, nothing had changed. The Germans' designated start date for the second defensive battle of Warsaw did not correspond with any of its own dates of course, since the STAVKA did not coordinate its campaign calendar with the *OKH* General Staff. The operational goal of Rokossovsky's First Belorussian Front remained the same—seizing bridgeheads on the western bank of the Vistula and along the critical junction of the Bug, Narew, and Vistula Rivers between Serock and Modlin. Once these bridgeheads had been consolidated and strengthened, they would be used as springboards for future operations aimed at Berlin, not towards the Baltic as the Germans still continued to believe—other Fronts of the Red Army would perform that secondary task from their positions in Lithuania and the border of East Prussia.

What would unfold over the next three weeks, although the *OKH* would later designate it as a single battle, were actually two separate and distinct battles. The first battle, the focus of this chapter, encompasses the period 31 August–9 September 1944, and will concentrate on the German withdrawal from Wołomin to an intermediate line and the battles north of the Narew, where elements of *IV. SS-Pz.Korps* fought in support of the *2. Armee* to contain the southernmost Soviet bridgehead on the west bank of the Narew north of Serock (see Map 7).

However, Rokossovsky had no intention of stopping there or allowing his enemy to reestablish a new defense line. Instead, he continued his attack, aiming at nothing less than the liberation of Praga and cutting off all German forces east of the Vistula, an operation that unfolded between 10 and 22 September, a phase of the fighting that is the focus of the next chapter. Seen in this light, this second battle of Warsaw would prove to be more critical than the first, with the stakes even higher for both sides. The fact that neither opponent completely succeeded in achieving his goal, despite the unbelievable carnage that ensued, meant that the defensive battle of Warsaw would drag on for three more months.

On 31 August, Rokossovsky's armies, including the VIII Guards Tank Corps, were all rather worn down after six weeks of attacking, but they still held the initiative and would continue as long as they had the means to do so. The immediate intentions of First Belorussian Front were clear. First, now that the Germans had evacuated Radzymin, Lt.Gen. Gusev's 47th Army on the left would continue its penetration to the southwest along the paved Radzymin–Warsaw highway which would lead them directly to Praga and the bridges over the Vistula. Second, in the center, Colonel General Vasily Popov's 70th Army, supported on the right by Lt.Gen. Alexander Luchinsky's 28th Army, would continue pushing through the forest between Benjaminów and Wólka-Radzyminska, with the goal of Nieporet,

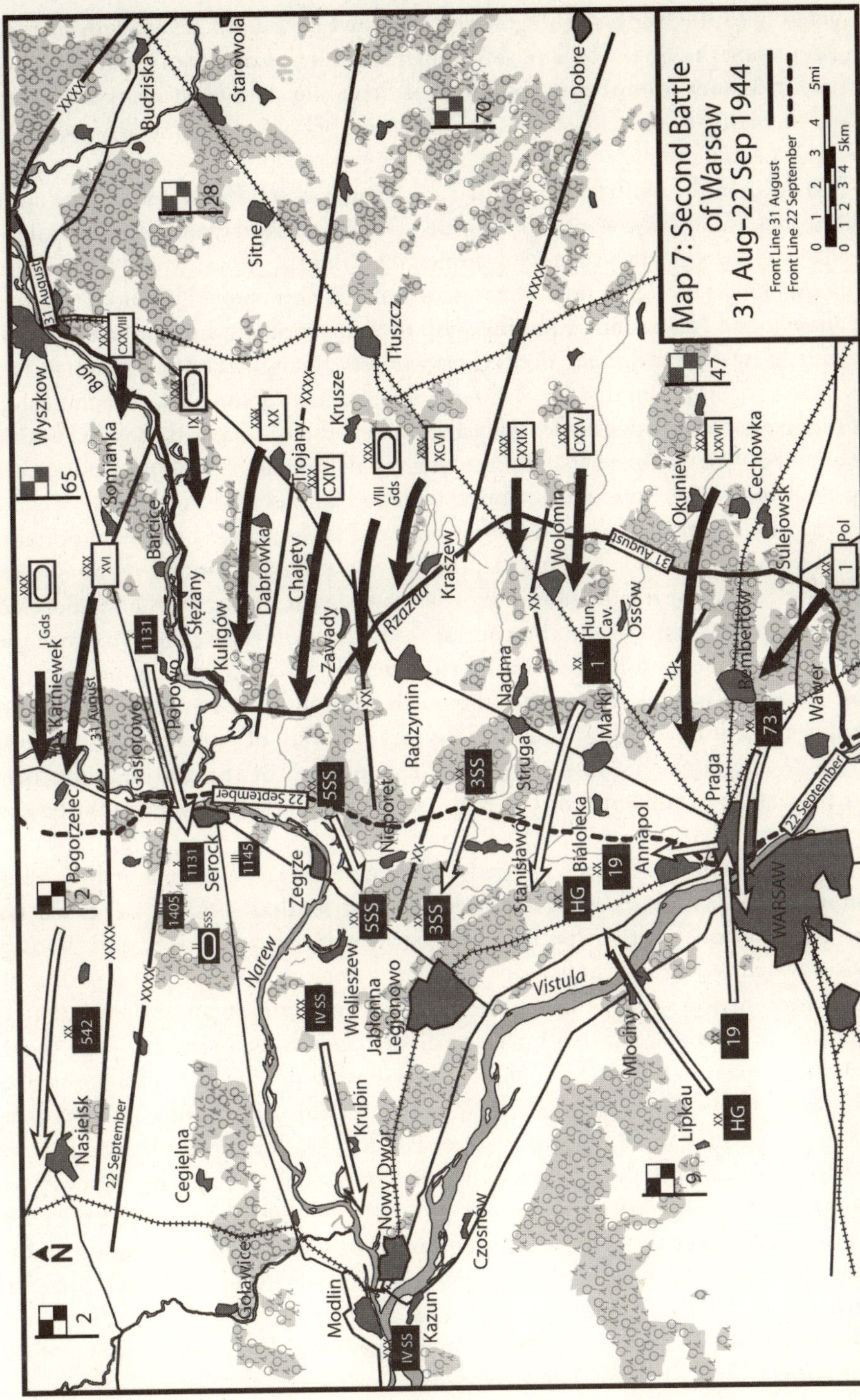
Map 7: Second Battle of Warsaw
31 Aug–22 Sep 1944
Front Line 31 August
Front Line 22 September
0 1 2 3 4 5mi
0 1 2 3 4 5km
Wyszkow
Bug
Somianka
Barcice
Słężany
Kuligów
Dabrowka
Chajety
Zawady
Trojany
Krusze
Tłuszcz
Sitne
Budziska
Starowola
Dobre
Kraszew
Rzazda
Radzymin
Wołomin
Ossów
Nadma
Marki
Struga
Okuniew
Cechówka
Sulejowsk
Rembertów
Wawer
Praga
WARSAW
Annapol
Białołeka
Stanisławów
Nieporet
Zegrze
Serock
Popowo
Gasiorowo
Karniewek
Pogorzelec
Narew
Wieliszew
Jabłonna
Legionowo
Vistula
Młociny
Lipkau
Krubin
Nowy Dwór
Czosnów
Kazun
Modlin
Goławice
Cegielna
Nasielsk
31 August
22 September
Hun Cav.
Pol
IV SS
5SS
3SS
HG
19
73
542
1131
1145
1405
CXXVIII
CXXIX
CXXV
LXXVII
XCVI
CXIV
XVI
65
28
70
47
2
9
Gds
VIII Gds
IX

the gateway to the bridges at Zegrze and Dabrowa. The 28th Army, with its right shoulder along the Bug, would push through Załubice to the Vistula, turn left, and outflank Nieporet from the north. South of Praga, the 1st Polish Army lay tightly coiled, preparing to strike. It was a comprehensive plan, backed up by an enormous amount of artillery.

Tied down in the south by the fighting at Magnuszew and Puławy, and in the north in Lithuania, *H.Gr. Mitte* would not be spared First Belorussian Front's attention for the next 10 weeks, and its two right-wing armies, the *2.* and *9. Armee*, would have to bear the brunt of most of it. This pressure meant that the *2. Armee* would be forced to slowly withdraw to the Narew and, if possible, leap over to its western bank, where it would establish a new defense line and do its best to prevent Rokossovsky's forces from seizing crossing sites. This meant that the *9. Armee* would have to continue the containment, if not elimination, of the two Soviet bridgeheads along the Vistula, while simultaneously crushing the Warsaw Uprising and protecting the right flank of *2. Armee* between the Bug and Narew Rivers, a task that would strain both armies to the utmost.

This critical junction between the two armies had become especially important, since if it was not defended as long as possible, Soviet units crossing over the Narew and Vistula from the north and south of Warsaw—a threat that constantly hovered in the background throughout this contest—could not only drive north towards the Baltic, cutting the German eastern defense line into two, but these forces, if they chose, could encircle *9. Armee* from the north and south. Preventing the southern contingency from occurring would be the responsibility of both *VIII. Armeekorps* and *XLVI. Pz.Korps*. The task in the northern portion of the army's sector, that is, defending the confluence of the Bug, Narew, and Vistula River, would be the responsibility of *Gruf.* Gille's *IV. SS-Pz.Korps*.

The *IV. SS-Pz.Korps* was not nearly as strong on 31 August as it had been a month earlier; over six weeks of constant, unrelenting combat had taken an enormous toll on both of its SS divisions. Though the *Totenkopf* and *Wiking* Divisions had performed uniformly well, they were in dire need of a period of rest and reconstitution. The lack of replacements had caused all of their infantry battalions to dwindle to 30–40 percent of their authorized strength (and those were the stronger battalions), forcing the survivors to fight even harder and make still greater sacrifices to carry out their missions. But the relentless attacks that Gille's corps had endured had also forced it to withdraw ever westwards into the narrow end of the funnel formed by the confluence of the Bug, Narew, and Vistula—that is, the farther his troops pulled back, the shorter their front line became, which meant a greater concentration of forces. This increasing troop density, spelt out in human terms as more men available to defend each meter of ground, paradoxically meant that the attacking troops of the 47th, 70th, and 28th Armies with their supporting armored forces would be facing more German troops, not less, the farther they advanced.

In regards to the performance of the corps' *Hauptquartier* itself, Gille's staff and corps units had performed remarkably well. Despite relocating its installations half a dozen times since 28 July, the corps headquarters had remained in firm control of its subordinate units throughout, despite occasional outages of its communications network. Supplies had been ordered and delivered, messages received and relayed, wounded troops evacuated, new defensive positions surveyed, and traffic regulated—in short, everything a corps headquarters was supposed to do, something taken for granted by the front-line combat troops. Much of the headquarters' work had been done in close proximity to the front line, while the Red Air Force constantly sought to locate and destroy it. The corps *SS-ARKO 104*, expertly led by *Oberführer* Brasack, had managed to get the most lethality out of its scarce artillery assets, including the incorporation of *Heer* artillery units into the corps' overall fire support plan. Frequently, the success of many of the corps' company- and battalion-level engagements had rested solely on the timely and deadly delivery of well-placed artillery fire.

The corps was still short of an ambulance company for its *Feldlazarett* (field hospital), its *Werfer Abteilung*, its *Artillerie-Abteilung*, and various and sundry other specialists, but in the main, it was functioning as efficiently as the circumstances permitted. Gille himself had been constantly on the move, following his daily schedule of visiting forward units in the morning, which usually meant going as far forward as division headquarters, then holding various meetings and conferences during the afternoon. Once a week, he and his staff could count on a visit by his army or army group commander, who would conduct command visits of their own. With a small security escort, Gille and his command group, usually consisting of his *O1* and *Begleitoffizier* accompanied by a radio car, would traverse the corps' sector to observe the battle and meet with division and regiment commanders.

These visits could be dangerous, of course, and the passengers in any vehicle had to be on their guard, even when behind friendly lines. Chance encounters with Polish partisans or roving Soviet units that had slipped through German lines were always a possibility, as was the unwanted attention of enemy fighter-bombers, ever alert for a staff car and escort vehicles raising a cloud of dust along a country road. That being a member of the corps staff or headquarters did not immunize one from harm is revealed by the casualty statistics. According to official reports, the corps staff and its affiliated corps units did not come through the months of July and August unscathed. Indeed, the *Hauptquartier* suffered the loss of one man killed in action, with seven more wounded seriously enough to warrant hospitalization. Two men from the corps' signal battalion, *SS-Nachr.Abt. 104*, were also reported as being missing in action.[1]

The most encouraging fact from which *IV. SS-Pz.Korps'* commander must have drawn some degree of comfort was that all of its divisions' artillery regiments were still intact, despite the concerted efforts of the Red Air Force during the past two weeks to locate and destroy its firing batteries and ammunition storage areas. An artilleryman himself, Gille would have been aware that his corps artillery assets were still below establishment, with only three units from the *Heer* having been allocated—*Einsatz-Bttr./Beob.Abt. 1*, *schw.Art.Abt. 154 (mot.)*, and *IV.Abt./Stellungs-Werfer Regiment 102*. All of these units had been with the corps since the beginning of August and had proved themselves to be very effective.

Though spread thin, *Obf.* Brassack's deft handling of these scarce assets allowed the corps artillery to repeatedly strike Soviet assembly areas and troop concentrations when front-line troops were too weak to intervene. The only limiting factor at this point in the battle was the availability of ammunition and the fuel to power the trucks to deliver it, which must have been a source of constant worry for Gille's *Ib*, *Ostubaf.* Scharff. The corps' artillery, coupled with the divisions' still-potent *panzer* regiments, time and again managed to avert catastrophe. During the second defensive battle of Warsaw, the situation would be no different.

Before describing the course of this second battle, it is worth taking a moment to get a sense of the front-line position occupied by the *IV. SS-Pz.Korps* on the morning of 31 August. *Grenadier Brigade 1131* defended the corps left flank on the northern bank of the Bug, where it had been stationed since withdrawing across the river after the fall of Ślężany on 27 August. Supporting the brigade was a platoon of three assault guns from *I. Abt./SS-Pz.Rgt. 5* and a platoon of Panthers from *Ostuf.* Flügel's *II. Abteilung*, as well as several *Alarm* companies hastily formed from various *Trossteile* from the *Wiking* Division. This collection of forces, under the tactical command of *Oberst* Söth, defended the northern bank of the Bug from Jackowo to Serock with the mission of preventing the Soviet forces on the other side from making any crossing attempts.

Söth's forces, now operating as a separate element of *IV. SS-Pz.Korps*, linked up with the rest of the corps nearly 10 kilometers to the west of the *Wiking* Division's left flank at the bridge over the Narew north of Serock, where the prewar bridge guaranteed the supply line to the right flank unit of *XX. Armeekorps*, held by the *5. Jäg.Div.* Here, south of the Bug, his brigade "shook hands" with *Gren.Rgt. 1145*, which was attached to *Staf.* Mühlenkamp's division. This regiment in turn held a thin screen line that stretched approximately 8 kilometers to the south where it linked up with the *I. Bataillon* of *Maj.* Alfred Nähring's *Pz.Gren.Rgt. 73* slightly to the north of Załubice. The area between the two regiments was ideally suited for defense, as it was mostly swamplands unsuited for tanks and bolstered by a north–south oxbow river tributary of the Bug. The only area suited as a high-speed avenue of approach was the narrow corridor that ran through Załubice itself. At this point, the battalion from *Pz.Gren.Rgt. 73* was positioned to block any Soviet attempt to break through.

Nähring's regiment defended the rest of the line from Załubice to Benjaminów, in what roughly corresponded to the center of the *Wiking* Division's front-line position. The *II. Bataillon* of *Pz.Gren.Rgt. 73* was centered on the village of Borki, which it had retaken for the second time the day before. Borki, located on a low hilltop, controlled several routes leading through the area as well as the southern approaches to Załubice which had to be taken by the Soviets before they could push on towards Zegrze. Here was the site of another vital bridge over the Bug, which the *Wiking* Division heavily relied upon for the movement of its supplies, so defending Załubice was vital. Borki would also be the scene of much heavy fighting during the next several days. To lend support to Nähring, Gille had attached *Maj.* Ritter's *Gren.Btl.z.b.V. 560* to his regiment the previous evening. Ritter's probationary battalion began moving into its new area of operations during the early morning of 31 August, and as events will soon show, it arrived in the proverbial nick of time.

South of *Pz.Gren.Rgt. 73*, two companies from the attached *II. Bataillon* of the *Eicke* Regiment from the *Totenkopf* Division were situated south of Borki, while *3. Kompanie* of *SS-Pz.Aufkl.Abt. 3* was positioned between it and Benjaminów. Here, they served as a connecting link between Nähring's regiment and the *Wiking* Division's two greatly weakened *Panzergrenadier* regiments. The fighting at Benjaminów was as heavy as elsewhere, and *Sturmmann* Gerd Kracht left a colorful description:

> Under heavy shellfire, we were told to dig deeper into the sandy soil. We were helped in this regard by the men of the probationary battalion who had just arrived. Our company commander, *Ostuf.* [Rolf] Wiethüchter, was standing with a few men a few feet behind me and was instructing them how to improve our positions, when suddenly a mortar shell burst nearby. He was killed immediately.

Ironically, only moments before he had been upbraiding his sergeants, telling them not to crawl between positions but to stand up while moving about in order to show the men that the shelling was nothing to fear. When the mortar round was heard coming in before it struck, everyone but Wiethüchter took cover. When they raised their heads from the dirt, he was the only one killed; everyone else escaped without a scratch.[2]

Obersturmbannführer Hans Dorr's *Germania* Regiment was positioned in the north between Benjaminów and Wólka-Radzyminska, while *Ostubaf.* Fritz Ehrath's *Westland* Regiment, which had recently returned from its hasty reconstitution, was to the south between Słupno and Cegielnia, forming the division's right-most unit and serving as the connecting link between it and the neighboring *Totenkopf* Division. The few remaining armored *SPW* and the crews of *III. Btl./Germania* were kept as division reserve, as well as the bulk of *II. Abteilung* of the *panzer* regiment and *Stubaf.* Hack's *SS-Pz.Aufkl.Abt. 5*. As for the *panzer* regiment's *I. Abteilung*, it had begun a four-week reconstitution period to the west of Serock and would not return to the front until mid-September. Its six remaining armored vehicles, which included three *Pz. IV* tanks and three *StuG IVs*, remained at the front and had been concentrated north of the Bug under the command of *4. Kompanie*.

Cegielnia lay astride the Radzymin–Warsaw highway, and after the *Totenkopf* Division was forced to give up Radzymin, keeping the Soviets out of this town and off the highway was vital for the defense. Fortunately, the *Totenkopf* Division's *panzer* regiment was still a powerful force and was kept in ready reserve behind the front lines. From Cegielnia, the *Totenkopf*'s position traced a wide arc west of Radzymin, curving around to the southeast, where it encompassed Wołomin before finally ending at Ossów, where *SS-Pz.Gren.Rgt. 5 Totenkopf* tied in with the left flank of the *1. ung.Kav.Div*. From thence, the corps' 80-kilometer-long front line turned abruptly west, to the portion of the line held by *Oberst* Hähling's *73. Inf.Div.* before it finally ended on the eastern bank of the Vistula at Zybtki.

A request by *9. Armee* to divert the newly activated *558. Gren.Div.*, recently arrived in the *H.Gr. Mitte* area of operations, to relieve the *Wiking* Division entirely was turned down by *Gen.Oberst* Reinhardt, who sent it elsewhere, but the critical manpower situation remained.[3] Towards that end, the *Westland* Regiment had returned to the front lines after a week-long rest period, where it had absorbed a small number of replacements intended to restore some semblance of combat power to its shattered ranks. Most of these "replacements" were men who had been combed from the various *Trossteile* (supply trains) of the division, men who only a day before had been driving trucks, mending uniforms, and typing requisition forms.

To date, no significant infusion of fresh SS replacements had arrived, despite both von Vormann's and Gille's constant requests. Ironically, one SS replacement unit, *SS-Grenadier Ersatz und Ausbildungs Bataillon 3*, had been quartered at the *Stauffer Kaserne* in Warsaw before the fighting, but had been thrown into the fighting south of Praga alongside the *73. Inf.Div.* during the last week of July instead of providing replacements to the *Totenkopf* and *Wiking* Divisions as it was designed to do. Incorporated into an emergency unit known as *SS-Kampfgruppe Kröner*, the green SS recruits suffered heavy casualties against the veterans of the 2nd Tank Army and the survivors shortly afterwards were incorporated into *Gruppe von dem Bach* fighting the Polish insurgents in Warsaw.[4]

The only question mark in the corps' order of battle was the Hungarian Division; its reliability and that of every other Hungarian unit in *9. Armee* was a subject of much discussion at the corps and at army headquarters as well. Gille was instructed by von Vormann on 25 August to keep a ready reserve force handy to take its place in the line should it withdraw without authorization.[5] To be fair, the vulnerability of their homeland to Soviet attack after the collapse of *H.Gr. Südukrain* must have weighed heavily on the minds of even the staunchest members of the *Honvéd*.[6] Over the next several weeks, nearly all of the Hungarian units under *H.Gr. Mitte* control would gradually be pulled out and replaced by German units, then sent back home via railroad to rejoin their own armies assembling for the defense of their country. Another factor that weighed on the minds of the German high command was the alleged sympathy the Hungarians had for the Poles, which in the opinion of the

OKH, *H.Gr. Mitte*, and even the *9. Armee* rendered them unsuited to carry out harsh retaliatory measures against the civilian population should those prove necessary.[7]

Regardless, most German commanders must have breathed a sigh of relief when the last of the Hungarian divisions departed by the end of October 1944. One of the most sacrosanct principles in combat was the necessity of trusting that the units on your left and right flanks would hold their positions; the recent events in Rumania, where entire army corps of the Rumanian Army went over to the Soviets or stood by and watched while they broke through must have sent a collective shudder through the ranks of the *Wehrmacht* and *Waffen-SS* whenever they were brigaded alongside an allied unit, which at this stage of the war meant only the Hungarians, since nearly all of the others—the Finns, Rumanians, Bulgarians, and Italians—had already departed the Axis coalition. Thus were Gille's forces arrayed at dawn on 31 August. In this respect, the *IV. SS-Pz.Korps*' mission had not changed: hold the current front line at all costs. In retrospect, this was a near-impossible task but as Gille himself was wont to say, "*Befehl ist Befehl*" (orders are orders).

The morning of 31 August began with surprisingly little enemy activity. Although the troops of the First Belorussian Front had continued their attacks in the area west of Radzymin begun the previous evening, particularly in the Aleksandrów area, the sun's first rays dawned over a nearly silent battlefield. Gille's corps was not the only beneficiary of this nearly peacetime calm; throughout the rest of the *9. Armee*'s sector, things were quiet as well.[8] Of course, this was just a passing phenomenon—by late morning, a large concentration of Soviet troops and tanks were spotted assembling for an attack west of Radzymin in the area between Aleksandrów and Ciemne. For once, Gille's constant entreaties for air support through his corps' *Luftwaffe Fliegerverbindungsoffizier* (*Flivo*, who coordinated air assets in support of ground forces) were answered when a squadron of Ju-87 *Stukas* arrived on the scene at 12:30 p.m. to repeatedly strafe and bomb the Soviets "with good effect." This aerial attack was immediately followed by an equally effective corps artillery concentration fired by the *Totenkopf* and *Wiking* Divisions' artillery regiments, as well as rocket salvoes from *IV. Abt./Werfer-Regiment 102* that drove their enemy to ground, forcing them to delay their scheduled attack.[9]

On account of these preemptive attacks, the Soviet assault, primarily consisting of the 413th and 143rd Rifle Divisions, only got underway in the mid-afternoon, with most of their effort directed in a southwesterly direction along the Radzymin–Warsaw highway. They did not get far, having been brought up short by the *Totenkopf* and *Wiking* Divisions' strong defenses. The commander of the XCVI Rifle Corps, who was carrying out the operation, withheld most of the supporting armor from the VIII Guards Tank Corps in hopes that the infantry could achieve a breakthrough wide enough to allow the armor to conduct a deep penetration of the German defenses.

On this score he was to be disappointed. After his infantry battalions were repulsed six times with heavy losses, the most that the Soviet corps commander could show for his efforts was the village of Cegielnia, which the *Totenkopf* Division's *Begleitkompanie* was forced to abandon before sundown. Of more concern to *Obf.* Becker was a battalion-sized attack by the 185th Rifle Division supported by several tanks that was directed against his right flank at Duczki, a small town northeast of Wołomin. Here, a battalion from *SS-Pz.Gren.Rgt. Totenkopf*, supported by two tanks, carried out a counterattack and after hand-to-hand fighting retook the town, destroying two T-34s in the process.[10] Duczki lay astride the Wołomin–Praga highway, and just like the other major road leading southwest out of Radzymin, was another high-speed avenue of approach that Becker had to deny the enemy.

On the corps' left flank, the first concerted Soviet attack against Załubice was reported by *I. Btl./Pz.Gren.Rgt. 73* late that afternoon. Despite fierce German resistance, a battalion from the 76th Guards Rifle Division managed to penetrate the town's defenses on two occasions, though it was finally thrown out by nightfall after suffering heavy losses. This event was confirmed by a staff officer from *9. Armee* who was on the scene to witness the carnage. Overall, the day's fighting was a significant defensive success, with the 47th and 70th Armies failing to achieve any of the penetrations that they had sought. In recognition of this achievement, the *IV. SS-Pz.Korps* was singled out for praise in the *Wehrmachtsbericht* (German Armed Forces Daily Communiqué), which stated that:

> At the defensive battle taking place northeast of Warsaw, the *IV. SS-Pz.Korps* under the leadership of *SS-Gruppenführer* Gille with the *SS-Panzer* Divisions *Totenkopf* and *Wiking* along with attached units from the *Heer*, particularly distinguished itself by its unshakeable steadfastness and dashing counterattacks. The corps held back the onslaught launched by portions of three Soviet armies and a tank corps and during the period from 23 to 30 August destroyed 102 enemy tanks, 8 assaults guns, 53 heavy antitank guns and four aircraft.[11]

While this was an impressive defensive achievement, once again it must be noted that as far as Rokossovsky was concerned, it did not alter his intentions whatsoever. In fact, the events of 31 August were merely the curtain raiser for what was to follow. One indicator was a report from *73. Inf.Div.*, where Soviet front-line activity had been remarkably quiescent, that its observers had spotted signs that a troop buildup was occurring several kilometers to the south, where the Red Army's 175th Rifle Division and the neighboring 1st Polish Army were bringing up additional artillery and engineering troops. While this event was duly reported by Gille's corps to the headquarters of *9. Armee*, no one seemed unduly alarmed.[12] They should have been.

Another event reported by *IV. SS-Pz.Korps* to *9. Armee* in its *Abendmeldung* early that evening was the wounding (for the 11th time) of *SS-Ostubaf.* Dorr, commander of the *Germania* Regiment. Dorr, who had successfully led his regiment for the past four months, had been wounded in the right arm near Aleksandrów earlier that day while leading a counterattack to retake lost ground.[13] His wound was severe enough to warrant hospitalization and convalescence, which meant that he would not be declared fit for duty and allowed to return to the division until 27 September; until then, his position would be temporarily filled by *SS-Stubaf.* Helmut Müller, the veteran commander of *I. Btl./Germania*. Dorr, who had been awarded the Swords to his Knight's Cross with Oak Leaves on 9 July 1944 for his leadership during the battle of Kowel, had skillfully led his regiment during the heavy fighting of the past two months and his steady presence would be missed. The war would have to continue without him, but he would soon be back for the third and final battle of Warsaw in October.

The fighting that began late in the afternoon of 31 August continued throughout the night. While the *73. Inf.Div.* and *1. ung.Kav.Div.* reported scattered artillery and mortar fire but little else, both *Wiking* and *Totenkopf* Divisions had a hot time of it. The 143rd Rifle Division continued its attack down the eastern side of the Radzymin–Warsaw highway, and despite bitter counterattacks launched by *Obf.* Becker's troops to retake Cegielnia, its troops managed to force the SS to pull back 5 kilometers on their far left flank, necessitating a withdrawal to a new defense line 1.5 kilometers north of the town of Pólko.

A counterattack attempt launched later that evening by *II. Btl./Westland* from the opposite side of the highway to retake Cegielnia from the west also failed, which resulted in the decision by the *Wiking* Division's commander to pull back his right flanking unit to Słupno in order to maintain its connection to the *Totenkopf* Division's left flank. The fall of Wołomin was now only a matter of time, since it was obviously on the verge of being outflanked from the north, just as Radzymin had. On the *Wiking* Division's far left flank, *Pz.Gren.Rgt. 73* carried out aggressive nighttime patrolling to determine exactly where and how far the Soviets had penetrated during the past several days. Its patrols reported that several villages to its front were only lightly occupied, which was interpreted to mean that a renewed Soviet attack along the southern bank of the Bug was not imminent.[14]

The main Soviet thrust that everyone had been anticipating began shortly after sunrise on 1 September with an enormous artillery barrage against German positions arrayed along both sides of the Radzymin–Warsaw highway. Picking up where they left off the previous evening, Rokossovsky's 47th and 70th Armies abandoned any pretense of finesse and attacked directly into the defenses of the *Totenkopf* and *Wiking* Divisions with an overwhelming superiority in tanks and infantry. Close air support by the Red Air Force was starkly evident, adding to the sheer hell that the men in the front-line trenches and fighting positions were experiencing. Meter by meter, the Germans grudgingly fell back, until they reached the heights that stretched 5 kilometers between Slupno, held by *II. Btl./Westland*, and Nadma, held by the *Totenkopf* Division's *III. Btl./Eicke*. Supported by their own aggressively handled *panzers* and accurately delivered corps and division artillery, the German infantry held firm and fended off every attempt by several tank battalions from the VIII Guards Tank Corps to break through.[15]

To draw off German reserves, a supporting attack was launched at the same time by the 413th Rifle Division against the positions of the *Germania* Regiment between

Aleksandrów and Benjaminów, but this too was shot to pieces before it made any progress by *Ostubaf.* Dorr's old regiment supported by a tank company from *SS-Pz. Rgt. 5.* A few kilometers to the north, another attempt to wrest Borki from *Pz.Gren. Rgt. 73* by the 38th Guards Rifle Division also failed. The center of the *Totenkopf* Division's line was assailed at Marjanów, a northern suburb of Wołomin, but this too was repulsed "with heavy losses" by *II. Btl./Totenkopf* Regiment, assisted by a company from *SS-Pz.Jag.Abt. 3.*

Becker reported his division's success in a radio message to *IV. SS-Pz.Korps* headquarters at 1:40 p.m. that was monitored by staff officers at the headquarters of *9. Armee*. In his overheard message to his corps commander, which was transcribed to paper an hour later and added to the army's war diary, Becker stated that a "strong enemy attack was fended off at our final main defense line." After drawing a line under the word "final" on the piece of paper, the staff officer maintaining the army's *Kriegstagebuch* scribbled "? ? ha, ha!" sarcastically in the margin.[16] Clearly, *9. Armee* expected the slow but steady advance of the Soviets would continue and where the final German main defense line would be, no one, not even *9. Armee*, knew for certain.

On the *IV. SS-Pz.Korps*' right, very little enemy activity was reported that day by the *73. Inf.Div.* and the Hungarian division. Although the Germans had been forced to give up some ground along the front line southwest of Radzymin, the Soviet attack had failed terribly, with the heavy losses to prove it. That day, Gille's corps reported to *9. Armee* that it had destroyed 47 Soviet tanks, including 10 of the JS-II models, as well as seven heavy antitank guns and five aircraft. In exchange, eight German tanks were knocked out, including four *Pz. IV* and four *Pz. V* Panthers, but these could be recovered and repaired or used as sources for scarce spare parts. Once again, the *Luftwaffe* made an unexpectedly robust appearance, and the corps' *Flivo* reported that its fighters had shot down 15 Soviet aircraft with no losses of their own as it attempted to wrest control of the skies from the Red Air Force.[17]

Though Gille's corps had fought very well that day and had inflicted considerable losses upon the enemy, its own butcher's bill had not been insignificant. Both the *Totenkopf* and *Wiking* Divisions had suffered hundreds of casualties; men that it could not replace. This constant drain on its precious manpower, without having received any significant amount of replacements, could not be tolerated much longer. The *Totenkopf* Division's *SS-Pz.Rgt. 3* had also lost six tanks during the past two days—two *Pz. IV*, two Panthers, and two *StuG IV*. On that day, *Ostubaf.* Darges's *SS-Pz.Rgt. 5* had only 29 tanks, assault guns, and tank destroyers operational. With one of his tank battalion still being reconstituted, his regiment in effect was now fighting with one arm tied behind its back. The constant eroding of the strength of Gille's divisions, particularly the *Wiking*, continued to weigh heavily on von Vormann's mind.

Throughout the day, the *9. Armee* commander repeatedly attempted to convince *H.Gr. Mitte*'s commander to give him yet another infantry division (this time he asked for the *542. Gren.Div.*) so he could pull Mühlenkamp's division as well as the Hungarian cavalry division out of the line (the latter because he feared that it would collapse if struck hard).[18] Finally, *Gen.Oberst* Reinhardt replied that the best he could do was to offer *9. Armee* the Hungarian *5. ung.Res.Div.* (5th Reserve Infantry Division) in exchange for the *Wiking*'s relief, but only if Mühlenkamp's tanks and artillery regiment were left behind to support the Hungarians. Von Vormann, to his credit, declared this solution unworkable given the prevailing tactical situation, preferring to keep a weakened but reliable division instead of one that might dissolve in its first battle and threaten the survival of Gille's entire corps. Stymied again, von Vormann would continue trying to shore up Gille's corps.[19]

One bright spot that appeared on the horizon that day was the unexpected return of *SS-Flak-Abt. 5*, which was finally released from its attachment to *Gruppe von dem Bach* at noon after a month-long absence. Its battalion headquarters and two heavy batteries, with a total of 18 8.8cm *Flak* guns, would be replaced in Warsaw by *I. Abt./SS-Flak-Abt. Reichsführer SS*, which had been transferred from Berlin for that very purpose. The *Wiking*'s *Flak* battalion, led by *Stubaf.* Joachim Stoige, would rejoin his division by nightfall, and his two heavy batteries would be immediately put to work the next day countering Soviet air superiority as well as any ground targets that got within range of their powerful guns.[20]

Another encouraging sign was the arrival of *Fest.Inf.Btl. 1405*, a fortress infantry unit equipped with a larger than normal complement of heavy weapons, which would take over the mission of securing the Narew River bridges at Serock and Dabrowa, as well as the northern bank of the Bug. It would be joined the same day by *Festungs-Pak-Kompanie* (*Fest.Pak-Kp.*, or Fortress Antitank Company) *2/VI*, a newly raised unit of the *Heer* equipped with eight captured Soviet 7.62cm antitank guns.[21] These new additions to the corps' order of battle would finally allow the ad-hoc infantry battalion consisting of the *Trossteile* of the *Wiking* Division, almost all of them logistics and administrative personnel, to return to their normal duties and help alleviate that division's increasingly strained sustainment effort. The two *Sturmgeschütz* platoons from *4. Kp./SS-Pz.Rgt 5* would finally be allowed to cross over to the west bank of the Narew and rejoin their regiment, since *Fest.Pak-Kp. 2/VI* would take over the antitank duties from that point onwards.

While these additions were welcome, they would contribute little to the battle raging southwest of Radzymin. Here, despite their failure to break through on 1 September, the divisions of the 47th and 70th Armies redoubled their efforts to advance down the road towards Warsaw. On a day that would once again prove warm, humid, and cloudy, Rokossovsky's troops and tanks hurled themselves against the lines of their equally resolute opponents in the *Totenkopf* and *Wiking* Divisions. The day began with an alarming report that the *1. ung.Kav.Div.* was being attacked by a battalion-sized force that penetrated their front lines on the division's right flank west of Hill 108 between Ossów and Rembertów. After a few tense hours, with the assistance from a platoon of assault guns from *SS-Stug.Abt. 3*, the Soviets, most likely from the 234th Rifle Division, were forced back after losing three of their own assault guns and the front line restored. But this was a mere prelude.

After the Hungarians were attacked, the main assault against the inner flanks of the two SS divisions recommenced with only slightly less pressure than the previous day. Three divisions of the CXXIX Rifle Corps, supported by 30 tanks from VIII Guards Tank Corps, pushed south beginning at 9:30 a.m. towards Czarna and Nadma in the *Totenkopf* Division's sector, where they achieved minor penetrations, reinforcing the expectation that the encirclement of Wołomin was now only a matter of days away. During the back-and-forth fighting, tanks and troops of the *Totenkopf* Division knocked out 23 Soviet tanks and inflicted a number of casualties on the accompanying infantry before the attackers were finally stopped, though they hung on to the town's outskirts. Another attack directed towards Marjanów was also stymied by a counterattack by the *Totenkopf* Regiment.

One eyewitness to the bitter fighting during this period was *Ustuf.* Gosta Borg, the Swedish war correspondent who had joined the *Waffen-SS* in 1941. Attached to the staff of the *IV. SS-Pz.Korps*, he was in an excellent position to observe and write about what he saw. After the war, he wrote an account about his experiences, which included a dispatch he wrote that was used in a radio broadcast during the battle southwest of Radzymin:

> Things are nervous during the afternoon. To the east, the clouds of dust rise, the Soviet frontline infantry is active, fighting rages at several points. The corps staff officers are updated; reconnaissance pilots deliver their aerial photos that show that the roads on the enemy's side are filled with convoys, every wooded area is bristling with tanks, artillery and heavy formations of infantry. In the evening a [German] counterattack is launched to ease the pressure against a certain position. Prisoners are captured from a new enemy division, deserters tell about the roads from Bialystok being lined with artillery, guards units, T-34s and many new Stalin tanks and Stalin organs [12.2 cm multiple rockets launchers mounted on trucks] … During the night, the Soviet pressure increases; after midnight enemy batteries fire at crossroads, command posts and our own batteries. Our *Panzergrenadiers* are wide awake, digging and improving the fortifications and trenches, priming hand grenades and stacking piles of *Panzerfausts* and *Panzerschrecks*. At 03:00 in the night, the corps staff waits. Not yet … not yet … suddenly a gigantic flame appears over the eastern horizon. It is like looking at a forest bending before a storm. A curtain of shells rush up towards the red sky at dawn. At last!—Tensions ease on everyone's faces. It has begun! From the closest sniper trench, reaching six miles to our rear, rages a hurricane of fire.[22]

Borg would continue reporting until nearly the end of the war, and would be present during the even greater battle of Modlin during October 1944. But what left the greatest impression upon his memory was the fighting during the late summer of 1944, which he describes in graphic detail in other reports from the front.

On the opposite side of the highway from Czarna, the *II. Btl./Westland* reported a large concentration of enemy troops forming up in the Słupno area that was broken up by artillery fire and a repeat performance by the *Luftwaffe*, whose ground-attack aircraft effectively strafed and bombed Soviet troops and tanks. Flailed from both the air and the ground, this attack never got underway and the loss of nine tanks only reinforced the point. Nevertheless, the *Wiking* Division's troops were pounded by Soviet artillery fire and air attacks in return for most of the day, giving them little opportunity to observe their handiwork or improve their own positions.

On the corps' far left flank, a position held by a company from *Pz.Gren.Rgt. 73* at Trzianna 1.5 kilometers northeast of Borki was attacked by a Soviet infantry battalion, but after the enemy managed to penetrate into the village, a counterattack was immediately carried out that drove them back to their starting point. Along the Bug River position held by *Gren.Rgt. 1145*, both sides traded artillery fire, but other than that, little activity was reported. In other developments, *Maj.* Ritter's *Gren. Btl.z.b.V. 560* moved into a position between Borki and Benjaminów during the evening of 1–2 September, relieving *1. Kompanie* from *SS-Pz.Aufkl.Abt. 3*, which enabled it to rejoin the rest of its battalion over in the *Totenkopf* Division's defensive sector, as well as *II. Btl./Eicke*, which had been subordinated to the *Westland* Regiment.

In his report to *9. Armee* that evening, Gille expressed his satisfaction with his corps' defensive success that day, during which 35 Soviet tanks and 11 heavy antitank guns were knocked out and hundreds of enemy troops were killed or wounded. Exact body counts were impractical, since this would require Gille's troops to move forward across a rather active battlefield to tally the results. However, he was under no illusion that while his corps had defeated this latest Soviet attempt, it would certainly continue the following day in the same direction with the same amount of forces, if not more. While he did not openly advocate evacuating Wołomin, around which the jaws of a Soviet pincer were clearly forming, Gille painted the picture to his army commander that giving it up was something that he strongly advocated.

In his assessment that evening, von Vormann agreed with his corps commander, informing *H.Gr. Mitte* that the fall of Wołomin was only a matter of time, but if his army gave up the town now, it would free up forces (i.e., the bulk of the *Totenkopf* Division) that would be badly needed later. However, believing that Wołomin was central to the defensive effort east of the Vistula, Reinhardt demurred for the time being. Additionally, the commander of *H.Gr. Mitte* refused to send any more reinforcements than he already had and remained firm in his position that the only way the *Wiking* Division would be relieved was if it left all of its tanks and artillery behind for the *5. ung.Res.Div.* that he was still offering in exchange.[23] Von Vormann, to his credit, refused this offer once again, since this was a second-rate formation with a poor reputation. Besides, with most of the Hungarian units destined to be transferred to their home country in the immediate future, why insert it into the middle of a major battle, where it would most likely fail? *H.Gr. Mitte* also informed *9. Armee* that *SS-Jäg.Btl. 500* had finally been released from its attachment to *2. Armee* and would be sent to reinforce Gille's corps as soon as possible. Since it does not appear after that point in the corps' order of battle, it must be surmised that this battalion was disbanded and its men parceled out among the most needy grenadier battalions within the division. While it was only at 50 percent strength, its 297 men would be another welcomed addition to the corps' critical manpower situation.[24]

The fourth day of the offensive, 3 September, passed quietly for the rest of *9. Armee*, except within Warsaw itself, where *Gruppe von dem Bach*'s suppression of the uprising was gathering momentum, and east of the city, where the fighting southwest of Radzymin in the *IV. SS-Pz.Korps* sector showed no signs of abating. Overnight, the limited penetrations achieved by Red Army's CXXIX Rifle Corps the previous day between Czarna and Nadma were eliminated by a *Totenkopf* Division counterattack. Strong artillery harassing fire was reported throughout the entire corps sector, primarily directed against front-line and artillery-firing positions. Finally, the weather had begun to cool, the first time in over two months that the combatants would be granted a respite from the heat and humidity of what had been a long, hot, and dry summer.

While *Oberst* Hähling's *73. Inf.Div.* reported no action worth mentioning, the *1. ung.Kav.Div.* drove off a company-sized attack directed once again towards Ossów. On the corps' left flank along the Bug, no attacks were noted, with harassing artillery fire being the only enemy activity worth reporting. The center of the corps sector, as predicted, was once again the focus of the enemy's attention. Throughout the day, both the *Wiking* and *Totenkopf* Divisions confronted numerous regiment-sized attacks orchestrated by the 47th and 70th Armies, supported by an ample amount of artillery fire. As before, the intent to encircle Wołomin was clear, with most of the Red Army's effort being directed in the gap between Czarna and Nadma along ground that was favorable for the employment of armor. Another attempt to seize Nadma was made by the 76th Rifle Division, whose troops actually broke through the *Totenkopf* Division's defenses west of the town before they were thrown back by another counterattack.

The Soviet forces entrenched inside Słupno launched a daring company-sized reconnaissance-in-force against the German defenses west of the town on the evening of 2–3 September. Under the cover of darkness, they managed to penetrate the *Wiking* Division's main defense line near Hill 104 before they were tossed out before dawn by an SS counterattack. Based on the intelligence this foray gained, another large-scale attempt was made later that morning by Soviet infantry to move out of their assembly area and initiate their attack towards Hill 104 and the surrounding area. This hill, which sat at the top of a ridgeline southwest of the town, was held by *II. Btl./Westland* and dominated the southwest approaches leading out of Słupno. The attackers, consisting primarily of the 413th Rifle Division, were brought up short by a well-aimed barrage from the *Wiking*'s entire artillery regiment that stopped the Soviet assault before it could even properly begin.

On the corps' left flank, *Maj.* Nähring's *Pz.Gren.Rgt. 73* endured three battalion-sized attacks that afternoon directed against its defenses in Borki by the 76th Guards Rifle Division, but all of these were stopped by the *Panzergrenadiers'* intensive supporting fire, including that provided by the single artillery battalion left behind by its parent artillery regiment of the *19. Pz.Div.*, *Pz.Art.Rgt. 19.* A fourth attempt was made to take Borki and this one actually partially succeeded, albeit temporarily, penetrating into the town before it was finally stopped. A counterattack was launched by *I. Btl./Pz.Gren.Rgt. 73* after sundown and with the help of *Gren.Btl.z.b.V.560*, which came up on its right flank and joined in, cut off, and eliminated the Soviet troops that had broken through by 10 p.m. Nähring's troops counted 30 enemy dead and one prisoner who was sent to corps headquarters for interrogation.

No Soviet tanks were reported as having been knocked out anywhere on the corps' front that day, an indication that the VIII Guards Tanks Corps' units were purposely being held back or were undergoing a brief period of reconstitution. After all, Gille's corps had knocked out over 113 Soviet tanks during the past five days to add to those destroyed during the preceding week, and even the Red Army could not replace these vehicles and crews immediately, so a pause was inevitable.[25] Artillery fire also slackened throughout the day, another sign that either the Soviet gunners were low on ammunition, or it was being withheld for the next day.

That evening, von Vormann continued his daily entreaties to *H.Gr. Mitte* to transfer *Gren.Div. 542* to Gille's corps before it moved completely out of the *9. Armee* area of operations. Despite the arrival of portions of one regiment from this division, the remainder were loaded on trains and shipped out, to be followed several days later by one battalion from the single regiment remaining east of the Vistula, *I. Btl./Gren.Rgt. 1076*. This regiment had been positioned behind the *1. ung.Kav. Div.* for several days in expectation of effecting the relief in place of the latter. But before it fired a shot in anger, it was pulled out to rejoin its division at Pułtusk in the *2. Armee* sector, leaving the Hungarians still in their original position between the *Totenkopf* Division and the *73. Inf.Div.*[26]

Again, von Vormann's persistent badgering of his army group commander bore some fruit—Reinhardt ordered the release of a tank destroyer battalion from *H.Gr. Mitte* reserve, *Heeres-Pz.Jag.Abt. 743*, equipped with 34 brand-new *Pz.Jg. 38t* tank destroyers, later nicknamed the *Hetzer* (roughly translated as "Baiter"), an effective, low-profile armored vehicle based on a Czech tank chassis that had the potential to contribute substantially to the antitank defenses of *IV. SS-Pz. Korps*. Unfortunately, this battalion would not arrive on the eastern bank of the Vistula until 4 September.

Additionally, and perhaps more importantly, von Vormann's request to evacuate Wołomin was still not taken up for consideration by *H.Gr. Mitte*, whose commander evidently was prepared to wait and see how the battle played out before making a decision. A bold and decisive *G.F.M.* Model he was not. Another factor influencing the Germans' thinking, based on the direction that it was taking, was that the course of the Soviet offensive since 31 August seemed to be directed towards the relief of the faltering uprising in Warsaw. However faulty that assumption was, what happened during the next several days can be better understood by viewing German reactions in this light, explaining why the *H.Gr. Mitte* commander thought that holding on to Wołomin was so important.

On the evening of 3 September, per the *H.Gr. Mitte* standard operating procedure, *9. Armee* submitted its now-daily combat strength reports, one which consisted of the status of operational tanks, assault guns, tank destroyers, and antitank guns, and the other which provided the *Kampfstärke* of every division, separate brigade, and attached infantry unit operating within the field army's area of operations. The report for 3 September is illuminating, for it paints a dramatic picture of the declining personnel and armor strength of both of Gille's SS divisions. The good news, what there was, was reported in the tank strength report (as of 2 September), which stated that the *Totenkopf* Division still had 72 operational armored fighting vehicles—24 *Pz. IV* tanks, 26 *Pz. V* Panthers, three *Pz. VI* Tigers, and 19 assault guns and tank destroyers—in addition to its 14 heavy (7.5cm) operational antitank guns. The *Wiking* Division was a good deal weaker, due in part to the absence of its *I. Abteilung*, still undergoing reconstitution. That division reported three *Pz. IV*, 15 Panthers, and 14 *StuGs* and tank destroyers operational, for a total of 32 of all types. In addition, the *Wiking* Division still fielded 31 heavy antitank guns (part of these belonged to *Pz.Gren.Rgt. 73*) and eight medium antitank guns assigned to *Festungs-Pak Kompanie 2./VI*.

With regard to front-line infantry, armored reconnaissance, and combat engineer strength, the situation was dramatically worse, and would result in Gille ordering yet another reshuffling of the defensive sectors assigned to each division that evening. Once again, the *Totenkopf* Division was the stronger of the two SS divisions, with a total of 1,329 men reported within its eight battalions, averaging 173 fighting men in each battalion, though the actual strength varied (this of course does not include administrative and logistics personnel assigned to each battalion). This *Kampfstärke* was less than 40 percent of its authorized front-line strength, but due to the division's still-lethal *panzer* and artillery regiments, Gille felt that it required no additional attachments and was still capable of holding its own.

Within the *Wiking* Division, the situation was rather dire. Including the combat troops in all of the seven battalions it had on the field (*III. Btl./Westland* and its *Feld-Ersatz Bataillon* had still not arrived), the division had only 670 men still standing to hold its front line, with an average of only 95 men per battalion. The weakest battalion of all was *III. Btl./Germania*, which reported only 33 men still ready for battle. This may have been due to its status as the division's only *SPW* battalion, whose *Sd.Kfz. 251* armored personnel carriers and crews had been repeatedly used as part of the division's "Fire Brigade." While accompanying the tanks of *SS-Ostubaf.*

Darges's *panzer* regiment as it counterattacked and providing them the necessary infantry protection, this battalion, led by acting commander *SS-Hstuf.* Helmut Schumacher, had been badly shot up.[27]

None of its sister battalions had fared much better, except for *Stubaf.* Franz Hack's *SS-Pz.Aufkl.Abt. 5* with 322 men still listed under its *Kampfstärke*, but it had only returned to the front lines the previous week after a six-month reconstitution and training period. Even though it was considered an armored unit, its specially trained reconnaissance troops were frequently employed as substitutes for infantry and it had already begun to experience a daily decline in its fighting strength. The division's combat engineer unit, *SS-Pio.Btl. 5*, was in better shape than the infantry battalions, with 123 combat troops reported, but even that was less than one-third of its authorized front-line strength.

To make up for the shortage of troops, the various regiments and battalions attached to the division contributed another 2,265 men to its *Kampfstärke*—832 in *Gren.Btl.z.b.V. 560*, another 587 men in *Fest.Inf.Btl. 1405*, 568 men still fighting in *Gren.Brig. 1131*, and 287 men in the two battalions from *Gren.Rgt. 1045*. In addition, 309 men from *Pz.Gren.Rgt. 73* were still fighting with the *Wiking* Division in Borki, which brought the total number of attached front-line troops from the *Heer* to 2,574, versus only 670 men actually assigned to the *Wiking*, thus *Heer* troops outnumbered SS troops by a factor of nearly four to one. Of these attachments, only two were actually veteran units, Nähring's *Pz.Gren.Rgt. 73* and Söth's *Gren. Brig. 1131*. The rest, which constituted the bulk of this "borrowed manpower," were either newly raised (*Gren.Rgt. 1145*), second-rate (*Fest.Inf.Btl. 1405*), or one that consisted of convicts undergoing rehabilitation (Ritter's probationary battalion). A more permanent solution was therefore required, and that would mean the assignment of troops from the *Waffen-SS* replacement pool.

A variety of solutions to the manpower problem were being formulated at the *SS-Führungshauptamt* in Berlin, including the assignment of *Luftwaffe* troops and *Kampfwillige* ("willing to bear arms") Eastern volunteers, but this would take time to hammer out, especially concerning an agreement with the *Luftwaffe*. In the intervening weeks, the only thing that Gille could do, that he was indeed authorized to do, was to reallocate the defensive sectors for each division. While the portion of the *Hauptkampflinie* held by the Hungarians and the *73. Inf.Div.* would remain unchanged, the boundary between the *Totenkopf* and *Wiking* Divisions was to be shifted north of the Radzymin–Warsaw highway beginning on 4 September. While the far-right boundary of the *Wiking* Division had been Hill 104 south of Słupno, it would be re-established up to but not including the village of Wólka-Radzyminska, a shortening of nearly 6 kilometers.

The portion formerly held by the *Germania* and *Westland* Regiments would be taken over by *SS-Pz.Gren.Rgt. 5 Eicke*, commanded by *Staf.* Karl Ullrich, the future commander of the *Wiking* Division. The *Wiking* Division's new defensive sector would now stretch from the northern outskirts of Wólka-Radzyminska to Benjaminów, then to Borki and Załubice, finally ending at the Bug River at Dabrowa, where the 70-ton military bridge still stood. Preparations at *H.Gr. Mitte* were already being drafted that would direct the *9. Armee* to detach *Gren.Brig. 1131* from Gille's corps and assign it to *Gen.Oberst* Weiss's *2. Armee*, since its disposition on the northern bank of the Bug was of little use to the *IV. SS-Pz.Korps* defensive effort. Additionally, Söth's brigade was to be given the mission of securing the Narew bridge at Serock to facilitate the withdrawal of the right flank of *2. Armee* (*XX. Armeekorps*) to the west side of the river. This change of assignment was planned to take place on the evening of 4–5 September.

Like the previous day, 4 September was another cool, cloudy day, though dry. The other two corps in *9. Armee—VIII. Armeekorps* and *XLVI. Pz.Korps*—reported little combat activity taking place the previous evening other than a slight increase in Soviet artillery fire. Fighting inside Warsaw was undiminished. In the *IV. SS-Pz. Korps* sector, most of the fighting during the previous evening was confined to artillery fire on both sides. A Soviet force assembling in the forest north of Wołomin was hit by a barrage from the *Totenkopf* Division's entire artillery regiment and the *Wiking* Division duly reported the retaking of Borki by *Pz.Gren.Rgt. 73* during the night. Both the *73. Inf.Div.* and the Hungarian division reported sporadic artillery and mortar fire on their positions, as well as increasing Soviet patrols attempting, under the cover of darkness, to gather information about their locations and strength. These reconnaissance efforts were easily driven off, but such efforts to scout out the exact front-line positions of these two divisions would intensify over the next several days.

Compared to the activity between 31 August and 2 September, 4 September was also relatively uneventful for Gille's troops, just as the previous day had been, with a noticeable slackening of enemy pressure. Both sides conducted artillery duels with each other, with the Germans seeking out Soviet troop concentrations to forestall attacks while their opponent's artillery ranged up and down the German lines to harass and delay troop movements. Air activity had also eased noticeably. The day was not entirely quiet, however. Four company-level attacks (100–200 men) were launched against Borki, but all were driven off and the two *Pz. IV* tanks from the regimental reconnaissance platoon of *SS-Pz.Rgt. 5* sent to support *Pz.Gren.Rgt. 73* destroyed one T-34 and two SU-76 assault guns. The biggest action that day was on the corps' far left flank along the southern bank of the Bug River, where *Maj.* Ritter's *Gren.Btl.z.b.V. 560* carried out a highly successful attack against a reinforced Soviet infantry battalion.

This battalion from the 55th Guards Rifle Division had infiltrated the front lines defended by *Gren.Rgt. 1145* sometime during the previous evening and had occupied the villages of Arciechów and Stok, deep in the rear area of *IV. SS-Pz. Korps*. Arciechów lay on the east bank of the Narew, from where an enemy force could directly threaten the bridge at Dabrowa, which lay a mere 2 kilometers to the north. Traffic over the bridge had been stopped, since the Soviet force had blocked the road on the river's eastern bank. Something had to be done immediately lest this incursion turn into something more dangerous. Therefore, Ritter's battalion was pulled out of its position south of Borki at 6 a.m. and marched to the western outskirts of Załubice, where it linked up with a supporting armored reconnaissance company from *SS-Pz.AufklAbt. 5* and seven *Jagdpanzer* tank destroyers from *SS-Pz.Jäg.Abt. 5*. Here, it formed three separate assault groups that began moving forward before noon. To their surprise, as the German force approached Arciechów its men came under Soviet artillery and mortar fire. The enemy was thought to be at least 10 kilometers behind the German lines, so an artillery-supported incursion was even more serious than it had first appeared. While advancing, the spearhead came under heavy fire from Soviet antitank guns positioned between Stok and Arciechów.

Ritter, in command of the *Kampfgruppe*, ordered his battalion and the supporting armor to immediately attack. Fighting was heavy, and the employment of multiple rocket launchers in support of the beleaguered Soviet force was reported. Apparently, these deadly weapons were being fired from a launching site east of the oxbow lake on the other side of the German main defense line. This was yet another rude surprise, because it was believed that these weapons were usually held back to support major offensives. Finally, Ritter's battalion wrested control of the area from the enemy battalion by nightfall after heavy fighting, including hand-to-hand combat in Arciechów. Most of the Soviet troops were killed or captured, and 12 Soviet antitank guns were reported to have been taken. The supply route was also opened up once again, allowing supplies to move forward across the Narew River bridge and casualties to be evacuated.

After this success, *Gren.Btl.z.b.V. 560* was ordered to remain in place to prevent a similar situation from occurring and to occupy a new defensive position stretching from the Bug at Dabrowa to Arciechów, where it connected with the left flank of *Pz.Gren.Rgt. 73*. What happened to the unit from *Gren.Rgt. 1145* that was supposed to defend this area was not reported. No other significant actions by the 47th or 70th Armies were reported as having occurred that day. As puzzling as it might seem, given the high operations tempo displayed by the Soviets between 31 August and 2 September, the relative inactivity from 3–4 September in the *9. Armee* area of operations might be better understood in light of what was occurring at the same time in the neighboring sector defended by the *2. Armee*. Here, the situation had begun to deteriorate rapidly and would soon draw in elements of *IV. SS-Pz.Korps*. To his surprise, Gille would soon find out that his corps would have to fight two major battles simultaneously.

During the past several weeks, Weiss's three corps had been slowly and grudgingly withdrawing to the west from their previous defensive positions that were arrayed on the right along the opposite bank of the upper Bug River, stretched to the north encompassing Ostrow-Mazowiecki, and ending east of Lomza at the great bend in the Narew River where it linked with the *4. Armee* on the left. The *2. Armee* seemed to have the situation well in hand until 3 September, when the right flank of Rokossovsky's First Belorussian Front, comprised of the 28th, 65th, and 48th Armies, resumed the offensive after a relative period of inactivity. To enable this offensive, Rokossovsky had decided to shift the emphasis on logistics, engineering, and air support to that area of operations, which resulted in a corresponding decrease in the same level of support to his Front's efforts in the center and left flank, which of course was the area defended by von Vormann's *9. Armee*. This also meant that the Warsaw Uprising would receive no support whatsoever—it was simply not a priority and did not even factor into the STAVKA's long-range plans.

On 31 August, Weiss's weakened *2. Armee* lacked any *panzer* formations of its own except for four assault gun brigades and three army-level tank destroyer battalions. These armored fighting vehicles, numbering less than 150 that were actually operational, and of which only 117 were assault guns, were interspersed throughout the length of his entire front in support of his 12 infantry divisions and two mounted cavalry brigades. Against these forces, the First Belorussian Front's commander had marshalled the three aforementioned armies with 24 infantry divisions, the I Guards Tank Corps, the IX Tank Corps, and the I Mechanized Corps, and an enormous amount of artillery and antitank gun regiments.

The tank and mechanized corps would each have had approximately 270 and 246 vehicles, respectively, at their full authorized strength, giving the right wing of the First Belorussian Front nearly 800 armored fighting vehicles in these three corps alone. Each army would have also had one or two independent tank regiments, so the actual number was undoubtedly higher. The attacking force would have had an overwhelming numerical advantage over the *2. Armee* in every category. Without mobile forces of its own, the best that Weiss could hope to accomplish against this onslaught was to retreat in good order over the Narew while he still could.

The offensive by the right wing of the First Belorussian Front against *2. Armee* commenced on 3 September with a powerful artillery barrage that pulverized German field fortifications. That same day, five rifle divisions of the CXXVIII Rifle and III Guards Rifle Corps conducted successful river crossings of the Bug along both sides of Wyszków, forcing the *35. Inf.Div.* on the right and the *5. Jag.Div.* on the left—both from *XX. Armeekorps,* Gille's neighbor to the north—to rapidly withdraw to avoid being trapped. On the left flank of *XX. Armeekorps,* the *XXIII. Armeekorps,* which had been successfully holding the Soviets back along the old prewar Polish border defensive positions for the past two weeks, the 48th Army simply crushed the right flank regiment of the *541. Gren.Div.* and the left-most regiment of the *211. Inf.Div*, nearly reaching the Narew River south of Rózan by midnight.

The following day, *2. Armee* was granted permission by *H.Gr. Mitte* to withdraw over the Narew. The question that no one could answer in the German camp was who would get there first? Most of *2. Armee*'s units were infantry, meaning that most of the means of locomotion for its guns, supply wagons, and kitchen trailers were provided by horseflesh, so the rate of march for the withdrawing troops was as fast as their feet (or hooves) could carry them, not fast enough to outpace the onrushing tanks of the I Guards and IX Tank Corps. Once pontoon bridges had been thrown across the Bug, Soviet commanders wasted no time in introducing these highly mobile and lethal units into the fray. They rapidly bypassed the Germans and in many cases arrived at the Narew before their opponents did, but found no bridges over the river when they arrived. Though the Narew was not as wide as the Mississippi in the United States or even the Vistula, it was still 300–400 meters across, no small barrier.

It did not take long for Reinhardt to respond to this existential threat. The *6. Pz.Div.*, in army group reserve, as well as two *panzer* brigades (*Pz.Brig. 102* and *104*) were thrown into the fighting on 4 September, carrying out numerous counterattacks over the next several days designed to slow or at least blunt the most dangerous advances. Fortunately, the bridges at Ostrołęka (known as Scharfenwiese in German), Rózan, and Pułtusk were stoutly defended, allowing most of *2. Armee*'s units to reach the safety of the western bank of the Narew and set up their defenses before the Soviets completely closed up to the river line. But the one that most concerned *H.Gr. Mitte* as well as the *2.* and *9. Armee* was the bridge at Serock, which had been outflanked in the north by a river crossing over the Narew at Karniewek by 600 men from the 65th Army's CV Rifle Corps. Finding themselves unopposed at this point except for ineffectual rear area security units, the Soviets quickly constructed a pontoon bridge that would enable them to send troops and vehicles over it with the goal of enveloping Pułtusk from the south or Serock from the north. Regardless of which direction this force decided to attack, it had to be stopped.

By the evening of 4 September, it had become apparent to both Reinhardt and von Vormann that *2. Armee* could possibly collapse if it did not withdraw over the Narew quickly enough and that forces would need to be made available rather quickly to shore up the new Narew defensive line before it was too late. The speed of the Soviet advance out of Wyszków and the ease by which it swept aside any German resistance and pushed forces across the river between Pułtusk and Serock at Karniewek had a sobering effect that tended to wash away any reluctance to take extreme measures. One of *9. Armee*'s first actions was to order the army's *Waffenschule* (weapons training battalion), located in Modlin, to send all five of its antitank guns to Serock to bolster the defenses there and protect the bridge, beginning at 12:40 p.m.

The next step was to decide whether to redirect the *542. Gren.Div.* from its original destination of Pułtusk to Serock or to send it back to replace the *1. ung. Kav.Div.* south of Wołomin as was originally intended. One of its regiments had already been recalled, *Gren.Rgt. 1076*, but this still left an open question about the percieved need to replace the Hungarians. Another course of action aired was to order the *19. Pz.Div.* to turn around once again and march north, leaving its mission of attacking into the Magnuszew bridgehead to an infantry division of *VIII. Armeekorps*. Its *Pz.Gren.Rgt. 73*, which had been fighting with Gille's corps for several weeks, would be the first from that division ordered to redeploy, since it was the closest element. Accordingly, an assembly area for the division was planned for the area east of Modlin a few kilometers south of the Narew to be used as a staging area for a possible move north into the *2. Armee* area of operations.

The problem that *H.Gr. Mitte* faced was the need to counterattack and eliminate the danger as quickly as possible. The penetration had been made in the *XX. Armeekorps'* new sector on the west bank of the Narew, but this corps had no forces immediately available to carry out a counterattack. Its right-most division that bordered the *IV. SS-Pz.Korps*, the *35. Inf.Div.*, had retreated so quickly across the Narew bridges at Serock and Pułtusk that its disorganized forces could do little to stop the Soviets. Fortunately, *Gren.Brig. 1131* was still positioned north of the Bug and east of the bridge at Serock, but with its own left flank completely uncovered by its neighbor's hasty withdrawal, it could not stay where it was. Late that afternoon, one of the brigade's rearguards had already destroyed three approaching Soviet tanks, definitely not a good sign. In addition to Söth's brigade, *4. Kompanie* (four *StuG IV*) from *I. Abt./SS-Pz.Rgt. 5*, under the command of *Ostuf.* Eberhard Metzger, was still in reserve east of Serock and could be employed as a stopgap until the *19. Pz.Div.* or *542. Gren.Div.* arrived.

It took Gille time to digest these developments, understandably so since up to this point he had been strictly focused on the battle his corps was waging southwest of Radzymin. His evening report of 4 September gave no indication of any awareness of what was going on along the northern bank of the Bug. However, the morning report his operations section sent in to *9. Armee* at 4:30 a.m. revealed that a great deal had occurred overnight. While most of the rest of his corps' defensive sector had been relatively quiet, except for the usual artillery fire and reconnaissance probes, as well as a raid mounted by the *73. Inf.Div.*, the bulk of the morning report was dedicated to events taking place on Gille's far left flank.

The report noted, with some indications of alarm, that the corps' left flank was now completely uncovered, save for *Gren.Brig. 1131*, which in any case needed to get across the Narew at Serock as soon as possible before it was trapped east of the river. That same morning, Gille was ordered to disengage *Maj.* Nähring's *Pz.Gren. Rgt. 73* from the Borki defensive sector and assemble it at Nieporet, where it would be directed across the Narew at Zegrze and from thence to its new area of operations north of Serock. The regiment's place in the line would be taken over by Ritter's battalion, which would have to defend nearly 10 kilometers of ground, a task that far exceeded its capabilities. Fortunately, Ritter still had armor support provided by a tank destroyer company from *Stubaf.* Oeck's *SS-Pz.Jag.Abt. 5*.

Throughout the day, the rest of *IV. SS-Pz.Korps*' front line remained relatively quiet, but Gille noted with some concern in his evening report to *9. Armee* that based on reconnaissance and observation, the Soviets appeared to be preparing to take some kind of action between the inner flanks of the Hungarian division and its right-hand neighbor, *73. Inf.Div.* He also once again brought to von Vormann's attention the need to evacuate Wołomin. When the *9. Armee* commander brought the matter to the attention of Reinhardt that same night, to von Vormann's surprise the army group commander concurred, ordering it to be given up by the next morning. Whether based on von Vormann's arguments or the unfolding situation north of Serock, the decision to abandon Wołomin probably saved half of the *Totenkopf* Division from destruction.

The real drama on 5 September as far as *IV. SS-Pz.Korps* was concerned was the unfolding action taking place between Serock and Pułtusk on the western banks of the Narew. In what had become a standard operating procedure, elements from as many as three Soviet divisions (the 193rd and 394th Rifle and 44th Guards Rifle Divisions) had been rushed across the river at Karniewek and immediately began to expand the bridgehead as rapidly as possible, followed by an undetermined number of tanks from the I Guards Tank Corps. In mid-afternoon, a regiment-sized enemy force supported by tanks advanced as far as Hill 108 overlooking the town of Dzierzenin, a mere 7 kilometers north of Serock and only 4 kilometers north of the 70-ton bridge over the Narew on the town's northern outskirts. From all appearances, that seemed to be the Soviet troops' ultimate objective.

Until *Pz.Gren.Rgt. 73* arrived, the only effective German force available to prevent this from happening was *Gren.Brig. 1131* and the platoon of assault guns from the *Wiking* Division. The *9. Armee* issued an order at 12:45 a.m. that directed *IV. SS-Pz.Korps* to take these two units as soon as they crossed over the Narew and place them under the tactical control of *XX. Armeekorps* of *2. Armee*. In the case of the *panzer* unit from the *Wiking* Division, this would only be a temporary measure until the arrival of the *19. Pz.Div.* In the case of *Gren.Brig. 1131*, it was to be a permanent one, to become effective at midnight on 5 September. In recognition of the achievements of Söth's departing brigade, von Vormann penned a proclamation at 7 p.m. that evening that was to be read to the troops. In it, he stated:

> Soldiers of *Grenadier Brigade 1131*! Today your brigade is departing the *9. Armee* area of operations. Since 30 July, when you arrived directly from the homeland as a young, inexperienced and hastily-raised unit, you have fought in one of the most critical battles of the Eastern Front. Through your efforts, you have helped bring the Bolshevist offensive directed towards Warsaw to a complete stop. You can be especially proud that your operations with the *IV. SS-Pz.Korps* on 2 September received the highest form of praise as a result of the corps being mentioned by name in the *Wehrmacht* daily report. The recognition bestowed upon the SS divisions applies completely to you as well.[28]

The new mission of Söth's brigade was to defend Serock by attacking in a northerly direction along the west bank of the Narew, destroying any enemy troops encountered along the way in cooperation with the *35. Inf.Div.*, which was to attack from the north. The new boundary between the *2.* and *9. Armee* would be set along the Bug River, with the dividing line between the armies located along the line Modlin–Serock. On the upside, at least Gille would no longer have to worry about any units from his corps being trapped on the wrong side of the Bug—but he now had to worry about them being trapped on the wrong side of the Narew.

One thing that Gille did have to ensure, however, was that the bridges over the Narew at Serock and Dabrowa were not to be allowed to fall into the hands of the enemy under any circumstances. The one at Dabrowa he still needed, but a small bridgehead on the eastern bank of the Narew at Serock was to be maintained as long as possible to keep it open as a lifeline for any remaining elements of either Gille's corps or *XX. Armeekorps* to retreat across. By 7 a.m., the last German stragglers made it across the bridge, screened by Metzger's four assault guns. With a Soviet spearhead bearing down on them, he was ordered to withdraw his guns across the bridge five minutes later. At 7:10 a.m., Gille's *Korps-Pionierführer* (senior engineer officer, also known as *Stopi*, *Stabs-Pionieroffizier*), *SS-Ostubaf.* Erich May, whose men had previously wired the bridge for demolition, ordered its destruction moments before Soviet troops from the 186th Rifle Division could seize it, not a minute too soon.[29]

The defense of Serock itself was left in the hands of *Fest.Inf.Btl. 1405* along with the fortress antitank gun company. Metzger and his assault guns would not be idle for long; in the intervening hour since the bridge was destroyed, he received new orders to seek, attack, and destroy the Soviet crossing site at Karniewek in conjunction with a *SPW*-mounted *Pionier* company from *SS-Pio.Btl. 5*. After rearming and refueling, at 8:35 a.m. he led three of his guns (the fourth having been sidelined with a mechanical problem) north along the Serock–Pułtusk highway where his unit linked up along the way with the *SS-Pioniere*. With no artillery or any other kind of support whatsoever, Metzer set off with his tiny *Kampfgruppe* in search of the enemy.

He did not have to go far. After passing through the defensive positions manned by troops from *Gren.Brig. 1131* near Weirzbica, his column began to draw Soviet artillery fire as it went through the northern outskirts of the village of Dzierzenin. While the engineer company swung to the left around Hill 81 to envelop the town of Pogorzelec on the left, Metzger ordered his three assault guns to attack directly into the enemy's defensive positions. After approaching to within 500 meters of the town, two of his vehicles, including his own, were disabled by enemy fire. While the crews of the two damaged vehicles arranged to have them towed to the rear for repair, Metzger climbed aboard the last surviving *StuG IV* and continued his attack.

Moving cross-country, his vehicle got as far as Hill 108 on the western edge of the town and from that point drove another kilometer east towards Karniewek, stopping and firing at selected targets all the while. Finding himself and his crew all alone and without support (what became of the attack by the combat engineer company is not recorded), and under increasing fire from Soviet infantry weapons, Metzger reluctantly decided at noon to turn around while he still could and return to his starting point at Dzierzenin. Incredibly, neither he nor anyone else in his crew was injured during his bold maneuver.[30] But he did confirm that the Soviets had occupied the area in force and were in the process of expanding their bridgehead when his force attacked. There was not a minute to waste.

In the meantime, four tanks from *7. Kp./SS-Pz.Rgt. 5* led by Finnish *Ustuf.* Ola Olin had arrived in Dzierzenin to reinforce Metzger. Along with a small number of infantrymen from *Gren.Brig. 1131*, Metzger and Olin's meager force resumed the attack towards Pogorzelec at 2:30 p.m. Fifteen minutes later, Olin's tanks, with infantry riding aboard, had already reached the outskirts of the town where they halted, but Metzer's two assault guns (one had been able to rejoin him) were stopped by heavy artillery fire at Hill 110.5 between Dzierzenin and Pogorzelec. The accompanying infantry refused to advance, so Metzger decided not to risk everything like he had earlier during the day but chose instead to wait for more forces to arrive. Another infantry force, either from *Gren.Brig. 1131* or the engineer company from *SS-Pio.Btl. 5*, attempted to make an enveloping maneuver through the hamlet of Dzbanice, just a kilometer north of Pogorzelec, but found it strongly occupied. Olin decided at that point to wait too, having been informed as Metzger had that reinforcements were on the way.

The reinforcements arrived in the form of four Panthers from *Ostuf.* Bauer's *8. Kp./SS-Pz.Rgt. 5*, which had been sent across the Narew to an attack position near Trzepowo, 2 kilometers northwest of Metzger's position at Dzierzenin. There were now 10 operational vehicles from the *Wiking* Division on the field, to be joined by more the following day. By nightfall, the bulk of *Pz.Gren.Rgt. 73* had also arrived. Now that Metzger and Olin, supported by troops from Söth's *Gren. Brig. 1131*, had halted the enemy's advance, *XX. Armeekorps* was directed to plan a counterattack to be carried out the following day to eliminate the Soviet bridgehead at Karniewek. In addition to the attack from the south carried out by *Pz.Gren.Rgt. 73* along with the tanks and assault guns of the *Wiking* Division, *Gren.Rgt. 1077* from the *542. Gren.Div.* would attack from the west and the *35. Inf.Div.*, supported by *Pz.Brig. 104* from *2. Armee* reserve, would attack from the north. According to the plan, all of them would advance in a concentric fashion to squeeze and entirely wipe out the Soviet bridgehead beginning the following morning, 6 September.

While this counterattack was being planned, the situation was uncharacteristically quiet throughout the rest of the *IV. SS-Pz.Korps* sector. The 47th and 70th Armies made no noteworthy sallies at all that day against the defenses of the *Wiking*, *Totenkopf*, *73. Inf.* and Hungarian Divisions. Reconnaissance probes appeared to be the order of the day, as witnessed by several Soviet attempts made to gather information on the defenses of the *73. Inf.Div.*, especially against its far right flank along the Vistula, but these were driven off by the defenders. Artillery fire, though constant, was relatively light in comparison to previous days, while most Red Air Force activity was directed against the Narew bridges at Serock and Zegrze. While tanks had been spotted and heard, none had gone forward to conduct any attacks except those operating north of the Bug.

Clearly, the attention of the First Belorussian Front was directed elsewhere on 5 September. The *Totenkopf* Division, except for a tank company from *SS-Pz.Rgt. 3* that was moving across the Narew at Zegrze to reinforce the *Wiking* Division's *Kampfgruppe* for the following day's attack, was preoccupied with the pending evacuation of Wołomin that was to take place that night. Since its right flank still tied in with the *1. ung.Kav.Div.* south of Wołomin, any withdrawal planning had to involve them, a thought that must have left *Obf.* Becker and his commanders feeling uneasy. Nevertheless, giving up Wołomin would avoid a trap and free up additional troops for the next phase of the battle.

Continuing what appeared to be a trend, the quiet across most of the *9. Armee* front prevailed throughout the evening of 5–6 September. The withdrawal from Wołomin by the *Totenkopf* and Hungarian Divisions that began at 9 p.m. took place without any interference worth mentioning, and all of the affected units were in their new positions west and southwest of Wołomin by 5:35 a.m. A Soviet attempt that night to insert a foot patrol into the area surrounding Wólka Radzyminska on the *Totenkopf* Division's far left flank was driven off without any further incident. The *Wiking* Division reported only sporadic artillery and mortar fire, with the occasional reports of Soviet night bombers operating in the airspace over its far left flank. In Warsaw, *Gruppe von dem Bach* had begun using *Sturmpanzer* (heavy assault guns) to destroy street barricades built by the Polish insurgents in order to facilitate the continuing German attack against the central core of the city begun the previous day.[31]

Across the Narew, things had not been as quiet. As the *2. Armee* prepared to launch its counterattack against the Karniewek bridgehead the next morning, it reported that under the cover of darkness enemy reinforcements including tanks had been spotted pouring across the pontoon bridges constructed by Soviet engineers. Attempts by German artillery to interdict traffic over the bridges were ineffectual. The implications of these sightings were born out later that day when the Soviets launched a series of strong counterattacks of their own in the late morning and early afternoon that managed to secure additional ground and push back the German forces attempting to hem them in by several kilometers. Although the past several days had been relatively uneventful ones for *IV. SS-Pz.Korps*, that trend would be reversed by the events of 6 September.

The most critical event that day, of course, was the fighting taking place in the *2. Armee* area of operations north of Serock, where the attack directed by *XX. Armeekorps* against the Karniewek bridgehead began to get underway mid-morning. In a race against time, *H.Gr. Mitte* sought to eliminate the Soviet forces being reinforced on the west bank of the Narew before they grew too powerful and threatened the entire Vistula–Narew defense line. With the recent experiences of the Magnuszew and Puławy bridgeheads in mind, where Soviet defenses had become so impenetrable that repeated German counterattacks had failed to destroy it, Reinhardt knew that this new one at Karniewek had to be destroyed before this pattern could be repeated. However, insufficient attention was paid towards the overall command and control of this counterattack. While it was a *2. Armee* operation, carried out by its *XX. Armeekorps,* little consideration appears to have been given to properly integrating both *Pz.Gren.Rgt. 73* and the *Wiking* Division's tanks into the overall scheme of maneuver. This left the responsibility by default in the hands of Nähring, who at any rate was fully occupied commanding his regiment. Gille also overlooked the need to establish a corps forward command post on the northern bank of the Narew to coordinate the actions of his own troops, since they had not been formally attached to *XX. Armeekorps* for this operation.

The attack launched from the south by both battalions of Nähring's *Pz.Gren.Rgt. 73*, in conjunction with the *panzers* and assault guns from *SS-Pz.Rgt. 5*, began shortly after 4:30 a.m. following a short artillery barrage on Soviet defensive positions on the western outskirts of Pogorzelec. On the right, the attack by one *Panzergrenadier* battalion progressed as far as the southern edge of Dzierzenin, before it stalled. The tanks from the *Wiking* Division kept moving without the infantry, bypassing enemy resistance before reaching a vantage point on the southern edge of Pogorzelec. Here, Olin's tanks and Metzger's assault guns were able to observe and shoot at the bridge over the Narew 1.5 kilometers away with their 7.5cm cannon, without doing much damage owing to the distance to the target.

Simultaneously, *Ostuf.* Bauer's *8. Kompanie*, with four more Panthers, supported the flanking attack by the other battalion from *Pz.Gren.Rgt. 73* at Trzepowo, located on the regiment's left. At 10 a.m., Bauer was ordered by *XX. Armeekorps* to detach three tanks and send them a kilometer northwest to assist the attack of a battalion from *Gren.Rgt. 1077*, which was attempting to seize Pogorzelec from the west. The distance between Bauer forces and those of Olin and Metzger was approximately a kilometer, and neither group was able to come to the aid of the other. At approximately 10:50 a.m., the German attack began to fall apart when a large battalion-sized Soviet force supported by two tanks advanced out of the bridgehead and attacked Pogorzelec.

As they attempted to rally their men and lead them forward to join the armor, both battalion commanders of *Pz.Gren.Rgt. 73* were killed in action. At that point, the infantry refused to go forward, much to Metzger's chagrin. This left Metzger in an exposed position, and the men in his four assault guns were soon fighting for their lives, simultaneously engaged from several directions by infantry weapons, antitank guns, and mortar fire. Metzer's vehicles engaged multiple targets with both their cannon and machine guns, and each one was hit several times by antitank rifles. One vehicle was struck in the right drive sprocket by a shell from an antitank gun, rendering it immobile. All attempts to retrieve it while under heavy fire came to naught and the vehicle was soon struck multiple times by antitank gun shells, setting it ablaze. Metzger, observing first-hand the movement of Soviet reinforcements into Pogorzelec, decided to order a withdrawal, though in the meantime six of his men were wounded by enemy fire, including Metzger himself.

As the German tanks withdrew, a much larger Soviet infantry assault was mounted from Pogorzelec at 11:55 a.m. towards Dzierzenin, but *7. Kompanie* under Olin was able to smash it with machine-gun fire and high-explosive shells from their tank's cannon. Another Soviet assault was launched at 1:15 p.m. and this one was driven back too, with Olin's tank platoon having been joined by Metzger's assault guns. Any further attacks towards the bridgehead at this stage of the battle seemed to offer little promise, as both *Panzergrenadier* battalions were in disarray following the death of their commanders and *Gren.Brig. 1131*, after the exertions of the past two weeks, was itself too depleted to be of much help. Complicating the situation was that Söth's brigade was now under the control of *XX. Armeekorps,* not Gille's.

Grenadier Regiment 1077's attack towards Pogorzelec from the west, spearheaded by Bauer and his tanks, appeared to have gotten nowhere either. No news was received about the situation north of the bridgehead at Karniewek, where *Pz.Brig. 102* and *35. Inf.Div.* were supposed to have begun their own attack. Gille, belatedly realizing that a firmer hand was needed to control the armored component of the southern *Kampfgruppe*, instructed the *Wiking* Division's commander to order the leader of *II. Abt./SS-Pz.Rgt. 5*, *Hstuf.* Flügel, to move his battalion's forward headquarters across the Narew to Marynino, 5 kilometers west of Serock. The situation required far more than a mere *SS-Hauptsturmführer*, as good a leader as Flügel was, to coordinate the activities of all these disparate units, some of which were under *2. Armee* control while others were still under *9. Armee* jurisdiction. In any case, *XX. Armeekorps* was ordered to make another attempt on 7 September. No one could have imagined the tank battle that would take place the following day.

While the events unfolding on the northern side of the Narew on 6 September might have been of vast importance in terms of *H.Gr. Mitte*'s overall situation, to Gille they may have been seen as merely a distraction. As far as he was concerned, based on his comments in his daily summary to *9. Armee* that evening, the situation following the withdrawal from Wołomin was far more relevant to his corps. He noted that Soviet forces, after belatedly realizing that both the *Totenkopf* and

Hungarian Divisions had escaped their trap, quickly filled the void created by the German withdrawal and began carrying out powerful attacks later that morning from the vicinity of Kobylka, a suburb 4 kilometers southwest of Wołomin. Based on radio intercepts, Gille believed that their objective was the town of Marki, one of the last towns along the Radzymin–Warsaw highway before it terminated in Praga. If this succeeded, it would effectively cut off both the Hungarian and *73. Inf.* Divisions.

More worrisome still, the previously quiet sector held by the *73. Inf. Div.* appeared to be undergoing a change, as a great deal of vehicular traffic was observed moving in and out of the area to its south, with more entering than departing. Especially disconcerting was the report that for the first time the enemy was using smoke screens to hide troop dispositions. Along the division's flank that it shared with the Hungarians, artillery and mortar fire had markedly increased. The Hungarians reported a battalion-sized infantry assault directed against its positions in the vicinity of Turow-Kobylka, just south of the Brest Litovsk–Warsaw railroad line. Supported by a tremendous amount of artillery fire, the Soviet force managed to penetrate the division's main defense line, an event that must have drawn Gille's immediate attention. Directed to launch an immediate counterattack, the Hungarian division, with the support of corps artillery, was able to throw the Soviet troops back before nightfall.

The *Totenkopf* Division reported enemy incursions all along its front line. The town of Nadma in the center of the division's sector fell that afternoon, forcing the regiment holding that portion of the line to fall back a kilometer to the Drewnica forest where they took up new positions. The division's artillery was kept very busy that day, engaging multiple targets, especially forward assembly areas near Nadma and Kobylka where Soviet troops were observed gathering to launch future attacks. No tanks were reported as having taken part in any fighting that day, another indicator that they were being held back in reserve.

In the *Wiking* Division's sector, most of the activity that day was taking place across the Narew as previously related, involving three of its tank companies. The greatest challenge reported by the division that day though was repositioning the units holding its left flank between Borki and Załubice in the wake of the departure of *Pz.Gren.Rgt. 73*. Not only were the units that replaced it not nearly as capable in terms of heavy weapons and other armaments compared to Nähring's regiment—e.g., Ritter's probationary battalion, the ragged *Gren.Rgt. 1145*, and newly arrived *SS-Jäger Battalion 500*—they also lacked the aggressiveness and esprit de corps displayed by his *Panzergrenadiers*. Fortunately, well-directed fire from *Ostubaf.* Bünning's *SS-Pz.Art. Rgt. 5* was able to keep the enemy off-balance that day by placing accurate artillery barrages on Soviet assembly areas east of Załubice while the other units took over the defensive positions recently vacated by *Pz.Gren.Rgt. 73*.

That night, in his evening report to the commander of *H.Gr. Mitte*, von Vormann, while fully aware of the critical nature of the battle being fought on the northern bank of the Narew, was far more worried about the situation brewing on the far right flank of the *IV. SS-Pz.Korps*, which was defended by the *73. Inf.Div.* According to the *9. Armee* commander, "..continuing enemy troop movements underscore the suspicion, that at this point, we believe that the enemy will soon begin his next powerful attack that will be accompanied by a resumption of his attacks against the army's northeastern flank," referring to Gille's position southwest of Wołomin and Radzymin.[32] The possibility that the center of the First Belorussian Front might make a push towards Warsaw via the bridges over the Vistula at Praga was not far from his mind. Except for the *73. Inf. Div.*, there were hardly any credible forces the Germans could use to stop any Soviet attempt to cross over to the western bank of the Vistula.

In view of this potential threat, the *9. Armee* commander ordered that the defenses along the western bank of the Vistula within Warsaw itself be reinforced. The continuing relentless attacks by *Gruppe von dem Bach* had pushed the Polish insurgents at many points so far back from the river's edge that German troops could now occupy a portion of the western bank without interference. This would be critical in stopping any Soviet or Polish crossing attempt. Furthermore, the big push by *Gruppe von dem Bach* against the city center had begun to bear fruit, as witnessed by the surrender of thousands of members of the *Armia Krajowa* that day as well as an equal number of civilians, who flooded out of the Vistula Quarter of the city as the area under General Bór's control continued to shrink. The defense of the newly occupied portion of the river's western bank would be assigned to *Ogruf.* von dem Bach, whose troops would briefly come under the tactical control of *IV. SS-Pz.Korps* a week later when it would be assigned responsibility for defending this portion of the Vistula defense line.

That night, the army commander also ordered that the four bridges over the Vistula at Praga be rigged for demolition should the worst case situation come to pass. One decision that von Vormann did make that would affect all the future plans of the *9. Armee* was that the *19. Pz.Div.*, except for its *Pz.Gren.Rgt. 73*, would not, after all, be transferred across the Narew to combat the Soviet bridgeheads being established north of Serock. That would remain the problem of *2. Armee*. Instead, von Vormann decided that *19. Pz.Div.*, once it handed over its positions around Magnuszew to the neighboring *17. Inf.Div.*, would become the *9. Armee* mobile reserve. Most of it by this point had arrived at the previously designated assembly area northeast of Warsaw, where it could be switched either to reinforce Gille's corps on the east bank of the Vistula or the *VIII. Armeekorps* or *XLVI. Pz.Korps* to the south, which were keeping the Soviets penned up in the Magnuszew and Puławy bridgeheads respectively. It would soon prove to have been a providential decision.

The following day, 7 September, began much the same as the previous one. Except for occasional harassing fire by Soviet artillery and low-level reconnaissance activity, all of the corps within *9. Armee* had very little out of the ordinary to report. In its own morning report, the *IV. SS-Pz.Korps* stated that Soviet attempts to gain information about the defenses along the inner flanks of the *73. Inf.Div.*, the Hungarian cavalry division, and the *Totenkopf* Division were undiminished. These patrols, however, were easily driven off by either small-arms fire or well-placed artillery strikes. German aerial reconnaissance reported that 130 Soviet artillery batteries had been spotted in position in the Radzymin area, a sure sign that something was imminent. Again, tank noises—rattling tracks, revving engines, etc.—were heard opposite the lines of the *73. Inf.Div.*, but no attack occurred. The weather, while dry and warm, grew very windy as the day progressed, accentuated by a partly cloudy sky.

Almost all of the action occurring that day took place on the northern bank of the Narew between Serock and Pogorzelec, where the tank crews of the *Wiking* and *Totenkopf* Divisions found themselves confronted by Soviet armor for the first time. Having failed to eliminate the Soviet bridgehead over the Narew at Karniewek the previous day, German forces had intended to make another attempt on 7 September. However, like so many other times during the past two months, the Red Army beat them to the punch. First, during the early morning before sunrise, an infantry company from the 186th Rifle Division made a surprise crossing of the Narew at Gasiorowo, a town on the east bank of the river a mere 4 kilometers north of Serock. Infiltrating the thin security line on the right flank of *Pz.Gren.Rgt. 73*, this force was able to penetrate as far as the village of Klusek a kilometer west of the river by 4 p.m., while their comrades in Gasiorowo feverishly labored to build a pontoon bridge to hasten additional forces across.

Simultaneously, a force of 20 Soviet tanks originating from the bridgehead at Karniewek broke through the *Panzergrenadiers*' main defense line at Dzierzenin and reached the town of Małe, 5 kilometers south of Pogorzelec. The apparent mission of this tank battalion was to reinforce the new bridgehead being established at Gasiorowo by linking up with the infantry holding Klusek, since this latter village was a mere 2 kilometers east of Małe. Clearly, neither *2. Armee* nor *9. Armee* could allow the Soviets to establish yet another bridgehead so close to Serock.

Immediate steps were taken to wipe out this force of 20 T-34s, approximately a battalion, before it could widen and reinforce the bridgehead at Gasiorowo. The greatest danger was that this battalion would help the bridgehead's defenders merge it with the larger one already established at Karniewek. This would create a much bigger bridgehead that would in turn enable a much larger number of Soviet units to be assembled on the west bank of the Narew, where they would be able to conduct deep attacks into the *H.Gr. Mitte* rear area. The responsibility for destroying it was assigned to *Hstuf.* Flügel and his tiny armored *Kampfgruppe*, most of which had already been fighting in the area for the past three days. Flügel acted quickly. He dispatched Metzger and three of his remaining *StuG IV* to reinforce the defenses of *Pz.Gren.Rgt. 73* to prevent any additional breakthroughs originating from Pogorzelec.

Then he ordered Olin with three Panthers to hasten to the village of Murowanka, 2 kilometers northeast of Małe, to strike the Soviet force in the flank. Two more Panthers were to move to the western outskirts of the village and prevent the 10

Soviet tanks reported there from going any further. Flügel, with one Panther and one assault gun, established his forward headquarters at Debinki, 2 kilometers southwest of Małe. Six Panthers from *I. Abt./SS-Pz.Rgt. 3* from the *Totenkopf* Division that had joined him were positioned between Serock and Małe. As the Soviet armor moved forward, the Germans opened fire. Tank-on-tank duels immediately broke out, and for the next two hours both sides fired and maneuvered as they sought an advantage over the other. But the outcome was rather one-sided. Olin and his crew knocked out 11 tanks, while two other Soviet tanks were abandoned by their crews and captured by the Germans. The remaining tanks retreated or were knocked out by antitank guns of *Pz.Gren.Rgt. 73*. None of the tanks from *SS-Pz.Rgt. 5* operating north of the Narew were destroyed or damaged that day.

The new Soviet bridgehead between Klusek and Gasiorowo was pounded throughout the day by *SS-Pz.Art.Rgt. 5* in an effort to prevent more troops from crossing the Narew. At one point, it was reported that the bridgehead had been wiped out, but this was false. In turn, German positions were struck by Soviet artillery as well as by ground-attack aircraft. Troops from the XLVI and CXIV Rifle Corps had closed up to the eastern bank of the Narew and were able to provide direct fire support for their comrades enduring the German counterattacks on the opposite side.

The soldiers from *IV. SS-Pz.Korps* defending the western bank of the Narew inside of Serock itself, *Gren.Brig 1131* and *Fest.Inf.Btl. 1405*, kept their heads down and probably wondered when it would be their turn to be attacked. An additional fortress antitank gun unit, *Fest.-Pak Kp. 4./II*, arrived in Serock that day, where it set up positions oriented to the north with its 14 guns. While Flügel and his tanks, supported by *Pz.Gren.Rgt. 73*, had been able to temporarily halt any further Soviet advance from taking place, they were under no illusions that it would resume the following day.

That evening, Gille's corps staff evaluated the various information they had received from the corps' major subordinate commands in order to calculate its available combat power to report it to *9. Armee* headquarters. They were able to do this efficiently even though the day before, the entire corps headquarters had moved to its new location on the west bank of the Vistula in the Warsaw suburb of Młociny. The battle area east of the river had become so crowded with units coming and going, and the front lines had drawn so close, that Gille had no choice but to order his *Hauptquartier*'s displacement. Fortunately, the situation east of the Vistula remained relatively calm that day, which allowed this movement to take place with a minimal amount of enemy interference and disruption of the corps' command and control apparatus.

Despite the infusion of new units, the manpower drain brought on by incessant combat continued. The *Wiking* Division reported that it had only 482 infantrymen and combat engineers of its own, while the remaining 1,146 men were assigned to either *Gren.Rgt. 1145*, *Fest.Inf.Btl. 1405*, or *Pz.Gren.Rgt. 73*. The *Totenkopf* Division still had 1,839 of its own men comprising its *Kampfstärke*, while the *73. Inf.Div.* had 3,082 men, including 242 serving in Ritter's *Gren.Btl.z.b.V. 560*, which had been attached to *Obf.* Becker's division the previous day as a reinforcement. The strongest division by far, in terms of available combat strength, was the *1. ung.Kav. Div.* with 3,946 men. In all, the *Kampfstärke* of Gille's corps boasted 10,495 men to defend its 57-kilometer front line, which equated to 184 foot soldiers to hold each kilometer of ground. This was an improvement over the previous month, but was largely due to the fact that its frontage had shrunk due to its steady withdrawal since 18 August, rather than to additional manpower.

The number of operational tanks available to the corps on 7 September had remained relatively constant, with the *Wiking* Division reporting 35, of which 17 were assault guns or tank destroyers. The *Totenkopf* Division's *panzer* regiment was much stronger, with 44 operational tanks (four of which were *Pz. VI* Tigers) and 24 assault guns and tank destroyers reported, for a total of 68 vehicles. Both divisions had more vehicles in short- or long-term repair, but those did not contribute to a unit's daily combat strength. While it had yet to be committed to battle since it was technically still the *9. Armee* antitank reserve, *Heeres-Pz.Jg.Abt. 743* with 32 operational *Jg.Pz. 38t* represented a considerable armored asset. All four of Gille's divisions, including attachments, had a considerable amount of serviceable antitank guns available, 91 in all, ranging in size from 5cm *Pak 38* to 8.8cm *Pak 43*.

In a related vein, 7 September proved to be a milestone for the *Wiking* Division's *panzer* regiment, for on that day, it recorded its 500th tank kill since its combat debut on 29 March 1944, when it went into battle during the relief of Kowel. In a regimental special order signed that very day by its commander, *Ostubaf.* Darges, not only were the number of destroyed Soviet tanks announced, but also the 1,050 antitank guns, 395 artillery pieces of various calibers, and four aircraft that the regiment destroyed. The announcement also mentioned that during this same five-month period, *SS-Pz. Rgt.* 5 had accounted for 26,735 enemy dead. Considering that it never had more than 100 of its own tanks operational at any given time during this period, and that it rarely fought as a consolidated unit but usually was dispersed to provide support to the infantry, this was quite an achievement. In closing, Darges commended his men for their "unique successes" and looked forward to the time in the near future when the regiment would be able to report its 1,000th tank kill. During the next five months, it would not lack the opportunity to do so.

The strength of the corps' artillery was roughly the same as it had been two weeks before, with four divisional artillery regiments and two separate corps artillery *Abteilungen*, for a total of 17 battalions with approximately 51 firing batteries. Additionally, the corps' multiple rocket launcher capability had been augmented by *SS-Hstuf.* Otto Krosta's *SS-Werfer Bataillon 104*, which had finally joined the corps artillery on 7 September after a long journey from the Kurmark training area in Brandenburg. Its four 12cm rocket launcher batteries would have been a very welcome addition to the *SS-ARKO 104*'s available firepower, though it was initially tasked to provide fire support to *Gruppe von dem Bach* as it fought its way into the

Zoliborz suburb of Warsaw. In order to fight the upcoming Soviet main attack, which based on intelligence reports would be heavily weighted against the corps' right flank, the corps' *ARKO*, *Obf.* Brasack, developed a plan that would allow him to quickly shift corps artillery fire to the most affected area. For his fire support plan to succeed, Brasack would have to ensure that the artillery planning of the *1. ung.Kav.Div.* and the *73. Inf.Div.* would be closely coordinated and integrated into the overall corps fire support plan.

During this same period, the first record of the on-hand strength of the *IV. SS-Pz.Korps* headquarters and corps troops was reported to the *SS-FHA* in Berlin. On 5 September, Gille's staff stated that it only had 1,520 troops assigned, against an authorized number of 4,348. Thus, his headquarters, corps field hospital, signal battalion, *ARKO*, *flak* battery, escort company, and service and support battalion were all greatly understrength, though this number did not include *SS-Werfer-Abtilung 104*, which arrived two days later. The addition of this unit to Gille's headquarters organization increased its overall number to 2,167 men by 10 September. Part of the shortfall in numbers was caused by the continuing lack of the corps heavy artillery battalion, *SS-schw.Art.Abt. 104*, which was still being activated, and its artillery observation battery, *SS-Beob.Bttr. 104*, still fighting in Holland with *II. SS-Pz.Korps*. Most disconcerting of all was the overall shortage of officers, there being only 67 assigned against 200 authorized. Without these specialists, the burden on those who were actually assigned was consequently greater. Fortunately, Gille's corps signal battalion, *SS-Nachr.Abt. 104*, was still at 86 percent strength, which allowed it to function nearly at its maximum capacity.

That evening, Gille expressed his best guess as to what the morning would bring, predicting that the Soviet 47th, 70th, and 28th Armies would initiate their attack. He was less concerned with what was occurring on the north side of the Narew River, concentrating instead on what he expected to happen in the center and right flank of his defensive sector, primarily southwest of Wołomin and between the inner flanks of the *Totenkopf* Division, the Hungarian division, and the *73. Inf. Div.* All that *IV. SS-Pz.Korps* could do north of the Narew at the moment was to harass and disperse Soviet troop concentrations with artillery. The commander of the *9. Armee* saw things differently than his SS corps commander, believing that the situation north of Serock was where his real concerns lay, at least for the moment. Although the Magnuszew and Puławy bridgeheads were still dangerous, they were temporarily contained and the Warsaw Uprising was being slowly squeezed to death. On that day, nearly 20,000 Polish civilians passed through the lines of *Gruppe von dem Bach* from the old city, a sign of the flagging public support for the *Armia Krajowa*, whose situation was becoming increasingly desperate. The evacuation of civilians from Praga on the other side of the Vistula was also begun that day, in anticipation of the battle to come.

In his commander's summary that evening, von Vormann mentioned that two *panzer* divisions from the army group reserve—the *24. Pz.Div.* and *25. Pz.Gren. Div.*—were being sent by *H.Gr. Mitte* to bolster the defensive efforts of *2. Armee* along the Narew, local efforts having failed to eliminate the Karniewek bridgehead and the other one at Rózan north of Pułtusk. Along with the *542. Gren.Div.* and the *35. Inf.Div.*, these divisions would lead a counterattack against the slowly expanding bridgeheads, which had grown to an 84-square kilometer area now occupied by no less than six rifle divisions. No date had been set for this attack, it being dependent on the arrival of the two divisions from *H.Gr. Mitte* reserve. It was hoped that this would restore the situation along the Narew so von Vormann could focus attention solely on his own area of responsibility.

As for Gille, his army commander directed that his corps carry out as many combat patrols as possible the next day to collect prisoners to gather intelligence about Soviet dispositions. Von Vormann was still very concerned about the rightmost flank of the *73. Inf.Div.* along the Vistula. He also knew, as Gille did not, that when the long-awaited attack came, it would at least be launched without the support of the VIII Guards Tank Corps, which had been withdrawn for reconstitution on or about 6 September after it had suffered heavy losses during the past two weeks of combat.[33] Its whereabouts on that day were still unknown. In his closing paragraph, von Vormann estimated that Soviet forces would most likely in the very near future be able to close up to the Vistula opposite Warsaw at Praga, either to assist the insurgents or to seize the bridges for future operations. In any event, the *9. Armee* commander foresaw that responsibility for defense of the west bank of the Vistula in this area would soon devolve upon *IV. SS-Pz. Korps*. In this he was not wrong.

Friday, 8 September began with little action other than the usual artillery exchanges and aggressive patrolling activity by both sides. The warming trend continued, and like the previous day it was windy and partly cloudy but with no rain reported overnight. Fighting in the capital city continued with undiminished intensity, with the insurgents grimly defending their ever-shrinking enclave against the inexorable advance of *Ogruf.* von dem Bach and his polyglot force of SS, *Polizei*, *Wehrmacht*, and foreign troops. Despite having to give up ground, General Bór's forces continued to strike in unexpected places, and launched two battalion-sized attacks during the night against the Stauffer *Kaserne*, the German barracks located on the northern edge of the Warsaw suburb of Mokotów along Rakowiecka Street, where *Ostubaf.* Walter Bellwidt's *SS-Ersatz und Ausbildungs Bataillon 3* was located. They were barely repelled after several desperate hours of close-quarters fighting, including hand-to-hand combat. While the uprising was beginning to show signs of weakening, the *Armia Krajowa* was still clearly capable of lashing out and striking telling blows against unsuspecting German forces. Perhaps their morale and fighting spirit were still being sustained by the hope that the First Belorussian Front was finally preparing to come to their aid. Time would tell.

During the course of the day, Soviet activity in the *IV. SS-Pz.Korps* sector east of the Vistula markedly increased, while events north of the Narew, where *Hstuf.* Flügel and his battalion was fighting, continued to develop as the Soviet 65th Army expanded its large bridgehead at Karniewek while attempting to defend its other smaller one north of Serock at Gasiorowo. In the *73. Inf.Div.* sector, its antitank guns knocked out two Soviet tanks that tried to breach its main defense line near Hill 119. This came as a surprise, since it was the first time in nearly a month that any Soviet tanks had been reported in that division's area. Both the *73. Inf.Div.* and the Hungarian division carried out aggressive infantry patrols against the enemy lines as instructed.

The *73.Inf.Div.* also reported that its former commander, *Gen.Maj.* Hermann Böhme, captured in the Crimea on 13 May 1944 after surrendering a portion of the division in Sevastopol, had been conducting propaganda broadcasts and distributing surrender leaflets on behalf of the Soviets. He had been convinced to join the *Nationalkomitee Freies Deutschland* (National Committee for a Free Germany) while in captivity and had been employed for the past few days urging the soldiers of his former division to cross over and join the Red Army.[34] No desertions of men from the *73. Inf.Div.* were reported, though it is now impossible to assess how many would have liked to have accepted Böhme's offer.

One patrol from *Gren.Rgt. 186* in *Oberst* Hähling's *73. Inf.Div.* sector captured several prisoners and brought in three Soviet machine guns as booty. The Hungarians' combat patrol discovered that the Soviet 234th Rifle Division had established forward attack positions, including approach trenches, concealed a short distance in front of the Hungarians' own front lines. These were soon reported as having been engaged and destroyed by their division's artillery. Both of these divisions, as well as the *Totenkopf* Division, soon found themselves occupied throughout the day repelling strong reconnaissance patrols launched by their adversaries, but besides that and the omnipresent artillery and mortar fire, very little happened that day out of the ordinary.

The troops, of course, did not idle their time away; far from it. Most of their day when not standing watch was spent improving their defensive positions, cleaning weapons, laying minefields, and stringing barbed wire so that when the anticipated large-scale attack came, they would be as prepared as possible. Troops designated as a reserve or reaction force, located several kilometers behind the front lines, trained and rehearsed their battle drills as time permitted, or performed long-deferred maintenance of their vehicles and crew-served weapons. Staff personnel typed up official reports, award recommendations, requisition forms for ammunition, clothing, or other supplies, while *Kriegsberichter* prepared reports for propaganda broadcasts or newspapers back home in the *Vaterland*. Company or battalion commanders wrote many condolence letters to the families back home whose sons, fathers, or brothers were killed or seriously wounded during the past several weeks of fighting.

These activities applied to the main body of the *Wiking* Division just as well, spread out as it was between the Bug on its left and the Aleksandrów collective farm on its right, where it linked hands with the *Totenkopf* Division. Here, the tactical situation remained static too, other than the aforementioned Soviet artillery and mortar fire. From his new division headquarters in the town of Wieliszew, which only weeks before had been the site of Gille's headquarters, Mühlenkamp's primary focus that day was concentrated on what was taking place on his division's left flank at the confluence of the Bug and Narew at Serock, where nearly half of his operational tanks and assault guns were committed in support of *XX. Armeekorps.* The previous day had seen a great deal of fighting west of the Narew and it would see just as much this day as well.

Early that morning, a Soviet infantry company moving south along the west bank of the Narew managed to approach the front lines of *Gren.Brig. 1131* concealed by the morning fog. Sentries failed to detect them until it was too late, and the Red Army riflemen quickly managed to break through the German defensive positions, where they got as far as the northern outskirts of Serock by 4 p.m. Here, near the western approaches of the destroyed bridge over the Narew, the same infantry company took over a series of German foxholes and trenches and prepared to hold their ground until reinforced by more troops coming from the bridgehead at Gasiorowo. At roughly the same time, 200 Soviet troops along with an undetermined number of antitank guns were reported as having advanced as far as the village of Duza, one kilometer west of Małe.

Most of the tanks and assault guns from *Hstuf.* Flügel's battalion, including those attached from the *Totenkopf* Division, were oriented towards the north and west, where they were positioned alongside *Pz.Gren.Rgt. 73* to defend against another large incursion emanating from the Karniewek bridgehead, which failed to materialize. Upon hearing of the enemy's presence at Serock, Flügel sent three of his Panthers to the northwestern edge of the town to keep an eye on them. Meanwhile, *Oberst* Söth organized a counterattack late that afternoon with his greatly understrength brigade that managed to evict the Soviet company from the northern edge of Serock, but was unable to continue advancing due to the approaching darkness. To prevent the enemy from reinforcing his positions, the area north of Serock along the western bank of the Narew was fired upon throughout the night by the *Wiking* Division's artillery. Thus ended the combat activity for the day.

The army commander had other worries, the biggest being that he had been told the day before by the *H.Gr. Mitte* chief of staff that he would have to temporarily surrender his *XLVI. Pz.Korps* headquarters to *2. Armee* within the next several days in order to control the counterattack being planned against the Karniewek bridgehead involving the two mechanized divisions, *24. Pz.Div.* and *25.Pz.Gren. Div.* What was just as bad was the notification from *H.Gr. Mitte* that *9. Armee* would definitely have to give up its only mobile reserve, the *19. Pz.Div.* for this attack. To command the forces which up to this point had been controlled by

Gen.d.Pz.Tr. von Lüttwitz's *XLVI. Pz.Korps*, von Vormann would have to order *VIII. Armeekorps* to temporarily take over that portion of the Vistula defensive position, which would give it an incredibly long front line to defend, stretching from an area immediately south of Warsaw for over 120 kilometers, which was beyond an infantry corps' ability to control.

To prevent this, *H.Gr. Mitte* added the headquarters of the *391. Sich.Div.* to von Vormann's order of battle. The *8. Armee* commander then designated it as *Gruppe Sieckenius* (after its commander, *Gen.Maj.* Rudolf Sieckenius) and directed it to take over responsibility for the defense of the portion of the Vistula defense line immediately south of Warsaw previously controlled by *XLVI. Pz.Korps*. Most of the *XLVI. Pz.Korps'* units, including *Fs.Pz.Div. Hermann Göring*, were reassigned to *VIII. Armeekorps*. This decision only partially alleviated the problem for *9. Armee*. Although the bulk of *Gruppe Sieckenius* would be composed of the full-strength *5. ung.Res.Div.*, it was a second-rate unit that was never intended for front-line service against a combined arms army. The most that could be expected of it was to continue manning the defenses along the Vistula and keep an eye on the Soviet and Polish troops disposed along its eastern bank. It was buttressed by two German infantry battalions and 44 antitank guns, which at least would give it some antitank capability. Additionally, the Vistula at this point was nearly a kilometer wide, which further discouraged crossing attempts, at least during daylight hours.

Von Vormann was also very concerned about the ability of *IV. SS-Pz.Korps'* right flank to hold when the offensive finally struck, which he knew by now was only a matter of days away. The army commander was most concerned about the ability of the *1. ung.Kav.Div.* and *73. Inf.Div.* to withstand the coming storm, especially the Hungarians. Although von Vormann was confident that the *Totenkopf* Division would fight well, the transfer of the 28th Army with its three rifle corps from its old position along the Bug to an assembly area east of Wołomin, confirmed by prisoner interrogations and aerial photos, worried him a great deal. There was also the matter of the 130 Soviet artillery batteries identified east of Radzymin the day before. Aerial reconnaissance had also confirmed that the VIII Guards Tank Corps, after three days of absorbing replacements, had been identified moving into an assembly area in the vicinity of Stanisławów, the same area where Gille's corps had defended only a month before.

The only thing that the *9. Armee* commander could do at the moment, with so many of his forces tied down and the *19. Pz.Div.* having begun its movement north, was to transfer two additional multiple rocket launcher battalions from *XLVI. Pz.Korps* to *IV. SS-Pz.Korps*. He also ordered Gille to start planning a *Sehnenstellung* (a bowstring, or intermediate defensive line) that would stretch across the triangle formed by the confluence of the Narew and Vistula Rivers between Zegrze and Różopole, with its apex to the west at Modlin. This decision would have a tremendous impact on the course of the fighting that would take place during the third defensive battle of Warsaw, but no one could have foreseen this at the time.

Most of the action in the *9. Armee* area of operations on the last day before the Soviet offensive east of the Vistula resumed took place north of the Narew. Here, *XX. Armeekorps,* aided by SS *panzers* and *Pz.Gren.Rgt. 73* from *IV. SS-Pz.Korps,* continued its efforts to contain the burgeoning bridgehead at Karniewek. The other two corps in von Vormann's army reported very little Soviet activity during the previous evening, though in Warsaw the fighting was as fierce as ever. All four of Gille's divisions reported a great deal of fighting, including night bombing attacks by the Red Air Force against the front lines of the *73. Inf.Div.* Both the 70th and 47th Armies had increased the number of their nighttime combat patrols, as reported by Gille's divisions, and were becoming increasingly aggressive. Artillery and mortar fire continued throughout the night, ensuring that hardly anyone could get any sleep.

Combat north of Serock also continued throughout the evening of 8–9 September. A counterattack by *Gren.Brig. 1131*, supported by flamethrowers, killed or captured nearly all of the Soviet troops who had managed to penetrate as far as the German trenches along the Narew north of Serock, forcing the survivors to fall back to the village of Wierzbica directly opposite the river from Gasiorowo. The entire area between Gasiorowo and Klusek was pounded all night by the *Wiking* Division's artillery, which was doing its best to eliminate the new bridgehead by their fire alone. Surprisingly, the leading regiment of the 186th Rifle Division abandoned its bridgehead at Gasiorowo by midnight on 9 September, with the survivors pulling back across the Narew. Although there were further attempts to repair the bridge over the Narew, German artillery fire made the effort nearly impossible, until the Soviet engineers finally gave up and retreated to the river's eastern bank.

Perhaps it had become evident to Soviet commanders that there were insufficient resources to reinforce both the bridgehead at Karniewek and Gasiorowo simultaneously. Another reason why the bridgehead was not reinforced with the usual determination was because all available resources were being marshalled for the impending assault by the center armies of the First Belorussian Front. For the first time, German defenders in Serock also reported large-caliber Soviet artillery fire being directed at their location, a sure sign that the XLVI Rifle Corps' artillery brigade had finally caught up with its advance. Flügel's armored *Kampfgruppe* also suffered from this barrage, when one of *Ostuf.* Metzger's assault guns was knocked out near Debinki by a direct hit from an artillery shell. Though no one in the crew was killed, the vehicle burned out and was a complete loss.

The situation concerning the German response to the Soviet bridgehead between Serock and Pułtusk would remain uncertain for the next several days. A reflection of the confusion was illustrated by the vague command and control relationships between *IV. SS-Pz.Korps*, *2. Armee*, and *9. Armee*, and where the exact boundary between the two armies lay. While Flügel's armored *Kampfgruppe* was fighting north of the Narew, it was technically under the operational control of *2. Armee*'s *XX. Armeekorps,* but still under the administration of Gille's corps for supplies. There was no overall command element from the *Wiking* Division on the northern bank of the Narew except Flügel's battalion headquarters, and exactly who controlled *Pz.Gren.Rgt. 73.* was still a source of contention. So much so, that on 9 September von Vormann sent a message via *Hellschreiber* to Gille in which he demanded a report of the course of the fighting so far, where the troops were disposed, and what, exactly, was the command relationships, especially in regards to *Pz.Gren.Rgt. 73.*[35] Gille's response is unknown, but in a few days, the situation north of the Narew would be overcome by events, resulting in the recall of both Flügel's tiny force and *Maj.* Nähring's *Panzergrenadier* regiment.

That evening, the commander of *H.Gr. Mitte* ordered von Vormann to send the *XLVI. Pz.Korps* headquarters across the river the following day, which he reluctantly did. The *19. Pz.Div.* was to stay where it was in the assembly area near Modlin for the time being, but it was understood that it would soon follow. Nähring was alerted that his regiment would finally be reunited with *19. Pz.Div.* once it had crossed over the Narew. The *9. Armee* commander was certain that all signs pointed to a large-scale attack by the First Belorussian Front against the right flank of the *IV. SS-Pz.Korps* that would unfold within the next two or three days. At a time when he needed the greatest amount of available combat power to fight the battle he knew was coming, some of von Vormann's most powerful assets were on the verge of being taken away. While it was true that the situation in the *2. Armee* sector was very grave indeed, von Vormann also knew that his own army would soon find itself in a similar situation.

Fortunately, Gille agreed with his assessment, and had positioned his four divisions accordingly to gain the maximum advantage from its available assets as well as what the terrain offered. However, the commander of the *IV. SS-Pz.Korps* was still worried about the Hungarian division's reliability (though events would soon show that he need not have worried). Everything that could have been done to improve German defenses east of the Vistula had been done and the troops were as ready as they ever would be. The *73. Inf.Div.* appeared to be well up to the challenge. One of von Vormann's last-minute steps to reinforce Gille included moving the *9. Armee*'s last reserve, *Sturmbataillon AOK 9*, commanded by *Maj.* Wolfgang Meinhold, from the *Armee-Waffenschule* (*A.W.S.*, the battalion-sized army weapons school), from its training area to an assembly a few kilometers south of Warsaw where it could react to threats emanating from the north or south of the city. All that Gille and the 60,000 troops of his *IV. SS-Pz.Korps* could do now was to wait and see what the next day would bring.[36]

CHAPTER 9

The Second Defensive Battle of Warsaw Part II: 10–22 September 1944

Upon reviewing the events of the past 10 days, *Gruf.* Gille concluded in his daily report on the evening of 9 September that all signs were pointing to a major attack occurring the following day. Except for the fighting unfolding north of the Narew near Serock which involved almost half of the operational tanks of *SS-Pz.Rgt. 5*, an event that he viewed in any case as a distraction, his corps' main defensive line east of the Vistula had been relatively quiet since the evacuation of Wołomin during the night of 5–6 September. Believing that the main attack was imminent, he focused his attention towards ensuring that his four divisions were doing their utmost to prepare for it.

Between 5 and 9 September, he made it a point to visit each division at least once each day, visits that included inspections of front-line defenses, alternate positions, reserve assembly areas, and artillery firing positions. Adding to the urgency of the preparations was the identification of approximately 1,300 Soviet motor vehicles gathering in assembly areas around Radzymin, as verified by *Luftwaffe* photographic reconnaissance as well as by artillery spotters who simply counted the headlights of the vehicles as they moved in at night.[1] Whether these were tanks could not be verified, of course, but it did reveal that the Red Army was not concerned at this point in time with *Maskirovka* (operational deception).

Gille's corps engineer officer, *Ostubaf.* Erich May, was doing his best to lend whatever assistance he could, advising the divisions on the best locations to place obstacles, where best to emplace the available stocks of landmines and antitank mines, and how to construct front-line and alternate fighting positions, using the diagrams provided by the *9. Armee* staff engineer officer. Since manpower was scarce, units could hardly be expected to denude their front-line positions where they were in daily contact with the enemy simply to provide manual labor. The corps had already been augmented by *9. Armee* with the addition of three *Bau-Pionier* battalions—the *9.*, *421.*, and *737.*—to help construct positions behind the lines. To lend additional manpower, these battalions had been given control of over a thousand impressed Polish civilian laborers from Praga, who did most of the pick- and shovel-work.

Further augmentation was provided by *Feld-Straf-Gefangen Abteilung 1*, a battalion consisting of unarmed German Army prisoners who had been reduced in rank and sentenced to perform manual labor under dangerous front-line conditions until they had been deemed "rehabilitated," or had been killed or wounded in action.[2]

Gille's greatest concern was the corps' southern flank held by the *73. Inf.Div.* along the Vistula south of Praga, and both sides of Wołomin, where the largest concentration of Soviet forces from the 70th and 47th Armies had been identified. Efforts to remove German minefields had already been detected in front of their units. Gille anticipated a supporting attack aimed at rolling up his right flank along the river, with the main attack striking the *Totenkopf* Division in a southwesterly direction towards the bridges at Praga along the Warsaw–Wołomin highway, where the Soviets had already been conducting aggressive reconnaissance for the past several days against German defenses.

If the Soviet attack succeeded, both the *73. Inf.Div.* and the Hungarian division would be encircled, along with roughly half of the *Totenkopf* Division. Gille also believed that any attack aimed against his left flank held by the *Wiking* Division would be a feint, though he had to have a contingency plan should it develop into the Soviets' main effort. One thing he had learned as a corps commander during the past two months was that the Red Army of 1944 was quick to exploit any success, no matter how small, a far cry from the "stumbling colossus" that the *Wehrmacht* had encountered on 22 June 1941 that was easily outthought and outfought.

From north to south, the disposition of Gille's forces had changed little since 31 August (see Map 7). In the north, *Staf.* Mühlenkamp's *Wiking* Division still held the defensive sector from the Bug River at Rynia to Wólka Radzyminska, with half of its *panzer* regiment's remaining tanks operating in the *2. Armee* area of operations. *Obf.* Becker's *Totenkopf* Division defended from there to Zielonka; from that point towards Wesola was held by *Maj.Gen.* Mihály Ibrányi's *1. ung.Kav.Div.*; and on the right flank from Wesola to Zbytki along the Vistula stood *Oberst* Hähling's *73. Inf. Div.* To hold this 57-kilometer main defense line, Gille had 10,989 front-line troops, which equated to approximately 192 men per kilometer, a greater troop density than average, a reflection of his shrinking front line more than an increase in the strength of individual infantry battalions. His corps also fielded over 100 operational tanks, assault guns, and tank destroyers, not including the 12 operating north of the Narew with *Hstuf.* Flügel's force, and he still had 33 uncommitted *Pz.Jäg. 38t* as the corps reserve from *Pz.Jäg.Abt. 743*.

The strongest German division in *IV. SS-Pz.Korps*, in terms of manpower at least, was still the *73. Inf.Div.*, with 3,084 front-line troops, while the weakest was the *Wiking* Division, with only 480 of its own men remaining in its order of battle, which had necessitated the attachment of four other units from the *Heer* to provide a semblance of strength. The *Totenkopf* Division reported 1,898 men in its *Kampfstärke*, while Ibrányi's division counted 3,721, though his battalions were underequipped with heavy weapons and had no tanks of their own. Gille poured more resources into supporting the *73. Inf.Div.* than his three other divisions, since he viewed it as holding the most threatened sector, but still rated it as being capable of handling the looming challenge. What worried him the most was not Hähling's division, but the Hungarians, whose fighting abilities were still suspect, although they had successfully defended their position for over two weeks. Despite these misgivings, most of the corps' troops had nearly a week to prepare for the onslaught and Gille was confident that they would do well.

In the rear of his corps on the opposite bank of the Vistula, the fighting in Warsaw had taken a seemingly positive turn, when the *Armia Krajowa*, under General Bór's direction, sent two parliamentaries under a white flag across German lines on 9 September to negotiate a cease-fire. In return, *Ogruf.* von dem Bach offered to treat the insurgents as prisoners of war in exchange for their surrender.[3] Fighting in the isolated ancient "Old City" (designated as the *Altstadtkessel* by *Gruppe von dem Bach*) had ended when Polish resistance collapsed on 2 September, leading to the aforementioned exodus of tens of thousands of civilians who sought to escape the fighting. Undeterred, the insurgents continued resisting in other parts of the city, especially Zoliborz and Mokotow. Portions of the west bank of the Vistula, where the four bridges connecting Warsaw to Praga were located, had finally been cleared of insurgents. With his corps' rear area now secure and his supply routes over the Vistula back under firm German control, Gille must have felt some sense of relief, though it would only be a brief reprieve.

Another positive sign, as least with regard to the manpower situation, was the reappearance of the *Wiking* Division's field replacement battalion, *SS-Feld-Ersatz Bataillon 5* (*SS-Feld-Ers.Btl. 5*), which arrived by train in Modlin at 11 a.m. on 8 September.[4] Fortuitously, it was not inserted into the front lines, but was allowed to set up within Modlin to perform its stated function, which was to receive recruits being forwarded from its field training battalion, *SS-Feld-Ausbildungs-Bataillon 5* (*SS-Feld.Ausb.Btl. 5*), then located at the *SS-Truppenübungsplatz* Kammwald in Bohemia-Moravia. Once assigned to one of the four companies within *SS-Feld-Ers. Btl. 5*, the new arrivals would then be sorted out and parceled as soon as possible to a unit in the division that had the greatest need, corresponding to each soldier's specialty. It would also serve as the division's *Kampfschule* (combat school), providing *Lehrgänge* (specialty training) to already assigned personnel, such as *Unterführer* candidates, snipers, and combat engineers.

For example, newly trained grenadiers could be assigned to either the *Germania* or *Westland* regiments, radio operators to the division signal battalion, artillerymen to the artillery regiment, tank crewman to the *panzer* regiment, and so on. The available records do not indicate whether *SS-Feld-Ers.Btl. 5* arrived with any replacements, only that the number of assigned cadre who remained with the battalion was at 90 percent strength, or approximately 150 men. Since the battalion did not appear in the division's monthly combat strength reports between September and November 1944, it can be safely assumed that it was moved to Modlin without any replacements assigned, nor was it placed in the front lines, perhaps in anticipation of receiving some of the thousands of ex-*Luftwaffe* personnel then flooding into the division's field training battalion in Kammwald. Usually, once the replacements had completed training and were forwarded to their new units in the division, the battalion was disbanded until new recruits were received and only the division's *Kampfschule* remained.

These replacements were badly needed, as has been previously related. In addition to the present-for-duty strength already discussed, the *Wiking* Division had only received 125 replacements since 1 August 1944, including 44 medical convalescents who had been returned to duty. The *Totenkopf* Division was in a similar shape, though its field replacement battalion had been on board for several weeks. *Reichsführer-SS* Heinrich Himmler, aware of the shortfall of replacements for the *Waffen-SS*, had taken several steps to alleviate the situation. One of these resulted in an order issued on 2 August 1944 that directed *Reichsmarschall* Hermann Göring, chief of the *Luftwaffe*, to begin transferring up to 26,000 personnel deemed "excess" to the native German divisions of the *Waffen-SS*, where they would exchange their blue uniforms for field gray.[5] The only caveat was that these personnel, sarcastically nicknamed *Hermann-Göring-Spende* (Hermann Göring's donation), would retain their *Luftwaffe* rank and appropriate assignments would be found to match the skill sets and qualifications for each man, such as an artillery or antitank gun crew for former *Flak* crewmen and the division signal battalions for former *Bordfunker* (aircraft radio operators). Most, however, were destined for the infantry, but these troops would not begin arriving at the division's field replacement battalions until early October after a brief training period with an *SS-Feld-Ausbildungs-Bataillon*.

The other step taken by the *Reichsführer-SS* would have more immediate consequences. Taking into account the current dire manpower situation at the Warsaw front, he ordered that as many as 1,500 Ukrainian volunteers then in training as replacements for the *14. SS-Freiwilligen Grenadier Division der SS* (*galizische Nr. 1*) be shipped from their camp near Kladno in Bohemia and Moravia to Modlin, beginning on 10 September. After a three-day rail journey, they were trucked across the Narew to Jablonna-Legjonowo, where they were parceled out to the *Wiking* and *Totenkopf* Divisions at the height of the battle. At the front lines, four or five of these *Waffenwilligen*, or *Wawis* (the designation for foreign volunteers willing to fight), would be assigned to each infantry squad.[6] With little or no knowledge of German, and no front-line experience to speak of, these troops may have increased the *Kampfstärke* numbers of each division, but not necessarily their effectiveness. While many of these men would soon give a good account of themselves, experience would quickly prove that this addition made only a marginal contribution to the fighting and created an additional burden to already stressed front-line leaders.[7]

With the *9. Armee* commander's attention divided between the fighting in Warsaw, events taking place to his north across the Narew, the looming Soviet attack east of the Vistula against Gille's corps, and the continuing containment of the bridgeheads at Magnuszew and Puławy, it is a wonder that *Gen.d.Pz.Tr.* von Vormann was able to make any effective decisions at all. To add to the stress he was under, von Vormann's performance was under ever more scrutiny by Adolf Hitler, who had become increasingly distrustful of his generals since the assassination attempt of 20 July, especially of those like von Vormann who were beginning to display "defeatist" tendencies. Nevertheless, the *9. Armee* commander had done everything possible to advantageously position his forces for the approaching battle. He had already complained bitterly, with no effect, about the transfer of *Gen.d.Pz.Tr.* von Lüttwitz's *XLVI. Pz.Korps* to *2. Armee* along with *Gen.Lt.* Källner's *19. Pz.Div.* to lead the fight against the Soviet bridgehead between Pułtusk and Serock, an attack scheduled to begin on 13 September.

Lead elements from Källner's division were already preparing to cross the Narew at Serock, but as of midnight on 9 September, they had not yet crossed over, nor had von Vormann done anything to speed up their departure from his army's area of operations. Perhaps he was hoping that events would soon turn in his favor that would result in its recall, but von Vormann had done all he could as a field army commander. As for the rest of Gille's preparations for the upcoming fight, ammunition and scarce fuel had been stockpiled, and mines, barbed wire, and other barrier materials delivered to the corps. What few reserves that *9. Armee* possessed were made available to Gille, should he need them. One unit that was standing by was his army's elite *Sturmbataillon AOK 9*, which was moved from *Gruppe Sieckenius*, where it had been in a rest area, to a reserve position in the southern Warsaw suburb of Wolica. Here, on the western bank of the Vistula, it would be able to move quickly across the river if needed.[8] Like von Vormann, all that Gille could do as 9 September came to a close was wait to see what the next day would bring.

Arrayed against Gille's four divisions was an incredibly powerful force comprising the center of Marshal Rokossovsky's First Belorussian Front. Two of his field armies—the 47th and 70th, reinforced by the VIII Guards Tank Corps—would lead the attack. The 28th Army would not participate after all, contrary to German expectations, since it had begun its movement to support the offensive being planned against East Prussia. Lt. Gen. Zygmunt Berling's 1st Polish Army on the 47th Army's left flank would conduct a supporting attack along the Vistula. Both the 47th and 70th Armies had been in action for nearly two months by this point, and were considerably understrength, though Berling's Polish Army was nearly at full strength with over 57,000 men.[9] In all, the First Belorussian Front would commit seven rifle corps with 19 infantry divisions, one artillery division, eight separate artillery regiments, two tank brigades, and three tank destroyer brigades, with probably in excess of 150,000 men against the *IV. SS-Pz.Korps*. In addition, the VIII Guards Tank Corps, after a brief reconstitution and re-equipping period, fielded three tank brigades, a mechanized infantry brigade, a separate heavy tank regiment, and two separate artillery regiments, with nearly 200 tanks and assault guns.

To ensure that there were sufficient amounts of fuel and ammunition to keep the offensive in the center going once it began, attacks being conducted on the left and right wings of First Belorussian Front (north of the Narew at Karniewek and Rózan and along the upper Vistula between Magnuszew and Puławy) would be temporarily halted, and all operations being conducted at these locations would temporarily transition to the defense. Contrary to modern misperceptions about the Red Army's inexhaustible resources of men and materiel, it could not mount simultaneous offensives everywhere, but had to limit resupply to some of its army groups in order to funnel resources elsewhere. In the case of operations around Warsaw during September 1944, these had been assigned a secondary priority so that ongoing operations in what were deemed by the STAVKA as more important sectors, such as the ongoing East Prussian offensive and the clearing of the Balkans, could proceed uninterrupted.

Although he was forced to limit operations north and south of Warsaw to economize on ammunition and fuel, Rokossovsky still had the relatively fresh 1st Polish Army, which had been occupying a quiet sector along the Vistula south of the *73. Inf.Div.* for over a month. This army would contribute four infantry divisions, a tank brigade, a separate artillery regiment, and a tank destroyer brigade to the impending offensive. This summary, of course, does not include Front forces, which would send additional artillery, antiaircraft, antitank, and combat engineer units to the fray. The II Guards Cavalry Corps was also available as Rokossovsky's Front reserve if needed.

In all, some 180 artillery batteries would contribute their artillery firepower towards the ground battle, ranging in size from the 7.6cm M1927 regimental gun all the way up to the powerful 20.3cm M1931 howitzer. Several battalions of rocket artillery equipped with the 13.2cm BM-13 *Katyusha* multiple rocket launcher system (also nicknamed the *Stalinorgel*, or "Stalin's Organ" by German troops) were also included in the artillery order of battle. With such firepower in support, concentrations of assault troops along narrow frontages in designated breakthrough areas would give the Soviets a four- or even five-to-one numerical advantage over the defenders during the initial stages of the operation.[10] The Red Air Force's 16th Air Army, in direct support of the First Belorussian Front, increasingly ruled the skies and made life miserable for the German defenders by launching hundreds of sorties by ground-attack aircraft that bombed and strafed troop assembly areas, supply depots, and road convoys. In the skies above, Red Air Force Yaks and *Lavochkin* fighters tangled with the *Focke-Wulfs* and *Messerschmitts* of the *Luftwaffe*, frequently fighting them to a draw.

Rokossovsky's intentions, as well as the STAVKA's, had not significantly changed since the tank battle of Praga, but for one exception. The Red Army still sought to possess the crossing sites over the Narew and Vistula Rivers at Serock, Zegrze, Modlin, and Praga. These locations had to be taken by the First Belorussian Front in order to establish the preconditions for future offensives aimed at the heart of Germany, then in the early planning stages. Even though the actions of the previous 10 days had not gained these objectives, Rokossovsky's troops had seized two bridgeheads over the Narew at Karniewek and Rózan, and had gained advantageous jump-off positions needed for the favorable beginning for the next phase of the offensive along that portion of the front. But in addition to these tasks, a new one had been added—the belated assistance of the Warsaw Uprising, which would be carried out by Lt. Gen Berling's 1st Polish Army.

Although the Polish Home Army forces fighting in Warsaw under Generals Bór and Monter took their orders from the exiled Polish government in London, and had not notified the Soviet Union about their intentions to begin their uprising, Stalin, after offering no assistance at all during August, belatedly realized that if for no other reason than maintaining good public relations with the Western Allies, he had to order his forces to do something (or at least appear to be doing something) to assist them.[11] It was perhaps already too late; during the previous week, thousands of Bór's troops had surrendered and the remainder had begun to lose hope that help would ever come. Many of the insurgents had already begun to suspect that this was all part of Stalin's scheme to eliminate any democratic competition for postwar rule of Poland that might upset Soviet plans for the puppet government that he had already assembled and installed in Lublin.

Ordered by Stalin to formulate a plan, Rokossovsky was loath to commit his own forces to fighting the Germans in the city, where he feared they might become bogged down in house-to-house fighting. He decided instead that the best way to liberate the city was to encircle it from the north and south, trapping the remaining German forces or forcing their withdrawal.[12] Air drops by the Red Air Force would soon begin to provide the insurgents with badly needed food and ammunition. Since Berling's 1st Polish Army had been positioned on the eastern bank of the Vistula opposite the southern suburbs of Warsaw for nearly a month, Rokossovsky ordered him to begin preliminary planning to seize Praga and then conduct a river crossing and fight his way into Warsaw to relieve Bór's forces, depending on how the fighting progressed. With any luck, his troops might capture one of the Vistula bridges at Praga; at the very least, Berling could drive the Germans out of that suburb of Warsaw entirely, thus allowing the First Belorussian Front to close up along the entire eastern side of the Vistula.[13]

Regardless of how the relief of the Warsaw Uprising would turn out, Rokossovsky was confident in achieving success in taking Praga, forcing the Germans back across the river, and seizing control of the indicated crossing sites. However, he also knew that the Germans would resist his offensive bitterly and would move armored reserves to block or slow it down. Auspiciously, almost all of the available German armor was already tied down in defensive fighting, including *Fs.Pz.Div. Hermann Göring*, the *Totenkopf* and *Wiking* Divisions. The transfer of the *XLVI. Pz.Korps* along with the *19. Pz.Div.* across the Narew to assist the *2. Armee* counterattack between Pułtusk and Serock gave Rokossovsky the window of opportunity that he was looking for. His forces were prepared and already in their jump-off positions. The next phase of his offensive would begin before dawn the following morning, 10 September, and would rage uninterrupted for the next 12 days. When it was over, both sides would be completely exhausted and no closer to a decisive outcome than they had been before it began.

Sunday, 10 September promised to be a bright and sunny day; conditions very favorable for air operations. A lull in the fighting had set in after the Red Air Force's night attacks against the Hungarian division and *Oberst* Hähling's *73. Inf.Div.* had concluded, with little noticeable damage except to the men's nerves. Despite all the defensive preparations that had been made, the Germans and Hungarians were surprised when the entire main defense line of the *IV. SS-Pz.Korps* was enveloped by Soviet artillery, mortar, and antitank-gun fire at 5:49 a.m. The barrage, which lasted an hour and a half, blanketed German front-line, reserve, and artillery firing positions, which had been painstakingly identified over the past several days by Red Army reconnaissance troops, often at great cost.

Most of the Soviet barrage was focused on the positions of the *Totenkopf* Division southwest of Radzymin, particularly those in the Słupno and Hill 104 area. The right flank of the *Wiking* Division also received its share of the shelling, with the bulk of it falling upon the positions between Borki in the north and Wólka-Radzyminska in the south. Despite its intensity, this bombardment caused little damage, owing to the sturdy construction of most of both divisions' fighting positions. The same was true in the defensive sector held by Ibrányi's Hungarians. At first light, large numbers of Red Air Force ground attack aircraft began making their strafing and bombing runs on the defenders' positions, giving the German *Flak* crewmen plenty of targets to shoot at. Oddly, the positions of the *73.Inf.Div.* were not included in this initial bombardment.

The ground attack, when it came, lacked any semblance of tactical finesse and was solely a frontal-assault affair that developed substantially along the lines that Gille had predicted. Dispelling any notion that it might have been overlooked, the first recipient of Rokossovsky's attention was the *73. Inf.Div.*, which was attacked at 7:15 a.m. after only a 10-minute artillery preparation, which was unusual in comparison to what the rest of the corps was experiencing. Catching the defenders by surprise, a regimental-size attack (500–1,000 men) by the 175th Rifle Division rolled up along both sides of the Otwock–Wawer railway line in the direction of Praga before it was temporarily halted after taking the factory at Zastów. The

Red Air Force provided rolling close air support to the attackers, adding to the difficulties faced by the German commanders and troops. A supporting attack between the railroad line and the Vistula quickly took the villages of Kuligów and Zerzeń, forcing the defenders back half a kilometer along the rolling dunes of the riverbank. This first attempt, however, did not result in the penetration the Soviet commanders sought, and by early afternoon it appeared that Hähling's division had endured the worst of it.

This was not to be, and shortly afterwards a much more powerful attack developed in the same direction, only this time with tank support. In this case, Soviet troops attacked after another heavy artillery barrage and kept pushing north, reaching as far as the southern edges of the towns of Las, Wawer, and Glinki, a gain of nearly 5 kilometers. The village of Zastów, including the large factory on its southern outskirts, and the town of Anin soon fell to the Soviets. Elements of one battalion from *73. Inf.Div.* were cut off in Zerzeń when the rest of the regiment it belonged to was forced to withdraw. As a precaution, von Vormann ordered the immediate evacuation of the huge *9. Armee* ammunition dump at Rembertów, where a large quantity of artillery and small arms ammunition earmarked for Gille's corps were stored.

In order to prevent a deeper Soviet penetration and to enable the complete removal of the ammunition dump, at 5:45 p.m. Gille authorized the commitment of the corps' powerful reserve, consisting of *I.Btl./Gren.Rgt. 70* from the *73. Inf. Div.*, *Maj.* Meinhold's *Sturm-Btl. AOK 9*, *1. Kp./SS-Pz.Rgt. 3 Totenkopf* under *Ostuf.* Erich Schramm, and one company of *Hetzer* from *Pz.Jag.Abt. 743*, as well as one *Pionier-Kompanie*—in all over 2,000 troops. This counterattack, led by the division commander himself, was able to throw the Soviets back several kilometers, regain much of the lost ground, and rescue the force cut off in Zerzeń, though the troops from the 175th Rifle Division were able to hold on to the factory at Zastów. Three Soviet tanks were knocked out in the course of the action, which was over by 8 p.m. During the counterattack, which would prove to be only a temporary reprieve since it was unable to restore the original main defense line, Hähling was wounded in action. Soviet attempts to keep pushing his division back continued throughout the night, but it appeared, based on preliminary reports, that the division had the situation well in hand.

Except for having to wait out the same one-and-a-half hour artillery barrage that the *Totenkopf* and *Wiking* Divisions had been forced to endure, the *1. ung. Kav.Div.* only reported that it had detected a Soviet attempt to remove portions of the extensive minefield emplaced on the division's right flank shortly before noon. This attempt, the division went on to report, was smashed and scattered by its own artillery. Otherwise, the only thing worth reporting was that its positions continued to attract the attention of the Red Air Force, which carried out numerous bombing and strafing sorties throughout the day. So well dug in were the Hungarians that these attempts to disrupt their defensive preparations seemed to rise only to the nuisance level.

Not every division was so fortunate, as illustrated by the heavy fighting taking place in the *73. Inf.Div.* sector. The *Totenkopf* Division, after the Soviet artillery preparatory fire had lifted, immediately found itself under attack at numerous points along its front line by battalion-sized enemy formations. Most of the attention of the three attacking divisions of the CXXIX Rifle Corps seemed to be directed against *Obf.* Becker's division's right flank between Słupno and Struga, the scene of heavy fighting during the previous week. Enormous pressure was exerted against the positions atop Hill 104, which controlled access from Słupno along the road through the forest linking it to the village of Stanisławów. Beyond that, there were numerous paved roads that would allow Soviet mechanized units to approach Praga from the north or Serock and Modlin from the south, and attack both the *Wiking* and *Totenkopf* Divisions from the rear. Clearly, the Germans had to prevent a breakthrough here at all costs.

Commencing at 9:30 a.m., a regimental-sized force supported by tanks advanced out of Słupno and attacked directly into the teeth of the *Totenkopf* Division's defenses centered on Hill 104. Disregarding its losses, which included two tanks, this force attacked up the hill and managed to punch through the German positions after subduing the defenders on either side of the road. This force then kept on pushing through the woods, paying no need to the fighting that had broken out behind them. In response, the *Totenkopf* Division immediately launched a counterattack that managed by early evening to seal off the penetration and prevent any additional forces from breaking through. Repeated Soviet attempts out of Słupno to reinforce their penetration were stymied by well-placed artillery fire and effective usage of battalion- and regimental-level heavy weapons in the *Panzergrenadier* regiments. The bulk of the Soviet unit that had broken through, consisting of 150 men and six tanks, were surrounded in the vicinity of the forester's house a kilometer west of Hill 104 and prevented from escaping. Becker informed Gille that he hoped to eliminate this trapped enemy force that evening by another counterattack.

In the *Wiking* Division's sector, the situation was just as tense on 10 September as it was with its southern neighbor. Heavy artillery and mortar fire ranged the length and breadth of the division's area, distributed in such a way that it was impossible to tell where the main Soviet effort would fall. When it did, a battalion-sized attack spilled out of the forest near Rejentówka towards Borki, while a similar-sized supporting attack originating from the forest northeast of Wolica attempted to cross the lower Rzadza River and seize Rynia, a village situated on the east bank of the Narew. Both of these attacks were stopped in their tracks and driven off by well-aimed fire from *SS-Pz.Art.Rgt. 5* and infantry weapons from the troops holding that portion of the front. North of the Narew, the elements from *IV. SS-Pz.Korps* still positioned there, including Flügel's armored battlegroup, reported heavy Soviet artillery fire on Serock, including antitank-gun fire being directed at German positions from across the river, a mere 300 meters away. No new attempt by the Soviets to push troops across the Narew at Gasiorowo was reported, however. While neither the *Totenkopf* nor the *Wiking* Divisions had been seriously threatened by any of these attacks, one thing was certain; both divisions had been tied down throughout the day in heavy fighting and were unable to send any appreciable forces to assist the *73. Inf.Div.* had they been ordered to do so.

In his corps commander's assessment that evening, Gille reported that the long-anticipated continuation of the Soviet offensive had begun. He assessed that Rokossovsky's intent was to push through to Praga, cross the Vistula, and relieve the insurgents fighting von dem Bach's troops in Warsaw. He also interpreted that the flag of truce used by Gen. Bór's parliamentarians the day before was merely an attempt to deceive German commanders and lull them into a false sense of security. In addition, Gille thought this indicated that very close communications existed between the insurgents and the First Belorussian Front, though we now know that this was not the case. In fact, there had been very little communication or coordination at all between the two parties, let alone with the STAVKA in Moscow.

After reviewing the situation, Gille concluded that the attack would continue throughout the evening hours as the Red Army sought to physically link up with the Polish forces fighting in Warsaw. He can be forgiven for his incorrect assessment of the situation at the time, since all indications seemed to be pointing in that direction. However, as it is now known, Rokossovsky always saw the relief of Warsaw as a secondary effort at best, with the main thrust still being directed towards Zegrze, Serock, and Modlin. What Gille did not anticipate was that once Soviet forces broke through the front of the *Totenkopf* Division southwest of Wołomin and Radzymin, instead of continuing to push directly towards Praga, they would instead execute a right turning movement and drive northwest towards the confluence of the Narew and the Vistula. It would take several days for that realization to play out. In the meantime, much hard fighting remained.

In his evening commander's report to *H.Gr. Mitte*, von Vormann was not as optimistic as Gille. He was very concerned about the situation in the *73. Inf.Div.* sector and noted that the attackers were in a good position to continue their advance the following day, as well as the fact that many of the smaller penetrations in the division's sector, such as one between Glinki and Nowy Rembertów, had not yet been pinched off. It was becoming increasingly evident that Hähling's operations staff did not have a very solid grasp of the enemy's precise location. The vulnerability of the large ammunition dump in Rembertów was also a source of great worry, and as far as von Vormann was concerned, it could not be evacuated quickly enough. Its removal also meant that the flow of ammunition to front-line units and artillery batteries would be interrupted at a critical moment in the battle.

The division's commander had been wounded far more seriously than was first reported, so was incapable of further command, at a time when the *73. Inf.Div.* badly needed a firm hand in control. This unforeseen development forced the *9. Armee* commander to appoint a replacement that very evening. The choice turned out to be *Oberst* Franz Schlieper, the dynamic young commander of *Gren.Brig. 1132*, which was positioned to the south on the west bank of the Vistula in the *VIII. Armeekorps* area.[14] Upon notification of his new appointment, Schlieper had to turn over his brigade to another officer, then be driven nearly eight hours through Warsaw, across the river at Praga, and join the division he was destined to lead somewhere southeast of that city. He would arrive shortly before dawn to take over the division at a time when the battle was reaching a crisis point.

Unlike Gille, von Vormann correctly recognized that the effort by the Soviet 70th Army to break through the *Totenkopf* Division's positions west of Słupno was not aimed at driving towards Praga from the north, but was instead the main effort going for the bridges north of Warsaw across the Narew. Should Col.Gen. Popov's army break through the *Totenkopf*, or the *Wiking* Division's defenses for that matter, there would be very little standing in their way between them and the long sought-after bridges. Influencing von Vormann's assessment was the fact that elements of the VIII Guards Tank Corps had not yet been spotted, a sign that it was still being held back in reserve until the right conditions for its commitment had been achieved. Sensing the danger, he contacted *Gen.Oberst* Reinhardt that evening, briefed him on the situation, and urgently requested that the *19. Pz.Div.* be returned to *9. Armee* control before it was too late. He stressed that lead elements of *Gen.Lt.* Källner's division, bound for the *XLVI. Pz.Korps* where it was scheduled to take part in the big counterattack being planned against the Soviet bridgehead south of Pułtusk, were on the verge of moving north across the Narew and needed to be recalled immediately before it was too late.

Von Vormann also believed, unlike Gille, that the *73. Inf.Div.* was a very brittle organization and that if struck hard it would collapse and lead to the fall of Praga unless something was done. After all, the division had collapsed once before during the last week of July 1944 when it attempted to stop the 2nd Tank Army from reaching Praga, and had been hastily and incompletely rebuilt with troops transferred from replacement levies destined for other divisions, men from penal units, and other disciplinary cases. Although it had performed adequately while defending from a fixed position, how it would fight in a major land battle had yet to be seen. Clearly, von Vormann was not optimistic.

A large portion of Källner's *19. Pz.Div.*, including the division headquarters, was still in an assembly area north of Praga, though the tank regiment was being moved up by rail from its former position near Magnuszew and had not yet arrived. Placing the *19. Pz.Div.* back under *9. Armee* control would allow it to be used either for blocking any attempt by the 70th Army to seize Narew River crossings or to prevent the 47th Army from seizing Praga. To von Vormann's relief, Reinhardt relented and authorized the return of the division that evening. Von Vormann immediately issued an order that recalled the lead elements from across the Narew, and directed the rest of the division's scattered units to move via *E-Transport* (express rail), reassemble in the vicinity of Praga, and prepare to conduct operations the following day.[15] Its commander was ordered to prepare plans that would address its commitment on either side of the Vistula. Once the *19. Pz.Div.* was assembled near Jablonna-Legjonowo, it would be immediately subordinated to *IV. SS-Pz.Korps* as its reserve.

The *9. Armee* commander also issued an order that evening that directed Gille to refuse his right flank, which meant that the portion of the corps' front line encompassing the *73. Inf.Div.* and the *1. ung.Kav.Div.* would begin pivoting to the north, so that when complete, both divisions would be facing south. The new right flank of the *73. Inf.Div.* would then be re-established less than 2 kilometers southwest of Praga's southern outskirts. This move would not only prevent both divisions from being outflanked, but would create a shorter, more defensible front line that would be easier to hold and buy more time to enable the rest of the ammunition stored at Rembertów to be evacuated. Upon reading von Vormann's report, one gets the impression that he anticipated the impending collapse of the *73. Inf.Div.* and the ensuing commitment of the *19. Pz.Div.* to shore up that portion of the front.

Clearly Gille did not share this assessment, since his own report seemed to portray a tactical situation well in hand, not one that was spinning out of control on the first day of the attack. It was apparent that both he and *Ostubaf.* Schönfelder, his chief of staff, needed to sharpen their sense of intuition, but at this point Gille had been serving as the corps commander for less than six weeks and still had a lot to learn. This was one of the few times when Gille's and von Vormann's assessments of the situation widely diverged from one another. Glossed over in the daily situation report, besides the loss of terrain in the *73. Inf.Div.* sector, the *IV. SS-Pz.Korps IIa* and *IIb* staff (which tallied officer and enlisted personnel status) reported that the number of casualties suffered within the corps between 9 and 10 September amounted to 2,072 men killed, wounded, and missing, a very high number for two days of fighting.[16]

In Warsaw itself, with the sound of a major battle on the eastern bank of the Vistula clearly evident, the Polish Home Army redoubled its efforts to keep *Gruppe von dem Bach* at bay, fiercely resisting German attacks. Whether they were aware of the impending Soviet offensive is difficult to tell even today, but the Germans perceived the Polish attempt to bargain for a cease-fire the day before as a trick and reacted with predictable fury. While *Ogruf.* von dem Bach's troops had fought during the past month with a degree of cruelty and callousness rarely seen even in the Third Reich's armies, they redoubled their efforts as they resolved to crush the Warsaw Uprising once and for all. The casualties suffered by both sides soared as a result, with 119 German troops and foreign auxiliaries reported by *Gruppe von dem Bach* as being killed or wounded on 10 September alone.[17] Two additional SS police regiments, *SS-Pol.Rgt. 17* and *Pol.Schtz.Rgt. 34*, were thrown into the battle in the city that same day to reinforce the effort to reduce the area under insurgent control. By this point, the city was suffering through its 40th day of fighting, far longer than anyone in the *Armia Krajowa* had anticipated. It would last for three more weeks. The day concluded with a cold downpour, soaking the battlefield and making living conditions in the trenches and dugouts on both sides miserable.

When the next day dawned, the outcome of the German counterattacks carried out during the previous evening were revealed more clearly in the *IV. SS-Pz.Korps'* morning report. In the *73. Inf.Div.* sector, it had become evident that the commitment of the corps reserve had slowed, but had not "pinched out" the Soviet penetration south of Rembertów as had been previously reported. Other Soviet penetrations were reported, though after midnight offensive operations by the 47th and 70th Armies seemed to have ceased. After regrouping the battalions on its right flank that had been scattered during the fighting, the *73. Inf.Div.* reported that it expected to retake the ground lost the previous day. With a new division commander at the helm, how that would transpire had yet to be seen. Otherwise, the rest of its position was relatively quiet except for occasional artillery and mortar fire.

The *Totenkopf* Division attempted throughout the night of 10–11 September to destroy the Soviet tank-infantry element that had taken up a defensive position around the forester's hut in the woods west of Hill 104, but in the darkness this was difficult. It also attempted to close the 800-meter gap on either side of the hill with its infantry. Both of these efforts ultimately failed as well, though not for lack of trying. The division destroyed four additional Soviet tanks and warded off numerous enemy counterattacks, which prevented the two *Panzergrenadier* battalions from linking up and re-establishing the old defensive line. The best that Becker's division could do at this point was to control the gap with artillery and antitank fire, which succeeded for a few hours.

On the *Totenkopf* Division's left flank, the *Wiking* Division reported a Soviet foray in the direction of Borki, but this was driven off by artillery fire. The only other noteworthy event that took place in the *Wiking*'s area on 11 September was the change of command of *SS-Pz.Gren.Rgt. 10 "Westland." Obersturmbannführer* Fritz Ehrath, who had been skillfully leading the regiment since 17 May 1944, was replaced by *Stubaf.* Franz Hack, who up to that point had been the commander of the division's armored reconnaissance battalion. Hack had been a very successful battalion commander and was well respected within the *Wiking* Division for his positive outlook and tactical acumen. Ehrath returned to Germany, where he temporarily was assigned to the *SS-FHA Führerreserve*. In turn, Hack was replaced as commander of *SS-Pz.Aukl.Abt. 5* by *SS-Hstuf.* Otto Borchert, succeeded several months later by *SS-Stubaf.* Heinz Wagner.

The Hungarians reported that the only action worth mentioning was an attempt by a small Soviet assault troop to seize one of their defensive positions in the center of its sector, but this was warded off too. Surprisingly, the Hungarians were proving themselves to be quite adept at waging defensive warfare, a development that none of their German allies had anticipated. Perhaps sharing a defensive sector alongside the *Totenkopf* Division, one of the most highly motivated of all the SS divisions, might have influenced them to perform at a higher level. Additionally, their status as an elite unit within the Hungarian Armed Forces may have influenced their performance—after all, they had an image among their fellow countrymen that they had to uphold. Aside from what had been reported, including events in the Hungarians' sector, the situation along the entire corps front line was unaccountably quiet after that, with nothing being reported until the early afternoon.

Another event that occurred that evening was the long-awaited extraction of *Maj.* Nähring's *Pz.Gren.Rgt. 73* from the front north of Serock, where it had been fighting alongside *Hstuf.* Flügel's tank battalion for over a week. The effective strength of its two battalions had been reduced to a combined total *Kampfstärke* of only 177 men out of the 535 that it had started with a month before. It was practically burnt-out from weeks of uninterrupted fighting and had suffered the loss of both battalion commanders, though the regiment had consistently performed well. It began marching south before dawn across the Narew, where it would finally be reunited with its parent *19. Pz.Div.* The division itself began moving at the same time into Praga, including the second battalion of its panzer regiment, *II. Abt./Pz.Rgt. 27*, and *Pz.Art.Rgt. 19.* The rest of the division, which were still being brought up from the Magnuszew area, would join it as soon as possible. *Gen.Lt.* Källner quickly established his new division headquarters in the Jablonna district in Praga, 800 meters south of the railroad bridge. To ensure the security of the bridges over the Vistula and to prevent it from falling into the wrong hands, two additional battalions, *Gren.Ausb. Btl. 458* and *Sturm-Pionier Bataillon 500*, were moved from Warsaw itself, where they had been fighting against the Warsaw Uprising, and subordinated to the *19. Pz.Div.* As events would soon demonstrate, *19. Pz.Div.* arrived at the right moment and had time to erect a supplementary defense line behind that of the *73. Inf.Div.* before the storm broke.

The eerie quiet at the front continued until noon, when Soviet artillery fire erupted with an intense barrage across the front of Gille's corps, the usual prelude to an attack. Once again, the corps' right flank received the brunt of it. Numerous company-sized forays by Soviet troops were reported by the *19. Pz.Div.*, which had taken over this portion of the line early that morning from the *73. Inf.Div.* This force, which was advancing along the eastern bank of the Vistula, oriented itself along the Vistula shore's elevated roadway but was brought to a halt by the guns of *Pz.Art.Rgt. 19.* The *73. Inf.Div.* reported that another force supported by six tanks was spotted advancing to the west towards Praga along the railroad line southwest of Rembertów. This force, too, was driven back by artillery and ground fire, and four tanks were reported destroyed.

In the center of the Soviet assault, a column of brown-clad troops and tanks originating from a position near the fork in the highway at Wawer and Anin managed to push 2 kilometers up the paved highway towards Praga to their northwest before they too were forced back by a counterattack launched by the *19. Pz.Div.* Despite their losses, the Soviets were unrelenting in their attacks and kept pushing against the German defenders. At the same time that Källner's division had managed to restore the line in its sector south and southeast of Praga, to its left a much larger Soviet tank-infantry force punched through central Rembertów itself, precipitating a momentary crisis in the *73. Inf.Div.* sector, but this force was driven back. Even Ibrányi's Hungarian division found itself under attack, when a battalion-sized Soviet force from the 132nd Rifle Division attempted to break through its front line southwest of Kobylka on the division's far-left flank. After heavy fighting, the Hungarians threw this force out of its positions and restored its old front line at that point.

On Ibrányi's northern flank, the *Totenkopf* Division warded off numerous attacks against its position west of Słupno, which were complicating its efforts to finally close the gap on either side of Hill 104. In the *Wiking* Division's sector, no large-scale attacks were reported, though the artillery regiment successfully engaged and scattered a large Soviet force assembling in the Załubice area. Overall, the attacks by the 47th and 70th Armies seemed to be general in nature, though their main efforts, as they were the day before, seemed to be aimed at the area west of Słupno and south of Praga along the eastern bank of the Vistula. Fortunately for the rest of the German units arrayed along the Visutla in the *9. Armee* area, the Soviets were surprisingly passive, though of course in Warsaw proper, fighting had resumed with undiminished fury. Worryingly for the Germans, Soviet artillery fire was reported in the southern outskirts of Warsaw and in the vicinity of the bridges over the Vistula, the first sign of the approaching forces of the First Belorussian Front, which gave new hope to the embattled men and women of the Polish Home Army.[18]

In his evening situation report, Gille outlined the course of the fighting that day, division by division. What becomes clear is that were it not for the timely arrival of the advance elements of the *19. Pz.Div.* the previous night, the Warsaw suburb of Praga would have fallen to Rokossovsky's forces. The weakened *Pz.Gren.Rgt. 73* and *II.Abt./Pz.Rgt. 27*, after heavy fighting, had successfully stopped the approaching troops of the 175th Rifle Division and had even thrown them back 2 kilometers. The new acting commander of the *73. Inf.Div*, *Oberst* Schlieper, who had installed himself in his new division headquarters at Zabki, had been able to pull his troops back to the new line that he shared with his division's new neighbor, *19. Pz.Div.*

One of his regiments, *Gren.Rgt. 186*, was hard pressed by pursuing Soviet troops during the withdrawal to the new line, where they were located on the division's left flank, and barely managed to occupy their positions in time before they were attacked. Although they forced the Soviets back in this instance, it was a sign that not all was well within the division. To reinforce the shattered *Gren.Rgt. 70*, which had borne the brunt of the fighting on the right flank along the Vistula for the past two days, Schlieper's division received the aforementioned *Gren.Ausb.Btl. 458* and *Sturm-Pio.Btl. 500*, which should have been sufficient to shore up its defenses with enough troops to man a solid front line.

Attacks against the *73. Inf.Div.* in the Rembertów area continued throughout the afternoon and into the evening, with increasing numbers of company-sized attacks being reported against the division's new front-line positions. The situation was still very unclear and Schlieper was receiving conflicting reports from his three regiments, making it difficult for him to determine what was really happening. A large concentration of Soviet troops and tanks was observed gathering near the town of Wesola, several kilometers east of Rembertów along the paved highway. This target was shelled by the division's artillery, but without any observed results due to the approaching darkness. Artillery and heavy mortar fire was reported all along the division's front line.

The *1. ung.Kav.Div.* reported that Soviet incursions against its front line had tapered off, especially after a rifle company that had penetrated the positions of one of its battalions was wiped out in a spirited counterattack. The rest of the day was marked by an artillery duel between Hungarian and Soviet gunners, with neither side gaining an advantage but sufficient enough for the Hungarians to prevent any large-scale enemy ground attack from succeeding. The Red Air Force was as busy as always, seeking to attack and destroy any artillery positions or troop concentrations it could spot from the air. As the German line contracted, it was becoming apparent that Ibrányi's division would soon be pinched out of the line, which would create an opportunity for it to be finally relieved and sent back to Hungary, as both von Vormann and Gille were advocating. So far it had fought well and had prevented any breakthroughs from occurring, which was no small feat.

In the *Totenkopf* Division's sector, the fighting showed no indication of slowing down, with artillery fire and air attacks occurring continuously in the background. Throughout the day, a *Kampfgruppe* from the division had sought repeatedly to close the gap west of Słupno at Hill 104, and at 4:00 p.m. finally succeeded after eliminating the Soviet infantrymen holding the ground. The other group trapped around the forester's hut in the woods west of Hill 104 was slowly being whittled down by German artillery and tank fire. Stymied and denied his goal of breaking through at Słupno, the Soviet commander on the scene from the CXIV Rifle Corps decided to order another tank-supported infantry regiment to go around this strongpoint by moving southwest along the Radzymin–Warsaw highway. First, this force would have to remove the extensive barbed wire barriers and concrete obstacles emplaced by the *SS-Pio.Btl. 3* during the past week. While thus engaged, the Soviet vanguard was struck repeatedly by German artillery and mortar fire with good effect, forcing it to retire after achieving nothing and losing a number of men in the process.

The *Wiking* Division was also denied the chance of resting on its laurels. While Becker's troops fought unrelentingly, *Staf.* Mühlenkamp's "Vikings" had to launch another counterattack at Rejentówka to forcibly eject a company-sized enemy force that had once again penetrated into the woods on the town's outskirts. The division also had to repel three other penetrations of its front line at Borki, Siwek, and Rynia the same day using troops from Ritter's *Gren.Btl.z.b.V. 560* and *Gren.Rgt. 1145*. The division's artillery regiment was kept busy that day, firing uninterruptedly across the division's sector. Once again, von Vormann's directive to use artillery sparingly during lulls in the action was paying dividends, as there now seemed to be ammunition aplenty at a time when it would have its greatest effect. Across the Narew, *Hstuf.* Flügel had nothing new to report, other than continuing Soviet artillery fire that seemed to be designed to prevent any movement of German units from taking place. While the artillery fire on German positions was indeed heavy, it did not prevent the displacement of *Pz.Gren.Rgt. 73* to Praga.

In his commander's summary concluding his report, Gille stated that based on the interrogation of Soviet prisoners, it was apparent that the boundary between the 47th and 70th Armies was being shifted to the south, signifying that Lt.Gen. Gusev's 47th Army was going to concentrate more of its forces towards the operation aimed at Praga, while the 70th Army seemed to be focusing on tying down the bulk of *IV. SS-Pz.Korps* and prevent it from taking any part in the defense of that city. Gille restated his assertion that his opponent's goal remained the liberation of Warsaw and believed that attacks to achieve that would continue the following day.

During the past two days, Gille's corps had destroyed 13 enemy tanks and his air defenses had shot down one IL-2 *Sturmovik*, while the *Totenkopf* Division had lost two Panthers and *schw.Pz.Jäg.Abt. 743* had lost two *Jg.Pz. 38t* tank destroyers. He expressed no real concern about the ability of his *IV. SS-Pz.Korps* to continue defending successfully. For the next day's operations, he had ordered the *73. Inf.Div.* to withdraw several kilometers to the more defensible line a kilometer west of Rembertów. He also ordered his corps engineer to reconnoiter a fallback defense line that would run from the southern edge of Praga in a northeasterly direction towards Struga along the Radzymin–Warsaw highway. The situation appeared to be under control, at least based on his evening report.

With Gille's daily report in hand, von Vormann wrote his own army commander's report that evening. Although *IV. SS-Pz.Korps*' front line had held, especially in the sector defended by the hard-pressed *Totenkopf* Division west of Struga, the *Hauptkampflinie* had been pierced at numerous points along its right flank, especially in the sector defended by the *73. Inf.Div.* In his opinion, only the timely intervention by advance elements of the *19. Pz.Div.* had prevented the front between Praga and the Vistula from collapsing. He wrote that had the Soviet assaults been better coordinated that day instead of being conducted in a piecemeal fashion, they would have been able to drive the entire way into Praga, whether the *19. Pz.Div.* stood in their way or not. While Källner's panzer division seemed to have the situation south of Praga well in hand, the area west of Rembertów seemed to be the source of most of von Vormann's concern. He noted, with a hint of surprise, that the infantry of Schlieper's division seemed to have lost "the will to fight," based on their poor performance so far during the past two days of fighting. Individual soldiers from the division had already begun appearing without authorization in Praga, necessitating the establishment of *Versprengte* (straggler) collection points, where such men would be dragooned into a *Marsch-Einheit* by the field police and sent back to the front lines.

Based on this assessment, von Vormann informed his army group commander that evening that he did not feel confident that the *9. Armee* front could continue to hold if the *19. Pz.Div.* was pulled out and sent back across the Narew as originally intended. Therefore, the *9. Armee* commander told *Gen.Oberst* Reinhardt that he had no choice but to keep the division in Praga longer than anticipated until the crisis had passed. At the risk of weakening the rest of his army's front line, he ordered two more rocket batteries moved from their positions around the Magnuszew bridgehead to take up firing positions in the southern quarter of Warsaw, where they could fire directly into the flanks of the Soviet units arrayed across the river. Another source of worry for von Vormann was the whereabouts of the 1,300 motor vehicles observed moving into position around Radzymin on the evening of 9 September. So far, this force had not made its presence known, and until it did, he had no idea where Rokossovsky's main effort would fall. Although there had been many reports of tanks operating among the attacking infantry forces, no general attack by the VIII Guards Tank Corps had yet been reported.

Von Vormann also used his evening report to voice his misgivings about the arrival of 1,500 Ukrainian and Galician *Wawis* to reinforce the *Totenkopf* and *Wiking* Divisions. He noted that it was a bad idea to introduce these green recruits to combat at this time, when both of these divisions were engaged in heavy fighting against the enemy. He believed that instead of being the badly needed reinforcements that both divisions required, they would prove to be a burden to the commanders, since they would have to exercise greater care when employing them. Rather, they should have been introduced to combat conditions slowly, in a location where there was little or no fighting.

The *9. Armee* commander also stated that he was not sure whether they would fight or simply run away, taking into account the overall deteriorating situation on the Eastern Front at that time. After all, the Ukraine had already been reoccupied by the Red Army and it was doubtful that these men would ever see their homes again unless as prisoners. But since it was an SS matter, there was little he could do except express his misgivings. All 1,500 of them went into the front lines and took up their positions alongside their German comrades. There was very little von Vormann could add except to praise the performance of the Hungarian cavalry division, which had fought much better than expected. The next day would determine how well he and Gille had positioned their forces. One of the last things that von Vormann did before he went to bed, was to issue a warning order to the *Fs.Pz.Div. Hermann Göring*, positioned at that time near the Puławy bridgehead near Radom, that it was to begin making movement preparations so it would be able to reinforce the Warsaw *Kampfraum* at a moment's notice. As events were to show, only one regiment was immediately affected, and this one, *Fs.Pz.Gren.Rgt. 2 Hermann Göring*, was soon designated the *H.Gr. Mitte* reserve, removing it from *9. Armee* control before it could depart for Warsaw.

The next day, 12 September, was to prove the most critical moment during the entire second defensive battle of Warsaw and would see German fortunes change for the worst. It began in an orderly enough fashion, with the withdrawal by the *73. Inf.Div.* and *1. ung.Kav.Div.* to their new defense line stretching between Praga, Rembertów, and Zielonka proceeding more or less according to plan, even though the former division had been harried here and there by the pursuing Soviets. Both divisions reported that they were set in their new positions by 4:58 a.m. The *73. Inf.Div.* was able to establish a rudimentary defense line 5 kilometers wide between Zielonka and Rembertów, with most of its troops being positioned on the eastern edge of the Drewnica forest. The other operation planned that morning was the counterattack by the *19. Pz.Div.* and the corps reserve to re-establish the front line south of Rembertów, the scene of the previous day's breakthrough by the 175th Rifle Division. Other than the usual heavy Soviet artillery and mortar fire that seemed to herald each day's impending action, the only other incidents worth reporting were the numerous sorties flown the previous evening by the Red Air Force, which conducted numerous night bombing missions throughout the *IV. SS-Pz.Korps* sector.

The first sign that things were not going as planned was the inability of the counterattack launched by the *19. Pz.Div.* to make any headway. Instead of clearing up the breakthrough from the day before and pushing further south to the highway leading east out of Praga to Rembertów as planned, the division reported at 7:14 a.m. that its forces were counterattacked by an even larger Soviet armored force. Surprised by this development, the *Kampfgruppe* leading the assault, which had barely begun its own attack, was pushed back several kilometers to a position northwest of Rembertów, beyond their original starting point. A few hours later, an even more powerful armored Soviet assault, originating from the old Rembertów artillery training area between Ossów and Wesola, slammed into the defenses of the *73. Inf.Div.* arrayed between Zielonka in the north and Stary Rembertów in the south, after its troops had been in their new positions for less than six hours.

Following a tremendous artillery barrage that forced the German troops to seek cover in the recesses of their foxholes, a force estimated to be at least a tank brigade initiated the most consequential attack of the day. Lieutenant General Popov's VIII Guards Tank Corps, the whereabouts of which had been an open question until now, had finally made its presence known. Another event that was recorded occurring at roughly the same time that day was the appearance of 120 four-engine bombers over Warsaw, where they were observed dropping supply canisters over the portions of the city in the southern area thought to be still under the control of General Bór's insurgents.

What followed next was something rarely seen on the Eastern Front—rarely seen anywhere, for that matter. A large portion of the *73. Inf.Div.*, a unit consisting of native-born Germans, simply broke and ran under the pressure of this tank assault. Many of the men in four of the division's six grenadier battalions threw down their guns, abandoned their positions and heavy weapons, and fled to the rear as fast as their feet would carry them. Efforts by their officers to rally them were fruitless, as the panicked men stumbled headlong towards the presumed safety of Praga. The only units that did not run were *I. Btl./Gren.Rgt. 70*, which was still part of the corps' reserve force. and another from *Gren.Rgt. 186* in the forest immediately southwest of Zielonka that was isolated from the fighting.

The panic-fueled flight of the bulk of the division's infantry left a 5-kilometer-wide gap in the German lines between the *1. ung.Kav.Div.* and the *19. Pz.Div.* Ironically, before the attack, the division had possessed more than ample means to effectively resist the Soviet tanks, having 16 of its own antitank guns in its *Pz.Jäg.Abt. 173* and 12 additional heavy antitank guns from the attached *Fest.-Pak Kp. 2./VI.* Most of these weapons were simply abandoned and captured intact, though the latter unit managed to haul off five of their guns in the resulting tumult. Schlieper, in command of the division for less than two days, attempted to stop the flood along with his division *Ia*, *Maj.* Otto Becker, but to no avail.

Through this gap poured the vanguard of a tank brigade, driving as rapidly as possible towards Praga with little to bar their advance. The Red Air Force flew numerous sorties in support of the attack, concentrating on any German reserves moving up or the few remaining centers of resistance. One tank spearhead, led by 25 T-34s, followed by troops of the LXXVII Rifle Corps, reached the crossroads northeast of Zabki by noon, less than 3 kilometers from Schlieper's command post, while another, operating 5 kilometers to its south, blasted its way through the village of Kawęczyn and was reported to be approaching Praga via the railway line from Rembertów, reaching the suburbs of Ultrata and Kozia Górka by late afternoon. The *19. Pz.Div.*, reinforced by the timely arrival of its *Pz.Gren.Rgt. 74* and half of *I. Abt./Pz.Rgt. 27*, launched an immediate counterattack that checked the advance on Praga and attempted to regain the ground lost that morning.

His right wing now completely exposed by the collapse of the *73. Inf.Div.*, Lt.Gen. Ibrányi ordered his southernmost regiment to refuse its right flank by swinging back to the north to prevent the Soviets from enveloping his division. One Hungarian cavalry squadron, together with an armored *Kampfgruppe* from the *Totenkopf* Division, carried out a series of counterattacks that retook the crossroads east of Zabki, while another Hungarian squadron was engaged in eliminating a penetration by Soviet infantry into the area southwest of Zielonka. Throughout the day, the entire front line of the *Totenkopf* Division was subjected to a series of battalion-sized tank-supported infantry attacks, evidently designed to relieve the unit encircled west of Słupno as well as to tie down *Obf.* Becker's division to prevent it from assisting its neighbors. This effort failed on all counts, and the only thing that the 70th Army could show for its efforts was a lengthening casualty roll. Not only did the *Totenkopf* Division ward off each attempt to penetrate its front, but it was able to use its division reserve to assist the Hungarians in stopping the Soviet effort to break through near Zabki, knocking out 16 T-34s in the process. The *Wiking* Division reported numerous company-sized attempts to penetrate its defensive positions, but all were successfully warded off.

The joint *Totenkopf*–Hungarian division attempt only accounted for the northern Soviet spearhead; a few kilometers to their south, a tank battle was raging between the other Soviet force from the CXXV Rifle Corps and the *19. Pz.Div.* east of Praga. This action was precipitated by an order issued by *9. Armee* at 10:30 a.m. that directed *IV. SS-Pz.Korps* to immediately attack and re-establish its old front line south and east of Praga, and then defend it at all costs.[19] This was to prove a tall order, as events soon demonstrated. Complicating the preparations for the German counterattack, Praga itself was subjected to intense shelling by Soviet heavy and super-heavy artillery, while an estimated 100 medium bombers from the 16th Air Army pounded the city from the air. Nevertheless, *Gen.Lt.* Källner's division commenced its attack late that afternoon and managed by nightfall to throw the Soviet force back nearly 3 kilometers, but could go no further because many of tanks from *I. Abt./Pz.Rgt. 27* became mired in the swampy area south of Zabki. At the same time, the corps reserve, consisting of *Maj.* Meinhold's *AOK 9 Sturmbataillon, I. Btl./Gren.Rgt. 70, Panzergruppe Schramm* from the *Totenkopf* Division, and *Pz.Jag.Abt. 743*, conducted its own counterattack from Zabki to the south, reaching an area only 500 meters north of Kawęczyn before darkness fell, leaving a gap only half a kilometer wide between it and the vanguard of the *19. Pz.Div.* One more push and the Soviet force would either be cut off completely or forced to withdraw, a task left for the following day.

During the late afternoon, the situation remained in the balance until the German counterattacks could re-establish a continuous front line. The complete collapse of the *73. Inf.Div.* was something that not even the pessimistic von Vormann had contemplated. It came as a shock not only to him, but to the commander of *H.Gr. Mitte* as well. Had *G.F.M.* Model still been in command of the army group, he would probably have driven to the scene and by force of personal example would have tried to halt the panic all by himself. The monocle-wearing field marshal would probably have resorted to the most extreme measures, such as summary execution on the spot, to provide examples to other leaders of the *73. Inf.Div.* of the consequences of "cowardice in the face of the enemy." He had done it before. *Gen.Oberst* Reinhardt was not that kind of commander and did not possess the personal ruthlessness that such actions required, but he was to attempt to make an example of the division in a different way.

In the meantime, the bulk of the division's infantry, having fled from their positions, began to show up on the streets of Praga and a group of them were reported to be marching towards the bridges over the Vistula. Not only did they want to extricate themselves from the battle, but were apparently trying to get out of the war entirely. This massive act of collective disobedience, even cowardice, could not be ignored, and the *9. Armee* commander ordered the *Feldgendarmerie* and *Auffangkommandos* (special straggler collection units) to stop them and do whatever was necessary, including *Schärfste Massnahmen* (extreme measures) such as shootings to keep them away from the bridges.[20] The next step was to arrest and detain the hundreds of stragglers found throughout the city. After sorting them out, they were organized into a battalion-sized unit that was led out of the city to occupy a blocking position between the village of Elsnerów, Hill 89, and the western outskirts of Zabki.

One of the immediate consequences of the collapse of the *73. Inf.Div.* front line was that many of the division's support elements that depended on the infantry holding their positions for protection were now completely exposed to armored attack. The firing batteries of the division's *Art.Rgt. 173* were particularly vulnerable, having been emplaced in the 10-kilometer square area between Zabki and Praga. During the late morning of 12 September, they found themselves in the path of the approaching tanks of the VIII Guards Tank Corps. This particular artillery regiment had been evacuated from the Crimea the previous May as an intact unit and had therefore not been affected by the wholesale collapse of morale in the infantry regiments. Its individual gun crews stood their ground, and some in the attack's direct path engaged the approaching tanks with direct fire. The rest began to limber up their guns and prepared to depart, an action that would have deprived the division of artillery support when it needed it the most.

At this point, *Obf.* Kurt Brasack, the *IV. SS-Pz.Korps*' artillery commander, appeared on the scene. After hearing the initial reports of the unfolding disaster, he acted on his own initiative, left the *ARKO* command post, and hurried to the area southwest of Zabki in his staff car. Upon arriving, he assessed the situation and took personal control of the regiment, since its commander was nowhere to be found. Driving up to the forward batteries as they were preparing to depart, he ordered each of the badly shaken gun crews to stop, unlimber their guns, and resume firing. He personally "laid in" several of the guns, orienting them towards their targets. Some of the individual batteries he found entirely without any officers in charge, and took control of them himself until someone could be found to exercise command. In the citation for the German Cross in Gold that Gille bestowed upon him the following month for his exploits that day, it stated, "To the members of the *Wehrmacht*, he served hereby as an example of bravery and willingness to fight." Due to his decisive actions, Brasack prevented most of the regiment's guns from falling into the hands of the enemy and contributed substantially to stopping the Soviet breakthrough as well as the establishment of a new defense line.[21]

Gille quickly determined that the *73. Inf.Div.* was no longer capable of functioning as a division, ordering its remnant to be placed under the command of *Gen.Lt.* Källner of the *19. Pz.Div.* As for Schlieper, he received none of the blame for his division's collapse, since he had not been there long enough to know his subordinate commanders' strengths and weaknesses or to learn about the actual front-line conditions within his command, much less what had brought about its failure in combat. The fact that he and his *Ia* (who had been wounded in action during the battle) had attempted to rally or at least stop the troops from fleeing the front lines was seen as evidence of their determination to keep fighting. Gille next ordered Schlieper to take steps necessary to assemble what battle-ready troops he still possessed, form them into a *Kampfgruppe*, and put them at Källner's disposal for the defense of Praga. His division's former front line was taken over by the *1. ung.Kav.Div.* and *19. Pz.Div.*, which were tasked with closing the remaining gap between them the following day.

In his summary of the day's action submitted to the *9. Armee* commander that evening, Gille wrote that he believed the 47th Army, with supporting armor, would continue their attempt to seize Praga and push across the river into Warsaw proper to relieve the insurgents still fighting there. He wrote that due to the failure of the *73. Inf.Div.* to defend its position, the entire southern portion of his corps' front line had been compromised, enabling the enemy to seize key terrain east of Praga and south of Zielonka. Gille wrote that while the *19. Pz.Div.*, joined by the corps reserve, the *1. ung.Kav.Div.*, and the armored *Kampfgruppe* from the *Totenkopf* Division would still carry out the attack to finish closing up the hole in the front the following day, the approaching 1st Polish Infantry Division, which was detected late that afternoon on the southern outskirts of Praga, might complicate things. Time would tell. On the plus side, Gille's corps had at least prevented the loss of Praga and destroyed 19 Soviet tanks that day, as well as six heavy antitank guns, in exchange for the loss of two tanks and two tank destroyers of their own, though this could not compensate for the dissolution of the *73. Inf.Div.*[22]

In his own commander's report that evening, von Vormann concurred with Gille's actions, stating his belief that were it not for the complete collapse of the *73. Inf.Div.*, the 47th Army would have been kept at bay on 12 September. He fully expected a new front line to be established the following day, though von Vormann acknowledged reality when he stated that it was beyond the capabilities of Gille's corps to expect that it could retake the old front line that had existed on 10 September. This was a task that the *H.Gr. Mitte* commander had ordered carried out, but von Vormann told him it was impossible. Reinhardt's response is not recorded, though he too was experienced enough to know that his army commander was correct, despite what he had previously directed.

What affected von Vormann the most though, what baffled him, was how an experienced German division that had sufficient manpower and heavy weapons could have folded so easily. While it had only recently been rebuilt, it had spent the past six weeks holding a front-line position where its troops had been in daily contact with the enemy. It had been given plenty of opportunity to train, build up its formations, and achieve the kind of internal cohesion necessary to withstand the shock of a major battle. Clearly, it was a problem of leadership more than anything else, because such events rarely happened to all-German units. Von Vormann wrote that in order to prevent this kind of panicked outbreak from reoccurring, harsh measures were called for. The measures he had in mind included flying courts martial for on-the-spot judgement while the fighting was still occurring, but more official measures would soon be taken after the fighting had died down.

However, he did exhibit sympathy for the rank and file. In his report that evening, he wrote:

> The *73. Inf.Div.* … was shattered in the Crimea and re-formed anew using men returning from leave. The development of the greater situation on the Eastern Front did not permit a longer period for reconstitution of the division. Without complete re-equipping with weapons, which had to be sent to them while they were still 'on the march,' the division had to be thrown into battle east of Warsaw in July, where it found itself involved in heavy fighting and where it was partially encircled. In the nearly two months since, where the division occupied a quiet period on the southern flank of the Army's front lines, the division was not able to develop the firm inner cohesion and confidence in its own strength that it needed.

He went on:

> Even before this, the old members of the division, who had lived through the fighting in the Crimea, had already displayed a minimal ability to stand firm in a crisis. The officer corps of these regiments consists overwhelmingly of company commanders between 18–22 years of age, whose life experiences up to this point lacked any combat exposure. These officers were neither in the position to lead their troops under these worsening circumstances nor had they themselves grown to the point where they could master a critical situation. So the minimal combat power of the division has been shown to be due not only to the three-fold numerical superiority of the enemy, but above all, to its past history and inability to forge a new tradition for itself, which only it could create.

He also knew that, however much sympathy he had for the men in the division, its failure had jeopardized the security not only of its corps, but *9. Armee* as well. Von Vormann concluded by writing:

> This situation has put the army in the position where it cannot count on the infantry of this division to contribute anything to our strength of arms. Currently east of the Vistula River in the Praga area the only force we can count on is *19. Pz.Div.*, whose *Pz.Gren.Rgt. 73* was drastically weakened during previous fighting while attached to *5. SS-Pz.Div. Wiking*. The defensive success of the past few days has been achieved only because of our tanks. The course of the fighting on the eastern bank of the Vistula leads us to expect that in the foreseeable future, the Vistula itself will become the new front line.

The subject of most concern to von Vormann was what the loss of Praga would mean to the ongoing fighting in Warsaw, which had reached a new height as the *Armia Krajowa* fought desperately to hold out long enough to be rescued by Rokossovsky's forces. Soviet artillery fire on German positions in the city was now commonplace and a river crossing could occur at any time.

The four bridges over the Vistula in Praga had already been rigged for demolition, and the senior officer on the scene, *Oberst* Meyer, had been granted authority by the commander of *9. Armee* to blow them up should the Soviets show any sign of making an effort to seize them. This was no decision to be taken lightly, since only the army group commander had the authority to delegate this responsibility. Earlier that day, it had appeared as if the southernmost bridge, the one closest to the Soviet spearhead, might actually fall into enemy hands, but the counterattack launched later that afternoon by *19. Pz.Div.* had just barely prevented this from happening.[23]

Should all four bridges be blown up, supplies for Gille's corps could still be sent across the Narew at Modlin and Zegrze, and a temporary 12-ton bridge was being constructed at Młociny, but the loss of Praga meant that Soviet troops would only be separated from Warsaw by a few hundred meters of water. To make the situation even more serious, only a thin screen of security troops from *Gruppe von dem Bach*, with no heavy weapons worth mentioning, secured the west bank of the Vistula, and could only report, not repel, any kind of river crossing attempt. To their rear, these security troops still had to reckon with the *Armia Krajowa*, leaving them in a sense "between the devil and the deep blue sea."

Nearly everything else available within *9. Armee* had been committed to completing the suppression of the Warsaw Uprising. Furthermore, the phased withdrawal of Hungarian units from the army's *Kommandanten für das rückwärtige Armeegebiet*, or *Korück* (army rear area command)—where they had been performing security duties, including defending rail lines and depots against partisan attack—meant that the few remaining German security and *Landeschützen* units would have to spread their assets widely and would thus be unable to contribute to securing Warsaw. Von Vormann had thinned out the corps troops of *VIII. Armeekorps* as much as he dared, and had even begun taking assets from *Gruppe Sieckenius* as well, which had very little to spare. Fortunately, the Soviet 8th Guards Army arrayed against von Vormann's southern front west of Magnuszew had displayed no initiative, nor had it carried out any offensive operations worth mentioning, which allowed the army commander to move troops out of that sector. But the forces needed to build up a new defense line along the Vistula on the eastern side of Warsaw would have to come from somewhere else.

That "somewhere else" was the *2. Armee*'s front along the Narew west of Pultusk, where the understrength *25. Pz.Div.* was idling as the *Heeresgruppe* reserve as it awaited the beginning of the long-awaited counteroffensive by the *XLVI. Pz.Korps* to eliminate the Soviet bridgehead located between that city and Serock. The commander of *9. Armee* had been trying to pry that division away from *2. Armee* for the past several days, but until 12 September, von Vormann had no luck. The collapse of the *73. Inf.Div.* and the corresponding threat of a river crossing at Warsaw was all it took to sway Reinhardt's decision: the *25. Pz.Div.* was ordered to begin moving south before dawn. It would not, however, cross the Vistula. Rather, it would go directly into Warsaw and fight its way through the city, if need be, all the way to the western bank of the Vistula, where it would relieve *Gruppe von dem Bach* of the responsibility for defending against any attempt by the First Belorussian Front to cross the river. In turn, *Gruppe von dem Bach* would be able to redirect its forces that had been outposting the river line and have them attack the Polish insurgents from the east.

The *25. Pz.Div.*, commanded by *Oberst* Oskar Audörsch, had just undergone a month-long reconstitution period at the Schieratz training area near Lødz and was not yet at full strength, being short one of its *Panzergrenadier* regiments and most of its tank battalion. But even in its weakened state (it was designated *Kampfgruppe 25. Pz.Div.* for administrative purposes), Audörsch's battle-hardened division still had more combat power than all of von dem Bach's forces put together.[24] It received its movement orders from the *H.Gr. Mitte* operations staff before midnight, and immediately leapt into motion. Its wheeled elements reached the northern Warsaw suburb of Młociny before dawn, where the division's commander reported to Gille's headquarters to receive his orders. Here, Audörsch learned that he and his men would serve under the *IV. SS-Pz.Korps* for the next three days. Meanwhile, the tracked elements moved via rail, arriving at the division's assembly area at Bielany by noon.

Audörsch's orders stated that the following morning, on 14 September, his division would conduct an attack in a southerly direction along the western bank of the Vistula through the suburb of Zoliborz, clearing it of any remaining members of the Polish Home Army. Since Zoliborz was one of the few remaining strongholds of the insurgents, some of the division would have to be posted there while the remainder would continue advancing south along the river bank. During this maneuver, the division would touch bases with troops from *Gruppe von dem Bach* already positioned there until Audörsch's troops finally linked up with the northern element of *Gruppe Sikenius* positioned on the southern outskirts of Warsaw at Sielce.

Then, with a solid line of combat troops arrayed along the entire western bank of the Vistula, the *9. Armee* would be in position to ward off any attempted river crossing at Praga by the First Belorussian Front. The *25. Pz.Div.* expected to have several days to get settled in before that happened. However, it would soon find itself involved in heavy fighting for Zoliborz. In the meantime, the most important action would continue to take place across the river, where the 47th Army and Polish 1st Army continued pressing forward their attacks against the right wing of Gille's corps, with its immediate goal of taking Praga.

On the morning of 13 September, Gille had found himself having to fight three battles at once—the holding action north of the Narew, where *Panzergruppe Flügel* was still engaged north of Serock with half of the *Wiking* Division's remaining tanks, one in the center involving the rest of the *Wiking* Division and the *Totenkopf* Division, and the most important one on his right flank involving the *19. Pz.Div.* and *1. ung.Kav.Div.* For all intents, the *73. Inf.Div.* was out of the fight, except for one battalion, with the rest of the division being hastily reorganized north of Praga into a *Kampfgruppe*. The *9. Armee* commander was keenly interested in the events unfolding in Praga and records indicate that von Vormann involved himself far more in the tactical dispositions there than he normally would have. There are no indications in the records that Gille protested von Vormann's interposition, since it is clear that he had his hands full with the fighting taking place between Borki and Struga, where the 70th Army was continuing its efforts to break through the *Totenkopf* Division's main defense line west of Słupno.

Surprisingly, the night of 12–13 September passed without any significant fighting, except for continuous and heavy Soviet artillery and mortar fire throughout the corps sector. Once again, the Red Air Force kept up with its night attacks, resuming its bombing and interdiction efforts against the Hungarians, who to everyone's surprise were proving to be a very tough nut to crack indeed. The *Wiking* Division's artillery regiment, *Ostubaf.* Hans Bünning's *SS-Pz.Art.Rgt. 5*, successfully engaged and dispersed an enemy troop concentration east of the old battleground at Załubice, thus forestalling an attack. The only significant development that evening was the shift of the boundaries between the *Wiking* and *Totenkopf* Divisions, with *Staf.* Mühlenkamp's division shifting to the south to enable *Obf.* Becker to free up forces to continue reinforcing his right flank alongside the Hungarians. The *19. Pz.Div.* was able to close the gap that night between Zabki and Elsnerów, which allowed *Gen.Lt.* Källner to report that a tenuous front line now ran from Zielonka, where his division linked up with Ibrányi's division, all the way to the Vistula on the southernmost outskirts of Praga.

It was a thin line, interspersed with a battalion from the *73. Inf.Div.* (*I.Btl./Gren.Rgt. 186*) and other *Alarm* units, and covered in some places only by heavy weapons and tanks, but Källner expected to continue building it up as the rest of his division arrived after its move, so long as it did not become bogged down in Praga itself. Stragglers in the city from the *73. Inf.Div.* were still being rounded up by the *Feldgendarmes*, quickly organized into ad-hoc infantry companies, and marched back to the front line. Amazingly, the Germans had managed to repair much of the damage that they had suffered the previous day, but they would not be afforded a moment's rest because neither the 47th Army nor the 1st Polish Army were quite finished yet with their offensive.

In fact, it was only beginning. In his daily report, von Vormann himself remarked that he realized late in the evening on the previous day that he expected 13 September would prove to be an "especially hot day" with regard to the fighting that was to come. He was proven to be quite prophetic, for it would mark the pivotal point for the second defensive battle of Warsaw. This battle would soon prove itself to be just as fiercely fought as the tank battle of Praga had been a month before, with many of the same divisions taking part. Generals von Vormann's and Gille's biggest concern was the impending loss of Praga, a major city in its own right, and the danger posed by the bridges across the Vistula possibly falling into enemy hands. Compounding the problem was the lack of infantrymen in the *19. Pz.Div.*, which was badly understrength to begin with and could not allow itself to be drawn into city fighting, which typically requires many more troops to cover the urban terrain.[25] The various *Alarm* units, the transport security battalion, and the assault engineer battalion positioned in Praga under the division's control were only temporary expedients and would be no match for tank-supported Soviet infantry, which would begin their attack outnumbering them by a factor of four to one.

The only bright spot in the otherwise gloomy situation was that the Soviet forces occupying the bridgeheads at Magnuszew and Puławy, the 8th Guards and 69th Armies, were unaccountably inactive, save for patrolling activity and random artillery fire. With the enemy pressure against the *VIII. Armeekorps* thus eased somewhat, von Vormann could now consider taking risks that would normally have been tactically unsound, including "borrowing" even more units from it to be used in the fight inside Praga or to build a new front line north of the city should it fall into enemy hands. One unit the army commander had his eyes on was *Fs.Pz.Div. Hermann Göring*, the most powerful division in his entire army, which was holding a portion of the static perimeter at Magnuszew. It would soon figure prominently in the fighting taking place 80 kilometers to the north.

After a slow night, action started up again along the entire front line of the *IV. SS-Pz.Korps*, with most of it, as anticipated, occurring in and around Praga. The weather seemingly cooperated with the attackers, proving to be a sunny, dry, and cool day that enabled good observation and attacks by the Red Air Force, as well as movement by mechanized forces along the dirt roads and highways in the area. Troops from *Gruppe Sieckenius*, arrayed south of Warsaw along the Vistula, observed long columns of enemy vehicular traffic headed north towards Praga on the opposite side of the river, but could do little except fire the occasional round from its limited stocks of artillery ammunition and report the results to *9. Armee* headquarters.

The storm broke first on the *19. Pz.Div.* at dawn, when Källner reported that his entire front line between Zabki in the north and Kepa Gocławska on the Vistula in the south was enveloped by artillery and rocket fire. Swarms of infantry from the 76th and 175th Rifle Divisions and the 1st Polish Infantry Division, supported by tanks of the 1st Polish Tank Brigade and rolling attacks by close support aircraft, surged forward against Källner's defensive positions. On his right flank, his troops were able to bring the Soviet assault to a halt outside the village of Gocław, but the situation in his center, held by *Pz.Gren.Rgt. 74*, quickly grew critical. A powerful thrust along the railroad line leading into the city, consisting of four infantry battalions supported by tanks, soon fought its way to the railway and highway intersection on Praga's outskirts 3 kilometers east of the river, where it collided with the troops from *II. Btl./Pz.Gren.Rgt. 74*. During the fighting, the German battalion was temporarily surrounded and its commander killed in action, and its remaining men were unable to prevent Polish troops from taking the industrial area of Utrata and the Praga switching yard south of the rail intersection on the city's eastern edge.

With the Poles having firmly established a foothold in the city, the situation soon devolved into house-to-house fighting, with Polish troops engaged in hand-to-hand combat with Källner's *Panzergrenadiers*. Losses were described as heavy on both sides, but the German defenders, lacking sufficient troops to hold out against a numerically superior foe in an urban environment, were ordered to fall back. Fearing that the Poles were about to seize the southernmost Poniatowski bridge by a *coup de main*, von Vormann ordered his corps engineer *Oberst* Meyer to have it blown up, but a lucky artillery shell hit the bridge before the charge could be ignited and set off two-thirds of the explosives. Though damaged, it could still be crossed by foot soldiers, so troops from *Sturm-Pio.Btl. 500* hastily reset the charges and dropped the rest of the span into the river with an enormous explosion. On orders from the army commander himself, the demolition charges on the neighboring railroad bridge were set off at 1:35 p.m. Now only two bridges remained across the Vistula and the loss of Praga was a forgone conclusion.

Since Gille had not yet received the order to abandon Praga, with von Vormann's approval he directed a withdrawal by the *19. Pz.Div.* northwards into the center of the city, a move that would shorten the lines. This action would free up forces for a counterattack that would relieve the immediate pressure being exerted by the enemy against the part of Praga still held by German troops. The new temporary line would run from the eastern edge of Saska Kapa to the eastern edge of the city's main railroad station. This would not only lead to the abandonment of the eastern, southeastern, and southern portions of the city, but also meant that holding on to the remainder, even for a brief period, would require that the point where the Radzymin–Praga highway intersected with the main railway line on Praga's northeastern outskirts be retaken. The counterattack, launched shortly after noon, was led by *I. Btl./Pz.Gren. Rgt. 74* attacking from the south, supported by a *Panzergruppe* from *Pz.Rgt. 27* attacking from the north. It was successful at first, striking the flank of a regiment from the 76th Rifle Division and pushing them back over a kilometer as far as the northern outskirts of the Targowek suburb. Ten Soviet tanks were destroyed in the course of the fighting, including four of the powerful Su-152 assault guns.

With the front around Praga temporarily stabilized, the evacuation of remaining non-combat units and supplies from the city began. Since the two southernmost bridges had been destroyed earlier in the day, this withdrawal meant that the troops concerned had to detour through the center of Praga to cross over the two surviving northern bridges, which were already set for demolition. Meanwhile, house-to-house fighting continued along the eastern and southern fringes of Praga, as Polish and Soviet troops struggled to clear the Germans from their cellar and upper-floor defensive positions. All four of the *Panzergrenadier* battalions from the *19. Pz.Div.* were by now seriously depleted, and even with the reinforcements they had been sent, it was only a question of time when the city would have to be given up for good.

Action that day was not limited to Praga. On the left flank of the *19. Pz.Div.*, Källner's forces maintained a tenuous connection throughout the day with the neighboring *1. ung.Kav.Div.* Consisting mostly of tanks from *Pz.Rgt. 27* and the division's reconnaissance battalion, this front line, nicknamed the *Panzer Hauptkampflinie*, or *Pz. HKL*, ran along the highway between Zacisze and Marki where the division's far left flank tied in with the Hungarians. Very little activity was reported as having occurred along this portion of the front line held by *Pz.Rgt. 27* that day, except for supporting the counterattack against Targowek carried out earlier in the day by *Pz.Gren.Rgt. 74*. Had any concerted Soviet attack been attempted on 13 September against this thinly held line, there would have been very little to stop them, especially in view of the success the Soviets achieved in the same area the day before when the *73. Inf.Div.* collapsed in the face of the CXXV Rifle Corps' attacks.

The situation with the *1. ung.Kav.Div.* was quite different. Its positions between Siwki and Marki were attacked early in the morning, including those held by the attached *I. Btl./Gren.Rgt. 186*. The only remaining intact battalion from the *73. Inf.Div.*, now temporarily attached to Ibrányi's division, it was pushed back as far as the southern edge of Marki by the 143rd Rifle Division, a move that threatened to separate *19. Pz.Div.* from the Hungarians. To avert this danger, Ibrányi ordered his *Hussar Regiment 3*, supported by tanks from the *Totenkopf* Division armored battlegroup, to carry out an immediate counterattack beginning at 8 a.m. This quickly restored the front line and recaptured Marki, though repeated Soviet attacks against the Marki area continued throughout the day without success.

The ferocity of the fighting in this area can be illustrated by the destruction of 25 Soviet tanks that day, against the loss of one of the *Totenkopf* Division's *Pz. VI* Tigers and a *Sturmgeschütz*, as well as the loss of three *Jäg.Pz. 38t* from *Heeres-Pz.Jäg. Abt. 743*. The Hungarian division fought so well on 13 September that the *9. Armee* commander recommended that it be mentioned in the daily *Wehrmachtsbericht*, which occurred the following day. In a personal letter to Ibrányi, von Vormann congratulated him on his division's admirable performance, stating, "*Herr* General, please convey to the men of your division my personal thanks and my desire to let them know that I have requested that they be especially recognized for their achievement."[26]

As it had for the past several days, the *Totenkopf* Division continued its defensive battle in the Wólka Radzyminska–Słupno area. Although the morning had begun quietly, at noon the division's sector was enveloped in heavy artillery, rocket, and mortar fire, signaling another Soviet attempt to breach the defensive line west of Słupno and drive to the Vistula via Stanisławów. After a 45-minute barrage, the assault force, estimated to be at least 400–500 men strong, attacked in a southwest direction between Hills 104 and 100. After overrunning the *Totenkopf* Division's forward outpost, this force surged through the 500-meter gap and a portion of it managed to get behind the small body of *Totenköpfler* holding Hill 104, forcibly ejecting them after hand-to-hand fighting.

Due to the heavy losses in personnel his division was suffering and the additional necessity of supporting the Hungarian division with an armored *Kampfgruppe*, Becker asked his corps commander whether the *Wiking* Division could extend its front line even further past Wólka Radzyminska, which would free the division of having to defend nearly 2½ kilometers of the front line and allow Becker to concentrate the bulk of his forces between Słupno and Struga. Gille duly approved the request and Becker immediately shifted the troops who were now available to complete the destruction of the encircled Soviet forces trapped in the woods west of Hill 104.

By nightfall, when this operation was completed, the *Totenkopf* Division reported that it had finally destroyed this force, capturing 12 heavy antitank guns and five infantry howitzers in the process. Becker's troops also counterattacked and retook Hill 104, which by this point had changed hands four times in bitter fighting. By nightfall, the situation had returned to the normal kinds of front-line activity everyone on both sides was accustomed to—random shelling, patrolling activities, repositioning, and provisioning.

In the *Wiking* Division's sector, this sort of task was the order of the day. In addition to shifting its boundary to the right to assist its sister division, the activity of Mühlenkamp's division was confined to having the guns of *Ostubaf.* Bünning's *SS-Pz.Art.Rgt. 5* fire at Soviet troop concentrations detected at Rejentowka, Rynia, and Arciechów, three positions that by this point ringed in the perimeter of the *Wiking* Division's left flank. Division artillery also conducted counter-battery fire missions at suspected Soviet artillery and mortar positions, "with good effect." During the past week of relatively static warfare, the *Wiking* Division had put the time to good use by concentrating on improving the readiness rates of its armored vehicles and incorporating some of the hundreds of Ukrainian *Waffenwilliger* into the ranks of its *Panzergrenadier* companies. Many of its veterans had returned to the division from hospitals in Germany and elsewhere, and a small number of replacement troops were beginning to trickle in from the division's newly installed *SS-Feld-Ers.Btl. 5*, though not nearly enough to fill the enormous gaps in its ranks.

Gille had continued to resist the *9. Armee* diktat that directed him to transfer greater numbers of able-bodied troops from the logistics and administrative services into front-line positions. So much so, that only the day before, von Vormann had passed on to Gille a message from *H.Gr. Mitte* ordering the *IV. SS-Pz.Korps* commander to explain the discrepancy between the number of men listed in his reports as being assigned in each of his two SS divisions' *Iststärke* report, compared to the number shown as part of each division's *Kampfstärke*. Apparently, in the considered opinion of the commander of *H.Gr. Mitte*, the ratio of men in the *Tross* was still too large, and more of these "available" soldiers needed to be transferred immediately to the front-line troops.[27] Gille's earlier arguments about the necessity of a smoothly running logistics and administrative system to ensure that each division functioned at peak proficiency had evidently fallen on deaf ears.

As a consequence, Gille was to report to *H.Gr. Mitte* by 17 September the number of men remaining in the *Tross* of both the *Totenkopf* and *Wiking* Divisions, plus the number of men in each of their reported *Kampfstärke*. He was also instructed to be able to explain what he had done to balance these supposedly out-of-kilter ratios or why he had chosen not to follow this directive. While the *H.Gr. Mitte* commander may have been trying to control the flow of *Waffen-SS* replacements, his concerns might also be explained by his desire to answer the continuing pleas by Gille for more personnel. As it was, over half of the *Wiking* Division's infantrymen holding its front line were from attached units of the *Heer*, a fact which *H.Gr. Mitte* and the *OKH Personalamt* (Personnel Department) must have been aware of.

These attached troops were badly needed elsewhere, and both *9. Armee* and *H.Gr. Mitte* had been attempting to take them away from the *Wiking* Division for weeks so they could be returned to their parent units or reconstituted as an army reserve. Despite the back-and-forth with its higher headquarters, the tank regiments of Gille's SS divisions had put this period of relative inactivity to good use—the *Wiking* Division's readiness rate had risen to 43 operational tanks, assault guns, and tank destroyers and the *Totenkopf*'s to 58, with about half that number in short-term repair.[28] Although the infantry strength of both divisions, the literal "boots on the ground," was still dwindling, with regard to armor and antitank weapons, they were still relatively strong.

As the day lengthened, it began to dawn on von Vormann that he would not be able to prevent the worst case from happening, that is, the loss of Praga and its four bridges. Two of the bridges had already been destroyed, and the remaining two soon would be. The problems he faced as the fighting continued that day were how to prevent Gille's right wing from being enveloped should Praga fall to the Soviets or Poles and where to find troops to defend the west bank of the Vistula, all the while having to continue the suppression of the Warsaw Uprising. The arrival of the *25. Pz.Div.* would solve one problem, that of defending the western bank of the Vistula against a river crossing attempt, and the other, the suppression of the insurgency, would be solved in due course. While the insurgents of General Bór's *Armia Krajowa* were fighting stubbornly and inflicting heavy casualties on *Gruppe von dem Bach*, they were clearly on their last legs and the destruction of the bridges at Praga would deprive the approaching Polish 1st Army of an easy crossing. This threat would resolve itself once the last bridge dropped into the river.

The other problem facing Gille's corps was a much larger, more complicated challenge. Not only did the corps lack sufficient troops to hold its present line, in order to escape destruction it would soon be forced to withdraw to another one north of Praga that was within its defensive capabilities. Even so, there would be barely sufficient troops to hold this new line. Gille forcibly made this point to Reinhardt when the latter paid a visit to his corps headquarters in the afternoon. Reinhardt later informed von Vormann that he was astounded to see how unfavorably the situation was developing in the *IV. SS-Pz.Korps* sector, and came away convinced of the need to pull out of Praga as soon as possible to a new defense line. Reinhardt's visit to Gille's headquarters and his on-the-spot decision to order the withdrawal saved about 12 hours, the time that it would normally have taken to make such a radical change in course had he not seen the actual situation with his own eyes.

There would still be a lot of staff work required to translate Reinhardt's decision into operational orders, which would first be transmitted to the *9. Armee* operations staff. There was understandable concern among both the *9. Armee*'s and Gille's staff about the future security of the lifeline across the Vistula. The *IV. SS-Pz.Korps* and its divisions could still be supplied across the bridges at Modlin and Zegrze, though the latter one would have to be blown up soon due to the inexorable expansion of the Pułtusk bridgehead north of Serock. Work continued on building a temporary 12-ton pontoon bridge at Młociny, north of Warsaw, but it would be unsuitable for tanks. All of the corps' critical food, fuel, and ammunition stored in several depots located on the eastern bank of the Vistula and in the Praga area would also have to be evacuated, which would take one or two days. After weighing the risks and considering Gille's advice, von Vormann and his operations staff developed a plan within two hours. After securing Reinhardt's final approval, von Vormann issued the order at 5:30 p.m. instructing *IV. SS-Pz.Korps* to begin displacing the following evening to an intermediate defensive line stretching from Annopol, a town 5 kilometers north of Praga, to Zegrze, a distance of approximately 20 kilometers. The movement was directed to be completed by the morning of 15 September.[29]

This *Riegelstellung*, or intermediate defense line, effectively bisected the triangle formed by the Vistula and Narew Rivers and would require that Gille's left wing pivot to the west nearly 10 kilometers, with both the *Wiking* and *Totenkopf* Divisions abandoning the defensive positions they had held for the past three weeks. The order implied that many if not most of the *Trosseinheiten* of Gille's corps' rear echelon and that of his four divisions would need to be transferred to the western bank of the Vistula, where they would be safe from direct assault. The *IV. SS-Pz.Korps* would assume responsibility for control of vehicular traffic over the bridges at Modlin and Zegrze. Gille would also transfer his corps headquarters from Młociny to the old Polish fortress at Klein Kazuń, directly across the Vistula from Modlin. Here, his *Korps-Hauptquartier* would be better positioned to exercise effective command and control of his corps units, even though they would still be on the opposite side of the river. The remaining portion of Praga under German control would be held as long as possible until the withdrawal was completed, when the surviving two bridges would be destroyed and rear guards deployed northwards to safety.

Since the suburb of Zoliborz was proving to be much more difficult to eradicate than anticipated, the *25. Pz.Div.*, less its *Pz.Gren.Rgt. 146*, was ordered to focus on its elimination using its combat engineer, armored reconnaissance, and antitank battalions, as well as the newly arrived *SS-Werf.Abt. 104*, which had been temporarily attached to *Oberst* Audörsch's division for the operation.[30] The *25. Pz.Div.* would then be attached in two days' time to *Gruppe von dem Bach*, a corps-equivalent headquarters that would assume responsibility for defending the portion of the west bank of the Vistula between *Gruppe Sieckenius* in the south and *IV. SS-Pz.Korps* in the north. The bulk of Gille's corps would still be fighting on the eastern side of the Vistula and would most likely have to withdraw further "up the funnel" towards Modlin, whereupon it would occupy a final defensive position, designated as the *Fuchsstellung* (the "Fox" position), at a point in time to be determined, as if any defensive position by this point in the war could ever be called final.

That evening, when the fighting had finally died down, von Vormann composed his thoughts at his desk in his headquarters in Żyrardów, where he wrote his daily report to *H.Gr. Mitte.* He expressed his confidence that the plan to evacuate Praga and build a new defense line would succeed. He also expressed his regret that Gille's corps had suffered a large number of casualties, but was satisfied that the opposing forces had suffered even more heavily. For example, he mentioned that the *IV. SS-Pz. Korps* claimed to have destroyed 37 Soviet and Polish tanks that day, a very high number indeed. Most of these tanks had been claimed by the *Totenkopf* Division's *panzer* regiment, which had been heavily engaged in fighting elements of the VIII Guards Tanks Corps between Zielonka and Marki alongside Ibrányi's Hungarians. Two IL-2 *Sturmoviks* were also shot down. He stated in his report that it was his belief that on Gille's right flank, the *19. Pz.Div.* and the *1. ung.Kav.Div.* had reported a noticeable lessening of the severity of the enemy's attacks.

Two additional issues that drew von Vormann's attention had arisen during the hours between sending the withdrawal order to Gille at 5:30 p.m. and submitting his commander's report later that evening. The first was the receipt of a warning order that evening from *H.Gr. Mitte* to begin detaching the *1. ung.Kav.Div.* from Gille's corps and prepare it for rail shipment to Hungary in three days' time.[31] This had been expected, but not for another week at the earliest. The second was precipitated by the first. The previous day, von Vormann had been ordered to transfer the *H.Gr. Mitte* reserve, *Fs.Pz.Gren.Rgt. 2* from the *Fs.Pz.Div. Hermann Göring*, from its assembly area near Radom and send it via a wheeled road march to Weiss's *2. Armee* to replace the *25. Pz.Div.* as that army's reserve.

A too-rapid departure of Ibrányi's division at this point in the battle could create a gap in Gille's front line between the *19. Pz.Div.* and the *Totenkopf* Division that could not be filled with existing forces, creating a potentially catastrophic situation that von Vormann wished to avoid at all costs. He would attempt to delay the movement of the Hungarians for a few days, until the withdrawal to the new intermediate position was complete. By this point they would no longer be needed since the *Riegelstellung* would be nearly 10 kilometers shorter than the current front line and could be defended by the three other divisions of the corps. Taking advantage of his army group commander's new-found understanding of the tactical situation in the *IV. SS-Pz.Korps* sector, von Vormann requested that the transfer of the regiment from the *Fs.Pz.Div. Hermann Göring* to *2. Armee* be cancelled and that new orders be issued to divert it to the Warsaw area instead.[32] This request was quickly approved and the movement of the 708 combat troops (not counting support elements) from the two *Panzergrenadier* battalions of *Fs.Pz.Gren.Rgt. 2 Hermann Göring* from the Radom area to Pułtusk was modified so they would be sent to the Warsaw suburb of Włochy.[33] Here, the regiment went into an assembly area, where it would be available to reinforce *IV. SS-Pz.Korps* or *Gruppe von dem Bach* at a moment's notice should that prove necessary.

The other item remaining before von Vormann turned in for the night was to instruct Gille to take the remaining troops from the *73. Inf.Div.* and form battalion-sized *Kampfgruppen* from each of its three infantry regiments. Once this had been completed, the division would be temporarily subordinated to the *19. Pz.Div.* until a decision had been made with regard to its future. Both Generals Reinhardt and von Vormann recommended to *Generaloberst* Heinz Guderian, chief of staff of *OKH*, to disband it entirely, but Hitler demurred, believing it would be better to reform it under new leadership. Of course, any further steps would have to wait until the current crisis had passed. The actual losses of the division's infantry amounted to approximately 60 percent, with *Gren.Rgt. 186* alone losing over 76 percent of its *Kampfstärke*, with only 180 combat troops remaining in its ranks. The artillery regiment had lost nearly half of its guns, and were it not for the efforts of *Brig.Fhr.* Brassack, it would have lost them all. Just as disconcerting was the loss of 14 of its 16 7.5cm antitank guns. Clearly, the division was a wreck and Gille estimated that it would need at least three days for its commander to reorganize it to conform to the new guidance.

Although the army commander and probably the commander of the *IV. SS-Pz. Korps* had both gone to bed after a long and tiring day, the fighting in Praga did not diminish. While combat activity throughout the rest of Gille's corps had noticeably decreased except for the usual artillery and mortar fire, house-to-house fighting continued in Praga all night, with fresh Polish and Soviet troops pushing back the defenders block by block. The units attempting to hold the city had been fighting without pause for several days and were approaching breaking point. As the Germans were being pushed inexorably back, it became obvious that the fall of the rest of Praga was now only a matter of hours away, and that unless measures were quickly taken, the two remaining bridges would soon fall into enemy hands.

Permission to blow them up had already been granted by *H.Gr. Mitte*, which had relayed this information to *9. Armee*, which in turn notified *Gruppe von dem Bach*'s engineer officer in charge of the demolition. Consequently, after midnight the order to demolish the bridges was given and was promptly carried out; the *Stadtbrücke* (city bridge) was blown up at 1:00 a.m., while the northernmost railway bridge followed 90 minutes later.[34] The lifeline for the *IV. SS-Pz.Korps* and Gille's 60,000 men now ran across the Vistula at Modlin and the Narew at Zegrze. Though work was still underway on the temporary bridge at Młociny, it would not be available until 17 or 18 September at the earliest.

Prior to their demolition, some of the 136 survivors of *Sturm-Pio.Btl. 500* who had been guarding the bridges crossed over to the west bank and were temporarily subordinated to *Gruppe von dem Bach*.[35] The rest of the battalion remained with *19. Pz.Div.* Nearly all of the Vistula had now become the front line, except for a small portion from the northern outskirts of Praga to Modlin held by *IV. SS-Pz. Korps*. With most of Praga now in the hands of the CXXV Rifle Corps, Soviet and Polish troops directly faced those from *Gruppe von dem Bach*, with nothing but a thousand meters of water separating them. A river crossing to relieve the pressure against the Warsaw Uprising was now a near certainty and German forces began to scramble to prepare their defenses to be ready for it.

That would take several days; in the meantime, fighting would continue from 14–22 September, although the immediate crisis had passed. During the early hours of 14 September, except for the *19. Pz.Div.*, the other three divisions in *IV. SS-Pz. Korps* reported the usual nocturnal activity, including Soviet artillery and mortar *Störungfeuer* (disruptive fire), infantry patrols, and in the case of the *Totenkopf* Division, a successful counterattack by one of its companies that retook Hill 100. This minor action resulted in *Obf.* Becker's troops being almost immediately surrounded by a large Soviet force, which in turn necessitated the launching of an even larger battalion-sized German attack to restore communications with the unit holding the hill. This counterattack was still underway when the corps' morning report was submitted to the *9. Armee* operations section at 6:15 a.m.

Throughout the day, fighting seesawed back and forth outside of Praga between Elsnerów and Wólka Radzyminska. Several Soviet tank-supported infantry attacks against the *Panzer-HKL* held by *Pz.Rgt. 27* between Zacisze and Marki were successfully driven back, with *19. Pz.Div.* claiming the destruction of five Soviet tanks. Fighting in the *1. ung.Kav.Div.* sector was equally fierce, with the attacking troops from the LXXVII Rifle Corps achieving a 400-meter-deep penetration in its lines east of Marki that was only eliminated by a counterattack launched in conjunction with the armored *Kampfgruppe* from the *Totenkopf* Division. Though this was successful, *SS-Pz.Rgt. 3* lost six tanks, including one *Pz. VI* Tiger when the counterattack encountered a Soviet *Pakfront* northwest of Zielonka.

As for the *Totenkopf* Division itself, fighting swirled around the area between Hills 104 and 100 west of Słupno for most of the day, and it was becoming increasingly obvious that this position could not be held much longer. A large Soviet force managed to penetrate the position north of Hill 104, fought its way through the forest, and advanced 500 meters to the paved highway linking Słupno to Nieporet, which necessitated further counterattacks by both the *Totenkopf* and *Wiking* Divisions to keep the road open. That afternoon, both Becker's and Ibrányi's division began slowly displacing westwards in conformance with the withdrawal order issued the night before.

The artillery regiments of both divisions fired incessantly to cover the withdrawal, while local counterattacks by the rear guards kept the pursuing Soviets at bay. In the *Wiking* Division's sector, the divisions of the CXIV and XCVI Rifle Corps persisted in their attempts to infiltrate *Staf.* Mühlenkamp's front lines, though without success, once again stymied by the accurately delivered artillery fire of *SS-Pz.Art.Rgt. 5* that stopped the attempted advance on Nieporet dead in its tracks. The Red Air Force's 16th Air Army relentlessly continued its attacks against German ground targets, though these were not controlled by any forward observers or air–ground liaison teams, rendering them less effective. The antiaircraft fire by the Germans defenders was intense, with Gille's corps reporting that three IL-2 *Sturmoviks* were shot down on 14 September alone.

In Praga, Soviet and Polish forces continued pressing the troops under the command of the *19. Pz.Div.* further and further north, such that by sundown, only the northern railway switching yards, the factory at Lewicpol, and the enormous cemetery at Bródnowski were still under German control. For all intents and purposes, Praga had been liberated and Polish troops from their 1st Infantry Division now stood on the banks of the Vistula opposite the city center of Warsaw, a mere 1,000 meters away. It might as well have been 1,000 miles, for there were no means at hand to effect an immediate river crossing attempt and begin the relief of the increasingly beleaguered troops of General Bór's *Armia Krajowa*.

With rescue in sight, the insurgents intensified their efforts to hold out, and continued to inflict heavy losses on the forces arrayed under *Gruppe von dem Bach*, resulting in an agonizingly slow advance. Were it not for the heavy weapons which the insurgents lacked, the various units under *Ogruf.* von dem Bach's command, including units composed of Turkomen, Azerbaijanis, Russian renegades of the Kaminski Brigade, *Landeschütz*, *Polizei*, *Luftwaffe*, *Heer*, and the *Dirlewanger* Brigade from the *Waffen-SS* would have made little progress. As it was, the fighting was quickly reducing Warsaw to a vast sea of rubble that would take years for the populace to reconstruct. Undirected Soviet artillery fire was increasingly falling among both German and Polish positions, adding another dimension of hell to an already shattered landscape.

One German unit that did enjoy a fair amount of success in Warsaw that day was *Oberst* Audörsch's *Kampfgruppe 25. Pz.Div.* After belatedly discovering that the insurgents were defending the Warsaw suburb of Zoliborz in strength despite reports from *Gruppe von dem Bach* to the contrary, Audörsch's troops commenced their attack at 11:45 a.m. with its division reconnaissance battalion, *Pz.Aufkl.Abt. 25*, reinforced by troops from its *Pz.Pio.Btl. 87* and 20 tanks and assault guns from *Pz.Rgt. 9*. Since its *Pz.Gren.Rgt. 146* was still fighting to the south under the control of *Kampfgruppe Rohr*, the shortage of infantrymen was made up by the attachment of a Cossack Brigade from Bronislav Kaminsky's *Russkaya Osvoboditelnaya Narodnaya Armiya* (or *RONA*, the Russian National Liberation Army).

In a two-pronged attack, Audörsch's troops, with armor and *Stuka* dive-bomber support, pushed back the insurgents into a narrow area around the Opel factory and managed to link up with German troops holding out in the old czarist fortress (the *Zitadelle*) along the riverbank. Many of the insurgents had taken up positions within concrete high-rise buildings in the area, forcing the Germans to take them out one at a time by having their tanks direct their cannon at each suspected position. Fighting was heavy, and losses due to Polish sniper fire were considerable, with one battalion commander and two company commanders falling victim, as well as many other troops.[36] Nightfall forced the withdrawal of the supporting armor, since the Cossacks could not be depended upon to protect them, but the insurgents remaining in Zoliborz were now completely cut off and isolated, not only from their comrades fighting in the city center. However, they still held a strip of land several hundred meters wide, running along the river opposite from the Soviet or Polish forces on the other side, giving the Polish insurgents hope that it might make a suitable landing site for a river-crossing operation.

That evening, much of the German activity on the eastern bank of the Vistula was directed towards the withdrawal to the new defense line stretching from Annopol in the south to Zegrze on the Narew. The *Totenkopf* Division managed to seal off the penetration west of Słupno and was able to withdraw to its new main defense line in good order, as did the *Wiking* Division. The *1. ung.Kav.Div.* began to pull its troops out of the line in increments as it prepared for its impending transfer, though it would continue to hold a diminishing portion of the new defense line until its movement was complete. Though attacked throughout the night, *Gen. Lt.* Källner's *19. Pz.Div.*, now able to take advantage of its long-range fire since it was no longer tied down in Praga, inflicted heavy losses on Soviet and Polish units attempting to penetrate its new position north of the city. The remnants of the *73. Inf.Div.* also began that evening to collect in their new assembly area near Henryków, where it would spend the next three days reorganizing before it would be committed to battle again.

In his report that evening to *Gen.O.* Reinhardt, von Vormann was satisfied that at least for the time being, the danger of the bridges falling into the wrong hands at

Praga had been averted and that the *19. Pz.Div.* and the rest of the *IV. SS-Pz.Korps* had been able to begin withdrawing to the new defense line without being pressed too closely. Additionally, during the past four days Gille's divisions had been able to destroy or immobilize 87 Soviet and Polish tanks and other armored vehicles, which von Vormann estimated to be roughly half the established strength of a tank corps.

On that same day, 14 September, the *25. Pz.Div.* reported dozens of Allied bombers and cargo aircraft flying over Warsaw to drop supply bundles, but most of it landed within German lines, allowing the men of *Gruppe von dem Bach* and other units to sample American food supplies and equip themselves with American small arms, such as the much-sought-after Colt .45 semiautomatic pistol. Von Vormann also succeeded in convincing the *H.Gr. Mitte* commander to delay the final transfer of the *1. ung.Kav.Div.* until 17 September, which would give the *IV. SS-Pz.Korps* the breathing space it needed to get set in its new positions.

Most of the fighting that took place the following day in the *IV. SS-Pz.Korps* sector involved *Kampfgruppe 25. Pz.Div.*, which continued its attempt to clear the Zoliborz area of insurgents. The fighting for the Opel factory and concrete workers' high-rise quarters grew so intense that the division had to resort to using its artillery regiment's *Hummel* self-propelled 15cm howitzers to fire point-blank into Polish defensive positions. This technique, combined with two *Stuka* dive-bomber attacks, managed to suppress the defenders enough to allow German troops and Cossacks to slowly overcome resistance house by house, though the vast Opel complex was heavily damaged in the process. Coordinating its action with the German troops defending the riverside *Zitadelle*, it appeared that the *25. Pz.Div.* almost had the upper hand, though fighting would continue until the end of the month. *Gruppe von dem Bach*, which would assume control of the division the following day, in the meantime was engaged in consolidating its control of the western bank of the Vistula.

Despite the fact that *Ogruf.* von dem Bach's forces controlled most of the riverbank, Polish insurgents still held some of the heights overlooking their positions, rendering movement by German troops during the day a hazardous undertaking, especially in light of the skill of Polish snipers. Polish forces on the east back of the river, now firmly in control of Praga, fired directly into German positions using antitank guns and artillery. The one notable German success scored that day in Warsaw was *Kampfgruppe Rohr*'s storming of the southern Warsaw suburb of Sielce, taken after two weeks of heavy fighting despite interference by the Red Air Force and Soviet artillery from the opposite bank. With this significant achievement, *9. Armee* finally established solid control of the Vistula north and south of Warsaw. The first Soviet attempt at a river crossing occurred that morning, when two amphibious vehicles on a reconnaissance mission tried to cross the Vistula opposite of Sielce. One vehicle was shot up and set on fire, while the other lost its steering and slowly sank. It would be the first of many such attempts.

As for the rest of Gille's corps, most of the action that day consisted of shelling Soviet assembly areas, as the troops of the 47th Army and 1st Polish Army moved in to fill the vacuum left by the withdrawing Germans and Hungarians. For his part, Marshal Rokossovsky seems to have been taken by surprise by this sudden movement, since his forces did not press the Germans closely, as was their usual tactic. Instead, most of the Soviet action that day appeared to be directed towards assembling troops, tanks, and artillery for yet another push that would take place as soon as ammunition, fuel, and food had been brought up and distributed. Forward observers from the *19. Pz.Div.* reported that up to 30 Soviet tanks and a number of other vehicles were spotted assembling south of Annopol. Attempts to feel out Kallner's front-line positions, most likely by the 60th and 132nd Rifle Divisions, with infantry patrols were reported, beginning at 9:20 a.m., prompting the division to engage them with artillery fire. Additional artillery ambushes were carried out against Soviet armor assembly areas, resulting in the destruction of four T-34s, which were set on fire by German shells.

In the rapidly diminishing sector still held by the *1. ung.Kav.Div.*, most of the several Soviet forays were beaten back by artillery fire, though one attempt at Tomaszów succeeded when a large Soviet force supported by 25 tanks attacked during the early evening and broke through the division's outer defensive line. A crisis was narrowly averted after this penetration was partially "ironed out," though the division was forced to pull back its front line several kilometers to a more favorable position. It took a Hungarian night counterattack, in conjunction with another by the neighboring *Totenkopf* Division's reserve, to relieve the pressure being exerted upon its forces as they withdrew. Overall, the division was still on track to achieve its mission of disengaging and beginning rail movement to Hungary beginning on 17 September.

Neither the *Totenkopf* nor *Wiking* Divisions reported any major engagements with the enemy that day, except the counterattack the *Totenkopf* launched in support of the Hungarians. Both divisions were still in the process of moving to their new positions, with their withdrawal covered by armored units and artillery. Their artillery regiments successfully stymied Soviet attempts to closely pursue their troops as they displaced, though on at least two occasions Mühlenkamp and Becker's troops had to turn around and fight minor engagements at Stanisławów and Aleksandrów, respectively.

The *Wiking* Division blocked yet another attempt by the Soviets to push towards Nieporet, a place that was destined to play a major role in the next defensive battle. A large concentration of enemy troops at Stanisławów was engaged with artillery fire from both divisions at 3:30 p.m., which undoubtedly dispersed what was intended to be a night attack against German positions. Neither division's tank regiments were forced to engage the enemy, since these threats were taken care of by artillery fire. Much of the credit for the success enjoyed by Gille's artillery that day is due to his

ARKO, expertly handled by *Obf.* Brassack, who achieved a rare level of coordination between the corps artillery and four division artillery regiments under his direction, sequentially concentrating the fires of over 100 guns against several large Soviet troop assembly areas throughout the day.

In Gille's own report to *9. Armee* that evening, he wrote that the major threat he anticipated for the following day would be a large-scale attempt by the 47th Army to continue pushing back his right flank to the north, including both the *19. Pz.Div.* and the Hungarians, with the intention of rolling up the eastern bank of the Vistula and cutting off both divisions at Modlin. He also foresaw a major tank-supported push along the seam between the *Totenkopf* and Hungarian divisions in the vicinity of Tomaszów, but was confident that he would be able to contain it with his own forces should that attack occur.

The only other item of note that occurred that day was the arrival of *Heeres-Beob. Abt. 21*, sent to replace *Einsatz-Bttr./Beob.Abt. 1* as the *ARKO*'s artillery observation battalion. This was necessary, since the latter unit was too small for its assigned tasks, and also because the corps' own observation battalion, *SS-Beob.Abt. 104*, was still serving with the *II. SS-Pz.Korps* in Holland. The corps' dedicated rocket artillery battery, *SS-Werfer-Abteilung 104*, had arrived from its training area in Germany on 7 September, but had been immediately attached to *Gruppe von dem Bach* to lend its considerable firepower towards the upcoming operation designed to wrest the Warsaw suburb of Zoliborz from the insurgents. It would not rejoin the corps until 17 September, in time to participate in the third defensive battle for Warsaw on 10 October.

As for von Vormann's evening report to *H.Gr. Mitte*, he mentioned the successful withdrawal of Gille's corps to the new intermediate position between Annopol and Zegrze, but was clearly under no illusions that this would be anything but a temporary solution, and that Soviet attacks would continue as soon as the bulk of 47th Army had shifted north of Praga. He still believed that the 70th Army, supported by the VIII Guards Tank Corps, would continue its westward push towards Nieporet, and that the Vistula sector from Praga to the south would be completely taken over by the 1st Polish Army, which in turn would most likely initiate crossing attempts. Already, he reported, pontoons and water craft had been spotted being assembled on the riverbank south of Praga, which were addressed by several artillery concentrations fired by *Gruppe von dem Bach*, with little success. A major crossing attempt was only a matter of time.

Fortunately for *9. Armee*, Soviet inactivity at both the Magnuszew and Puławy bridgeheads continued, a weeks-long run of luck that would not continue forever. Recognizing this, von Vormann asked Reinhardt that *Gen.d.Pz.Tr.* von Lüttwitz's *XLVI. Pz.Korps* headquarters, which had been moved north of the Narew to the Serock area two weeks before to coordinate the counterattack by *2. Armee* against the Pułtusk bridgehead, be returned immediately to his control. Since it no longer had any *panzer* divisions to call its own, with both the *25. Pz.Div.* and *Fs.Pz.Div. Hermann Göring* having been returned to *9. Armee*, this corps headquarters no longer served a purpose and could be put to better use once again south of Warsaw along the Pilica River. Not only would this allow von Vormann to relieve *Gruppe Sieckenius* of that responsibility, but would give him a *panzer* corps headquarters to control the fighting in that area that he knew would be inevitable.

The *9. Armee* commander was genuinely saddened at the prospect of losing the *1. ung.Kav.Div.*, which despite all preconceptions, had fought extremely well east of the Vistula. It also could not be immediately replaced. The *73. Inf.Div.*, once it had been reconstituted, would be reinserted again into the front line, but until this occurred, he knew that Gille would have to assume a great deal of risk, since it was clearly evident that his three *panzer* divisions (the *Totenkopf*, *Wiking*, and *19. Panzer*) lacked the infantry strength to hold the intermediate position. This disparity in forces would have to be temporarily balanced by the increased use of artillery as a substitute for ground troops, but only infantry could, in the final analysis, seize or defend terrain. The next several days would prove a time of great stress.

The evening of 15 September passed relatively quietly, with the exception of a number of Allied air resupply drops being reported all over Warsaw. Intended to support the insurgents of Bór's army, most of these Red Air Force parachute canisters landed among the troops of *Gruppe von dem Bach*. Intermittent artillery and mortar fire, combined with night raids and reconnaissance activity, was reported throughout the *9. Armee* sector along the Vistula between Zegrze and Warka. The next day, 16 September, began with a powerful artillery concentration being fired upon the new front lines of the *1. ung.Kav.Div.* at 6:05 a.m., focused primarily in the area around Tomaszów, where fighting had raged the previous day. This was the prelude to a large infantry attack, which followed closely upon the heels of the barrage and resulted in a breakthrough that Ibrányi's troops could not address with their own reserves, which would force Gille to commit his corps reserve, the armored *Kampfgruppe* from the *Totenkopf* Division.

That morning also witnessed a change in Gille's order of battle. At 9 a.m, control of *Kampfgruppe 25. Pz.Div.* passed from *IV. SS-Pz.Korps* to *Gruppe von dem Bach*, ending its rather brief period of service under Gille's leadership. Its mission had not changed though, and Audörsch's division would continue the fight to subdue the insurgents holed up in the Opel factory in Zoliborz. By the time this action had concluded over a week later, the factory and surrounding high-rise buildings had been reduced to rubble, though this, as with the rest of the fighting in Warsaw proper, most likely would not have concerned Gille at all, since by this point his corps was focused exclusively on the fighting east of the river, particularly that occurring in the Hungarians' sector.

Several other units attached to Gille's corps had been notified that they would be departing from his order of battle as well, including four antitank gun companies from *Fest.Art.Pak-Abt. 1061*, which had suffered heavily during the past two weeks due to their relative immobility, not possessing prime mover vehicles of their own. Another unit that had been notified that day that it was to be transferred was the *9. Armee* weapons school's *Sturm-Btl. AOK 9*, which would be moved to the area north of Warka to be reconstituted as the army reserve the following day. It had been serving as part of the *IV. SS-Pz.Korps'* reserve since 9 September, fighting alongside the armored *Kampfgruppe* from the *Totenkopf* Division for the past week.

Most of the action that day centered around two key areas—between the right flank of the *1. ung.Kav.Div.* and the left flank of the *19. Pz.Div.*, and in the center of the *Totenkopf* Division's new defensive line on both sides of Stanisławów. The first attack was by far the most serious, led as it was by a force of 40 tanks with infantry escorts from the VIII Guards Tank Corps. After a devastating artillery barrage, this force made a penetration 2 kilometers wide in the Hungarians' primary front-line positions during the late morning west of the village of Białoleka. Before this force could reach the railroad line 8 kilometers west of the front line, it was brought to a temporary halt at the division's secondary defensive positions thanks to the intervention of *I. Btl.(gep.)/Pz.Gren.Rgt. 74* from the *19. Pz.Div.* Later that afternoon, a division-led counterattack, composed of *I. Abt./Pz.Rgt. 27*, the division's *SPW* battalion, *Pz.Jäg.Abt. 19*, and its armored artillery battalion, *I.Abt./Pz.Art.Rgt. 19*, crashed into the flank of the attackers, and in the ensuing tank battle drove them back to the original *HKL* after destroying 26 Soviet tanks, while losing only one of their own.[37]

The attack against the *Totenkopf* Division's lines was carried out just as violently as that against the Hungarians', though with fewer tanks. At 6:30 a.m., a force consisting of approximately 1,500 infantrymen supported by six tanks managed to penetrate the division's lines on the southeastern edge of the village of Rembelszczyzna (referred to as Rembelsz in German reports), 3 kilometers west of Stanisławów, and pushed the defenders back to the town's outskirts. A counterattack was immediately carried out by *III. Btl./Pz.Gren.Rgt. Eicke*, supported by *2. Kp./SS-Pz.Jag.Abt. 3* and the Tigers of *9. Kp./SS-Pz.Rgt. 3*. After several hours of see-saw fighting, this force managed to eject the attacking Soviets out of the village, destroying five T-34s in the process. One Tiger taking part in the counterattack, commanded by *SS-Ustuf.* Neff, suffered a direct hit by a Soviet shell during a counter barrage, setting it ablaze and killing three of the crewmen, though Neff survived.[38]

At 3 p.m., the Soviets tried again, attacking immediately following an artillery barrage that blanketed the entire division main defense line. This attack, too, was driven off, with the support of the *Totenkopf*'s artillery regiment as well as rockets fired by *II. Abt./Stellungs-Werfer Regiment 103*. Several other smaller attacks were reported, and though at least two managed to break through the German lines, they were all "ironed out" by nightfall. Further attacks were forestalled by artillery concentrations on observed assembly areas, which dispersed troops and tanks gathering to launch them.

One squad from the *Totenkopf* Division's *SS-Pio.Btl. 3* observed an attempt spearheaded by Soviet tanks to roll up the left flank of the Hungarian division near Tomaszów. Watching in horror from their foxholes in the woods a few hundred meters north of their neighbors, the squad leader, *SS-Uscha.* Flatow, later reported that:

> [A]s the tanks approached, the Hungarians attempted to flee. We fired our machine gun into the Russians' flank until its barrel glowed red-hot. We then saw a Hungarian officer attempt to rally his men and compel them to return to their positions. Into this group the Russian tanks pressed forward, and began carrying out a wild massacre. Two of the tanks changed direction and began approaching our position. One of my men screamed that we had to get out of there right away! I told him to shut up, and that we were staying put.[39]

Miraculously, one of tanks got stuck, and came no further, while the other one backed off and turned around. Flatow credited their survival to God's intervention, but in reality it was a counterattack launched at that very moment from the north by *I. Abt./SS-Pz.Rgt. 3* of the *Totenkopf* Division and one from the south by a portion of I. *Abt./Pz.Rgt. 27* from *19. Pz.Div.* This attack, supported by *Stuka* dive-bombers, quickly closed the gap, drove off the attackers, and re-established the old main defense line between Tomaszow and Białoleka.

That same day, the *Wiking* Division suffered primarily from heavy artillery and mortar fire that pinned its units inside their defensive positions. Division artillery drove off several Soviet attempts to penetrate its front lines by company-sized reconnaissance patrols. One such patrol managed to evade German defensive positions and penetrate deep into the large forest east of Nieporet, but was engaged nearly every step of the way by well-aimed artillery fire from *SS-Pz.Art.Rgt. 5*, which finally drove it back. Another attempt to slip through German lines at Pilawa on the division's left flank was likewise driven off. On the northern bank of the Narew, where the *Wiking* still maintained a small force, its observers noted additional Soviet forces being ferried over upriver from Serock, scene of heavy fighting the week before. This indicated that a resumption of the Soviet offensive from the bridgehead south of Pułtusk was now only a matter of time, though this was something for the *2. Armee* to worry about. All *Staf.* Mühlenkamp's troops could do in this situation was observe and report.

The day ended with the troops of *IV. SS-Pz.Korps* holding the same ground that they had held that morning, though losses, especially in the Hungarian division, had been heavy.[40] The troops from the 47th Army's CXXIX and LXXVII Rifle Corps had undoubtedly suffered heavy losses as well. Thirty-one tanks from the VIII Guards Tank Corps had been destroyed, having nothing to show for their efforts. In his evening report, Gille stated that his intention for the next day was to defend his current position, eliminate any remaining penetrations of his front line, and continue preparing the two intermediate defensive lines that his corps would occupy in what would become known as the "Wet Triangle"—the *Marder* (marten) line and the *Iltis* (ferret) line. With the imminent departure of the Hungarians, his corps would soon be bereft of enough infantrymen needed to hold either of them. His tanks could simply not do it by themselves. Though the *73. Inf.Div.* had been earmarked to replace Ibrányi's division in the line, it had not yet completed its hasty reorganization and would not be ready for recommitment for several more days. Reinserting it now, Gille believed, would only result in a repeat performance of its failure of 12 September.

Furthermore, Gille added, his *ARKO* had been notified by *Luftwaffe* reconnaissance that there were indications of a large-scale Soviet troop build-up in the vicinity of Praga, including at least three large artillery-firing concentrations being constructed, signs that another set-piece attack was in the planning stages, possibly, in his opinion, including a large-scale attempt to cross the river and aid the Warsaw Uprising. Gille closed by stating that he did not believe, with the forces he had available, that he could hold his current line much longer unless he was reinforced, and requested that a fresh division be quickly brought forward to buttress his right flank before the Hungarians pulled out.[41]

In his own report that evening to *H.Gr. Mitte*, the *9. Armee* commander took a broader perspective. Not only did he have to take into account the events that took place in Gille's sector that day, he also had to concern himself with what was happening in the rest of his army's area of operations. Fortunately, the situations in the *VIII. Armeekorps* and *Gruppe Sieckenius* sectors were still relatively unchanged, though the fighting in Warsaw was visibly approaching its climax. And it was he, not Gille, who was the most concerned about an enemy crossing of the Vistula. But like Gille, he was also painfully aware that he lacked sufficient forces to adequately defend his entire front line. Von Vormann knew that the favorable situation opposite the Magnusziew and Puławy bridgeheads was only temporary and would not stay quiet forever, so he had to begin planning for the day when they would once again erupt. The return of *XLVI. Pz.Korps* headquarters that day was one of the first elements of that plan that began to fall into place, taking over the sector formerly held by *Gruppe Sieckenius* beginning at midnight.[42] *Gruppe Sieckenius* itself would fall under the command of the *panzer* corps headquarters and function as a division-level command.

Besides describing the day's fighting east of the Vistula in his evening commander's report, von Vormann also wrote that he believed that it had yet to reach its zenith, which he expected to occur during the next several days. He also mentioned the progress of the fighting in Warsaw proper, including an account of the fighting for Zoliborz as well as the first serious attempt by Polish troops to cross the river late that evening to aid their fellow countrymen.

Aimed at reaching Czerniaków, the southernmost portion of the city nearest the Vistula still held by General Bór's forces, the operation, which included the use of a smoke screen to conceal the approach of the landing boats, was shot up by troops from *Kampfgruppe Rohr* from their defensive positions along the riverbank as well as by well-aimed artillery fire. Most of the boats that survived turned back and only a few carrying a battalion from the 3rd Polish Infantry Division's 9th Infantry Regiment reached the western shore, not nearly enough to have any influence on the fighting.[43] This would only be the first of several attempts that were to follow.

Another factor that weighed upon von Vormann's mind, one that Gille seemed to be unaware of, was the growing realization that something would have to be done about the Polish partisans gathering in the huge Kampino forest northwest of Warsaw, a mere 20 kilometers south of Gille's *Hauptquartier* at Klein Kazun. This forest, located in the *Kommandanten für das rückwärtige Armeegebiet 532* (*Korück 532*, or army rear area command) area of responsibility, had become the base of operations for an estimated 8,000 members of the Polish Resistance, whose attacks against German rear area support installations and transportation networks had begun to reach alarming levels, beyond the ability of rear area security units to overcome.

The *9. Armee* commander feared that this large body of men, if it began to operate in concert with elements of the advancing First Belorussian Front, might be able to isolate the *IV. SS-Pz.Korps* from the rest of the army and facilitate the seizure of Modlin and its crossing sites over both the Narew and Vistula from the rear. Should this occur, the specter of a renewed attack towards East Prussia might once again become a reality. To address this growing threat, he directed his army's *Ia* staff section to begin developing an operations plan that would be put into effect once the ongoing Soviet offensive died down, which he believed would happen in late September, as soon as both sides fought themselves to exhaustion. This operation, which would be known as *Unternehmen Sternschnuppe* (shooting star), would aim at the total eradication of this looming threat, and would impact every corps under von Vormann's command.

Lastly, echoing Gille, he informed *H.Gr. Mitte* that the continuing shortage of troops in the *IV. SS-Pz.Korps* sector would make any effective defense of the Annopol-Zegrze line nearly impossible unless something was done quickly. The something that he recommended to Reinhardt was the castling once again of the *Fs.Pz.Div. Hermann Göring* from the *9. Armee* far-right flank at Puławy along the boundary between it and the *H.Gr. Süd* far left flank, held by *4. Pz.Armee*, to the north in order to buttress Gille's corps on his army's own left flank. Reinhardt gave his preliminary approval to carry out this plan, but he warned von Vormann of the risk he would incur should something happen in the bridgehead during its absence. The *9. Armee* commander also asked that the *3. Pz.Div.* be transferred to his army from *4. Pz.Armee* as a temporary reserve, but his army group commander disapproved this request. In the meantime, for several days at least, Gille and his corps, primarily the *Totenkopf*, *Wiking*, and *19. Panzer* Divisions, would have to do the best they could until the *73. Inf.Div.* was declared ready for battle, or at least until all or a portion of the *Fs.Pz.Div. Hermann Göring* arrived.

Sunday, 17 September, began quietly enough, with most fighting having died down during the last evening. It started as a cold and windy day, with temperatures at freezing point, as troops from *Gruppe von dem Bach* and *Kampfgruppe Rohr* scoured the western bank of the Vistula searching for any Polish or Soviet troops who had survived the failed river crossing attempt the previous evening. The situation in the *VIII. Armeekorps* sector was quiet, as was that in the sector defended by *Gruppe Sieckenius*, which was in the process of handing over control to the recently returned *XLVI. Pz.Korps*. The *IV. SS-Pz.Korps* reported at 6:02 a.m. that it was experiencing only sporadic artillery and mortar fire upon its positions, and that the *Totenkopf* Division was preparing to carry out its own local counterattacks designed to wipe out several smaller Soviet penetrations near Rembelsz that it had not had time to address the previous day.

The *1. ung.Kav.Div*, with approximately half of its troops still occupying its front-line positions, reported light artillery fire and a suspected Soviet troop concentration including several tanks forming near Białoleka. The division still had four days to go before all of its elements were withdrawn, and would still experience some hard fighting before the last unit marched back to the trains to take them safely home to Hungary. Besides reports of the enemy's continuing efforts to concentrate his forces for yet another attack, the only other item of significance was the *Wiking* Division's report that the bridge across the Narew at Zegrze, previously wired for demolition, blew up when it suffered a direct hit from Soviet artillery fire. Due to the amount of damage it had suffered, combined with the fact that the Soviets were now too close to safely use the bridge, Gille ordered the division to completely dismantle what remained using explosives and to burn the rest in order to deny any possible future use by the enemy.[44] Where there had previously been eight bridges over the Vistula and Narew to resupply Gille's corps, now there were only three—the bridge at Modlin, which could accommodate tanks, the adjacent one over the Vistula at Nowy Dwór, and the temporary 12-ton bridge at Młociny. These three bridges would now become *IV. SS-Pz.Korps'* lifeline for the next month.

The *9. Armee* midday report for 17 September states "*An der gesamten Armeefront ruhiger Verlauf des Tages*," ("along the entire Army front, the day passed uneventfully"), much like the phrase "all quiet on the Western Front." One explanation for this unexpectedly uneventful situation can be found in Soviet and Polish postwar accounts, which describe the next several days as being used to bring up additional forces, reposition existing units, and in general to give the units time to rest after over two weeks of continuous operations. Some of the new units, including the 1st Polish Infantry Division, had suffered heavy casualties during the battle for Praga between 10 and 15 September, listing 353 men as being killed in action, 1,406 wounded, and 109 missing, nearly 2,000 men in all. Although it claimed to have killed 613 German troops and captured a quantity of war materiel, this division too was in need of rest.[45]

To the soldiers on the front lines, of course, their days could be described as anything but uneventful. For the troops in Gille's corps, this meant having to endure seemingly unending harassment by artillery and mortar fire, warding off the nightly reconnaissance forays by the enemy, and repairing their old positions or building new ones. In the early morning, a large Soviet scouting party managed to penetrate the *Wiking* Division's main defense line near Zagroby only a few hundred meters from the bridge at Zegrze before it was driven off by a counterattack, leaving 25 of its own dead behind. Actions like this were typical and few soldiers in Gille's divisions got any restful sleep. Ground-attack aircraft of the Red Air Force were constantly overhead both day and night. Close attention had to be given to camouflage, lest their positions by spotted by the ever-alert Soviet reconnaissance aircraft and shortly afterwards be targeted by artillery fire or aerial bombardment.

This was also the day when all the units within *9. Armee* had to submit their weekly personnel *Kampfstärke* and *panzer* status reports. While most of the army's units had suffered hardly any casualties, with the exception of *Gruppe von dem Bach*, the losses suffered by the units comprising *IV. SS-Pz.Korps* were cast in bold relief, reinforcing the validity of Gille's demand for additional infantrymen, reconnaissance troops, and combat engineers to hold his new defense line. For example, between 10 and 17 September, the *Kampfstärke* of the *73. Inf.Div.* declined by at least 997 men, a figure which does not include any losses suffered by units of the division's regimental, battalion, or company *Tross*. The *19. Pz.Div.* suffered a decline of 509 men, a figure that once again does not include any support troops, nor does it reflect the heavy losses incurred by officers and NCOs.

The *Totenkopf* Division had suffered a net loss of 275 men, while the *Wiking* Division in contrast reported a net gain of 642 men, but neither of these figures reflects actual losses, since both divisions received an infusion of 1,000–1,500 recruits from the *14. SS-Freiwilligen Grenadier Division* replacement battalion the week before. How many Ukrainian volunteers each division received is still a matter of dispute, though what cannot be doubted is that this influx of men, however well trained, did increase each division's reported fighting strength and partially compensated for the enormous losses suffered during August. The actual number of casualties would not be reported until the end of the month, though these preliminary figures are indicative of the severity of the fighting.

All told, as of 17 September the combined *Kampfstärke* for Gille's corps stood at 10,125 men, approximately half of what was authorized, had its units been at full strength.[46] With this force, Gille would be responsible for defending a front line that was approximately 23 kilometers long, which worked out on average to be 440 men per kilometer of front. Even with the departure of the Hungarian division, this still meant that Gille would have 317 men to cover the same amount of ground, a troop density greater than anything his corps had yet enjoyed, a factor that would have a great deal to do with his corps' defensive successes in October and November.

With regard to the strength of the corps' armor and antitank forces, the situation was even more positive. As of 17 September, the *19. Pz.Div.* still had 58 operational tanks, assault gun, and tank destroyers, plus 12 operational heavy antitank guns. In comparison, the relatively weak *73. Inf.Div.* reported eight operational antitank guns, while the *1. ung.Kav.Div.* reported having seven, though it fielded 14 *Jg.Pz. 38t Hetzers* from the attached *Heeres-Pz.Jäg.Abt. 743*. The *Wiking* Division reported 44 operational tanks, assault guns, and tank destroyers, along with nine heavy antitank guns.

The *Totenkopf* Division was the strongest of all, with 80 operational tanks, assault guns, and tank destroyers, including three *Pz. VI* Tigers, as well as 11 heavy antitank guns. In all, Gille's corps still fielded 22 operational *Pz. IV* tanks, 64 *Pz. V* Panthers, three *Pz. VI* Tigers, 98 assault guns and tank destroyers, and 59 antitank guns, counting guns deployed by three smaller attached units.[47] With a total of 198 tanks, assault guns, and tank destroyers, as well as those still in short-term repair, *IV. SS-Pz.Korps* was in a good position to fight Soviet armor on nearly even numerical terms, but it was the number of infantrymen manning foxholes, plus the quality of supporting artillery, that would define the outcome of the fighting that would take place over the next five days, when the second defensive battle of Warsaw would draw to a close.

In addition to tallying the actual combat strength of his corps, Gille had to bid farewell to *Sturmbataillon AOK 9*, which began loading out that very day at the railroad yard in Jablonna-Legjonowo for a trip via *Eiltransport* to its new assembly area near Warka. This elite battalion, which had been fighting as part of the *IV. SS-Pz.Korps* reserve for the past week, would undergo a rapid reconstitution that would see it recommitted to battle once again as the *9. Armee* reserve force. While Gille no doubt did not wish to see this unit depart, nor did he want to see Ibranyi's division leave his order of battle, this loss was balanced by the good news that *III. Btl./Pz.Gren.Rgt. 10 Westland* had nearly completed its training period and would soon be on its way to rejoin its parent division, after leaving the year before to be fully rebuilt. Its projected arrival date by rail was 23 September, and though that was six days away, it would be a welcome addition once it arrived.

While Gille's staff, situated as it was behind the thick walls of the ancient Klein Kazun fortress, tackled the minutiae of tallying quantities of supplies, gallons of fuel consumed, and the number of replacements needed to fill the ranks of its units, fighting went on that day, though at a much lower scale than recently. The most important action that occurred on 17 September was the *Totenkopf* Division's aforementioned counterattack to complete the retaking of Rembelsz. Before the SS men could consolidate their positions, the Soviets launched another tank-supported counterattack of their own at 6:30 a.m. that retook a portion of the town. When the regiment and tanks from *Obf.* Becker's division began forming up for yet another attempt to retake the town, it came under fire from Soviet artillery, which made any further attempt in daylight nearly impossible to carry out. Another attempt would be made that evening. Even so, two Soviet JS-II heavy tanks were destroyed in the fighting for Rembelsz, while another one was knocked out in the *1. ung.Kav.Div.* sector by a cavalryman wielding a *Panzerfaust*. The Hungarians' antiaircraft battalion also downed an IL-2 *Stumorvik* that day.

In closing his report, Gille stated that his intention for the following day was to continue to defend, eliminate any remaining Soviet penetrations of the intermediate defense line, and carry on developing the intermediate positions in the Vistula–Narew Triangle, the so-called *Marten-* and *Iltistellung*. A number of construction engineer battalions and local civilian labor levies had been brought in by the *9. Armee* to build these positions, envisioned to be the intermediate lines in front of the main defense line, the *Fuchsstellung*, that would keep the area southeast of Modlin out of the enemy's hands. These defense lines incorporated a large number of dugouts, bunkers, reinforced fighting positions, minefields, artillery firing positions, outpost lines, and trenches. Built more like a World War I defensive system than one conducive to mobile operations, it would be a strange position for a *panzer* corps to occupy, but over the next several months it would prove nearly impregnable.

The *9. Armee* commander's report that evening reflected the changes in fortune that occurred earlier in the day.[48] First, he recalled that his request for the release of the *Fs.Pz.Div. Hermann Göring* to assist *IV. SS-Pz.Korps*, though tentatively approved in concept by *H.Gr. Mitte*, had been overruled by *OKH*, which probably meant that Hitler himself had made the decision. Later that evening though, *Gen.O.* Guderian, the *OKH* Chief of Staff, arguing on von Vormann's behalf, gave *Gen.O.* Reinhardt permission at 11:15 p.m. to move the division, commanded by *Gen.Maj.* Wilhelm Schmalz, provided that the *25. Pz.Div.* also be moved immediately to support the *2. Armee*, whose commander feared an eruption of Soviet forces out of the bridgehead south of Pułtusk.[49]

While *Gen.d.Pz.Tr.* von Vormann was grateful that his request had finally been approved at the highest levels, he wrote that moving *Oberst* Audörsch's division at this inopportune time would make it extremely difficult to counter any amphibious landing along the river bank a few hundred meters east of Zoliborz, since he was counting on the *25. Pz.Div.* to hold that portion of the Vistula defense line. He also begged to be allowed to keep the *1. ung.Kav.Div.* for a few days longer, but once again that request was denied.

Additionally, and perhaps most importantly, von Vormann reported that he strongly believed that the Warsaw Uprising would soon reach its culminating point—not only was the Polish Home Army itself nearly at the end of its ability to continue fighting due to lack of ammunition and food, but the Soviet and Polish efforts on the opposite bank, including the continuing attempt to dislodge Gille's *IV. SS-Pz.Korps* and the impending large-scale river crossing operation to relieve the *Armia Krajowa*, were also about to reach a crescendo. This assessment was based on reports of additional troop movements and concentration of 90–100 Soviet tanks assembling southeast of Praga.[50] The *9. Armee* commander noted that the international press had finally begun paying attention to the battle, and felt that the pressure being exerted upon Stalin by "world opinion" (a term that was still fresh in the public lexicon) via newsreels, radio, and print would soon force the Soviet dictator to take more visible action. *H.Gr. Mitte* was in agreement on this point, but instead of sending additional troops to aid *9. Armee*, Reinhardt directed von Vormann to order von Lüttwitz's *XLVI. Pz.Korps* to assume responsibility for defending Warsaw against an amphibious assault.

This action would require that von Lüttwitz extend his corps' left flank up and into the city, a point beyond where *Gruppe Sieckenius* had previously defended. Evidently, Reinhardt believed that *Ogruf.* von dem Bach was not up to the task of fighting a conventional battle against the Red Army; at least in this regard, most historians would agree. Additionally, Reinhardt directed von Vormann to determine whether a regimental-sized *Kampfgruppe* could be formed from any still-reliable elements of the *73. Inf.Div.* to use as a stopgap for the next several days. But the *9. Armee* commander demurred, stating that even should such elements be assembled, it would take an additional 10 days before such a battlegroup would be ready to take over the sector held by the Hungarians.[51] By then, of course, it would be too late. Gille would simply have to hang on until the *Fs.Pz.Div. Hermann Göring* arrived, a move that would take two days at the earliest. There was so much heavier fighting occurring on the northern portion of *H.Gr. Mitte*'s area of operations on the Eastern Front, particularly that taking place on the border of East Prussia and around Memel, that it seems as if the situation in Warsaw was receding in importance, at least in the mind of Reinhardt.[52]

The nineteenth day of the second battle of Warsaw, 18 September, witnessed a renewed offensive attitude among the ranks of the First Belorussian Front, especially the corps and divisions of the 47th and 70th Armies and the 1st Polish Army. Once again, while most of the *9. Armee* front line was relatively quiet that evening—with the exception of Warsaw proper, where the Poles attempted another unsuccessful small-scale river crossing—the *IV. SS-Pz.Korps* did not get a day of rest. Most of the action that did occur that day took place on the corps' right flank, as it had for most days since 12 September. A pattern of the Soviet and Polish attacks was beginning to emerge, and it was becoming increasingly evident that the effort to roll back the front lines of the *19. Pz.Div.*, the *1. ung.Kav.Div.*, and the *Totenkopf* had two primary goals. The first was to force *Gen.Lt.* Källner's panzer division to the north in order for the 1st Polish Army and left flank of the 47th Army to control all of the east bank of the Vistula directly opposite the areas in Warsaw which still contained a large number of insurgents This, of course, was prerequisite for conducting any kind of successful large-scale river crossing operation. The second goal was to punch through the inner flanks of the Hungarian division and the

Totenkopf Division in order to seize the railroad yard at Jablonna-Legjonowo and push all the way to Modlin, which would completely cut off Gille's corps and gain control of the confluence of the Narew and Vistula Rivers, which was imperative for any successful follow-on operation.

The troops of Gille's corps once again awoke to experience heavy artillery and mortar fire upon their positions, which by now had become routine. While the *19. Pz.Div.* and the remaining cavalry regiment of the Hungarian division still in the line were not attacked until noon that day, a large-scale attack by the 328th Rifle Division with only a tank company in support struck the *Totenkopf* Division beginning at 5:30 a.m. This attack was aimed at SS positions at Grabina and Michałów, as well as yet another attempt to retake Rembelsz. Seizing the latter town would have opened the way for the Soviets to attack Jablonna-Legjonowo, a task that would be made easier by the well-developed paved highway network running through and around it, hence the reason for the bitter defense mounted by the *Totenkopf*.

After the division carried out several successful counterattacks to force the Soviets out of Rembelsz and the surrounding area, fighting shifted to the south, where the enemy sought to punch through German positions at Hills 103 and 101 after a brief drumfire artillery barrage that began at 10:15 a.m. Once the attackers from the 328th Rifle Division had successfully fought their way through the gap between these two strongpoints, they pushed through the forest east of Rożopole, an event that created something of a crisis within Becker's sector, forcing him to commit his division reserve. This force, composed primarily of tanks from *SS-Pz.Rgt. 3* and *III. Btl./SS-Pz.Gren.Rgt. 6 Eicke*, drove the attackers back several kilometers and restored the front line as far east as the town of Szamocin. Soviet tanks accompanying the attack refused to become engaged, preferring to withdraw instead, leaving only dead infantrymen to be counted by Becker's troops. It was not without cost to the Germans, however. During the counterattack against Soviet positions near Hill 101, 24-year-old *SS-Ostuf.* Erich Schramm, commander of *1. Kp./SS-Pz.Rgt. 3*, was killed in action. Nearly two months later, he was posthumously awarded the prestigious *Ehrenblattspange der Waffen-SS* (Honor Roll Clasp of the *Waffen-SS*) for his achievements that day.[53]

By noon, the fighting had shifted to the south, being aimed primarily at the *19. Pz.Div.*, though Ibrányi's remaining cavalrymen received their share of attention. Most of the focus of the attacking troops from the 2nd Polish Infantry Division appeared to be directed at the German positions between the town of Annopol and the Vistula, a clear indication of their desire to establish control over the east bank of the river opposite the insurgent-held enclaves still remaining at Zoliborz and Marymont. This attack got nowhere near either, and was driven back by a combination of well-directed German tank and artillery fire. Later that day, *Pz.Rgt. 27*, *Pz.Jag.Abt. 19*, and *Pz.Aufkl.Abt. 19* combined to launch a division-level counterattack to relieve pressure being exerted against their Hungarian neighbors, hitting the attacking 175th Rifle Division in its left flank and destroying four T-34s, an event that forced the surprised Soviets to halt their attack and hasten back to their line of departure near Białoleka.

The most serious event of that day was an attack against the remaining positions held by the *1. ung.Kav.Div.*, sandwiched as it was between the *19. Pz.Div.* and the *Totenkopf* Division. Centered around the village of Tomaszów, the Hungarians were struck hard by a tank-supported rifle regiment from the 143rd Rifle Division originating from the Szamocin area. After being pinned in their positions by a short but heavy artillery barrage, the attacking Soviets quickly punched through the Hungarian lines and, ignoring the defenders, made a beeline towards the town of Płudy which lay astride the Praga–Modlin railway line. The Hungarians quickly launched a counterattack using one of its regiments that was preparing to march to the railhead at Jablonna-Legjonowo, augmented for this purpose by *Pz.Jag. Abt. 743*. After destroying one T-34, the Hungarians, assisted by the two German divisions on its left and right, forced the remainder of the attackers back, though it was a very close call.

This narrowly averted crisis created quite a stir in Gille's headquarters. Płudy was in the same area where the *73. Inf.Div.* was being reconstituted, and two battalion-sized *Kampfgruppen* from *Gren.Rgt. 170* and *186* were ordered out of their encampments to form a hasty reception line east of Henryków to block any attempts by the Soviets to continue their drive. Fortunately, none of the enemy troops made it that far. The rest of their day was spent holding the line while the *Totenkopf* Division on their left and the *19. Pz.Div.* on their right attacked to close the gap, along with the previously mentioned counterattack carried out by the Hungarians. Neither Gille nor von Vormann had any confidence that the *73. Inf.Div.* would stand its ground, since it was obvious to both that it was not yet ready to return to combat, despite its ability to turn out two battalions at a moment's notice. At least for now the division, its reputation scandalized by its previous collapse, had earned a brief respite.

For the *Wiking* Division, 18 September was almost a quiet day, notwithstanding the constant artillery and mortar harassing fire that ranged across the entire thinly spread division sector from the village of Wolica in the north to Aleksandrów in the south. East of Nieporet lay the division's main defense line, blocking access to the paved highway leading from Słupno to Zegrze. Fortunately, the opposing XCVI Rifle Corps, which had suffered heavy losses during the past two weeks, confined its activity to the aforementioned artillery fire and intensive ground reconnaissance activity, with one such attempt being successfully warded off by the *Wiking* Division's troops north of Aleksandrów. *Ostubaf.* Darges, the commander of *SS-Pz.Rgt. 5*, carefully husbanded his few remaining tanks, keeping *5.* and *6. Kompanie* of his *II. Abteilung* in reserve west of Nieporet, while the *7.* and *8. Kompanie* under the command of *Hstuf.* Flügel were in action north of the Narew, where it was still acting as the *9. Armee* far-left flank unit, linking up with *XX. Armeekorps* at Serock. Action there had been sporadic, with most activity being confined to Soviet artillery fire.[54]

Besides describing the course of the fighting, Gille in his evening report wrote about a singular event that he and many of his contemporaries witnessed that day. Beginning at 1:40 p.m., approximately 145 American four-engine bombers (evidently B-17s, since the German reports described them as "Fortresses") escorted by dozens of P-51 Mustangs from the Eighth Air Force, flying at high altitude, began dropping hundreds of supply canisters over the entire corps' area of operations. Initially described as being enemy paratroopers, the *Flak* battalions of the *3.* and *5. SS-Pz. Div.*, *19. Pz.Div.*, the *1. ung.Kav.Div.*, and the corps headquarters' own *Flak* battery reacted vigorously, shooting at the American aircrews with 8.8cm, 3.7cm, and 2cm antiaircraft guns. Gille's troops claimed to have shot down four of the aircraft (the U.S. reported only two lost) and to have captured one American bomber's radio operator after he bailed out.[55]

In its after-action report, the American bomber wing that flew the mission reported that the 110 B-17s taking part in the mission dropped 1,284 containers of food, ammunition, clothing, and weapons, claiming that they were delivered with "excellent results" to the embattled Poles within Warsaw. In truth, the bombers widely missed their intended targets, and over 80 percent of the resupply canisters were reported as landing within German lines, while some landed within Soviet lines.[56] This mission, which initially raised the hopes of the inhabitants of Warsaw, was a failure. Many Poles who believed that it heralded the long-awaited rescue operation by the Polish Airborne Brigade had their hopes dashed yet again when they saw most of the multi-colored parachutes with their precious supplies drift behind German lines. For many of the insurgents, it was a bitter disappointment. The Germans, however, rejoiced to have received such unexpected manna from heaven, since many of the canisters were packed with American canned food, sweets, and other items in short supply.

In his summary of the day's events of 18 September that evening, Gille reported that his corps would continue to defend its present position, straighten out the intermediate line by ironing out any remaining penetrations or retaking lost ground, and prepare the final defensive lines across the Narew–Vistula triangle. Based on his observations from the previous day, he believed that the Soviets were holding back their armor for the major attack which he believed could come at any time, in the next several days at the latest. He noted that his divisions reported that there were relatively few tanks supporting the attacks that day by the 1st Polish Army and elements of the 47th Army, another indication, he believed, that Rokossovsky was carefully holding back his armor in anticipation of a breakthrough by the rifle divisions.

Overall, the *IV. SS-Pz.Korps* had fought well that day, though it would soon have to bid farewell to the hard-fighting *1. ung.Kav.Div.* This realization was lightened somewhat by the knowledge that von Vormann had approved Gille's request to keep *Gren.Btl.z.b.V. 560* for a few days longer, at least until *III.Btl./Pz.Gren.Rgt. 10 Westland* arrived on 23 September. This probationary battalion, whose 550 men were badly needed to hold the division's extended front line, had earned the respect of the *Wikinger* for its tenacity and *esprit de corps*, primarily due to the dynamic leadership of its commander, *Major* Ritter. In addition to the foxhole strength it brought to the corps' combined *Kampfstärke*, its three heavy antitank guns and two light infantry howitzers were also very welcome.[57]

In his own summation of the day's activities, von Vormann echoed Gille's concerns about the movement of Soviet armor to the south, away from the German front lines east of the Vistula to an assembly area southeast of Praga. He also believed that this regrouping was a sign that the III Tank Corps had returned for yet another large-scale attack against the *IV. SS-Pz.Korps*' positions or to take part in the build-up at the Magnuszew or Puławy bridgeheads. Though Gille and von Vormann's were legitimate concerns, what was actually taking place was that Lt.Gen. Popov's VIII Guards Tank Corps, and not the III Tank Corps as they believed, was being pulled back for a brief period of rest and reorganization after nearly three weeks of unrelenting combat. During one 10-day period alone, Popov's corps had suffered the loss of 105 tanks and assault guns destroyed or badly damaged, plus an unknown number rendered inoperable for mechanical reasons. In addition, it suffered the loss of 640 men killed, wounded, and missing, with another 93 captured. Given the operational tempo of the past three weeks, this rest period was well overdue, though the corps would soon be back in action during the third and final defensive battle of Warsaw.[58]

Although von Vormann was rightly concerned about what occurred that day on the eastern side of the Vistula, what he was mostly focused on in his report was the attempted landing that took place shortly after midnight across the river from Zoliborz. Heralded by a heavy artillery barrage intended to suppress any German defenses, the Polish landing force of approximately battalion size managed to get at least 120 men across before German artillery responded in kind and shut down the operation. Another attempt was made at 2:30 a.m. on 19 September but the defenders, primarily troops from Audörsch's *Kampgruppe 25. Pz.Div.*, forced it to turn back. German efforts to wipe out the tiny bridgehead failed when it too began receiving heavy artillery fire upon their positions.

With the return of the *XLVI. Pz.Korps* into the *9. Armee* order of battle, which was scheduled to take over command of the sector from *Gruppe Sieckenius* at 10 a.m. on 18 September, the Germans would finally be able to establish a unified, coherent Warsaw defense line under the competent leadership of a combined arms headquarters along the entire western bank of the Vistula, though it was still very thin in places and in some spots the insurgents were still able to access the river.[59] After the failure of the landing attempt the night before, both sides traded artillery and direct-fire weapons across the river at each other's positions without achieving much except the further destruction of Warsaw's and Praga's buildings and landmarks.

Meanwhile, *Gruppe von dem Bach*, freed from responsibility for defending along the river, continued its grim business of reducing the ever-shrinking parts of the city still under the control of General Bór's forces. The spectacular failure of the American air supply drop the previous day had affected Polish morale in the city quite adversely, though the insurgents hung on with a growing sense of desperation. A worrying sign that the Polish partisans outside of the city were beginning to cooperate with Soviet forces on the other side of the river and inside the city itself was a report that an attack had been launched against German security forces southeast of the Kampino forest by the increasingly assertive Polish partisans organizing within the forest. This development gave a greater sense of urgency to the *9. Armee* plan to eradicate this growing menace as soon as possible, though at the moment it had no forces to hand with which to do so. The Kampino forest would have to wait.

Another issue that began to worry von Vormann that day was the indication that the Soviet troops inside the Magnuszew and Puławy bridgeheads were finally beginning to show signs of renewed activity, illustrated by heightened infantry patrolling and increased use of artillery and mortar fire reported by *VIII. Armeekorps*. However, Soviet air activity over German positions in the southern sector of the *9. Armee* area of operations remained unchanged and there were still no signs that an attack was imminent. At least for the time being, the *9. Armee* commander could still focus the bulk of his attention on the battle inside Warsaw as well as the battle raging east of the city and what future operations might entail.

With regard to future operations, von Vormann stated in his report that he intended to move Schmalz's *Fs.Pz.Div. Hermann Göring*—less its *Pz.Gren.Rgt. Hermann Göring 2*, which would remain as the *H.Gr. Mitte* reserve in Warsaw—to the eastern side of the Vistula, where it would assume responsibility for the sector defended by the *19. Pz.Div.* and the *1. ung.Kav.Div.* The *19. Pz.Div.*, despite its excellent performance, was considered to be in need of a period of rest and reconstitution. Though its strength in armor was still formidable, both of its *Panzergrenadier* regiments were terribly short of personnel, as illustrated by the weekly strength report that indicated that *Maj.* Nähring's *Pz.Gren.Rgt. 73* only had 93 men as its *Kampfstärke*. While its sister regiment, *Pz.Gren.Rgt. 74*, was slightly better off, the combined fighting strength of both regiments was only about 25 percent of what was authorized. Losses in battalion, company, and platoon commanders had been very high, to the point that the units themselves could no longer be led efficiently unless replacements were provided.[60]

March orders for the *Fs.Pz.Div. Hermann Göring* were issued that night, stating that it was attached to the *IV. SS-Pz.Korps* forthwith and would begin moving via rail and highway the following day. When it had assembled in the Jablonna-Legjonowo area, it would begin replacing the *19. Pz.Div.* as quickly as possible. Movement of the Hungarian division would proceed uninterruptedly as planned, and Ibrányi would turn over his positions to Schmalz's troops as soon as they arrived. Another order that von Vormann's headquarters issued was one directing that the *73. Inf.Div.* begin moving to the western side of the Vistula to complete its reorganization. This was seen as necessary in order for this process to continue undisturbed. Though it had stood in the breach earlier that day when the Soviets broke through the Hungarians' main defense line, no one was under any illusions that the two *Kampfgruppen* would have stood their ground had the attack actually reached their positions, which was merely an unprepared screening line unsuitable to defend against a tank assault.

The status of this ill-starred division had become quite a topic of contention among the *9. Armee*, *H.Gr. Mitte*, and *OKH*. *Generaloberst* Reinhardt, who had previously informed Guderian at *OKH* that he intended to disband the division completely and distribute its remaining reliable elements throughout the other units within the *9. Armee*. Guderian once again refused to grant him permission to do this, based on a standing order from Adolf Hitler that expressly forbade the dissolution of existing German divisions. Instead, Guderian ordered that the division would be fully rebuilt, the unreliable elements weeded out, and new leaders installed. The most stringent disciplinary measures were authorized, with those leaders most liable for the collapse tried by a military tribunal. Those found guilty would be executed by firing squads or demoted and assigned to a disciplinary battalion. The division commander, *Oberst* Schlieper, was not charged, since he had only taken over the division two days before it collapsed and was deemed not to be responsible for what happened. He was allowed to remain in command and was charged with the reconstruction of his division, including the incorporation of hundreds of replacements and dozens of new company, battalion, and regimental commanders.

One beneficiary of the reorganization of the *73. Inf.Div.* was the *IV. SS-Pz.Korps'* medical establishment. Besides receiving new leadership and replacement personnel and equipment, many of the division's constituent elements were also required to conform to its new *K.St.N.* that would strip them down and streamline them in an administrative action that would make the "new" *73. Inf.Div.* appear more similar to a *Volks-Grenadier* division than its old *Kriegsetat 1944* infantry division structure. As briefly mentioned in a previous chapter, to comply with the directive, the division had to shed one of its field dressing stations, *1./San.Kp. 173*, and a motorized ambulance platoon, *Kr.Kw.Zug 1./173*. Both units were assigned to Gille's corps to fill the existing shortage of these capabilities, where they retained their function though not their title.[61]

Von Vormann did not operate in a vacuum, of course, and spent a certain amount of time each day in conversation with his army group commander. Most of these conversations are not found in the *9. Armee* records, but in the *H.Gr. Mitte* war diary some of these are briefly summarized. For instance, we learn that on 18 September, von Vormann balked at Reinhardt's request to immediately give up *Kampfgruppe 25. Pz.Div.*, which was holding a vital sector along the Vistula's western bank. Reinhardt wanted to use it, along with the *3. Pz.Div.*, to support the long-planned but oft-delayed counteroffensive by the neighboring *2. Armee* against the Pultusk–Serock bridgehead. The *9. Armee* commander would agree to that move, provided that he be allowed to use the one regiment of the *Fs.Pz.Div. Hermann Göring* stationed in Włochy, part of the army group's reserve, to take over the sector held by Audörsch's division.[62]

This Reinhardt refused to allow, responding that von Vormann would have to hold the river line with his existing forces, minus *Kampfgruppe 25. Pz.Div.*, and that under no circumstance could he deploy the *Fs.Pz.Div. Hermann Göring* in the city, fearing that it would become enmeshed in suppressing the Warsaw Uprising. In his rejoinder, von Vormann stated outright that without the *25. Pz.Div.* or a comparable-sized unit, holding Warsaw was "absolutely impossible" should the Poles and Soviets launch a full-scale river crossing operation, and hinted that a withdrawal from the city might become necessary. He reminded his superior that most of the troops fighting in the city proper were a mish-mash of units with a wide variety of capabilities, and were totally unsuited to carry out a deliberate defense along the river without a conventional unit such as the *25. Pz.Div.* to provide the backbone. Reinhardt forcefully ended the conversation by stating that Hitler felt that retaining Warsaw was of the highest strategic importance and that *9. Armee* would hold the city "at all costs." In place of Audörsch's division, Reinhardt directed his subordinate to use *Gren.Btl.z.b.V. 560* as a substitute. This, of course, was an impractical idea because this particular battalion, though well-led, simply lacked the number of heavy weapons and troop numbers to mount any kind of sustained defense across such a wide sector. Finally, worn down by his subordinate's persistence, Reinhardt allowed *9. Armee* to keep the *25. Pz.Div.* for a few more days.

To re-emphasize the importance of holding Warsaw though, Reinhardt directed von Vormann to issue an order to his troops the following day repeating the existing *Führerbefehl* (an order from Adolf Hitler himself), which stated that the defense of the Vistula line, especially the city of Warsaw, was the duty of each and every unit leader, and that they would be held personally responsible for holding his assigned sector "at all costs."[63] This order, of course, would not have caused any hesitancy on the part of the *IV. SS-Pz.Korps* commander, since to Herbert Otto Gille, *Befehl ist Befehl*. One result of the back-and-forth between Reinhardt and von Vormann was that the *Fs.Pz.Div. Hermann Göring*, so long as it was not used within the city itself, could be employed east of the Vistula as Gille saw fit, with no strings attached. This was good news indeed, because Schmalz's division would soon be put to good use. Thus ended 18 September.

The next day began as almost a repeat of the previous one, with the exception of early morning rain. In the *IV. SS-Pz.Korps* sector, attacks against the corps' right wing continued, though few tanks were in evidence. Most of the attacks were directed against the same strongpoints that the Soviets had attacked the previous day and the day before that. Infantry assaults were reported against Białoleka, Rembelsz, Hill 103, and Aleksandrów. Local penetrations were ironed out by immediate German counterattacks and strong artillery fire continued throughout the day. By midday, it was apparent that the primary focus of the Polish and Soviet attacks was the *19. Pz.Div.*, which was once again subjected to numerous attacks between Białoleka and Tomaszow. Despite the orders for it to begin displacing across the river, Gille was forced to order elements of the *73. Inf.Div.* back into the line, where the *Kampfgruppen* from the *170.* and *186. Gren.Rgt.*—to everyone's surprise—performed remarkably well, capturing 24 Soviet stragglers and four abandoned T-34s found near Hill 96.

A notable achievement that day was the smashing of numerous Soviet attempts to prosecute their attacks towards Annopol by the concentrated application of the artillery from the *19. Pz.Div.*, as well as corps artillery by Kurt Brassack's *SS-ARKO 104. Brigadeführer* Brassack, working with the artillery regiments of each of the four remaining divisions in corps (including that of the *73. Inf.Div.*) had conceived an intricate plan whereby a number of actual or suspected Soviet assembly areas were located and mapped as targets, followed by the assignment of one or more gun battalions to mass their fires to "service" that particular target. In this manner, with few firing commands given, the guns of a division could be augmented very rapidly by those from other divisions or corps artillery and rocket batteries, which would conduct the fire mission and then just as rapidly switch to other designated targets as required. This procedure was practiced several times during the day with stunning effect, often stopping large-scale Soviet attacks before they could even begin. Though not as sophisticated as the U.S. Army's use of massed artillery fire in Western Europe, it was a close approximation and something that the troops of the 47th Army had rarely encountered. This was borne out by reports from forward observers who witnessed the results of several artillery strikes upon assembly areas that saw Soviet troops abandoning their vehicles and running away in panic to escape the shelling.[64]

The *Totenkopf* Division was struck hard again that day. Its headquarters reported that its front line was hit repeatedly by numerous company- and battalion-sized infantry attacks, with small numbers of tanks in support. The greatest crisis of the day arose when a force of approximately 200 riflemen broke through the *Totenkopf*'s position at Michałow, forcing the employment of the division reserve to wipe them out. In the fierce fighting that ensued, the division claimed three T-34s and two T-70 light tanks destroyed near Hill 96 west of Tomaszów, though some of these might have been the same tanks that the *73. Inf.Div.* reported as having been captured at about the same time. According to the VIII Guards Tank Corps war diary, none of the Soviet tanks lost that day were from any of its brigades; most likely they were from tank battalions organic to the 47th Army, which had several of these independent units. Aside from combating Soviet artillery concentrations with its own artillery regiment using the procedures described above, the *Totenkopf* Division's *SS-Flak. Abt. 3* also shot down two IL-2 *Sturmoviks*.

Things had begun to heat up in the *Wiking* Division's sector too. Weathering the usual daily heavy artillery fire, the division reported increased Soviet daytime patrolling activity, with several attempts being made to penetrate the division's extended front-line positions. Most of these were driven off with artillery fire. In the area north of Serock, where *Hstuf.* Flügel was leading the *Wiking*'s *panzer* contingent in support of *Fest.Inf.Btl. 1405*, his battalion reported hearing a great amount of Soviet tanks moving about on its far left, where an attack seemed to be underway against its left flank neighbor from the *XX. Armeekorps.* There was little they could do about it except report it, since it was too far away for their guns to reach and they had no artillery of their own to employ, also being too far from the guns of *SS-Pz.Art.Rgt. 5*. The other thing of note of that day was that one of the division's infantry companies captured a wounded soldier from the 160th Rifle Division, who had been shot while attempting to cross German lines posing as a deserter. In reality, he had been performing a reconnaissance mission when apprehended.

The Hungarians, now dwindled to less than a brigade in strength, had to endure several hours of a drumfire barrage upon its position, though no infantry attack materialized. Lt. Gen. Ibrányi had departed along with most of his staff, leaving the one brigade headquarters with several squadrons and some artillery behind. Most of the division's soldiers had departed by this point, and many of its remaining troops were fearful that they would somehow be trapped and not be able to return to their homeland like their comrades in the division's other cavalry regiments, an attitude that their German liaison officer commented on when he submitted his own separate report to *9. Armee* headquarters that evening.

Across the corps front, the ground attack aircraft of the 16th Air Army, which had sent many of its squadrons away to support operations elsewhere within the First Belorussian Front's area of operations, returned with a vengeance, making life as miserable for the average German and Hungarian soldier as it had throughout the previous month. In addition to bombing and strafing enemy front-line positions, its aircraft also paid a great deal of attention towards the 12-ton temporary pontoon bridge at Włochy, attacking it repeatedly throughout the day, though without success. All the Red Air Force had to show for its efforts was the loss of two IL-2 *Sturmoviks*, shot down by the *Flak* battalion of the *19. Pz.Div.* Its aircraft also attacked the positions of the *XLVI. Pz.Korps* along the western bank of the Vistula. Except for carrying out several strikes that day by a *Stuka* squadron, the *Luftwaffe*'s fighter aircraft were nowhere to be seen, a sign that its few remaining fighter assets were being shifted increasingly to the West to combat the Allied bomber offensive.

Gille stated his intentions for the following day, which were identical to the previous one: continue defending, iron out local breakthroughs, and keep working on the final defense line so they would be completed in time. He closed by providing his recommendation that that the *19. Pz.Div.* should be mentioned in the *Wehrmachtsbericht* for the following day in honor of its outstanding performance since falling under his command the week before. In his recommendation Gille stated:

> During the heavy defensive fighting in the Praga area, the *19. Pz.Div.* under the leadership of *Gen.Lt.* Källner was employed as the [corps'] main effort … through its unshakeable steadfastness and decisively-led counterattacks, it once again especially proved itself, inflicting heavy losses in manpower and materiel upon the enemy.[65]

That evening, Gille's corps reported the arrival of the assault battalion and combat engineer battalion from *Fs.Pz.Div. Hermann Göring*, a sign that the rest of the division, minus one regiment, was on its way. The news could not have come at a better time.

While von Vormann was no doubt cheered by the defensive successes of that day on the eastern bank of the Vistula, his main concern was repelling the first serious river crossing attempt by the Polish 3rd Infantry Division, which began at 4 p.m. The division, using its entire 8th Infantry Regiment, began crossing the Vistula between the columns of the destroyed Central and Poniatowski bridges under the protective cover of a smoke screen. Further supported by a heavy artillery barrage and substantial fighter-bomber attacks, the lead battalion quickly seized a bridgehead on the opposite shore 1,000 meters wide and 500 meters deep. To repulse this major threat, the *9. Armee* commander authorized the attachment of *Pz.Gren. Rgt. Hermann Göring 2*, the *H.Gr. Mitte* reserve, to augment the *Kampfgruppe 25. Pz.Div.*, which lacked much infantry of its own since its *Pz.Gren.Rgt. 146* was still attached to *Kampfgruppe Rohr*.

Gen.d.Pz.Tr. von Lüttwitz, whose *XLVI. Pz.Korps* had taken over this defensive sector along the river earlier that morning on Gille's right flank, ordered his subordinate units–*25. Pz.Div.*, *Gruppe Sieckenius*, and *Kampfgruppe Rohr*—to launch an immediate counterattack. Even troops from *Gruppe von dem Bach* participated. By nightfall, the Germans had eradicated most of the Polish units that had made it safely ashore and sank 26 of the landing boats that tried to cross with reinforcements, throwing 150 troops into the water to swim or drown. Of the men from 1st and 2nd Battalions of the 8th Infantry Regiment, 370 of them were reported as being killed in action, with another 300 taken prisoner.[66] Despite this reversal, the survivors clung desperately to their narrow bridgehead and hoped for reinforcement the following day. In response, von Lüttwitz ordered his units that evening to wipe out any remaining resistance and mop up any survivors they found along the riverbank, and to be prepared to repel more such attempts. So far, none of the Poles' several attempts to cross the river and relieve their fellow countrymen had been successful, though small pockets of Polish troops were involved in house-to-house fighting against German forces along the water's edge. Undaunted, the Polish 1st and 3rd Infantry Divisions would try again.

That night in his commander's report to *H.Gr. Mitte*, while describing his satisfaction with the defensive success that day along both banks of the Vistula, von Vormann expressed his apprehension that unless his army was reinforced, Warsaw could not be held much longer. Though he did win approval of his request to keep the *25. Pz.Div.* until 23 September, this was not enough in his mind to make a measureable difference. With the Warsaw Uprising dragging on into its seventh week, he felt that his army could not both defend Warsaw and complete the suppression of the Polish Home Army at the same time. To illustrate the challenges he faced regarding manpower, von Vormann told his army group commander that *Regiment Nöthe* from *Gruppe von dem Bach* had to be employed along the riverbank, a mission for which it was totally unsuited, consisting as it was of thrown-together police, home guard units, and various *Alarm* battalions with no heavy weapons and weak leadership.

In closing his brief (for once) report, von Vormann stated that *Gen.Maj.* Sieckenius would be appointed as the investigating officer for the courts martial presided over by the commanding officer of the *19. Pz.Div.*, *Gen.Lt.* Källner, who would try officers of the *73. Inf.Div.* accused of cowardice during the division's collapse of 12 September. In furtherance of this responsibility, Källner was granted the authority to have those found guilty executed by a firing squad to serve as examples for the rest of the division.[67] The results of the trial were to be reported to von Vormann by 23 September, though the army commander had the final say on any recommended executions. These trials would occur under Gille's watch, since the *73. Inf.Div.* was still attached to his corps. What Gille thought of the proceedings is unrecorded, though in his daily report of 12 September he did state in no uncertain terms that this unit had "betrayed" the other divisions in his corps and had put their very survival at risk.

That night, the contretemps between von Vormann and Reinhardt over the future employment of the *Kampfgruppe 25. Pz.Div.* continued. Reinhardt categorically stated that the division must be completely withdrawn and sent to *2. Armee* by 23 September, with the first element beginning their movement by rail on the morning of 20 September. He emphasized that without this division, the attack against the Soviet bridgehead north of Serock would not succeed. The *9. Armee* commander countered by stating that if the division was pulled out, the Polish river-crossing operation would succeed and Warsaw would fall. Reinhardt proposed taking the *19. Pz.Div.* instead, prompting von Vormann to respond that if he did so, Gille's corps would collapse, since the forward elements of *Fs.Pz.Div. Hermann Göring* were only just arriving and it would take several days before the entire division could be assembled. Von Vormann then told Reinhardt that in his opinion, the commander of *H.Gr. Mitte* was not assessing the situation of the *9.*

Armee as seriously as the situation warranted. So it went, back and forth, until late in the evening.[68]

Clearly, the *9. Armee* commander's stubbornness was doing his case no good, for Reinhardt telephoned Guderian at *OKH* headquarters that night and informed him of his desire to replace von Vormann with someone more cooperative as soon as possible. While the situation in Warsaw was important, Reinhardt had other far more serious crises to deal with, including the ongoing offensive in East Prussia and the planned counteroffensive against the Soviet bridgehead between Serock and Pułtusk, as well as the other one at Rózan. Guderian agreed with his assessment, but told the *H.Gr.Mitte* commander that only Hitler could approve a change in commanders at this level, but that he would pose this question to *der Führer* the following morning. When Reinhardt asked him who he recommended as von Vormann's replacement, Guderian immediately proposed von Lüttwitz, commander of *XLVI. Pz.Korps*, as the new *9. Armee* commander.[69]

Another issue that cropped up during one of the discussions that evening between von Vormann and Reinhardt concerned the *IV. SS-Pz.Korps*. When von Vormann complained that Gille's corps did not have sufficient manpower to hold its extended intermediate position between the Bug River confluence with the Narew at Serock and the Vistula at Annopol, Reinhardt asked him about the 1,500 replacements that had just been sent in Gille's direction for his two SS divisions. Von Vormann replied that only 500 of them were German recruits, while the other 1,000 were Ukrainians and Galicians, so-called *Waffenwilliger*. Though Gille had welcomed the German replacements, von Vormann told Reinhardt that his subordinate SS corps commander wanted to send back the foreign volunteers, since in Gille's opinion, probably based on his own recent experience employing them, they were "of limited combat value." Forcefully concluding the discussion, Reinhardt stated that, if necessary, he would issue an order demanding that Gille employ these troops as intended.[70] None of these developments boded well for von Vormann, who must have felt that he was treading on thin ice.

What probably ended von Vormann's chances of continuing as commander of *9. Armee* was a bleak radio message he sent to the *H.Gr. Mitte* commander on 19 September, which stated:

> Only Division 'Hermann Göring' can be said to be fully adequate with regard to combat strength and battle-competence. The hard-tested SS Divisions 'Totenkopf' and 'Wiking'—as well as the *9. Armee*—have, during the past several weeks of combat, become so decimated that at this present juncture, they are only equivalent to a very mediocre fighting force.[71]

This statement, coming from an army commander, would have set off alarm bells among the senior staff officers of the army group, who could only interpret this as a loss of will. Regardless of whether or not it was true, it went against the prevailing National Socialist orthodoxy, where blind obedience was becoming a more prized asset than military competence. Von Vormann's statement must have reeked of sheer defeatism, at least in their perceptions.

Wednesday, 20 September, which would prove the last day that the *IV. SS-Pz. Korps* would be under the command of Nikolaus von Vormann, witnessed a further decrease in the intensity of attacks by the First Belorussian Front. Aside from the ever-present artillery and mortar fire throughout the corps' front line and rear area, the only action the corps thought worth mentioning in its morning report was the result of attacks and counterattacks occurring the night before in the *Totenkopf* Division's sector. *Oberführer* Becker's troops were having difficulty clearing up the battalion-sized breakthrough from the previous afternoon at Michałow, and found themselves having to ward off another determined attack against Hill 101 using artillery fire and infantry weapons. The *19. Pz.Div.* and the last Hungarian brigade from *1. ung.Kav.Div.* reported engine noises, signifying a large convoy to the southeast of Bialoleka, but could not observe any movement. In the *Wiking* Division's sector, it reported artillery duels with Soviet batteries, artillery strikes against assembly areas, and unsuccessful attempts by the Soviets to employ loudspeaker teams broadcasting entreaties from the "National Committee for a Free Germany."

Though it began with a cold wind, as the day grew longer it warmed to a pleasant 62 degrees Fahrenheit. The fighting grew warmer too, especially concerning the amount of artillery being employed by both sides. The *Wiking* and *Totenkopf* Divisions both reported increased enemy ground reconnaissance activity, which was simply driven off by artillery fire. The corps' *ARKO* also did his best with deep artillery strikes to interrupt or disrupt the large amount of vehicular traffic that could be observed with the naked eye passing along the road network between Radzymin and Praga. What this signified could only be guessed at, but the consensus seemed to be that it signified yet another large-scale offensive being prepared. A Soviet prisoner of war captured that same day seemed to confirm this suspicion, stating that the main effort would be aimed at the area north of Aleksandrów in the direction of Nieporet, squarely in the *Wiking* Division's area of operations. A tethered Soviet observation balloon was reported at Stare Grodno, but a few shots from the *Totenkopf* Division's artillery regiment forced the balloon's ground crew to quickly reel it in.

The only tactical action worth mentioning on 20 September in the *IV. SS-Pz.Korps* area was primarily confined to the *Totenkopf* Division's sector, where its long-struggling counterattack to regain Michałow finally succeeded by the middle of the afternoon, only to see the division's positions between Hills 101 and 96 fall to the enemy at 5 p.m. after a 15-minute artillery barrage. A counterattack was immediately launched to regain the lost ground, that was still ongoing when darkness fell. The division's artillery ranged across its front, striking targets estimated to be located in the forest east of Rembelsz and Aleksandrów. *SS-Pz.Art.Rgt. 3* was rewarded when one of its shells struck a target in the woods, setting off several large explosions in quick succession. Evidently it had hit an ammunition storage area.

While this low-level fighting continued, a variety of units were moving in and out of Gille's sector. The Hungarians finally bid farewell that evening, marching to the railroad yard at Jablonna-Legjonowo to join the rest of their comrades after their shrinking defensive sector was taken over by the special assault battalion from *Fs. Pz.Div. Hermann Goering*. The bulk of the *73. Inf.Div.* began moving westwards across the Vistula over the pontoon bridge at Młociny that afternoon towards its new assembly area south of Warsaw near Mokotow, where it would continue its rebuilding process. Remaining behind were the *Kampfgruppen* from *Gren.Rgt. 170* and *186*, most of the artillery regiment, and the division's reconnaissance battalion, *Füs.Btl. 173*, all of which would be temporarily placed under the control of the *19. Pz.Div.*

By midnight, additional elements from the *Fs.Pz.Div. Hermann Göring* began arriving behind the front lines, including its division reconnaissance battalion and one battalion from *Fs.Pz.Gren.Rgt. 1 Hermann Göring*. Once the rest of the division had arrived (excluding *Fs.Pz.Gren.Rgt. 2*, which was fighting under the *25. Pz.Div.* along the western bank of the Vistula), it would move into the front lines and conduct a relief in place of the *19. Pz.Div.*, which would itself begin moving westward across the river to prepare for its new assignment. After correcting the previous day's report that *19. Pz.Div.* had destroyed an additional three Soviet tanks and 12 artillery pieces than had been previously reported, Gille closed his evening report by stating his intentions for the next day with his usual laconic, "Will defend the same as before.[72]

The heaviest fighting that day took place not in the *IV. SS-Pz.Korps sector*, but in Warsaw itself. Much of the combat involved the efforts by the *XLVI. Pz.Korps* to destroy the enemy forces that had managed to cross the river and establish themselves on the opposite bank. With the *25. Pz.Div.* attacking to the south along the riverbank, *Gruppe Sieckenius* supported by *Kampfgruppe Rohr* attacking to the north, and with every available German artillery piece in Warsaw firing at the landing sites, the Polish troops caught in the middle soon found themselves trapped in a vice with no way to escape, since most of the landing boats had been sunk. By 8:30 p.m, *Gen.d.Pz.Tr.* von Lüttwitz's corps headquarters reported that most of the western bank was back in German hands and that over 300 Polish troops had been captured along with a great deal of war materiel, including antitank guns, mortars, and machine guns.

In the aftermath of the fighting that day, over 283 enemy dead were physically counted, with 800 more estimated to have drowned in the Vistula. This was a significant victory, much like the one scored on the Western Front at Arnhem a week later, signifying that perhaps Germany's fortunes were changing for the better. It also demonstrated that the Germans now had the wherewithal to mount a formidable defense against any serious attempts by the First Belorussian Front to cross the river. *Gruppe von dem Bach*, besides assisting with the elimination of one of the Polish landing attempts that day, finally captured a key element of the *Armia Krajowa*'s inner defense line in the city nearest to the riverbank, a block of houses between

Wielanowska Street and the Wasserstrasse. While *Ogruf.* von dem Bach may have boasted of his small contribution to the ultimate German victory, it did not come cheap, for his forces suffered the loss of 38 men killed in action and another 217 wounded. But to the butcher of Warsaw, human life, whether German or anyone else's for that matter, was a cheap and expendable commodity.

Besides the drama taking place along the eastern and western shores of the Vistula, another one was playing out at *H.Gr. Mitte* headquarters. Reinhardt had been notified by Guderian that Hitler had approved the replacement of von Vormann by von Lüttwitz. In his evening report, which would prove to be his last, the man who had commanded the *9. Armee* since 27 June for three critical months recounted the successes achieved that day, and stated that in his opinion, *9. Armee* had turned the corner and would survive the current crisis, at least for the time being. He outlined a proposal for the continued suppression of the Warsaw Uprising that would begin in the south near Mokotow and end with the final elimination of the stubborn holdouts in Zoliborz, which despite the best efforts of the *25. Pz.Div.* was still controlled during the night by the insurgents. In von Vormann's final report, he recorded to his disappointment that Reinhardt had disapproved this plan, evidently having another in mind.

Another topic von Vormann stressed in this last report was the urgent need to do something as soon as possible about the growing partisan menace in the Kampino forest, which was beginning to adversely impact the movement of supplies across the river to Gille's corps. On account of the partisans' occupation of the forest, half of Gille's corps rear area support elements and the *Trossteile* of the *Totenkopf* and *Wiking* Divisions were on the northern bank of the Vistula in the *2. Armee* rear area, while the other half, including the division trains for the *19. Pz.Div.*, *73. Inf.Div.*, and the incoming *Fs.Pz.Div. Hermann Göring*, were located south of the forest. He informed *H.Gr. Mitte* that the *9. Armee* staff had drawn up a comprehensive plan to deal with the partisans for good, once the major fighting for Warsaw had decreased to the point where combat troops could be withdrawn from the front lines for that purpose. Von Vormann stressed that something had to be done to eliminate the threat as soon as possible. This last recommendation of his, at least, would be acted upon. The start date for *Unternehmen Sternschnuppe* was set for 27 September.

That afternoon, Reinhardt flew to von Vormann's headquarters west of Warsaw to inform him in person that on account of his inability to agree with his army group commander on the basic outlines for the continuation of the defense of Warsaw, he had lost confidence in his subordinate's ability to perform his duties and von Vormann was to be relieved of command. He was told that he would hand over the reins of *9. Armee* the following day to one of his subordinates, the current commander of *XLVI. Pz.Korps*. For his part, von Lüttwitz was reportedly quite surprised by his elevation in command and did not learn of his promotion until he was flown to army group headquarters that same day for a personal audience with Reinhardt.

Here, Reinhardt congratulated him on his new position and quickly outlined how he wanted *9. Armee* to conduct future operations.[73] His promotion to *General der Panzertruppe* was backdated to 1 April 1944. In turn, von Lüttwitz would hand over his corps command to *Gen.Lt.* Walter Fries, who had only recently given up command of the *29. Pz.Gren.Div.*[74]

Before von Vormann departed his command post and returned to Germany to join the "Führer Reserve" of unemployed general officers, he signed a last flurry of orders that day, which would impact the *IV. SS-Pz.Korps* directly. The first, issued at 2 a.m. on 20 September by *Gen.Maj.* Helmut Staedke, the *Ia* of *9. Armee*, was a warning order informing Gille that he was to form four *Alarm* battalions from the constituent elements of his corps, not to exceed a total of 1,000 men, for the purpose of operating on the western side of the Vistula in order to clear a route through the eastern edge of the partisan-infested Kampino forest to allow the safe passage of supplies. These four battalions were to be formed from division *Trossteile* and supply units and had to be ready for deployment by 25 September. This was Gille's first official notification that *Unternehmen Sternschnuppe* was about to get underway.

The second order, issued at 2:25 p.m. that same day, detailed how the *73. Inf. Div.* was to be reorganized in the wake of its collapse on 12 September. It described how new leadership would be brought in to whip the division back into shape at regimental level and below, how miscreants and cowards were to meted justice by a firing squad after the aforementioned courts martial had taken place, and how the reorganization was to proceed. It laid out requirements to list the numbers, ranks, and arms of service that needed replacement personnel, what equipment was required, and how many weapons that had been lost had to be replaced. It also stated that since it had disgraced the *Führer*, the entire division would be treated like a *Bewährungseinheit* (probationary unit), similar to *Gren.Btl.z.b.V. 560*, but on a much larger scale. All home leaves would be cancelled, no awards handed out, and no promotions would be allowed until the division had redeemed itself in battle. *Oberst* Schlieper was ordered to submit his plan that described how he would accomplish these tasks to *9. Armee* headquarters four days hence. However, his immediate predecessor, *Oberst* Hähling, and the division's *Ia*, *Oberstlt.* Becker, were both to be tried by the military tribunal (both were acquitted).

The third order, issued at 8:05 p.m. that evening—von Vormann's last—was a comprehensive plan describing how each corps or corps-level unit in the *9. Armee* order of battle would be reorganized in the coming days so they could more effectively wage the battle for the Vistula defense line. The *9. Armee* staff correctly assumed that the Warsaw Uprising would soon be completely defeated. After two months of combat, the subordinate elements of the *9. Armee* had become a confused mish-mash of units, including smaller units that had been attached to larger units, companies and battalions that had been scattered throughout the army's area of operations and throughout Warsaw itself, and other units that had no higher headquarters of their own, that had become virtual "orphans" of the battlefield.

This order was designed to dispel the chaos and restore some kind of logic to the organization of the *IV. SS-Pz.Korps* and *XLVI. Panzerkorps*, and *Korpsgruppe von dem Bach*. It laid out a time frame to carry forth the reorganization, what the left and right corps boundaries were, which sub-unit answered to which corps, and what was to become of *Splitterteile* (splinters or fragments of units) that had been operating on an ad-hoc basis since joining the *9. Armee*.

Carrying out the order would be a challenging task, but it had to be fully executed by 26 September to ensure that every combat unit operating in the northern sector of the *9. Armee* area of operations could play its part in the successful defense of Warsaw and the Vistula defense line.[75] It would involve four divisions moving simultaneously across the Vistula; three crossing to the western bank, with one replacing them to the east. Several "splinter" units would be disbanded or returned to their parent organizations. The *IV. SS-Pz.Korps* would detach the *73. Inf.Div.*, the *19. Pz.Div.*, and any remaining elements of the *1. ung.Kav.Div.* beginning on 20 September, actions that were already under way.

In turn, the *Fs.Pz.Div. Hermann Göring* would replace all three, taking up the entire defensive sector on the right of the *IV. SS-Pz.Div.* main defense line that the three other divisions had previously held. The *Wiking* and *Totenkopf* Divisions would not be affected, but would hold their present sectors. They would, however, have to detach several of the units from the *Heer* that had been operating under their umbrella since early August. This particularly impacted the *Wiking* Division, whose dwindling infantry strength had been bolstered by the addition of several battalions from the Army. In addition, *Heeres-Pz.Jäg.Abt. 743*, which had been assigned to Gille's corps since mid-August, would cross over to the west with its remaining *Jg.Pz. 38t* tank destroyers and revert to *9. Armee* control no later than 23 September.

Upon arrival on the western bank of the Vistula, both the *19. Pz.Div.* and the *73. Inf.Div.* would come under the control of the *XLVI. Pz.Korps*. The *73. Inf.Div.* would be allocated a quiet sector on the southwest edge of Warsaw where it would continue its reconstitution as previously described, while the *19. Pz.Div.* would take over most of the responsibility for defending the river line on the eastern edge of Warsaw. In doing so, it would relieve the *Kampfgruppe 25. Pz.Div.*, which would be withdrawn *en echelon* and moved north via rail to the area north of Serock, where it would take part in the effort to reduce the Soviet bridgehead as part of the *2. Armee* concept of operations. The artillery regiment of the *73. Inf.Div.* would remain in place until all of its firing sections had been replaced by those from one of the *Fs.Pz. Div. Hermann Göring* artillery battalions. This would ensure the maximum number of gun tubes available for fire support missions. The last unit scheduled to move would be *Fs.Pz.Pio.Btl. Hermann Göring*, which would replace *Pionier-Bataillon 173* of the *73. Inf.Div.* by 26 September.

This intricate maneuver, involving dozens of battalions, would occupy the attention of the new *9. Armee* commander and the commanders of the three corps involved for the next several days. Fortunately, the operations tempo on the front line had noticeably decreased, due to a reorganization going on within the Soviet order of battle and scattered reports that front-line Soviet infantry units were digging in, a possible sign that they were preparing to switch over to a defensive posture. With the exception of the *Totenkopf* and *Wiking* Divisions, which were still engaged in ongoing combat, and the continued suppression of the Warsaw Uprising by *Gruppe von dem Bach*, the rest of the *9. Armee* area of operations had remained comparatively quiet.

That night, von Vormann's aide-de-camp packed his bags and prepared to accompany his general back to Germany. The former *9. Armee* commander would not languish very long in the *Führerreserve* of senior officers, for on 5 October he was recalled to serve as the *Oberbefehlshaber* of *Festungsberich Süd-Ost* (Fortress Command Southeast), where he would be responsible for fortress troops in southeastern Europe within the *H.Gr. E* area of operations, a position he held until 4 May 1945.[76] His last assignment, only days before the war ended, was his appointment to command the so-called *Alpenfestung* (Alpine Fortress), a last-minute organization created to continue the war in the mountains of southern Germany. This assignment never came to pass, since by that point it was little more than sheer fantasy. After being released from a POW camp, he settled in Berchtesgaden and made a living as an author. He died there on 26 October 1959. Although belittled by Hitler and discredited by his army group commander, *Gen.d.Pz.Tr.* Nikolaus von Vormann had achieved the almost impossible task of slowing down and then stopping the seemingly unstoppable offensive by Marshal Rokossovsky's First Belorussian Front between July and September 1944, while a major uprising was simultaneously taking place inside of Warsaw. Whether von Lüttwitz could claim to be as successful had yet to be proven.

Amazingly, both 21 and 22 September passed without any significant fighting reported anywhere along the *9. Armee* front line, with the exception of the continuing fighting in Warsaw between *Gruppe von dem Bach* and the Polish Home Army. The units of *XLVI. Pz.Korps* continued mopping up along the western bank of the Vistula where the various river crossing attempts had been made the past several days by the Polish 1st and 3rd Infantry Divisions. East of Zoliborz, *Pz.Pio.Btl. 86* of the *25. Pz.Div.*, aided by *Fs.Pz.Gren.Rgt. 2*, attacked the dune area on the riverbank at Potok and brought in 218 prisoners on 21 September alone, including a large amount of weapons, such as mortars, antitank guns, and machine guns. Further efforts by the Poles to transport more troops across the river were unable to get underway due to heavy German artillery fire on the crossing sites. Three boats that tried to cross the Vistula were shot up on the early morning of 21 September by *Gruppe Rohr*, which sank one and drove off the other two. Clearly, the attempts to relieve General Bór and his weary rebels had failed completely, though the bravery of the Polish troops involved was unquestioned.

This day, 21 September, also marked Smilo von Luttwitz's first day in command of the *9. Armee*. A highly experienced leader of armored and mechanized troops, he had previously led a motorized infantry regiment and then a motorized infantry brigade on the Eastern Front, and had spent two years as the commander of the *26. Pz.Div.*, which he helped to form and lead into battle on the Italian Front. A recipient of the Knight's Cross with Oak Leaves and Swords, he had served as a corps commander under von Vormann for nearly a month and had gained a good grasp of the operational and tactical situation of the *9. Armee*, as well as a thorough understanding of the capabilities of the First Belorussian Front. Apolitical, he was a realist who would soon prove himself a very good army commander. He was also an excellent tactician with an unflappable demeanor, traits that would serve him well during the trying times to come.

Most of the focus during the first two days of his army command was the large-scale transfer of troops from the eastern bank of the Vistula to the western side, and vice-versa. Despite ineffectual attempts by the three enemy armies concerned (47th and 70th Armies and the 1st Polish Army) to interfere with this large-scale transferral operation with artillery and air attacks, the *19. Pz.Div.*, along with the two attached *Kampf* battalions from the *73. Inf. Div.*, managed to make their way across the river in good order and filed into their new positions without incident. The battalions of the *19. Pz.Div.* relieved those of the *25. Pz.Div.* in a sequential manner, ensuring that there were no gaps between the departure and arrival that might be exploited by the Polish insurgents or the 1st Polish Army on the other side of the river. By the evening of 21 September, elements of the *25. Pz.Div.* began moving north to their new area of operations, a movement that would be completed two days later.

The last battalion of the *1. ung.Kav.Div.* also departed that evening, having been replaced by the *Fs.Pz.Pio.Btl.* of the *Hermann Göring* Division, which was to complete its takeover of the defensive sector of the *19. Pz.Div.* by 1 p.m. on 22 September. In the same sequential manner, the elements of Schmalz's *Luftwaffe* division arrived and began relieving the two *Panzergrenadier* regiments of Källner's division without any incidents worth mentioning. At one point, as the leading elements of *Fs.Pz. Div. Hermann Göring* began moving into their new positions, the tail end of the division, including the supply, medical, and transportation units, were departing their old positions in the southern sector of the *VIII. Armeekorps* area of operations nearly 100 kilometers away. That this highly complex operation was carried out as smoothly and efficiently as it was is a testament to the skill and dedication of the German Army's general staff officers, who had worked long hours to ensure that the operation happened exactly as von Vormann had intended.

That the Soviets had done so little to disrupt this operation has already been commented on, though they continued exerting pressure upon the *Wiking* and *Totenkopf* Divisions during this period. Fortunately for the Germans, most of the Soviet action consisted of harassing artillery and mortar fire, as well as aggressive infantry patrols that continually probed German lines in search of weak points that could be exploited later. In turn, both SS divisions sent out their own foot patrols to determine Soviet strengths and intentions, as well as to see how far forward their front-line positions extended. An important task for most of these patrols was to bring back a prisoner for interrogation to determine the identities of enemy units opposite and to learn of any impending Soviet attacks. One *Wiking* Division patrol brought in a prisoner who proved to be a member of the 38th Guards Rifle Division. Several patrols from *Staf.* Mühlenkamp's and *Obf.* Becker's divisions were fired upon during these operations, which usually were carried out at night, and on one occasion a patrol from the *Wiking* Division blundered into a newly laid Soviet minefield that woke up the Soviet infantry in a nearby trench, forcing the patrol, carrying its wounded, to beat a hasty retreat.

The last combat patrol by troops from *Kampfgruppe Gren.Rgt. 170* of the *73. Inf. Div.*, attached to the *19. Pz.Div.* until the evening of 21 September, managed to capture and bring back three Soviet antitank guns that night, dragging their trophy into the division's front-line positions. All of Gille's divisions reported hearing sounds of continued digging on the Soviet side, further indications that their enemy was constructing entrenchments. The use of artillery interdiction tactics was continued on both sides, and on 21 September, *SS-Pz.Art.Rgt. 5* of the *Wiking* Division reported that one of its salvoes had struck a Soviet ammunition dump east of Aleksandrów that began erupting like a volcano. The gunners from these two divisions' artillery regiments also claimed to have destroyed two Soviet tanks, 11 artillery pieces, 13 antitank guns, and 45 machine guns with their accurate firing.

The only tactical action worth mentioning was the continuing struggle by the *Totenkopf* Division to retake and hold the village of Michałow, which had changed hands several times during the past week. Clearly, the Soviets intended to own this churned-up piece of real estate and had suffered heavily for it. Each time the men of Becker's division thought they had taken it, they would be driven out by an enemy counterattack. On several occasions, the SS men holding Michałow and Hill 101 reported the clatter of tank tracks and the roar of their engines, as did front-line troops of the *Wiking* Division, though no armored attack materialized. Like his men, Gille and his staff also anticipated that Rokossovsky would resume his offensive at any time, and were bracing for it, but mysteriously, it did not materialize.

Meanwhile, work continued on the *IV. SS-Pz.Korps*' intermediate defensive works being constructed behind the front line, the *Iltis* and *Marder* positions. Gille's quartermaster staff, led by his corps' *Ib*, Hans Scharff, labored with their division counterparts to help them stockpile food, fuel, and ammunition for the battles to come. Covered positions for the artillery, bunkers and troop accommodations for the infantry, revetted positions for tanks and other armored vehicles, and depots for supplies were all built behind the front lines by construction troops and impressed civilian labor for the purpose of preserving as much of the corps' strength as possible. The entire area in the triangle formed by the confluence of the Bug, Narew, and Vistula was slowly being transformed into what a veteran of World War I would recognize as a sign of looming trench warfare, as well as a symbol of the shift in battlefield fortunes that was beginning to impact the rest of the defensive battle for Warsaw.

Friday, 22 September was much like the day before. The weather had turned warm and dry, allowing the continued movement of thousands of troops from both sides to take place without being affected by adverse road conditions. Soviet activity once again was limited to artillery and mortar fire, reported as being weaker than usual, and there was limited air and ground reconnaissance. On the opposite bank, the *XLVI. Pz.Korps* anticipated another river assault, and the newly returned *19. Pz.Div.* braced for it, as well as the other units in the corps, including *Gruppe Rohr* and *Gruppe Sieckenius*, but it did not transpire. *Gruppe von dem Bach*, now freed of its responsibility for holding a defensive sector along the river, was able to fully devote its efforts towards eradicating the remainder of the *Armia Krajowa*, which still clung to its ever-shrinking perimeters within the remaining enclaves at Mokotow and Zoliborz. Despite the growing realization that their cause was hopeless after the failure of the relief attempt by the 1st Polish Army, the insurgents continued to resist bitterly, killing and wounding hundreds of Germans and their allies for another week.

Although *Gruf.* Gille was pleased to have the *Fs.Pz.Div. Hermann Göring* rejoin his corps' order of battle, he complained in his evening report to von Lüttwitz on 22 September that he believed this was not going to be enough to strengthen his corps sufficiently for the large-scale Soviet attack that he believed was imminent. He did have a point—while his corps had gained the *Hermann Göring* Division, this unit was still short one of its two *Panzergrenadier* regiments, as *Fs.Pz.Gren.Rgt. 2* was still in Warsaw fighting under *XLVI. Pz.Korps* along the Vistula. In return, he had given up the *19. Pz.Div.*, the *73. Inf.Div.*, and the Hungarian division, as well as *Sturm-Pio.Btl. 500*, *Tr.Sich.Btl. 384*, *I./Art.Abt. 154*, *Heers-Pak-Art.Abt. 1061*, three independent antitank gun companies, and an independent tank destruction company equipped with the 8.8cm *Panzerschreck*. He felt that on balance, he had less combat power than before the transfers took place. Regardless, he closed his evening report with one word summing up his intentions for the following day: "Defend."

That evening, von Lüttwitz composed his own report for *H.Gr. Mitte*'s commander, which was considerably less verbose than those of his predecessor. He noted the calm that seemed to have descended on the *9. Armee* front line, which, with the exception of Warsaw, appeared to signify that the Soviets were either too exhausted to keep fighting or were preparing for a continuation of their offensive aimed at encircling Warsaw from the north and south in a pincer movement. This, he wrote, would occur within the next several days. He also wrote that he expected that the Polish forces in Praga would continue their efforts to cross the Vistula and help the insurgents liberate Warsaw. In this assessment, von Lüttwitz was incorrect. The 1st Polish Army had given up any hope of launching further riverine operations after suffering crippling losses during their previous attempts.[77] Von Lüttwitz noted that *Gruppe von dem Bach* had enjoyed a considerable amount of success that day, having finally eliminated the southernmost area of Warsaw still held by the insurgents (designated as the *Südkessel*) and capturing 470 of them who had literally fought until the last bullet. In closing, he noted that the *19. Pz.Div.* had taken over the sector along the Vistula formerly held by *25. Pz.Div.*, which had moved out, and that the *Fs.Pz.Div. Hermann Göring* had taken over the *19. Pz.Div.* sector in *IV. SS-Pz.Korps*.[78]

As far as the *H.Gr. Mitte* operations section was concerned, the only action occurring in the *9. Armee* area of operations that day was the continuing fighting in Warsaw itself against the Polish insurgents. Aside from a mention of the operation planned to retake the Mokotow area of the city beginning on 26 September, the army group's chief of staff, *Oberst* Peter von der Groeben, stated his belief that it would be best to limit further attempts at retaking the remaining portions of the city still under Polish control to local counterattacks only; it was becoming clear that the Warsaw Uprising was on its last legs and it would be a waste of men and resources retaking every single block when the end was in sight. No mention was made of action occurring on the opposite bank of the Vistula or of the *IV. SS-Pz.Korps*. The army group's focus was still on operations unfolding to the north in East Prussia and preparations at eliminating the bridgehead between Pułtusk and Serock, and the other one at Rózan, in the near future.[79] It had become evident, at *H.Gr. Mitte* headquarters at least, that things had quietened down considerably along the Vistula Front.

Thus ended the second act of the second defensive battle of Warsaw. What was to follow was nearly three weeks of relative calm, a period both sides used to replenish their ranks, repair their vehicles and equipment, and stockpile supplies, especially ammunition, for the next round of fighting. Though the Germans claimed victory during this battle, it is worth remembering that despite the heavy losses it had suffered since it resumed the offensive on 31 August, the First Belorussian Front still held the initiative on the battlefield, not *H.Gr. Mitte*, and certainly not the *9. Armee*.

Throughout the past three weeks, Rokossovsky's troops, primarily those assigned to the 47th and 70th Armies, the 1st Polish Army, and the VIII Guards Tank Corps, had pushed the Germans back relentlessly, liberated Praga, and controlled almost the entire eastern bank of the upper Vistula, except for the portion that stretched from the northern suburbs of Praga to Modlin. While acknowledging its own casualties (during September 1944 alone, the 47th and 70th Armies suffered nearly 21,000 men killed, wounded, and missing), the First Belorussian Front had inflicted significant damage to the divisions in Gille's corps, especially the *73. Inf.Div.* and the *Wiking* Division. Rokossovsky could still attack wherever he wanted and at a time of his own choosing, but in the battle to come, he would unwaveringly stick to his objectives—crushing the *IV. SS-Pz.Korps* and seizing the triangle formed by the confluence of the Vistula and the Narew. On 12 September, he had come very close to realizing this objective. All that stood in his way now were a few thousand SS men, *Heer*, and *Luftwaffe* troops who were determined to resist his forces with every last ounce of their strength.

CHAPTER 10

An Unexpected Lull in the Action 23 September–9 October 1944

When the second defensive battle of Warsaw ended inconclusively on 22 September 1944, very little had changed in an operational sense, although the First Belorussian Front had made significant territorial gains since it began the battle on 31 August. While the Warsaw suburb of Praga had been liberated and the *IV. SS-Pz.Korps* had been pushed back over 20 kilometers, the Germans still hung on tenaciously to a foothold on the eastern bank of the Vistula, thus denying Marshal Rokossovsky's objective of seizing the Vistula and Narew crossing sites at Modlin. Furthermore, the daring river crossing and relief attempt of the *Armia Krajowa* in Warsaw by the 1st Polish Army had failed miserably with great loss of life, sealing the fate of the Warsaw Uprising, which would soon run out of ammunition and food. Huge expenditures of Soviet artillery ammunition and aerial bombs and the loss of hundreds of tanks, as well as the deaths and crippling of thousands of the Red Army's soldiers, had failed to shake the resolve of *Gruf.* Gille's troops, who had suffered nearly as much as their opponents had.

During the past three weeks, both sides had fought themselves to exhaustion. What happened next was something that the Germans, at least, had not anticipated—a near complete cessation of large-scale operations along the entire Vistula front line. Rather than the rapid resumption of the great Soviet offensive that Generals Gille, von Lüttwitz, and Reinhardt had been expecting and dreading for the past several days, what happened instead was an 18-day pause in major combat operations. Between 23 September and 9 October, the *9. Armee* reported that no significant enemy action took place, other than the usual low-level type of activity that always occurred daily along the front line between two opponents, such as patrolling, laying wire and minefields, and artillery and mortar harassment fire. As noted by Rokossovsky himself in his memoirs, "A lull had set in at Warsaw, the enemy having assumed the defensive along the whole front."[1] In fact, both sides had gone over to a defensive posture along the entire upper Vistula between Modlin and Puławy. This was borne out by numerous reports from all three corps in the *9. Armee* order of battle that testified to the sights and sounds of Red Army troops of the 8th Guards,

69th, 47th, and 70th Armies, as well as the 1st Polish Army, digging in, improving their fighting positions, and even conducting training exercises.

The only heavy fighting taking place during the first half of this period of relative calm was the continuing effort by *Gruppe von dem Bach* to complete its mission of eliminating the Polish resistance forces in Warsaw and re-establishing control of the entire city. With the failure of the Polish 1st Army's river crossing attempt, the only significant areas of the city still under insurgent control was the suburb of Zoliborz, which still stubbornly held out, the southern suburb of Mokotow, and the ever-shrinking *Südkessel* (Southern Pocket). Though German losses—especially among the rabble of SS foreign volunteer units, Police, and the *Dirlewanger* Brigade—had been astronomical, the addition of heavily armed front-line combat troops from the *19. Pz.Div.* and *Fs.Pz.Div. Hermann Göring* quickly began systematically reducing the resistance block by block in these remaining areas. The failure of aerial resupply efforts, despite the heroic action of American and Soviet aircrews, had adversely affected the morale of the Polish population as well as the resistance fighters. Once the city was finally secure, which was now only a matter of days away, the Germans would refocus their efforts on building up and strengthening the Vistula defense line to prevent any future river crossing attempts before the river froze over during the winter.

For Gille and the divisions under his command in the *IV. SS-Pz.Korps*, this pause in operations was a Godsend. Just as the troops of the First Belorussian Front put this time to good use resting and reorganizing their armies, corps, and divisions, so did the Germans. The past six weeks of nearly non-stop combat had taken their toll, not only in terms of men killed or wounded and equipment damaged or destroyed, but also in an emotional sense. Lack of sleep, infrequent meals, and physical exhaustion brought on by the need for constant activity had worn down the mental resilience of the survivors, especially in the *Wiking* and *Totenkopf* Divisions. Fortunately, large numbers of *Waffen-SS* replacement troops were finally on their way, though most would not start arriving until the beginning of October.[2]

The heretofore slow trickle of replacements had forced the remaining SS men in infantry, reconnaissance, and engineer units to do the work of several men. No matter how much each man was individually motivated by the mythical SS spirit at this stage of the war, no human being could stand this sort of punishment indefinitely. Therefore, the pause in the First Belorussian Front's operations could not have come at a more fortuitous time. While the *Hauptkampflinie* between Zegrze and Annopol still had to be actively defended, the pause in battle allowed units to be rotated in and out of their positions for brief periods in a rest area behind the lines. Here, they were able to clean their weapons and equipment, read their accumulated letters from home, and above all, catch up on their lost sleep. Importantly, tanks and other armored vehicles that had been the mainstay of the defense for the past month could now be moved to the rear area as well, where they could receive long-overdue overhauls and repairs to damage suffered in battle.

On 23 September, the elements of Gille's corps were disposed as follows, from north to south: on the opposite side of the Narew stood the *Wiking* Division's *Kampfgruppe Braune*, consisting of two tank companies from *II. Abt./SS-Pz.Rgt. 5* (the *7.* and *8.*) under *Hstuf.* Flügel, *3. Kp./SS-Pz.Pio.Btl. 5*, *Fest.Inf.Btl. 1405*, one battalion from *Gren.Rgt. 1145*, and *Fest.Pak-Art.Kp. 1/VI*, which defended Serock and blocked the route to Zegrze; then the main body of the *Wiking* Division, reinforced by *Gren.Rgt. 1145* and *Gren.Btl.z.b.V. 560*, which held the line running from Rynia to Aleksandrów; the *Totenkopf* Division, which defended from south of Aleksandrów to Hill 101 east of Rożopole; and on the right flank in the south, the newly returned *Fs.Pz.Div. Hermann Göring* held the line between there and Zeran along the Vistula.[3]

The last train carrying the remaining elements of *Gen.Lt.* Ibrányi's *1. ung.Kav. Div.* had finally departed for home on 23 September, making Gille's corps now an all-German formation.[4] The corps commander ordered that strong armored reserves of at least a tank battalion and a *Panzergrenadier* battalion from each division be positioned where they could quickly launch counterattacks yet remain out of range of Soviet artillery until committed to battle. German corps and division artillery, still numerically inferior, had been placed in concealed positions where their batteries could fire and displace quickly to alternate firing positions based on the fire support plan developed by *Brig.Fhr.* Brasack's *SS-ARKO 104*. These included the divisional artillery of the *19. Pz.Div.*, then occupying a portion of the Vistula defense line on the river's western bank, though the division itself was not under Gille's corps.

For the most part, German troops were able to occupy the defensive positions that had been under construction for the past several weeks by the engineer battalions from both SS divisions as well as by Army construction troops and conscripted civilians. These positions, built to exacting specifications as laid down by the *9. Armee Stopi* (*Stabs-Pionieroffizier*, or corps engineer officer), consisted of camouflaged outposts, communications trenches, command posts, observation posts, dugouts, heavy weapons firing positions, troop bunkers, and underground ammunitions storage areas. Nearly all had been dug in to a depth of 2–2½ meters, with roofs reinforced by several layers of logs covered by at least a meter of soil. Proof against anything but a direct hit by a large-caliber shell, these shelters would save many lives in the days ahead.[5]

Flandernzaun (barbed wire entanglements), "Spanish riders" (wooden crossbeam arrangements laced with barbed wire), minefields, and other obstacles had been incorporated into virtual "devil's gardens" by the corps' combat engineers, making any approach by Soviet foot soldiers a hazardous and deadly undertaking. Fields of fire to a depth of 500 meters were also created, requiring the clearing of any trees, shrubs, or undergrowth that might conceal the approach of enemy foot soldiers. Antitank guns had been sited along every possible avenue of advance that might be taken by Soviet tanks, and antitank mines had been cleverly placed to channel tanks into kill zones. Antiaircraft guns had also been positioned to take maximum advantage of their killing power, whether against the Red Air Force or ground targets. Everything had been done that could be done to strengthen the front lines to withstand a 20th-century siege by an opponent with overwhelming firepower.

This operational pause was not entirely without a certain amount of fighting in the *9. Armee* area of operations; indeed, three instances are worthy of note, including the aforementioned effort to finally eliminate the Warsaw Uprising by *Gruppe von dem Bach*. The other two were *Unternehmen Sternschnuppe*, designed to eradicate the Polish partisans in the Kampinos forest, and the support for the *2. Armee*'s major counteroffensive against the Serock–Pultusk bridgehead, code named *Unternehmen Sonnenblume* (Sunflower). While neither of these operations required major commitment of forces on the part of *9. Armee*, elements of the *IV. SS-Pz.Korps* did play a major role in both, the first time troops of the corps would go on the offense since the tank battle of Praga ended eight weeks before. Though the fighting that ensued could be considered small-scale within the greater context of the Eastern Front, for the several thousand men of Gille's corps who took part, these two engagements must have seemed significant, at least within their 100-meter view of the fighting that took place.

Unternehmen Sternschnuppe began as scheduled on 27 September. Under the overall control of *Gruppe von dem Bach*, this operation incorporated elements of the *IV. SS-Pz.Korps*, *XLVI. Pz.Korps*, *VIII. Armeekorps*, *Gruppe von dem Bach*, and *Heerestruppen* from *9. Armee*, a force comprising approximately 4,000 men. The tactical command on the scene would be exercised by *Gen.Lt.* Friedrich Bernhard, commander of the *9. Armee Korück 532*, with a temporary staff provided by the *391. Sich.Div. Oberst* Gerhard Klein, the commander of the *9. Armee Waffenschule*, would serve as the commander of the northern attack force, designated *Gruppe Nord*, while the commander of the southern attack force, *Gruppe Süd*, would be *Major der Schutzpolizei* Nachtwey, commander of *Pol.Schtz.Rgt. 34*.

The overall intent of the operation was to eliminate the several thousand Polish partisans thought to be assembling in the forest, who had been harassing German logistical efforts in the rear area for the past several weeks and were believed to be constructing fortifications to withstand a German assault. In essence, *Unternehmen Sternschnuppe* would consist of a concentric attack into the 25-square-kilometer forest, with most of the attacking force (the "hammer") advancing on foot from the east to the southwest. This was intended to compress the partisans into an increasingly small area until they were forced against the units holding an interception line on the southwestern edge of the forest (the "anvil"). Finally, through the use of overwhelming firepower, including *Stuka* support, the partisans would be annihilated. The *9. Armee* chief of staff estimated that this operation would only take three or four days. Once it was concluded, the troops involved would be released to their parent units and the entire forest, when cleared of Polish partisans and the civilian population, would be turned over to *Maschinegewehr* (*M.G.*) *Btl. 23* to secure.

The bulk of the assault troops would come from Gille's corps and *Maj*. Nachtwey's *Pol.Schtz.Rgt. 34* of *Gruppe von dem Bach*. For the purpose of this operation, Nachtwey's regiment would be reinforced by a Cossack battalion and a Ukrainian *Schuma* battalion. The *IV. SS-Pz.Korps* was tasked to provide three *Alarmbataillone* totaling 1,000 men, to be formed from rear area troops from the *Tross* of each of the corps' three divisions, which would operate as part of *Gruppe Nord*.[6] In addition, Gille's corps was tasked to provide six armored car platoons with a total of 18 vehicles that would come from *Hstuf.* Borchert's *SS-Pz.Aufkl.Abt. 5*, and six light *Flak* platoons. Artillery, mortars, antitank and multiple rocket launcher units would come from the entire 9. *Armee* area of operations, as well as a company of *Pz. IV* tanks from the *19. Pz.Div.* and 15 operational *Jgd.Pz. 38t* tank destroyers from *Heeres-Pz.Jg.Abt. 743*.[7]

A tremendous amount of firepower would be applied against the partisans, who lacked any heavy weapons of their own except machine guns and mortars. The fact that such an effort would soon be directed against these Polish patriots is an indication of the severity of the threat the *9. Armee* commander felt that they posed. Due to the relative inactivity being displayed by the troops of Rokossovsky's First Beloruissian Front, *Gen.d.Pz.Tr.* von Lüttwitz must have determined that such a large number of German troops could be confidently brought together to carry out the operation without fear of an immediate Soviet response. Had Rokossovsky decided to carry out even a limited attack against the Vistula defense line, most of these German units would have been involved in defensive operations instead and the outcome of *Unternehmen Sternschnuppe* may well have been different.

The operation began on schedule on the morning of 27 September and made rapid progress. The elements of both *Gruppe Nord* and *Gruppe Süd* encountered heavy resistance initially, and even had to call on *Luftflotte 6* to provide a squadron of *Stukas* to bomb some of the more solidly built Polish field fortifications near the town of Wiersze on the northern edge of the forest. These came as a rude surprise because the Germans had not expected such sophisticated defenses on the part of mere partisans. The bodies of 13 partisans were found, against the loss of one German and six Cossacks killed in action. A group of 140 civilians hiding in the forest were discovered and evacuated.

The following day, the attack began to pick up steam, and both *Gruppe Nord* and *Gruppe Süd* pushed ahead several additional kilometers, against initially determined resistance that melted away once heavy weapons were brought to bear. Twelve enemy dead were counted, though the German advance was not without cost, for three SS men from *Gruppe Nord* were killed and a further two seriously wounded. *Gruppe Süd* discovered a large bunker complex consisting of eight well-constructed bunkers, but upon approaching them, they were found to be empty. A local inhabitant volunteered the information to *Pol.Schtz.Rgt. 34* that a large group of 1,000–2,000 partisans had broken out during the evening before heading in a northwesterly direction.

Though both *Gruppe Nord* and *Süd* were powerful *Kampfgruppen*, there were simply not enough men to cover every meter of such a large area. That evening, the units comprising the western interception line were also widely dispersed and unable to see, much less stop, partisan units intent on exfiltrating the forest during the night.

On 29 September, the operation's third day, the advance continued, though there was little enemy contact. The few German casualties by this point were being caused by land mines that were laid as the partisans withdrew. Most of the Polish fighters, except for civilians, had vanished and the local inhabitants—as many as 640 men, women, and children, along with 22 cows—were evacuated after being searched. Everything left behind was burned and the Kampinos forest would become a no-man's land once the operation was completed to prevent any recurrence of partisan activity. With the forest nearly restored to German control, the *Totenkopf*s *Alarmbataillon*, the tank company from *19. Pz.Div.*, and four of the armored car platoons of the *Wiking* Division were released and allowed to return to their parent units.

No enemy contact was reported at all on 30 September, when it seemed as if the several thousands of Polish partisans had simply disappeared into thin air, though in reality nearly all of them had slipped through the noose being drawn around them. A number of booby-trapped bunkers and fighting positions on the forest's western edge were encountered, though all were unoccupied. By the following day, 1 October, *Gruppe Nord* and *Süd* had reached the western limit of their final objectives along the Bzura River. While the anticipated pitched battle with the partisans in the forest never materialized, the woods at least were now clear of the enemy. This was no doubt a welcome development as far as the command and staff of *IV. SS-Pz.Korps* was concerned, because its supply lines had been the most affected by the partisan threat; most of them passed through or along the forest's outskirts, and the northeast corner of the *Kampinowald* was less than 10 kilometers away from the corps *Hauptquartier* at Klein Kazun.

However, during the night of 30 September, a large group of partisans who had managed to escape the net closing around them were reported to have reached the northern outskirts of Żyrardów, a town nearly 30 kilometers southwest of the Kampinos forest that also housed the headquarters complex of *9. Armee*. Recognizing the immediacy of this threat, the alarm was sounded throughout the town, and the various staff elements promptly activated their respective close defense plans. According to established procedure, these *Alarm* units would have operated under the overall direction of *Maj.* Helmut Stammler, the *9. Armee* headquarters commandant, aided by *Oblt.* Johann Wenzel, commander of the guard force. Fortunately for the Germans, the partisans chose not to attack, opting to conceal themselves in homes and buildings, evidently hoping to continue their escape when darkness fell.

While the *9. Armee* staff anxiously waited to be attacked, the call went out for reinforcements to drive the partisans out of the town. Within a few hours, mobile units of *Gruppe Süd*, consisting of a battalion from *Gren.Rgt. 70*, two armored car companies, and a tank platoon from *19. Pz.Div.*, had rushed to Żyrardów to render assistance. After the Polish resistance fighters were spotted by German security forces combing through the town's northern outskirts, the relief force immediately attacked and overwhelmed them. Once the fighting subsided, the relief force learned that a number of partisans had escaped to the northwest, though the bodies of over 400 of their comrades had been left behind as well as most of their heavy weapons and horse-drawn vehicles.[8]

On 2 October, *Unternehmen Sternschnuppe* was declared officially concluded and most of the units were allowed to return to their divisions, including any remaining men of the *Totenkopf, Wiking* and *Hermann Göring* Divisions still serving with *Oberst* Klein's *Gruppe Nord*. In terms of actual fighting, very little took place; though in terms of the number of men and resources committed to it, *Sternschnuppe* was a major undertaking that did accomplish its main goal, the restoration of freedom of movement of supplies and reinforcements within the *9. Armee* rear area.

The second operation to unfold during this period leading up to the third battle of Warsaw, *Unternehmen Sonnenblume*, was the long-anticipated effort by *Gen.Oberst* Weiss's *2. Armee* to eliminate the Soviet bridgehead across the Narew stretching from the area south of Pułtusk to a few kilometers north of Serock. Delayed at least twice by the transfer of units out of its sector, including the *XLVI. Pz.Korps* and *19. Pz.Div.*, two weeks before, the counteroffensive would now be carried out instead by *Gen.d.Art.* von Roman's *XX. Armeekorps*. Though not a *panzer* corps, von Roman's headquarters had been directing the defense of this section of the Narew line ever since Col.Gen. Pavel Batov's 65th Army had seized a bridgehead across the Narew on 6 September and they were well informed about Soviet defensive preparations. To accomplish *H.Gr. Mitte*'s intent of destroying this ever-growing threat and restoring the front line along the Narew, *XX. Armeekorps* had been reinforced with two *panzer* divisions (the *3.* and *25. Pz.Div.*), a *panzer* brigade (*Pz.Brig. 104*), two heavy tank battalions (*s.Pz.Abt.505* and *s.Pz.Abt.507*), and the *252. Inf.Div.* They would attack along with the corps' veteran *542. Gren.Div.* and *35. Inf.Div.* The "Sunflower" offensive was scheduled to begin on the morning of 4 October.

The *IV. SS-Pz.Korps* would again play a supporting role in the upcoming operation, not a major one. *Obersturmbannführer* Dorr's *Germania* Regiment, minus its *II. Bataillon*, had replaced *Kampfgruppe Braune* on the northern bank of the Narew on 2 October and would conduct a limited attack using *Hstuf.* Flügel's *Panzergruppe*, consisting of approximately 12–15 operational Panthers, to pin down and then encircle Soviet forces still occupying the shallow bridgehead at Gasiorowo. This would aid the attack by the neighboring *542. Gren.Div.* by preventing the Soviet XX Rifle Corps from reinforcing their comrades in the north who lay in the path of the *XX. Armeekorps* offensive. All of the *Wiking* Division's artillery would be dedicated to supporting this mission, including the suppression of Soviet artillery emplaced on the eastern bank of the Narew. In furtherance of this objective, *SS-Stubaf.* Gunter Bernau's *I. Abt./SS-Pz.Art.Rgt. 5* had been moved across the Narew to increase the artillery regiment's ability to fire at deep targets.[9]

The attack began that morning on schedule, and Flügel's tanks quickly took the town of Pobylkowo by 10 a.m., followed shortly by the seizure of the neighboring town of Male, where they had fought the month before. By 4:30 p.m., they had driven the Soviets out of the town of Debinki and had taken the commanding height of Hill 135.8, encircling a large number of Soviet troops in the process, who were systematically dealt with by the *542. Gren.Div.* After laagering for the night, on the morning of 5 October Flügel and his tanks began firing on Soviet traffic crossing the bridge over the Narew at Gasiorowo, less than a kilometer away, with "good effects." After a short pause, the *Panzergruppe* continued its envelopment to the south at 9 a.m., reaching the northern outskirts of Serock after encircling and destroying another large group of Soviet infantrymen who were caught in the open by the tank attack. After the fighting subsided that evening, in his report Flügel claimed to have killed between 400 and 600 Soviet troops, captured over 300 rifles and machine guns, and destroyed 12 antitank guns. No Soviet tanks were encountered. After this date, the portion of *IV. SS-Pz.Korps* north of the Narew transitioned to the defense.

To the north of Serock, the main effort of *Unternehmen Sonnenblume* also enjoyed initial success. The attack, involving over 200 German tanks and assault guns, "took the 65th Army completely by surprise," according to Rokossovsky in his memoirs.[10] He admitted that on that first day, the *XX. Armeekorps'* attack had driven Col.Gen. Batov's units back to the Narew, where in some places Batov's troops were holding on "by the skin of their teeth." Bad weather had prevented the 16th Air Army from flying any ground-attack missions, enabling the German tanks to mass and attack with impunity. According to Rokossovsky, the 65th Army was able to withstand the powerful German assault only with the assistance of artillery emplaced on the eastern bank of the river that employed direct fire to keep the *panzers* at bay.

The 65th Army did indeed take a pounding; in addition to destroying 34 of its tanks between 4 and 9 October, the *XX. Armeekorps* assault troops also captured 903 Soviet soldiers and destroyed or captured 85 artillery pieces and antitank guns. The number of Soviet troops killed and wounded are not known, but based on the amount of crew-served weapons and small arms captured, their losses must have numbered in the thousands. German losses had been comparatively light, at least during the first four days of the offensive. Only 15 tanks and assault guns were reported as being completely destroyed or unrecoverable, including five of the powerful *Pz. VI* Tigers.

By now thoroughly alarmed, Rokossovsky and his staff drove to Batov's headquarters to assess the situation two or three days after the attack had begun. This particular bridgehead figured prominently in the plans for the winter offensive being developed by the STAVKA, and had to be held at all costs since it was a necessary jump-off point for the operation. After consulting with Batov,

Rokossovsky decided to shift as many Front reserves that could be spared to aid the 65th Army, including the I Guards Tank Corps, antitank regiments, and additional artillery. These began arriving on 7 October and their impact was soon felt by the attackers, whose assault began to lose momentum as it encountered fresh troops, heavy artillery counterbarrages, and hundreds of well-emplaced antitank guns. That same day, the weather cleared, enabling the Red Air Force to harass German ground troops and target individual tanks. Realizing the futility of continuing the attack, *Sonnenblume* was suspended the following day, 8 October, and *XX. Armee-Corps* transitioned to the defense.

Fierce counterattacks carried out by the 65th Army's XVIII, XLVI, and CV Rifle Corps, as well as by the aforementioned I Guards Tank Corps, between 10 and 12 October managed to regain at least all of the ground lost during the German offensive.[11] However, the net effect of Rokossovsky's focus on assisting Batov with reserve forces, additional ammunition, and supplies meant that there would not be as much available for the impending attack by the 47th and 70th Armies slated to begin on 9 October. As far as *9. Armee* was concerned, *Sonnenblume* had also been a waste of precious tanks, ammunition, and troops that had accomplished relatively little, burning up scarce resources that would soon be needed elsewhere along the Vistula defense line.[12] But it had, if nothing else, diverted some of the Soviet combat power away from *Gruf.* Gille's corps, which may have affected the outcome of the third battle of Warsaw.

The third and perhaps most important fighting affecting the *IV. SS-Pz.Korps* that took place during this period was the final suppression of the Warsaw Uprising. Between 22 and 30 September, *Gruppe von dem Bach*, now assisted by *XLVI. Pz.Korps*, slowly but steadily crushed the remaining resistance. On 23 September, the *Südkessel* held by General Bór's troops near the western end of the destroyed New Bridge over the Vistula was eliminated, bringing the last remaining portion of the riverbank firmly under German control. The large-scale assault against the southern suburb of Mokotow began the following day. By 27 September, resistance in Mokotow finally collapsed, leading to the surrender of 2,000 men and women of the Polish Home Army and the evacuation of 5,000 civilians. On 28 September, surrender negotiations began with Bór, who was commanding the forces in the inner city.

The next morning, 29 September, another large-scale attack against holdouts in the Zoliborz area, codenamed *Wolfsangel* (an ancient German runic symbol believed to ward off wolves), was initiated by the *19. Pz.Div.* in the *XLVI. Pz.Korps* area of operations. Spearheaded by three infantry battalions supported by tanks of *Pz.Rgt. 27*, the attackers steadily overcame fierce Polish resistance after destroying numerous bunkers and improvised fighting positions emplaced in the concrete housing blocks. Combat engineer units were deployed under the covering fire of antiaircraft guns to lay explosives at the base of several high-rise buildings, designed to cause their collapse. By the end of the day, resistance began to crumble. On 30 September, the last remaining Polish insurgents were holed up in a small block of buildings on the northern edge of Zoliborz. They were offered unconditional surrender that evening. A large group of Polish fighters refused these appeals and attempted to break out that night and swim across the Vistula, but were intercepted by German troops positioned on the riverbank. Most of them were killed or captured. That left only the inner center still under the control of the insurgents.

On 1 October, capitulation discussions resumed in earnest between Generals von dem Bach and Bór for the unconditional surrender of all remaining members of the Polish Home Army. At 8:20 p.m. on 2 October, the Polish delegation, led by Bór, finally signed the document of capitulation. Its terms included an immediate cease-fire, the surrender of all remaining members of the *Armia Krajowa*—including all of their armaments and supplies—and the release of all German prisoners of war. Over the next several days, under the watchful eyes of the troops from *Gruppe von dem Bach* and *XLVI. Pz.Korps*, 13,668 members of the *Armia Krajowa*, including a number of women fighters, their heads held high, marched into captivity. Over 153,519 civilians were eventually evacuated from the areas under insurgent control at the time of the ceasefire.[13] The Warsaw Uprising was over.

Though it did not play an active role in the latter stages of the Warsaw Uprising, its participation being limited to less than three days when the *25. Pz.Div.* was briefly attached to it, the *IV. SS-Pz.Korps* benefitted from the end of the fighting in Warsaw like all other elements of the *9. Armee*. Supplies and reinforcements could once more flow unimpeded throughout the city. Thousands of troops who had been fighting as part of *Gruppe von dem Bach*, *Gruppe Rohr*, and other extemporaneous organizations could now be released. Additionally, Gille's troops no longer had to worry about being attacked from behind by Polish freedom fighters lurking in the city or in the Kampino forest. *Unternehmen Sternschnuppe* and the elimination of the *Armia Krajowa* in Warsaw itself had seen to that.

Now that the city, which Hitler had already declared a *Festung* (fortress) as early as 27 July, was considered secure, preparations by *9. Armee* began immediately to transform it into an impregnable bastion. The ancient inner city of Warsaw was to be completed razed to the ground, with nothing left but ruins. Most of the inhabitants who had been evacuated were sent to work for the rest of the war in German labor camps spread throughout Eastern Europe. The survivors of the *Armia Krajowa* were sent to prisoner of war camps in Germany, where they sat out the rest of the war. The 11,668 male survivors of the *Armia Krajowa* who asurrendered (the female members, estimated to be 2,000, were not included in this figure) were treated as legitimate POWs in accordance with the Geneva Convention. Evacuated to the network of German POW camps spread throughout Germany, they received the same treatment as prisoners from Western countries, including the receipt of Red Cross parcels, and most survived the war. A few were accidentally shipped to concentration camps. After the war, their greatest fear was how they would be treated should they decide to return to their home country, now occupied by Soviet forces. The rebuilt *73. Inf.Div.* and the *5. Kgl.ung.Res.Div.*, the last remaining Hungarian unit in the *9. Armee* order of battle, began moving into new defensive positions along the western bank of the Vistula, replacing elements of the *19. Pz.Div.* and other armor units operating in the city.

In addition to the limited fighting taking place within its area of operations as described above, *Gen.d.Pz.Tr.* von Lüttwitz also directed the *9. Armee* to embark on the wide-ranging shuffling and reorganization of its units planned by his predecessor, which began on 24 September. Taking advantage of the general lull that had set in after the end of the second battle of Warsaw, a number of companies and battalions that had been separated from their parent regiments and divisions since the reintroduction of the *9. Armee* into the *H.Gr. Mitte* order of battle on 14 July were set in motion to rejoin their units. *Versprengte* (straggler) companies and *Alarmeinheiten*—composed of men separated from their units or those returning from home leave, hospitals, or schools in Germany—were dissolved and its members reunited with their old *Haufen* (gang) at the front, after in some cases being separated for over two months.

Several battalion-sized *Kampfgruppen*, whose ranks were filled with an assortment of *Luftwaffe*, *Heer*, and *Waffen-SS*—as well as members from civilian organizations such as the *Bahnschutz* (railway guards), *Postschutz* (post office guards), and *Ordnungspolizei* (Order Police)—were disbanded and its members sorted out and sent back to their units. Most of the remaining Hungarian units in the army's area of operations, except the *5. Kgl.ung.Res.Div.* which remained behind in Warsaw, were shipped back home to participate in the defense of their own country. Von Lüttwitz had already been anticipating the dissolution of *Gruppe von dem Bach*, which was the worst-off in terms of being a polyglot organization, born of the need to suppress the Warsaw Uprising with every available man capable of bearing arms.

The *9. Armee* commander was especially keen to remove from his army's order of battle the foreign or SS units nominally under *Ogruf.* von dem Bach's control, particularly the *Dirlewanger* and *Kaminski* Brigades, Cossack and Azerbaijani units, as well as other "Eastern" troops, including Ukrainian police battalions. These units had committed some of the worst excesses throughout the Warsaw Uprising, including the rape and murder of innocent Polish civilians—thought to number in the tens of thousands—as well as unrestrained looting and wanton destruction of property. With the suppression of Bór's forces nearly complete, these outlaw units would soon become a liability, since they were thought to be virtually useless in battle against a conventional enemy and had a proven reputation of being undisciplined and difficult to control. With the situation in and around Warsaw steadily stabilizing, *9. Armee* could soon afford to be rid of them.

The general reshuffling and reorganization of units during this period also affected the *IV. SS-Pz.Korps*. The first unit to depart the corps' order of battle was *Maj.* Ritter's *Gren.Btl.z.b.V. 560*, which began displacing on 22–23 September for its new assignment under *XLVI. Pz.Korps*. Two days later, it had assembled on the western bank of the Vistula southwest of Mlociny. After a brief period of rest and integration of a new shipment of replacements, it would be committed to the battle for the final elimination of the Warsaw Uprising. The next unit to depart was *Gren.Rgt. 1145*, which was detached from Gille's corps on 29 September and sent north by train to rejoin its parent unit, the *562. Gren.Div.* then assigned to the *LV. Armeekorps* in the *4. Armee* sector. It had been emplaced on the right flank of the *Wiking* Division, sharing a boundary with *Obf.* Becker's division. Its positions would be taken over by *Pz.Gren.Rgt. Totenkopf.* The last unit to depart, *Fest.Inf.Btl. 1405*, which had been defending Serock for nearly a month, was detached on the evening of 1–2 October and sent to buttress the defenses of the neighboring *2. Armee*.

All three of these units had been attached to the *Wiking* Division for several weeks to compensate for its lack of infantry. Their absence would be sorely missed. *Fest. Inf.Btl. 1405* would be temporarily replaced by the *Alarm-Btl.* from the *Totenkopf* Division, after it had just completed its participation in *Unternehmen Sternschnuppe*. It would now be attached to the *Wiking* Division instead of being allowed to return to its own division until Gille was able to replace it with *II. Btl./Germania*.[14] While this cleaned up the corps' order of battle, at least from an administrative standpoint, the departure of over 1,300 infantrymen from these units complicated Gille's task of manning his main defense line that included not only the Zegrze–Annopol position stretching between the Narew and the Vistula, but the defensive position north of the Narew at Serock too. On 23 September, he felt that he simply lacked enough troops to do so, especially with a major Soviet attack anticipated.

Fortunately for Gille as well as the *Wiking* Division, on 23 September, *III. Btl./ SS-Pz.Gren.Rgt. 10 Westland* finally arrived via train from the *SS-Truppenübungsplatz Böhmen* (the *Waffen-SS* training area in Bohemia and Moravia). The 820 men of the battalion, led by veteran *Stubaf.* Alfred Nedderhof, had been undergoing a complete rebuild after its remnants were withdrawn from the division the previous autumn.[15] Fully equipped and at near full strength, these men (of which 536 comprised its *Kampfstärke*) were viewed as a Godsend not only by Gille, but by their division commander, *Staf.* Mühlenkamp. After disembarking from their two trains at Modlin, the men of the battalion marched across the Narew bridge towards their new positions in the Jablonna forest southwest of Nieporet, where they conducted a relief in place of *Gren.Btl.z.b.V. 560* by midnight.

The division viewed this position in the forest as being vitally important for the defense of the town of Nieporet, and it was certain that this area would receive a great deal of attention should the Soviets decide to attack. At least Nedderhof and his men, most of whom had never experienced combat before, would have two weeks to "acclimatize" themselves to front-line combat. But even the arrival of this battalion was still not enough to fill every gap in the front line; Gille made this point known at every opportunity, but the *9. Armee* commander and his staff did little to address the problem, most likely because the entire army along the Vistula Front was overstretched and undermanned. Besides, the army's chief of staff and *Ia* had been badgering Gille for weeks to ruthlessly comb through his *Tross* elements to glean more manpower, a move that the corps commander had been successfully resisting, though the *9. Armee*'s authority could only extend so far. Matters involving manpower and replacement personnel were still an SS affair, so Gille could ignore the Army's dictates if he felt the need to do so, so long as the *SS-FHA* backed him. He also knew that thousands of new replacements from the *Luftwaffe* were en route, thanks to the so-called *Hermann Göring Spende*.

Although *IV. SS-Pz.Korps* had received as many as 1,500 Ukrainian replacements originally earmarked for the *14. Waffen-Gren.Div. der SS* that had arrived as early as 10 September, these *Wawis* had not been enough to solve the manpower problem. In addition, the language barrier had often made their employment problematic, so their attachment to *IV. SS-Pz.Korps* was a mixed blessing. Additionally, their attachment to the *Wiking* and *Totenkopf* Divisions was never meant to be permanent, but was understood to be a short-term solution to the overall corps manpower shortages that would last until enough *Deutsche* and *Volksdeutsche* SS replacements could be assigned. Once they did, these Ukrainians would then be shipped to Bohemia and Moravia to rejoin their own division, at the moment re-forming after being virtually destroyed following the breakout from the Brody Pocket in July.

Some of these Ukrainians, occasionally derided as "*Hiwis*" by their German overseers, had complained that they were being used for dirty jobs thought to be beneath their dignity, such as recovering and burying the dead from the battlefield or digging fighting positions. But all front-line troops, Germans included, had to perform these duties, and the SS men from the *Totenkopf* and *Wiking* Divisions who had been fighting east of Warsaw without a break for the past two months probably felt it was someone else's turn to do this kind of exhausting, dangerous work, so why not make the Ukrainian recruits do it?

According to Yaroslav Dermenda, one of the Ukrainian soldiers serving with the *Wiking* Division as an interpreter, some of the Ukrainians even threatened to begin a hunger strike, but apparently this plan never came to fruition. That it did not was mostly likely due to the beginning of the third battle of Warsaw, which saw both German and Ukrainian SS troops fighting for their very lives. In such a situation, there was no time for such peacetime tactics as staging hunger strikes or writing petitions. Even had there been a strike, Gille would most likely have dealt with it harshly, just as Heinrich Himmler had when one battalion from the Bosnian Muslim SS division, the *13. Waffen Geb.Div. "Handschar"*, mutinied in France the previous year.

Some of these petitions were addressed to the commander of the *Wiking* Division requesting to be sent back to their parent division, and some of the men's complaints even reached the ears of the representatives of the Ukrainian Central

Committee, a social welfare organization whose delegation was located in Berlin. Established in 1941, it saw as its mission the need to look after Ukrainian national interests and deal with issues concerning Ukrainians working for the Third Reich, including those serving in the *Waffen-SS*. Himmler was also well disposed towards the "Galician" division, though he saw it more as a source of acceptable manpower than as a forerunner of a national Ukrainian army. While the correspondence from the Ukrainian volunteers was being evaluated by the Committee, fighting resumed east of Warsaw, an event that immediately consumed the attention of everyone in the *IV. SS-Pz.Korps*. The survivors would not finally be withdrawn from Gille's corps and shipped to the Galician division's training area at Žilina in Slovakia until 3 November.[16]

But the arrival of the Ukrainian recruits was but a foretaste of the flood of replacements that was to come. The *IV. SS-Pz.Korps' IIa, Stubaf.* Schulze, had been notified on 16 September that 10,000 replacements from the *Luftwaffe* were finally going to be shipped to the Warsaw front, with an anticipated arrival date of 19 September. The message stated a blindingly obvious fact, that "for ground combat operations, a general retraining period of three to eight weeks … will be necessary." It concluded by informing the *IV. SS-Pz.Korps* that the *SS-Führungshauptamt* would ensure that these men would be first shipped to the divisions' respective *Feld-Ersatz* battalions where their training would be conducted.[17]

Most of them were initially shipped to newly activated *Feld-Ausbildungs* (field training) battalions established by each division for this purpose. The movement of these troops was duly carried out, and by15 October, 1,762 men had received initial training by the *Totenkopf* Division's *Feld-Ausb.Btl. 3*, located in Freystadt in West Prussia, before being shipped to the division's *SS-Feld-Ers.Btl. 3*. Another 1,302 men had been processed by the *Wiking* Division's *SS-Feld-Ausb.Btl. 5* at the Kammwald training area near Straschitz in Bohemia and Moravia. By 15 October, the remaining men—some 6,936 in all—were still with the newly established *Feld-Ausbildungs* battalions, where they were still undergoing various kinds of courses of instruction designed to transform them from airmen into infantrymen, artillerymen, and so forth.

The reason they were not all sent at the same time was primarily due to the limited capacity of both *Feld-Ersatz* battalions to train and process so many men at once. Most of the transferred airmen arrived at the training camps at Freystadt and Kammwald still wearing their *Luftwaffe* uniforms, which they had to exchange for the field gray of the *Waffen-SS*. This in turn required the establishment of a clothing issue facility at each of the two camps. Furthermore, since neither SS division was authorized a field training battalion, they had no approved table of organization that allowed them to draw upon equipment depots from the *Heereszeugamt*.

Since none of the new replacements came with any small arms or heavy weapons, both the *Totenkopf* and *Wiking* Divisions had to provide them from their own limited stocks in order to supply the necessary weapons and equipment for the new recruits to train with. To compound the problem, in order to fill out the training and administrative positions required for both field training battalions, both divisions had to detach scarce officers and NCOs from their field units or field replacement battalions. Officers and NCOs convalescing from wounds and not yet fit to return to their units were also frequently used as instructors or administrative staff.

The net effect of this temporary expedient was to temporarily drain the combat power of both divisions, since the men needed to train the new *Luftwaffe* transfers had to come from somewhere. This situation highlights the impact that the explosive growth of the *Waffen-SS* during the summer of 1944 had on its ability to sustain the field units with replacement personnel, equipment, weapons, and vehicles. Unlike the *Wehrmacht*, which had a mature, robust, and fully developed individual training and replacement system, the *Waffen-SS* had to devise one from scratch that was forced to rely on a ramshackle system of expedients to fulfill the requirement to not only activate and train new units, but to provide the manpower needed for the units already in combat.

According to official records, these former *Luftwaffe* personnel were transferred to the *IV. SS-Pz.Korps* beginning in mid-September 1944, but most did not go directly to the front around Warsaw. They were first sent to either of the divisions' *Feld-Ausbildungs* battalions, then after two to eight weeks of basic ground combat training, would be shipped to a *Feld-Ersatz* battalion located in the divisions' rear area, where after less than a week (more if they were to receive additional specialty training) they would be transported to the front lines and allocated to regiments, battalions, and companies. This flood of replacements began arriving in early October, some prior to the third defensive battle of Warsaw, and by the end of November nearly all of them had been processed and were serving with their units. Both *Feld-Ausbildungs* battalions were disestablished by late November, with the field training and replacement functions being resumed in their entirety by each division's *Feld-Ersatz* battalions.

While the transition of junior enlisted men from airman to *Waffen-SS* soldier went relatively smoothly, once they had recovered from their culture shock, the transition of *Unteroffiziere* and *Feldwebeln* to *Waffen-SS* NCO was more problematic. Due to Göring's insistence that these men keep their current *Luftwaffe* ranks, they soon proved a burden to the two divisions in Gille's corps, who had no choice but to assign them to junior leadership positions commensurate with their rank and time in service, which in their case meant squad or platoon leaders. Here, these former airmen were at a distinct disadvantage because they had to unlearn what they had previously known and acquire tactical leadership skills in a brief period of a few weeks, skills that usually took months or even years of combat to learn. Many did not make the transition satisfactorily and became yet another distraction for company and battalion commanders, who already had enough manpower problems to worry about. That is, if the newly minted *Waffen-SS* NCOs survived their first exposure to combat.

One of these young men, Albert Vogt, later recounted his experiences as a "Hermann Göring Donation" in *Der Freiwilliger*, the *Waffen-SS* veterans' magazine. He recalled how he regretted having to exchange his blue *Luftwaffe* uniform with the yellow collar tabs for the field gray drab of the *Waffen-SS*. Shortly before he was to make his first operational flight against the enemy, he wrote:

> The entire squadron was disbanded and its members transferred into the infantry and assigned to the *SS Panzer Division Wiking*. All of us had come from combat or transport squadrons of the *Luftwaffe*, for which we had volunteered, and where we had enjoyed some wonderful days, but now we had to become acquainted with the life of an infantrymen. On 17 September 1944, we travelled via Vienna to Budapest, ending up at the Kammwald training area near Piesnik in the Protectorate of Bohemia and Moravia. We were then shipped that same day to Straschitz. Here we were assigned to the *5. Kompanie* of *Feldersatzbataillon 5* of the *SS-Panzerdivision Wiking*, where we underwent infantry training, which was nothing new to us. We had to get accustomed to a much smaller ration of food, no cigarettes and living quarters that were barely adequate. After eight days, we were split up and given our future assignments, divided into infantry, combat engineers and specialist jobs like radio operator. Because I had volunteered as an officer candidate [while in the *Luftwaffe*], I was given 14 more days of infantry training to prepare me for my future duties as an *Unterscharführer*. But I preferred to stay with my old squadron comrades who were all radio operators like me ... From Straschitz we were then sent to Horschowitz, where we were quartered in a movie theater ... finally, on 4 October, we were shipped to Modlin, but the trip took 14 days because our train was missrouted to Gross Strehlitz in Upper Silesia, where were sat on the railroad siding for three days. Finally, on 19 October we arrived in Modlin, and marched from the train station in pouring rain to the fortress. Early the next morning, we were loaded on trucks, which drove us through *Bugmünde* [Nowy Dwór], and from there to Okunin, where I finally was assigned to *2. Kompanie* of *SS-Panzer-Nachrichten Abteilung 5*. For the first time I found myself in the front lines.[18]

Not surprisingly, all of these *Luftwaffe* transfers did not go directly to the *Totenkopf* or *Wiking* Divisions. Many of them, perhaps several hundred, were parceled out amongst the corps units, such as the *Hauptquartier*, *SS-ARKO 104*, the corps' *Flak* battery, the *Nachschubdienste* (supply services), and medical units, who were all short of their authorized strength.

This partially explains why the total strength of the *IV. SS-Pz.Korps* headquarters and headquarters units expanded from 1,520 men on 5 September to 2,198 two weeks later. Despite this infusion of manpower, the corps headquarters never reached its authorized (*Ist*) strength, being still 2,150 men short of establishment by the end of the month.[19] In this regard, the *IV. SS-Pz.Korps* was not alone. Records indicate that none of the 18 *Waffen-SS* corps headquarters established by the end of the war ever reached their authorized strength; the demand was just too great for the ever-dwindling number of men available, not to mention the increasingly scarce general staff-qualified officers need to efficiently lead them.

One of the *Luftwaffe* airmen who was assigned to the corps *Hauptquartier* was construction engineer *Oberfeldwebel* Willy Kirschmeier, born on 23 October 1906 in the town of Hornburg, who was transferred to the *Waffen-SS* on 18

August 1944. After a two-week transition period with *1. Kp./SS-Pz.Gren.Rgt. 40* of the *18. SS-Pz.Gren.Div. "Horst Wessel"* he spent another week with *SS-Pz. Gren.Ers.Btl. 18* until 9 September. During this assignment, he was promoted to *Oberscharführer*, the SS equivalent of his former *Luftwaffe* rank. On 10 September he was shipped out to join *1. Kp./SS-Feld-Ausb.Btl. 3 Totenkopf* where he remained until 10 October, when he was reassigned to *6. Kp./SS-Feld-Ausb. Btl. 5 "Wiking."*

After two-and-a-half months of being bounced from one SS training and replacement unit to another, he was finally assigned on 5 October to the *Kommandant Hauptquartier* (headquarters company) of *IV. SS-Pz.Korps*. It remains unclear whether he served in the headquarters company itself or as a member of one of the corps staff elements, but due to his age (38) and seniority (he had joined the *Luftwaffe* in January 1940), he was certainly not suited to be an infantryman. He served with the corps headquarters throughout the remainder of the war, was awarded the *Kriegsverdienstkreuz* (War Service Cross) 2nd Class by Gille himself on 30 January 1945, and survived to march into American captivity at Fürstenfeld, Austria, on 8 May.[20]

Reinforced somewhat by the addition of *Luftwaffe* replacement personnel such as Willy Kirschmeier, between 23 September and 9 October many of the corps headquarters units were redesignated as *Sondertruppen des Reichsführung-SS* (Special Troops of the SS Command, as outlined in Chapter 3) by a special order dated 4 October, but in reality this did not change day-to-day operations. It simply meant that in theory, these heretofore "corps troops" were now considered to be similar to *Heerestruppen* (field army troops) and could be shifted from corps to corps, as the operational situation dictated. With regard to the *IV. SS-Pz.Korps*, several units were affected. The *SS-Werfer-Abteilung 104* was redesignated as *SS-Werf.Abt. 504*, *SS-Lazarett 104* became *SS-Lazarett 504*, and *SS-Krankenwagen-Zug 104* became *SS-Krankenwagen-Zug 504*.[21]

Two of the corps' dedicated artillery units, *SS-schw.Art.Abt. 104* and *SS-Beob. Bttr. 104*, were similarly renumbered, though neither was present with the corps at this time, the artillery battalion still undergoing activation and training, while the observation battery was serving in Arnhem with *II. SS-Pz.Korps*. *SS-Werf.Abt. 504*, led by *Hstuf.* Otto Krosta, had returned to Gille's corps on 15 September after a brief period of service in Warsaw in support of the attack against Zoliborz by the *25. Pz.Div.* and would be available to deploy its *Nebelwerfer* multiple rocket launcher batteries in support of the next battle, where they would prove very important in combating Soviet massed assaults with their lethal salvos.[22]

The cumulative impact of these new units being added to the corps, as well as the influx of all the *Luftwaffe* and Ukrainian replacements, was soon borne out in the weekly *Kampfstärke* reports required to be submitted by all division-sized units in the *9. Armee* area of operations. For example, on 2 October, the *Totenkopf* Division had only 972 remaining front-line soldiers of its own who were reported as its *Kampfstärke*, as compared to 2,591 men on 13 August, but by 9 October that number had risen to 1,567. The change in the *Wiking* Division's *Kampfstärke* was even more dramatic. On 9 September, its combat strength was reported as only 480 men, compared to 1,597 on 13 August. By 9 October that number had mushroomed to 3,070 troops, almost all of them coming from the much-maligned *Hermann Göring Spende*. Small wonder that Gille had argued so loudly to be reinforced by another infantry division when the Hungarian division departed. Howsever, with this influx of replacements, he no longer had grounds for complaints.[23] The divisions of the *Heer* were also being flooded with new men at the same time.

While the *Totenkopf* and *Wiking* Divisions issued awards to deserving individuals during this lull in the action, the corps headquarters did the same for its soldiers and those from attached units. Between 23 and 30 September, Gille's headquarters awarded four Iron Cross, 2nd Class medals to members of corps headquarters troops; 40 to soldiers from *Gren.Brig. 1131*, as well as 10 Iron Cross, 1st Class; five to deserving individuals from Ritter's probationary battalion; 14 to soldiers from *Heers-Art.Abt. 154*; 15 to men in *Heeres-Pz.Jag.Abt. 743*, including five Iron Cross, 1st Class; and one repeat award of the Iron Cross, 2nd Class to *Rittmeister* Bruno Pabst, a World War I veteran assigned to *Bau-Pionier Btl. 421*. One soldier assigned to the liaison detachment working with the *1. ung.Kav.Div.*, *Obergefreiter* Heinz Gummersbach, was also awarded the Iron Cross, 2nd Class. More would be handed out before the third battle of Warsaw had ended.[24]

During this same period, both of the SS divisions were required to submit their end-of-month readiness reports for September to the *OKH* Inspectorate of Armored Troops in Zossen. The *Totenkopf* Division's report, dated 4 October, reflected its end-of-month actual strength (15,948 men) and its losses for the month (1,750 men, including 268 killed in action, 1,216 wounded, 72 missing, and 134 men sick or otherwise absent). It also reported that it had received 4,438 replacements throughout the month, though many of these, while assigned, were *Luftwaffe* replacements still undergoing training in either *SS-Feld-Ausb.Btl. 3* or *SS-Feld-Ers.Btl. 3*.[25]

However, the division's total strength, 89.6 percent of its authorized number, was deceiving. It had only two-thirds of the required number of NCOs and was short of 38 percent of its officers, of whom an indeterminate amount were serving in the division's replacement and training pipeline, meaning that even fewer were available for front-line service. An infantry company was fortunate to have more than one officer assigned, but that was the exception to the rule. Nearly illegibly written on the bottom of the page of *Anlage 1* (enclosure 1) was the statement that there were 480 *Hiwis* serving within the ranks of the division's combat troops. Whether they were Ukrainian combat troops or other volunteers was left unsaid.

Regarding armored vehicles and heavy weapons, the report was more positive. The division still had 34 assault guns (23 operational), 27 *Pz. IV* tanks (18 operational),

30 *Pz. V* Panthers (22 operational), 24 *Jagdpanzer IV* tank destroyers (18 operational), and six operational *Pz. VI* Tigers, making a total of 121 serviceable armored fighting vehicles. Additionally, it had 18 heavy antitank guns and 59 artillery pieces of all types, as well as a dozen 12 cm mortars. Even more encouraging was that it still had enough tracked prime movers (121) to tow all of its heavy weapons and enough trucks to carry 86 percent of its basic load of supplies in one lift. However, the shortage of MG-42 machine guns was alarming, for the division had only 488 on hand, as compared to the 1,204 it was authorized by its *K.St.N.* This equated to one MG-42 per platoon, or two at the most, roughly only half of what they needed.

The report concluded with the commander's assessment. *Obf.* Becker evaluated his division as being suited for a defensive mission, but no longer suitable to serve in an offensive capacity due to the shortages of trained grenadiers. While he assessed that the overall training level of the division was good, he felt that the newly arrived replacements from the *Luftwaffe* would need two more weeks of training before they would be ready for combat. He added that his division was suffering from a widespread shortage of small arms, such as rifles, machine guns, pistols, and machine pistols. While he felt that he had enough motor transport, the shortage of tires was beginning to impact the readiness of his trucking fleet. He also bemoaned the crippling shortage of light and medium *SPW* and *Panzerspähwagen* (armored reconnaissance vehicles), having only 45 on hand against 330 authorized. Overall, he believed that based on these figures, his division could be rated as only 48 percent mobile. In conclusion, Becker emphasized in his "Commander's Special Concerns" paragraph that "the division is still lacking a large number of front-experienced officers and NCOs."

The *Wiking* Division's report, submitted at the same time as the *Totenkopf*'s, also reflected the large influx of *Luftwaffe* replacements that had begun to pour in from its field training and field replacement battalions. It had far in excess of its authorized number of 17,797 men, with 19,153 reported as being assigned at the end of September. As many as 1,760 of these were moving through the field training and replacement pipeline, but the division's personnel readiness was definitely improving. These new troops were badly needed, because the division had lost 798 men during September, of which 110 were reported as being killed in action with another 443 wounded. Unlike the *Totenkopf* Division's report, the *Wiking's* does not mention how many of its troops were Ukrainian volunteers from the SS Galician Division, only that it had 309 of its 949 authorized *Hiwis*.[26]

With regard to vehicles of all types, the *Wiking* Division was not nearly so well off as the *Totenkopf*. In the armored fighting vehicle category, it had only nine assault guns (eight operational), 23 *Pz. IV* (20 operational), 32 *Pz. V* Panthers (26 operational), and 13 operational *Jagdpanzer IV*, for a total of 77. It had 249 *SPW* and reconnaissance vehicles on hand, roughly 72 percent of its authorized amount. It still had a good number of heavy weapons, reporting

23 serviceable antitank guns, 52 artillery pieces of all types, twelve 8.8cm antiaircraft guns, and 19 self-propelled 3.7cm antiaircraft guns. The number of cargo vehicles of all types had improved due to deliveries of new vehicles, to the point where it could carry 87 percent of its daily requirement of all classes of supply and no longer needed augmentation by *Transport-Brigade Speer*. The number of machine guns on hand in the division, as with the *Totenkopf*, were only half of the authorized amount.

Staf. Mühlenkamp, the division's commander, had a lot to say in his "Commander's Special Concerns" paragraph. In it, he wrote:

> On account of the newly arrived enlisted replacements, the personnel situation had improved. There has been no appreciable amount of replacements to fill the vacant officer and NCO positions though, which accounts for the difficulties encountered in training the enlisted replacements. The Division has exhausted the possibilities for finding new leaders, having already combed through its transportation and supply units for NCOs, as well as having conducted training courses for junior NCOs. I do not expect the situation to improve until the middle of October, at the earliest. The requirement for junior officers can no longer be fulfilled by the division."

He also commented critically about the Ukrainians attached to his division, stating:

> The replacement of our manpower shortages by 650 *Wawis* [volunteer Ukrainian soldiers] was carried out by the end of September when they were parceled out to the units. Most of them appear to be willing [to fight]. We are experiencing tremendous language difficulties. Their reliability in a major battle cannot yet be evaluated; we have already had one deserter.

Discouraged by the shortages facing his new command, he wrote

> The material situation has not noticeably improved. The number of combat-ready weapons and vehicles has risen, on account that the reduced operational tempo of the last few days has made it possible to carry out fundamental maintenance. We also took possession of 17 Panzer IV [note: this marks the arrival of the reconstituted *2. Kompanie* of the *panzer* regiment's *I. Abteilung*]. Furthermore, we lack sufficient machine guns and tanks, although we have enough crews available to operate them. Besides this, we still do not have enough vehicles in the division's supply column."

Finally, Mühlenkamp closed his report by stating:

> The Division is not suited to conducted offensive operations, on account that the newly-received [and still enroute] flood of new replacements from the *Luftwaffe* still have not completed sufficient training, such that the *Germania* and *Westland Panzergrenadier* Regiments cannot be considered at all to be combat-ready. For the conduct of defensive operations, only *SS-Pz. Art.Rgt. 5*, *SS-Pz.Rgt. 5*, *SS-Pz.Jg.Abt. 5*, and two *Panzergrenadier* battalions can be considered ready for employment. *SS-Pz.Aufkl.Abt. 5* is completely prepared for combat."

Although it was not to serve alongside the *Totenkopf* and *Wiking* Divisions during the upcoming October battles, the *Fs.Pz.Div. Hermann Göring* had fought alongside them several times during August and September and had endured its share of victories and losses. At the end of September, it was attached once again to *IV. SS-Pz.Korps* and was required to submit its monthly report through its headquarters just like the other two divisions. During the past two months, it had suffered just as heavily as the *Wiking* and *Totenkopf* Divisions, losing 4,481 men, including 585 killed in action, 2,240 wounded, and 405 men missing. Like the *19. Pz.Div.*, it had been shuttled several times between the Warsaw front and the Magnuszew or Puławy bridgeheads, each time arriving in the nick of time to avert the front's collapse. In turn, it had received 3,724 replacements directly from its own *Ausbildungs-Regiment Hermann Göring* during the same period.[27]

Regarding the status of its armored fighting vehicles at the end of September, it had a total of 34 *Pz. IV* tanks serviceable, of which 24 were reported as being operational on 1 1944. Its *Pz. V* Panther battalion, *I. Abt./Fs.Pz.Rgt. "HG"*, had not yet arrived from Germany since it was being re-equipped with new tanks and would not begin rejoining the division until the following month. It also had 19 *Jagdpanzer IV*, of which 13 were operational, 181 *SPW*, seven self-propelled antitank guns, 27 towed antitank guns, and 62 artillery pieces of various calibers, of which 50 were operational. *Generalmajor* Schmalz, the division commander, rated the *Kampfwert* (combat value) of his formation as having a Category I, or "*Zu jeder Angriffsaufgabe geeignet*" ("fully capable of carrying out offensive operations"), and its mobility at 80 percent.

On 24 September, the division received an order that would result in its transfer to the Radom area, where it would serve as the foundation for the establishment of a second division named after the *Reichsmarschall*, *Fs.Pz.Gren.Div. 2 Hermann Göring*. Schmalz's division would provide the leadership cadre for this new *Panzergrenadier* division, requiring it to effectively give up half of its remaining officers and NCOs, as well as a number of specialist personnel. Between 2 and 8 October, the division began displacing in phases from the east of Warsaw and once more across the Vistula, being replaced incrementally for the second time by the *19. Pz.Div.*, a division that would mark its third period of service under Gille's corps.[28]

After the reorganization, which included the establishment of a new corps headquarters as well as the aforementioned second division, the now-renumbered *Fs.Pz.Div. 1 Hermann Göring* lost its elite character and would never be the same unit again. Additionally, the infusion of thousands of excess *Luftwaffe* aircrew watered down the division's battle effectiveness, just as it had with the two SS divisions it would soon bid farewell to. In his commander's comments at the end of his monthly readiness report for October, Schmalz acknowledged this when he stated, "On account of the influx of involuntarily transferred replacements, the troops have temporarily lost their old *Schwung* [offensive spirit]."[29] Its reorganization and activation in Radom was still ongoing when the new *Fs.Pz.Korps "Hermann Göring"* and its two divisions were ordered to the East Prussian front beginning on 6 October, with most of the elements arriving four days later and immediately going into action. None of its elements would fight alongside Gille's troops again.

As mentioned above, the *19. Pz.Div.* was brought over the Vistula for a third time to replace the *Fs.Pz.Div. Hermann Göring*, beginning on 2 October, when its advance elements came under the control of *IV. SS-Pz.Korps*. This marked the last major movement of troops in and out of Gille's corps until the third defensive battle of Warsaw was over. Freed up for employment elsewhere due to the surrender of the Polish Home Army that same day, *Gen.Lt.* Källner handed over his division's positions in Warsaw to the newly rebuilt *73. Inf.Div.* and began conducting a relief in place of the *Fs.Pz.Div. Hermann Göring*, whose combat engineer battalion immediately began moving out to its new assembly area near Radom that evening. By the end of the day on 6 October, the movement of both divisions was relatively complete.

Källner's *19. Pz.Div.* was no stranger to *IV. SS-Pz.Korps*, of course. Though it had been fighting in Warsaw against the last holdouts in the Zoliborz suburbs for most of the past two weeks, the division's leadership had used the time wisely, taking advantage of the opportunity for its battalions and regiments to absorb replacements and install new officers to replace the dozens of platoon, company, and battalion commanders who had been killed or wounded during the past two months of heavy fighting along the Vistula Front between Praga and Magnuszew. Källner's readiness report for September 1944, dated 1 October, gives an indication of what his division had endured.

During September alone, *19. Pz.Div.* had suffered 1,162 casualties, including 80 out of its 313 authorized officers. During the same period, it had received 1,332 replacements, bringing it close to its authorized full strength of 14,821 men, including 476 *Hiwi*. Regarding armor, though it was still short of the required amount, the division still fielded 21 *StuG III* assault guns, 42 *Pz. IV* tanks, and 41 *Pz. V* Panthers, for a total of 104 AFV—of which 73 were operational—along with 225 *SPW* of all types. It had all of its authorized amount of artillery pieces (42), most of its antitank guns (11), and sufficient wheeled and track vehicles to haul the daily amount of supplies it needed to stay in fighting trim.[30]

In his commander's comments, Källner rated the division as having a *Kampfwert* of "I" (the highest), meaning fully capable of carrying out any offensive assignment. He also stated in his report that he was satisfied with the division's overall level of training, that the troops' morale was good, and that the division was 90 percent mobile. On the negative side, he reported that replacements arriving from the *Ersatzheer* were insufficiently trained to fulfil their fundamental individual skills of their particular branch of service, which had to be made up for in the limited time available by mandating further training that placed additional strain on the division's already-overtasked junior officer and NCO leadership.

His biggest complaint was saved for the situation the division faced concerning replacement parts for tanks, in particular motors and tracks for the *panzer* regiment's *Pz. IVs*, which had sidelined 16 of them. He also noted that the division possessed only one operational recovery tank (*Bergepanther*) for the entire tank regiment, that 30-Watt radio transmitters were in short supply—thus hindering the artillery regiment's communications—and there was a shortage of tires (3,000) and repair parts for his trucks, as well as several other minor shortages that were impacting the division's readiness. However, despite these minor issues, the *19. Pz.Div.*, upon arrival in its new defensive sector, automatically became the most powerful division in Gille's order of battle.

It would have to hasten its preparations though; the *19. Pz.Div.* would only have four days to position itself to weather the storm that was about to break upon its newly occupied main defense line. To compensate for the division's inherent lack of *Panzergrenadier* battalions to cover its frontage, *Gren.Btl.z.b.V. 560*, still under the command of the indefatigable *Maj.* Ritter, was once again transferred across the Vistula from its assembly area in Warsaw on 5 October, taking up a new position on the division's left flank adjacent to the *Totenkopf* Division.[31] Two days later, Ritter's battalion was placed under the tactical control of *Obf.* Becker's division, and the boundary between it and the *19. Pz.Div.* was subsequently redrawn, resulting in a narrower frontage for Källner to defend.

Clearly, the lull between the second and third battles of Warsaw had been anything but uneventful for everyone concerned, but judging by the records, this time had been put to good use by both sides. As was usually the case, the front-line troops would have been surprised if anyone had told them that things were quiet; their daily lives were filled with outpost duty, raids, small-scale local counterattacks, artillery barrages, constructing fighting positions, cleaning weapons, filling sandbags, emplacing mines and barbed wire obstacles, laying communications wire—the myriad duties of soldiers on both sides who were practically living nose-to-nose with their opponent.

Sniper duels, raids, and reconnaissance forays were the order of the day during this so-called "lull" in the action. In the *Fs.Pz.Div. Hermann Göring* sector, 21 confirmed sniper kills were recorded by its regiments on 24 September alone. Thirty-two additional Soviet *Frontovnik* (Russian slang for front-line soldiers) were killed by German snipers five days later. Soviet snipers took a similar toll, killing or wounding anyone careless enough to expose themselves during daylight. A company-sized raid launched by the *Totenkopf* Division during the early hours on 25 September east of Hill 101 bagged 20 Soviet prisoners and brought in a large number of captured weapons.

In return, Soviet units stepped up their own efforts to gather prisoners and information, often using rifle battalions for that purpose, though these were usually heralded by concentrated artillery fire on German forward positions, warning the defenders that their opponents were up to something.[32] Three of these battalion-sized actions took place against the right flank of the *Fs.Pz.Div. Hermann Göring* on 30 September, but each of these Soviet attempts were driven off by a combination of infantry weapons and artillery counterfire. Forty dead Soviet soldiers were counted afterwards and 32 prisoners were taken during the German counterattack that threw the remaining Soviets out of the forward positions they had temporarily taken possession of.

A large counter-raid by the *Totenkopf* Division on 27 September penetrated the Soviet forward defense line east of Rembelsz, rolled up the trench line on either side, destroyed several bunkers, and killed a number of troops from the 328th Rifle Division before making good their escape. This same raid also brought back two Soviet prisoners for interrogation. A similar attempt by the *Wiking* Division the following evening to replicate the *Totenkopf*'s performance ran foul of alert Soviet defenders near Rynia, who forced the SS men back to their own lines after discovering their approach. When they encountered heavy rifle and machine-gun fire that killed and wounded a number of the men in the raiding party, the surprised *Wikinger* beat a hasty retreat. And so it went, day in, day out, with both sides determined to find out their opponent's intentions. In the front-line trenches between Zegrze and Annopol, boredom was seldom, if ever, an option.

The lives of staff officers and NCOs at the levels of battalion, regiment, division, and corps were just as busy, though perhaps not as dangerous as living in a front-line trench. They had to endure artillery barrages and air attacks too. And of course, commanders at all levels were fully occupied with leading their units, visiting the troops at the front, attending briefings at their respective higher headquarters, meeting with their staffs, and writing reports at the end of the day. Somewhere in their busy schedule they would snatch a few hours of sleep. At all times, they had to maintain their persona as a strong leader and display the proper optimistic view of things to keep up morale. If the commander was a general officer, his *Begleitoffizier* and enlisted aid ensured that he was fed and his uniform was immaculate.

During this period, there also arose a controversy involving the Gille's *Ib*, or *Quartiermeister*, *Ostubaf.* Scharff, the corps' logistics officer since July. According to an official complaint lodged by Johann Arens, the *Amtskommisar* (District Commissioner) of Modlin, a Nazi Party appointee, on behalf of Erwin Leffler, the *Kreisbauernführer* (Agriculture Supervisor) of Plöhnen, Scharff had authorized the units within the corps' area of operations to requisition farm animals, grain, potatoes, and other crops for their own troops without securing permission first from the local Nazi Party leadership. While combat troops were authorized to requisition anything within their immediate *Gefechtsgebiet* (area encompassing the front lines), anything beyond that point, extending into the field army's *Korück*, was strictly forbidden. Concerned that German troops had acted in a high-handed manner and had potentially upset the fall harvest schedule, on 3 October these local officials complained to the commander of *Korück 532*, *Gen. Lt.* Bernhard, who presented the sticky situation to *Gen.d.Pz.Tr.* von Lüttwitz at *9. Armee* headquarters for resolution.[33]

Not desiring a confrontation with the Nazi Party's chain of command, since he had far more pressing matters to worry about, he penned a note to the commander of *IV. SS-Pz.Korps* on 8 October that amounted to a personal reprimand. In his letter, von Lüttwitz stated:

> To the Commanding General of the *IV. SS-Panzerkorps*, I draw your attention to the various explicit orders given by this army, which prohibit the unauthorized seizure or confiscation of livestock, food, and other commodities. You are to investigate these incidents in detail, and must report back to me what occurred. In addition, I ask that you provide information about the measures that you have taken, which would ensure future compliance with the previously issued army orders."[34]

No record of Gille's response can be found in the existing historical material.

However, it does not appear that Gille did anything to punish his enterprising staff officer, much less issue him a reprimand. There was little that Reinhardt could actually do other than demand disciplinary action be taken, since SS personnel and disciplinary matters, again, were not under his purview. Shortly afterwards, Gille recommended Scharff for the award of the German Cross in Silver for his personal service on behalf of the corps' troops, ensuring that "1,300 tons of potatoes and 70 tons of green vegetables were provided from areas near the front," which "maintained them in an exemplary state of combat readiness" during a period of heavy defensive fighting. Gille pinned the award on Scharff on 10 February 1945 while the corps was fighting in Hungary, after it had been approved by the *SS-FHA* in Berlin.[35] While Scharff's actions probably did not earn him any friends among the local *Bonzen* (German slang for the Nazi Party bosses), it likely did earn him the respect if not the affection of the men in the divisions and corps troops of *IV. SS-Pz.Korps*, who might have gone hungry without the requisitioned food.

Throughout this period of relative calm, the normal rotation of commanders and staff officers in and out of their positions continued, unlike the enlisted men, who more often than not would serve throughout the entire war in the same platoon or company. The most important change of command that occurred between 23 September and 9 October 1944 was the appointment of *Staf.* Karl Ullrich to command the *Wiking* Division. Ullrich, who up to that point had been serving as the commander of *SS-Pz.Gren.Rgt. 6 Theodor Eicke* of the *Totenkopf* Division, had been fighting alongside the neighboring *Wiking* as a regimental commander for the past two months and was already well acquainted with its subordinate leadership and staff.

Ullrich, born on 1 December 1910 in Saargemünd, was a college-educated engineer who joined the *Pionier-Bataillon* of the *SS-Verfügungstruppe* in June 1934 after two years of service as an NCO in the *Allgemeine-SS*. He graduated from the first course taught at the *SS-Junkerschule* in Braunschweig in 1936 and was immediately posted as a platoon leader of the engineer battalion in Dresden. By 1938, he was serving as a *Hauptsturmführer* and company commander in the *SS-Pioniersturmbann*, leading it through the Western Europe campaign in 1940. In

May 1941, he was transferred to the *Totenkopf* Division as a company commander in its *Pionier-Bataillon*, being elevated to its commander less than a year later. He fought with the division during the battles of Staraja-Russa, Demyansk, Kharkov, and Kursk, where he repeatedly distinguished himself with his leadership ability.

After serving briefly as the *Stopi* (corps engineer officer) of *Ogruf.* Hausser's *SS-Panzerkorps*, he assumed command of *III. Btl./SS-Pz.Gren.Rgt. 6 Theodor Eicke* on 18 March 1943. Six months later, he took over leadership of the entire regiment from *Obf.* Becker and was promoted to *Standartenführer* on 29 July 1944. A brave and decisive leader, he had already been awarded the Knight's Cross on 19 February 1942 and the Oak Leaves on 15 May 1944, which were bestowed by Hitler himself at the Wolf's Lair headquarters in East Prussia on 29 July. Considered by former division commander *Obf.* Otto Baum to have been the best officer that ever served under him, Ullrich was well chosen to succeed Mühlenkamp as the division's leader and would not disappoint his corps commander, Gille, who had known him since both men had served together in the pre-war *Verfügungstruppe*.[36]

Upon Ullrich's departure, command of *SS-Pz.Gren.Rgt. 6 Theodor Eicke* was assumed by *Ostubaf.* Franz Kleffner. Kleffner had previously served in the *Totenkopf* Division and most recently as the commander of *SS-Pz.Rgt. 10* of the *Frundsberg* Division, until he was relieved of command for alcoholism on 2 June 1944. He was transferred from house arrest in Bad Saarow, where he had been undergoing detoxification, on 25 September to take over the command of *SS-Pz.Rgt. 5* from Fritz Darges, who was junior in rank.[37] He arrived at the front on 4 October, but instead of going to the *Wiking* Division, he was diverted to Ullrich's former regiment on 6 October, formally taking command of *SS-Pz.Gren.Rgt. 6* on 9 October.

Ullrich made quite a dramatic appearance upon his arrival that same day at the forward headquarters of the *Wiking* Division in the town of Jablonna-Legjonowo, where the headquarters of the *Westland* Regiment was also located. One day before the beginning of the great Soviet offensive, *Staf.* Mühlenkamp had summoned all of the division's regimental and battalion commanders to his headquarters to officially welcome Ullrich to the *Wiking*, but while Ullrich was on his way to the gathering in one of the division's *SPW* an intercepted radio message was received that informed everyone that a Soviet artillery barrage upon Jablonna-Legjonowo was expected at 2:30 p.m. Arriving in a cloud of dust at that very hour, Ullrich and the *SPW*'s other occupants rushed into the house and immediately took shelter in the basement, while a hurricane of shells burst outside. No one was injured, and once it became clear that the barrage was over, everyone went back upstairs, where the planned program took place as if nothing had happened.[38]

Although he was officially designated as the new leader of the *Wiking* Division effective from 9 October, the evidence indicates that he did not actually take up the reins of division command until 23 October. Until that time, it appears that he served as Mühlenkamp's "understudy," acting in the capacity of a deputy division commander. Because the third battle of Warsaw began the very next day, having Mühlenkamp remain in place as the commander until the crisis passed would have been in keeping with Gille's philosophy of leadership. Briefly summarized, it expressed itself in his care for his men and desire to do everything possible for his new subordinate commanders to succeed by thoroughly preparing them for their responsibilities. Having Ullrich serve under his predecessor for two weeks until the worst of the fighting was over would have done just that.

From a more practical point of view, it was also wise for Gille to keep Mühlenkamp at the helm for a few more days as an insurance policy, since no one knew once the Soviet offensive began how it would unfold; it made no sense to place such an important leadership position in the hands of someone who had yet to prove himself as a division commander. With two months' experience successfully leading a *panzer* division during three large-scale battles already behind him, Mühlenkamp would have instinctively known what to do and would have made a superb mentor to Ullrich. For example, on 10 October, he personally directed the actions of *SS-Pz.Rgt. 5* during the division's initial defensive efforts to prevent a Soviet breakthrough east of Nieporet.[39]

For his following assignment, Mühlenkamp had been named as the next head of the *Inspektion der Panzertruppen der Waffen-SS* (Inspector of SS Armored Troops) in Berlin, where he would be responsible for overseeing the training and equipping of all armored units in the *Waffen-SS*. Instead of departing for Germany after the formal handover of command to Ullrich, Mühlenkamp evidently remained in the division's area until at least 23 October, when he personally awarded the *IV. Stufe* (4th Grade) of the *Panzer-Kampfabzeichen in Silber* (Panzer Assault Badge in Silver) to *SS-Hstuf.* Willy Hein, the acting commander of the *I. Abteilung*, at the *panzer* regiment's headquarters.[40] After that date, he no longer appears in the division's records.

Three months after assuming his new duties in Berlin, on 30 January 1945, Mühlenkamp was appointed to serve as the acting commander of the newly-created *32. SS-Freiwilligen-Gren.Div. "30. Januar,"* then deployed on the Oder River Front where it was undergoing activation. He served in that capacity for nearly a week, helping to form and train the division, which was created from various odds and ends of the SS replacement system and other scrapings from the bottom of its manpower barrel, until he was relieved by its duly appointed commander, *Staf.* Joachim Richter, on 5 February. He then returned to his previous position as Inspector of SS *Panzer* Troops. Near the end of the war, Mühlenkamp was captured by U.S. troops on 3 May while he lay in an Innsbruck military hospital after being wounded again (for the sixth time) on 16 April.[41]

The uncommonly long pause in the fighting from 23 September along the *9. Armee*'s Vistula Front would not last forever, and it duly ended on 10 October. However, during the previous 18 days, the corps and division under von Lüttwitz's command had done their utmost to make the best use of the time they had. Not only had it been used to crush the Warsaw Uprising once and for all, but the lull in large-scale operations had also enabled the army to simultaneously eliminate the threat posed by the large grouping of Polish partisans inhabiting the Kampinos forest and to support the neighboring *2. Armee*'s ultimately unsuccessful counteroffensive north of the Narew River. Units throughout the army's area of operations, including the *IV. SS-Pz.Korps*, had reorganized as much as the time allowed, incorporated thousands of replacements into their ranks, stockpiled ammunition and fuel, and prepared for the major Soviet offensive that everyone knew was coming. All they could do now was wait.

CHAPTER 11

The Third Defensive Battle of Warsaw 10–28 October 1944

The Soviet offensive against the bridgehead held by the *IV. SS-Pz.Korps* between the Narew and Vistula that officially began on 10 October 1944 cannot be described as anything other than a throwback to the battles fought on the Western Front during World War I. Tactically and operationally uninspired, it was not Marshal Rokossovsky's most brilliant battle, and seems to have been launched reluctantly. Rokossovsky admitted as much in his memoir, where he wrote that the position could only be taken by a "head-on assault." He recognized before the battle even began that the Germans had constructed a nearly impregnable position, strongly supported by artillery located on the high ground on the opposite banks of each river that would enable them to fire directly into the flanks of the attacking units. "Orders, however, were to deny the enemy any foothold on the eastern bank," he wrote.[1] This was to be the last significant offensive action taken by the First Belorussian Front until January 1945, though smaller-scale attacks would be tried a month later during the siege of Modlin.

To be fair, the Front commander had few other options. He had sent much of his artillery to support the fighting north of Serock, where the 65th Army was still locked in a deadly struggle with the *XX. Armeekorps,* and he was uncertain as to German intentions concerning the Magnuszew and Puławy bridgeheads on the upper Vistula.[2] The knowledge of the movement of the *Fs.Pz.Div. Hermann Göring* to Radom had not eased his worry either. Did the transfer of this still-powerful division presage yet another German attempt to wipe out either bridgehead? In truth, if he did have orders instructing him to eliminate the SS *panzer* corps occupying what had become known as the "Wet Triangle" between the Narew and Vistula, there was only one way to do it—and that was by a direct assault. He could not outflank it, nor could he ignore it. The only way to go about it was to crush it with as much overwhelming force as his army group could muster.

The two armies chosen to lead the attack, the 47th and 70th, supported by the VIII Guards Tank Corps and the 1st Polish Army, had already been fighting east of Warsaw for the past two months. Neither the 47th nor 70th Armies were at full strength—in fact, during August and September the First Belorussian Front's 8th Guards, 28th, 47th, 65th, 69th, and 70th Armies and 2nd Guards Tank Army had lost 246,000 men killed, wounded, and missing, including 11,000 soldiers from the 1st Polish Army in September alone.[3] Roughly half of these losses had been replaced before the offensive began on 10 October. Therefore, the six rifles corps—with a total of nine Soviet rifle divisions and one Polish division, with five more rifle divisions in reserve—had slightly more than half of their authorized strength assigned, mustering between 6,000 and 7,000 men per division.[4] This did not apply to the artillery, rocket artillery, or armored formations, which were still nearly at full strength.

Though each of these rifle divisions had been replenished with new troops, weapons, and ammunition as much as conditions permitted, they were anything but refreshed, having occupied front-line trenches opposite some very active German defenders for the past two weeks. The addition of the now-rested VIII Guards Tank Corps, once again mustering over 200 tanks and self-propelled guns, made it the most powerful element in the attacking force, but both armies were still short of infantry. Still, even in its weakened state, Rokossovsky's offensive would hurl approximately 100,000 men against Gille's estimated 50,000.[5] Even this was not considered adequate. Given the tactical advantage generally enjoyed by the defender, much more was needed to even the odds than mere manpower. Therefore, the available rifle divisions would have to be concentrated along a very narrow front in order to have the desired mass to achieve a breakthrough. In his own assessment of Soviet strength before the battle, Gille estimated that 12–14 rifle divisions had been positioned to attack along a zone only 10–12 kilometers wide, a judgement later borne out by both Soviet and German intelligence maps.[6]

To compensate for this unaccustomed shortage of infantrymen, the First Belorussian Front would ensure that the 47th and 70th Armies were reinforced with as much artillery and rocket artillery as could still be mustered. The 16th Air Army would also be providing support, though when the offensive began its main effort would still be directed against the fighting taking place between Serock and Pułtusk. Once the German counteroffensive to the north was defeated—as appeared certain by 9 October—and the lost ground regained, additional artillery and air power would be immediately shifted to the south, but until then, the 47th and 70th Armies would have to do the best they could. Still, that would be quite enough. The lethal and omnipresent artillery fire would long be remembered afterwards by German survivors of the battle as one of their most vivid memories of the third defensive battle of Warsaw.

As far as *H.Gr. Mitte* and *9. Armee* were concerned, they were not expecting an offensive against the Narew–Vistula defense line at all. *Generaloberst* Reinhardt, as well as von Lüttwitz, confidently believed that the Soviet buildup spotted by aerial reconnaissance and agents operating behind the lines had nothing to do with the *IV. SS-Pz.Korps*, but were instead signs that the First Belorussian Front intended to launch a massive counteroffensive from the Pułtusk and Magnuszew bridgeheads, designed to converge upon and encircle the entire Warsaw–Vistula defense line from the north and south, respectively. The encirclement of Warsaw, they believed, would be a prelude to a much larger offensive aimed at a breakthrough to the Baltic designed to cut off and isolate East Prussia, based on intelligence estimates provided by the *Fremde Heere Ost* (Foreign Armies Intelligence Office).[7] The reemergence of Soviet activity within the Magnuszew bridgehead during the first week of October, seen as a precursor to offensive intentions, seemed to confirm both Reinhardt's and von Lüttwitz's suspicions.

The only commander objecting to this scenario was Gille, who repeatedly reminded his senior commanders between 1 and 9 October of the visible signs of a Soviet buildup occurring just a few kilometers beyond his own front lines. Tanks were seen or heard assembling, new artillery batteries were spotted arriving, and the movement of large numbers of troops into front-line positions had been ascertained by nightly raids and reconnaissance forays. Artillery fire upon Gille's three divisions was noticeably increasing, much of it appearing to consist of registration fire conducted to lay-in new artillery batteries with their predesignated targets. German signal and aerial reconnaissance indicated that facing the 42 artillery batteries within the *IV. SS-Pz.Korps* sector, with about 150–175 guns of their own, were approximately 235 Soviet batteries, with roughly 900–1,000 guns.[8] Prisoners brought in by foot patrols also confirmed the presence of newly arrived divisions, a fact confirmed by a German agent parachuted behind Soviet lines who had observed their movement towards the front at night.[9]

Yet all of Gille's concerns, when aired at *9. Armee* or *H.Gr. Mitte* headquarters, were downplayed. Most distressing was the *9. Armee's* refusal to allocate his corps more than the normal amount of artillery ammunition, which it would need to compensate for his shortage of troops.[10] In Gille's daily report for 8 October he wrote that, based on heightened Soviet activity and all of the previously mentioned indicators, he expected the long-awaited offensive would begin any day.[11] When even this report drew no encouraging response from von Lüttwitz or his staff, who were at the time planning another counteroffensive to eliminate or reduce the Magnuszew bridgehead, Gille and his staff knew that for the moment at least, when the battle finally did begin his corps would initially be fighting alone.[12]

Gille had already sent his chief of staff, *Ostubaf.* Schönfelder, to von Lüttwitz's headquarters on 6 October to convince the army's commander and his staff to take the matter more seriously, but all he encountered was "total disbelief."[13] The *9. Armee* commander told Schönfelder that he thought Gille was being far too pessimistic, that there was nothing to fear, and that his front would stay quiet.[14] After the war, Gille wrote, "As I had been unsuccessful in convincing *AOK 9* of the correctness of my assessment, as I saw it a catastrophe in my Corps' sector would inevitably take place which would result in the loss of Warsaw, which again could not fail to have an effect on the overall situation on the Eastern Front."[15] It would take the events that would soon play out over the next several days to convince his chain of command otherwise.

Ominously, on the evening of 8 October, Soviet communications networks on the eastern side of the Vistula between Zegrze and Warsaw fell silent. Rokossovsky had evidently imposed radio discipline, a typical practice used immediately prior to an offensive to deny the Germans any opportunities to divine relevant information about an impending attack. German aircraft were forced to keep their distance that day by omnipresent Soviet fighter aircraft, so no overhead reconnaissance photographs could be taken between 8 and 10 October that might reveal the enemy's intentions. Attempts by foot patrols from the *19. Pz.Div.*, the *Totenkopf*, and the *Wiking* Divisions to scout Soviet front-line positions were met with volleys of small arms and artillery fire that drove the men back to their starting point. On the evening of 8 October, *9. Armee* finally began to take Gille's concerns seriously, but too much valuable time had been lost. Frustratingly, von Lüttwitz and his staff were still fixated on the long-awaited Soviet attack out of the Magnuszew bridgehead, which never materialized until three months had passed, so a great deal of time was lost in supplying *IV. SS-Pz.Korps* the additional artillery ammunition it had requested before the attack began.

In his evening report that night, the *9. Armee* commander predicted that the attack against *IV. SS-Pz.Korps*, if it came in the next day or two, would be a two-pronged affair, with the 47th Army attempting a crossing of the Vistula a few kilometers north of Warsaw, while the 70th Army would conduct a supporting attack via Nieporet towards Modlin aimed at seizing the bridges there and sweeping south to encircle Gille's corps before investing Warsaw. In this assessment von Lüttwitz was incorrect; both armies would push through the Wet Triangle in tandem and attempt to destroy Gille's corps before seizing crossing sites over the Vistula and Narew at Modlin, but then would go no further. Von Lüttwitz did not know that Josef Stalin had decided that Warsaw's liberation could wait, especially now since there was no longer an uprising to assist or a civilian population to rescue. *Ogruf.* Erich von dem Bach had done Stalin's dirty work for him.

Gille, in consultation with his corps' *Ic*, *Stubaf.* Jankuhn, had predicted the same day that the attack would be launched on the morning of 9 October. He was correct, for that was exactly when Rokossovsky had directed it to take place. Using the limited time available, Gille, working with his *ARKO*, *Brig.Fhr.* Brasack, devised an artillery ambush for that evening, to be carried out using every available gun in the corps area. Brasack, with Gille's permission, had amassed a reserve of artillery ammunition, approximately one-third of its daily allocation, by hoarding shells during the quiet period of the past two-and-a-half weeks. These were then distributed throughout the divisions' artillery regiments and corps artillery battalions. Though infantry company and battalion commanders in the front lines might complain about insufficient fire support being available to combat small-scale Soviet incursions, this tactic would more than pay for itself that evening.

Based on intelligence information gained during the previous weeks, as well as sights and sounds clearly heard that day on the opposite side of the lines—including tank tracks, revving motors, and dust plumes indicating the movement of many motor vehicles—Brasack's artillery fire coordination center in his *ARKO* headquarters had gained a good idea of where the guns should fire for best effect. The targets were Soviet command posts, troop and tank assembly areas, ammunition dumps, and fuel depots. Forward artillery and rocket artillery firing positions would also receive their share of attention. Firing coordinates were distributed throughout the corps, and the guns were made ready for action.[16]

In its first major conventional engagement, *SS-Werfer-Abt. 504*'s 24 *Nebelwerfer* launchers would soon contribute to the inferno with hundreds of 15cm high-explosive rockets. The amount of shells expended in this attack by the corps artillery units was considerable. For example, the *Wiking* Division's artillery regiment, *SS-Pz.Art.Rgt. 5*, fired roughly a third of its authorized daily allocation of artillery ammunition; its neighboring divisions fired a similar amount. In all, over 353 tons of ammunition would be fired that night and during the early morning at Soviet targets, mostly artillery, rocket, and mortar shells of all calibers, roughly 7.5 percent of the corps' authorized daily stockage level of 4,235 tons.[17]

Twice before midnight, at 8 p.m. and 9:30 p.m., and once again during the early hours, all of *IV. SS-Pz.Korps*' available artillery and rocket artillery simultaneously hammered key Soviet positions with short but violent pinpoint barrages. The effects were immediate; primary and secondary explosions lit up the night sky and the sound of the detonations reverberated far and wide. The sights and sounds would have buoyed the spirits of German troops manning front-line trenches and machine-gun positions, who naturally rejoiced to see the enemy on the receiving end of a massive barrage for a change. Soviet prisoners taken the following day, along with intercepted radio messages, indicated that the preventive strike had indeed been effective.[18]

Another sign that the artillery ambush had succeeded was the fact that the offensive widely expected to begin on the morning of 9 October did not materialize; the shelling had so disrupted Soviet communication lines that the attack was rescheduled for the following day to allow time to put the command and control networks of the Soviet front-line divisions back into operation. Rokossovsky himself admitted as much, when he wrote:

> Thousands of shells rained on our troops from beyond the Narew and Vistula and from the fortress [of Modlin]. Guns of all calibers, including heavy fortress ordnance, mortars and six-barrel rocket launchers let loose a hurricane of fire. The enemy used up shells unsparingly, as though bent on showing what he was still capable of. Obviously, we could not hope to liquidate the enemy bridgehead until this artillery system was suppressed … I ordered the signal calling off the attack to be given, and over the telephone told Generals Gusev and Popov that the offensive was off.[19]

Gille ordered two similar preventive barrages to be carried out the following night, but too much ammunition had been fired during the evening of 8–9 September to achieve the same level of success. The corps' remaining artillery ammunition would be needed to repel the ground attack when it came. Though these two artillery strikes also inflicted a considerable amount of damage on the Soviet formations massing for the attack, it was not enough to cause the same degree of disruption as the previous night.[20] The Soviet attack would go forward as scheduled during the early morning of 10 October.

As 10 October dawned, the divisions of *IV. SS-Pz.Korps* were arrayed as follows, from north to south: the *Wiking* Division, with two battalions of the *Germania* Regiment deployed on the north bank of the Narew and one on the south, defended the area between Serock and Aleksandrów, with the focus of its defensive effort, consisting of the *Westland* Regiment and *SS-Pz.Aufkl.Abt. 5*, lying east and southeast of Nieporet; to its south, the *Totenkopf* Division defended from Aleksandrów to Tomaszów with its *Totenkopf* and *Eicke* Regiments; and the refreshed *19. Pz.Div* was responsible for defending the area running from Tomaszów to the Vistula at Żerań.[21] In all, the corps was responsible for holding 27 kilometers of the Vistula Defense Line with a combined front-line *Kampfstärke* of 7,409 men. The *panzer* regiments of all three divisions occupied reserve positions close to the main defense line, where they could quickly swing into action when required.

This equated to a rather favorable troop density of 274 men per kilometer, the highest the corps had enjoyed up to that point, but this was still less than half of what was doctrinally called for. This unaccustomed high German troop density would be a telling factor in the fighting to come. Despite this welcome development, on the eve of battle the commander of *9. Armee* rated Gille's corps as only being "moderately strong enough in tanks to fight a defensive battle, but since it burns up its infantry so quickly, its front line strength is very thin." Although von Lüttwitz recognized Gille's predicament, he still intended to withdraw the bulk of the *19. Pz.Div.* as soon as the rest of the newly arrived *Luftwaffe* replacements were incorporated into the corps' two SS divisions.[22]

Lined up opposite Gille's three divisions were 15 Soviet divisions—10 divisions in the first attacking echelon, with five more in the second, or follow-on, echelon. The *Wiking* Division directly faced three Soviet divisions—the 38th Guards Rifle and 160th and 413th Rifle Divisions of the 70th Army; the *Totenkopf* was also up against three—the 132nd, 260th, and 328th Rifle Divisions of the 47th Army; while the *19. Pz.Div.* was opposed by four—the 143rd, 234th, and 76th Rifle Divisions and the 2nd Polish Division, also of the 47th Army (the Polish unit was under the tactical control of the 47th Army for this operation). The night before the attack, the forward outposts of the *19. Pz.Div.* reported hearing the sounds of Red Army troops singing and raising cheers in their assembly areas, signs that alcohol had been issued to stiffen their morale.[23]

General Popov's VIII Guards Tank Corps would divide its brigades between both armies, with most of his tanks oriented on the boundary between the *Totenkopf*

The *Totenkopf* Division Fighting at Siedlce, 27–31 July 1944

The following photographs were taken by *SS-Kriegsberichter* Hermann Grönert on 29 July 1944, when a *Kampfgruppe* consisting of *SS-Panzergrenadier Regiment 6 Theodor Eicke*, along with the *Pz. V* Panther-equipped *I. Abteilung/SS-Panzer Regiment 3 Totenkopf* from the *3. SS-Pz.Div. Totenkopf* fought in and around the town of Siedlce. For five days, the *Totenkopf* held this town, designated as an *Eckpfeiler* (cornerstone) by the commander of *H.Gr. Mitte*, against repeated assaults by the 11th Tank Corps from 27–31 July 1944 to enable the bulk of *2. Armee*, including the *Wiking* Division, to withdraw to a new defense line and get into position for the tank battle of Praga which began on 1 August (All photos courtesy of the Günther Lange Archive; other sources include Red Army war diaries revealed in the online article, "In the Footsteps of the Siedlce "IS" by Igor Zlobin, 18 September 2019).

A squad of *Panzergrenadiers* from *SS-Pz.Gren.Rgt. 6 Theodor Eicke* staring with awe at a Josef Stalin II (JS-II) heavy tank from the 50th Guards Separate Tank Regiment that has just been knocked out at approximately 1:40 p.m. on the northwestern outskirts of Siedlce by *Stubaf.* Erwin Meierdress's Panthers. The JS-II had only been introduced to battle during the late winter of 1944 and was initially assigned only to special separate heavy tank regiments. The early model of the tank weighed 51 short tons, was equipped with a 12.2cm main gun, and had a crew of four. Each heavy tank regiment was equipped with 21 of these vehicles, consisting of four companies of five tanks each, with one for the battalion commander. Its emergence posed a considerable threat to existing German armor.

Having examined the immobilized giant, the soldiers turn towards the cameraman as they prepare to move on to the next objective. In the background, a T-34/85 from the 20th Tank Brigade burns after being struck by the 7.5cm armored-piercing shells fired by Meierdress's Panthers. On the left, the squad's machine gunner looks on calmly at the photographer, as he rests his weapon, a *Maschinegewehr* (machine gun) model M.G. 34 on the ground. The desperation of the fighting is stamped on all of their faces, as is the fatigue they must have felt after undergoing several days of sustained heavy combat in stifling heat.

A close-up image of the *Panzergrenadiers* from the previous page depicts the squad leader, armed with an *Maschine-Pistole* (submachine gun) model *M.Pi. 40* urging his men to move, including the machine gunner who has picked up his weapon. Interestingly, most of the men in this photograph sequence appear to be wearing white neck scarves but no camouflaged outer garments. On the far left, another knocked-out T-34/85 burns fiercely after being struck by German shells.

Two *Panzergrenadiers* from the *Totenkopf* Division rush past the burning T-34. Both of them appear to be carrying a minimal amount of equipment, although the soldier in the front has a bundle wrapped in his camouflaged *Zeltbahn* (shelter quarter) strapped on to his equipment suspenders. The summer heat during the last several days of July 1944 was intense, causing many men from both sides to go into battle with as little extraneous equipment as possible.

Two *Panzergrenadiers* from the *Totenkopf* Division rush past an immobilized Soviet T-34 from the 20th Tank Brigade of the 11th Tank Corps on the outskirts of Siedlce, 29 July 1944 while a destroyed tank burns in the background. (Photo by Hermann Grönert)

Another infantry squad from the *Totenkopf* Division closely examines a T-34/85 from the 1st Battalion of the 20th Tank Brigade abandoned on the outskirts of Siedlce. According to the Soviet after action report, "The 1st Tank Battalion of the [20th Tank] Brigade rushed into the city of Siedlce and began fighting against enemy tanks, artillery and infantry. Due to the lack [of our own] infantry and artillery cover, the battalion was withdrawn to the southwestern outskirts of Siedlce." During fighting on 29 July 1944, according to its own report, 18 tanks of all types, including T-34s, several JS-IIs, and M-4 Shermans, were destroyed in and around the city by the troops of the *Totenkopf* Division, including several knocked out by troops using *Panzerfaust* anti-tank weapons.

T-34/85 number 210, seen in the image above, has been placed into operation by its captors. With its red star marked out by white chalk, and a hasty *Balkankreuz* (the Balkan Cross, recognition symbol of the German armed forces) sketched on the side of the turret, its new owners sample some of the goods found inside, including a bottle of wine. Operation of captured enemy equipment in such fluid combat situations always entailed certain risks, because other armored vehicles frequently fired at vehicle outlines rather than waiting for visual confirmation of whether it was actually friend or foe!

A Volkswagen *Schwimmwagen* (amphibious scout car) from *SS-Pz.Aufkl.Abt. 3* of the *Totenkopf* Division drives down a side street on the outskirts of Siedlce, 29 July 1944. A close examination of the photograph reveals that six soldiers are riding inside, including men who are possibly wounded. This specialized vehicle, intended to carry no more than four passengers, would have been overloaded by this point, but the shortage of ambulances often resulted in any available vehicles being pressed into service to carry wounded to the nearest field dressing station.

Three *Panzergrenadiers* from the *Totenkopf* Division examine holes in the turret and hull of a JS-II knocked out by Panthers of *Stubaf.* Meierdress's battalion. Turret number 111, according to Soviet wartime records, indicates that it was assigned to the 2nd Platoon of the 2nd Company of the 50th Guards Separate Tank Regiment. This particular tank was commanded by the platoon leader, Senior Lieutenant Alexander T. Sevastyanov, who was killed in action on 29 July. His was one of two JS-IIs destroyed that day, while a third one was knocked out but later recovered by the regiment and placed back in service after being repaired.

Here, several *Panzergrenadiers* from the *Totenkopf* Division are being issued *Panzerfausts* and additional ammunition before being rushed once again back into battle. Using weapons such as these and supported by tanks and assault guns, the SS troops from this division stalked the tanks from the 11th Tank Corps that had broken into Siedlce during the early afternoon. Initiating ambushes from side streets, houses and alleyways, the Germans inflicted heavy losses on the 20th Tank Brigade, the 12th Motorized Infantry Brigade, and the 50th Guards Separate Tank Regiment and drove them out of Siedlce on 29 July 1944, but Soviet forces resumed their attack with additional forces the following day.

Troops from the *Totenkopf* Division, most likely from one of the battalions of the *Eicke* Regiment, march towards their next objective, shrouded in smoke in the near distance. While the Soviet 11th Tank Corps suffered heavy losses during the fighting for Siedlce between 27 and 31 July 1944, the *Totenkopf* Division's were not insignificant. Contemporary Soviet reports claimed the destruction of four German tanks (including two Panthers), five antitank guns, and several vehicles carrying ammunition on 29 July alone. While the Germans reported their own losses as being considerable, the *Totenkopf* Division grimly held on to Siedlce until its regiments were ordered to withdraw on 31 July, having bought the time the rest of *2. Armee* needed to withdraw and concentrate its forces for the next phase of the campaign.

On the right, *SS-Ostubaf.* Erwin Meierdress, commander of *I. Abt./SS-Panzer Regiment 3*, confers with an officer from the division's reconnaissance battalion, while a Soviet tank burns in the background. (Courtesy of the Günther Lange Archive)

Fighting all day in hot, dusty conditions placed an enormous physical strain on the combatants on both sides. In this photo, two soldiers from the *Totenkopf* Division quench their thirst from canteens while standing in front of another knocked out Soviet T-34. Both of these men are veterans, evidenced by *Panzervernichtungs Abzeichen* (Tank Destruction Badge) on the upper right sleeve of the *Unterscharführer* (Sergeant) on the left. This award was presented to soldiers who had knocked out enemy armor using hand-held weapons, such as the *Panzerfaust* (a hollow-charge antitank projectile), antitank mines, or hand grenade bundles. Many of these awards were earned during the savage fighting for Siedlce, where the men of the *Totenkopf* Division fought for five days against hundreds of Soviet tanks attempting to take this important town. (Photo by Hermann Grönert)

An infantry squad withdraws through a swirling cloud of black smoke from a burning Soviet tank. The look of desperation on the soldier's face is indicative of the severity of the fighting. (Photo by *SS-Kriegsberichter* Hermann Grönert, courtesy of Angel Mansolas)

SS-Stubaf. Meierdress confers with an unnamed *SS-Hauptsturmführer*, the commander of an infantry unit, somewhere outside the town of Siedlce. (Photo by *SS-Kriegsberichter* Hermann Grönert, courtesy of the Günther Lange Archive)

and *Wiking* Divisions southeast of Nieporet in the 70th Army's area.[24] His corps, consisting primarily of the 58th, 59th, and 60th Guards Tank Brigades and the 28th Guards Motorized Rifle Brigade, was equipped primarily with T-34/85 tanks, as well as a large number of Lend-Lease M-4 Shermans, but the corps' 62nd Guards Separate Tank Regiment had been recently re-equipped with JS-II heavy tanks, having 21 of them as authorized by its table of organization. While the 47th and 70th Armies were augmented by separate tank regiments from the First Belorussian Front's reserves, it would be the task of the VIII Guards Tank Corps to exploit the breakthrough once it took place.

In order to understand the course of the battle that was about to begin, one must gain an appreciation of the important role that terrain would play and how it would influence the fighting. The first point to realize was that the area occupied by the *IV. SS-Pz.Korps* was not nicknamed the Wet Triangle in jest. Besides being bounded to the north by the east–west flowing Narew River and to the west and southwest by the north–south flowing Vistula, there were numerous smaller rivers and streams running in a north–south direction between Nieporet and Praga, as well as rivers and streams running southeast–northeast between Michałow-Grabina and Skrzeszew with swamps in between. Most of the southern bank of the Narew between Rynia and Wieliszew on the corps' left flank was poorly drained marshland and sand dunes, nearly unnavigable by tanks, but once any armor was able to traverse the paved highway connecting Zegrze on the Narew to Jablonna on the Vistula, the terrain flattened out and became considerably drier. The Soviet objective was to reach this highway, and once all their forces closed up they would advance in a line to Modlin.

In the center of the *Wiking* Division's sector ran the Krolewski Canal, while in the *Totenkopf*'s were the Brodnowski and Nowy Canals, both man-made drainage features that were serious obstacles to movement in their own right, which necessitated holding a number of bridges to guarantee freedom of movement or their destruction to avoid having them fall into enemy hands. Two highway bridges north of Nieporet along the Krolewski Canal had already been destroyed on 2 October to prevent them from being used by the Soviets. Much of the *Wiking* Division's main defense line was in swampy ground with a very high water table, which made digging foxholes a chore, hence the area's well-deserved nickname. Only the large forest east and northeast of Nieporet held any high ground. The *Wiking*'s primary mission was to block the enemy's attempt to use the high speed avenue of approach running up the corridor connecting Nieport to Zegrze.

The *Totenkopf*'s front line was similarly situated, but Becker had positioned much of his actual front-line defensive positions in the wooded heights in the forest west of the line running from Tomaszow to Rembelsz. His division's primary mission was to block the enemy from advancing northwest along the secondary movement corridor running from Rembelsz to Łajsk, a small town 5 kilometers north of the urban complex of Jablonna-Legjonowo, which had to be held at all costs. The forest in both divisions' sectors would channel most of the Soviet armor into kill zones; therefore in order to succeed, the enemy would have to overcome German defenses in the forest flanking these corridors before their armor could move freely.

Most of the *19. Pz.Div.* defensive sector was located in the built-up area encompassing Rożopole, Płudy, Henryków, and Żerań. Its right flank was secure, being anchored on the Vistula, but two high-speed avenues of approach ran through its area of operations—the rail line running from Praga to Modlin and the paved all-weather highway that ran parallel to the railway to Modlin. The terrain did not always work to the Germans' advantage. The Vistula River itself separated a portion of Källner's division from its main body, since he had to occupy a few kilometers of the western bank with *Pz.Aufkl.Abt. 19.* Once the battle was joined, this battalion would be effectively out of the fight due to its mission to defend along the river and secure the 12-ton pontoon bridge at Młociny.

Rokossovsky's staff took all of these adverse terrain factors into consideration and crafted a plan designed to negate the Germans' advantages and the terrain's negative influences upon the upcoming operation, including the addition of construction engineer battalions to repair roads and build field-expedient bridges as soon as they were taken by the infantry. However, success would ultimately depend upon close cooperation between the rifle divisions and tank brigades of the VIII Guards Tank Corps, supported by an overwhelming amount of artillery and rocket fire. Colonel General of Aviation Sergey Rudenko's 16th Air Army's fleet of fighter and ground-attack aircraft would be constantly overhead, doing everything in their power to keep the *Luftwaffe* at bay while harassing and bombing Gille's troop and supply installations.

The third battle of Warsaw began on a foggy morning at 9 a.m. on Tuesday, 10 October with an enormously destructive 100-minute artillery and rocket barrage that blanketed the front-line positions of all three of Gille's divisions, focusing on identified infantry and heavy weapons emplacements, including those protecting their machine guns, antitank guns, and mortars. These had to be eliminated or at least suppressed to facilitate the assault of the rifle battalions, which were vulnerable to their devastating fire during the few minutes it took to charge the last 500 meters of open ground that lay in front of the German forward positions. After half an hour of this bombardment, the Soviet fire lifted and immediately shifted to the next set of targets a few kilometers to the rear, consisting of command and observations posts, reserve positions, and communication centers. When this fire lifted, that was the signal for the infantry assault to begin.

To facilitate the attacking troops' movement to their line of departure, sappers had cleared lanes through German minefields the previous evening and obstacles were identified for demolition by follow-on combat engineers from the 57th Assault Engineer Brigade. Supported by waves of ground-attack aircraft from the 16th Air Army (the *19. Pz.Div.* reported 74 IL-2 *Sturmoviks* and Douglas A-20 "Bostons" operating in their air space alone at one point that morning), the Red Army infantry

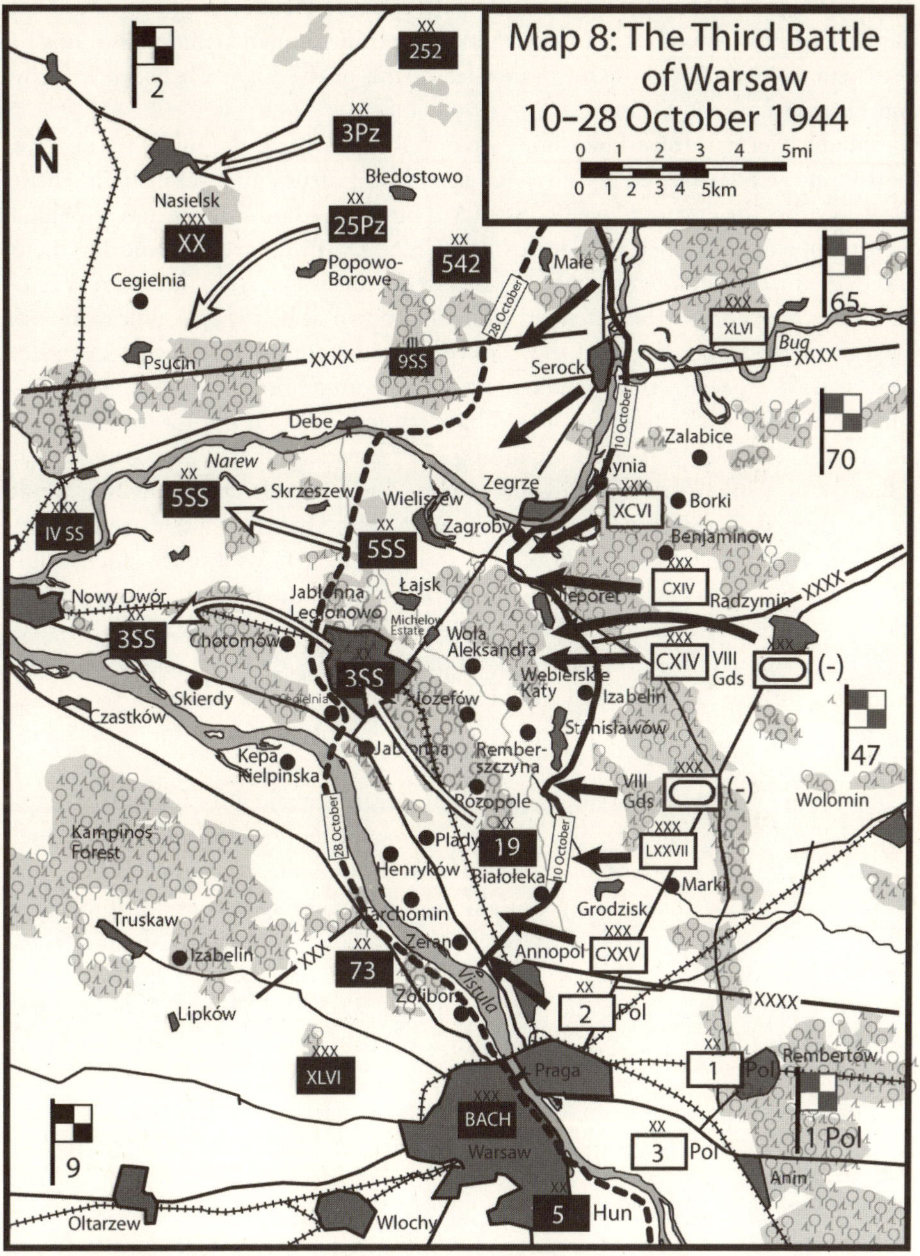
Map 8: The Third Battle of Warsaw 10–28 October 1944
0 1 2 3 4 5mi
0 1 2 3 4 5km
N
2
252
3Pz
25Pz
542
9SS
XX
Nasielsk
Błedostowo
Popowo-Borowe
Cegielnia
Psucin
Male
Serock
XLVI
Bug
65
70
Zalabice
Debe
Narew
5SS
Skrzeszew
Wieliszew
Zegrze
Zagroby
IV SS
XCVI
Borki
Benjaminow
Łajsk
Jabłonna
Legionowo
Nowy Dwór
3SS
Chotomów
Michelow Estate
Wola Aleksandra
Nieporet
CXIV
Radzymin
VIII Gds
(-)
47
Skierdy
Czastków
Józefów
Webierskie Katy
Izabelin
Stanisławów
Kepa Kielpinska
Jabłonna
Rember-szczyzna
Rozopole
Wolomin
28 October
10 October
Kampinos Forest
Plady
19
Henryków
Białołeka
LXXVII
Marki
Tarchomin
Grodzisk
Truskaw
Izabelin
73
Zeran
Annopol
CXXV
Vistula
Zolibor
2 Pol
Lipków
XLVI
Praga
1 Pol
Rembertów
BACH
Warsaw
3 Pol
Anin
9
5 Hun
Oltarzew
Wlochy

surged forward through the morning fog into the German front-line infantry positions before their enemy could recover from the shelling, in an effort to clear the way for the follow-on Soviet tank assault.[25] As the infantry fought one another, the Red artillery fire lifted again, this time targeting German artillery positions for destruction, including those on the western bank of the Vistula between Młociny and Dabrowa.

Though German front-line troops were well entrenched, the initial barrage was devastating. Characterized by survivors as reaching drumfire level in its intensity, the heavy shelling destroyed well-constructed bunkers, troop shelters, and individual fighting positions. Trench lines were buried, along with the troops manning them, and barbed wire and other obstacles obliterated. Communication lines were severed and roads plowed up. The defenders hunkered down as best they could; many had lived through such barrages on the Eastern Front before and knew what to expect. New arrivals, especially those who had been transferred from the *Luftwaffe* after just a few weeks of sketchy training, would have panicked were it not for the reassuring words and examples of the still-remaining *alte Hasen* ("old hares," slang for veteran infantrymen), who knew that anyone who tried to escape from the shelling would be slaughtered. Astonishingly, German morale held; after all, these three divisions were considered to be composed of elite troops, and that knowledge alone would have been enough to sustain them—as well as some of the residual "SS spirit" that the men of the *Totenkopf* and *Wiking* Divisions had been inculcated with since their inception. As the minutes passed, all three of Gille's divisions sat and took this pounding—there was little they could do except wait for the storm to pass. Then the real fighting would begin, when they would have to deal with the approaching Soviet infantry.

According to one historian, the Soviet infantry attacked with great courage, but "the units carrying out the fighting were noticeably undermanned, which negatively affected their combat ability. It was only thanks to the massive artillery bombardment that the infantry was able to make even small inroads during the attack's first hours."[26] German troops in the path of the assault, which affected virtually the entire front of the corps, do not seem to have noticed any slackening of their combat ability, for the soldiers of the 47th and 70th Armies attacked with their customary gusto and disregard for losses. The Germans suffered heavy casualties too; the *Totenkopf* Division, which was the focus of the initial Soviet *Schwerpunkt*, or point of main effort, saw some of its front-line infantry companies reduced in a matter of minutes from 80–100 men to platoons of only 25–30 men due to the devastating barrage.

By 10:10 a.m., as it began to rain, Gille's operations staff had reported to their counterparts at *9. Armee* that Rokossovsky's massive attack had already begun punching through the corps' front line in several locations. Penetrations up to several kilometers deep had been made by the 234th Rifle Division towards Tarchomin and Henryków in the sector held by the *19. Pz.Div.* Assisted by the Polish 6th Infantry Regiment of the 2nd Infantry Division and SU-85 assault guns from the 13th Artillery Regiment, the Soviet troops and their allies had managed to push as far north as the town of Wiśniewo, held by troops from *Maj.* Nähring's *Pz.Gren. Rgt. 73.* The *Totenkopf* Division was assailed from its Rożopole sector to Hill 101 west of Jósefów, and from there 10 kilometers north to Hill 90 southwest of Woła Aleksandra, where it linked up with the right flank of the *Wiking* Division, held by the *Westland* Regiment. At the same time in the *Wiking*'s sector, the Soviet attack had reached as far as the southern outskirts of Nieporet and was already beginning to advance into the large forest southwest of the town.[27]

In its midday report, Gille's staff stated that tank-supported counterattacks consisting of the last available reserves from his divisions were already underway to regain the lost ground, including several in the Wiśniewo area by the *19. Pz.Div.* and in the Tomaszów and Rożopole areas by the *Totenkopf* Division. *Hauptmann* Meier, the new commander of *I. Btl./Pz.Gren.Rgt. 74*, led a battalion counterattack that threw the Soviets out of Wiśniewo and pushed them back across the north–south railroad line towards Białoleka, until he was seriously injured when his *SPW* drove into a ditch while taking evasive action. Elsewhere in the division sector, the guns of *Pz.Rgt. 27* kept enemy tanks at bay, particularly in the Żeran area, and by nightfall the division's *HKL* has been restored to where it had been that morning. After the fighting, *Gen.Lt.* Källner reported that his division had taken 38 prisoners and counted 400 dead Soviet troops.[28]

This *Totenkopf* Division's largest counterattacks were directed that afternoon towards retaking Rożopole and preventing the Soviets from advancing on Jablonna-Legjonowo. After heavy fighting, the division was able to restore part of the old *Hauptkampflinie* southeast of Hill 101 near Jósefów using *Stubaf.* Eckert's *II. Btl./ SS-Pz.Gren.Rgt. 6 Eicke* and six Tiger tanks of *9. Kp./SS-Pz.Rgt. 3*. After heavy fighting, including the destruction of eight Soviet tanks that had attacked from the direction of Rembelsz, Becker's counterattack finally succeeded in restoring the division's *HKL* shortly before nightfall, though not without casualties.[29] Some *Totenköpfler* who had been presumed lost turned up later that day, revealing that their forward positions had been bypassed during the morning's initial attack and that they had to attack the Soviet troops from behind in order to regain their own lines.[30] Many other stragglers turned up that night as well, having evaded Soviet troops who had saturated the area.

Throughout the division's main defense line, its armor losses on this first day were relatively high, mostly consisting of five assault guns from *SS-StuG.Abt. 3* that were totally destroyed (*ausgebrannt*) by Soviet antitank guns while supporting infantry counterattacks, as well as one *Pz. IV* and a Tiger damaged. During the heavy fighting, the commander of *II. Btl./SS-Pz.Rgt. 3*, *Stubaf.* Fritz Biermeier, was seriously wounded when his command post was struck by enemy fire while he was observing his battalion's counterattack. Biermeier, who had been awarded the Knight's Cross the previous December, died the following day in the division's field hospital. Three months later, he was posthumously awarded the Oak Leaves in recognition of his and his battalion's achievements during the defense of the Vistula Line.[31]

Along the boundary between the *Totenkopf* and *Wiking* Divisions, things were just as hot as everywhere else in the corps' sector. A number of Soviet tanks were spotted assembling for an attack east of the village of Rembelsz, but these had been spotted by the *Luftwaffe* despite the rainy weather, and soon suffered a large-scale attack by German dive-bombers at 2:15 p.m. During this *Stuka* attack, several Soviet tanks were reported as being destroyed, relieving some of the pressure being exerted against the right flank of the *Westland* Regiment and alleviating the threat of a large-scale tank attack from unfolding along the Jósefów–Legjonowo corridor.[32]

While the *Totenkopf* Division was successful in preventing the Soviet advance from reaching Jablonna-Legjonowo and had succeeded in throwing them out of Rożopole and restoring much of its old front line, the *Wiking* Division was having serious difficulties. At roughly the same time as the *Stuka* strike, the *Wiking* Division reported that the advancing spearhead of the CXIV Rifle Corps had pushed into the Jablonna forest as far as 700 meters east of Hill 90, effectively skirting the far-right flank of the division and bypassing the defenses at Aleksandrów along the Krolewski Canal. These troops were only stopped by another *Totenkopf* Division counterattack. A few kilometers to the north, house-to-house fighting had already broken out in the southern outskirts of Nieporet by mid-afternoon.

Even more dangerous was the continuing westward advance into the Jablonna forest of the 38th Guards Rifle Division, whose spearheads had penetrated all the way through the woods from the church in Nieporet as far as a point 500 meters east of the Michalow estate, a mere 5 kilometers northeast of Jablonna-Legjonow. During this attack, *Stubaf.* Nedderhof's *III. Btl./Westland*, which had only been back with the division for less than three weeks, was overrun and its survivors scattered into the woods before they were collected and reorganized into their old companies once again. All of its company commanders had been either killed or wounded. Nedderhof's command post was cut off and isolated, though he and his headquarters group continued fighting. The reassembled battalion, supported by five Panthers from *Ostuf.* Lichte's *5. Kp./SS-Pz.Rgt. 5* and one *StuG IV* from *Ostuf.* Hans Weerts's *4. Kompanie*, then counterattacked and was able to reach the battalion's command post, rescuing Nedderhof and reestablishing a weak screening line in the forest. *Staf.* Mühlenkamp, still acting as the division commander though technically he had been replaced by *Staf.* Ullrich, showed up on the scene and directed the *Wiking* Division's response to the crisis himself.[33]

The *5. Kompanie* Panthers were then released to return to their reserve position when the remaining seven *StuG IV* of *4. Kompanie* arrived. Leaving four behind to support Nedderhof's troops in the forest, the rest of the assault gun company continued pushing to the south, attacking the Soviet troops in the flank, finally halting when they reached as far as the church in Nieporet on the town's western outskirts. Here, Weerts waited for reinforcements before continuing his assault. At 3:30 p.m., the *Wiking* Division's reserve, *2. Kp./SS-Pz. Rgt. 5*, commanded by *Ostuf.* Leopold Mittelbacher, and the *SPW*-mounted *10. Kompanie* of *III. Btl./Germania* began rolling south along the eastern edge of the wood line from their reserve position 5 kilometers away near the forester's house at Kontrowers. Mittelbacher's company had just returned from two months of reconstitution at the Debiča training area and was at full strength with 17 brand-new *Pz. IVH* models when it rejoined his battalion.

As this strong armored force approached Nieporet, it was fired upon by two separate Soviet *Pakfronts* that had been hurriedly emplaced along the town's northern and northwestern outskirts. In quick succession, five *Pz. IV* tanks were knocked out, as well as one of the *Panzergrenadiers*' armored half-tracks. Mittelbacher himself was wounded during the action and died later that day from his wounds. The remaining tanks and infantry pulled back to the safety of the woods, while the survivors from the damaged tanks made their way back on foot to join them (four *Pz. IV* were later written off as total losses). After linking up with the *4. Kompanie*, the *2. Kompanie*, now under the temporary command of *Ustuf.* Helmut Bauer, formed a screening line to prevent the Soviets from advancing any further. The *Westland* Regiment's reserve, its *I. Bataillon*, was brought up to the Kontrowers area and pushed south through the Jablonna forest, linking up with the tanks and establishing contact with the left flank of what remained of Nedderhof's shattered battalion. For the time being, the hole in the front caused by the Soviet push past Nieporet had been plugged, though most of the town itself was firmly in enemy hands.

On the division's left flank, the situation was far from rosy. Here, along the southern bank of the Narew, the 160th Rifle Division, shielded by a smoke screen, steadily worked its way towards the west, pushing aside the forward outposts of *Hstuf.* Borchert's *SS-Pz.Aufkl.Abt. 5* arrayed between the village of Bialobrzegi and Nieporet. As the reconnaissance battalion was forced back under Soviet pressure, losing two of its supporting *Jagd.Pz. IV* tank destroyers in the process, *Hstuf.* Franz Pleiner's *II. Btl./Germania* on Borchert's left, positioned on the other side of the river opposite the village of Rynia, had no choice but to withdraw as well, before it finally stopped at Zegrze. Here, the reconnaissance battalion dug in along the railroad embankment connecting Zagroby with Jablonna-Legjonowo, though since the bridge at Zegrze had already been blown up, they had no physical contact with Pleiner's troops. Meanwhile, the *II. Btl./Germania* established a new defensive line stretching from Zegrze to the north, where the rest of *Ostubaf.* Dorr's *Germania* Regiment, along with *Hstuf.* Flügel's two tank companies, reported nothing except strong harassing artillery fire throughout the day. Due to the smoke screen being laid on the southern bank of the Narew, they saw very little of the unfolding action taking place there.

The corps' artillery had been busy all day, firing accurate barrages on Soviet troop concentrations and attacking tank and infantry formations, as well as carrying out counter-battery fire against Soviet artillery groupings. The German batteries also had to endure both Soviet artillery fire and air attacks, which required that they change firing positions as frequently as possible, a contingency that the corps *ARKO* had insisted they prepare for. The most remarkable achievement that day was the heroic actions of one of the *Totenkopf* Division's artillery batteries when it was threatened with being overrun by Soviet infantry that had broken through the *Wiking* Division's right flank that morning. The unit, *8. Batterie* of *III.Abt./SS-Pz. Art.Rgt. 3*, commanded by *Hstuf.* Paul Grund, had kept on firing a pre-planned fire support mission with its six 10.5cm howitzers even after all wire communications with the infantry had been severed by Soviet shells.[34]

Suddenly, at 10:00 a.m., approximately 600 Soviet troops appeared from the woods only 500 meters in front of their firing positions and began charging in the direction of his battery, located a few hundred meters northeast of the Michałow estate. Having no infantry of his own for protection in such an eventuality, Grund ordered his artillerymen to depress their guns and fire over open sights instead of telling them to flee. On his instructions, shells were loaded with Charge 1 (the lowest possible propellant charge as it was virtually point-blank range) and fuses set to activate their explosives at only 80–100 meters after leaving the gun tubes. The result was carnage.

While some members of the battery fired at the approaching enemy troops with rifles and machine guns, and even engaged in hand-to-hand combat when some Soviet infantrymen reached the gun positions, the rest of the gunners sweated over their pieces, firing shell after shell into the closely packed masses of brown-clad troops. Several hours later, when the smoke finally cleared, Grund's battery had successfully held its ground. Fifty dead Soviet troops lay within the battery's position; there were so many enemy dead lying in front of the guns they could not be counted. Grund and his gunners remained in place throughout the rest of the day and continued firing missions in support of the various counterattacks that were carried out. Numerous similar examples of dedication to duty by the *Totenkopf*'s soldiers help to explain how the division withstood the nearly overwhelming Soviet attacks that day, and even managed to restore its old front line in most places.

Everywhere else along the *9. Armee*'s Vistula Front, nothing much was reported as happening except the usual random shelling and patrol activity. There were no available armor reserves to send anyway, since the army's only other *panzer* division, the newly redesignated *Fs.Pz.Div. 1 Hermann Göring*, had been shipped to East Prussia four days earlier. One tank battalion from *19. Pz.Div.* was positioned outside of Warsaw, but since it had been designated as part of the army group's reserve, it could not be touched without *Gen.Oberst* Reinhardt's permission. The only other unit that von Lüttwitz could possibly spare was the newly arrived *337. Volks-Gren. Div.*, but this was still undergoing training and was not yet completely equipped nor even remotely ready for combat. The only reinforcement that *Gen.d.Pz.Tr.* von Lüttwitz could send Gille's way that evening was the badly understrength *SS-Jäg. Btl. 501*, recently freed up for further employment when *Gruppe von dem Bach* was disbanded several days before.[35] This was to be *IV. SS-Pz.Korps*' own fight for the next week and a half.

That evening in his report to *9. Armee* for 10 October, Gille summarized the day's events and the countermeasures taken so far. He started his narrative by stating that the Soviet offensive that he had long predicted had finally begun, developing along the lines and in the strength that he had believed it would follow. His intelligence staff had identified eight rifle divisions and the sapper brigade, as well as three other previously unidentified divisions that had not yet been committed. The anticipated main effort of the offensive, which would be signaled by the commitment of the VIII Guards Tank Corps along the line stretching from Hill 96 west of Tomaszów to Rembelsz, had not yet unfolded, primarily due to the infantry's failure to break through the German defenses and roll up their main defensive line, a prerequisite to launching the tank brigades *en masse*, per Soviet doctrine.

The *IV. SS-Pz.Korps* had inflicted a great deal of damage against its assailants, claiming the destruction of 21 Soviet tanks (13 by the *Totenkopf* Division alone), comprising eight T-34/76, eight T-34/85, two JS-II, and three assault guns. It had also destroyed or captured four infantry howitzers, 15 antitank guns, and numerous machine guns and other small arms.[36] Thousands of Soviet troops had probably been killed or wounded, but neither had Gille's losses been unsubstantial. Though casualty reports for the first day are no longer available, his three divisions must have lost hundreds of men killed or wounded. Although the *19. Pz.Div.* and the *Totenkopf* Division had more or less been able to restore their main defense lines by the evening, the situation on the *Wiking* Division's right flank and center were very worrying, and there appeared little hope of restoring its old front line based on its rapidly declining strength.

To reinforce impressions of the severity of the fighting, Gille informed his army commander that his *Panzergrenadier* battalions had been so weakened, that even if his troops were able to restore the *HKL* to where it had been before the offensive began, they would be stretched so thinly that they would not be able to hold it in the face of another similar attack, which he expected the next day. He went so far in his report to chide von Lüttwitz and his staff by stating that if the *9. Armee* had provided him the forces that he had originally asked for, the Soviets would not have achieved any success at all that day. This point was debatable; given the severity of the initial barrage, which completely plowed up the corps' front-line positions, adding another division to his order of battle may have only increased the number of casualties suffered. As it was, Gille estimated, based on initial reports, that his corps had suffered the loss of 1,000 men on the first day alone, losses he could not spare.[37]

As it were, the only substantial combat power remaining in the *Totenkopf* and *Wiking* Divisions lay in their armored regiments (the *19. Pz.Div.* had not suffered nearly as much). Without them, Gille believed, none of his counterattacks would have succeeded. To further rub salt in the wound, Gille trumpeted the success of his preemptive barrage on the night of 8–9 September, and reminded the *9. Armee* staff that if he had been supplied with the extra ammunition he had requested, he might have been able to forestall the Soviet offensive indefinitely. This too was an exaggeration, although another preemptive barrage would have lessened the severity of the attack when it finally came.

Regarding Soviet intentions, Gille made it clear in his report that based on prisoner interrogations and the course of the fighting that had taken place so far, the First Belorussian Front definitely intended to establish a bridgehead across the Vistula near Modlin and to eliminate all German forces in the Vistula–Narew triangle. Mention of another bridgehead being established immediately north of Praga had dropped from his report, since it had become clear that neither the 47th Army nor 1st Polish Army was planning such an operation. He did close, however, by stating that several prisoners taken that day had said that their orders were to "keep advancing until they reached and crossed over the Vistula," but Gille believed that they had a far deeper operational goal than merely destroying his corps and crossing a river. This assessment essentially dovetailed with Rokossovsky's (and the STAVKA's) intentions, though Gille of course had no idea of the timeline for future Soviet operations.

In his own report to the *H.Gr. Mitte* commander later that evening, von Lüttwitz repeated much of what Gille had already said in his, adding that although enemy losses had been extraordinarily high, his own troops had unfortunately suffered correspondingly heavy casualties. The *9. Armee* commander, rather than wasting space in an official communication describing how Gille had been correct all along, was clearly more concerned about preventing the 47th and 70th Armies from crossing the Vistula.[38] There was not much else he could do for Gille, except continue providing him with the supplies that he needed, particularly ammunition and fuel for his *panzers*. Later that evening, the disturbing news arrived that the 12-ton pontoon bridge over the Vistula at Młociny had been damaged by a direct hit; this immediately affected the *19. Pz.Div.* Though still passable for foot movement, it would require further repair to allow vehicles to move across it once again. Such efforts were begun immediately. Fortunately for Gille, since 1 October, most of the supplies for his two SS divisions and corps troops were being provided by the *2. Armee Oberquartiermeister* via the bridges over the Narew at Modlin.[39]

To form a screening line along the west bank of the Vistula line between Warsaw and Modlin should the Soviets destroy Gille's corps, all that von Lüttwitz could scrape together were two engineer battalions and a *Pionier* regiment staff, to be augmented by *Art.Brig. 140*, and if needed, by the remaining tank battalion from the *19. Pz.Div.*, which still lay in army group reserve near Warsaw. At least this small force could observe and report any crossing attempts, and try to delay it until more forces could be brought to bear. He also enquired whether *2. Armee* could release the *25. Pz.Div.*, still fighting north of the Narew in the wake of the failed *Sonnenblume* offensive, but the *H.Gr. Mitte* chief of staff informed him that he would have to wait 24 hours for an answer. That would have to do, at least for now. The *9. Armee* commander's instructions for the following day to Gille were to continue with his defense and restore the former *HKL*. Assigning the first task was superfluous; Gille was planning to do that anyway. The latter was to prove impossible with the forces at Gille's disposal. One thing that did not change was that the initiative still lay with the enemy; the course of the next day's operations would prove a repeat of the first.

Fighting continued throughout the evening, particularly in the *19. Pz.Div.* sector. The key village of Marcelin, which lay alongside the Praga–Modlin rail line, had been retaken in a counterattack the previous afternoon, but fell again to a nighttime Soviet assault, which necessitated yet another counterattack by *Gen.Lt.* Källner's division reserve at 5:15 a.m.[40] As 11 October dawned, another wet, cold day, both sides prepared their attacks—the Germans to regain lost ground, the Soviets to resume their offensive at first light. Gille's corps artillery under *Brig.Fhr.* Brasack's direction fired two more preventive strikes at Soviet assembly areas designed to forestall the attack, but no noteworthy effects were observed. Soviet artillery fires had slackened noticeably at first light, a sign that their guns were being moved forward to provide continuing support to their forces as they advanced deeper into their zone of attack. The sounds of tanks moving up in the fog were reported at Marcelin and Tomaszów at 6:35 a.m.

At 10:00 a.m., another drumfire barrage of 20 minutes' duration (described by one survivor as a "hail of iron") was directed against each of the three divisions of the corps, a sign that the offensive had resumed.[41] By late morning, most of the heavy fighting was confined to the area between Tomaszów and Wiśniewo along the boundary between the *Totenkopf* and *19. Pz.Div.*, in the Rembelsz area, and in the woods on either side of Nieporet, where the *Wiking* Division observed a large Soviet force assembling. All of Gille's corps reserves had been committed by early morning, and except for any small reserve force his divisions could assemble, all that he could provide to help was artillery fire and ensure that ammunition and fuel kept flowing their way.

In the *19. Pz.Div.* sector, the town of Marcelin changed hands four times, while the neighboring village of Lejanów was lost and retaken six times, an indication of the intensity of the fighting. Masses of Soviet infantry were being thrown at the division's main defense line in an effort to break through and gain control of the railroad and highway leading to Modlin. Despite its heavy losses, Källner's troops prevented the Soviets from breaking through. When the *Totenkopf* Division attempted its own counterattack shortly after noon to restore the remaining portion of its old *HKL* between Rembelsz and Michałow, its troops collided with a renewed Soviet attack and quickly found themselves decisively engaged. Six Tigers from *9. Kp./SS-Pz.Rgt. 3* took part in this action, with four being "seriously damaged" but not totally lost to the guns of a Soviet *Pakfront*.[42] One infantry platoon led by *SS-Usha.* Zährl from *II. Btl./Eicke* taking part in the aborted counterattack was reduced to a mere 10 men, losing half of his troops during the attack and withdrawal.[43]

A major source of concern to Gille reported later that evening was the defeat that afternoon of *Gren.Btl.z.b.V. 560*, which had occupied the key position atop Hill 96 west of Tomaszów that tied together the inner flanks of the *19. Pz.Div.* and *Totenkopf* Division. The smashing and scattering of Ritter's battalion and the loss of this key terrain enabled the 185th and 260th Rifle Divisions to punch through Becker's right flank between it and Hill 101. With nothing to stop them, the Soviets pushed 800 meters through the woods and emerged east of the railroad line south of Rożopole, where, if they desired, they could have penetrated into the left rear of the neighboring *19. Pz.Div.*, which had its hands full at the moment in repelling another attack. Rather than continuing, however, the leading Soviet battalion inexplicably halted on the open ground, seemingly not sure what to do next. Incidents like this were reported as having occurred throughout the corps sector that day, an indicator that the mid-level Soviet leadership (regiment and division commanders) of the attacking formations had fragmented on account of heavy casualties or some other cause, such as loss of communications. Opportunities that had arisen repeatedly during the day that would have allowed the Soviets to make greater gains were not taken advantage of, much to the defenders' astonishment.[44]

While the attackers dithered, Becker was able to use the breathing spell to assemble a force consisting of *II. Abt./SS-Pz.Rgt. 3* and the survivors of Ritter's battalion to carry out an immediate counterattack from Rożopole, which successfully pushed the Soviets back into the woods. A number of enemy troops were captured during the assault, bringing the total number taken that day alone by the *Totenkopf* Division to 195, an unexpected bounty for the division's *Ic* interrogation team. Once the situation was cleared up, Becker ordered tanks of *II. Abteilung*, along with the reassembled *Gren.Btl.z.b.V. 560*, to establish a hasty intermediate position east of Rożopole and Płudy and prepare for any subsequent attacks. Any thought of restoring the old main defense line was abandoned, as it was apparent that this was now becoming a battle for survival. Just such a battle was being experienced that afternoon by *III. Btl./Eicke* when its positions south of Jósefów were attacked at 3:00 p.m., as related following the battle by *SS-Strm.* Hans Vengel.[45]

After enduring a strong artillery barrage upon its positions, the men of Vengel's company rushed from their troop shelters to reoccupy their fighting positions. They immediately saw a large body of enemy troops advancing towards them, supported by seven tanks. The tanks, festooned with mounted infantrymen, quickly broke through the battalion's defenses and reached as far as its command post, when two of them were knocked out by tank destroyers from *3. Kp./SS-Pz.Jg.Abt. 3.* Another T-34 was soon knocked out by a 7.5cm antitank gun, while two others were immobilized by hits on their running gear. When a sixth tank became stuck in an antitank ditch, a *Grenadier* attacked it with a magnetic mine, rendering it harmless. The last remaining tank, seeing the rest of its company destroyed, turned around and returned to its own lines. At that, the remaining German troops rose up with a cheer and attacked the now-unsupported Soviet infantry. After a brief hand-to-hand fight, the survivors fled, leaving the field in the possession of the Germans. Incidents similar to this were repeated throughout the division's entire sector.

As the see-saw fighting in the center and right flank of the corps continued throughout the day, the situation on its left flank worsened. A night attack to retake Nieporet from the north along the sand dunes by the *I.* and part of the *III. Bataillon* of the *Westland* Regiment failed when it ran into a curtain of enemy artillery and small-arms fire. At daylight, the Soviet assault continued from where it had left off the previous day, seeking once again to get behind the lines of the division reconnaissance battalion and the *Westland* Regiment. In response, *Kampfgruppe Hein*, consisting of the remaining tanks from *2. Kompanie*, a company from the *Westland* Regiment, as well as the battalion reconnaissance platoon, led by the acting battalion commander *SS-Ostuf.* Willy Hein, took up positions north of the town and warded off four Soviet attacks. This only had a temporary effect, because the enemy made a fifth attempt late in the afternoon that overran *9. Kp./Westland* and managed to get behind *3. Kp./SS-Pz.Aufkl.Abt. 5.*[46]

This development forced the German defenders to fall back as far as the Zegrze–Legjonowo railway line to avoid encirclement. In Zagroby, held by an element from *Hstuf.* Pleiner's *II. Btl./Germania* that had crossed over the river to ensure the connection with the rest of the division, nothing out of the ordinary was reported so at least the *Wiking* Division's left flank was secure. Most of the battalion was still positioned on the other side of the Narew to hold Zegrze, though the bridge there had been partially blown up and only allowed limited foot traffic across its shattered span. Ominously, the *Germania*'s forward outpost reported that a large amount of vehicle traffic, including truck-towed artillery and self-propelled rocket artillery, was assembling in the area east of Rynia and around Załubice, scene of heavy fighting during the previous month. This sighting was an indicator that a major attack by the 160th Rifle Division along the river's southern bank could be expected.

On the *Wiking* Division's right flank, a rather tenuous connection was maintained with the left flank of the *Totenkopf* Division by 11 *Pz. V* Panthers from *Ostuf.* Lichte's *5. Kp./SS-Pz.Rgt. 5.* Reinforced by a company from *Hstuf.* Schumacher's *III. Btl./Germania*, Lichte's small battlegroup had been switched back and forth from the left flank of the *Wiking* to its right during the evening, where it took up a defensive position at Hill 94.5 a few hundred meters northeast of the Michałow estate. Here, it served as a backstop to the *Totenkopf* as well as the *Wiking* Division, should the Soviets break through along the boundary between the two divisions, as had briefly occurred the previous day.[47]

In his report to *9. Armee* that evening, Gille confirmed the identification of nine rifle divisions, a tank brigade, and the sapper brigade, verified by the 237 prisoners his troops had taken during the past two days. He noted the lack of coordination that had been observed between the various Soviet corps and divisions, each of which seemed to be carrying out their own separate campaigns.[48] Only because of this, he believed, were his divisions able to carry out separate small-scale counterattacks with some degree of success; had the Soviet forces been under firmer control, he stated that it would have been difficult to stop them, due to his own losses and lack of a significant reserve to carry out large-scale counterattacks. His artillery had also played a significant role in slowing and even stopping some Soviet attacks; his two SS-divisions and corps artillery alone had fired 387 tons of ammunition at the enemy that day.[49]

Continuing in his narrative, Gille bemoaned the critical shortage of infantrymen due to heavy casualties suffered by shellfire. Without additional manpower, his corps could not hope to man a continuous defense line, only widely spaced strongpoints. He stated that if the attack by the 47th and 70th Armies continued the next day, which he knew would occur, he doubted that he could hold his *HKL* for much longer. Only his armor was holding everything together, he wrote, but that too had begun to show the signs of overcommitment. On that day alone, the *Totenkopf* Division had lost five Panthers, one *Jg.Pz. IV*, two *StuG III* assault guns, and nine heavy antitank guns, in exchange for only six T-34s. Tank readiness rates also began to reflect the decline. The *Totenkopf* only had 42 tanks, tank destroyers, and assault guns ready for action, less than half of what it had three days before. The *Wiking* had 67 tanks and assault guns still operational, but two of its tank companies were sitting idle north of the Narew in the *Germania*'s sector. The *19. Pz.Div.* in its *I. Abt./Pz.Rgt. 27* and antitank battalion could muster 45 tanks and assault guns, though its *II. Abteilung* with 38 *Pz. IV* was still positioned across the Vistula in *H.Gr. Mitte* reserve.[50] In addition to asking for more troops, Gille also requested that this tank battalion be immediately released to his control. Meanwhile, the Soviets still had at least 200 tanks available, with more undoubtedly on the way.

In his report that evening to *Gen.Oberst* Reinhardt, von Lüttwitz credited Gille with achieving a great defensive success during the past two days, though whether the Soviet offensive had run its course would not fully be known until several more days had passed. The *9. Armee* commander wrote that he could detect a lessening of the Soviet effort, though this statement would have come as a surprise to anyone involved in the fighting on the ground. In addition to acknowledging the legitimacy of Gille's demand for more troops to make up for his losses, von

Lüttwitz repeated his request for the release of the *25. Pz.Div.* Once again, his request to *H.Gr. Mitte* was denied—the *2. Armee* still needed it, he was told by *Gen.Maj.* Otto Heidkämpfer, the army group's newly-appointed chief of staff, in a telephone conversation at 9:50 a.m.[51]

As a measure of von Luttwitz's desperation, he then requested that the *Dirlewanger Brigade* be transferred to Gille's corps, for it too had been freed up after *Gruppe von dem Bach* was disbanded. This request was also turned down; not only was its employment an SS matter, but it was *en route* by rail at that moment to an SS training area in Bohemia and Moravia, where it would undergo conversion into an infantry division after absorbing several thousand replacements.[52] It could not be turned around, even for such a temporary assignment. This was probably a good thing; Gille would have gotten very little use out of this organization, which was a brigade in name only, consisting almost exclusively of new recruits fresh from the various *Wehrmacht* and SS prisons from which they had been granted a reprieve in exchange for "proving themselves" at the front. During the suppression of the Warsaw Uprising, it had suffered nearly 100 per cent casualties in its infantry companies, a reflection of the poor leadership at the company and battalion level, and its addition to Gille's order of battle would have made it a liability.

The only other infantry unit within the entire *9. Armee* area of operations that von Lüttwitz could spare was the army's own *Sturmbataillon AOK 9* from its *Waffenschule*, which had been the corps reserve of the *VIII. Armeekorps.* Orders were issued that night directing it to move from the Warka area across the Vistula first thing in the morning. Once it arrived in Gille's corps area, it would be positioned on the left flank of the *19. Pz.Div.* to act as insurance to prevent any Soviet breakthroughs and entrapment of that division against the Vistula. Whether the addition of a mere battalion with a *Kampfstärke* of 395 men would have made any difference in the correlation of forces was debatable, but it was better than nothing and its troops were first rate, unlike those of *Gren.Btl.z.b.V. 560.*

The last nugget of information that was revealed in von Lüttwitz's communication with *H.Gr. Mitte* was the fact that it had grudgingly agreed to allow *II. Abt./Pz.Rgt. 27* to be committed to aid Gille, though this had strings attached. Instead of sending the entire battalion to rejoin its parent division, it would send one company at a time and only in exchange for a company from the regiment's *I. Abteilung*, and only when that company had lost most of its tanks. The rest of the battalion would remain as part of the army group's operational reserve. This, of course, was not much of an addition to the combat power of *IV. SS-Pz.Korps*, but Gille was not in a position where he could be selective; he had to take what he was offered. These additions were the best he could hope for, at least for the time being.

Rather than easing up, as von Lüttwitz had predicted, the third day of the Soviet offensive proved to be one of its most destructive and dangerous yet. Apparently, the 47th and 70th Army commanders, perhaps encouraged by Marshal Rokossovsky, had taken some time to reorganize their communications network and instill in the corps and division leadership a better sense of their mission's purpose, as well as what was expected of them. The remaining divisions in reserve, all five of them, were also to be committed to the battle the next day, reinforced by the artillery that had been able to move forward several kilometers in order to strike more deeply into the *IV. SS-Pz.Korps*' rear area. The entire 70th Army, approximately 25,000 strong, would be tasked with attacking the *Wiking* Division through the Nieporet corridor, while the 47th Army would press forward against the whole line of the *Totenkopf* and *19. Pz.Div.*, with a focus of main effort against Rożopole. The rest of the VIII Guards Tank Corps would also be committed to battle on 12 October. Events would prove it to be a day of decision.

The day's beginning was deceptively calm. On another cloudy, rainy day that limited both sides' aerial activity, the only ground action initially reported was a small-scale attack by *III. Btl./Westland* before sunrise to retake some ground lost the previous day in the Jablonna forest west of Nieporet and the northern portion of Nieporet itself, and an armored raid carried out by *19. Pz.Div.* at 8:30 a.m. against a Soviet assault gun company, knocking out two and sending the rest scurrying to the rear. At 9:00 a.m., the corps artillery under Brasack's direction fired two additional preventive barrages upon known or suspected enemy assembly areas and troop concentrations that possibly delayed the onset of the offensive's resumption. No other significant action was reported until noon, when the Soviet artillery opened up with a tremendous 20-minute drumfire barrage opposite the positions they had taken the previous day. With the sky clearing somewhat, the Red Air Force soon made its presence again known, sending waves of IL-2 *Sturmoviks* to harass German artillery positions and supply convoys. Their infantry quickly followed the barrage, storming into the gaps at Rożopole, Jósefów, and Nieporet, which were only covered by widely dispersed infantry positions.

Gille's own artillery, including that of his three divisions and *Art.Brig. 140* firing from across the Vistula, immediately responded with a devastating response, shutting down the assaults aimed at the first two areas before they could even develop with well-aimed artillery and *Werfer* barrages. Even though the Soviet assault had been rocked back upon its heels, after recovering from the initial shock, the infantrymen from the 47th and 70th Armies kept attacking, absorbing heavy losses in their ranks. In many places, fighting in the *Totenkopf* Division's sector devolved into hand-to-hand combat, but by the end of the day, *Obf.* Becker's troops still held their positions, though the division's strength was rapidly ebbing.

The German preventive barrage, as effective as it was elsewhere, was not enough to stop the assault from Nieporet. Here, the 38th and part of the 76th Guards Rifle Division, supported by at least a company of tanks, were able to quickly achieve a deep penetration through the forest as far as the railroad line linking Zegrze with Jablonna-Legjonowo. Two tanks from *2. Kp./SS-Pz.Rgt. 5*, positioned north of the rail line, were hit by artillery during the bombardment and destroyed.[53] During the barrage, Nedderhof's *III. Btl./Westland*, which had been reassembled after being dispersed two days before, was nearly wiped out, leaving only a few survivors. His battalion, which had been over 800 strong when it arrived at the front on 23 September, was whittled down to a *Kampfstärke* of only 75 men. Still, the battalion's sacrifice had not been in vain, for it had managed to delay the enemy's movement through the woods long enough to give *Stubaf.* Hack, the regiment's new commander, sufficient time to generate a response.[54]

Gille's corps was now in great danger of being enveloped on its left flank should the 70th Army achieve the breakthrough that it had sought for the past three days. While the *19. Pz. Div* and *Totenkopf* Division fought a series of see-saw actions throughout the day that ultimately resulted in no significant gains for the Soviets, and where in some places the Germans were even able to restore the old *HKL* of 10 October, the *Wiking* Division desperately fought all day to deny the enemy the ground they sought. Since Hack's depleted *I.* and *II. Bataillon* were already tied up in fighting along the regiment's right flank between Woła-Aleksandra and Aleksandrów, and his *III. Bataillon* was effectively destroyed, there was little hope that the regiment's former main defense line could be restored. The only thing the *Westland*'s commander could muster to stop the Soviet advance before it crossed over the highway and railway was his headquarters company, regimental antitank company, and some stragglers from *III. Btl./Westland*. That proved to be enough.[55]

Taking advantage of the cover provided by the railroad embankment, Hack's scratch force, supported by his regimental infantry gun company as well as the division's artillery regiment, put up such a sustained wall of fire that the Soviet lead infantry elements shrank back, seeking cover in the forest from whence they came. Their tanks had yet to make an appearance, to the Germans' good fortune. On his left flank, Hack observed that his former command, *SS-Pz.Aufkl.Abt. 5*, was also holding its ground along the highway and railway leading to Zagroby. On Hack's right, Lichte's *5. Kp./SS-Pz.Abt. 5*, along with a company from *III. Btl./Germania*, had changed position and was now facing east towards the enemy-held Jablonna forest, shielding against any Soviet tank incursion in their direction.

With the assistance of *II. Btl./Westland*, Lichte's battlegroup had already forced one Soviet attack back, destroying four M-4 Shermans in the process. Two of these tanks were destroyed with *Panzerfausts* by the acting commander of *5. Kp./Westland*, *Ostuf.* Gerhard Lotze, who was mortally wounded during this action. Lotze had been on an inspection tour of the front that week while serving as an instructor from the *Junkerschule* at Bad Tölz and was not assigned to the *Wiking* Division at that time. Taking over when its commander was wounded, Lotze led the company for two days until his death on 12 October. On Lichte's right lay the positions of the two other battalions of Hack's regiment, which had changed their orientation to the east as well. But between Lichte and Borchert's reconnaissance battalion, Hack had hardly anything at all and could not reasonably hope to continue holding his ground unless reinforced.

Fortunately for Hack, among the forces he could count upon were units such as *4. Bttr./SS-Werfer-Abt. 504*, which had been moved far forward the previous evening into his regiment's sector to provide additional fire support. The battery's 70 men and their six *Nebelwerfer*, under the command of *SS-Ustuf.* Horst Bärwind, were positioned in a meadow on the edge of the Jablonna forest, with the rear of their firing position demarcated by the railroad line. Having dug several bunkers for shelter and emplaced its three machine guns to defend against any infantry, Bärwind's battery's prepared for action. That opportunity came the following day, when it was ordered to prepare a rocket salvo to fire against a Soviet troop concentration at 11:45 a.m., shortly before the Soviets began their own preparatory fire. The men waited besides their launchers, which were fully loaded and ready to fire. Finally, the order arrived by field telephone at noon, the same time the Soviet barrage began.

In one salvo, the battery launched 36 15cm high-explosive rockets, just as the first Soviet shells began to fall on its own position. The crews continued to load and fire their own launchers, as individual rocketeers fell dead or wounded all around them. Still, they continued firing, launching their deadly payloads at their enemy, who had learned to call them *brühlende Kuhe* (bellowing cows), the Russian counterpart to American G.I.s' nickname for the weapon, the "screaming meemie." When the order came to cease fire, the surviving crew members limbered up their four remaining rocket launchers (two had been completely destroyed) and had them towed by the few surviving vehicles across the railroad embankment to safety. Thirty-five of their number had been killed and wounded, fully half the battery. But despite their loss, the battery had earned the respect of the *Grenadiers* from Hack's regiment. Wherever they fought afterwards, they would hear the infantry say, "There goes the rocketeers—they're great guys! They kept firing even while they were being hit by artillery themselves!"[56]

Meanwhile, the *Wiking* Division's acting commander, *Staf.* Mühlenkamp, was assembling forces to come to Hack's aid. His first step was to order *Hstuf.* Flügel and his two tank companies (the *7.* and *8.*) to cross the Narew at Modlin and hurry with all possible speed to the village of Łajsk, 3 kilometers northeast of Jablonna-Legjonowo, where his dozen tanks would become the new division reserve once they arrived that evening.[57] The next was to order the division's *Alarmbataillon*, at that time located in Modlin, to hurry forward as quickly as possible to Hack's sector to reinforce him. Arriving at Hack's headquarters that evening, the battalion, under the command of *Hstuf.* Eberhard Heder, the division's new *Pionier* battalion commander, was positioned along the highway between the Michałow estate and the highway crossroads southwest of Zagroby, joining Hack's scratch force. Here, Heder's three *Alarm* companies, composed of truck drivers, mechanics, orderlies, and clerks, as well as a *Flak* battery from *SS-Flak-Abt. 5*, would acquit themselves admirably during the next several days.[58] Fortunately for the *Wiking* Division, Soviet attacks slackened off that evening, as it had elsewhere along the corps' front, except for the usual harassing artillery fire.

In the corps' evening report, written for Gille and signed by Manfred Schönfelder himself, the total number of Soviet divisions that had been identified had risen to 13, with one more apparently moving in to reinforce the attack's *Schwerpunkt*.[59] Jankuhn, the corps' *Ic*, estimated that there were five divisions engaged in the Rozopole sector against the *19. Pz.Div.*, four at Jósefów against the *Totenkopf*, and three or four more against the *Wiking* at Nieporet, including a Soviet *Straf* (punishment) battalion. Schönfelder described the effectiveness of the preventative artillery strike and how it had most likely delayed the resumption of the Soviet attack by at least three hours. Despite the thin screening line that both the *19. Pz.Div.* and *Totenkopf* had jury-rigged, both divisions, thanks to effective artillery supporting fire and the judicious employment of tank-led counterattacks, had kept the enemy at bay, in spite of the ever-increasing shortage of infantry due to their high loss rate from Soviet artillery.[60] Armor losses had continued, a reflection of their heavy use. In exchange for the destruction of 10 Soviet tanks and assault guns that day, Gille's corps had lost two *Pz. IV* tanks, both in the *Wiking*'s sector.[61]

Although the corps was experiencing a defensive success so far, its *Chef des Stabes* predicted that the enemy offensive would continue undiminished the next day, with emphasis being placed on the one area where the First Belorussian Front was achieving a measure of success—on the corps' left flank in the *Wiking*'s defensive sector. In other developments, Schönfelder noted the arrival of *Maj.* Meinhold's *Sturmbataillon AOK 9*, which had been positioned at Płudy under *Gen.Lt.* Källner's control, and that the exchange of tank companies from the fresh *I. Abteilung* of *Pz.Rgt. 27* to the battle-worn *II. Abteilung* had begun. Neither *SS-Pz.Rgt. 3* nor *SS-Pz.Rgt. 5* had a spare battalion to exchange with the other. They would have no alternative but to keep fighting and hope for a pause in the offensive long enough to repair and maintain their vehicles. Additionally, *SS-Jäg.Btl. 501* with an initial *Kämpfstarke* of only 46 men had arrived and been placed under the control of *Obf.* Becker's division. The corps commander's intent for the following day was to continue to defend and prepare to repel any Soviet attempt to envelope its left flank.[62]

The *9. Armee* commander's report to *H.Gr. Mitte* again echoed Schönfelder's report concerning the course of the fighting that day, but went a step further by stating with confidence that there were now two clearly identified points of main effort. The first, involving the 47th Army (based on prisoner interrogations), was to penetrate to the Vistula between Henryków and Jablonna and to effect a river crossing perhaps in the vicinity of Tarchomin, which would also cut off the *19. Pz.Div.* The second point of main effort was the attack by the 70th Army, but this, he felt, had been relegated to a mere supporting attack, covering the flank of its neighbor. In this regard, the assessment was diametrically opposite that of

Gille and Schönfelder, who believed that the 70th Army posed the greatest threat to their corps.

According to the army's *Ic*, there were at least three more rifle divisions that had not yet been committed, nor had the bulk of the VIII Guards Tank Corps. But in any case, von Lüttwitz and his staff agreed that the attacks would continue. The only other event occurring within the *9. Armee* area of operations was that the *337. Volks-Gren.Div.* had finally been moved into the Vistula defense line south of Warsaw, relieving the *5. ung.Res.Div.*, which immediately began preparing to move via rail to its native country for the defense of Budapest. In other matters, *H.Gr. Mitte* had still not decided whether to order the *2. Armee* to give up the *25. Pz.Div.* and send it across the Narew to aid Gille's corps.[63]

During that evening, while the *Wiking* Division's hastily assembled last reserve moved into position northwest of Nieporet, the only action that merited mention was an attempt by an enemy force to storm Hill 97 south of Jósefów in the *Totenkopf*'s sector, which was driven off with heavy losses. In the corps' morning report for 13 October, submitted at 6:35 a.m., Gille's forward command post's *Erster Schreiber* (Operations NCO), *Oscha.* Schlemmer, stated that the usual Soviet artillery and mortar fire had continued throughout the evening intermittently. He repeated Gille's assertion that the corps no longer possessed any reserves of any kind. With the *Wiking* Division's *Alarm* battalion now committed, everything that his corps had was in the line. The last bit of information Schlemmer related was to report that at dawn that morning, a Soviet tank platoon launched a probing attack towards the railroad line in the vicinity of the Wieliszew forest park on the western edge of the Letniska forest, where Hack's battle headquarters was located, but was driven off after one M-4 Sherman was destroyed. This was merely a prelude to a much larger assault that was gathering in the Jablonna forest on the other side of the Zegrze–Jablonna highway.

As had been the case during the previous three days, Gille again ordered Brasack to plan and execute two more artillery ambushes on the usual targets—Soviet assembly areas, known troop concentrations, and artillery firing positions, a sign that the restrictions on the use of artillery ammunition imposed earlier by *9. Armee* had evidently been lifted. The area was becoming so crowded with troops from both the 47th and 70th Armies, and VIII Guards Tank Corps, that it was hard to miss. One concentration was fired during the late morning, while the second followed during the mid-afternoon. Once again, this caused the Soviet commanders to delay the start of their assault, which finally got underway when the Red artillery began laying down an enormous barrage at 5 p.m. that lasted 90 minutes. Drumfire barrages crashed down repeatedly on German front-line positions, destroying the hastily constructed bunkers and foxholes that had been built during the past two days. To add to the defenders' misery, the 16th Air Army was present in force, taking advantage of the first clear weather in days. The First Belorussian Front's assault had definitely not yet reached its culminating point.

On the right flank, the *19. Pz.Div.* reported large-scale attacks directed against the area between Płudy and Marcelin that resulted in minor penetrations. Källner ordered immediate tank and infantry counterattacks to be carried out that erased the Soviet gains at Marcelin by nightfall. The Soviet unit that had broken through near Płudy was wiped out at the same time by an artillery barrage that blanketed its position. Ominously, division observation posts reported that large numbers of enemy vehicles, primarily trucks and tanks, were seen moving up the highway from Praga, indicating that another fresh Soviet unit was about to be thrown into the equation.

Unlike the *19. Pz.Div.*, which had enjoyed a good deal of success on 13 October, the *Totenkopf* Division had a very rough day. Once their opening barrage had lifted, enemy troops surged forward, backed up by at least a tank regiment. Here was a truly target-rich environment, but to prevent a major breakthrough, the division's *panzer* regiment was placed virtually into the front line, since there was hardly any infantry left to hold it. An enemy force of at least 600 men, estimated to be an infantry regiment, stormed through the *Totenkopf* Division's defenses at Wegierskie Katy, the linchpin between the inner flanks of the *Totenkopf* and *Wiking* Divisions. An armored counterattack was immediately launched and in the fighting that ensued, the commander on the scene reported that his men had killed or captured 60 percent of the Soviet regiment. On the division's flank it shared with the *19. Pz.Div.*, after the 6 p.m. artillery barrage was over, a tank-supported attack attempted to penetrate the boundary between Jósefów and Rożopole.[64]

Since the *Totenkopf*'s tanks were busy elsewhere, the defending infantrymen, employing their antitank guns, knocked out seven tanks and three trucks towing antitank guns, while the division's artillery regiment took care of the rest with accurately directed fire that smashed the assault and drove the invaders back to their own lines. Becker's division also appears to have garnered the majority of the Red Air Force's attention that day, with swarms of IL-2s, A-20 Bostons, and other ground-attack aircraft busily bombing and strafing front-line positions as well as artillery firing positions. The division's logistics base at Jablonna-Legjonowo was also heavily bombed, though *SS-Flak-Btl. 3* shot down two of the attackers, its fifth and sixth kill since 10 October.[65]

The fighting in the *Wiking*'s sector that day can only be described as a horror show. It began when the division ordered *Stubaf.* Hack and his regiment to conduct a counterattack that morning to throw the Soviets out of the Jablonna forest, a tall order for a unit that had suffered such heavy losses during the past three days. Nevertheless, after a brief preparatory barrage was laid down on the woods, Hack's battlegroup (it could no longer be described as a regiment), with *Hstuf.* Walter Schmidt's *II. Btl./Westland* serving as the main effort, launched its attack at 6:50 a.m., advancing southeast towards the forest from the general line of the Michalow estate to Wola Aleksandra. The remnant of *III. Btl./Westland* and *Hstuf.* Heder's *Alarm* battalion remained in position along the railroad line. When Schmidt and his troops reached the ridgeline capped by Hill 87, they encountered a large-scale Soviet attack consisting of at least a regiment approaching from the opposite direction. He immediately ordered his battalion to stop, take up firing positions, and engage the enemy. Soon, quite a battle had developed and Schmidt's battalion was in danger of being overwhelmed, but was able to hold its ground. The engines of large numbers of tanks could clearly be heard revving up in the forest behind the Soviet infantry, signs of an impending major attack.

The division's armored reserve, *II. Abt./SS-Pz.Rgt. 5*—once again re-formed as a complete battalion with 32 Panthers under the command of *Hstuf.* Flügel—launched a relief attack at noon with one company of 10 tanks from its assembly area at Łajsk to relieve the enemy pressure against *II. Btl./Westland*, still holding out along the ridgeline 5 kilometers to the southeast. Crossing the railroad and main highway, the company attacked until it had reached the line Hill 94.5–Hill 87, linking up with Schmidt's battalion after killing a number of Soviet troops and destroying several tanks.[66] This action only temporarily improved the overall situation; while it was unfolding, a large enemy tank and infantry attack was taking place 8 kilometers to the northeast in the vicinity of the church and cemetery on the edge of Letniska forest north of the main highway and rail intersection east of Wieliszew.

This Soviet advance actually broke through the German lines, severing the connection between the *Westland* Regiment and the reconnaissance battalion. Both forces had been positioned alongside one another following the railroad and main highway, and had to refuse their left flank to avoid being rolled up. One Soviet force then angled to the north and northwest in the direction of Zagroby, with the obvious intent of getting behind and encircling the bulk of the *SS-Pz.Aufkl.Abt. 5* located on the southern edge that town. The other attacking force veered left and plowed into the left flank of *Stubaf.* Hack's regiment, taking up a strong position along the woodline in the cemetery, where it halted. The remaining assault guns of *Ostuf.* Weert's *4. Kp./SS-Pz.Rgt. 5* launched a counterattack towards the rail overpass southwest of Zagroby in an attempt to restore the position along the rail line, but instead ran into a strong Soviet force before it was compelled to pull back after one of its *StuG IVs* was knocked out by artillery fire. Overhead, an air battle raged, as a small number of German fighter aircraft attempted to relieve the pressure being exerted by the Red Air Force, which at one point had 60 fighter-bombers and ground-attack aircraft operating against the *Wiking* Division alone.

During the next several hours, a back-and-forth struggle ensued which saw a Soviet tank brigade, supporting the two guards rifle divisions, attempting to get behind the Germans' left flank between Zagroby and Wieliszew, while the *Wiking* Division fought to prevent it. Both sides launched numerous attacks and counterattacks, while heavy artillery fire blanketed the landscape. On the right, *II. Btl./Westland* fought to keep the main body of Soviet troops from breaking out of the Jablonna forest; in the center, Hack's improvised force and Heder's *Alarm* battalion struggled to hold the new main defense line stretching between the Michałow estate and the forest cemetery southwest of Zagroby; and on the left, Borchert's reconnaissance battalion, now aided by elements of *I. Btl./Germania* that had crossed over the new bridge at Debe/Podebe, held Zagroby and counterattacked to restore the connection with Hack's regiment. Throughout, *Hstuf.* Flügel's *II. Abt./SS-Pz.Rgt. 5*, joined by the *2.* and *4. Kompanie* of *I. Abteilung*, thrust and parried, managing to keep the tanks of the VIII Guards Tank Corps from achieving the penetration which they sought, while knocking out 16 Soviet tanks in exchange for just two of their own.[67] Orchestrating the battle was *Staf.* Mühlenkamp, who arrived on the scene at 1 p.m. to ensure that the division's main effort was properly coordinated and supported as much as possible. He had previously managed situations every bit as dangerous as this one, and his steady hand and tactical acumen also succeeded on 13 October.

In his report to *9. Armee* that evening, Gille recounted the course of events that day, stating that the scale of the Soviet attacks had increased significantly, with entire regiments being thrown into attacks against German positions, where previously battalions had been used. The identification of two tank brigades from the VIII Guards Tank Corps had been reported, one at Nieporet and the other between Rożopole and Józefów. Rather than waiting for the infantry to achieve a clean breakthrough, evidently Rokossovsky had decided to use the tank corps for that purpose, a sign that the Front commander was growing impatient. In nearly every case, these tank and infantry attacks had been bloodily repulsed, with huge enemy losses being reported by Gille's divisions. The amount of ammunition expended and fuel consumed that day is another indicator of the intensity of the fighting. Excluding the *19. Pz.Div.*, Gille's corps fired 581 tons of shells on 13 October alone, an extremely high amount compared to the average daily delivery of 132 tons, while his tanks, other armored vehicles, and trucks had consumed nearly 100,000 gallons of gasoline, four times the replacement rate for fuel. His divisions were using these essential supplies so rapidly that the field army's logistical system was having difficulties in keeping up with these requirements.[68]

Several POWs revealed that many of their infantry companies had been reduced in size from an average strength of 50–60 men to only 15. Twenty-three Soviet tanks were reported as being completely destroyed that day, as well as three antitank guns. The *Totenkopf* Division had accounted for six of these, including three JS-II Stalin heavy tanks. The corps' own losses were reported as being "considerable," primarily inflicted by artillery fire and rolling air attacks. Large amounts of the *Totenkopf* and *Wiking* Divisions' small arms and heavy weapons (machine guns, infantry howitzers, mortars, etc.) and even a *Hummel* 15cm self-propelled howitzer, had been lost to enemy fire or captured.[69] The *IV. SS-Pz.Korps*, which had been fighting a successful battle so far, was slowly being bled white. In concluding his assessment of the day's fighting,

Gille stated that he fully expected the Soviet offensive to continue the following day, with even more enemy force being brought to bear, especially in the Nieporet area. He had given up asking for more support, apparently believing the *9. Armee* mantra that there was nothing left to give.

In his commander's narrative shared with Reinhardt's headquarters that evening, von Lüttwitz echoed Gille, stating that the weight of the Soviet offensive could be seen shifting to the north, within the *Wiking* Division's defensive sector along the Narew. The *9. Armee* commander recounted how the artillery counterstrikes by the corps' and division's artillery had been incredibly effective in denying the 47th Army any success in breaking through between Żeran and Jósefów, despite the initiation of regiment-sized infantry attacks supported by armor. Von Lüttwitz also expressed his admiration for the fighting abilities of the men of the *Totenkopf* Division, who despite their numerical inferiority, had managed to inflict extraordinarily heavy losses on the attacking Soviet troops, even while enduring drumfire artillery barrages and air attacks upon their positions. He then expressed his concern about the fighting at Nieporet and the possibility that the 70th Army might achieve the operational breakthrough that it sought, which in addition to striking towards Modlin, would include an envelopment of the *Totenkopf* and *19. Pz. Div.* and half of the *Wiking* Division by Soviet tank forces moving down the Zegrze–Jablonna highway.

To rectify the situation, von Lüttwitz, perhaps sensing a bit of desperation in Gille's report, had suggested attaching the fresh *337. Volks-Gren.Div.* to Gille's corps, but Reinhardt turned this down immediately, stating that it would be unwise to commit a new and untried division to such a major battle. The army's repeated request for the release of the *25. Pz.Div.* was also turned down yet again. Therefore, von Lüttwitz improvised. To keep the Zegrze–Jablonna highway clear of the enemy, he directed *19. Pz.Div.* to place its Panther battalion, *I. Abt./Pz.Rgt. 27*, in a reserve position in the Jablonna-Legjonowo area, where it could react if needed to any Soviet thrust down the highway from the northeast.[70]

To replace the *I. Btl./Germania*, which Gille had ordered to move across the river from Zegrze to reinforce the *Wiking*'s reconnaissance battalion, leaving most of the northern riverbank of the Narew unsecured, *Lds.Schtz.Btl. 649* was hurried across the Narew at Modlin. A light artillery battalion, *lei.Art.Abt. 430*, was also added to the *Wiking*'s artillery regiment to provide extra fire support. Additionally, the *Füsilier* battalion from the *73. Inf.Div.* in Warsaw was attached to the *19. Pz.Div.* that evening, relieving *II. Btl./Pz.Gren.Rgt. 74*, which had been temporarily posted on the western side of the Vistula, freeing it up to join the rest of its regiment on the other side. Lastly, one tank destroyer company from *Pz.Jg.Abt. 743* was detached from *VIII. Armeekorps*' reserve and set into motion towards Gille's corps. Any further diversion of resources would threaten the tactical integrity of *9. Armee*, but von Lüttwitz could rest knowing that he had done all he could for one day.

In addition to sending whatever reinforcements to *IV. SS-Pz.Korps* that could be spared, the *9. Armee* commander also spurred on the efforts of the army's construction engineer staff to complete work on the final defensive line for Gille's troops. This position, which was titled the *Fuchs* (Fox) position, would run from the Vistula bend to Chotomów, from there to Łajsk, and thence to east of Wieliszew/Zegrze. It would be constructed as a continuous series of field fortifications, taking advantage of the terrain where possible, and would have its left and right flanks secured by the Narew and Vistula, respectively. An additional *Bau-Pionier* battalion was attached to *IV. SS-Pz.Korps* that day, joining with several others (the *421.* and *728. Bau-Pio. Btle.*, as well as three other *Bau-Pionier* companies composed of Eastern volunteers) that were already at work.[71] Bolstered by the thousands of pressed civilian laborers, this construction crew worked while under enemy fire in some cases to have the new position ready within the next 10 days; that is, if Gille's troops could prevent the front from collapsing in the meantime.

The performance of the *IV. SS-Pz.Korps* during the fighting had not gone unnoticed, for it received a mention in that day's *OKW Tagesmeldung*, broadcast to all the German Armed Forces, which stated that, "in spite of heavy enemy artillery fire and the effects of continuous attacks by fighter bombers, today the divisions of the SS-Panzerkorps fought heroically, using the last ounce of their strength, to prevent the enemy from breaking through."[72] Though the announcement may have been a bit premature, since the offensive would last for at least another week, the men of Gille's corps must surely have appreciated it if they had heard.

Saturday, 14 October found both sides literally locked in mortal combat. That day, the 47th and 70th Armies would feed more of their reserves into the fight, while the VIII Guards Tank Corps sought the elusive operational breakthrough. With the battle between Pułtusk and Serock finally decided in the Soviets' favor, additional artillery assets would be transferred south to bolster the already impressive array of guns and rocket launchers in position. The 16th Air Army would also intensify its efforts, complicating the Germans' effort to keep their forward units supplied with the fuel and ammunition they required. The Red Air Force would provide an overabundance of targets for the ever-alert *Flak* troops.

In response, the three *panzer* divisions in the Wet Triangle of the Narew and Vistula were increasingly forced to employ their dwindling numbers of tanks and assault guns, sometimes without infantry support, to stop and hurl back numerous Soviet tank and infantry assaults. Little tactical acumen was required by Gille and his subordinate leaders, since most of these actions had devolved into battalion- and even company-level actions, carried out to defend or retake positions, often repeatedly. The few remaining infantrymen held the line as best they could, grimly standing by day and night as they awaited the next assault. Frequently, only the artillery, skillfully directed by *Brig.Fhr.* Brasack's *SS-ARKO 104*, was all there was preventing a Soviet breakthrough. Time and again, the enormously destructive power of the corps' 40–50 artillery and rocket artillery batteries shattered Soviet units as they advanced, stymieing their efforts to achieve their objectives.

The day began uncharacteristically with an early-morning Soviet attack launched against the right flank of the *Wiking* Division northwest of Nieporet. The neighboring *Totenkopf* and *19. Pz. Div.* reported numerous Soviet reconnaissance forays against their lines during the night, which were all driven off, and both were subjected to continuous artillery fire in the morning. German artillery fired in response, targeting the usual troop concentrations, tank assembly areas, and Soviet artillery firing positions. At 9 a.m., attacks were launched against German positions at Marcelin, Rożopole, and Jósefów, all scenes of previous heavy fighting that continued throughout the day. In every case, Soviet gains were nullified by immediate tank-led counterattacks, or were stopped before attacks could even get underway by German artillery fire. Losses on both sides were heavy. The heaviest fighting that occurred on 14 October took place, as Gille predicted, on the corps' northern flank. After a one-hour drumfire barrage against the hastily erected defensive positions of the *Westland* Regiment, a large-scale ground attack got underway at 5:15 a.m.[73]

This initiated a series of regiment-level tank and infantry attacks against the division, which continued virtually without pause until nightfall. Nearly all of the fighting took place in the area between Hill 87 south of the Michałow estate and the railroad viaduct southwest of Zagroby. All of the *Westland* Regiment, most of *SS-Pz.Rgt. 5*, and the division's reconnaissance battalion were involved, as well as *Alarm-Btl. Wiking*. The division's artillery regiment, augmented by *lei.Art.Abt. 430* and a 21cm heavy mortar battery from *schw.Art.Abt. 732*, fired uninterruptedly in support of the defenders. Most of the fighting that day centered around the northern edge of the Jablonna forest, around the Wieliszew railway station, and the cemetery on the northeastern edge of the Letniska forest. These locations changed hands numerous times, and *SS-Pz.Rgt. 5* carried out 18 separate counterattacks to hurl the Soviet troops back across the railroad line.[74] Heavy Soviet artillery fire was continuous and accurate.

At 4:10 p.m., 12 Soviet tanks with mounted infantry crossed over the railroad line southwest of Zagroby north of the forest and advanced towards Wieliszew proper, before being stopped and forced back with the loss of two tanks by a counterattack carried out by the *I. Abteilung* of the *panzer* regiment in conjunction with *I. Btl./Germania*. Red Air Force ground-attack aircraft were seemingly everywhere, bombing and harassing the *Wiking*'s *panzers* as they tried to assemble and move about the battlefield. By nightfall, most of the division's defenses along the railroad tracks had been restored and the enemy thrown back into the Jablonna forest, but there was no longer a continuous line of defending troops.

So heavy was the number of SS troops killed and wounded in the fighting that day, that the best that *Stubaf.* Hack and his commanders could muster was a series of widely spaced strongpoints, with the backbone provided by the tanks of *Ostubaf.* Darges's *SS-Pz.Rgt. 5*. Darges had been appointed the on-the-scene battle commander by *Staf.* Mühlenkamp himself, since the *panzer* regiment was the only unit remaining with any appreciable combat power. Hack's regiment had been reduced in size to battalion strength, so badly had it been depleted. *Hstuf.* Heder's *Alarm* battalion remained subordinate to Hack, who in turn took his orders from Darges. Nightfall found the *Wiking* defense line restored, with the exception of a Soviet battalion-sized force that had dug itself into a nearly impregnable position within the cemetery surrounding the forest church at Wieliszew. It would be attended to that evening, when a counterattack to clear the area of the foe was scheduled to be carried out. The German defenders were afforded no rest that evening, however, as Soviet artillery continued to fall upon their precarious positions all night.

That evening, Gille reported the day's events as usual, stressing the near-total dependence that the corps had placed upon both its artillery and armor for the continuing success of its defense. The Soviet attack, he said, was following the course that he had predicted, and he expected the offensive's main effort would remain in the north, where the tanks of the VIII Guards Tank Corps had very nearly achieved a breakthrough. Despite the corps' defensive success so far, it had come at a high cost, he wrote. The total number of casualties his units had suffered in the five days since the offensive began had risen to 5,000 men killed and wounded, compared to only 1,000 replacements received. Most of the losses had been suffered by the infantry and combat engineers, as was usually the case. Although both the *Totenkopf* and *Wiking* Divisions had over 1,000 men in each of their field replacement battalions, most of these men were recently arrived *Luftwaffe* transfers with little training and no front-line experience, and committing them to battle at this point was tantamount to murder.

The armor strength of *IV. SS-Pz.Korps* had also continued to dwindle. The *Totenkopf* Division, which had the longest frontage to cover, and correspondingly had to rely more on its armor than the other two divisions, was down to a mere 25 operational tanks, of which only three were Tigers. Were it not for its 24 remaining assault guns and tank destroyers, as well as its three surviving antitank guns, it would hardly have any armored strength at all. The *Wiking* was slightly worse off, with only 24 operational tanks as well as 11 assault guns and tank destroyers, but it still had 16 operational antitank guns, which compensated somewhat for the armor's weakness. Fortunately, the majority of its 20 or so non-operational tanks could be repaired, though *SS-Pz.Rgt. 5*'s maintenance services would need time. The *19. Pz.Div.* was the strongest, possessing 60 operational tanks and 14 tank destroyers, though half of *II. Abt./Pz.Rgt. 27* was on the western bank of the Vistula in reserve, while most of its Panther battalion had been pulled back in a reserve position in Jablonna-Legjonowo. The addition of the tank destroyer company from the *9. Armee* reserve would help the corps to redress the imbalance in armor, though the turretless *Hetzer* was no adequate substitute for a tank.[75]

Gille's most intriguing comment was that he had noticed that Soviet command and control of its troops had been significantly stiffened and their actions had become more unified, as witnessed by the increasing focus upon certain objectives rather than attacking everywhere at once. Gille expected this to continue. Although the efforts of the 47th and 70th Armies had not yet been crowned with success, Gille expected the offensive to continue until it had. The critical moment of the conditions needed to fully commit the VIII Guards Tank Corps had not arrived, despite the best efforts of the commanders concerned. The fact that only three Soviet tanks were destroyed that day was a sign that after losing so many tanks the day before, Lt.Gen. Popov, the corps commander, had decided—or had been instructed—to wait another day until the proper time to commit the rest of his corps.

Gille closed his report with the remark that in order to enable the artillery to do its job, the flow of ammunition had to be maintained. In light of the complete destruction that day of the recently repaired pontoon bridge over the Vistula at Młociny by a direct hit, this was ever-more critical. Now all of the supplies for *19. Pz.Div.* would have to be brought over the bottleneck at Modlin, as well as what was already required by the two SS divisions, which had fired over 525 tons of artillery rounds on 14 October. Continuing with the theme of ammunition supply, Gille also stated that the chronic shortage of 2cm and 3.7cm *Flak* ammunition was severely hampering the ability of the corps' and divisions' antiaircraft batteries to fight back against the increasingly effective Red Air Force squadrons operating in the air space above his *Kampfraum*. Though six IL-2 *Sturmoviks* had been shot down that day, this was little compensation for the fact that over 200 Soviet bombers and ground-attack aircraft had been harrying his troops on that day alone.

He also noted by way of emphasis that on that day, the *Totenkopf*s *Flak* battalion celebrated the destruction of its 200th and 201st Soviet aircraft. Gille concluded with the laconic statement, "Will continue defending by conducting counterattacks with tanks as well as combating the enemy with tightly concentrated artillery strikes against his troops and artillery." The army commander had experienced the devastating power of the Red Air Force's attacks himself that very day, when he travelled by staff car to Gille's command post at Klein Kazun. An enemy fighter-bomber had bombed and strafed his vehicle, and one of the car's occupants seated next to him was wounded by a shell splinter. Though von Lüttwitz was uninjured, it must have emphasized the knowledge of just how much the Red Air Force had improved since the early days on the Eastern Front, when the *Luftwaffe* ruled the skies and their opponents were a running joke. Things had indeed changed, and not in the Third Reich's favor.

In his own evening report for 14 October, von Lüttwitz emphasized the importance of the identification of the VIII Guards Tank Corps and what it signified as to

Rokossovsky's ultimate intentions in the Wet Triangle. But what worried him even more was the news that the 65th Army had broken out of the Pułtusk–Serock bridgehead and was pushing back the right flank of *Gen.Oberst* Weiss's neighboring *2. Armee*. To von Lüttwitz's way of thinking, this could only mean that Col.Gen. Batov's 65th Army was operating in conjunction with the 47th and 70th Armies and would envelope Modlin from the north, while Generals Gusev and Popov drove west to link up with the 65th Army at the ancient Napoleonic fortress from the south. In addition to this dire scenario, the *9. Armee* commander was pondering how this might fit into the ongoing battle for East Prussia and whether the First Belorussian Front would begin operating in concert with its fellow army group to the north, the Second Belorussian Front. This was the scenario that both he and Reinhardt had feared might happen for the past month, despite the fact that Rokossovsky had no intention of doing so.[76]

Aside from praising the miraculously unbroken offensive spirit of Gille's troops, von Lüttwitz informed his army group commander that the Soviets had made no significant gains at all that day, despite the introduction of more reserves and tanks to the fighting and, above all, the incredibly heavy artillery fire the troops had to endure. Despite that, like Gille, he also reckoned that the attacks would continue undiminished the next day. He also emphasized to the *H.Gr. Mitte* commander and staff how important it was that an uninterrupted flow of ammunition, especially that for the 10.5cm howitzer, be maintained for Gille'corps. The *9. Armee* commander stressed how vital artillery was for the continuing defensive effort east of the Vistula, not only in smashing Soviet attacks as they occurred, but while the enemy's assault troops were forming up behind their lines as well. Other than ensuring that the necessary ammunition to continue the defense was being provided, no additional reinforcements for Gille's corps were forthcoming from *9. Armee*. As for the other corps in his army, there was nothing new to report, other than the usual bombing, shelling, and patrolling activity, which permitted more of the *9. Armee* daily ammunition allocation to be diverted to *IV. SS-Pz.Korps*.

The next day, following a relatively quiet night, quickly developed into a repetition of the previous day's attacks, with the only significant exception being the *Wiking*'s successful night attack of 14–15 October against Soviet troops entrenched in the park village near the Wieliszew railroad station and cemetery. In their midday report, the corps' divisions' informed Gille's forward *Gefechtstand* that the attacks that followed an hour-long Soviet artillery barrage beginning at 8:40 a.m. had noticeably more force than before, an indication that nearly all of the First Belorussian Front's additional artillery had been thrown into the fight to prepare for VIII Guards Tank Corps' commitment.

Another difference detected on 15 October was that the 47th Army was directing more of its effort against the *19. Pz.Div.*, which heretofore had avoided most of the heaviest fighting. The division commander reported infantry attacks in regimental strength against the Marcelin–Lejanów sector, while another was underway further north at Płudy. A small penetration was achieved at Marcelin, forcing Källner to commit his division reserve to throw them back. Heavy air attacks occurred all day, complicating the forming up of the counterattacking force. After a back and forth battle, during which heavy casualties were inflicted upon the enemy, by sundown the old *HKL* had been restored at Marcelin and one T-34 destroyed in exchange for one of *II. Abt./Pz.Rgt. 27*'s *Pz. IV* tanks. At Płudy, the Soviet attackers had been driven back 800 meters beyond the initial jump-off point for their attack by the elite troops from *Sturm-Btl. AOK 9* after being pummeled by German artillery. That afternoon, Soviet artillery fire noticeably slackened.

The fighting that day in the *Totenkopf* Division's sector was the heaviest it had experienced since the offensive's beginning. The attacks by the 47th Army again seemed more focused than before and had fallen into a recognizable pattern. First, the attack would be heralded by an hour-long drumfire barrage upon the division's defensive positions, immediately followed by one or more regimental-sized infantry attacks supported by tanks. On 15 October, the positions at (from north to south) Wegierskie Katy, Woła Aleksandra, and Rożopole experienced such assaults, all of which appeared to be closely supported by ground-attack aircraft. During the fighting that day alone, 129 IL-2s, 60 A-20 Bostons, and 30 fighter-bombers were spotted roaming over the division's battlefield, and were frequently seen attacking the *Totenkopf* Division's forward line of troops and individual *panzers*. The guns of *SS-Flak-Abt. 3* shot down four aircraft that day, but this did very little to stop the Red Air Force's aircraft from carrying out their mission.

As before, immediate counterattacks by *SS-Pz.Rgt. 3*, with ample artillery support, managed to rectify the situation and restore the front line. The only breakthrough noted as having occurred that day took place in the vicinity of Wegierskie Katy, defended by *Hstuf.* Bachmann's *II. Btl./Totenkopf*, but this was cleared up by a pincer attack launched from north and south of the village. After expelling the Soviet infantry battalion that had broken through the village, the counterattacking armored *Kampfgruppe* counted 122 enemy dead on the field. In addition, the *panzer* regiment claimed the destruction of six Soviet tanks from the 70th Guards Tank Regiment in the corridor between Jósefów and Wegierskie Katy that day: three destroyed by the Tigers of *9. Kompanie*, while the others were knocked out by the Panthers of *I. Abteilung*. The antitank gunners of *2. Kp./SS-Pz.Jag.Abt. 3* also accounted for a gigantic JSU-152 assault gun.[77] Later that afternoon, Soviet artillery fire began to ease, just as it had in the neighboring *19. Pz.Div.* sector.

One Soviet assault from the 76th Rifle Division managed to push its way past the *Totenkopf*'s thin infantry screen line north of Rożopole and get as far as the railway embankment at Choszczówka, where its leading battalion came into contact with *3. Kp./SS-Pz.Aufkl.Abt. 3* manning a strongpoint there. After braving a hail of machine-gun and mortar fire, at least 120 Soviet troops surged into the German positions, where vicious hand-to-hand combat broke out. Using machine pistols, shovels, and hand grenades, the Germans fought back desperately for an hour and a half, though outnumbered three or four to one. One seven-man squad, led by *Uscha.* Alfred Titschkus, distinguished itself in the fighting. Though every one of Titschkus's men were wounded in the melee that followed, including himself, by the time it was over his squad had captured 16 prisoners and counted 25 dead Red Army troops within his position. A counterattack by the rest of the company, which had been ejected from its positions while Titschkus's squad remained, drove the rest of the Soviet troops back towards the old main defense line and rescued the squad from complete annihilation. For his heroic actions that day, Titschkus was awarded the Knight's Cross two months later.[78] He and his squad were also recognized for their steadfastness by their mention in a *Wehrmachts-Ehrenblatt* (Honor Roll of the Day) on 10 November.

On the *Totenkopf*'s left, the *Wiking* Division had another hot day of it. It began at 8:45 a.m. with a one-hour *Trommelfeuer* on the *Westland*'s positions at Hill 87, the Wieliszew railway station, and around the perimeter of the Letniska forest cemetery. When the barrages ended, each location was immediately assaulted by a battalion-sized Soviet force from the 38th Guards Rifle Division. While the attacks at the railway station and cemetery were repulsed, that against Hill 87, which included a number of Soviet tanks, managed to break through the defenses of *II. Btl./Westland* and reach the Michalow estate along the Zegrze–Jablonna highway, effectively severing the connection between the *Totenkopf* and *Wiking* Divisions. This generated a genuine crisis, forcing Gille to commit the corps' reserve, the Panther battalion from the *19. Pz.Div.* positioned in Jablonna-Legjonowo. This battalion of approximately 30 tanks joined up with the men of *Hstuf.* Schmidt's *II. Btl./Westland* and counterattacked. After several hours of fighting, by midday the old main defense line running along the ridgeline, including Hill 87, was back in German hands.

On the left, the situation unfolded quite differently. At 10 a.m., after creating a smokescreen with phosphorous shells that obscured their approach, a large tank-supported force consisting of at least an infantry regiment attacked out of the smoke and broke through the position at the highway intersection southwest of Zagroby held by Borchert's reconnaissance battalion. Here, the connection between it and *I. Btl./Westland* was severed, but a counterattack was immediately carried out by the two battalions, with assault gun support, that temporarily forced the Soviets back to their lines. Their opponent tried again at 5 p.m., broke through the right flank of *SS-Pz.Aufkl.Abt. 5*, and began rolling up its defenses, while another unit attacked the positions in Zagroby held by *I. Btl./Germania*. Once again, SS tanks came to the rescue, on this occasion two *Pz. IV* from the *panzer* regiment's own reconnaissance platoon. These joined with *Hstuf.* Borchert's battalion and forced the Soviets back yet again, losing two of their tanks to the *panzers*.[79]

The action shifted later that day back to the woods between the cemetery and the Wieliszew railroad station, where Soviet troops and tanks repeatedly attempted to break through. Much of the fighting centered around *Hstuf.* Heder's 400-man *Alarm* battalion, which was defending around a villa in the Wieliszew park in a hedgehog position. Heder and his men soon found themselves bypassed and subjected to repeated enemy attacks. For a brief period, Heder later related, their situation seemed hopeless. Finally, near nightfall, a counterattack launched by *Stubaf.* Hack's *Westland* Regiment, in conjunction with *I. Abt./SS-Pz.Rgt. 5*, threw back the enemy and rescued Heder and the 40 unwounded survivors of his battalion. During the fighting, *SS-Oscha.* Schweiss's *Pz. IV* destroyed four Soviet tanks, while *II. Abteilung* knocked out eight others, bringing the *Wiking* Division's score that day to 14, including two T-34s and six M-4 Shermans.[80]

The final act of the day was a continuation of Hack's assault against the last remaining Soviet position on the western side of the highway and railroad line, the cemetery and forest church located on the northeastern edge of the Letniska forest. After an intensive preparatory artillery barrage that included the regiment's heavy weapons and *Nebelwerfer* fire from *SS-Werf.Abt. 504*, the men of *I. Btl./Westland*—supported by *2. Kp./SS-Pz.Rgt. 5*—launched their attack at 9 p.m. After a violent struggle in the darkness, which devolved at some points into hand-to-hand combat, the cemetery and church were cleared of Soviet troops within an hour. Fifty enemy dead were counted and three Soviet antitank guns captured.

By 10 p.m., physical contact was once again made between the *Westland* Regiment and Borchert's battalion, and the *Wiking*'s left flank was secured, at least for the night. On the other side of the Narew, where *Ostubaf.* Dorr's regimental headquarters was positioned with part of *II. Btl./Germania* and the recently arrived *Lds.Schtz.Btl. 649*, nothing of note was reported except continuing artillery harassing fire. On the same day, the division's *SS-Flak-Btl. 5* shot down three enemy aircraft. Overall, the *Wiking* Division had fought a very successful defensive action that day, though it had to eliminate no fewer than four Soviet penetrations of its line.

That evening, Gille recounted the day's events, noting that far more Soviet tanks were reported on that battlefield than before, a sure sign that the VIII Guards Tank Corps was about to be fully engaged. Fortunately for the defenders, most of the ground in Gille's area of operations was unfit for the employment of armor, being too swampy, with the exception of the corridor on his left flank at Nieporet in the *Wiking*'s sector. He mentioned the introduction of the 76th Rifle Division and 70th Guards Tank Regiment, as well as the detection of the apparent movement of control boundaries between the 47th and 70th Armies, in which the 47th shifted its attack zone to the north, leaving only the Nieporet area in the 70th Army's zone.

With this shift, there were also signs that the 1st Polish Army was moving up its northern boundary with the 47th Army, which would introduce additional numbers of troops to the correlation of forces, which were still overwhelmingly in the First Belorussian Front's favor. Instead of diminishing, Gille stated that there were signs that Rokossovsky's offensive was continuing to intensify. The Red Army's rifle divisions, though depleted, would keep attacking relentlessly, with or without tank support. He repeated his assessment that, with the renewed clear and sunny weather, his troops were suffering almost as many casualties from air attack as they were from the Red Army on the ground, and that his corps would need more dedicated close air support than what it was receiving, as well as the previously requested antiaircraft gun ammunition.[81]

That evening, Gille saw no signs that the overall direction of the Soviet attack was changing, and believed that the following day would bring renewed attacks. He had no explanation for the scaling down of the Red artillery's supporting fire, except that perhaps his corps' own preemptive fire had begun to make Gusev's and Popov's artillery brigades exercise more caution in the selection of their batteries' firing positions in order to avoid the Germans' more accurate fire. The shift of effort against the *19. Pz.Div.* worried Gille, who knew that Källner's division defended the only high-speed avenue of approach to Modlin with the best highway network. Why Rokossovsky had chosen the Rożopole and Nieporet sectors to employ his armor must have puzzled him. Gille closed by repeating that his corps was continuing to suffer high casualties, particularly in infantry, but that he would aggressively defend against the following day's attacks.

Paradoxically, that evening the *9. Armee* commander expressed his optimism that the Soviet offensive east of the Vistula had reached its culminating point, despite the evidence to the contrary offered by Gille. The slackening that afternoon of the Soviet artillery fire was seen by von Lüttwitz as a sign that "the point in time has arrived where the long-awaited subsiding of the [Soviet] offensive can finally be seen approaching."[82] Perhaps this was wishful thinking on von Lüttwitz's part, but he had received some rather disturbing reports that day, based on aerial photoreconnaissance, which indicated that the Soviet 8th Guards Army had recently begun to increase the number of its artillery batteries in the Magnuszew bridgehead from the low 40s into the 80s, a doubling of the army's firepower. This, von Lüttwitz believed, was a clear sign that the offensive along his army's southern border in the direction of Radom was about to resume. This was also confirmed by reports from a German agent (a so-called *V-Mann*) operating on the east bank of the Vistula. Whether these reports were true or not (it could have been a classic example of Soviet *Maskirovka* deception), it prompted the *9. Armee* commander to begin contemplating the immediate transfer of the *19. Pz.Div.* out of Gille's corps to the *VIII. Armeekorps* to serve as the army's reserve should the 8th Guards Army resume its offensive activity in the near future.[83]

In a subsequent telephone conversation that evening after being informed that the *9. Armee* commander was seriously contemplating such a plan, Gille strongly protested this possible action, telling his army commander that if he withdrew

Källner's division at this point in the battle, his corps' front would collapse. In response, von Lüttwitz told Gille that his fears were misplaced and that all he had to do was to incorporate the several thousand *Luftwaffe* replacements he had received for his two SS divisions and that this, combined with his corps' withdrawal to the *Fuchsstellung*, would give him a troop density sufficient to continue his heretofore successful defense of the Wet Triangle. Gille retorted that these recruits could not be considered trained nor ready for intensive ground combat, and stressed that the *19. Pz.Div.* needed to stay where it was until the crisis had passed. Fortunately, von Lüttwitz agreed to think it over and would decide what to do at a later time.

Another event that day that occupied the *9. Armee* commander's attention was the visit to his command post by Reinhardt, who was making a tour of the army's front, visiting the headquarters of the *XLVI. Pz.Korps*, *73. Inf.Div.*, *19. Pz.Div.*, and the *IV. SS-Pz.Korps*. Among the many topics discussed, including Reinhardt's relaxation of the disciplinary measures against the *73. Inf.Div.* due to its commendable performance in battle since its reconstitution, was the keen interest expressed by both Reinhardt and von Lüttwitz in the future status of Källner's division. When asked by Reinhardt as to his opinion concerning the construction of the new defensive line in the Narew–Vistula triangle, to his credit Källner replied that it was in no way ready for occupation by the *IV. SS-Pz.Korps* and that it would be best to wait until the current Soviet offensive had run its course before moving his division west of the Vistula to take up its former position.

Reinhardt and von Lüttwitz then drove north to visit Gille's command post at the old Klein-Kazun fortress in Modlin. The first question Gille was asked by his army group commander was what he had done so far with the *Luftwaffe* replacements assigned to his corps. Gille reported that 1,762 men had already been incorporated into the *Totenkopf* Division since 23 September, with another 1,302 assigned to the *Wiking* Division. He also responded, when asked, that the *Feld-Ausb.Btl.* of the *Totenkopf* was in Freystadt, while that of the *Wiking* was in Lowitsch (Lowicz), 50 kilometers west of Warsaw. Several thousand other newly assigned replacements were undergoing infantry training between both locations. Gille further informed Reinhardt that none of them had arrived with weapons and that the overall level of training upon arrival was miserable, with most of them not even able to handle the standard Mauser *Karabine* 98K. Reinhardt then asked Gille about the leadership situation in his divisions. He responded that most of the combat elements of the infantry regiments and engineer battalions now lacked junior officers and NCOs, and that this had caused great difficulties in training the recruits as well as incorporating them while a major battle was still underway.

The topic then shifted to the status of the construction of the final defensive position on his corps' left flank near Zegrze (the *Fuchsstellung*). Gille responded that as far as the terrain was concerned, the position looked well laid-out and tactically promising, and would enable him to spare troops to be used to form a corps reserve. Reinhardt then drove the point home, asking. "Will the occupation of this position allow a division to be pulled out?" Gille replied, "No, because the [corps'] combat strength has sunk so low and the training level of my new replacements is so minimal, that this would not be advisable." Gille explained that even if his corps moved into a new defensive position with a shorter front line, he expected that the Soviets would still use the same number of troops that they were now using against his current position. Whether or not Gille's frank answers influenced Reinhardt's or von Lüttwitz's decision, it would be five more days before the *19. Pz.Div.* began to pull out. Gille had won a temporary reprieve.[84]

Back at von Lüttwitz's headquarters after their field inspection, he and Reinhardt privately discussed various courses of action before Reinhardt flew back to his headquarters at *H.Gr. Mitte*. Aside from discussing their mutual concerns about the situation developing near Radom in the *VIII. Armeekorps* sector and other related matters, they discussed what to do with the *IV. SS-Pz.Korps*: should it stay where it was or be withdrawn, abandoning the *Festungsdreick* (fortress triangle) of Modlin–Zegrze–Warsaw? Reinhardt suggested to von Lüttwitz that leaving the SS corps in its current location would make the *OKW* happy, since it would be better to keep SS troops there instead of *Wehrmacht* troops (with the implication that with the withdrawal of the *19. Pz.Div.*, it would become an entirely SS problem).

Another course of action they discussed was pulling all forces out of the Wet Triangle entirely, placing the security of the western bank of the Vistula north of Warsaw in the hands of the fresh *337. Volks-Gren.Div.* This proposal was discarded, since not only was the *337. VGD* inexperienced, but the corps holding the area, *XLVI. Pz.Korps*, would still be short a division needed to hold this line. The conversation ended with no decision being made. The *IV. SS-Pz.Korps* would stay where it was for the time being.[85] In retrospect, this was probably not a wise decision, because it made no sense to keep two elite *panzer* divisions in such a static situation where they could not employ their mobility to advantage; for a World War I-style battlefield such as the Wet Triangle had become, infantry divisions would have been far better suited than two tank divisions.

Elsewhere, the situation for the Third Reich had not noticeably improved, though on the Western Front the Allied advance had been slowed in Alsace-Lorraine, the Low Countries, and on the German border. The Italian Front was still holding, while most German troops had been successfully withdrawn from the Balkans in the wake of the defection of Rumania and Bulgaria. The Soviets were advancing inexorably on Hungary and in Slovakia, and had made initial incursions into East Prussia. *Heeresgruppe Nord* had been virtually cut off in Courland. The most distressing news that day was the report that Hungary's Regent, Admiral Horthy, had secretly been negotiating with Moscow to defect from the alliance with Germany. This would have a two-fold ramification: the first was the possibility that Hungary's armed forces would switch sides, as had the Rumanians, which led to the loss of two German field armies and the collapse of

H.Gr. Süd Ukraine; the other, more immediate, matter was the status of the several Hungarian units still operating under *9. Armee* control, whose men might feel more sympathy towards the Polish resistance than with the Third Reich. Certainly, von Lüttwitz and Reinhardt had a lot on their minds to consider, while "all" Gille had to worry about was how to fight the battle at hand.[86]

To Gille's surprise, but probably not to anyone on the staff of *9. Armee*, the next day, 16 October, saw a noticeable decrease in the size and scale of attacks by both Soviet armies facing *IV. SS-Pz.Korps*. Other than several minor company-sized attacks against the front lines of the *19. Pz.Div.* and *Totenkopf* Division, the only other action either division had to report was the usual harassing artillery fire (but no lengthy barrages) and increasing Soviet aerial reconnaissance. Even the bombing and strafing attacks by the 16th Air Army had lessened, a providential event, given that the corps was almost completely out of ammunition for its light and heavy antiaircraft batteries. The only offensive action in the *Totenkopf* Division's sector worth mention occurred when a 200-man force tried to take a hill north of Rożopole without success in the late morning, which Gille interpreted as an attempt to seize a more favorable attack position when the offensive resumed. Both the *19. Pz.Div.* and *Totenkopf* Division employed artillery ambushes and preventive strikes against newly identified Soviet assembly areas and troop concentrations.

Things were not as quiet in the *Wiking* Division's sector, where the fighting continued unabated. Here, the 70th Army continued its efforts to break through north and west of Nieporet, and as it had the day before, the fighting swirled around the Wieliszew cemetery and the Letniska forest church, Hill 87, the railroad and highway overpass, and the summer villas in the Wieliszew park. All of these locations changed hands several times that day, following what had become a pattern: the Soviets would attack, break through or seize a key terrain feature, the *Wiking* Division would counterattack with tanks supported by infantry from the *Westland* Regiment, and the Soviets would be thrown out again. Both sides were employing their artillery unsparingly, though the *Wiking*'s was more accurate. During the eight days of battle, including the preemptive attacks of 9 October, the *IV. SS-Pz.Korps* artillery and *Flak* troops had fired over 3,239 tons (6,478,000lb) of shells at the enemy, the equivalent of the loads of several dozen freight trains.[87]

The Letniska forest on the north side of the railway was devastated by the constant fighting, with hundreds of trees reduced to splinters by artillery fire or shorn of their tops by tank shells. On that day, one Soviet battalion was able to push across the railroad into a small glove-shaped wood a kilometer northwest of the Michalow estate; here a counterattack led by *Hstuf.* Flügel's Panther battalion, with infantry from *II. Btl./Westland*, overran their position and killed 143 of them, driving away the survivors, who left behind their 7.62cm antitank gun. On the left flank, a *Werfer* battery, joined by division artillery, blasted a Soviet assembly area spotted a few hundred meters southeast of the railway viaduct southwest of Zagroby. The best news for the Germans that day was that the *II. Bataillon* from the *Germania* Regiment had finally been brought over the river; except for the regimental headquarters and part of its *III. Bataillon*, nearly all of the *Germania* was now fighting south of the Narew. By midnight, all of the *Wiking*'s positions lost that morning had been retaken, with the exception of the forest cemetery at Wieliszew, which would have to wait for the following day. The severity of the fighting is reflected in the division's daily summary, which reported nine tanks destroyed, including six M-4 Shermans, and two IL-2 *Sturmoviks* as well as three LaGG-3 fighters shot down by *Flak* troops.[88]

Gille summarized the day's events, seeing the easing of Soviet attacks as a sign that the 14 infantry divisions that had now been identified were regrouping, and had not given up their offensive intentions, despite what the *9. Armee* commander and his staff believed. Indeed, Gille declared his certainty that the 47th and 70th Armies had merely paused to absorb replacements (as confirmed by POW interrogations), bring up more artillery, and shuffle their units in conformance to boundary changes drawn up by their Front headquarters. The *9. Armee* intelligence staff had reported that the 1st Polish Army had taken over a greater portion of the 47th Army's attack zone, enabling the latter formation to shift over to the north, while the 70th Army on its right decreased its attack frontage to 14 kilometers. The 47th Army reduced its frontage to the same width, enabling both armies to further concentrate their combat power for the next phase of the operation along very narrow attacking zones.

An additional Polish infantry division was observed moving north through Praga, as evidenced by the sighting of 600 trucks moving through the city, within the operational area of the 1st Polish Army. This was confirmed when the *337. VGD* captured 18 members of the Polish 4th Infantry Division who had crossed the river opposite Warsaw with the evident intent of deserting. With this addition to its order of battle, the 1st Polish Army could now employ two or three divisions against the right flank of the *19. Pz.Div.* The last item Gille reported was evidence that seemed to indicate that 150 tanks of the VIII Guards Tank Corps had taken up attack positions in the Jablonna forest west of Nieporet, based on POW interrogations, radio intercepts, and the disappearance of tanks from elsewhere along the corps' front, as reported by the *19. Pz.Div.* and *Totenkopf* Division. This could only mean, they thought, that the 70th Army had not given up its intention of seeking its operational breakthrough at that location and would use the VIII Guards Tank Corps for that purpose. Clearly, heavier fighting was ahead.

At army headquarters, von Lüttwitz agreed with Gille that based on the intelligence reports received that day, it did indeed appear that the attack against the corps' left flank would continue after all. However, he believed that the resumption of the offensive by the 47th and 70th Armies would probably not occur until 26 or 27 October, when Batov's 65th Army was expected to attack towards Modlin. In the meantime, *9. Armee* would continue to develop contingency plans to defend against the anticipated offensive from the Magnuszew bridgehead towards Warka.

It was still developing contingency plans should the 65th Army advance as far as Modlin, but it had no forces to spare in such an event. The *19. Pz.Div.* was intended to play a key role in the effort to contain any offensive towards Warka, and von Lüttwitz was anxious to remove it from Gille's corps as soon as it was safe to do so. A Soviet deserter had confirmed that the breakout from the Magnuszew bridgehead was scheduled to unfold on 27 October to coincide with the launching of Batov's offensive on that date.[89]

Other matters also drew the *9. Armee* commander's attention away from the east bank of the Vistula, such as the re-emerging partisan threat—this time posed by an elusive mounted Polish battalion that had risen from the ashes of *Unternehmen Sternschnuppe*—and the decision concerning the ultimate fate of the Hungarian troops remaining in the *9. Armee* area of operations. The latter troops, *H.Gr. Mitte*'s commander had decided the day before, would be disarmed and used to build defensive positions for the *IV. SS-Pz.Korps* and *VIII. Armeekorps*. This would be a temporary measure, designed to keep them otherwise occupied until some sort of a political solution had been found that would reconcile ongoing German–Hungarian political disagreements and clarify their military relationship; at such a point, the Hungarians would probably be allowed to go home and join their fellow countrymen in the defense of their nation. However, the bonds of trust that had existed between German troops and their Hungarian brethren had vanished, with unforeseeable consequences.

For the *19. Pz.Div.* and *Totenkopf* Division, 17 October unfolded much as the previous day. Aside from the ubiquitous artillery duels taking place throughout the day, especially a German strike against Soviet forces assembling at Rożopole, both sides conducted vigorous nighttime patrolling activity to gather prisoners, which in some cases resulted in vicious clashes when patrols from either side encountered one another in the darkness. Several raids conducted by the *Totenkopf* brought in 30 Soviet prisoners, who were immediately sent to the division's *Ic* for interrogation. In addition to the POWs, four Soviet deserters crossed into German lines, who, upon interrogation, also revealed further valuable information about enemy troops dispositions and intentions, which was shared with the corps' *ARKO*. Taking advantage of the brief lull in operations, both sides improved their fighting positions, cleaned weapons, and restocked ammunition. There was no time to rest, since it was evident that this pause would not be as long as the last one.

The troops of the *Wiking* Division had no opportunity to enjoy even this small luxury. Fighting continued uninterruptedly in the battle zone west and northwest of Nieporet, with the events of 17 October closely resembling those of the previous day, including fighting around the cemetery and the forest church, the railroad overpass southwest of Zagroby, and in the Wieliszew park. A Soviet attack during the early afternoon preceded by a short artillery barrage seized the German strongpoint atop Hill 87 southeast of the Michałow estate after eliminating all of the defending troops from *II. Btl./Westland*. A German counterattack launched shortly afterwards to retake the hill counted 600 enemy dead as it swept through the parkland. The division's artillery, augmented by the rocket launcher batteries of *SS-Werf.Abt. 504*, battered the woods west of Nieporet, where the VIII Guards Tank Corps was believed to be assembling. Though no tanks were observed and no effects could be immediately discerned, thick columns of black smoke could be seen afterwards.

Later that evening, the surviving troops of *Hstuf.* Heder's *Alarm* battalion were relieved in the line by *Hstuf.* Pleiner's *II. Btl./Germania* and disbanded. Heder himself resumed command of his *Pionier* battalion, which had been re-formed after each of its companies had been parceled out to the *Panzergrenadier* regiments for the past several weeks. Now designated the division's reserve, Heder would use the time to rebuild its battalion, which had suffered heavy casualties during the fighting. Its *2. Kompanie* alone had suffered 70 casualties during the past seven days, including 20 killed in action. When Heder returned, the *Kampfstärke* of his battalion had sunk to the strength of a weak company, though on that same day it received an influx of replacements, mostly ex-*Luftwaffe* troops fresh from two weeks at the *Feld-Ers.Btl. 5*, bringing its effective strength up to 381 men. However, most of his veteran officers and NCOs were gone. Two days later, when Pleiner of the *II. Btl./Germania* was wounded in action, Heder, who had a reputation as an excellent infantry leader, was placed in temporary command until another commander was appointed.[90]

Gille reflected the events of the day in his evening report, saving most of his comments for the portion reserved for his assessment. He interpreted the signs of the slowing down of combat activity as merely a prelude for the continuation of the offensive by 47th and 70th Armies, and believed the displacement of heavy artillery forward into the forest west of Nieporet was a sure sign of the enemy's intentions. Nor had his troops observed the removal of any Soviet artillery batteries, which would have been a clear sign that Marshal Rokossovsky had given up and planned to use his guns elsewhere. The number of firing batteries was unchanged, the *IV. SS-Pz.Korps* commander said.[91]

By this time, based on reports sent from *Ostubaf.* Hans Dorr's headquarters north of the Narew, Gille began to believe that the 65th Army north of Serock was also beginning to display more aggressive activity after all, his assessment falling in line with that of his army commander from the previous evening's *9. Armee* report. To add to Gille's suspicions, a large Soviet unit of undetermined type with several hundred vehicles was spotted moving through the town of Wyszków 70 kilometers to the east; its destination was unknown, but Gille believed that it could either be headed for Serock or be added to the forces arrayed against him. The combined effect of all this may have begun to play upon his own fears and insecurities; having to fight one enemy force while looking over his shoulder at another that might strike him in the flank or rear must have been an unsettling thought to contemplate.

That same day, all of the units reported their *Kampfstärke* to Gille's *IIb*, who relayed the numbers to his counterpart at *9. Armee* headquarters. Unsurprisingly, the strongest division in terms of manpower was the *19. Pz.Div.*, with a *Kampfstärke* of 2,278 men. Adding the 1,000 men of the other three infantry battalions attached to it that were positioned on the west bank of the Vistula, the division's strength was even higher, though these were not involved directly in the fighting. *Gen. Lt.* Källner's division still had 72 operational tanks and tank destroyers and 11 antitank guns, as well as an additional 15 heavy antitank guns assigned to *Art. Pak.Abt. 1061* stationed on the western bank of the river. It was no small wonder that von Lüttwitz wanted to bring it back across the Vistula while it was still nearly at full strength.

The weakest division in Gille's corps was the *Totenkopf*, whose *Kampfstärke* had shrunk to an astonishingly low 748 men. Its weakest battalion was *II. Btl./SS-Pz. Gren.Rgt. Totenkopf*, with only 25 effectives reported on 16 October. During the past week of bitter fighting, it had lost over half of its remaining infantry strength, necessitating the armor to play a more central role in the division's defensive plans. With regard to armor, the division reported only 55 operational tanks, assault guns, and tank destroyers, including four Tigers. Its antitank gun complement had shrunk to just three, the remainder being either destroyed or under repair. Not reflected in these reports were the numbers of other major weapons systems destroyed, but according to official *Ib* records, between 10 and 16 October, *Obf.* Becker's division had lost 12 7.5cm antitank guns, eight 7.5cm infantry howitzers, two other field howitzers, and several antiaircraft guns. Still, the morale of the division was good, and its low *Kampfstärke* had been compensated somewhat by the attachment of Ritter's *Gren.Btl.z.b.V. 560*, with 266 effectives, and the reinforced *SS-Jäg.Btl. 501*'s 154 men, bringing the division's total effective ground troop strength to 1,168 men, roughly one-third of its normal complement.[92]

The *Wiking* was far better off than its sister division, having recently received an influx of replacements from its *Feld-Ers.Btl. 5*. On 16 October, its *IIa* reported a *Kampfstärke* of 1,766 men and it had no troops attached from other units. Still, it was operating at only 50 percent of its authorized effective strength and many of its men were newly assigned replacements with no front-line experience. Regarding armor, the division could still count 44 operational tanks, assault guns, and tank destroyers, as well as 12 antitank guns. Like the *Totenkopf*, it had also lost a great deal of ordnance during the past week, including four 7.5cm antitank guns, five 7.5cm infantry howitzers, two self-propelled antitank guns, four 12cm mortars, and two self-propelled *Hummel* 15cm howitzers. Many of these weapons had been lost on account of air attacks carried out by the 16th Air Army. Though on paper the division still had a great deal of remaining combat power, it stood squarely in the path of the VIII Guards Tank Corps and the 70th Army, and would undoubtedly be whittled down even further in the fighting to come.

That evening, in his summary of the day's action for 17 October, the mind of the *9. Armee* commander was clearly elsewhere, for his report to *H.Gr. Mitte* began with the sentence, "The day passed with no fighting worth mentioning." This would have been news to the men of the *Wiking* Division, who were engaged the entire day in heavy back-and-forth fighting between Hill 87 and Zagroby. Von Lüttwitz assessed that while it appeared the fighting in the Vistula–Narew–Bug triangle had "virtually ceased," the build-up in the Magnuszew bridgehead appeared to be continuing. This, he believed, had confirmed his decision to take the *19. Pz.Div.* away from Gille and send it south to a reserve position near Radom. Preparatory orders were issued that night to *IV. SS-Pz.Korps* instructing Gille and his staff to begin planning the transfer at a date in the very near future, as determined by the tactical situation. One of the tasks Gille was assigned was to immediately begin making arrangements to move one of Källner's tank battalions, to be followed shortly thereafter by a further armored *Kampfgruppe*. The current front-line trace of the *19. Pz.Div.* would remain where it was, but at a point to be determined, the corps would then withdraw to the *Fuchsstellung*, and the rest of Källner's division would immediately follow. Clearly, von Lüttwitz believed that Gille with his two divisions would be able to manage with a shorter defensive line. The transfer of the tank battalion from *19. Pz.Div.* was directed to occur no later than 21 October.[93]

The *9. Armee* commander made no mention of developments across the Narew in the *2. Armee* sector. After the failure of *Unternehmen Sonnenblume*, the forces of *XX. Armeekorps* had shifted over to a defensive posture on 12 October, after having achieved nothing substantial in exchange for heavy losses in tank and troops. The First Belorussian Front's commander was planning a small-scale counteroffensive between Serock and Pułtusk, intended to seize favorable terrain needed for the grand offensive planned for January 1945, in which this Front would play a major role. However, there is no indication that either Batov or Rokossovsky were planning on using the 65th Army at that time to entrap the German forces defending the Wet Triangle by taking Modlin, unless the opportunity presented itself. That operation would come much later and would not involve Gille's corps.

Astonishingly, hardly any combat activity took place the following day, 18 October. Even in the *Wiking* Division's sector, very little was reported, other than the "usual" activity that the other two divisions were engaged in—artillery ambushes, preemptive strikes, aggressive patrolling, and repelling air attacks, while the Soviet forces arrayed opposite them did the same. One company-sized attack against a forward outpost of the *Totenkopf* Division at Wegierskie Katy was wiped out at 5:30 p.m., with 75 enemy dead counted afterwards. Four Soviet tanks were reported on the other side of the river north of Serock by *Ostubaf.* Dorr's headquarters, but these were so far away from the rest of the division that it could not have made much of an impression on Gille or his staff. Gille's assessment that evening remained unchanged from the previous day.

Another event that Gille did not mention but would have known about was that thousands of disarmed Hungarian troops had arrived in the corps' rear area to speed up the construction of the *Fuchsstellung*, upon whose completion the *9. Armee* commander depended as a precondition for moving the *19. Pz.Div.* out of the *IV. SS-Pz.Korps'* defensive sector.[94] It was also reported that the *Totenkopf* Divison's *Feld-Ers.Abt. 3* had finally arrived in Modlin and that three battalions (*1.* to *11. Kompanie*) of *SS-Feld-Ausb.Rgt. 5*, whose two training battalions provided replacements for both SS divisions' field replacement battalions, had nearly completed itheir movement to Löwitsch from the SS training area in Bohemia and Moravia.[95] Once they were set up and had placed their training program back into operation, these replacement and training units would considerably ease Gille's manpower problem.

In his evening report to *H.Gr. Mitte*, von Lüttwitz had very little to say regarding the *IV. SS-Pz.Korps*, except to mention that he had ordered the armored battlegroup from *19. Pz.Div.* forming around *Pz.Gren.Rgt. 74* to begin rail movement to its new reserve area near Warka beginning on the evening of 19 October. This was to be concluded by 21 October. In the meantime, the rest of the *19. Pz.Div.* would remain where it was, pending the withdrawal of Gille's corps to the *Fuchsstellung*. Earlier that day, von Lüttwitz had been instructed by Reinhardt, who had been informed by *OKH*, that he was not to disarm the Hungarians after all, but rather that they were to be gathered up, armed, and shipped by rail to the neighboring *4. Pz.Armee* to the south. Here, they were intended to be reinserted into the front line between two German divisions. Apparently, the *9. Armee* commander was not overly happy with this development, stating his belief that they would be far more gainfully employed as labor battalions rather than in the front line, where their performance had been less than satisfactory. As construction troops, he believed they were excellent.[96]

In the rest of his report, von Lüttwitz expressed his concerns about the future course that operations would take on the Eastern Front. He worried about a major offensive spilling out of the Magnuszew bridgehead and about having to hold the Wet Triangle when it was starting to become tactically pointless to do so. He was also concerned about what the 65th Army might do, and whether any future offensive towards Serock would be a prelude to a much larger offensive aimed at slashing to the northwest and cutting off East Prussia from the rest of Germany, the old familiar fear. In any case, there was little he could do should that occur, but the fact that his army possessed few appreciable reserves to stop or even slow down any major Soviet offensive beyond the Vistula was a legitimate concern.

His last order of business with Reinhardt was to discuss the future of Warsaw as a *Festung* (fortress city), and the need to place the *Festungskommandant* under the command of a field headquarters. This unenviable task befell *Gen.d.Art.* Felzmann's *XLVI. Pz.Korps*, which was currently defending the Vistula defense line south of Gille's corps between Warsaw and Augustowka. *Generalmajor* Hellmuth Eisenstuck was given the even less enviable position of serving as fortress commander under Felzmann.

Thursday, 19 October began as a rainy, quiet morning, after an equally quiet evening. It promised to be as uneventful as the previous two days, making it easy for the soldiers of both sides to believe that perhaps the Soviet offensive had after all been called off. The calm was illusory. In response to reports that morning from the *Wiking* Division that a large enemy force was once again attempting to move into the area of the Michałow estate, the corps reserve, *Hauptmann* Krammer's *I. Abt./Pz.Rgt. 27*, began moving to the east in the early morning darkness. At 6:20 a.m., he reported that his battalion shortly thereafter had run into a sizeable body of Soviet troops and immediately deployed for combat. Within minutes, the battalion's 36 Panthers had smashed the approaching enemy formation. With that, the third defensive battle of Warsaw was back in full cry.

German artillery and rocket batteries then began firing at prearranged targets based on their individual fire plans. The Soviet gunners responded in kind, and in greater volume, though not as quickly nor as accurately. Soon shells and rockets were falling heavily on both sides. Aside from artillery fire, the *19. Pz.Div.* had nothing to report except a company-sized attack against one of its position at Lejanów that was easily repulsed. Things were not so easy in the *Totenkopf*s sector, which had to endure a 90-minute artillery barrage from 7:45 a.m. that frequently rose to drumfire proportions. A battalion-sized attack at Rożopole was beaten back, and no fewer than seven separate large-scale assaults of 300–500 men each, with tank support, were carried out in the gap between Wegierskie Katy and Woła Aleksandra throughout the day. These were all unsuccessful, thanks to the intervention of the division's *panzer* and artillery regiments. One Soviet tank was reported as destroyed.

As may have been expected, most of the heaviest fighting took place in the *Wiking* Division's sector between Hill 87 and Zagroby, the scene of heavy fighting during the past week. The division had to endure the same 90-minute barrage as had *Obf.* Becker's, with most of the shells raining down on the 4-kilometer wide defense line extending from the Michałow estate to the Wieliszew park area, and upon the railroad viaduct/highway intersection southwest of Zagroby, two locations that evidence already indicated having been chosen as sites for the intended breakthrough attack by the VIII Guards Tank Corps. Hill 87 was quickly taken from *Hstuf.* Schmidt's *II. Btl./Westland*, whose survivors withdrew on the other side of the highway to rally and prepare a counterattack. Soviet artillery fire was continuous, making any German troop movement a dangerous proposition, but *Stubaf.* Hack and his *Westland* Regiment, now joined by *I. Btl./Germania*, had to retake the lost position at all costs.

A large number of Soviet infantrymen had seized the Wieliszew parkland again, this time reinforced by tanks. More see-saw fighting raged throughout the afternoon for possession of these key positions, which had been shattered and churned up so much by artillery fire that it became nearly impossible to see where the previous fighting positions had been located, so troops took shelter in the many shell craters dotting the area. German artillery fire kept most of the VIII Guards Tank Corps hemmed in the forest on the German left, preventing Lt.Gen. Popov's brigades from carrying out the attacks he sought. On the *Wiking*'s right flank, the breakthrough at the parkland was finally cleared up that evening, after three Soviet tanks were destroyed and the infantry forced back across the highway. In return, the division lost four of its armored fighting vehicles that day—two *StuG IV* assault guns from *4. Kp./SS-Pz.Div. 5* and two *Jg.Pz. IV* tank destroyers from *SS-Pz.Jag.Abt. 5*. One *StuG IV* was lost due to artillery fire, the other three vehicles to Soviet tanks and antitank guns.[97]

In his evening report submitted at 8:30 p.m., Gille assessed that the action by the 47th and 70th Armies that day had been carried out with the intent of securing favorable jump-off positions for the main attack, which he expected to happen the following day, 20 October. This attack, he reckoned, would be in conjunction with one by the 65th Army that the intelligence staffs of *9. Armee* and *H.Gr. Mitte* had expected would unfold at the same time on the northern bank of the Narew.[98] Gille still had forces positioned there, including the headquarters of Dorr's *Germania* Regiment, his regimental antitank and infantry howitzer company, one tank platoon, most of *III. Btl./Germania*, an artillery battalion, and an attached *Landeschutzen* battalion.

The most encouraging thing that Gille said that day was a phrase that he had not uttered in a while—that on this day, 19 October, he believed that his corps had achieved a notable defensive victory, something he rarely said. Not only had the enemy been denied the favorable positions he needed to launch his attacks on the following day, but Gille's troops had inflicted heavy, bloody losses on them. He ended his report with a warning, however. Unless the impending enemy offensive north of the Narew was stopped before it reached Modlin, he wrote, his current defensive success and those of the past several weeks would have been for nothing if his corps was surrounded. It would not matter how well the *Fuchsstellung* or several other intermediate defense lines were constructed if there was no viable avenue of escape for his divisions when or if the time came. Another object of his concern was the fact that despite the clear need to have it remain where it was, the armored *Kampfgruppe* from the *19. Pz.Div.*, including the *panzer* regiment's Panther battalion, began to pull out of the line that evening in preparation for its move by rail to the south. The trains had already been laid on and were waiting in Modlin for its arrival.

Although he acknowledged and agreed with Gille's reports about the resumption of the offensive by the 47th and 70th Armies, and even expressed his satisfaction with the results of the day's fighting in his evening report, the *9. Armee* commander was evidently far more worried about the resumption of the offensive by the 8th Guards Army from the Magnuszew bridgehead. Apparently, the First Belorussian

Front's *Maskirovka* had worked as intended upon von Lüttwitz's thinking, who expressed his fixation that evening with the immediate need to build up a large enough reserve for the *VIII. Armeekorps* and *9. Armee* from existing assets to be strong enough to handle the offensive when it came. The *Kampfgruppe* from the *19. Pz.Div.* figured prominently in his plan, but von Lüttwitz believed even that would not be enough. He wanted the entire division shipped south as soon as possible, and his anxiety about the slow pace of the construction of the *Fuchsstellung* for *IV. SS-Pz.Korps* clearly vexed him, though no fault of Gille's. The fact that *9. Armee* had been ordered to withdraw the Hungarian troops who had been helping to construct the fortifications must not have helped to ease his concerns.[99]

The *9. Armee* commander did express some concern about the initial reports that indicated the offensive by the 65th Army north of the Narew had already begun, his primary worry being that should Batov's attack reach as far as Serock and control the entire southern bank of the Narew, how would he be able to extricate Gille's corps? Without any bridges, his men would have to swim across the Vistula or surrender. The proposal by von Lüttwitz to *Gen.Oberst* Reinhardt to allow him to withdraw his army's right flank as far as Radom was categorically refused by *H.Gr. Mitte*, although this measure would have freed up forces to form an army reserve. By this point in the campaign, Hitler himself was increasingly meddling in decisions at the tactical level, and giving up ground without a fight was becoming heresy. Reinhardt was no Walter Model, and lacked the stomach to challenge Hitler directly. Even *Gen.Oberst* Heinz Guderian, Chief of Staff of the *OKH*, was finding it increasingly difficult to prevent Hitler's dilettantism from interfering with rational decision-making. The *9. Armee* would therefore not yield a foot of ground.

As predicted, the 47th and 70th Armies initiated their breakout attempt on 20 October. After a relatively quiet morning, save for occasional random artillery fire, in the early afternoon, after a brief but very powerful artillery barrage, Soviet troops in regimental strength (500–1,000 men), supported by tanks, attacked the *Wiking* Division's positions in the parkland on the northern side of the highway near the Wieliszew railroad station. At the same time, an equally strong force stormed the grounds surrounding the Letniska forest cemetery and regained possession of it after ejecting the defenders from *I. Btl./Westland*.

Because the *19. Pz.Div.* suffered only from occasional artillery fire that day, it was still able to withdraw the armored battlegroup without interference. This *Kampfgruppe*, consisting of *Pz.Gren.Rgt. 74*, *I. Abt./Pz.Rgt. 27*, and one artillery battalion, would begin loading in Modlin for their trip to the Warka area that evening. Once its trains had departed, it would be very difficult to recall them. The *Totenkopf* Division once again found itself the target of numerous battalion-sized Soviet attacks against its positions at Jósefów and Rożopole, which were all driven off with heavy loss to the enemy assault troops. Afterwards, *Obf.* Becker's men counted 85 enemy dead and two prisoners, as well as two Soviet deserters. Most of the damage the division suffered that day was primarily caused by artillery fire, which rained down upon its positions throughout the afternoon. Its own artillery had responded with the usual degree of accuracy, though the damage it inflicted upon the Soviet gunners is unknown.

Apparently believing that the time had come to employ the VIII Guards Tank Corps' spearheads, Col.Gen. Vasily Popov, 70th Army commander, unleashed Maj. Gen. Alexei Popov's corps in mid-afternoon, with the bulk of its tanks advancing in the gap between Zagroby and the woods to the south. While Soviet and German artillery fell heavily between the forest cemetery and the parkland, the infantry from both sides bitterly fought one another for possession of a few square kilometers of shattered woodland. The prize the 70th Army sought was the town of Łajsk, for once they had this key feature in their possession, this second mobility corridor would be opened up to support the other tank thrust that was taking place on the other side of the forest.

Despite the best efforts of the defending troops from the *Wiking* Division, they had no success in retaking the lost ground as they had the previous day. They simply lacked enough tanks and assault guns, let alone infantry, to do it. On the other hand, neither were the Soviet tanks able to achieve their breakthrough on 20 October—that would have to wait for the next day. The tanks from *II. Abt./SS-Pz. Rgt. 5* had been able to block all attempts by Soviet tanks to cross the highway west of the Michałow estate on the German right; similarly, the demolition of the railway overpass at the highway intersection southwest of Zagroby that afternoon had temporarily stymied the enemy's tanks on the left. The few remaining tanks and assault guns of *I. Abt./SS-Pz.Rgt. 5* waited in ambush for any Soviet armor that attempted to pass around the obstacle, but the attack did not come that afternoon, much to everyone's surprise. The *Pz. IV* commanded by *SS-Oscha.* Schweiss was knocked out that afternoon when he was supporting an attack by *I. Btl./Germania* against the forest cemetery, leaving only 10 operational *Pz. IV* tanks in the entire regiment. Schweiss survived his injuries, though the danger of operating in the forest without an infantry escort had once again been clearly illustrated.

What had changed in the equation to the Germans' disadvantage was that *I. Abt./Pz.Rgt. 27* was no longer there to influence the fighting, since it had been pulled out during the previous evening. While the *Wiking* Division could still defend, it was finding it increasingly difficult to counterattack and hold terrain without infantry. Even though over 1,000 new replacements, mostly *Luftwaffe* transfers, had been assigned to the regiments, they suffered a high casualty rate, as Gille had predicted. They were simply not prepared to fight in a major battle, having no time to become accustomed to its sights and sounds. On account of this shortage of foot soldiers, the *panzer* regiment's commander, *Ostubaf.* Darges, had to use his tanks in the front-line defenses, where they were vulnerable to attack by Soviet antitank teams.[100]

The most serious fighting reported by the *Wiking* Division that day, surprisingly, concerned events unfolding on the other side of the Narew, where *Ostubaf.* Dorr and his mixed bag of troops witnessed the onset of Batov's offensive out of the Serock–Pułtusk bridgehead. A Soviet attack of at least regimental size, supported by tanks, broke through west of Serock, still held by German troops, and headed west along the Serock–Modlin highway. Dorr, whose force had only one three-tank platoon from *II. Abt./SS-Pz.Rgt. 5* in support, fought back against this incursion as best he could, as well as another threat posed by an attempt to bridge the Narew at Rynia. Though Dorr's *Kampfgruppe* was able to smash this bridging attempt with its regimental infantry howitzers, a thrust by Soviet tanks reached the northern bank of the Narew as far as Zegrze, effectively splitting his force in half. Seemingly, there was very little that *Staf.* Mühlenkamp could do to support him.

With few tanks available to function as the division's reserve, and none to reinforce the units fighting north of the Narew, Mühlenkamp had ordered on 19 October that an antitank *Kampfgruppe* be formed from a heavy battery from the division's *Flak* battalion and sent across the river to assist the forces struggling there. This unit, led by its battery commander, *Hstuf.* Heinrich Grabner, was supported by an infantry *Alarm* battalion to help protect his guns from Soviet infantry. It went into action upon arriving in the town of Carolina southwest of Serock the following day, 20 October. When the lead gun crew spotted a group of 30–35 Soviet tanks approaching from the east along the main highway leading to Modlin, *Oscha.* Alois Schnaubelt, 23-year-old gun leader of an 8.8cm gun of *3. Bttr./SS-Flak-Abt. 5*, coolly ordered his men to begin firing.

Within an hour, Schnaubelt and his crew destroyed nine T-34s from a range of approximately 300 meters, while two other guns of his battery knocked out a couple more. Thus blocked, the enemy tanks withdrew out of range and took up defensive positions in the woods. By his action, his and the other guns prevented a Soviet breakthrough that day, which would have been catastrophic had the tanks reached Modlin. In recognition of his deeds that day, Schnaubelt was awarded the Knight's Cross by Herbert Gille himself three weeks later.[101]

Fortunately for Dorr, in addition to the *Flak* battlegroup that had stopped the tank brigade earlier that day, the *Kampfgruppe* from the *19. Pz.Div.* had arrived at its assembly area in Modlin on the northern bank of the Narew, where it awaited the trains that would transport it to Warka that evening. At around noon, both Gille and the army group commander appeared at the temporary headquarters in Modlin of *Oberst* Karl-Richard Kossmann, the regimental commander, and ordered him to carry out an immediate counterattack to the east to destroy any enemy forces he encountered and restore the connection with Dorr's regiment. After taking several hours to get organized while being subjected to air attack, Kossmann's attack got underway at 3 p.m. and made rapid headway. By 5 p.m., it had made contact with the *Germania* Regiment and relieved Serock, after encountering and destroying several Soviet tank units along the way. Since the threat was seen as continuing, at 8 p.m. the *Kampfgruppe* was ordered by *IV. SS-Pz.Korps* to establish a defense line between Dorr's forces and the *542. Gren.Div.* while it awaited the transfer of the rest of the division to the area.[102] Given the critical nature of the situation, Reinhardt's decision to employ von Lüttwitz's carefully husbanded reserve force made more sense than sending it down to the Warka area, where it would have sat for months while benefitting no one.

In that night's report, while Gille expressed his own satisfaction with how his former division had managed to stall the Soviet offensive in the Nieporet area earlier that day, he reserved most of his comments to the situation developing north of the Narew. Were it not for the speedy deployment of the *Flak Kampfgruppe* and the *19. Pz.Div.* battlegroup, which had been fortuitously sitting in Modlin awaiting transport, the spearheads of Col.Gen. Batov's 65th Army may well have reached the city that day. Prisoner interrogations had also revealed that the 1st Rifle Division had been moved into the Nieporet area from Rynia to reinforce Batov's effort to achieve a breakthrough there. Gille repeated his observation from the previous evening's report that unless the former front line north and west of Serock was restored, it would be inadvisable to leave his corps in its present location between the Narew and Vistula, and it should be pulled out instead.

As it was, Gille stated that the enemy had got so close to the *Dachsstellung* (Dachshund position), then being constructed as an intermediate position between Zagroby and the *Fuchstellung* ending at Skrzeszew, that construction work had to be stopped, and in any case the position no longer served any useful purpose unless the enemy pressure was relieved. Gille recommended that action be taken to push the enemy back into his former bridgehead between Serock and Rozan, though by this point this was impossible—neither *Gen.d.Art.* von Roman's neighboring *XX. Armeekorps* nor *Gen.Oberst* Weiss's *2. Armee* had any reserve forces strong enough to do this. Gille stressed the importance of continuing to hold the high ground along the Narew's northern bank that offered excellent observation as far as Warsaw; whoever held this key terrain would control what happened in the Vistula–Narew–Bug triangle. For the next day, Gille's intentions would be focused on continuing his heretofore successful defense; on that day alone, the *19. Pz.Div.* and the *Wiking* had destroyed a total of 22 Soviet tanks and knocked out six heavy antitank guns. Again, infantry losses on both sides were described as heavy.[103]

The *9. Armee* commander in his narrative submitted to *H.Gr. Mitte* that evening began with the laconic sentence ,"The situation along the army's northern boundary has gradually intensified." If anything, this was an understatement. While von Lüttwitz understood and agreed with the necessity of committing the *19. Pz.Div.* north of the Narew to stop the 65th Army's advance, he bemoaned the fact that the only significant mobile reserve left to him had been effectively taken away. No one, including himself, knew how long it would be employed there or whether he would ever get it back, though it was still "his" in the sense that it was operating under Gille's control. To straighten and simplify the command and control arrangements between his army and the neighboring *2. Armee*, von Lüttwitz proposed to Reinhardt that either the *2. Armee*'s southern boundary be shifted all the way down to the Narew or von Roman's *XX. Armeekorps* be moved under *9. Armee* control, enabling von Lüttwitz to take charge of operations as far north as Rózan.

To the army commander's disbelief, Reinhardt decided to let the situation remain as it was. This half-measure pleased no one, except perhaps Reinhardt, who gave no satisfactory explanation for his decision. In the rest of his narrative report, von Lüttwitz described several possible scenarios the Red Army could carry out, should Modlin fall. Would the First Belorussian Front turn north and cut off East Prussia? Or would it carry out a shallow envelopment of Warsaw with the aid of forces attacking out of the Magnuszew area? Or would they turn left and go south, in an attempt to cut off all German forces in Slovakia? Had Gille been in earshot of this argument, he probably would have shaken his head in wonderment. After all, what Gille wanted most was a clear, concise order that told him what to do—in his mind, there was little room for what he would have thought as mere speculation. He was first and foremost a man of action, not contemplation.

While very little of consequence occurred in the rest of the *9. Armee* area of operations that day (for example, the *VIII. Armeekorps* boasted about how many kills its division's snipers claimed that day), the *IV. SS-Pz.Korps* was involved in very heavy fighting on both sides of the Narew and east of the Vistula from morning until night. When the sun rose on 21 October, the 12th day of the third defensive battle of Warsaw, the evening before as well as the morning that followed had proven to be anything but quiet. The *Wiking* Division launched a counterattack against the Wieliszew parkland during the early hours that was still underway when it submitted its 5:55 a.m. report. Soviet infantry from the 70th Army launched their own attack at the same time to reclaim the ruins of the railway viaduct and highway intersection southwest of Zagroby that had stymied their armor the day before. This Soviet effort had been stopped and was being "cleaned up" by *I. Abt./SS-Pz.Rgt. 5* at the report's time.

Soviet artillery fire was typically heavy, which drew the usual German response. A mid-morning company-size attack against a *Totenkopf* position in Wegierskie Katy, thought possibly to be a reconnaissance in force, was driven back after a brief firefight, with the aggressors leaving behind 28 dead as they pulled back. The main body of the *19. Pz.Div.*, still holding its positions west of Marcelin, reported heavy shelling and multiple strong reconnaissance patrols attempting to penetrate its front line. Evidently, the 47th Army was intent on discovering just how much of *Gen.Lt.* Källner's division had been shifted to the northern bank of the Narew. It would be another long, bloody day, just as the previous days had been. How much longer the First Belorussian Front could endure beating its brains out against Gille's defenses for so little gain was anyone's guess.

In the *Wiking* Division's defensive sector south of the Narew, it was becoming obvious that it could not hold the enemy back from the highway along the line Zagroby–Jablonna much longer. It had exhausted its strength in defending and retaking the Michalow estate, the Wieliszew park, the Letniska forest cemetery, the church, and the woods west of it, as well as the open ground between Zagroby and the forest, including the highway and rail intersection. Too many of its junior officers and NCOs had fallen in the infantry companies, leaving few *Führer* and *Unterführer* remaining to effectively lead the inexperienced replacements from the *Luftwaffe*, who were being disproportionally killed and wounded as a consequence. That evening, Gille issued orders to the *Wiking*'s commander to be prepared to abandon his current line and withdraw to the next intermediate position. In the meantime, the *panzer* regiment had to do a great deal of fighting to provide cover as the grenadier battalions, or what was left of them, pulled out.

In addition to holding the line to prevent the enemy from breaking out of the areas already mentioned, the *2. Kompanie* of *SS-Pz.Rgt. 5* lost its second acting company commander in two days when Knight's Cross recipient *Ustuf.* Helmut Bauer sustained a head wound as he stood in the commander's hatch of his *Pz. IV*. Evacuated to the division's *Hauptverbandsplatz* (*HVP*, or main dressing station) in Modlin, he would soon be back in action after his wound was treated. One enemy attack against the flank of *I. Btl./Germania* was so serious that the *I. Abteilung*'s two headquarters *Befehlspanzer* (command tanks), joined by two assault guns from *4. Kompanie*, were committed to the fight to keep the enemy from overrunning the position long enough to allow the infantry battalion's survivors a chance to withdraw to the eastern edge of the forest.[104]

One tank and three tank destroyers from *Stubaf.* Oeck's *SS-Pz.Jag.Abt. 5* were committed later that afternoon to seal off a penetration of the reconnaissance battalion's front lines on the southern edge of Zagroby.[105] This victory was fleeting; by 5:30 a.m. the next day, Borchert's reconnaissance troops, as well as *I. Btl./Germania*, were forced to completely pull out of Zagroby and the woods south of the town to avoid encirclement. Once they had escaped, they established a screening line several kilometers to the west on the edge of the village of Rybaki, taking advantage of the hills west of Zagroby to build their new positions.

By the end of the day, *Bataillonsführer* (acting commander) Kurt Schumacher's *I. Abteilung* (Willy Hein had been evacuated to the *HVP* on 18 October for an inner ear infection) had been reduced to a mere nine vehicles: four *Pz. IV* tanks in the *2. Kompanie*, three *StuG IV* assault guns in the *4. Kompanie*, and two *Pz. IV* in the *Stabskompanie*, the lowest point ever reached during the battles for Warsaw. Despite the losses and grueling battle tempo, the battalion's morale was still reported to be high. One example of the unit's *esprit de corps* was the recovery of a damaged *Pz. IV* behind enemy lines by the battalion's assistant maintenance chief, *Hscha.* Rosenhauer, who managed to pull off this daring feat right under the noses of dozens of Soviet soldiers, who mistook his recovery vehicle for one of their own. These are other similar incidents providing a good illustration of what a predominately armored force, weak in infantry, had to go through in order to accomplish its mission in such a wooded environment. On more than one occasion, the tank crews had to provide their own security at night with no friendly infantry in sight. The experience must have been unnerving, to say the least.

As the bulk of the division began preparations to move back to its new defense line, heavy fighting continued across the river involving the *19. Pz.Div.* battlegroup and the *Germania* Regiment with its motley collection of troops. There, the 65th Army continued its attack at multiple locations towards the south and southwest in its attempt to reach the Narew behind the left flank of the *IV. SS-Pz.Korps.* At mid-afternoon, an infantry force of between 700 and 800 men, augmented by several tanks, broke through between the towns of Zegrzynek and Lodwinowo. Driving rapidly behind the position held by *Lds.Schtz.Btl. 998*, the Soviet force nearly reached the Narew before it was stopped by several counterattacks conducted by the battlegroup from *Pz.Gren.Rgt. 74*.

That same day, this group and the portion of *Germania* still under Dorr's control were combined into one task force, now named *Gruppe Kossmann* after the regiment's commander, *Oberst* Karl-Richard Kossmann, who was senior to Dorr. The situation in the town of Zegrze was unclear; no one knew whether German or Soviet forces held this key river town, but it was assumed to be lost. Contact with the neighboring unit from *XX. Armeekorps* was tenuous at best. Soviet air activity above that area of the front that day was also intense. *Gruppe Kossmann* reported that it came under attack by up to 90 Soviet aircraft in the afternoon, which enormously complicated carrying out movement even by individual vehicles. Though its attached *Flak* battery claimed the destruction of one aircraft that day, camouflage of vehicles and tanks ensured a better chance of survival, much as it then did on the Western Front, where the Allied air forces similarly ruled the sky.

Gille reported these events that evening to *9. Armee*, mentioning for the first time that two new units, the 71st Rifle Division and the 54th Guards Rifle Division, had been identified in his area based on prisoners taken that day. These divisions were assessed to be part of the 28th Army, which meant, if the reports were accurate, that another field army was being introduced into the equation. He also mentioned that several interrogated prisoners had reported that Stalin had apparently issued an order, known as a *Stalinbefehl*, which exhorted his troops in the First Belorussian Front to keep fighting until they reached the attack's objective of the Vistula, no matter how they did it, under whatever circumstance, and without consideration for casualties.[106] This would partly explain why Popov's and Gusev's troops had been fighting so determinedly.

But if the 28th Army was indeed on its way, as well as another guards mechanized corps as mentioned in agent reports, then Gille foresaw difficult days head for his corps. Still, orders were orders and he would keep using his remaining armor to buy time so the rest of his troops could pull back to the intermediate *Marder* defensive position beginning the following day. The *Wiking* would essentially pivot slightly to the north while retaining contact with the left flank of the *Totenkopf* Division, which would remain in its current positions. Fortunately, he now had most of the *19. Pz.Div.* back under his control. To the north of the Narew, *Gruppe Kossmann* would erect a screen line to intercept and delay the Soviet advance until more forces became available. It was not ideal, but it was a workable solution.

That night, von Lüttwitz agreed with Gille's recommendation to begin pulling back to the *Fuchsstellung*, and requested official permission from *H.Gr. Mitte* to start doing so the following day. There was little that Reinhardt could object to; unless he approved his subordinate's request, a portion if not all of Gille's corps could be lost. Not much help was available to send to the aid of the troops fighting north or south of the Narew, so approving the request was the least that *H.Gr. Mitte* could do. Gille was instructed to pull back in phases, and keep his armor in the line as long as possible to allow the infantry to make their withdrawals unmolested. Again, Gille was doing this anyway, having gained a great deal of experience in conducting withdrawals when in close proximity to his opponent, and had been doing so since mid-August, when *Unternehmen Brückenschlag* was carried out under similar circumstances, though his corps had been much stronger then.

Despite the evidence that he was interested in the events on his army's left flank, which seemed bad enough, for his part von Lüttwitz appears to have still reserved most of his concern for the developing enemy situation on his army's southern flank. Reinforcing his belief was an order he received that day from *H.Gr. Mitte*, which informed him that, "The front line at Magnuszew must be held." To Reinhardt at his army group headquarters, as wide as the rift between *9.* and *2.* Armee caused by the 65th Army's offensive might have seemed, to lose the continuity of the front between *Heeresgruppen A* and *Mitte* would have been catastrophic. Still, when this eventuality came to pass, nearly three months would have gone by and the *IV. SS-Pz. Korps* would be long gone.

At this point, day 12 of the battle came and went and it seemed nowhere closer to ending. The stubborn defense by the *IV. SS-Pz.Korps* had managed to thwart the Red Army's intentions, but the longer it continued in its current position, the more precarious its situation became. Hope was in sight, at least for Marshal Rokossovsky, with the unexpected good news that the First Belorussian Front's 65th Army was approaching the point where its forces north of the Narew could finally lever Gille's corps out of its defensive positions. All it had to do was to take control of the river's northern bank between Zegrze and Modlin, begin firing into their enemy's vulnerable northern flank with artillery, and make a few threatening small-scale river crossings. This would soon prove to be not as easy as it seemed at the time.

While 22 October proved to be another uneventful day for the *XLVI. Panzer* and *VIII. Armeekorps,* which carried out their normal defensive activities, it was anything but for Gille's corps. All three of this divisions reported heavy Soviet artillery fire upon their positions throughout the night and early morning, along with continuing aggressive patrolling activity by their opponents from 47th and 70th Armies and the 1st Polish Army. At first light, Soviet fighter-bombers and ground-attack aircraft bombed and strafed German positions along the front line as well as the artillery positions in the rear. While the *Totenkopf* Division sent reports that Soviet forces could be observed moving into assembly areas near the front lines, which they engaged with artillery fire, the *Wiking* reported that a strong enemy force had attacked the meager force from *I. Abt./SS-Pz.Rgt. 5* that was screening in front of the highway and rail intersection southwest of Zagroby, a town that was now in Soviet hands. North of the river, the tanks from *Gruppe Kossmann* engaged a large enemy force that was attempting to break through to the west between the towns of Szadki and Izpica.

As before, these actions were merely a prelude to what was to follow. By midday, the action had strongly intensified. The *Totenkopf* Division found itself attacked again by a battalion-sized force with tanks in the Wegierskie Katy area that was warded off with artillery fire and tank counterattacks by *SS-Pz.Rgt. 3*. The attacks against the left flank of the *Wiking* Division increased in intensity and scope, with the force reported at the highway intersection that morning having broken through and reached the town of Wieliszew proper. With this action, the 70th Army finally secured a portion of the Narew River wide enough for the neighboring 65th Army to conduct a river crossing operation. This would not be such an easy feat, since the German forces on that side of the river had something to say about it, namely that they would contest every inch of ground, even with artillery if that was all they had. *Gruppe Kossmann* conducted a number of attacks and counterattacks designed to slow or bring to a halt the numerous Soviet spearheads from the 65th Army's I Guards Tank Corps as they attempted to penetrate its front line; at one point, one unit from *Ostubaf.* Dorr's regiment was briefly encircled in the town of Skubianka before a tank-led counterattack freed it. It was touch and go for several hours.

By late afternoon, a force of 25 Soviet tanks and an infantry regiment had joined in the attack, which managed to break through the German positions by nightfall and appeared poised to drive all the way to Modlin until it was finally stopped by a night counterattack from *Oberst* Kossmann's armored battlegroup. Two enemy tanks were destroyed and 11 prisoners reported as being taken that day by Kossmann's troops, and one Soviet aircraft was shot down. In return, nine Panthers from *I. Abt./Pz.Rgt. 27* were completely destroyed by enemy tank and antitank gun fire, a heavy loss.[107] In recognition of the magnitude of the threat, Gille recognized that the *IV.*

SS-Pz.Korps' forces north of the Narew were insufficient, and directed the *19. Pz.Div.* to send another tank company and an armored *Pionier* company across the river to reinforce Kossmann. Complicating the situation was that the neighboring *XX. Armeekorps* had its hands full coping with the main Soviet assault and could spare nothing to help Gille's corps. It was everything that Kossmann's nearest neighbor, the *25. Pz.Div.*, brought in to assist the *542. Gren.Div.* could do just to maintain contact with its southern neighbor.[108]

As it had for nearly a week, the main effort by Rokossovsky's armies in the Wet Triangle was directed at the *Wiking* Division's eroding left flank. While the *Totenkopf* Division successfully defended its sector between Jósefów and Rożopole against several battalion-level attacks by the 47th Army, the *Wiking* had to endure even larger ones launched by a reinforced 70th Army as well as increasing pressure from the VIII Guards Tank Corps, which was aggressively seeking to break out into the clear and race to Modlin. Although a thin *Gefechtsvorposten* (screening force) composed of remaining infantry from *II. Btl./Germania*, buttressed by what was left of *II. Abt./SS-Pz.Rgt. 5*, held the enemy at bay along the line Michałow Estate–Wieleszew park–Letniska forest cemetery, most of the *Westland* Regiment fell back to occupy the just-completed *Fuchsstellung* west of Lajsk along the Bródnowski canal. Soviet artillery fire was continuous, further weakening the already decimated infantry companies. Enemy losses had been heavy as well, as the 70th Army's advancing elements from the 1st Rifle Division and the 16th, 54th, and 38th Guards Rifle Divisions ran into a hail of German defensive fire, including 7.5cm tank cannon and 2cm *Flak* being used in a ground support role. Forward artillery observers expertly called in supporting fires, blanketing the terrain in front of the defenders' positions with timely and accurate barrages of 10.5cm and 15cm high-explosive shells.

But this was merely a holding action, designed to buy time to allow the new alternate line to be manned and its defenses activated. Most of the decisive action took place that day along the southern bank of the Narew, where *Ostuf.* Schumacher's *I. Abt./SS-Pz.Rgt. 5* with his eight remaining tanks and assault guns (one command tank had been left behind to protect the battalion's new headquarters at Skrzeszew), joined by a few tank destroyers from *SS-Pz.Jag.Abt. 5*, fought to deny the VIII Guards Tank Corps the breakthrough it had sought for over a week. Augmented by the few surviving troops from the division's reconnaissance battalion and *I. Btl./Germania*, this battlegroup, under the overall command of *Ostubaf.* Darges, fought all day to keep the division's left flank from collapsing, destroying three Soviet tanks and one heavy antitank gun during the day.

At 11:30 a.m., a platoon from *I. Btl./Germania* that was positioned along the southern bank of the Narew River was fired upon from the opposite side by a battalion from the 28th Guards Motorized Rifle Brigade of the VIII Guards Tank Corps that had crossed the Narew on the recently completed pontoon bridge at Rynia. Apparently it was operating in concert with the I Guards Tank Corps.

Schumacher then positioned two of his tanks there to provide support, which immediately took the enemy troops across the river under fire. In the meantime, the town of Izbica, northwest of Wieliszew on the opposite bank of the Narew, had been completely occupied by the enemy, who began to emplace antitank guns and heavy infantry weapons that soon began firing at the troops manning the thin screening line of *I. Btl./Germania* positioned to the south. Leaving two assault guns behind at the Łajsk–Wieliszew road junction that afternoon to serve as a back-stop for the withdrawing infantry, Schumacher, with four remaining tanks and an infantry platoon, boldly attacked the town of Wieliszew proper following the main east–west road from Kałuszyn.

Upon reaching the town's western outskirts without encountering any resistance, he saw that the Soviet battalion that had just taken the town was forming up to continue its attack. Striking quickly, Schumacher's force smashed the enemy assembly, forced it to disperse, and just as quickly withdrew back to safety. His action had bought a few hours of breathing space for the withdrawal to the *Fuchsstellung* to continue unmolested, though the enemy force was merely temporarily scattered, not destroyed.[109]

Surprisingly, fighting died down after the counterattack at Wieliszew. The *Wiking* Division's outpost line west of the Letniska forest slowly withdrew to the new intermediate line along the Bródnowski canal, giving ground grudgingly while forcing the pursuing attackers to repeatedly stop and deploy their troops. On the right, the *Wiking* Division's connection to its neighboring division, the *Totenkopf*, remained firm at the hinge point linking the two divisions between Łajsk and Jablonna-Legjonowo, while *Obf.* Becker's division had not yielded a meter of ground that day. Most of the decisive fighting that day was taking place across the Narew, while the fighting in the Wet Triangle, except on its northern boundary, was becoming something of a deadly sideshow. Despite their limited gains on the ground, the three armies arrayed against Gille's corps kept up a steady volume of artillery fire throughout the length and breadth of his shrinking perimeter, while the Red Air Force maintained its unceasing tempo of attacks against ground targets. The *Luftwaffe* was conspicuous for its absence; its *Stukas* were sorely missed. While the bad weather that day may have been a factor in its failure to support the troops, no one could have failed to notice that rain and fog had not deterred the Red Air Force from its operations.

There was very little for Gille to say in his evening report. He had recognized early that day that most of the heaviest fighting was going to take place north of the Narew, and until the I Guards Tank Corps could be brought to a halt, the situation between Skubianka and Izbica would remain tense. Gille was puzzled about the continuing timidity of the VIII Guards Tank Corps—why had it not attacked in force? Perhaps, he thought, it was going to wait for the I Guards Tank Corps on its right flank to clear the northern bank of the Narew as far as Izbica before the bulk of its tank forces swung into action. What was urgently needed, he recommended to his army commander, was to assign either the *XX. Armeekorps* or *IV. SS-Pz.Korps* responsibility for defending north of the Narew. The divided command arrangement, split between two corps from two different armies, could not possibly lead to a unified effort and needed to be rectified as soon as possible, lest the opposing forces seize the victory they had long sought. Gille had done what he could do to assist Kossmann by sending him the reinforcements he needed. In the meantime, the *19. Pz.Div.* and *Totenkopf* would hold their current positions while the *Wiking* pulled back to the new line. Given no other options or orders to the contrary, he would continue defending, as a *Nur-Soldat* should.[110]

At the end of what had been a cloudy, rainy day, von Lüttwitz pondered his situation. While Gille's troops had once again successfully held their ground, events across the Narew, where *Gruppe Kossmann* was fighting stubbornly to keep the advancing columns of the I Guards Tank Corps at bay (and in some instances pushing them back), were mostly beyond his control. The direction of the 65th Army's attack had been unanticipated and as a result the situation was, as he related, "tense." Fortunately, the armored battlegroup of the *19. Pz.Div.* had been awaiting its trains in Modlin at the time the Soviet breakthrough at Serock happened the previous day; otherwise, there would have been nothing there to stop them except rear area security units. The remaining tanks of the *IV. SS-Pz.Korps* were tied up battling the enemy south of the Narew, and removing them to address the threat on the other side of the river might have led to the collapse of Gille's front in the Wet Triangle. It could have been a lot worse. Von Lüttwitz was puzzled by the apparent slackening of Rokossovsky's attacks towards Modlin, but he believed that the relative pause of the last two days was most likely due to the Soviet army commanders' need to resupply and reposition their forces, rather than a general cessation of the offensive. Like Gille, he fully expected the attacks against the *Wiking* Division south of the Narew and those along the northern banks of the river by the 65th Army would continue undiminished.[111]

Nevertheless, the *9. Armee* commander was very dissatisfied with the development of the tactical situation that day. His request to withdraw the rest of the *19. Pz.Div.* across the Vistula to serve as his army's new reserve force south of Warsaw was disapproved by his army group commander, who knew that Gille was not ready to give it up until he had fully occupied the *Fuchsstellung*. Von Lüttwitz and his operations staff were still fixated on a possible offensive bursting out of the Magnuszew area. Though the 8th Guards Army had been quiet for the past several days, aerial reconnaissance indicated that more Soviet artillery batteries had been moved into Chuikov's bridgehead. The *9. Armee* commander even modified his request to move *Gen.Lt.* Källner's division so that it would be positioned north of Warsaw, so it could be employed either in support of *2. Armee* or south against the Magnuszew bridgehead. Again, Reinhardt turned down his suggestion. Instead, von Lüttwitz was ordered by *H.Gr. Mitte* to move the rest of Källner's division beginning that night, minus the tank regiment, to the northern bank of the Narew to join *Gruppe Kossmann*.

This stay-behind element, which officially became known that morning as *Gruppe von Hake* after the new commander of *Pz.Rgt. 27*, *Oberst* Friedrich von Hake, consisted of the regimental headquarters, its *II. Abteilung* (minus one company), one *Panzergrenadier* battalion, *Gren.Btl.z.b.V. 560*, *Sturm-Btl. AOK 9*, an artillery battalion, 17 guns from *Art.Pak-Abt. 1061*, and other supporting arms, making his a very potent force. Its mission was to take over the defensive sector previously held by the entire division, stretching from Marcelin on the left to the Vistula on the right near Tarchomin. Since Soviet and Polish activity along this front had been ineffectual, Reinhardt evidently believed that moving the rest of the division was a risk worth taking, given that the Soviet advance north of the Narew was a far greater danger to the army group's defensive effort. The *9. Armee* commander could not have been pleased with this development, for right before his eyes his coveted army reserve was in his opinion being frittered away and removed from his control. The portion of the west bank of the Vistula that had previously been part of the *19. Pz.Div.* sector was handed over to *Heeres-Pio.Btl. 46*, thus freeing *Oberst* von Hake from that responsibility.

The most that von Lüttwitz could do was to ensure that Gille got as much support as his army could still provide—but even most of the supplies for *IV. SS-Pz.Korps* were now being provided by *Gen.Oberst* Weiss's army, which was beginning to experience difficulties of its own in providing sufficient fuel and ammunition due to the disruptions in its own supply chain. Ammunition deliveries to Gille's corps, for instance, fell from 390 tons on 21 October to 184 two days later, while his corps troops and divisions were expending on average 320 tons per day.[112] Weiss could not expect support from his fellow army commander either. In the last sentence of his evening report, von Lüttwitz wrote, "The *9. Armee* can only provide support [to the *2. Armee*] by weakening its own defensive power that it will soon need for the expected future offensive from the Magnuszew bridgehead."[113] One thing must have brightened his mood somewhat, and that was the departure that day by rail of most of the rest of the Hungarian troops. Only one regiment remained, scheduled to leave the following day. While von Lüttwitz had a low opinion of their fighting abilities, he did miss their talent in building field fortifications.

By this point in the fighting, just about every conceivable pattern of attack–defend–counterattack had been demonstrated, although both sides still had some tricks up their sleeve that were on display on Monday, 23 October. The first was a series of counterattacks on the far left flank of the *Wiking* Division, carried out by *Ostuf.* Schumacher's *I. Abt./SS-Pz.Rgt. 5*, with the help of some troops from *I. Btl./Germania* who had been manning the thin screen line stretching between the town of Wieliszew and Łajsk. Attacking after a brief artillery barrage that each time caught the defending Soviet troops napping, Schumacher's tanks on several occasions that day managed to reach the old *HKL* on the edge of Wieliszew and along the highway, and shot up the Soviet forces assembling there before the enemy's overwhelming numerical superiority soon forced his tiny task force to withdraw to the point where it had started that morning. After reassembling his daring force, he would lead them forward on another identical foray a few hours later with the same results.

While unsuccessful in terms of throwing the enemy back, his audacious attacks had momentarily knocked the Soviets off balance and gained valuable additional time. This tactic, which became known 30 years later within the North Atlantic Treaty Organization as "active defense," depended as much on the mobility of armor as its firepower, as a way to continually rob the enemy's attack of its momentum, giving up ground temporarily only to inflict greater losses later on.[114] Despite the disappointing results of his counterattack that day, Schumacher was summoned to the regiment's headquarters in Skrzeszew at 7:30 p.m., where much to his surprise, his erstwhile division commander, *Staf.* Johannes Mühlenkamp, was waiting for him. Here, his former battalion and regiment commander, whom he had served under since May 1942, personally awarded him the Tank Assault Badge in Silver, 4th Grade, in recognition of the 75 days he had accumulated in armored combat.[115] After shaking his hand and congratulating him, Mühlenkamp departed the division forever, allowing *Staf.* Karl Ullrich to finally take up the reins of command.

Another unexpected move that day was carried out by Soviet troops, whose 328th Rifle Division launched a surprise early morning attack against *Totenkopf* Division troops near the right flank it shared with the *19. Pz.Div.* at Rożopole using flame throwers in an effort to roust them from their fighting positions. Though the Red Army troops were thrown back by the defenders on this occasion, it was an unnerving experience for SS men who had not been confronted by this tactic before. The rest of the day was quiet until the late afternoon. Heralded by a 75-minute drumfire barrage that began at 4:45 p.m., the Soviets attacked the *Totenkopf* Division's left flank, this time with a combined tank and infantry force that attempted to penetrate through a 1½ kilometer gap blown in the *Totenkopf*'s defensive line. This force was stopped and driven back by a counterattack by *SS-Pz.Rgt. 3*, which managed to knock out a JS-II Stalin tank as well as two antitank guns.

Heavy fighting took place at the same time in the vicinity of Łajsk, where *II. Abt./SS-Pz.Rgt. 5* fought to hold the hinge position where the *Wiking* Division maintained its connection on the right with the *Totenkopf* Division. After the barrage ended, a battalion-sized enemy force attempted to advance down the Zagroby–Jablonna highway into the *Totenkopf*'s left flank via the Michałow estate, but *Hstuf.* Flügel's battalion, with the aid of the division's *SS-Pz.Art.Rgt. 5*, forced them back. However, Flügel and his men had to endure heavy artillery fire upon their position that destroyed three of his Panthers, leaving his battalion with only 19 operational tanks. Fortunately for the *Wiking* Division, enemy activity quietened down that night, allowing it and its two neighboring divisions an opportunity to catch their collective breaths. The usual nighttime patrolling activity and random artillery fire continued, including one infantry raid by the *Totenkopf* Division against Soviet trenches east of Wegierskie Katy that netted several prisoners and killed at least 30 of the enemy.

Most of the decisive action that day took place north of the Narew, where the *19. Pz.Div.*, including *Gruppe Kossmann* (which was reincorporated as *Pz.Gren.Rgt. 74*) and Dorr's *Germania* battlegroup, fought to bring the I Guard Tank Corps' advance to a halt. To make up for the absence of *Pz.Gren.Rgt. 73*, which remained in the division's former position along the Vistula, at some point during the day, Källner's division was augmented by *II. Btl./Pz.Gren.Rgt. 394* of the *3. Pz.Div.*, which lay in a reserve position in the rear of the *2. Armee* undergoing reconstitution after its rough handling during the waning days of *Unternehmen Sonnenblume* two weeks earlier. By late morning, the reinforced division, which officially took command of the defensive sector at 11:00 a.m., had struck Soviet positions at the village of Izbica, where bridging equipment was being brought up to cross the Narew, and threw the defending infantry out after heavy fighting. On its left flank, Källner's troops had managed to establish contact on the left with the *25. Pz.Div.*, which had been withdrawing in disarray since that morning when the commander of the attached *Sich.Btl. 350* was wounded while trying to maintain the connection on the right with *Gruppe Kossmann*. After restoring the line and consolidating its positions, Källner's units were heavily shelled by Soviet artillery and rocket barrages, as well as suffering unremitting attacks by Soviet aircraft. One IL-2 was shot down by the division's *Flak-Art.Abt. 272*.

That evening, Gille expressed his concern about the portion of the west bank of the Vistula that was still within his area of operations. With the withdrawal of the right flank of *Gruppe von Hake* to the Vistula at Tarchomin, the entire riverbank between Annopol and Tarchomin was now uncovered, a sector approximately 10 kilometers wide, that was immediately occupied by Polish forces. This gave rise to his belief that it offered the 1st Polish Army an opportunity to carry out another river crossing operation, directed across the narrowest portion of the Vistula at Młociny, previous site of the corps' 12-ton pontoon bridge that had been destroyed several days before. To augment *Heeres-Pio.Btl. 46*, which was insufficient for a defensive task of this magnitude, Gille directed that the *19. Pz.Div.* be prepared to detach its armored reconnaissance battalion to assist it when ordered to do so. He seemed to be satisfied that the situation on the north bank of the Narew was under control, and said nothing about the fighting that took place that day inside the Wet Triangle, a sign that perhaps the crisis had passed.[116]

In his own report that evening, von Lüttwitz evidently agreed with Gille's assessment, stating that the pressure along the boundary between his army and *2. Armee* had "noticeably decreased," thanks to the previous fighting by *Gruppe Kossmann*, the successful action of the *Wiking* Division's *Flak Kampfgruppe*, and the arrival of the main body of the *19. Pz.Div.* He repeated his previous belief that the slackening of pressure against Gille's corps by the 47th and 70th Armies did not signify that the offensive was over, rather that the pause was only due to their need to reform their units, replenish their ammunition, and reposition their forces in order to be more advantageously positioned to continue their attacks. In this sense, he had completely come around to Gille's way of thinking.[117]

This feeling was perhaps reinforced by the news that the three armies involved—the 47th, 70th, and 65th—had once again initiated a radio blackout, a sign that something was up, perhaps the arrival of another corps or even a field army to restore the offensive's momentum. This, of course, led von Lüttwitz to begin voicing his concerns about the lack of an operational reserve to send to the southern flank of his army. Concerning the good news from *H.Gr. Mitte* that the *19. Pz.Div.* might soon be pulled out again once the *3. Pz.Div.* was reinserted into the line in its place, the *9. Armee* commander was disappointed to learn that while the *19. Pz.Div.* would go into a reserve position northwest of Warsaw, it would become the army group's reserve, not his. Fortunately, enemy activity in the Magnuszew and Puławy bridgeheads continued to be limited to the usual shelling, patrolling, and sniping.

By the time 24 October dawned, the *IV. SS-Pz.Korps* had already been carrying out operations for the past several hours. In addition to the raid on the Soviet trenches by the *Totenkopf* Division already mentioned, *Gruppe von Hake* displaced several kilometers to the north to its new defensive line beginning at midnight, a maneuver that it carried out in conjunction with the *Totenkopf* Division, which also shifted its right flank. The tanks of *II. Abt./Pz.Rgt. 27* began moving to Modlin, where the battalion had been ordered to join the rest of the *19. Pz.Div.* across the Narew. The division's reconnaissance battalion, *Pz.Aufkl.Abt. 19*, also moved to the western bank of the Vistula to take up position, and *Sturm-Btl. AOK 9* was moved to Jablonna-Legjonowo as the corps' reserve force.

Oberst von Hake no longer had any tanks to call his own, but he and his tank regiment headquarters would soon depart the area to rejoin his division anyway, leaving the responsibility of defending this area to *Oberst* Günter Zugehör, commander of the division's *Pz.Art.Rgt. 19*. Consequently, the *Kampfgruppe* was renamed *Gruppe Zugehör*, which would continue covering the corps' right flank along the Vistula. Regulation of the enormous amount of two-way traffic moving across the bridges at Modlin and Nowy Dwor 24 hours a day was controlled by the field police of *Hstuf.* Kurt Schliep's *SS-Feld-Gen.Kp. 104*, which had to endure daily attacks by the Red Air Force, which sought to destroy both bridges or at least disrupt and delay traffic. Antiaircraft protection at the bridges was provided by *Ostuf.* Adolf Eberhard's *SS-Flak-Kp. 104*, with its nine deadly self-propelled 3.7cm *Flak* guns that successfully warded off enemy air attacks.

Before sunrise, foot patrols from the *Wiking* were sent out between Łajsk and Wieliszew, avoided enemy contact, and were able to ascertain that Soviet forces had only lightly occupied their new outpost line and were seen digging in. By that point, nearly all of the

Wiking's infantry, except the few troops supporting the *panzer* regiment, had occupied the new main defense line along the Bródnowski canal, where they now oriented in a northeasterly direction towards the town of Wieliszew. The *19. Pz.Div.* reported that some fighting was relayed as having occurred north of the Narew, including a Soviet night assault on Izbica, but this was driven off. Throughout the corps' area of operations that night and early morning, enemy harassing fire fell without much damage and Red Air Force U-2 night bombers operated with impunity, though the only effect of these aircraft, nicknamed *Nähmaschine* ("sewing machines") by the Germans for their rattling sound, was to keep Gille's troops awake.

If German commanders thought that the battle was tapering off, then the events of 24 October must have come as a rude shock. After a slow start, the day witnessed Gille's front ablaze from the northern bank of the Narew to the western bank of the Vistula, a distance of over 30 kilometers, along which nearly every part of his front line was involved in heavy fighting. The first unit to feel the effects was *Gruppe Zugehör*, which began moving again to another intermediate line early that afternoon. As it withdrew it was at first pursued hesitantly by the 1st Polish Infantry Division, which grew increasingly aggressive as the day wore on. At one point, Zugehör's rear guard was attacked by eight Polish assault guns, forcing it to stop and fight back, destroying four of them. Employment of the division's artillery, which laid down several effective barrages, forced the pursuing Polish troops to keep a safe distance until the Germans had reached their next phase line, where they turned around and dug in. Enemy artillery fire fell throughout the *Kampfgruppe*'s sector, while Soviet fighter-bombers ranged across Zugehör's narrow defensive sector, though his attached *Flak* did not remain passive, managing to shoot down one IL-2 *Sturmovik*.

From 9:45 a.m. until 11 a.m., a drumfire barrage was laid upon the entire front line of the *Totenkopf* Division's defensive position. Two powerful Soviet tank-led attacks were immediately launched against the defensive sectors, centering around Rożopole on the flank shared with *Gruppe Zugehör* and the mobility corridor centered on Woła Aleksandra, where the attackers were still trying to work their way up the seam between the *Wiking* Division and the *Totenkopf* and the hinge point at Łajsk. Both attacks were broken up by artillery fire, with the gunners of *SS-Pz.Art.Rgt. 3* claiming the destruction of five tanks. The division's artillery also broke up Soviet troop assembly areas at Hill 97, three kilometers south of Jósefów, and another forming in the woods north of Rożopole. Like elsewhere, Soviet artillery, including the heaviest calibers, fell throughout the division's sector and the Red Air Force was very active, conducting no few than 18 separate raids on the division's rear area between Rożopole and Łajsk, losing one IL-2 to the *Totenkopf*s *Flak*. The division's tank regiment experienced little fighting, leaving that up to the artillery on account of its dire need for tanks and crews to rest and repair their vehicles. Fortunately, *Ostubaf.* Josef Swientek's artillery regiment was up to the task, continually delivery lethal and accurate fire throughout the day that smashed and drove back every enemy assault.

The *Wiking*'s new front line stretched from Łajsk northwest along the Brodnowski canal to Poniatowski, where the temporary *Dachshund* position then bent to the northeast, running another 8 kilometers to the Narew opposite Izbica.Nearly all of the division's main defense line was under heavy artillery fire during the late morning, and its troops experienced a drumfire barrage at the same time as the *Totenkopf* Division's troops, with most of it falling on the positions held by *Hstuf.* Borchert's reconnaissance troops. East of that portion of the line, the eight remaining tanks and assault guns of the *I. Abteilung* of Darges' regiment continued their hit-and-run tactics, but Schumacher's battalion withdrew when a large enemy attack burst forth from the town of Wieliszew early that afternoon. This force was dealt with by artillery, while another Soviet force attacking Łajsk had earlier been driven back by the *5. Kompanie* of *Hstuf.* Flügel's battalion after suffering heavy losses.[118]

That afternoon, an interesting report reached *Staf.* Ullrich's new division headquarters at Krubin, a small village 15 kilometers east of Nowy Dwór. The *I. Btl./Germania*, holding the division's left flank along the river from Poddebe to the hills 5 kilometers northwest of Wieliszew, reported that a group of approximately 150–200 Soviet troops coming from the direction of Izbica had made a successful river crossing using rubber rafts and begun to dig in on the opposite bank. The battalion from *Germania* called in artillery fire upon the Soviet troops, who were dispersed when they later tried to infiltrate the German lines at sundown, but more men kept crossing the river all night. This would merely be the first successful crossing attempt.[119] As elsewhere, Soviet aircraft made their presence manifest, forcing Ullrich's troops to employ both active and passive defensive measures, which meant in most cases extensive camouflage featuring foliage and other materials to break up vehicle outlines, artillery firing positions, and supply depots.

While the fighting throughout the corps defensive sector between Wieliszew and Tarchomin was relatively heavy in comparison to previous days, that taking place north of the Narew involving the *19. Pz.Div.* was the heaviest of 24 October by far. Here, the division was engaged in mobile operations, fighting to prevent the I Guards Tank Corps from breaking through and racing to the Modlin. Enduring the same drumfire barrage that struck the SS divisions and *Gruppe Zugehör* that morning, Källner's forces had to contend with one attack on its far left flank that caused it to lose contact with its left-hand neighbor, the *25. Pz.Div.* This enemy attack managed to penetrate into the division's rear area, forcing it to pull its left flank back as far as the village of Debe, site of the sole remaining bridge over the Narew besides those at Modlin that provided a connection between the *Wiking* and the *19. Pz.Div.* In the division's center, one enemy force managed to penetrate as far as Izbica (a portion of which had already crossed the river on rubber boats earlier that day, as related above) before the division was able to wipe it out. From the bridgehead at Debe, the division's *panzer* regiment struck north, fighting its way through wooded terrain until it was finally able to restore contact with the neighboring division near Stanisłowowo, clearing the Serock–Modlin highway of the enemy once again. The bridge at Debe was damaged by a Soviet shell or bomb dropped by an aircraft, limiting its use by Källner's division.

Gille's commander's report that evening at 8:30 p.m. was brief. After relating the tactical events of the day, he wrote that he expected the fighting north of the Narew involving the *19. Pz.Div.* and other German units engaged there would continue to grow in severity. To make it easier to logistically support Källner, he ordered the bridge at Debe to be repaired and the bridgehead north of the town expanded in order to keep the bridge out of range of Soviet artillery. He described how he saw the attacks against the *Totenkopf* Division that day as a precursor to an even larger assault the next day, or the day after that, in an effort to seize favorable jump-off positions for an attack up the middle of Gille's corps.

The fighting that day in the *Wiking*'s sector, he related, was also a foretaste of the attack he expected would occur in conjunction with the one against the *Totenkopf* in an attempt to punch through its defense line between Lajsk and the dune-covered area east of the town. Should this occur, it would give the 70th Army the opportunity to get behind the new *Fuchsstellung* with mobile forces, which would cause Gille's defenses to collapse. However, he did not seem overly worried that this might happen, especially now that he knew the *Totenkopf* Division had managed over the past several days to increase the number of operational tanks in its *panzer* regiment to 72, including seven Tigers. Though weak in infantry, the *Totenkopf* was still a powerful force to be reckoned with. All told, on 24 October Gille's corps fielded 111 operational tanks, 51 assault guns and tank destroyers, and 40 antitank guns. Just as important was the fact that his corps' artillery was still almost completely intact.[120] While losing none of its armored vehicles to enemy fire, it did claim the destruction of nine Soviet tanks and assault guns that day.[121]

In his turn, the army commander in his daily report expressed his surprise that the 70th Army had not more aggressively pursued the withdrawal of the *Wiking* Division to the hybrid *Fuchs-* and *Dachsstellung* more closely. As weak as Ullrich's division was, the Soviets had sent only a few tanks after it, a missed opportunity in von Lüttwitz's mind. He also marveled at the fact that the 47th Army had not taken advantage of the long, overexposed front lines of the *Totenkopf* Division, which stretched in an arc from Rożopole all the way to the northwest to Lajsk, where it tied in with the right flank of the *Wiking*. All of the attacks against it that day had been battalion-sized or smaller, and none had been mutually supporting, making it easier for *Obf.* Becker's troops to deal with. Given the relatively few numbers of front-line troops the division had to hold this extended line, there was not much that the division commander could have done to prevent a breakthrough, had they made a concerted effort. But if the Soviets did ram a regiment-sized or larger force through his thin line, his division still possessed the power to cut it off and kill it with his *panzer* and artillery regiments.

Most of the rest of his report focused on a discussion of command relationships and boundary issues arising between his forces operating north of the Narew and those of the *2. Armee*, whose *XX. Armeekorps* was also under great pressure from the 65th Army. He opined that unless the *25. Pz.Div.* could help the *19. Pz.Div.* to restore and hold the old defensive line that had existed before 19 October, then the left flank of the *Wiking* Division would have to swing further back. The way the situation developed that day, the *Wiking* now had to secure an increasingly long left flank along the Narew. With insufficient forces at hand should the 65th Army, in conjunction with the I Guards Tank Corps, make a concerted attempt to cross the river behind it, Ullrich's troops would either have to fall further back or accept encirclement. None of these choices could have been very appealing.

The only other comment he felt worth mentioning was that he felt Gille's corps was using too much artillery ammunition and that part of the resupply problem was due to his division's liberal usage of shells. On that day alone, Gille's artillery had fired 433 tons of explosives, the third greatest usage rate recorded thus far. The *9. Armee* commander closed his evening report by mentioning that additional artillery had been spotted moving in firing positions throughout the 8th Guards Army's Magnuszew bridgehead, enabling its commander, should he choose, to mass between 120 and 145 guns per kilometer in the areas where his army could potentially carry out a breakthrough. Considering the fears that he had already expressed about the future course of fighting on his right flank, von Lüttwitz would have become even more concerned upon receiving this unsettling report.[122]

The next day, 25 October, would soon prove to be another trying day for the troops of the *IV. SS-Pz.Korps*. By this point in the battle, most of Gille's men had been in combat for two weeks with little respite. They certainly got little rest during the night or early morning. All four of the corps' major units—*Gruppe Zugehör*, the *Totenkopf* and *Wiking* Divisions, and the *19. Pz.Div.* —reported numerous attempts by their opponents to reconnoiter their front lines, seeking weak points. In some instances, Soviet units even carried out battalion-sized reconnaissances in force designed to seize German positions if the opportunity presented itself. The *Wiking* Division reported one such attempt, which forced all of its units holding the *Fuchs-* and *Dachsstellung* to respond. Two SU-76 assault guns backing up another attempt to probe *Gruppe Zugehör*'s lines in the south were destroyed by antitank-gun fire and the rest of the force driven back. Soviet artillery increased in tempo as dawn approached, when aircraft of the 16th Air Army began their own attacks. The clear, dry weather that day would favor the attacking air force, while once again the *Luftwaffe* was nowhere to be seen.

In *Oberst* Zugehör's sector along the right bank of the Vistula, his troops fended off a mid-morning attack against his task force by Polish troops. Undeterred, the Poles kept attacking all afternoon. After a 30-minute drumfire barrage that began at 1 p.m., Zugehör's entire main defense line was confronted by several tank-supported battalion-sized attacks. One of these penetrated the lines on his left flank, but was thrown back in a counterattack. Elsewhere his lines held, although his men had to endure at least 15 air attacks. Polish troops attempting to infiltrate his right flank along the river were driven off by artillery fire. Overall though, at the end of the day *Gruppe Zugehör*'s lines were in the same positions that they had been that morning.

The attacks against the *Totenkopf* Division were a repeat of the previous day, but stronger. After a quiet morning, a drumfire artillery barrage rained down upon the division's entire front line, beginning at 2 p.m. Again, the main Soviet effort was directed against *Obf.* Becker's left flank, where several battalion-sized attacks, with tanks in support, tried to break through his positions along the line from Jósefów to Woła Aleksandra and ending at Stanisławów. Several local penetrations were reported, though with the aid of artillery fire from *SS-Pz.Art.Rgt. 3* these had all been ironed out by nightfall. Soviet fighter-bombers ranged up and down the division's lines, supporting the ground assault by strafing and bombing German positions in an effort to destroy or disrupt their defenses.

To the *Totenkopf*s north, the *Wiking* Division found itself under unremitting attacks that day too, including a drumfire barrage at the same time that its neighbor did. However, instead of blasting the division's entire front line like it did against the *Totenkopf*, the Soviet artillery's effort was directed against *Staf.* Ullrich's left flank along the Narew. It and the ground attacks that followed focused on the area between the town of Wieliszew and the *Dachsstellung*, the intermediate position stretching from the bend in the Brodnowski canal at Poniatowski to the Narew, 5 kilometers east of the bridge at Debe. Clearly, the enemy was still attempting to turn the division's flank along the river.

Although a battalion-sized Soviet attack from Wieliszew was driven off by artillery fire, the troops from *I. Btl./Germania* holding positions along the riverbank were shelled from the opposite shore by enemy antitank guns, which pinned them down while more Soviet troops were ferried across the river. Eventually forced to fall back from the river, the battalion was able to fend off a company-sized attack that evening. Like everywhere else, the *Wiking*'s troops endured harassing artillery fire and numerous attacks by the Red Air Force throughout the day. No Soviet tanks were reported taking part in the ground attacks, allowing the *II. Abteilung* of the tank regiment a day of rest, though the division did lose one *Jgd.Pz. IV* to enemy antitank fire when Schumacher's battalion attempted a counterattack towards Wieliszew.[123]

As it did the day before, most of the critical action that day was taking place north of the Narew, where Källner's *19. Pz.Div.* and the neighboring *25. Pz.Div.* fought shoulder-to-shoulder against the I Guards Tank Corps. At 12:50 p.m., an hour-long drumfire barrage enveloped its entire front line in smoke and clouds of dust, immediately followed by tank attacks at several locations, ranging between Stanisławów on the left to Izbica on the right. When *Pz.Rgt. 27* launched a counterattack to retake Izbica, which had fallen to the enemy after an infantry assault, it ran into a large Soviet tank force that was advancing to the west. In the engagement that followed, *Oberst* von Hake's tanks knocked out four T-34s for the loss of none of their own, but his *Kampfgruppe* was unable to retake the town. The net effect of the fighting that day was that the 65th Army now controlled the entire north bank of the Narew, from Serock at the mouth of the Bug River all the way to Izbica. In recognition of this development as well as to the approaching darkness, Källner ordered his division to fall back several kilometers while retaining contact on his left with the *25. Pz.Div.* at Bolesławowo, and on the right with the bridgehead at Debe, though this town would soon be in direct-fire range of the attackers who had already permanently ensconced themselves in Izbica, only a couple of kilometers away. That evening, action by both sides seemingly ground to a halt.

In his assessment that evening, Gille was primarily concerned with the events on his left, where he saw the continuing advance by the 70th Army along the southern bank of the Narew and that by the 65th Army along the north as a threat to the continuity of his defense line. Not only was there a danger that his corps could be split in two by this development, but he was doubly concerned that the still incomplete *Fuchsstellung* could be outflanked by a series of shallow river crossings that would lead to the collapse of the *Wiking* Division's effort. The *Dachsstellung* was already nearly outflanked and would last for only two more days, at the most. Soviet artillery and antitank shells fired from Izbica were already falling behind the lines of the Dachshund position, creating havoc among the troops entrenched there.

Therefore, he urged his army commander to grant him permission to move his troops completely into the *Fuchsstellung*, whether it was completed or not, before it was too late. However, he cautioned, this was not an action that could take place in a vacuum. Should the *Wiking* execute this movement, it would in turn expose the left flank and rear of the *Totenkopf* Division, so any move into the *Fuchstellung* would in turn require Becker's division to withdraw into the *Marderstellung* 24 hours later, an action that would force the abandonment of the major town of Jablonna-Legjonowo.

Ideally, both divisions would move at the same time into the *Fuchsstellung*, designated as the final main defense line for the Wet Triangle. Further complicating the situation would be the enemy's response. Should Marshal Rokossovsky get wind of the pending displacement, an attack at the wrong moment might allow his forces to drive straight down the highway to Jablonna, cutting off both the *Totenkopf* Division and *Gruppe Zugehör* before they could respond. However, issuing an order for a general withdrawal was not something that Gille was empowered to do; for anything of this magnitude, only the *9. Armee* commander, or even the commander of *H.Gr. Mitte*, could issue the order. The fact that his troops had destroyed eight enemy tanks and assault guns and four heavy antitank guns must have done little to boost his spirits, given his corps' future prospects for survival, which must have appeared slight at this point in the battle. Still, he would continue the defensive effort to the best of his ability.[124]

That evening, von Lüttwitz saw the actions unfolding on Gille's left flank as merely a prelude to the offensive he felt certain would burst forth any day from the Magnuszew bridgehead. The absence of any appreciable activity by the VIII Guards Tank Corps was assessed as being a deliberate act by Rokossovsky, who von Lüttwitz believed was waiting to commit it to battle if not tomorrow then the day after. The heavy fighting reported by the *IV. SS-Pz.Korps* in its sector that day was viewed by the *9. Armee* commander as only being of a "local, limited" nature. The only action that drew his attention was the inability of the *19. Pz.Div.* to retake Izbica; otherwise, he seemed satisfied with how the fighting had run its course that day.[125]

More important was the future status of the *19. Pz.Div.* Von Lüttwitz was informed by the *H.Gr. Mitte* chief of staff that an order had been issued that day directing Källner's division to be withdrawn from the front no later than 28 October and moved into a position in the Kampinos forest north of Warsaw, where it would become the army group's reserve. On the same date, all the other various *Kampfgruppen* and *Alarm* units would move back across the Narew and rejoin their units, except *Ostubaf.* Dorr's *Pz.Gren.Rgt. 9 Germania* and *Hstuf.* Grabner's *Flak Kampfgruppe*, which would remain in place. The *25. Pz.Div.* would temporarily stay where it was until it too was relieved shortly thereafter by the *542. Gren.Div.*, whose *Gren.Rgt. 1077* would once again become *Ostubaf.* Dorr's neighbor to the north. Dorr had already become acquainted with its regimental commander, *Maj.* Walter Kopp, and their cooperation would be essential if both *2. Armee* and *9. Armee* were to continue holding the new defensive line. To buttress Dorr's *Kampgruppe*, Ritter's *Gren.Btl.z.b.V. 560* would be attached as soon as it could be released on 28 October.

The good news in this was that the *25. Pz.Div.* would be moved to an assembly area west of Magnuszew, where it would be reconstituted and then become the *9. Armee* reserve force. Though this development would certainly have pleased von Lüttwitz, who would finally get the army reserve he had long sought, the defense of the narrow sector north of the Narew would still be his responsibility, and by extension, Gille's too, until some point in the future. Developments that day also included a kernel of good news for Gille, for von Lüttwitz had been given permission for *IV. SS-Pz.Korps* to move all of its units into the *Marderstellung* by 28 October. Of course, it would have to give up *Gruppe Zugehör*, but the final position would be narrow enough (and supposedly impregnable enough) to allow it to be held by just the two SS divisions. Once this move was complete, for all intents and purposes, the third defensive battle of Warsaw would come to an end. Until it did, there were still three more days of hard fighting remaining.

The night of 25–26 October was anything but quiet. The front lines seemed to be alive with artillery fire, night bombing raids by the Red Air Force, and foot patrols from both sides seeking to gather prisoners and feel out front-line positions. The

I. Btl./Germania carried out two nighttime assaults against Soviet positions along the southern bank of the Narew that brought in several prisoners. *Gruppe Zugehör* fended off a night assault by the Poles during the early hours, destroying two more of their assault guns and chasing the survivors back to their lines with artillery fire. The situation overall was tense. Would today be the day when the VIII Guards Tank and I Guards Tank Corps finally launched their long-awaited and dreaded main attack? If the attack came that day, the odds were that it would fall on the *Wiking* Division's left flank, along the corridor between Zagroby and Wieliszew and along the highway connecting Serock to Modlin on the northern bank of the Narew.

The fighting grew in intensity throughout the day. *Gruppe Zugehör* withdrew on schedule to its intermediate position in the north, avoiding a one-hour artillery barrage that fell on its old positions. No enemy assault followed, contrary to expectations. Still, Soviet and Polish harassing fire fell upon the *Kampfgruppe*'s rear area, particularly against its artillery, which in turn was engaged in shelling known and suspected Polish assembly areas. The Red Air Force bombed and strafed the area along the east bank of the Vistula all day, making life hazardous for anyone driving a motor vehicle along the highway between Jablonna and Choszczówka.

The following day, 26 October, was nearly a repeat of the *Totenkopf* Division's experiences of the previous day. Heavy artillery fire fell along the division's entire 15-kilometer front line. During mid-morning, enemy assault troops were observed assembling to prepare for attacks near Hill 97, Rożopole, Jósefów, Michałow Grabina, and Hill 90.1. Just as they were preparing for their assault, the division's entire artillery regiment, supported by artillery and rocket fire from the corps' *SS-ARKO 104*, launched a massive preemptive barrage of their own, smashing and scattering the concentration of enemy troops with great loss of life. The few attacks that day were mostly company- to battalion-size, and achieved no discernable results. A *Totenkopf* antitank gun destroyed one JSU-152 assault gun. An artillery observation balloon spotted near the village of Izabelin, over 10 kilometers away, was shot down by a German fighter, the only mention of the *Luftwaffe*'s appearance that day.

The *Wiking* Division was similarly tormented that day by heavy enemy artillery fire, which at one point reach drumfire proportions on the forward positions held by *I. Btl./Germania* and *SS-Aufkl.Abt. 5* west of the town of Wieliszew. Attempts by Soviet forces attacking from Wieliszew through the sand dunes area west and southwest of the town were forced back by heavy defensive fire. Although they were able to achieve one minor penetration of the Germans' defensive positions, this was quickly eliminated by a local counterattack. However, the Soviets did successfully take the large wooded area on the southern bank of the Narew across the river from Izbica, where heavy artillery and antitank fire forced the defenders to retreat. When this same force, probably a battalion, attempted to push towards the defensive positions held by *I. Btl./Germania* along the *Dachsstellung*, a counterattack by *I. Abt./SS-Pz. Rgt. 5* forced them back into the woods. More enemy troops were seen crossing the river upstream from Debe, increasing the size of the force that had been compelled by *Ostuf.* Schumacher's attack to begin digging foxholes inside the woods. Slowly but steadily, the forces of the 70th Army were nibbling away at Gille's flanks.

As it had for the past several days, most of the dramatic action unfolding on 26 October involved the *19. Pz.Div.*, which, despite the assurances from *2. Armee* that the 65th Army's attacks were beginning to slacken, found no such evidence of this taking place along the northern bank of the Narew. After enduring a heavy artillery barrage beginning at 9:45 a.m, several attacks ranging in size from battalion to regiment attempted to break through the division's thin screen line. Supported by rolling air attacks, which included 91 sorties by IL-2s and Douglas A-20 Bostons, the main attack got moving in the early afternoon when an infantry regiment, supported by five tanks, attempted to pierce Källner's line along the main highway leading to Modlin. In the ensuing battle, two Soviet tanks were destroyed and the remainder fled, along with the infantry who could not stand up to the accurate artillery barrage that was laid upon them. After mopping up the few local breakthroughs, the division's line was restored by nightfall. Throughout the day, its forces observed the various crossing attempts of the Narew between Izbica and Jachronka, but was unable to engage them with anything but artillery. Two gun boats on the Narew that were observed firing into the German lines west of Izbica were engaged and driven off by indirect fire. One IL-2 was shot down, in itself a minor victory, but *19. Pz.Div.* was decreased in size when *II. Btl./Pz.Gren.Rgt. 394* was ordered to return to its parent *3. Pz.Div.*

In reviewing the day's events, Gille focused primarily on two topics. While noting the day's defensive successes, he was concerned that the planned withdrawal of *Gruppe Zugehör* to its next phase line had shortened the enemy's front line and had correspondingly freed up three rifle divisions—the 143rd, 234th, and 185th. Once his corps had completed its withdrawal to the *Fuchsstellung*, even more enemy divisions would become available, including perhaps most of the 47th Army. In turn, this force, including the Polish 1st Army, would be available to conduct a deliberate river crossing operation anywhere between Tarchomin and the bend in the river at Jablonna, a width of nearly 20 kilometers. Should Rokossovsky decide to order such an operation, there were not many German troops available to hold the western bank of the Vistula. The purpose served by keeping Gille's corps tied down in the Wet Triangle was becoming ever more elusive.

The second topic that drew his more immediate attention was the approval of his request to begin withdrawing in stages to the *Fuchsstellung*, which was to be completed by 28 October. The first stage was to take place that night, when *Gruppe Zugehör*, together with the entire *Totenkopf* Division, would begin withdrawing from their current positions to a general line running 500 meters east of the Jablonna–Zagroby highway up to Hill 77, where the line bent back to the north and the right flank of the *Wiking* Division began. For *Gruppe Zugehör*, this was a comparatively easy task; all it had to do was fall back, as it had been doing the past few days, and stop at the southeast corner of Jablonna, which it had to control in order to deny the enemy access to the paved highway that paralleled the Vistula. It would only have to remain in this new position for one day; on the night of 27–28 October it would be completely withdrawn and sent back across the river to join up with its parent division in its assembly area in the Kampinos forest.

The *Totenkopf* Division's task was much more challenging. Not only did it have to withdraw a greater distance, but it still had troops in contact with the enemy along a 15-kilometer-wide front, which it would have to vacate while drawing as little enemy attention as possible. In addition to that, most of its artillery would have to displace from the Jablonna-Legjonowo area, and many small ammunition dumps would have to be moved as well. The artillery had already developed contingency plans for this to ensure that fire support would be available throughout, even though some of the batteries would be displacing at any given time and hence not available to fire unless it was an emergency. Fortunately, *Obf.* Becker's staff had been planning this operation for at least a week, and some of these activities would have already been doned. Since the withdrawal would take place at night, the division at least would have the cover of darkness to help it avoid detection.

As for the enemy's intentions, they had not apparently changed much at all based on examination of captured documents and the interrogation of numerous POWs and deserters carried out by Gille's *Ic*, *Stubaf.* Jankuhn, and his staff during the last several days. The results indicated overwhelmingly that 47th and 70th Armies were still striving towards Modlin, with a river crossing to be carried out somewhere along the Vistula. The disposition of the VIII Guards Tank Corps, which had been strangely quiet for several days, was still unknown. In closing, Gille informed his army commander that he expected the offensive to continue, and that his corps' withdrawal would be carried out as ordered; even while this was occurring, his corps would continue to defend as it had been doing for the past two weeks.[126]

In his own narrative of the day's events, von Lüttwitz continued to remark upon what he saw as the continued easing of pressure against *IV. SS-Pz.Korps*, with the only exceptions being the attacks against the left flank of the *Wiking* Division at Wieliszew and the combat north of the Narew involving the *19. Pz.Div.*, but neither of these seemed to have been a source of concern, probably because the *2. Armee* was being reinforced with sufficient forces to address the threat posed by the 65th Army, whose own attack appeared to be slowing down. The fact that the *Germania* Regiment had been left on the northern bank of the Narew did not seem to be anything he was concerned about either. What vexed von Lüttwitz the most that day was the information he received from the *VIII. Armeekorps* that indicated the number of artillery batteries being moved into the 8th Guards Army's bridgehead at Magnuszew may possibly have been greatly exaggerated.[127]

Whether he knew he had been the target of a large-scale operational deception is unknown, but he did question the accuracy of the aerial photographs taken before and after, such as whether there was some kind of trick on the eyes caused by the lighting of the photos, or if the batteries had been clever decoys, and so forth. If the number of batteries was less than half of what he had believed, and the threat exaggerated, then the danger posed by Chuikov's army was not nearly as great as had been thought. To confirm the reports, he ordered additional aerial photos taken the following day. Until these results were made available, he would reserve judgement as to the true nature of his enemy's intentions. In this regard, at least from the vantage point of three-quarters of a century, the *9. Armee* commander seems to have been attempting to reassure himself that his initial estimates of the enemy's strength were correct.

Another development that concerned him greatly was the implications of the withdrawal of Gille's corps, including the inevitable detachment of *Gruppe Zugehör* from the corps' right flank along the Vistula. While von Lüttwitz knew that this battlegroup would return to the *19. Pz.Div.* the following day and rejoin it in its new reserve position, the ensuing vacuum would require that the defensive line held by *Gen.d.Art.* Felzmann's *XLVI. Pz.Korps* along the Vistula in front of Warsaw be extended to the north by nearly 20 kilometers. Gille's corps was not strong enough to take on this mission, so the only option remaining was for the two divisions in Felzmann's corps—the *337. VGD* and *73. Inf.Div.*—to extend their lines to the north out of the city as far as Kepa-Kielpinska at the bend in the river, opposite the Polish and Soviet forces that had occupied the eastern bank as soon as *Gruppe Zugehör* had withdrawn. These units had already begun to engage German outposts on the opposite side of the river with sporadic artillery fire, a reminder that although the Vistula was nearly 2 kilometers wide at this point, the enemy was not very far away at all.

The *ad hoc* engineer task force that had previously held this sector was obviously insufficient, so most of the responsibility would befall *Oberst* Schlieper's *73. Inf. Div.*, which had not completely redeemed itself after its collapse on 12 September. Temporary manpower was to be provided by the attachment of *SS-Pol.Rgt. 17* and *Sturm-Btl. AOK 9*. If a river crossing were to occur in its sector, if need be, Felzmann could in theory turn to the *19. Pz.Div.* for help, since Källner's division would be located only a few miles away in its reserve position, so long as it had not already been committed elsewhere. These and other similar considerations probably gave von Lüttwitz a great deal to worry about, but there was little he could do about it in any case. At least the news that *H.Gr. Mitte* had issued an order to the *25. Pz.Div.* for it to begin moving by rail to the Warka area the following day must have offered some consolation.

Friday, 27 October— the second to last official day of the third defensive battle of Warsaw—began as a sunny but cool and windy day. True to their pattern, the artillerymen of the 1st Polish, 47th, and 70th Armies began the day with harassing fire, increasing in volume and intensity as the day grew long. Most of it landed on empty positions, however, since from midnight the three units arrayed across the Narew–Vistula triangle began withdrawing as ordered to their intermediate defensive line. The *Totenkopf*s units reached their intermediate line, which its commander had designated as the *Uhustellung* (owl line), while the *Wiking* Division withdrew in an orderly manner to the *Fuchsstellung*. Other than having to stop and fight off Soviet reconnaissance patrols, which were dealt with by mobile rear guards that remained in the old positions until midday, all units reported their arrival at their new positions by 8 a.m.

On the opposite side of the Narew, the day began for the *19. Pz.Div.* with disruptive fire and artillery ambushes upon its positions, but it would have to endure these attacks for only two more days. As it grew brighter, Soviet aircraft became increasingly active, with bombing runs and strafing attacks against anything that attracted their attention. Although these were not as intensive as those being carried out by their Allied counterparts on the Western Front, the Red Air Force could still inflict considerable damage on any force that underestimated its ability and failed to practice good camouflage discipline.

For *Gruppe Zugehör*, on its last day in the line as part of *IV. SS-Pz.Korps*, the only thing it had to contend with on 27 October was enemy artillery fire. At one point, it used its own artillery to engage and disperse a Soviet unit it had observed on the left attempting to envelop the right flank of the *Totenkopf* Division. Around midday, when Soviet commanders began to realize that Becker's SS troops had withdrawn, their units were ordered to immediately attack at several points along the old main defense line with their supporting armor and attempt to exploit and penetrate the new defensive line before it was fully ready. This lead to heavy fighting between these onrushing troops and the *Totenkopf*s *Nachhut* (rear guard), which was almost exclusively composed of Becker's armor. Supported by artillery fire that attempted to suppress the German artillery, the Soviets launched multiple attacks in their attempt to push their way past the rear guard, get into the *Uhustellung*, cut them off, and disrupt the division's entire defensive scheme. Only at one point were they able to do this, when 160 men and four tanks got behind the *Nachhut*. An order was issued to reverse course and counterattack, which one of the tank battalions did, dispersing the Soviet infantry and destroying three of the tanks, capturing three soldiers in the process.

Though the *Wiking* Division's morning passed relatively uneventfully, shortly after noon it too was subjected to a series of attacks by infantry forces supported by a few tanks. In one instance, a battalion of approximately 300 men with some tanks attacked from the direction of Wieliszew along the highway leading towards Modlin. A combined counterattack by *I. Abt./SS-Pz.Rgt. 5* and the division's reconnaissance battalion halted and then repulsed this attempt to penetrate the *Fuchsstellung*. After that, the day degenerated into one artillery duel after another. Fortunately for the *Wiking* Division, the distance covered during the withdrawal placed its new front lines beyond the range of the Soviet heavy artillery and rocket launcher battalions, which would need a day or two to move and occupy new firing positions closer to their front lines.

During the day, one of *Ostuf.* Schumacher's *Pz. IVs* broke down and had to be blown up by its crew to keep it from falling into enemy hands because there was no prime mover to tow it. Another was damaged in the fighting and had to be abandoned in no-man's land, with the intention of returning that night and recovering it. However, it was spotted and set alight by Soviet troops and was completely destroyed. That day, *Hstuf.* Flügel's *II. Abteilung* with his 10 remaining operational Panthers were ordered back across the Narew to augment Dorr's *Kampfgruppe*, replacing *Pz.Rgt. 27* of the *19. Pz.Div.*, which was being pulled out that night.[128] Flugel's new headquarters was established in the village of Orzechowo on the southern bank of the Narew opposite his old one at Skrzeszew. As Flügel established contact with the *19. Pz.Div.* to determine the enemy's locations, he found that division engaged in defensive activity but little else. It was not under attack except by random and inaccurate artillery fire and the occasional fighter-bomber attack, giving the impression that Källner's men were evidently ready to leave. After nearly a week of grueling tank warfare, they had earned a rest, having not only defeated a numerically superior opponent, but prevented the I Guards Tank Corps from reaching Modlin, the lifeline of the *IV. SS-Pz.Korps*.

After reviewing his troops' performance that day, Gille was satisfied that things had gone so well. The withdrawal to the new line had gone relatively smoothly, as by the time his opponents had woken up to discover that his troops had pulled out, it was too late for them to launch any effective attempt to interdict the movement. He remarked upon the noticeable ineffectiveness of the Soviet artillery that day, which seemed not to know where best to employ its tremendous firepower. That problem would be solved directly. His greatest concern was now that he knew most of the 47th Army was no longer in contact, where would it go next? He pondered whether it would go into reserve and reconstitute its heavily depleted units, attempt a river crossing operation, or be pulled out and inserted into the line somewhere else, perhaps north of the Narew. He had no answer, and *9. Armee* could not provide one either. He closed his commander's report with the comment that his intentions for the next day were to continue to defend, while ensuring that all units had fully closed up on their new positions the next day and occupied all of the field fortifications that had been constructed for them for the past two months.[129]

That evening, an equally thoughtful *9. Armee* commander pondered the Soviets' next steps. Von Lüttwitz praised withdrawal that had been carried out the night before as being "flawlessly" executed, though he noted that once the enemy had finally discovered that Gille's troops had pulled out, they reacted strongly and aggressively.

The fact that Marshal Rokossovsky had decided not to fully commit the VIII Guards Tanks Corps against the *IV. SS-Pz.Korps'* positions may have been a clue that it was not going to play a huge role in the offensive after all. Evidence actually indicates that it was withdrawn at some point after 22 October and became part of the First Belorussian Front's operational reserve. Although the expected large-scale offensive had yet to manifest itself, and the scaling down of artillery forces was puzzling, von Lüttwitz restated his belief that Rokossovsky's intent remained the same—launch a massive attack from the Magnuszew bridgehead in combination with another towards Modlin and across the Vistula into Germany. He was more correct than he knew, but this would not occur for another two months.[130]

Von Lüttwitz did not seem concerned about Gille's new positions in the Wet Triangle, knowing that it was a strong main defense line and would be difficult to crack for the time being. Most of his worry that day was still focused on the inconclusive aerial photos taken that morning of the artillery positions in the Magnuszew bridgehead. To him, they still seemed inconclusive, with not enough evidence for him to change his mind. He also fretted about his left flank, which was being handed over to the *Wiking* Division as the *19. Pz.Div.* withdrew into army group reserve. Von Lüttwitz did not believe that the 65th Army's offensive had run its course, having seen reports of Soviet troops digging in and of the arrival of additional units to swell the size of the force in the Pułtusk-Serock bridgehead.

To further strengthen what he assessed as a vulnerable position, he directed Gille to send another tank or assault gun reinforced battalion to the area northeast of Modlin, where it would serve as a reserve force for his left flank, no later than 30 October. Here, it could block any attempt by the enemy to take Modlin and envelope *9. Armee* from the north. As he wrote that report, the first elements of *19. Pz.Div.* began to arrive in the Kampinos forest to take up their new quarters, while the *25. Pz.Div.* began moving through his army's rear area towards Warka. It had been a long time since *9. Armee* had enjoyed the luxury of having two uncommitted *panzer* divisions in its area of operations, which must have created a feeling, for once, of security for the army commander.

The last day of the third battle of Modlin was later officially designated as 28 October. The only significance of this date is that it was when the *IV. SS-Pz.Korps* completely closed into its new defense line, which thereafter became known as *Festung Modlin* (Modlin fortress). The *Fuchsstellung* was not really a fortress of course, but a series of strong field fortifications that had been laboriously constructed during the past two months by Polish laborers, Hungarian soldiers, German construction engineers, and Soviet POWs. Whether it would hold for any length of time had yet to be determined. As the troops of the *IV. SS-Pz.Korps* withdrew they were probably happy to see its barbed wire entanglements, obstacles, and minefields, as they would be safer behind its trenches and bunkers than they had been during the past two weeks, when they had occupied hasty defensive positions that provided little protection. Here they could repair and clean their weapons and equipment, and perhaps get some rest.

It was also the last day of *Gruppe Zugehör*, which had already begun withdrawing during the early morning and, by midnight, was completely back across the river operating again under its old name—*Pz.Gren.Rgt. 73*. Its acting leader resumed his command of *Pz.Art.Rgt. 19*. Although its name had changed, its artillery continued firing up to the last minute against Soviet positions and traffic along the road leading from Praga to Jablonna. Even if the *19. Pz.Div.* was going into reserve, its artillery regiment would continue firing in support of Gille's corps from across the river since he needed all the firepower he could get. From its positions in the eastern edge of the Kampinos forest, it could still range and fire its heavier guns at the 1st Polish Army and the left flank of the 47th Army.

At midnight, the *Totenkopf* Division finally displaced to the *Fuchstellung*, withdrawing from the intermediate *Uhustellung* while under Soviet pressure. A counterattack against Soviet tanks attempting to get behind one of its withdrawing units resulted in the destruction of three T-34s. By 3:30 a.m., the division had closed into its new location, except for rear guards that had lagged behind to cover the movement. The *Wiking* Division was already in the *Fuchsstellung*, so most of its attention was focused north of the Narew, where nearly half of the division's remaining combat power was positioned—most of the *Germania* Regiment, one tank battalion, a *Flak Kampfgruppe*, an artillery battalion, and the attached probationary battalion of *Maj.* Ritter's. Soviet artillery fire throughout the evening and early morning was described as light, with some scattered disruption fire. At 5 a.m., command of the sector north of the Narew was officially handed over from the *19. Pz.Div.* to *Kampfgruppe Germania*. The only other significant act on Källner's part that day was to release *Sturm-Btl. AOK 9* from its attachment to his division and send it on its way to Warsaw, where it would augment the *73. Inf.Div.* on the Vistula defense line.

In the *IV. SS-Pz.Korps* sector that day, the pursuing Soviet troops wasted no time in reconnoitering the new German defensive line and probing to find its weak points. Enemy artillery fire was sparse and sporadic; it was evidently awaiting information about where its new targets were going to be as well as finishing moving forward to be within range. The most serious incident that day occurred in the *Totenkopf* Division's new sector, where a significant enemy force of approximately 400 infantrymen and eight tanks attempted to advance up the Jablonna–Modlin highway. When they reached the outskirts of the town of Chotomów, they were fired on by the *Totenkopf*'s own tanks as well as by artillery. The enemy battalion was soon forced to retreat after losing one tank and a number of its men. The Soviets on the *Wiking*'s flank were even less aggressive. Every attempt to probe the new positions was driven back by *SS-Pz.Art.Rgt. 5*'s guns. Soviet air activity was also described as light. On the other side of the Narew, even *Kampfgruppe Germania* was left relatively unmolested, except for occasional artillery fire.

In his own memoir, Marshal Rokossovsky states that he had originally intended to continue the offensive beyond that point, as Stalin had ordered him to "deny the enemy any foothold on the eastern bank" of the Vistula. Aware that the forces of the 47th and 70th Armies had already suffered heavy losses of men and materiel, and that continuing the offensive the following day would only add to the long casualty list while most likely only delivering meager results, he decided before the next day's attack to travel to the front lines to see the situation for himself. After reviewing the plans at his command post for continuing the offensive that evening, the next morning Rokossovsky, accompanied by two of his staff officers, traveled to visit a front-line battalion from a rifle division belonging to the 47th Army. Here, he was briefed on the situation by the local unit commander.[131] Shortly thereafter, the preparatory barrage by the 47th Army's artillery to support the attack began, signaling the resumption of the offensive.

It was a powerful barrage, but as before, the Germans responded just as strongly. Based on what he had just experienced, and aware that his troops had been suffering under the same accurate German fire for weeks, he decided on the spot to call off the attack scheduled for that morning. Notifying army commanders Gusev and Popov of his decision, Rokossovsky called Moscow upon returning to his own command post to tell Stalin. Knowing what the consequences might be if he displeased the notoriously unpredictable dictator, he was relieved when Stalin told him over the telephone that he agreed with the decision and he wanted the First Belorussian Front to transition from the offense to a defensive posture. No doubt Stalin was thinking ahead to the next operation planned for the winter and, like his Front commander, agreed that there was no point wasting Rokossovsky's striking power on such a minor objective. Rokossovsky's decision may well explain why the 47th and 70th Armies did not pursue the *IV. SS-Pz.Korps* more aggressively as it withdrew, but both of Gille's divisions still felt the pressure as Soviet forward units pressed them closely.

Reviewing the day's activities that night, Gille seemed satisfied with how operations had gone. His corps of three divisions and all of his corps troops—nearly 50,000 men—had successfully broken contact with the enemy, withdrawn between 10 and 15 kilometers, and occupied a new defensive position without any significant enemy interference. Any one of these operations would have been difficult in itself. The fact that all three had been carried out in less than 48 hours was a testament not only to the quality of his division's leadership, down to the company and battalion level, but also to the proficiency and professionalism of the corps and division staffs, who had spent many sleepless nights planning the move, estimating ammunition and fuel required, and myriad other details involved in managing such a complex withdrawal.

Gille pondered the significance of the apparent cessation of Rokossovsky's offensive. Had the Soviet commander merely postponed it for a few days in order to bring up more troops and ammunition, or had he cancelled it entirely? And why had the VIII Guards Tank Corps not been fully committed? To determine his opponents' intentions, Gille directed that Becker's and Ullrich's division both launch a series of aggressive combat patrols that evening to gather prisoners.[132]

At *9. Armee* headquarters that evening, the army commander evinced a sense of relief that the withdrawal to the *Fuchsstellung* had gone so well. Apart from the attempt by Polish troops to get around the *Totenkopf* Division's right flank at Chotomów that was successfully repulsed, there had hardly been any ground fighting that day. Given the significant amount of air and ground reconnaissance that had taken place, von Lüttwitz assessed that the 1st Polish, 47th, and 70th Armies were attempting to feel out where the *IV. SS-Pz.Korps*' new front line was and to take advantage of any gaps or weaknesses before Gille's troops could consolidate their positions. He also confirmed in his own mind the belief that the offensive in the Narew–Weichsel triangle was over, based on the absence of any large-scale attacks that day, and that there would be no large-scale offensive north and south of the Narew after all, despite Gille's belief to the contrary.[133]

Freed of the dread that this possibility might have imposed on his thinking, the *9. Armee* commander, with almost a sense of relief, turned his eyes towards his right flank, where he anticipated the great offensive from the Magnuszew bridgehead occurring any day. Unaccountably, this sector had been dormant for the past two months and he needed to find out why. Therefore, he must have been disappointed when he learned the results of the aerial photo reconnaissance mission he had ordered flown the previous day to confirm or dispute the initial reports about the number of Soviet artillery batteries detected.

To his surprise, the photos revealed that there were now even fewer evident than in the previous ones, with only 50 batteries detected instead of 80, far less than he anticipated. The *VIII. Armeekorps* commander, *Gen.d.Art.* Walter Hartmann, believed that these photographs, combined with prisoner interrogations and observations from his own front-line divisions, signified a de-escalation of tensions. Hartmann correspondingly ordered a cessation of the state of alert his troops had been operating under for the past several weeks, which must have created a sense of relief within the four divisions under his command.

In the remainder of his narrative, von Lüttwitz focused on the disposition of the two *panzer* divisions that were being placed in reserve within his area of operations—the *19. Pz.Div.*, which at the moment had been designated as the *H.Gr. Mitte* reserve and already occupying the Kampinos forest northwest of Warsaw, and the *25. Pz.Div.*, which would become his own army's armored reserve once it completed its move to its reserve position at Białobrzegi near Warka. The latter division, which had served with the *9. Armee* before under von Vormann's tenure, was well-known to von Lüttwitz's staff, but at that point, it hardly constituted a formidable reserve. Still missing its second *Panzergrenadier* regiment, *Pz.Gren.Rgt. 147*, which was undergoing activation and training, the rest of the division had been roughly handled during the *Sonnenblume* offensive against the Rózan–Serock bridgehead and had suffered heavy losses in men and materiel. Upon its arrival, it could only field seven operational tanks and 10 assault guns. It would need at least a month to be restored to full operational capability.

He made no mention at the time that the third defensive battle of Warsaw was over. The announcement that would officially name the campaign and the three battles of Warsaw comprising it would have to wait several more months. But in a real sense, the withdrawal of the *IV. SS-Pz.Korps* into the *Fuchsstellung* brought a sense of closure, marking an end to the First Belorussian Front's offensive that had begun on 13 August. For the past three months, Marshal Rokossovsky and his armies had been trying furiously to leap over the Vistula and destroy the *IV. SS-Pz. Korps* east of the river.

The fact that they had not been able to do so was a testament to the leadership ability and stubborn determination not only of *Gruf.* Herbert Gille, but of his division and regimental commanders as well, such as Mühlenkamp, Ullrich, Becker, Schlieper, Källner, Schmaltz, and Ibrányi. Not to be overlooked was the superb performance of the officers and enlisted men—*Wehrmacht*, *Waffen-SS*, and Royal Hungarian Army—who had stood shoulder-to-shoulder and withstood some of the most savage fighting ever seen on the Eastern Front. While they had yielded much ground, Gille's troops had done so at great cost to their enemy, yet retained the same high morale, if not the fighting lethality, they had displayed at the beginning of the campaign.

It had been a very costly campaign in terms of lives and materiel for both sides. During the third battle of Warsaw alone, Soviet losses in killed, wounded, and missing had been 13,582 men in the 70th Army and 16,225 in the 47th Army, while the Polish 1st Army had lost 1,600 men in battle, an overall total of 31,407 men who would have to be replaced.[134] In August and September, beginning with the tank battle of Praga, the Soviet and Polish armies committed in the Warsaw area had lost a total of 246,000 men, including 11,000 Polish troops. Adding the 31,407 men lost in October provides the staggering number of 277,407 men (the German official tally for enemy losses was between 30,000 and 35,000 men for October). This number is staggering when compared with the number of troops that Rokossovsky's Front started with on 17 July 1944: 410,162. Of course, roughly two-thirds of his casualties were replaced, but his army group finished the operation much weaker than when it started.[135]

Tank and armored fighting vehicle losses had been just as staggering. According to the First Belorussian Front's official records for the period from 1 August to the end of October 1944, 1,739 tanks, assault guns, and self-propelled artillery were knocked out, of which 1,169 were tanks. Of this number, only 369 were declared to be totally destroyed, i.e., written off, while the remainder were either deemed repairable on the spot or suitable for being shipped back to the USSR to be rebuilt.[136] During the

19 days comprising the third defensive battle of Warsaw within the Wet Triangle and along the southern bank of the Narew, a total of 131 tanks were destroyed (the official German number was 138).[137] Additionally, *IV. SS-Pz.Korps' Flak* gunners had shot down 22 Soviet aircraft.[138] Perhaps Rokossovsky best summed up the results of the failed offensive himself, stating in his memoirs, "Units of the 70th and 47th Armies attacked the bridgehead but in spite of heavy losses and expenditure of large quantities of ammunition they were unable to dislodge the enemy."[139]

During this same period, excluding the month of October, the units of the *2.* and *9. Armee*, with approximately 250,000 men, suffered a total of 91,595 casualties, including 27,422 killed, wounded, and missing in the *9. Armee* area of operations on the front east of the Vistula, while another 8,951 men were lost in Warsaw during *Ogruf.* von dem Bach's repression of General Bór's uprising, excluding SS and Police casualties.[140] Approximately half of these German losses were replaced. A quick tally of the casualties suffered by the *Wiking* and *Totenkopf* Divisions reported for the month of October reveals that they lost 4,057 and 2,114 men respectively, totaling 6,171, including 979 confirmed dead. Of the 1,223 reported as missing in action, this number undoubtedly includes many solders taken prisoner, though most were killed and their bodies not recovered.[141] In return, by the end of the month both divisions received a total of 4,033 replacements, nearly all of them recent *Luftwaffe* transfers. Losses in the *19. Pz.Div.* were also high, totaling 1,623, including 240 killed in action. During the 19 days of battle, Gille's corps lost 57 tanks and assault guns deemed total losses, including 20 Panthers. Undoubtedly, many others were damaged and either repaired by the division's maintenance services or shipped back to Germany for factory-level repair or rebuild. Regardless of the outcome, the third defensive battle of Warsaw had been enormously destructive for both sides.

One other item must be mentioned, and that is the First Belorussian Front's purported lack of action in coming to the aid of the Warsaw Uprising. Since the fall of the Soviet Union, a veritable cottage industry has sprung up blaming Stalin and the Red Army for the failure to help the insurgents, an assertion just as vigorously denied by Russian historians. However, the facts are clear. When the 2nd Tank Army began its drive towards Praga on 27 July 1944, there was no intention of immediately liberating Warsaw and no arrangements had been made to coordinate with the Polish Home Army. Furthermore, the Polish government-in-exile had injudiciously failed to notify the Soviet government of its plan to rise up against its German overlords on 1 August. Rather, evidence indicates that Rokossovsky had assumed that once his army group succeeded in cutting off and destroying the *9. Armee* east of the Vistula in early August, the city would fall into his hands as a matter of course, without much fighting being needed. The Warsaw Uprising surprised the Red Army as much as it did the Nazis.

The German response to Rokossovsky's gamble, as evidenced by their astonishing success during the resulting tank battle east of Praga, cut short those dreams, leading to three months of heavy fighting that forced the First Belorussian Front's armies to crawl their way to the Vistula. It was not Stalin's decision to punish the western-oriented Polish *Armia Krajowa* by having his armies halt at the gates of Warsaw while *Gruppe von dem Bach* devastated the city and brutally crushed the Polish resistance. Rather, it was the incredibly skillful and determined German resistance, including the contributions of five elite *panzer* divisions, that brought the First Belorussian Front's offensive up short. It was not for lack of trying that they failed; the 277,407 casualties that Rokossovsky's forces suffered—more than a quarter of a million men—attests to that.

While it can be argued that in September the Soviets could have provided more support to the 1st Polish Army's river crossing attempt, and probably should have, it must be remembered that the liberation of Warsaw did not fit into STAVKA's overall strategy for defeating Nazi Germany. Diverting a large number of troops towards that goal, which would involve a large-scale river crossing operation followed by a costly house-to-house battle in the city itself, would have undeniably cost the Soviet Union thousands of lives and unknowable amounts of materiel, and more importantly, would have disrupted plans for the liberation of Poland in January 1945 as well as the Berlin operation in the spring of 1945. Attempting an attack on the scale needed to liberate the city would have drawn a commensurately large German response, which again would have led to heavy losses. In summation, liberating Warsaw simply was not a Soviet priority and did not fit into their overall plan for the defeat of Nazi Germany. Historians, no doubt, will continue to argue the point, but for the soldiers on either side, whether German, Soviet, Hungarian, or Polish, the first, second, and third battles of Warsaw were some of the hardest and bitterest ever fought during the annals of World War II.

CHAPTER 12

The Battle of Modlin 29 October–25 November 1944

By midnight on 28 October 1944, the bulk of the *IV. SS-Pz.Korps* was behind its new main defense line, officially designated by the *9. Armee* as the *Fuchsstellung*. With the exception of the screening force positioned forward to provide early warning, as well as the *Germania* Regiment's *Kampfgruppe* fighting north of the Narew, most of Gille's 50,000 men were now safely behind one of the most formidable defensive barriers ever constructed on the Eastern Front. Roughly 20 kilometers wide, this new position, stretching from the village of Rajszew on the Vistula across the Polish countryside to its terminus 300 meters west of Poddebe along the Brodnowski canal, had been made into a virtual fortress, complete with strongpoints, stoutly constructed bunkers, machine-gun positions, antitank obstacles, barbed wire fencing, and extensive minefields. This position, almost immediately nicknamed "Fortress Modlin" by Gille's troops, would be the corps' home for the next two months. Taking advantage of every fold in the ground and terrain feature, the *9. Armee Pionierführer*, *Oberst* Meyer, had designed it with an eye towards making it as impregnable as possible (see Figure 4).

To hold it, each of the corps' two remaining divisions, the *Totenkopf* and the *Wiking*, was assigned a defensive sector only 10 kilometers in width, a front so narrow that they did not have to use all of their troops to defend it. This permitted them to amass a tactical reserve as well as provide opportunities to pull their men out of the line for rest and training periods. Though the *Germania* Regiment (minus one battalion) and most of the *Wiking* division's *panzer* regiment were positioned north of the Narew to secure the corps (and *9. Armee*) northern boundary with the *2. Armee*, the rest of Ullrich's troops, primarily the *Westland* Regiment, occupied the northern half of the Narew–Vistula triangle, with the division headquarters located north of the Narew in the village of Nowy Modlin, 5 kilometers northeast of the old fortress at Modlin. Its initial reserve consisted of *SS-Pz.Aufkl.Abt. 5*, positioned a few kilometers northeast of Nowy Dwór. Ullrich's neighbor, his old *Totenkopf* Division, held the southern half, with Becker's own right flank, held by the *Eicke* Regiment, resting on the Vistula, his left flank held by the *Totenkopf* Regiment

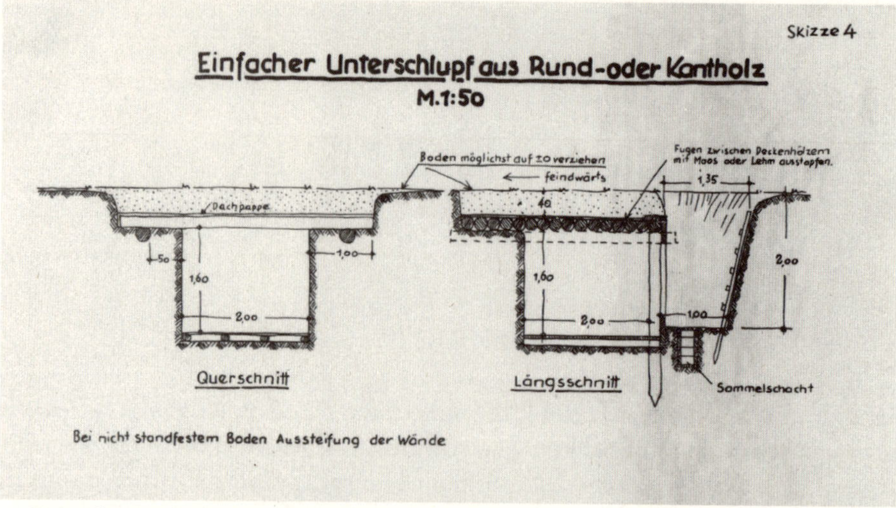

Figure 4. Example diagram of a front-line troop shelter for the Vistula Defense Line, July 1944

next to the *Wiking* near Derlacz, with his headquarters located in the tiny village of Boza Wola, 6 kilometers southeast of the Nowy Dwór railroad station. Nearly all of *SS-Pz.Rgt. 3* was designated as the division reserve.

The corps' logistics lifeline ran through the town of Nowy Dwór, renamed *Bugmünde* in 1939 by the Germans, crossing over the two-level road and railroad bridge across the Narew River to the fortress town of Modlin in the north or across the Vistula at Kazuń Niemiecki to the south. Over these two bridges flowed all of the supplies needed by both divisions and corps units, as well as replacement troops and weapons. The *Wiking* Division depended upon the paved all-weather *Rollbahn* (main movement route) running from Okunin through Krubin, terminating near the front line in the village of Kałuszyn. The *Totenkopf* Division's *Rollbahn* was the paved highway running from Nowy Dwór along the eastern bank of the Vistula through the village of Skierdy, ending just short of Rajszew. If it needed to, the division could also use the railroad that bisected its sector to bring up supplies, beginning at Modlin and terminating just short of Chotomów, the end of the line. To ensure the connection in the Vistula bend area on the western bank with the neighboring *Gren.Rgt. 186* of the *73. Inf.Div.*, Becker positioned *SS-Aufkl.Abt. 3* around the town of Kepa Kielpinska, with *7. Bttr./SS-Pz.Art.Rgt. 3* co-located to provide direct fire support. Here it would undergo rest and recuperation while it performed its security duties along the river bank, alert for any attempt by the enemy to cross.

In the opposite direction along these *Rollbahn* flowed the wounded, who went into the field hospitals, and the dead, who were interred in the new corps cemetery established inside of Modlin. Supplies were occasionally delivered by riverboat sailing

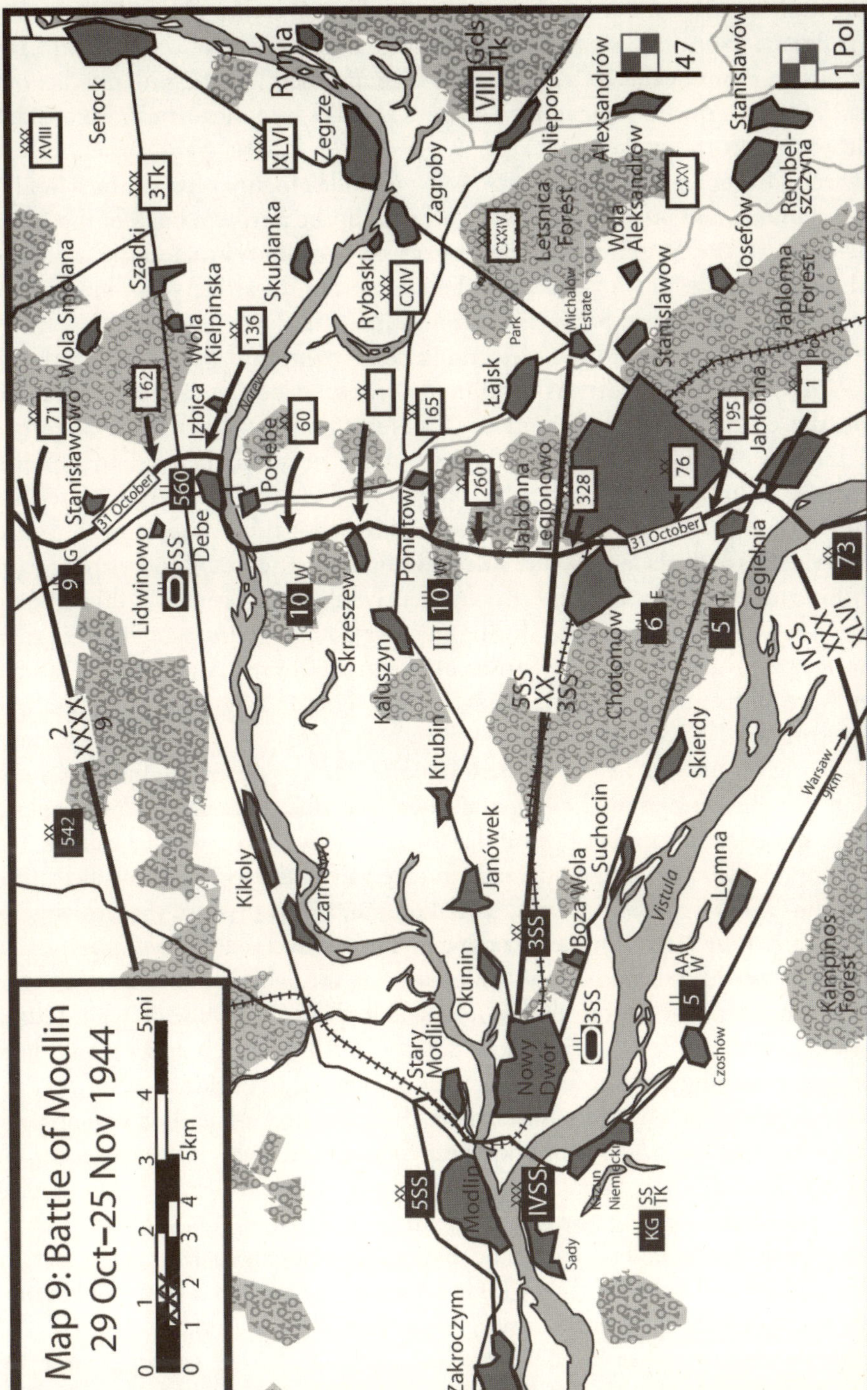
Map 9: Battle of Modlin
29 Oct–25 Nov 1944
5mi
5km
Serock
Rynia
Zegrze
Zagroby
Nieporet
Alexsandrów
Aleksandrów
Stanislawów
Rembel-
szczyzna
Josefów
Wola
Aleksandrów
Letsnica
Forest
Michalow
Estate
Park
Stanislawow
Jablonna
Forest
Jablonna
Łajsk
Rybaski
Skubianka
Szadki
Wola Smolana
Wola
Kielpinska
Izbica
Stanisławowo
Podebe
Poniatow
Jablonna
Legionowo
31 October
Lidwinowo
Debe
Narew
Skrzeszew
Kaluszyn
Chotomow
Cegielnia
Krubin
Skierdy
Janówek
Suchocin
Boza Wola
Okunin
Lomna
Vistula
Kikoly
Czarnowo
Stary
Modlin
Nowy
Dwór
Modlin
Zakroczym
Sady
Niemiecki
Czoshów
Kampinos
Forest
Warsaw
9km
XVIII
3Tk
XLVI
VIII Gds Tk
CXIV
CXXIV
CXXV
47
1 Pol
71
162
136
60
1
165
260
328
76
195
1 Pol
560
5SS
9 G
10 W
6 E
5 T
73
2
9
542
3SS
5SS
IVSS
KG SS TK
5 AA W
IVSS
XLVI

along the Vistula from the river ports of Thorn (Toruń) or Bromberg (Bydgoszcz) in West Prussia. None of these main supply routes were a secret, of course, to the First Belorussian Front or the 16th Air Army, which did their level best to interdict or at least slow down the movement of troops and supplies into the fortress. Accordingly, much of the corps' and some of the *9. Armee*'s *Flak* assets were concentrated in and around Modlin and Nowy Dwór. Most of Gille's logistics installations holding food, clothing, and other supplies were located on the northern bank of the Narew north and west of Modlin or on the western bank of the Vistula in the vicinity of his headquarters at Kazuń-Niemiecki, though most of the artillery ammunition was located in several dumps between the front lines and Nowy Dwór.

German veterans' accounts describing the two-month period when the *IV. SS-Pz.Korps* occupied Fortress Modlin are scanty at best, as are official records from the corps itself, which end on 25 November 1944, giving a researcher the impression that not much of consequence occurred beyond that point.[1] However, although major offensive operations by the Soviets had ceased—as confirmed after the war by Rokossovsky himself—there was a great deal of activity that took place on both sides, enough for the *OKH* to award a name for this phase of the war in the East: defensive battles east of Modlin. Though few of the engagements fought during this period rose to the same level as those that occured during the three battles of Warsaw between August and October, they were still significant events in their own right and figure prominentally in the history of *IV. SS-Pz.Korps*.[2]

One such event was the reorganization of the *Wiking*'s *panzer* regiment, plans for which were announced on 29 October. In essence, due to the lack of new tanks to replace those lost in combat but still having sufficient crews to man a full-strength regiment, Fritz Darges proposed a plan to take half of the regiment's soldiers, form them into a *Lehrabteilung* (training battalion), and ship them to the Schieratz SS training area near Litzmannstadt (Łódź) in the Nazi-governed *Generalgouvernement*, where they would continue to train while awaiting the delivery of replacement tanks and assault guns. The first battalion would send its *1.* and *3. Kompanie*, while Flügel's *II. Abteilung* would send its *7.* and *8. Kompanie*. All four companies would hand over any remaining tanks to the other four companies left behind—*2.*, *4.*, *5.*, and *6. Kompanie*—which would remain under the current two-battalion organization. *Obersturmführer* Karl Nicolussi-Leck, an experienced and highly respected leader, was appointed as the acting commander of the *Lehrabteilung*, which would be shipped out by rail beginning on 9 November.[3] Before they departed, Darges held an award ceremony at the battalion's command post in Zakroczym to recognize deserving individuals as well as to bid farewell. He expressed his hope that they would return soon with a full complement of tanks, but in fact they never did.

Besides ensuring that his divisions had properly carried out their orders to occupy the new defense line, Gille and his corps staff were keen to determine the corps' actual condition after nearly three weeks of uninterrupted combat. Partly this was due to the corps commander's duty-bound need to know how much combat power was available to him for the next phase of the campaign that he knew lay ahead; the other reason was that he had to submit his monthly status report to the Inspector of Armored Troops in Berlin at the end of the month. He already knew much from Ullrich's and Becker's daily status reports that highlighted their daily *Kampfstärke* and combat fighting vehicle readiness, but he also had to know the internal condition of his two divisions and how his subordinate commanders rated their organizations. This was of vital importance. It also provided him with a tool to measure their performance as division commanders.

Unfortunately, the readiness report of *IV. SS-Pz.Korps*' headquarters and corps troops can no longer be located, though records indicate that the only element of the corps that suffered significant losses during this period was *SS-Werfer Abt. 504*, which lost 74 men between 1 September and 31 October, including 18 killed in action, as well as the loss of three launchers from the *4. Batterie*.[4] In contrast, the reports of both the *Totenkopf* and *Wiking* Division are still on file at the U.S. National Archives in College Park, Maryland, and at the *Bundesarchiv* in Freiburg. Like those from the previous months, the reports for October reflect the cumulative effects of three months of nearly unbroken combat, save for the 18-day grace period from 23 September–9 October.

At the end of October, Becker's *Totenkopf* Division reported 20,740 men actually assigned to its ranks. Of these, over 4,316 were ex-*Luftwaffe* transfers, of which 2,227 were still undergoing training in either the corps' *SS-Feld-Ausb.Rgt. 5* or its own *SS-Feld-Ers.Btl. 3*, resulting in an actual strength after these were subtracted of 18,513 men.[5] This, of course, must be seen in the light of the 2,114 men lost during the same period, as discussed in the previous chapter. As was usually the case, the most critical manpower shortage was in its officer and NCO ranks, where the division lacked 531 men out of the 4,537 leaders authorized. While this represented only a 12 percent shortage, it must be emphasized that most of the officer replacements it had received during the past two months had also come from the *Luftwaffe* or the *Allgemeine-SS*, which in either case meant men who were not trained or enured to ground combat.

Regarding equipment, Becker's division had suffered a significant erosion in its armored fighting vehicle strength, as well as in heavy weapons, since the end of July. Of the 190 tanks it was authorized (both *Pz. IV* and *Pz. V* Panther) by the *K.St.N.*, it possessed only 30 *Pz. IV*s (of which only 18 were operational) and 27 *Pz. V*s (15 operational). Though not authorized, the division still had 10 *Pz. VI* Tigers on its establishment, including eight that were operational, and 33 *StuG III* assault guns (11 operational), giving the division a total number of 100 tanks and assault guns, of which 52 were operational, a readiness rate of only 52 per cent. It also fielded 14 of its authorized 31 *Jg.Pz. IV* tank destroyers, with another four in short-term repair, boosting the division's number of combat-ready AFVs to 66 out of 118.

It was still woefully short of the 330 armored half-tracks it was authorized, with only 80 on hand, and of these, only 62 were operational. Of the 3,054 trucks of all types the *K.St.N.* called for, it had 2,390 on hand, but the mix of types was so varied, with larger capacity trucks being substituted for smaller ones, that the amount of tonnage they were capable of carrying in one load was 4,279 metric tons (4,717 short tons), compared to the required load of 4,674 metric tons (5,152 short tons). Given that many of the all-terrain trucks in the division would have been used in the *Panzergrenadier* regiments as substitutes for armored half tracks, this shortage was actually worse than it appeared. However, since the division was occupying a static defensive position at the end of a very short supply line, this lack of trucks would not have posed much of a problem during this period in the division's history.

Perhaps the most glaring shortage of weapons was the actual number of antitank guns on hand, with only eight reported as being operational (with one in repair), compared to the 28 that were authorized. Many of these had been lost during the fighting of the last two months, either to artillery fire or during Soviet infantry assaults that overran their positions before a prime mover could be brought up to tow them and their crews to safety. The same situation applied to heavy mortars, with only 10 12cm mortars servicable, and one in repair, compared to the 26 authorized by the *K.St.N.* The artillery regiment was still in good shape though, with 50 guns of all calibers reported as operational and eight in repair, leaving the *Totenkopf* Division only one gun short of its authorized amount.

As always, the most interesting comments were reserved at the end of the report, where the commander gave his personal assessment of his divison's overall level of readiness. As was usually the case with Becker's assessments, his comments were short and succinct, frequently consisting of one or two words or a sentence at the most. In regards to its assessed *Kampfwert* (overall combat power), Becker wrote, "Suited for defensive missions, only conditionally ready for offensive ones on account of the insufficient training of the *Luftwaffe* replacements." He considered the overall level of training of the division to be "sufficient to good." As to the status of the training being administered to the new recruits, he rated it as only being sufficient, in other words, barely adequate. He rated troop morale and conduct as being "very good."

In regards to his division's weapons situation, he noted the continuing shortages of light and heavy machine guns, medium mortars, and even rifles to equip the new replacements. Concerning the stockage levels of ammunition, he felt that it was good, that there was a sufficient amount on hand, and that other equipment of all types (radios, maintenance equipment, etc.) was "sufficient." Becker did note the continuing shortage of armored half-tracks and reconnaissance vehicles, which hampered his division's mobility, which he rated as only 67 per cent. In the last category of the report, under the heading *Besondere Schwierigkeiten* (special problems or challenges), he wrote that the new replacements his division had been receiving lacked front-experienced officers and NCOs.[6] Overall though, considering what his division had endured for the past three months, it was in remarkably good shape. It would use the next several weeks wisely, as its commanders and staff would do their utmost to restore the division to its former level of lethality, even while remaining in the front line, and to revive the legendary "SS spirit" that the *Totenkopf* Division was known for.

Ullrich's division status report, submitted the same day as Becker's, depicts a unit that had been battered even more in terms of lives and equipment. While the *Wiking* Division had suffered the loss of 4,057 men killed, wounded, and missing, these had been more than compensated for in raw terms by the 4,996 replacements it had received during the same period. Of this enormous number of "Göring's finest," 2,284 had been incorporated into the division by 26 October, leaving 2,712 still undergoing training in the rear. By the end of the month, this had left Ullrich's division with a total strength of 20,112 men, more than 113 per cent of its authorized amount, with 17,400 actually serving in the field, with the exception of those who were sick or attending specialist schools in Germany.[7]

Most of these replacements went directly to the *Germania* and *Westland Panzergrenadier* Regiments; those who had been sent to the *Wiking* during the height of the battle had quickly been killed or wounded. In contrast, it appears that Becker had held his replacements back until the worst of the fighting was over, when the conditions for their introduction to ground combat were a little less intense. Apparently, Gille granted his division commanders some discretion in deciding when to have their replacements moved into the front lines. While Becker's course of action for the *Totenkopf* Division may seem to have been the wiser one in retrospect, in the *Wiking*'s case, it was heavily involved in combat at the same time, and Ullrich may have felt the need to keep sending replacements forward to provide his front-line units with the manpower they needed to continue holding the line outweighed other considerations.

In terms of combat fighting vehicles, the numbers looked grim. Of the 211 tanks, assault guns, and tank destroyers the *K.St.N.* called for, only seven *Pz. IV*s, 15 *Pz. V* Panthers, three *StuG IV*s, and nine *Jg.Pz. IV*s were operational, with another 11 in short-term repair, a total of just 34 vehicles, a woeful roughly 16 per cent of its full-strength establishment. Much hard work remained to get the 11 damaged or broken down vehicles operational again; in two months' time, the division would need every one of them. It did have 195 armored half-tracks and armored cars operational, with another 34 in repair, giving it the ability to mechanize at least one of its *Panzergrenadier* battalions, the *III. Btl./Germania*, and its reconnaissance battalion, *SS-Pz.Aufkl.Abt. 5*.

With regard to trucks and other motor vehicles, the situation was far less rosy than the *Totenkopf*s, though it too had the luxury of short supply lines and close proximity to its logistics depots. Only *Kampfgruppe Germania* and the *panzers* operating north of the river had an extended supply line, but like the rest of Gille's corps, most of its supplies were coming from *Gen.Oberst* Weiss's *2. Armee* quartermaster's department. Authorized 3,042 trucks of all types, including the half-tracked *Maultier*, Ullrich's division only had 1,916 on hand, leaving a shortfall of 1,126, roughly 56 percent of establishment. However, Ullrich rated it as able to carry 90 per cent of its basic load of food, fuel, and ammunition. Again, this is misleading, since many of these trucks intended for logistics purposes were being used instead to ferry infantry into battle, which unsurprisingly resulted in a high loss rate. The *N.S.K.K.*'s *Transport Brigade Speer* had been withdrawn in September, so the division could no longer count on it to carry its supplies, and thus *SS-Hstuf.* Dr. Heinz Fischer, the *Wiking*'s *Ib*, had to use his remaining trucks judiciously.

The *Wiking* Division was more fortunate with regard to heavy weapons, which it could still count on to make up for the lack of trained infantry, including *SS-Stubaf.* Hans Bünning's *SS-Pz.Art.Rgt. 5*, which still had 41 operational pieces, with 10 more in repair. Besides the artillery regiment, the division's *Flak* battalion also had 13 operational 8.8cm and 17 3.7cm antiaircraft guns, 19 antitank guns were present in the *Panzergrenadier* regiments and *SS-Stubaf.* Oeck's antitank battalion (of which nine were in repair), and four 15cm infantry howitzers were rated as being operational in Dorr's and Hack's regiments.

Unlike his former division commander at the *Totenkopf*, Karl Ullrich spared no words in his commander's comments concluding his monthly report. He wrote:

> The division's personnel situation has been improved on account of the transfer of 5,000 replacements from the *Luftwaffe*, of which 70 percent have already been sent down to join their units. Due to the tactical situation that existed at the beginning of the month, I had no choice but to send the best trained and most suitable of the replacements directly to the front lines, where they suffered heavy casualties due to drumfire barrages and constant counterattacks. Units already engaged in combat can only carry out the further training that these men need on a very limited basis. To continue in such a manner wastes valuable manpower in exchange for only an imperceptible increase in combat strength.

Ullrich was also unimpressed by the transfer to his division of so many former *Luftwaffe* NCOs in their existing ranks and specialties. He wrote, "The transfer from the *Luftwaffe* of 1,200 *Feldwebel* und *Unteroffizier* [senior and junior NCOs] allowed us to fill most of the vacant *Unterführer* positions [squad leader through to platoon sergeant], although most of them, except for a very small number, could not be usefully employed as such in their former ranks." He remarked that because the reconnaissance battalion during the past month had suffered particularly heavy losses of vehicle gunners and radio operators, urgent replacements for these specialties were needed.

Lastly, the division commander focused on the condition of the *Wiking*'s materiel. He emphasized again the high losses of armored vehicles and heavy weapons his division had suffered, and felt that he needed to provide an explanation for it. He said, "Due to the heavy number of casualties suffered by the troops as well as by the back and forth attacks and counterattacks, the armored vehicles had to be overly committed to compensate for the manpower shortage, making constant [armored] counterattacks necessary." Ullrich then mentioned that the division urgently needed more machine guns, since it only had 553 of the 1,204 it was authorized by the *K.St.N.*, less than 50 per cent of its requirements. Because there were not enough of the Mauser 98K rifles on hand, it made it impossible to arm all of the new replacements, who had arrived from the depots in Germany without weapons of their own. In addition, Ullrich wrote, the division was short of the necessary amount of personal equipment, such as helmets. In addition to this, he decried the shortage of replacement tanks, stating that he had enough trained crewmembers on hand to man all of them and bring the *panzer* regiment up to full strength. By that point, his division had received no new Panthers since 17 April. Despite his entreaties, his division would not receive any replacement *Pz. V*s until 1 April 1945, and merely a *Bergepanther* (recovery tank) at that.

In closing, Ullrich simply stated, "the division is only conditionally suited to conduct defensive operations." Clearly, the division had been terribly weakened by the fighting, just as had the *Totenkopf*. It too would have to undergo a rebuilding program, and would have to do so while still serving in the front lines, like its sister division, in a situation where fighting could interrupt any unit training program or reconstitution at any moment. Unlike the *Heer panzer* divisions in the *9. Armee*, neither the *Totenkopf* nor the *Wiking* could be pulled out and sent to a rest area behind the front lines to be rebuilt; there was no time and the SS had no such resources available for that, so they had no choice but to do the best with what they had.

Fortunately, the *IV. SS-Pz.Korps* commander and his staff would do their utmost to provide them with as much of what they needed as possible, ever mindful that the tactical situation along the *9. Armee* front could erupt at any time. The *Oberquartiermeister* of both *2. Armee* and *9. Armee* would also do their part to ensure they got whatever supplies and other materials they still had the means to provide, which, after five years of war, was becoming increasingly difficult to do. As for armored vehicles, the *SS-FHA* would have to deal directly with the *Heeresrüstungsamt*, an office that still mistrusted the *Waffen-SS* and was chiefly concerned that the Army's *panzer* divisions first got what they needed in preparation for the massive *Wacht am Rhein* counteroffensive that Hitler was planning for December in the Ardennes.

The materiel requirements for this grandiose operation, which *der Führer* believed would change the direction of the war in Germany's favor, would require German industry to make one last heroic effort that autumn to produce enough tanks, half-tracks, infantry weapons, and ammunition to newly outfit or re-equip the two dozen *panzer* and infantry divisions destined to play their role in the drive to Antwerp. To meet this enormous demand, many of the replacement vehicles originally intended for the Eastern Front would be diverted by the *Heeresrüstungsamt* to *Generalfeldmarschall* Model's *H.Gr. B.* This reallocation of resources would ensure that neither of Gille's divisions would ever reach their full strength again, or even receive replacements for the few armored fighting vehicles they had left.

So while the *Totenkopf* and *Wiking* Divisions would do their utmost to make good the manpower and materiel losses of the past three months, the fighting along the Vistula Front in the *9.* and *2. Armee* area of operations had by no means ended. Though Gille's corps had successfully withdrawn into its *Fuchsstellung* by 28 October, an event marking the end of one campaign, the First Belorussian Front was not operating by the same calendar as the *Wehrmacht.* It continued conducting its own attacks until 7 November, at which point all of its armies arrayed along the Narew and the Vistula transitioned to the defense, punctuated occasionally by several army-level operations intended to seize more advantageous positions for the upcoming January offensive, or to wear down and tie up the forces of the *IV. SS-Pz.Korps*.

Why it was deemed to be a good idea to keep two of the Third Reich's premier armored divisions committed to wage a World War I-style campaign of attrition on an essentially static battlefield has never been adequately explained. The shortage of infantry formations on the Eastern Front during this phase of the campaign was probably one of the reasons, since most of the new *Volks-Grenadier* divisions created from August–October 1944 were being sent to the Western Front in preparation for the Ardennes offensive instead of to the East. However, the need for mechanized forces to serve as operational reserves, especially in view of the inevitable Soviet winter offensive, was even greater. Perhaps either Guderian at *OKH* or the *H.Gr. Mitte* commander felt they had no other choice but to order them to stay put. And stay put they did.[8]

The commander of the First Belorussian Front, no doubt aware that the *IV. SS-Pz.Korps* was pulling back into a new defensive position, evidentally decided that if Gille could not be outflanked or a bridge seized behind him, his forces could still be forced to withdraw across the Vistula if enough pressure was applied, thus achieving the results that Stalin had demanded when the offensive was launched in mid-August,without having to initiate a large-scale operation. In pursuit of this goal, the 47th and 70th Armies, tired as they were, continued their probing attacks on the morning of 29 October before the German defenses could be solidified. Both the *Wiking* and *Totenkopf* Divisions fended off weak early morning attacks, with Becker's troops stopping one directed along the Jablonna–Modlin *Rollbahn*.

The *Wiking* Division reported that two of its foot patrols, sent to feel out enemy positions on its right flank in the vicinity of Poniatów, were driven back under heavy fire without any prisoners, but at least the division now knew where two Soviet positions were. Soviet artillery and mortar fire was reported falling throughout the area, but apparently the amount was not considered out of the ordinary. Gille's intelligence officer, Herbert Jahnkun, working with his *9. Armee* counterpart, *Major i.G.* Hermann Kesselheim, was able to identify five Soviet divisions in the line opposite the corps.

Based on aerial reconnaissance, prisoner interrogations, and deserter testimony, these were (from south to north) the 175th, 328th, 260th, 1st, and 60th Rifle Divisions, all of whom had been in daily contact with Gille's troops for the last three weeks.

The number of Soviet company-sized attacks intensified throughout the afternoon, as well as Soviet and Polish artillery fire. Under Kurt Brasack's expert direction, the corps and division artillery batteries fired back in response, as well as upon known or suspected troop concentrations in the Jablonna-Legjonowo area—the *Totenkopf*s former logistics base—and in the forest east of Derlacz along its left boundary shared with the *Wiking* Division. At 2:45 p.m., after an artillery barrage was fired to pin down the defenders, a 200-man infantry assault was mounted against the *Totenkopf*s positions located around the Szybalin estate, a kilometer northwest of Derlacz, but was driven off.

The situation in the *Wiking*'s sector was much the same, with similar Soviet forays reportedly attempted along both sides of the Narew. A company-sized force supported by one tank attempted to penetrate *I. Btl./Germania*'s positions at Skrzeszew on the southern bank of the Narew, before it too was forced to retreat by indirect fire. On the northern bank, *SS-Pz.Rgt. 5* and the *II. Abteilung* engaged two Soviet battalions of 300 men each, which were attempting to bypass an obstacle thrown across the Serock–Modlin highway. As each rifle battalion tried to work its way around the regiment's right and left flanks at 2:40 p.m., Flügel's Panthers engaged them with 7.5cm high-explosive and machine-gun fire, forcing both battalions back beyond the road obstacle, where they turned and began to dig in.[9]

Most of these were merely continued attempts to feel out the *Wiking*'s and *Totenkopf*'s positions within the *Fuchsstellung*. For a change, no air attacks were reported, though a number of reconnaissance planes were spotted overhead throughout the day. In his summary of the day's activities for 29 October, Gille wrote that he expected the strong reconnaissance attempts like those carried out that day would continue along the corps' entire front for the foreseeable future. Based on POW interrogations, radio intercepts, and aerial reconnaissance, he assessed that due to the contraction of his front lines, up to five Soviet divisions had been withdrawn from their positions, with their current whereabouts unknown. Lastly, he reported that the Soviet artillery commands of either army had not yet determined where the *IV. SS-Pz.Korps*' key installations were located, based on the randomness of the artillery and mortar fire upon his positions that day. His intention for the next day was unchanged: defend.

At *9. Armee* headquarters, most of the commander's concerns were focused on the situation on his right flank in the south, fretting once more about the number of Soviet artillery batteries identified by aerial reconnaissance, and where best to position his scanty reserves once the offensive burst forth from Magnuszew. He was clearly anticipating the arrival of the *25. Pz.Div.*, which he expected would be released to his control once the Soviet offensive went forward. At that moment, the only reserve that the *VIII. Armeekorps* could muster was one infantry regiment from the *17. Inf.Div. General der Panzertruppe* von Lüttwitz was also concerned about any attacks originating from the Puławy bridgehead several dozen kilometers further to the south along the boundary shared with the *4. Pz.Armee* of *H.Gr. A*. Any action there by *VIII. Armeekorps* would have to be taken in concert with the *LVI. Pz.Korps*, the leftmost corps of *4. Pz.Armee*. With regard to Gille's corps, all the *9. Armee* commander had to say was, "Except for a few company-sized enemy reconnaissance probes against the *IV. SS-Pz.Korps*, there was no combat activity worth reporting."

Though there was a certain amount of Soviet artillery fire and small-scale reconnaissance activity reported, including one attempt directed against the boundary between Gille's two divisions west of Jablonna-Legjonowo, the night of 29–30 October passed quietly. Dawn brought a cold and cloudy day, which limited air activity by both sides. Once again, on 30 October most of the combat action was carried out by each side's artillery arm, directed against targets on both banks of the Narew and Vistula. Based on the increasing accuracy the Germans observed, it was becoming apparent that not only had Soviet gunners found the new ranges to their targets, but they had also accurately identified the locations of the most important targets, allowing them to be prioritized.

One example of this trend was the targeting that day of a battery from the *Totenkopf*'s artillery regiment as it was moving into its new firing position west of Cegielnia. During the ensuing barrage, two guns and two towing vehicles were destroyed by shellfire. That same day, the target acquisition battery from the *Totenkopf* Division discovered that the Soviet artillerymen had begun using delayed-fuse projectiles, a feature that allows shells to bury themselves deep into their targets before detonating. This made them much more effective against field fortifications or concrete bunkers, and hence more dangerous, especially to the men occupying them in shelters positioned along the rear slopes of the *Fuchsstellung*.

On the northern bank of the Narew, *SS-Pz.Rgt. 5* reported five Soviet tanks moving into the riverside town of Izbica, while a company-sized infantry force attempted to infiltrate the town of Stanisławówo on the regiment's left flank, but both attempts were driven off. That evening, three tanks from Schumacher's *I. Abteilung* arrived to reinforce Flügel's battalion. Besides this, the only other item Gille thought worth reporting to *9. Armee* that evening was the intelligence gleaned from POW interrogations that the 70th Army's sector opposite the *Wiking* Division had been narrowed even further. The POW also stated that 70th Army had not called off its offensive at all, but appeared to be preparing to assault the fortifications at Skrzeszew on the division's left flank. That evening, for the first time in weeks, the *9. Armee* had nothing to add, a sure sign that the crisis of October had passed.

Tuesday, 31 October passed much as the previous day had, with the exception that a 600-man Soviet force, supported by four tanks, assaulted the *Totenkopf*'s center and flank positions near the town of Chotomów during the late morning. Preceded by a powerful artillery barrage that struck the division's entire front line, the enemy force had worked its way to the forwardmost positions of the *Totenkopf* Regiment until German defensive fire stopped and then hurled them back to their jump-off positions. Two T-34s and two antitank guns were knocked out by defensive fire. On the division's right flank along the Vistula, another Soviet assault began to move forward after an artillery barrage, but in turn was stopped and driven to ground by accurately delivered SS artillery fire. At the same time, a similar-sized assault took place on the northern bank of the Narew, where Dorr's *Kampfgruppe* and Darges's *panzer* regiment lay in wait for the next Soviet attack. This was broken up by German artillery fire as well, before it got close enough to the defenders to do any damage. To cover their withdrawal, Soviet gunners fired smoke shells that prevented the Germans from delivering any additional observed fire.

Evaluating the events of the day, Gille's perception of the separate attacks carried out against his corps' outer flanks was that they were possible warning signs of a much larger one that would most likely be carried out under the central control of the 47th Army. Clouding this assessment was whether the movement of the fresh 71st Rifle Division across the Narew, identified as having taken place that day, was a sign that it had left the 65th Army's area either to reinforce the neighboring 70th Army or the 47th Army. Depending on where this division eventually landed, then the *Ic* of both the *IV. SS-Pz.Korps* and the *9. Armee* would be able to predict where the next major Soviet attack might take place. This would, of course, be of great use to Gille and his *Ia*, who would then be able to position corps assets to be better prepared to respond to it. Other than that, Gille reported very little except to repeat a proclamation he issued to his corps that same day, which read as follows:

> During the enemy's third attempt to break through the *IV. SS-Pz.Korps* in the area northwest of Warsaw between 10 and 28 October, he threw against our positions two armies and part of another with 19 rifle divisions or Guards rifle divisions, a motorized rifle brigade, two assault engineer brigades, one Guards tank corps and several independent tank regiments, supported by a massing of artillery of over 230 batteries and between 150 and 200 multiple rocket launcher batteries, as well as constantly rolling air attacks. Our defenses, in day-long battles, were able to form an unbreakable ring around our positions using tightly concentrated artillery fire and counterthrusts by our tanks and grenadiers that were able to stop the enemy within our main defense line by destroying or capturing 138 tanks, 22 aircraft, five artillery pieces, 123 antitank guns, 14 mortars … and capturing 540 prisoners and 134 deserters, as well as counting 4,233 enemy dead and inflicting an estimated 30,000 to 35,000 additional casualties.

While von Lüttwitz acknowledged in his report the fighting that had taken place that day in the *IV. SS-Pz.Korps*' area of operations, which he must have deemed to have been a minor affair in comparison to the levels it had reached during the previous two weeks, he focused primarily on the two *panzer* divisions that had moved into his army's area. All of *Oberst* Audörsch's *Kampfgruppe 25. Pz.Div.* had finally arrived in its assembly area at Białobrzegi, joining with the still-forming *Pz.Gren.Rgt. 147*, where it would then begin completing the division's reorganization and training in preparation for its next assignment.

The *19. Pz.Div.* had been in its new assembly area in the Kampinos forest for four days, and except for its artillery regiment, which was engaged in support of the *IV. SS-Pz.Korps* and the *XLVI. Pz.Korps* from its firing positions on the west side of the Vistula, the remainder of the division was enjoying a well-deserved rest, having taken part in nearly every consequential battle in and around Warsaw since the end of July. That same day, von Lüttwitz's chief of staff, *Gen.Maj*. Staedke, and his *Ic* had travelled to Radom to meet with their counterparts from the neighboring *4. Pz.Armee* to discuss an upcoming action they were planning to address the threat posed by a band of mounted Polish partisans threatening the security in the *Korück* (rear area command) of both armies.

Looking back from today's standpoint, we know that in early November 1944, Stalin had ordered a cessation of major offensive activity along the entire Vistula Front in order to marshal his forces for the big operation slated to begin in early January 1945. At the time, however, it must have seemed to the German commanders defending this portion of the Eastern Front that another major Soviet offensive could break out at any moment. Undoubtedly, part of their perceptions was influenced by Soviet *Maskirovka*, which the First Belorussian Front conducted to deceive the enemy as to the exact date, time, and location of its impending grand offensive. Skillful use of camouflage, decoy positions, simulated radio transmissions, and double agents working for the Red Army (the so-called "V" men) successfully misled German intelligence officers, whose task it was to identify indicators or signs of future Soviet intentions, into looking elsewhere than where the real attack was going to take place.

This period in the history of the *IV. SS-Pz.Korps* during November 1944 is a story punctuated by many false alarms, artillery barrages, small-scale attacks, large numbers of foot patrols, and even battalion-sized raids carried out by both sides to determine each other's relative strengths and troop dispositions. While it is true that no large-scale attacks occurred while defending Fortress Modlin, the troops in the front line from the *Totenkopf* and *Wiking* Divisions would not have thought so because they were constantly having to respond to their opponents' attempts to disrupt their defenses or capture prisoners.

The troops were denied the sleep they so badly needed by *Iwan*'s constant indirect fire, nighttime air raids, or loudspeaker broadcasts. Of course, the Germans would also attempt to do the same, but by early November, it became increasingly difficult for either side to do so. Both had dug elaborate defensive positions, laid extensive barbed wire obstacles, and emplaced deadly minefields. The only way to approach each other's lines was at night, and any foray designed to take a prisoner or feel out their defensive positions was a high-risk operation that frequently ended in failure. To lead such operations, brave and intelligent men were needed, preferably those with a great deal of front-line experience who could "read" a battlefield and understand what the sights, sounds, and even the smells signified. For example, the odor of Russian *Machorka* (a coarse, homegrown tobacco) wafting from a trench meant that Soviet troops were somewhere nearby. Incoming or outgoing shelling had sounds all of their own, and the ability to distinguish between them could spell life or death.

Although large-scale combat activity did not happen, this period was filled with other less warlike activity. Units were frequently rotated in and out of the lines, moved into or out of a reserve position, or occasionally had to take up arms to repel enemy incursions. The weather increasingly began to influence operations as winter approached. As November neared its end, heavy downpours, cold temperatures, and snow and sleet became everyday occurrences, making life in the trenches miserable. Keeping warm in such conditions meant that troops living in bunkers at the front lines needed a source of heat, such as trench stoves, but had to judiciously ration their fuel lest the resulting smoke draw Soviet artillery fire. Troops in the rear areas generally enjoyed better living accommodations but in turn had to worry about the Red Air Force, not to mention the ever-present Soviet artillery that could strike at any moment, transforming a peaceful farmyard 10 kilometers behind the front into a charnel house in a matter of seconds.

Throughout this period, *Pioniere* continued laying minefields and repairing roads, *Lastkraftwagenfahrer* drove their trucks—often laden with ammunition and fuel—over rutted roads, while *Kompanieschreiber* (clerks) in company dugouts typed up reports and updated personnel records. In short, many of the usual peacetime activities continued without pause, with a rifle, submachine gun, or *Panzerfaust* always within reach being one of the many signs that these men were performing their duties in an active combat zone instead of in their home *Kaserne* (barracks).

Graves registration teams recorded the names of the dead while supervising work crews of Soviet prisoners, Polish civilians, or men from German punishment battalions (one such battalion was attached to Gille's corps), who dug the graves and buried the bodies. Occasionally, if there were enough dead to bury at one time, a ceremony might be held over the graves, with a stirring speech delivered in honor of the memory of the dead, led by a company commander or a more senior officer. There were no chaplains in the Germanic *Waffen-SS* divisions, and graves would usually be marked by a wooden marker instead of a cross. Inscribed upon it would be the soldier's name, rank, date of birth—marked by an inscribed *Lebensrune* (life rune)—and date of death, denoted by the accompanying *Todesrune* (death rune).

One such ceremony, albeit on a much larger scale, took place on 9 November outside the old fortress in Modlin, attended by division and regimental commanders as well as senior staff members. Here, the *IV. SS-Pz.Korps* had established the cemetery for the fallen from the various divisions and brigades that had served with the corps since late August 1944, including units from the *Heer* such as the *19. Pz.Div.* and *Gren.Brig. 1131*. Eventually, the number of men buried here would reach 2,679

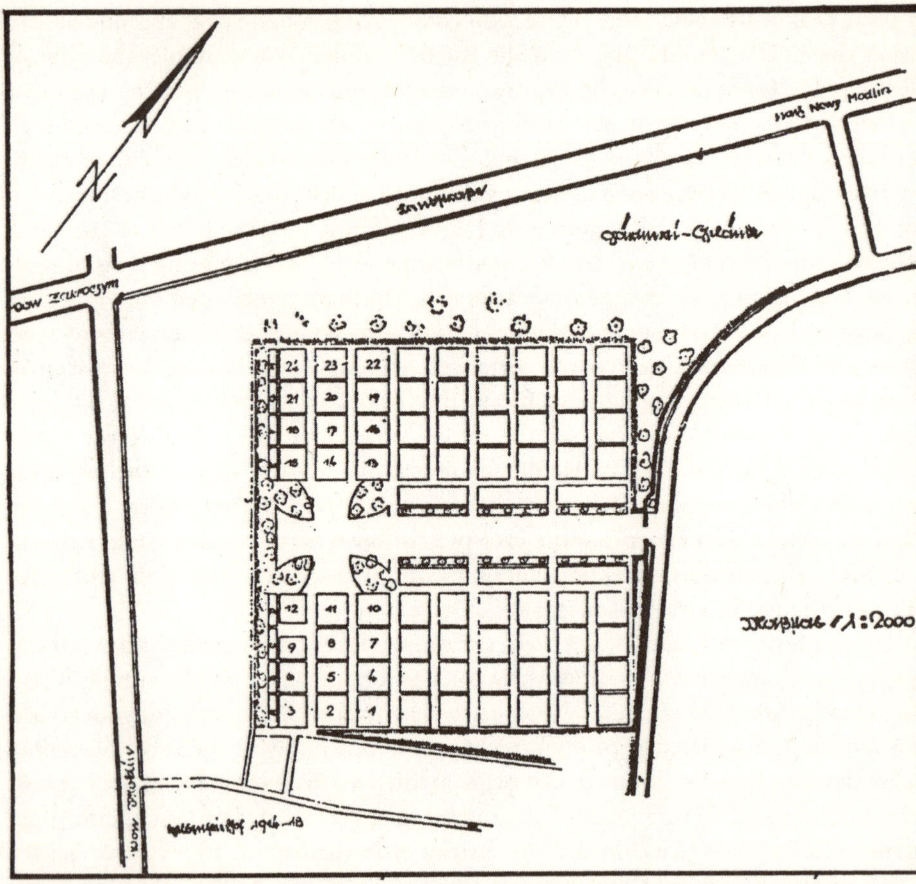

Figure 5. Diagram of the *IV. SS-Panzercorps* Cemetery in Modlin, dedicated 9 November 1944 (Courtesy of Günther Lange Archive)

before the corps was transferred to Hungary at the end of December (see Figure 5 for diagram of cemetery).

To tend the graves and ensure that burials were carried out properly, the corps' *Ib*, *SS-Stubaf.* Schulze, appointed *Hascha.* Theo Rexilius as its graves registration officer. The dedication ceremony featured a soldier's choir, who sang the funeral dirge by Werner Altendorf, "The Heavens are Gray and the Earth is Brown," poetry readings, and music by the *IV. SS-Pz.Korps' Musikkorps* (military band), which played suitably nationalist tunes such as the *Deutschlandlied*, *Deutschland, heiliges Wort* (a popular Hitler Youth song), and the *Rienzi Overture*.[10]

The corps commander then gave a suitably somber speech to mark the occasion, closing with a quote from Hitler, "Peoples free themselves not by inaction, but rather by sacrifice." The choice of 9 November was no coincidence, for it marked the 21st anniversary of the failed 1923 "Beer Hall" Putsch attempt in Munich, where 16 of Hitler's compatriots were gunned down by German police as they marched to seize control of the town hall. Following the dedication ceremony, Gille escorted his guests to the garrison chapel of the old fortress, where a reception had been set up to provide refreshments. The day also marked Gille's promotion to *SS-Obergruppenführer und General der Waffen-SS* (*Ogruf.*, equivalent to a *Generalleutnant* in the *Heer*), which became effective on 9 November. After that, Gille's subordinates took their leave and returned to their units.[11]

Such field cemeteries were needed in Modlin, Warsaw, and elsewhere to accommodate the ever-increasing number of German soldiers who were either killed in action or died because of their wounds in field dressing stations or in the *Feldlazarett* (field hospitals). Although the intensity of fighting had diminished since 28 October, the number of casualties both sides suffered continued to mount. Death or injuries by artillery and mortar fire, snipers, mines, booby traps, antitank weapons, air attacks, or infantry weapons continued throughout November, challenging the division field replacement battalions to keep pace with men to take the place of the fallen.

Another thing that must be borne in mind from this period was the apprehension that the resumption of the First Belorussian Front's October offensive could happen at any moment. Any Soviet incursion, however minor, could be, and frequently was, interpreted as a sign that renewed attacks could be expected to happen that very day, or the next at the latest. This weighed on the minds not only of the *Landser* in the front line, but upon division commanders, staff officers, and even Herbert Gille himself. Between 1 and 5 November, constant movement of Soviet troops was observed taking place several kilometers behind the front lines, but since the traffic was in both directions, it was difficult to discern whether they were reinforcements for the expected offensive, worn-out units being relieved in the line for rest periods, or being transferred somewhere else entirely. However, according to the *9. Armee* intelligence officer, the Soviet attack was expected to occur on 7 November at the earliest, so all of these troop movements reinforced the prevailing thinking among Gille and his staff.

One of the first alarms that a large-scale attack might be imminent was the shelling of the old Modlin fortress on 3 November by a large-caliber weapon of 20cm or larger, most likely from one of the First Belorussian Front's independent artillery brigades or the 22nd Artillery Penetration Division. Thirty shells struck Modlin, shaking the walls of the fortress and rattling the nerves of those inside seeking shelter. In response, *Beob.Abt. 21*, working under *SS-ARKO 104*'s direction, located the source of the shelling using sound- and flash-ranging equipment that pinpointed the enemy battery in a patch of woods on the northern edge of Jablonna-Legjonowo. That evening, once it had grown dark, the corps' own artillery batteries conducted a counter-fire mission, firing a brief but powerful barrage of 15cm and 17cm shells at the suspected location. Large fires and detonations were immediately seen and heard, a sign that the German gunners had hit their target or at least had hit an ammunition dump.

Although only a few large-scale actions occurred during November, several are worth mentioning. On 4 November, a 50-man enemy raiding party attempted to penetrate the front lines of the *Totenkopf* Division before it was driven off by mortar and machine-gun fire. Later that same day, the *Wiking* Division's forward observers on the north bank of the Narew witnessed a large number of Soviet troops attempting to cross the river using rubber boats a few kilometers upstream from their position near Debe. They quickly called in artillery fire, which promptly scattered the Soviets and forced the attempt to be abandoned, at least during daylight. Interestingly, this was an indication that the destroyed bridge at Zegrze had not yet been rebuilt; otherwise why would troops attempt such a dangerous operation? The army group commander visited von Lüttwitz's headquarters that afternoon, but Reinhardt offered no further information about Soviet intentions, other than discussing the movement of the *19. Pz.Div.* to the south.

That night, the *Totenkopf* sent out a raiding party of its own, creeping through no-man's land and killing 20 enemy soldiers before bringing back one very valuable prisoner. On 5 November, eight large-caliber shells fell upon the small military airfield a kilometer north of Modlin, a sign that either more heavy artillery had been brought forward or that the corps' artillery had failed to destroy the guns two days before after all. That same day, the *Totenkopf*s prisoner whom they had snatched in their raid, upon interrogation by their *Ic*, revealed that a relief in place was indeed taking place in all of the 47th Army's rifle divisions and that each burned-out division was being replaced, battalion by battalion, by a fresh one. This could be interpreted in several ways, one of which was that this signified Gusev's army was preparing to continue its attack. It could also have meant something completely opposite—that it was not planning an attack, but that it signified only the rest and recuperation of units that had been in constant battle since mid-July. Muddying the water somewhat was the result of a *Luftwaffe* aerial reconnaissance mission flown the previous day, which brought back photographs indicating more artillery batteries being moved out of the Narew–Vistula triangle, with a total of 132 identified between the rivers and 48 more north of the Narew. This was considerably less than what had been employed previously against the Germans during the height of the October offensive.

These events occurred on the same day that Gille was directed to provide a mobile reserve for *9. Armee*, whose commander had learned on 2 November that the *19. Pz.Div.* had been designated that same day as the new *OKH* reserve for the Eastern Front and would soon be shipped to the Warka area, where it would join the *25. Pz.Div.* in reserve. With both of the *panzer* divisions he was counting on for emergencies within his army's area of operations now removed from his immediate control, von Lüttwitz had no recourse but to form another reserve using elements from his remaining forces. Burdened by the *OKH*-imposed requirement to garrison and equip *Festung Warschau*, an order that forced him to strip most of the remaining available fortress and security troops from *Korück 532*, the *9. Armee* had no recourse but to turn to Gille's corps for the forces he needed.

Accordingly, Gille, upon receipt of the order, tasked Becker to provide this force, which he would form using *I. Abt./SS-Pz.Rgt. 3* with its remaining 14 operational Panthers, and most of the *Totenkopf* Regiment, along with its *I. Btl. (gep.)* and *II. Btl./SS-Pz.Gren.Rgt. 5*, minus its third battalion. That evening, these troops would begin their movement across the Vistula bridge at Nowy Dwór and then into their new reserve position on the river's west bank at Lomna Niemiecki, a town 25 kilometers southeast of the corps headquarters in Kazun. To compensate for the loss of one of Becker's *Panzergrenadier* regiments, Gille ordered Ullrich to shift his division's boundary south to a new line running 700 meters to the west of Derlacz. Here, Hack's *Westland* Regiment would take over the sector being vacated by one battalion from the *Totenkopf* Regiment by extending its lines to the south. With only two days remaining before the Soviet offensive was expected to resume, Gille had now lost a significant portion of his own remaining armor reserve.

This was not the only unwelcome news that Gille received that day. Because *9. Armee* had been directed by *H.Gr. Mitte* to move its boundary with Weiss's *2. Armee* several kilometers to the north to fill the vacuum caused by the impending withdrawal of the *3. Pz.Div.*, the *IV. SS-Pz.Korps*, as von Lüttwitz's northernmost corps, had to take over that assignment as well. This meant that Dorr with his three battalions, comprising two from the *Germania* Regiment and Ritter's *Gren.Btl.z.b.V. 560*, had to extend the width of its front line several kilometers to the north. To serve as Dorr's backstop, all except one company of *SS-Pz.Rgt. 5* was positioned north of the river. Gille was no doubt keenly aware that if the attack did fall on 7 November as predicted, he would have only one understrength tank battalion to ward off any Soviet armor that managed to break through his front lines.

On the early morning of 6 November, one day before the expected blow was supposed to fall, a seemingly random artillery barrage ranged over the division's entire sector, including eight more shells from heavy guns that once again struck the Modlin airstrip, which had heretofore been used to fly litter-born patients to hospitals in Germany. The *Westland* regiment reported later that morning that up to 300 additional ground troops with heavy weapons, including an antitank gun, had been observed moving into the front lines opposite its positions in the vicinity of Poniatów, indicating that they were moving up to prepare for the next day's attack. At 5:25 p.m., this same enemy force attacked along the Poniatów–Kałuszyn road in an attempt to breach the *Westland*'s lines. Aided by accurate artillery fire, Hack's troops were able to drive back the Soviet troops.

That evening, based on the day's event, Gille was reinforced in his belief that the big attack was imminent. He did not know yet that Popov's 70th Army had been withdrawn that evening; had he known, he would probably have slept a little easier. In other developments, the corps' rear command post, responsible for handling logistics and personnel matters, moved out of Modlin that day and into the Smoszewo Palace 25 kilometers west of the fortress, where Gille's *Ib*, *Ostubaf.* Scharff, and his *IIa*, *Stubaf.* Schulze, could conduct their business of supplying the corps with manpower and materiel without undue influence by the enemy.[12]

Tuesday, 7 November was the long-anticipated day that the 47th Army's offensive was expected to resume. The morning began quietly, other than the usual harassing artillery and mortar fire. In the *Totenkopf* Division sector, a Soviet combat patrol penetrated the front-line positions of the *III. Bataillon* of the *Totenkopf* Regiment near Chotomów. In the heavy fighting that ensued, the battalion commander, *Stubaf.* Hermann Buchner, a Knight's Cross recipient and one of the few remaining original members of the division, was severely wounded, dying at the *Feldlazarett* in Modlin 10 days later. Shortly thereafter, he too was interred in the *IV. SS-Pz.Korps* cemetery in Modlin alongside his men.[13] On the left flank, a night raid by a company of the *Germania* Regiment against Soviet positions near Bolesławowo on the north bank of the Narew was driven off by heavy defensive fire from the unit from the 65th Army holding the position. Enemy artillery fire intensified throughout the day, but with no definite *Schwerpunkt* identified.

It began to rain, first lightly, but then by the middle of the day it had changed to a cold downpour. In the distance, more Soviet troops could be seen moving up to the front lines from Wieliszew and Jablonna-Legjonowo. Both of *Ogruf.* Gille's divisions south of the Narew braced for the attack that they expected would be unleashed against them at any moment. But nothing happened. Even the Red Air Force was reported as being relatively inactive that day, probably due to the heavy rain. In his assessment that night, however, Gille stuck to his belief that since the attack did not unfold that day, then it would on the next. For his part, von Lüttwitz did not seem to be concerned at all, reporting that the day passed "relatively quietly."

That night, the *Wiking* sent out two combat patrols to collect prisoners, but despite killing an indeterminate number of Soviet troops, came back empty-handed. The night passed quietly in the *Totenkopf*s sector. As 8 November began, heavy downpours and artillery fire were reported, as well as increasing enemy troop movements into the area inhabited by the 47th Army. The Red Air Force, despite the weather, launched a number of reconnaissance aircraft, which roamed the sky out of range of most German *Flak*. Again, the offensive did not materialize. Gille was undaunted; his mission for the next day: defend!

At *9. Armee* headquarters, von Lüttwitz and his staff were concerned about matters such as warning signs of a possible river-crossing attempt north of Warsaw in either the *Totenkopf*s sector or that of *73. Inf.Div.*, which never materialized. They also continued their efforts to convince *H.Gr. Mitte* of the necessity of transferring an infantry division for the defense of *Festung Warschau* instead of having to place too much reliance on less-capable fortress and security troops. By midnight, the last train carrying troops from the *19. Pz.Div.* departed the railroad yard in Warsaw, leaving *9. Armee* with the meager force from Becker's division—little more than a reinforced mechanized infantry battalion supported by a single tank company—as its only mobile reserve. Everywhere else along the army's front, things were relatively quiet—at this point, the Vistula still posed a formidable natural barrier, and were it not for the two bridgeheads Rokossovsky's troops had seized in August at Magnuszew and Puławy, von Lüttwitz would have had little to worry about until the river froze over in December.

The next day, 9 November, was another cold, rainy day. Early that morning, troops from the *Eicke* Regiment drove away two Soviet raiding parties attempting to penetrate their lines. Artillery and mortar fire was weak and sporadic at first, growing stronger as the day progressed but never reaching barrage or drumfire proportions. Brasack's *SS-ARKO 104* had begun focusing its efforts on identifying and eliminating Soviet artillery observation posts using precision fires in a cat-and-mouse game designed to make the enemy's artillery less accurate and hence less effective. Otherwise, German use of artillery was minimal, with only 21 tons of ammunition expended that day, part of the continuing effort to rebuild stocks levels of shells to replace what had been used up during the previous month.[14] The Red Air Force, for once, was absent from the skies overhead. A foot patrol from the *Germania* Regiment, operating north of the Narew, was able to snatch a prisoner from a Soviet position, who under interrogation revealed to his captors that 30 tanks had recently moved into the forest near Szadki in preparation for the offensive; all they were waiting for, he said, were reinforcements and then the long-awaited attack would begin. That night, Gille had little to add, other than to state that his mission and intentions for the following day remained unchanged.

Headquarters of *9. Armee* simply stated in its evening report for the day, "Along the entire Army front, no combat activity worth mentioning." In his comments, von Lüttwitz acknowledged receipt of an order issued by the *OKH* that directed all divisions of the *Heer* and *Waffen-SS*, except for armored divisions, to undergo a mandatory 10 per cent reduction in strength below what was currently authorized by their various *K.St.N.* in a bid to economize on Germany's dwindling reserves of manpower. The situation had grown so dire by the fifth year of the war, that the Third Reich was forced to increasingly rely on Poles of German descent and other ethnic German minorities of southwest Europe—the so-called *Volksdeutsche*—to fill its ranks. It had even begun to recruit Poles of non-German descent to act as *Flakhelfer* (auxiliary) for the *Luftwaffe* and as construction troops in the rear areas, playing on their justified fears of the approaching Red Army as an inducement to volunteer.[15] Amazingly, by 25 November, 845 Poles had volunteered to work in a military capacity in support of the *9. Armee* logistics troops as uniformed *Hiwis*, and 110 boys between the ages of 15 and 17 had volunteered to serve as *Flakhelfer* for the *Luftwaffe*, but none of these volunteers were sent to serve in the *IV. SS-Pz.*

Korps.[16] No reason was given why; perhaps they rightly feared any association with the SS, considering how other SS units had behaved towards the civilian population of Warsaw during the uprising.

The rain continued throughout the following day, making movement along unpaved roads nearly impossible, except for tracked vehicles. Fog and occasional snow showers contributed to the overall gloomy atmosphere on that Friday, 10 November. That evening, the *IV. SS-Pz.Korps* reported random Soviet artillery fire falling throughout its defensive sector, with several large-caliber shells impacting close to the bridges at Modlin and within Nowy Dwór, but otherwise causing no damage. In reply, corps and division artillery batteries fired on known and suspected Soviet troop concentrations, road junctions, and communication sites. Except for a 50-man patrol that unsuccessfully attempted to penetrate the front lines of the *Eicke* Regiment near Jablonna, nothing out of the ordinary was reported. It was the quietest day in weeks.

That same day, the commanders of *H.Gr. Mitte* and *9. Armee* paid a visit to Gille's headquarters, to notify him in person of the ongoing discussions between Guderian and Reinhardt concerning the future disposition of *IV. SS-Pz.Korps*. Apparently, both men had agreed that Gille's corps would be transferred to the *2. Armee* sometime in the near future, but would remain in its present location, taking over responsibility for a portion of Weiss's right flank. They mentioned that in exchange, *9. Armee* might then be able to shift its focus more to the south, assuming control of the *LVI. Pz.Korps* from the neighboring *4. Pz.Armee*, but the date this would be done was undecided. Unless this was carried out at the same time that Gille's corps departed von Lüttwitz's order of battle, *9. Armee* would once more be unable to form any appreciable armored reserve. This issue would arise again the following day. Following their meeting with Gille, Reinhardt and von Lüttwitz visited the forward headquarters of the *Wiking* Division to speak with *Staf.* Ullrich and his regimental commanders.

The rain continued to fall throughout the following day. Most roads, except for paved highways, had become rivers of mud, making travel virtually impossible. Again, most of the activity on 11 November was limited to artillery exchanges, with Soviet gunners aiming at the town of Chotomów and southwest of Jablonna-Legjonowo in the sector defended by the *Eicke* Regiment. No ground attacks materialized, however, to the relief of Becker's troops. They had not remained passively sitting in their troop shelters, and *Totenkopf* snipers recorded 16 confirmed kills that day, reinforcing the lesson that anyone who attempted to move around in the open in broad daylight would soon fall victim to the ever-alert marksmen of both opposing camps. At 2 p.m., the *Westland* Regiment warded off a Soviet reconnaissance party near the Szybalin farm with mortar and small-arms fire. Shortly afterwards, two deserters were apprehended by troops from the *Westland* Regiment after they attempted to make their way through German lines. When questioned, both men said that they had seen four dug-in tanks in the woods southwest of Poniatów on the northern outskirts of Jablonna-Legjonowo. They also volunteered the information that the 47th Army's offensive had been postponed until the following day, news that was immediately transmitted to Gille at his headquarters.

Of course, Gille passed this information just as quickly to *9. Armee*, but von Lüttwitz apparently was unconcerned, noting in his evening report to *H.Gr. Mitte* that other than heavy artillery fire being directed at locations within the *IV. SS-Pz.Korps'* front lines, very little worth mentioning by way of combat activity had happened throughout his army's area of operations. What did concern him was a report from the *H.Gr. Mitte Ic* that the world's press outlets had been repeatedly circulating the news that the *Schwerpunkt* of the impending "great Russian advance" would take place north of Warsaw and that Soviet units designated to take part in this attack had already been notified of the "big task" awaiting them. Whether this was another case of the U.S.S.R.'s ongoing strategic deception effort can only be surmised, but what the news outlets did not report was when this great advance was supposed to take place. Still, based on the tone of von Lüttwitz's narrative comments, he took this news to be of genuine import, and the impending transfer of Gille's corps to *2. Armee* must have filled the army commander with apprehension.

The last piece of information that von Lüttwitz shared with Gille that evening was the unwelcome news that his corps would take over an additional slice, over a dozen kilometers' worth in fact, of the *2. Armee*'s southern flank the following day, including a major portion of the sector held by the *XX. Armeekorps*. How Gille perceived this new assignment can only be surmised; faced with what he believed to be an imminent large-scale attack against his center and right flank, he was now being ordered to divert additional forces north of the Narew, where hardly anything was happening at all. His only corps reserve was the *Totenkopf*'s armored reconnaissance battalion, and that was on the west bank of the Vistula watching the river flow by. He had already given up the *Totenkopf* Regiment and a tank battalion as the *9. Armee* reserve. For his part, von Lüttwitz echoed Gille's fears, pondering the imminent loss of *IV. SS-Pz.Korps*, along with the mobile reserve it was providing, and how it would leave his army with nothing to counter any large-scale Soviet action.

For the troops of the *IV. SS-Pz.Korps*, the next day began with the expectation that the Soviet attack would unfold at any moment. It certainly had all of the classic warning signs—heavy artillery fire along the front lines, attempts by Soviet obstacle-clearing parties in company strength to clear barbed wire obstacles, and troops moving forward into the trenches from assembly areas in the rear. Heavy shelling of Modlin and its bridge, as well as the one at Nowy Dwór, was reported, though again there was no appreciable damage. Along the banks of the Narew, troops from both the *Germania* and *Westland* Regiments experienced heavy Soviet barrage fire at Debe, Woła Kielpinska, and Ludwinowo. Even the corps' reserve on the opposite bank of the Vistula reported that it was being fired on by four Soviet assault guns emplaced inside Jablonna castle. The only thing missing to make the

An die Führer, Unterführer und SS-Männer der SS-Pz.-Division „Wiking"

Soldaten des Todes!

Schaut Euch um! Ihr gehört zu einem Haufen, dem aus der jüngsten Vergangenheit nur die Nummer noch geblieben ist.

Ihr gehört zu einer Totendivision!

Die Zahl Eurer Toten ist um das mehrfache größer als die der Lebenden.

Euer Kampfgefährte, Euer Führer ist der Tod!

Die eigentliche Wiking-Division wurde im Februar in dem Kessel von Korsun (westlich Tscherkassy) vernichtet. Tausende Eurer jungen Kameraden fielen im sinnlosen Kampf, betrogen durch Hitlers Entsatzversprechungen, verraten von ihren Führern. Der Kommandeur der Wiking-Division, der Gruppenführer Gille, sein Ia Obersturmbannführer Schönfelder und Ic Hauptsturmführer Main-Kuhn flohen mit einem «Fiesdler Storch» aus dem Kessel, nachdem sie ihre Soldaten verräterisch dem Untergang preisgegeben hatten.

Ihr meint, sie kamen vor das Kriegsgericht als Feiglinge und Verräter? So seht Ihr aus! Gille, der Mörder und Verräter seiner Soldaten, erhielt die Schwerter zum Eichenlaub des Ritterkreuzes. Auch die anderen Lumpen wurden ausgezeichnet.

Dafür sorgte Hitler — Hitler, der diesen verbrecherischen Krieg vom Zaun gebrochen, Hitler, der Jahr für Jahr Euch mit Siegesversprechungen und von Größenwahn überschäumenden Reden betrogen und verhetzt hat, Hitler, der Millionen deutscher Männer seinen wahnwitzigen Eroberungsplänen opferte, Hitler, der diesen nunmehr vollkommen aussichtslosen, verlorenen Krieg bewußt verlängert und Euch und Eure Heimat ins Verderben mitschleppt, nur um seine und seiner Mordgesellen Galgenfrist in die Länge zu ziehen.

Eben zu diesen Mordgesellen Hitlers, die auf Kosten Eures Blutes durch Euren sinnlosen Tod ihren eigenen unvermeidlichen Niedergang zu vertagen suchen, gehören auch Eure Kommandeure. Sie haben Tausende Eurer Kameraden im Kessel von Korsun gemein betrogen, verraten und dem Tode preisgegeben. Jetzt führen sie auch Euch in den Tod

Figure 6. Surrender leaflet dropped on *Wiking* Division troops, August 1944 (Courtesy of Günther Lange Archive)

scene complete was the Red Air Force, grounded due to weather so bad that even its pilots could not fly into such a storm of rain and snow.

Still, no attack came. In its place, loudspeaker broadcasts were heard along the corps' front lines, enticing Gille's men to surrender with appealing descriptions of how easy their life would be in a POW camp if they deserted. If they continued fighting for Hitler, the broadcasts announced, they would face certain death when the attack came. One soldier from Ritter's probationary battalion, positioned on Gille's far left flank in *Kampfgruppe Dorr*, evidently took these entreaties to heart and deserted in the early evening hours as *Germania* extended its left flank to the north to take over more of the *542. Gren.Div.* sector in the *XX. Armeekorps'* area of operations. None of the SS men gave themselves up, though some surreptitiously tucked surrender leaflets into their pockets when no one was looking (see Figure 6 for example of Soviet surrender leaflet).

The *9. Armee*'s reaction to the events that took place that day was rather blasé, with its *Ia* stating in its war diary that, "Once again, the day passed without any action worth mentioning." It certainly had not seemed that way to the men of the *IV. SS-Pz.Korps*, who had to endure yet another day in anticipation that it would be their last. The only good news that Gille received from von Lüttwitz that day was the notification that he would no longer have to take over the neighboring *XX. Armeekorps'* sector, other than the ground that he had already occupied with Dorr's troops. Apparently, the army group commander had still not yet decided upon his next course of action. Von Lüttwitz was relieved, as he would be able to rely for the foreseeable future on the army's mobile reserve provided by the *Totenkopf* Division.

It also happened that 12 November was the date for the *9. Armee*'s corps and divisions to report their available *Kampfstärke*. The numbers provide an indication of the growing strength of Gille's corps, improved by the influx of large numbers of replacement troops from the *Luftwaffe*. On that date, the *Totenkopf* Division reported 2,840 men serving in it, not counting the 620 from the *Totenkopf* Regiment on the other side of the river acting as the *9. Armee* reserve. The number also included 1,068 men in its *Feld-Ersatz Bataillon*, even though it was not occupying a front-line position but was in training near Modlin. The division's strongest grenadier battalion was *II. Btl./Eicke*, with 361 combat-effective troops reported; the weakest was its sister battalion, *I. Btl./Eicke*, with only 248. While these numbers may seem rather low in comparison with their authorized full combat strength of 546 men, they must be seen in the light of those reported on 16 October, when their *Kampfstärke* was 97 and 108 respectively. The attached *SS-Jäg.Btl. 501*, which was disbanded on 9 November and its few remaining men incorporated into the division, reported only 46 men in its *Kampfstärke*. The division also reported 90 operational armored fighting vehicles, including 20 Panthers, 10 Tigers, 36 assault guns and tank destroyers, and 24 *Pz. IV*s.

The *Wiking* Division had also seen a remarkable improvement in its manpower situation. It reported 3,195 men in its *Kampfstärke*, not counting the 530 serving as the corps' reserve from *SS-Pz.Aufkl.Abt. 5*, having exchanged places with the *Totenkopf*'s reconnaissance battalion on the other side of the river. It also still had Ritter's *Gren.Btl.z.b.V. 560* attached, with another 379 men reported, a considerable amount for that period. Like the *Totenkopf* Division, the *Wiking* also had a large number of troops in *SS-Feld-Ers.Btl. 5*, with 1,334 men reported. Regarding to tanks, assault guns, and tank destroyers, it had only half as many as the *Totenkopf*, reporting just 47 operational vehicles, including 26 Panthers and nine *Pz. IV* tanks. As a substitute for its lack of armor, the division's antitank defenses had been buttressed by the attachment of *Art.Pak Abt. 1061*, with 18 Pak 43/41 8.8cm antitank guns. By all accounts, Gille's corps was growing stronger and he was increasingly confident that his troops would give a good account of themselves when (or if) the anticipated Soviet offensive resumed.

While no action worth mentioning occurred on 12 November, the situation on the following day was somewhat more intense. Enemy artillery fire increased both in volume and accuracy, with observers reporting far more shelling occurring than usual. Shells from heavy batteries fell near the bridges over the Narew and Vistula, though luckily neither were hit. In both *Wiking*'s and *Totenkopf*'s sectors, movements by truck of large numbers of enemy troops close to the front lines were reported by forward observers, who promptly called artillery fire down upon them. A 15-minute drumfire barrage was directed against the *Eicke* Regiment's front lines between the railroad line and the village of Chotomów, immediately followed by a company-sized force of 150 men who attempted to fight their way into the defenders' forward positions. After directing an artillery barrage of their own, the Germans counterattacked and drove the Soviet troops from their position, counting 40 bodies and capturing one antitank gun left behind after the action was concluded.

The *Wiking* Division reported that the Soviets made multiple small-scale attempts to probe its front lines on either side of the Narew. One such patrol nearly penetrated the outpost line west of Podebe on the southern bank of the Narew, but *I. Btl./Germania*, defending that position, was able to drive them back with the aid of mortar and machine-gun fire, supported by infantry howitzers. The situation never reached the point where either division felt compelled to launch counterattacks using their armored reserve. While no large-scale attack developed that day, Gille stated in his evening report that he expected that it would begin the next day, and that the events of 13 November were a warning sign that confirmed in his mind his opponent's intentions.

Other than recounting the events of the day taking place in his other two corps and *Festung Warschau*, which except for the *IV. SS-Pz.Korps* were very uneventful, von Lüttwitz had little to add, other than to state that he did not believe that the attacks of the day signified anything out of the ordinary. He focused much of his report on emphasizing the importance of placing artillery forward observers inside tanks or assault guns so that supporting fire could be called down even when enemy artillery fire was heavy. This was a lesson learned from a report he had recently received, which detailed how the initial barrage heralding a Soviet attack usually wiped out or suppressed German forward observation posts. By placing observers inside a tank or other armored vehicle, von Lüttwitz wrote, the forward observer would be protected from everything but a direct hit. While this made eminent sense, and had already been common practice in many armored units, it was something of a technical challenge as any vehicle put to such use had to have the standard artillery 30-watt radio sender installed instead of the more common vehicle radio set. It is unknown whether Gille followed up on this lesson; as an artilleryman, he would already have been aware of such tactics.

The only other item von Lüttwitz mentioned that evening was to note that his army could expect in the near future the attachment of *Volkssturm* units, most likely of battalion size. The *Volkssturm* organization was the brainchild of Josef Goebbels, the minister of propaganda, who saw it as an opportunity for the Nazi Party to have its own civilian militia that would operate under its control, while being tactically directed by the Army like the *Waffen-SS*. Members of the *Volkssturm* were usually teenagers and men deemed too old for active field service, haphazardly equipped and poorly trained. As experience would soon demonstrate, they were more of a liability than an asset, which the *Wehrmacht* saw as a waste of both manpower and scarce weaponry. Fortunately, Gille's corps would not have to deal with these poorly trained amateurs, at least while it occupied the Wet Triangle north of Warsaw.

Another significant event that took place that day, of which the Germans were unaware, was the transfer of Marshal Konstantin Rokossovsky. He had been directed by Stalin himself to assume command of the Second Belorussian Front, his immediate neighbor to the north, replacing Army General Ivan Yefimovich Petrov, who in turn had been posted to command the Fourth Ukrainian Front. Initially disappointed that this signified a demotion and that he would not be able to complete the liquidation of the German troops in the Narew–Vistula Triangle, he was reassured by Stalin that it was indeed a promotion, since he intended to have the Second Belorussian Front play a key role in the upcoming strike against Berlin.[17] He was replaced as commander of the First Belorussian Front by Marshal Georgy K. Zhukov, who was already well known by Gille and the veterans of the *Wiking* Division, having orchestrated their encirclement in the Cherkassy Pocket 10 months previously.

As if to contradict von Lüttwitz's assertion that a major attack was not imminent, 14 November began with an early artillery barrage that struck throughout Gille's sector. The Red Air Force made a strong appearance, dropping bombs in the vicinity of key installations and strafing any traffic moving along the roads in the divisions' rear areas. More enemy troop movements were spotted, and forward observers from the *Eicke* Regiment reported a great deal of track noise in Jablonna, possibly signifying the approach of a Soviet tank unit. To combat the relentless artillery fire, *SS-ARKO 104*, in conjunction with *Beob.Btl. 21*, located two heavy enemy artillery batteries within Jablonna-Legjonowo and directed fire upon their locations, resulting once again in heavy secondary explosions and flames leaping into the sky, a sign that they had indeed hit something.

Becker's and Ullrich's troops braced themselves for most of the day for the attack they believed would come at any minute. It would start with a drumfire barrage upon their positions, followed by screaming hordes of Soviet troops advancing with fixed bayonets through the snow, joined shortly by tanks. The few remaining veterans knew what to expect, but for the hundreds of new replacements from the *Luftwaffe* that the divisions had no recourse but to incorporate into their ranks, this would be something altogether new. A scouting party from the *Eicke* Regiment found the body of a Soviet officer killed the previous day during the attack near Chotomów. His papers revealed that he belonged to the 132nd Rifle Division, a heretofore unidentified unit. Nothing else happened that day to cause Gille to change his mind—for him, these attacks provided mounting evidence that his opponent was ready to strike. So it must have come as a surprise to him when he was ordered to detach *Gren.Btl. z.b.V. 560* that night and send it back to Modlin the next day, where it would be loaded onto trains and shipped to *H.Gr. Mitte*, becoming part of Reinhardt's operational reserve.

That evening, the *9. Armee* commander had to admit that the signs did indicate that a Soviet attack seemed imminent, though not against Gille's corps. Instead, von Lüttwitz read the signs and concluded that an attack was far more likely in the next few days to originate from the Magnuszew or Puławy bridgeheads, although the situation in both areas had been relatively quiet for weeks. In addition, he foresaw an imminent attack from the Baranow bridgehead, a much larger concentration of Soviet forces that lay inside the northern boundary of the neighboring *4. Pz.Armee*. He based his conclusion on the upsurge in enemy air reconnaissance, the movement of troops into all three bridgeheads, and photo reconnaissance that seemed to indicate the Soviets were adding additional numbers of artillery batteries to both areas. Von Lüttwitz did do one thing that day to support Gille that he would have greatly appreciated, the transfer of 1,700 new Mauser 98K rifles to *IV. SS-Pz.Korps*. This would make up for the shortage of small arms for the new replacements, who still had not been issued any firearms despite being so close to the front. However, Gille's corps would not receive any of the new *Maschinepistole M.p. 44* assault rifles issued to *9. Armee* that day—these were only to go to newly raised or newly redesignated *Volks-Grenadier* Divisions, such as the *337. VGD* or the renamed *45. VGD*.

Despite Gille's premonition, no large-scale attacks took place in his corps sector on 15 November either, except for the usual activity. During the night, the *II. Btl./ Germania* relieved Ritter's battalion, which was picked up by a truck column and transported back to Modlin to catch its trains. On the southern bank of the Narew, the *I. Btl./Germania* was relieved by *II. Btl./Westland*. Besides these actions, Soviet troop movements were widely reported, foot patrols scouted German forward positions and minefields, the sound of tank tracks were heard, and artillery fire fell randomly, but as the sun rose, no attack took place. Gille concluded that night that his opponent had made all of the necessary preparations to launch his attack, and was now only waiting for the word to go.

His soldiers made maximum use of the opportunity provided by the lull in operations that day to further improve their positions, lay more mines, and clean weapons. The operations staff at *9. Armee* headquarters reported to *H.Gr. Mitte* that the day had passed quietly. The only thing that von Lüttwitz added was to announce that a training exercise would happen the following day for various rear-echelon units slated to play a defensive role as *Sperrverbände* (blocking units) to thwart or slow any large-scale Soviet offensive. This event was to occur several dozen kilometers west of Warsaw and would not involve Gille's corps. The only other issues occupying his attention that day were ensuring that the remnants of *Pz.Brig. 104* were incorporated into the *25. Pz.Div.*, for whose logistics his army was responsible even though he had no command authority over it, and that the newly assigned legion of security and fortress battalions were being properly billeted and incorporated within the order of battle of *Festung Warschau*.

By 16 November, a pattern in the enemy's activity during the past week had become clearly recognizable. The divisions of the 47th Army maintained the pressure against the *IV. SS-Pz.Korps* in such a way that the Germans could never lower their guard, keeping them continually wondering when the blow would fall. Would *Iwan* attack or not? Constant activity in the form of day and night attempts to penetrate front-line positions, daily random shelling, barrages with no follow-up attack, aerial reconnaissance or bombing, and the sounds of tank tracks coming and going all seemed calculated to strain Gille and his troops to the utmost. The daily records indicate that Gille believed all these actions confirmed that the offensive was imminent and that he was deeply worried that when it came, he would not have sufficient forces to defend or counterattack.

Another sign that confirmed Gille's belief was that Soviet troops were heard singing and playing music opposite the *Totenkopf* Division's front lines at Jablonna-Legjonowo. Experience had taught Becker's veterans that this usually meant commanders had issued troops with their alcohol ration, something that traditionally occurred immediately prior to a large-scale attack. That same day, a large raiding party stormed one of the *Wiking* Division's trenches and, after a brief but violent firefight, departed with one SS prisoner. The heavy rains, snow, and high winds that day had facilitated this raid, enabling the assailants to approach the front lines undetected. He was the first man from the *IV. SS-Pz.Korps* ever taken prisoner in such a manner; he would not be the last. But again, no attack came.

With the benefit of hindsight, the actions by 47th Army can now be clearly seen as a *Maskirovka* operation intended to tie down Gille's corps in a static position. By making it appear that an attack was imminent, *9. Armee* or *H.Gr. Mitte* could not withdraw it and employ it elsewhere, testimony to the fear and respect that the Red Army had developed for the *IV. SS-Pz.Korps* based on its sterling performance during the past four months in combat.

In contrast, while Gille expected the attack to occur at any moment, von Lüttwitz was beginning to see the situation differently. After analyzing the various intelligence reports coming in with his key staff, the *9. Armee* commander concluded that the odds of an attack beyond this point were dwindling, not increasing. As before, his biggest concern was the lack of reserves available to counter any offensive, especially one originating from the Magnuszew area. To clarify the enemy's intentions, von Lüttwitz ordered Gille to have his divisions seize more prisoners, beginning that evening. On the same day, *H.Gr. Mitte* ordered that the northern boundary with the *2. Armee* be shifted a few kilometers further north once again, which forced the *Wiking* Division, in particular its *Germania* Regiment, to extend its line even more. Fortunately for Dorr and his regiment, enemy activity was limited to the actions already described.

Beginning on 17 November, both of Gille's divisions, as ordered, carried out nocturnal infantry raids against their opponents' front line positions to collect prisoners. All came back empty-handed, having been driven off by alert Soviet sentries. Later that morning, loudspeaker propaganda designed to induce Becker's and Ullrich's troops to surrender, punctuated by aerial-delivered leaflets, once again resumed, though the loudspeaker teams frequently drew artillery fire from German batteries. By mid-afternoon, the *Totenkopf* reported heavy artillery fire upon its front-line positions, but no attacks. In the *Wiking*'s sector, the situation appeared ominous. Ullrich reported the heaviest artillery fire his division had experienced in several weeks.

Particularly worrying was his report that *Stalinorgel* fire had been used to suppress the *Westland* Regiment's positions near Kałuszyn, immediately followed by another report that 15 Soviet tanks had been spotted assembling near Poniatów, less than 2 kilometers from the *HKL*. Gille's headquarters received multiple reports stating that groups of 200–300 Red Army infantrymen were spotted moving into forward positions outside Wieliszew and Poniatów. Finally, as if these reports were not sufficient to illustrate the enemy's intentions, eight rubber assault boats were spotted on the northern bank of the Narew near Rybacki ferrying troops across the river. Upon weighing this evidence, Gille was convinced that the attack could happen at any moment.

Once again, this did not occur. Except for artillery fire, the front quietened down, muffled somewhat by the heavy snowstorm that afternoon. Both the *Wiking* and *Totenkopf* Divisions dutifully sent out patrols that evening in hopes of capturing some prisoners, but again all returned with nothing to show for their efforts except a few more wounded men to add to the casualty list. That evening, the *9. Armee* headquarters reported no combat activity worth mentioning throughout the army's defensive sector, except that the *Wiking* Division had experienced heavy artillery fire and spotted 15 enemy tanks. In his follow-up commander's commentary, von Lüttwitz had nothing to add.

After all of the excitement of the previous day, 18 November passed relatively quietly, except perhaps for exchange of artillery fire, sniper duels, and attempts by both sides to grab prisoners, which were uniformly unsuccessful. Only 30 tons of artillery ammunition were expended that day, less that 10 per cent of the usage during the height of the October battle. The only event out of the ordinary was a report from the *Germania* Regiment on the north bank of the Narew that mentioned how a Soviet motor boat had approached the site of the demolished bridge at Debe under the very noses of the sentries posted there to keep an eye out for such things. After reaching the ruins of the bridge, the boat turned around and only belatedly was engaged by German machine-gun fire. By then, it had escaped. This event even raised the eyebrows that night of the watch officer at *9. Armee* headquarters, who scribbled on the report in pencil, "how were they able to get away?"

This event did not seem to interest the army commander, who focused instead on his intention to require front-line divisions to also form *Sperrverbände*, just as he had directed units operating in the army's *Korück*. These special units were to consist of no less than a full-strength *Pionier Kompanie* held in reserve and equipped with appropriate demolitions and other engineer equipment that would enable them to quickly block roads, blow up bridges, and construct obstacles to constrict an advancing enemy force's movement. In real terms, this meant that Becker and Ullrich each had to pull an engineer company out of their *Panzer-Pionier* battalions and move them to the western bank of the Vistula to stand in readiness should a Soviet breakthrough occur. With regard to the *9. Armee* reserve from the *Totenkopf* Division, at that time still occupying an assembly area on the west bank of the Vistula, on that date *II. Btl./Totenkopf* was allowed to return to its parent division, leaving only *I. Abt./SS-Pz.Rgt. 3* and *I. Btl.(gep.)/Totenkopf* as von Lüttwitz's mobile reserve.[18]

During the night of 18–19 November, combat patrols from both of Gille's divisions were sent out, but only one launched by Becker's division was crowned with success, bringing back two prisoners after killing several Soviet troops in the process. Their opponents immediately launched a counterattack to rescue the two men, but heavy German fire drove them back. Upon interrogation, the prisoners reported that a Polish unit was moving in to take over their position, an indication that the boundary between the 47th Army and the 1st Polish Army was being shifted to the north. Thick ground fog made accurate targeting by artillery difficult, forcing German and Soviet gunners to shoot at preregistered targets with unobserved results. In the *Wiking* sector, heavy vehicular traffic could be heard but of course could not be seen on account of the fog. Despite the weather, the Red Air Force flew over the northern bank of the Narew, dropping surrender leaflets on *Kampfgruppe Germania*.

The *Luftwaffe* was also active during this period flying reconnaissance missions. One photo-reconnaissance mission flown the previous day upon Gille's request revealed that there were 249 enemy artillery batteries arrayed against his corps between the Vistula and Narew and in the narrow sector he held north of the Narew. Another interesting piece of information, provided by Dorr's troops, was the identification of the 162nd Rifle Division, which had apparently been brought in to replace the 153rd Fortified Region, the Red Army's version of a *Sperrverband* designed to free up combat troops for other missions. If a rifle division was being brought in to replace an essentially static unit, what did this signify?

Pondering the day's events that night, von Lüttwitz was clearly trying to understand what the intelligence gained from the prisoners seized that day meant. Was the 1st Polish Army's front line being increased to allow the 47th Army to narrow its zone of attack and form a *Schwerpunkt*, or was it doing so to allow more units of the 47th Army to be taken out of line and given a rest? Since he could not reach a firm conclusion, the *9. Armee* commander tasked his acting *Ic*, *Oberstleutnant* Lange, to provide more information. Soviet radio transmissions had markedly decreased and the static front-line situation made it difficult for German agents to safely travel behind the lines to spy on troop movements. Otherwise, von Lüttwitz outlined his plans for the next several days, taking account of the "prevailing pause in battle" to conduct an inspection tour of rear area units, particularly several *Festungs-Pak* companies, to determine their level of readiness.

Even though attempts by *Ogruf.* Gille's two divisions to bring in prisoners on 20 November were unsuccessful, their failure was more than made up for by the arrival of eight Soviet deserters from the 185th Rifle Division, who had somehow walked right into the *Eicke* Regiment's front lines at Derlacz before sunrise. Under interrogation, they stated that the major attack everyone was expecting was supposed to occur "any day now" between the area bounded by Derlacz in the south and Skrzeszew in the north, oriented along the boundary between the *Totenkopf* and *Wiking* Divisions. This only confirmed in Gille's own mind that the attack was indeed truly imminent. A prisoner taken the previous day confirmed the information that the 76th Rifle Division was in the process of being relieved by a Polish division, which was subsequently confirmed by a German signal intelligence unit that indicated that the division had indeed been moved to the Radzymin area.

Trying to make sense of the conflicting intelligence reports, weighing the results of the recent prisoner and deserter interrogations, the news from the international press, and what his own intelligence services were providing, von Lüttwitz could not decide which to believe. Direct observations of the front, combined with reports of troop movements in and out of the area and the slackening of Soviet artillery activity tended to indicate that the First Belorussian Front in general and the 47th Army in particular had backed off on their intentions to immediately pursue the goals of their offensive.

Unfortunately, he wrote, the bad flying weather that day had grounded all of the *Luftwaffe*'s reconnaissance assets, making it impossible to know for sure. Von Lüttwitz requested that another photo-reconnaissance mission be flown the following day, weather permitting. He also acknowledged the fact that *Gren.Btl.z.b.V. 560*, the only other viable reserve that the *9. Armee* could claim besides the *Kampfgruppe* from the *Totenkopf* Division, had finally been shipped north to serve as the *4. Armee* operational reserve. Should Gille's corps be reassigned to *2. Armee* as Reinhardt was considering, von Lüttwitz would soon have no reserve force at all.

More combat patrols were sent out on the evening of 20–21 November to bring in more prisoners to enable a more complete picture of the Soviets' order of battle to be painted. The *Totenkopf* succeeded in bringing back one live prisoner, while both of the *Wiking*'s patrols were forced to turn back before they reached enemy lines. The constant background music of artillery and mortar fire exchanges continued throughout the day. Though only 19 tons of ammunition were expended on 21 November, *SS-ARKO 104* still registered some successes, relying more on accuracy than massed fire to achieve the desired destructive effects. For example, on that day *Beob.Btl. 21* located two Soviet artillery observation posts, one atop Hill 86.3, three kilometers north of Derlacz, and the other positioned 300 meters southwest of the Ludwisin farm. Firing data was relayed to one of the corps' artillery battalions, most likely *schw.Art.Abt. 154*, whose 15cm field howitzers quickly destroyed both sites using high explosive shells.

The *9. Armee Tagesmeldung* submitted for 21 November that evening to *H.Gr. Mitte* was one of the shortest ever sent, merely stating, "The day passed uneventfully." In his own report, von Lüttwitz concluded that based on available information, including Soviet POW and deserter interrogations, the repositioning of their units, radio intercepts, captured documents, and agent reports, the earliest the 47th Army could be expected to attack was 1 December. Although this date could not be confirmed with absolute certainty, the *9. Armee* commander was confident that his analysis was correct. What the data did confirm, at least in his mind, was that the offensive, when it came, would primarily erupt from the Magnuszew bridgehead against his *VIII. Armeekorps,* and from the Baranow bridgehead in the neighboring *LVI. Pz.Korps* of the *4. Pz.Armee* sector, with a smaller supporting attack conducted from the Puławy bridgehead, now known as the *Nahtbrückenkopf* (seam or boundary bridgehead) because it was positioned along the boundary between *H.Gr. Mitte* and *H.Gr. A.*

Von Lüttwitz clearly believed that any threat to the *9. Armee* would not come from the Vistula–Narew area, which he seemed confident could be successfully defended, but from Soviet mechanized units advancing to the northwest out of the Magnuszew area attacking his army from the rear. Consequently, he began to place even more emphasis on the readiness of units populating his army's *Korück*, with an emphasis on antitank defenses, employing *Sperrverbände*, and teaching tactical fundamentals to logistics and administrative troops who were not normally expected to play key defensive roles in a major battle. Von Lüttwitz then directed his *Armee-Waffenschule* to set up specialized courses to begin training the commanders of these units by the end of November.

The next day, 22 November, proved full of portent, not because of any tactical action, but because of events that would soon directly impact the future of the *IV. SS-Pz.Korps*. On the front line, the situation remained stable, with no major attacks reported and nothing out of the ordinary occurring. Another Soviet artillery observation post was destroyed by timely and accurate counter-battery fire, and two infantry patrols carried out that night by the *Wiking* Division were forced to turn back without any prisoners taken. The weather continually worsened, as the snow melted only to be replaced by heavy rain showers, followed by freezing temperatures at night. Life in the trenches became more miserable than ever, but at least platoons and companies could be rotated in and out of the lines, spending two or three days at a time in sturdy bunkers up to a kilometer behind the *HKL*, where they could rest, repair clothing and equipment, and get deloused. Mail would be delivered again and troops could line up at field kitchens to eat a hot meal in relative peace. Then, back into the line they would go. Though it was still dangerous up front, casualties were dramatically less during November in comparison to the previous month, with only 1,007 casualties due to combat, including 270 killed in action or dying from wounds. This was approximately 16 percent of the casualties lost during October.

While the *9. Armee* operations staff reported that most of the army's front lines remained relatively quiet, even in the *IV. SS-Pz.Korps* sector, the army commander mulled a number of developments that had occurred that day during a conference conducted at *H.Gr. Mitte* headquarters, attended by his chief of staff, *Gen.Maj.* Staedke, as well as by other key staff officers, including several from *H.Gr. A*. The focus of the conversations revolved around the future course of the fighting on the Eastern Front. Staedke reported that the participants agreed with the *H.Gr. Mitte Ia*, Oberst Peter von der Groeben, who informed them that the Soviet offensive, when it began, would most likely come from two primary directions, in the north through East Prussia and the south from the Baranov and Magnuszew bridgeheads, forming a giant pincer to trap the bulk of *Heeresgruppen A* and *Mitte*. Importantly, he predicted that the offensive, when it began, would probably not occur until late December or even early January 1945. In the meantime, the situation along the Vistula Front would probably remain stable, with the Red Army conducting nothing but local attacks conducted to gain better positions for future operations.

Attaching *9. Armee* to *H.Gr. A* was a proposal developed by von Lüttwitz and put forth by Staedke as one of the ways to prepare both army groups to counter this threat. If approved, it would place the responsibly for defending the entire Vistula line under one army group, instead of two as it was presently. That night, von Lüttwitz, who did not attend the conference, evaluated the advantages and disadvantages of this proposal in his narrative and forwarded his recommendation to *H.Gr. Mitte*. He suggested that his two southern corps—the *XLVI. Pz.Korps* and *VIII. Armeekorps*—remain with *9.*

Armee and move with it to join *H.Gr. A*, while Gille's corps would remain where it was. This would require *IV. SS-Pz.Korps* to be formally transferred to the control of the *2. Armee*, a move that would push the right flank of Weiss's army further to the south to a point just above Warsaw. All von Lüttwitz could do now was to wait and see if his recommendation was approved.

The commander of *IV. SS-Pz.Korps* did not find out about the results of this conference until the following day, 23 November, when he was informed that photo-reconnaissance had confirmed that nearly all of the First Belorussian Front's artillery, less those forces possessed by 47th Army and its subordinate corps and divisions, had been removed from the area opposite his corps. This development meant that without the forces to create an artillery *Schwerpunkt*, there could be no breakthrough attack against Gille's corps in the near future. It was obviously being sent somewhere else to reinforce an attack in a different area, but Gille still thought that perhaps these assets had only moved to an area behind 47th Army and that the *9. Armee* might be too hasty in its decision to give up his corps.

That night, von Lüttwitz disagreed with Gille, believing that *9. Armee* could well afford to be shed of the *IV. SS-Pz.Korps* if it improved the army's overall defensive posture. He then ordered several army-level assets to be brought back under *9. Armee* control, including *II. Abt./Art.Brig. 732*, which had been operating north of the Narew in support of Dorr's and Darges's regiments. The reasoning behind this decision was that if Gille's corps was going to be transferred to another army, why give up any assets that technically belonged to *9. Armee* anyway? Orders were sent out accordingly and during the next two days, several units moved out of the Wet Triangle and Modlin areas, crossed the rivers, and returned to the army's control. In turn, elements of *2. Armee* began to arrive in their place, including the relief of *10. Bttr./Stellungswerfer-Rgt. 102* by *9. Bttr./Stellungswerfer-Rgt. 103*. The only thing Gille did not yet know was when the decision to attach his corps to *2. Armee* would take place, but it would undoubtedly happen within the next several days, if the exchange of *Heerestruppen* was any indicator.

Action at the front that day was light, with the poor weather once again influencing the pace and outcome of operations. Both sides carried out sporadic artillery activity, infantry patrols, and sniping competitions. In the area west of Jablonna and southeast of Chotomów, the *Eicke* Regiment, using infantry weapons, repulsed two attempts by the Polish 2nd Rifle Division to probe its front lines. In the *Wiking* Division's sector held by the *Westland* Regiment, its troops called in artillery fire upon Soviet sappers attempting to construct an approach trench opposite German positions on the northern bank of the Narew. Air activity was minimal and only 16 tons of artillery ammunition was fired that day at the "Comrades from the opposite *Feldpost*." Trench warfare was reinforcing the impression learned during World War I that this kind of warfare was a dull yet dangerous business.

Regardless of what the future held, Gille did his best to ensure that his troops would be as prepared as possible for any large-scale Soviet attack, whenever or from whichever direction it finally came. Sufficient food, fuel, and ammunition of all types had been stockpiled on both sides of the Narew to provide adequate resupply, including up to six days of solid food, up to eight days of bread, 110,500 gallons (418,000 liters) of gasoline and diesel fuel, and 4,782 tons of ammunition. At least when the transfer did take place, *2. Armee* would still remain the provider of the bulk of the supplies for *IV. SS-Pz.Korps*, as it had already been doing since 1 October.

The next day witnessed additional changes when *I. Btl./Gren.Rgt. 70* arrived to begin taking over the sector held by the *Wiking*'s *SS-Pz.Aufkl.Abt. 5*, which had been defending the western bank of the Vistula, along with a battery from *SS-Pz. Art.Rgt. 5*. The battalion from the *73. Inf.Div.* was far less capable than the one it was replacing, but *9. Armee* had nothing else it could send that could match it. Except for the *19.* and *25. Panzer* Divisions, von Lüttwitz had no armor to call his own. Both of these powerful formations were located in the *9. Armee* area but were, for command and control purposes, either in *H.Gr. Mitte* or *OKH* reserve and hence untouchable except in dire emergencies, and only with the explicit approval of *der Führer*. With the transfer of Gille's corps to *2. Armee* still pending, *9. Armee* continued pursuing additional steps to be ready when the order finally came.

Throughout the day, there were signs indicating that the enemy's artillery *Schwerpunkt* had indeed been transferred elsewhere. Instead of the super-heavy artillery of either 20.3cm or 28cm type that had been bombarding Modlin, the bridges over the Narew and Vistula, as well as other rear area installations during the past several weeks, smaller and less powerful 12.2cm and 15.2cm howitzers were being used instead. Multiple rocket launcher batteries, another indicator of offensive intent, had also disappeared. The front line was still dangerous of course, where the usual activity continued as it had before. The 1st Polish and 47th Armies had not gone away either, and kept up their own nightly raids, artillery ambushes and attempts to infiltrate German positions.

That evening, von Lüttwitz's headquarters notified Gille that the transfer of control for the west bank of the Vistula between *IV. SS-Pz.Korps* and Felzmann's *XLVI. Pz.Korps* would occur at 6 a.m. the following morning, by which point the handoff between the outgoing unit from the *73. Inf.Div.* and the *Wiking* should be complete. Gille found out later that night when the *9. Armee* commander notified him by telephone that he would be reporting to *Gen.Oberst* Weiss of the *2. Armee* from midnight the following day, 25 November. *Ogruf.* Gille had previously served under Weiss's command from 17 July until the end of the tank battle of Praga in August. They had enjoyed a good working relationship with each other then, and Gille hoped that it would continue during this next assignment.

This transfer meant that the *9. Armee* mobile reserve provided by Becker's *Totenkopf* Division would also be departing from the army's area, leaving von Lüttwitz with no army reserve whatsoever. Von Lüttwitz was mollified somewhat by the news from *H.Gr. Mitte* that Headquarters, *XL. Pz.Korps* was being considered as the controlling headquarters for both the *19.* and *25. Panzer* Divisions, but would first have to be moved from its present position in the northernmost sector of *H.Gr. Mitte.* Should there be any Soviet breakthrough attempt from Magnuszew, Reinhardt told him, this new corps would probably be assigned to *9. Armee* as a countermeasure.

Throughout 25 November, the remaining *Heerestruppen* supporting Gille's corps returned to the new *9. Armee* area of operations. In addition to four construction battalions that had been building fortifications and repairing roads, *schw.Art.Abt. 154* also returned to the *9. Armee ARKO*'s control but was not immediately replaced. Combat operations proceeded without pause, though no large-scale actions were conducted by either side, limiting their activities to the usual artillery and mortar harassing fire, combat patrols, and sniper competitions, which seemingly neverending. On 25 November alone, the last day Gille's corps was under *9. Armee* control, the *Totenkopf* Division claimed bragging rights after its sharpshooters recorded 29 confirmed kills, while those of the *Wiking* Division had only shot 10. As sanguinary as this sounds, sniping was a necessary evil, forcing the enemy to stay under cover at all times, especially leaders, who depended on the force of their personal example to lead men into battle. Of course, Soviet snipers were just as eagerly involved and as good if not better than the Germans, perhaps claiming as many if not more kills. Temperatures hovered just above freezing, while scattered thunderstorms and rain showers added to the gloomy atmosphere that day. Soldiers in the front lines would not have known, nor would have particularly cared if they did hear the news, that at midnight they would become part of *2. Armee*. All that mattered to them was that they were able to keep warm and dry, and that their *Haufen* (heap or group of friends) survived the next round of fighting.

At midnight on 25 November, *IV. SS-Pz.Korps* officially became part of *2. Armee* once again. To mark the occasion, von Lüttwitz issued an order thanking Gille and his troops. His order was read out to the troops as follows:

> Commanding General, *9. Armee*
>
> To the men of the IV. SS-Pz.Korps:
>
> On 26 November 1944, after nearly four months of assignment to the *9. Armee*, you will be departing from my command. With pride and satisfaction the *9. Armee* looks back upon this time in which the *IV. SS-Pz.Korps* under the always-steady leadership of your commanding general, *SS-Obergruppenführer und General der Waffen-SS* Gille, has again brought glory and honor upon your banners. As exemplary comrades in arms, the SS divisions and the divisions of the German and Hungarian armies under his command repeatedly broke the onslaught of an overwhelmingly superior enemy force in three heavy defensive battles east and north of Warsaw The *3. SS-Pz.Div. "Totenkopf"* and the *5. SS-Pz.Div. "Wiking"* can both rightfully claim their share in these successes. With my appreciation and gratitude for your brilliant feats of arms, I extend my warmest wishes for the future of the *IV. SS-Panzerkorps*. Our fight continues until the end!
>
> Heil Hitler!
>
> Signed, *Gen.d.Pz.Tr.* von Lüttwitz

Von Lüttwitz did not exaggerate the corps' accomplishments. It had indeed done all of those things and more, almost always at a numerical disadvantage and in highly fluid tactical situations where individual initiative at the lowest levels of leadership, a high standard of training, trust in their weapons and in each other, and above all, their legendary "SS spirit" had seen them through.

During each of the battles the corps fought, including the tank battle of Praga, the three defensive battles of Warsaw and the siege of Modlin, Gille's men had kept their unit integrity and had prevented major breakthroughs. Though they had been forced to give up ground, they prevented a crossing of the Vistula, which, had this happened, would have threatened the integrity of the entire Eastern Front. By any military standard, the corps had succeeded in all of its missions. Not only had it blocked the road to Warsaw and bought time while additional forces could be assembled, it had fought to a standstill numerically superior enemy forces led by one of their most skilled practitioners of the operational art.

This achievement had come at a considerable cost. Since joining the *9. Armee* at the beginning of August 1944, the two SS *panzer* divisions had lost an incredible combined total of 15,398 men, of whom 2,592 were killed in action, 10,827 were wounded, and another 1,979 listed as missing in action. During August and September, neither division had received any replacements, except for a small infusion of Ukrainian volunteers at the end of September. The bloodbath of October was unprecedented, with the divisions losing over 6,171 men. Though the records of the corps headquarters and corps troops are incomplete, they indicate that at least 86 members of the *Waffen-SS* were killed, wounded, or listed as missing. Losses of attached *Heerestruppen* are not available, though they must have been proportionally as great. Losses on this scale cannot be sustained for very long, and indeed the heaviest losses were of experienced junior officers and NCOs, who were responsible for the successes of myriad individual platoon- and company-level actions.

These men were well-nigh irreplaceable. They had progressed through the various stages of the *Waffen-SS* training and replacement system since the late 1930s and had gained, through several years of combat, the necessary experience and knowledge required to not only succeed in their mission, but to keep as many of their men alive as possible. The nearly 10,000 *Luftwaffe* replacements the *Totenkopf* and *Wiking* Divisions received in October and November, although creating the illusion of strength, merely watered down the quality of the replacements that had been received up to that point, not only because these men from the oft-mocked *Hermann-Göring-Spende* had no ground combat experience worth mentioning, but they lacked the fundamental "SS spirit" that had been inculcated in *Waffen-SS* recruits since the mid-1930s.

Now, 12 years later, these new recruits lacked the fundamental *Härte* (hardness) needed to mentally cope with the extreme conditions prevailing on the Eastern Front, especially during the period of the war when it was evident that Germany was losing the conflict. The old "SS spirit," as well as their belief that they were an elite military force, had sustained the more senior men who had seen conditions just as bad or worse. But this spirit was lacking in the new recruits, who, despite the veterans' best efforts, soon demonstrated that they were not up to the challenge of waging intense and bitter battles against a remorseless and unrelenting enemy. Though the first signs of what could be called a "rot" in the quality of the average SS man had begun to appear during November 1944, this phenomenon would manifest itself in a far more serious manner four months later when the Eastern Front began to collapse.

But at the end of November 1944, all things still seemed possible. The corps was safely behind a formidable defensive barrier that their powerful enemy had not yet been able to breach. Supplies were still sufficient and enough weapons were on hand, save for new tanks to replace the older ones which had been lost during the past four months. Their artillery had performed magnificently, repeatedly proving its ability to throw up a protective steel curtain in front of the infantry's positions, halting many a determined Soviet ground assault. Their battalion, regimental, and division commanders, and above all their corps commander, were men of proven worth, calm in crises, and tactically savvy.

New recruits were flowing into their shattered ranks, and a few weeks of careful instruction by veteran corporals—the legendary *Reichs-Rottenführer*—during the next two months of relative calm would do much to restore the *esprit de corps* and combat power of their divisions.[19] Just as importantly, commanders at all levels who valued their men's lives did what they could during this rebuilding period to prevent them from being needlessly sacrificed. Some of the veterans even received up to two weeks of home leave, especially those who had gone a year or more without seeing their loved ones. Other veterans began returning from hospitals, eager to get back to their squads or platoons to rejoin their old gang. Sadly, on too many occasions they would find only a few of the familiar faces. Much had changed since the corps had been activated and sent into action at the end of July 1944, but many more changes still lay ahead. But on 26 November, there was still room for hope. Perhaps *der Führer* could still perform a magic trick and restore Germany's fortunes after all.

APPENDIX A

Command and Staff (August 1943–May 1945)

Commanders: *SS-Ogruf. und Generalleutnant der Waffen-SS und Polizei* Alfred Wünnenberg, *SS-Ogruf. und Generalleutnant der Waffen-SS* Matthias Kleinheisterkamp, *SS-Ogruf. und Generalleutnant der Waffen-SS* Herbert Otto Gille

O5 (*Begleitoffizier*): *SS-Ostuf.* Günther Lange

Chef des Stabes: SS-Ostubaf. Peter Sommer, *SS-Oberfüher* Nikolaus Heilmann, *SS-Ostubaf.* Manfred Schönfelder

O6 (*6. Ordonnanz Offizier*): *SS-Ustuf.* Joachim Barthel

Tactical Group (*Führungsabteilung*)

Ia (*1.GenStabsOffz.*): *SS-Stubaf.* Richard Pauly (acting), *SS-Hstuf.* Werner Westphal (acting), *SS-Stubaf.* Wilhelm Klose, *SS-Stubaf.* Fritz Rentrop (captured after being wounded in action, died or executed by Soviets 2 February 1945), *SS-Stubaf.* Friedrich Rauch

O1 (*1. Ordonnanz Offizier*): *SS-Hstuf.* Werner Hartmann, *SS-Hstuf.* Werner Westphal (acting), *SS-Hstuf.* Heinrich Fockenbreck, *SS-Hstuf.* Hans Velde

Ia (*Mess*): *SS-Ostuf.* Karl Tönnies

Id (*Offizier für Verkehrsregelung*): *SS-Ostubaf.* Wilhelm Honsell

Ic (*3. GenStabsOffz.*): *SS-Hstuf.* Werner Reimer, *SS-Stubaf.* Herbert Jankuhn, *SS-Hstuf.* Werner Müthel-Patzig

O3 (*Gehilfe des Ic*): *SS-Ostuf.* Ludwig Fuchs

Ic Dolmetcher (Translator): *SS-Ostuf.* Heinz Maus

O4 (*4. Ordonnanz Offizier*): *SS-Ostuf.* Fritz Grond

Korps Pionier-Führer: *SS-Stubaf.* Erich May; *SS-Ostubaf.* Fritz Braune

Korps-Nachrichten-Führer: *SS-Hstuf.* Martin Müller, then *SS-Stubaf.* Karl Krüger (until February 1945); *SS-Stubaf.* Hubert Hüppe

Korps-Kartenstelle 104: *SS-Ostuf.* Karl Tönnies

Wehrgeologen-Einsatzzug 104: Unknown

Korps-Gasabwehroffizier (*Gabo*): *SS-Stubaf.* Hermann Baldauf

Supply and Administrative Group (*Quartiermeisterabteilung und Intendantur*)

Ib Quartiermeister (*2. GenStabsOffz.*): *SS-Ostubaf.* Hans Scharff

O2 (*Gehilfe des Ib*): *SS-Hstuf.* Otto Bauman

Korps-Nachschubführer: *SS-Ostubaf.* Christian Steinmetz, *SS-Ostubaf.* Wilhelm Honsell

WaMun (*Korps-Feldzeug-Offizier*): *SS-Stubaf.* Erich Olbrück, *SS-Stubaf.* Walter Schmiedecke

IVa (*Korpsintendant*): *SS-Ostubaf.* Erwin Tschentscher, *SS-Ostubaf.* Rudolf Klotz

IVb (*Korpsarzt*): *SS-Oberführer* Dr. Bruno Rothardt, *SS-Stubaf.* Dr. Walter Weyand (m.d.F.b.)

IVc (*Veterinär*): *SS-Ostubaf.* Dr. Heinrich Wich

IVd (*Zahnarzt*): *SS-Stubaf.* Dr. Paul Reutter

IVz (*Zahlmeister*): *SS-Ostuf.* Heinz Grashorn

Korps Apotheker: *SS-Ostubaf.* Hans-Joachim Loennies

V Korps-Ing./TFK (motor transport): *SS-Stubaf.* Waldermar Krüger, *SS-Stubaf.* Otto Brandt, *SS-Ostubaf.* Paul Barnekow, *SS-Ostubaf.* Friedrich Schuster, *SS-Feldpostamt 104*: *SS-Ostuf.* Ludwig Viktor

Personnel (*Adjutantur*) Group

IIa: SS-Ostubaf. Dr. Walter Schneevoigt, *Stubaf.* Karl-Willy Schulze

IIb: SS-Ostuf. Fritz Kramer, *SS-Ostuf.* Wilhelm Burkhardt

III (*Korpsrichter*): *SS-Stubaf.* Hans Heinz

VI (*NSFO*): *SS-Stubaf.* Adolf Kleffel, *SS-Hstuf.* Dr. Franz Wehofsich, *Kriegsberichter Mitarbeiter: SS-Ustuf.* Kristian Zarp

Corps Headquarters Troops

Kommando des Hauptquartier: *SS-Stubaf.* Hans Kasten (acting), *SS-Hstuf.* Ferdinand Zachmann

SS-Nachr.Abt. 104: *SS-Stubaf.* Georg Janensch, *SS-Stubaf.* Karl Krüger; *SS-Stubaf.* Hubert Hüppe

SS-Fla.Kp. 104: *SS-Ostuf.* Adolf Eberhard, *SS-Ostubaf.* Wilhelm Fuhrländer (*SS-Fla.-Abt. 104/504*)

Kommandeur der Korps-Nachschubtruppen: *SS-Ostubaf.* Otto Wagenknecht, *SS-Ostubaf.* Christian Steinmetz, *SS-Ostubaf.* Wilhelm Honsell

SS-Kraftfahr-Kp. 1./104: *SS-Hstuf.* Erich Dielmann

SS-Kraftfahr-Kp. 2./104 (*1. und 2. Züge*): Unknown

SS-Kfz.-Instandsetzungs-Zug 104: *SS-Ustuf.* Walter Glöckler

SS-Bekleidungs-Instandsetzungs-Kp. 104/504: *SS-Hstuf.* Alfred Häusser, *SS-Ostuf.* Aloys Thome

SS-Sicherungs-Kompanie 104: Unknown

SS-Feldgendarmerie-Trupp 104: *SS-Hstuf.* Kurt Schliep

Corps (*later Army*) Troops:

SS-ARKO 104/504: *SS-Brigadeführer* Peter Hansen, *SS-Brigadeführer* Kurt Brasack, *Oberst* (*Heer*) Klucke (March 1945)

Adjutant: *SS-Ostuf.* Richard Postier

schwere-SS-Artillerie-Abteilung 104/504: *SS-Stubaf.* Alfred Neuwirth, *SS-Ostubaf.* Wilhelm Leppert

SS-Werfer-Abteilung 104/504: *SS-Hstuf.* Otto Krosta

SS-Beobachtungs-Batterie 104/504: *SS-Hstuf.* Ernst Schandara, *SS-Ostuf.* Peter Ostwaldt

SS-Santitäts-Abteilung 104/504: *SS-Stubaf.* Dr. Fedor Sibeth, *SS-Stubaf.* Dr. Walter Weyand

SS-Feldlazarett 104/504: *SS-Ostubaf.* Dr. Peter Metzmacher, *SS-Stubaf.* Wilhelm Giese

SS-Pz.Korps Santitäts-Kompanie 104/504: *SS-Stubaf.* Fritz Polzer

SS-Pz.Korps. Kr.Kw.Zug 104/504: Unknown

APPENDIX B

IV. SS-Pz.Korps Battle and Campaign Participation Credits awarded for the period 27 July 1944 to 8 May 1945

2. Armee (*Generaloberst* Walter Weiss) 27 July–5 August 1944

Defence and withdrawal battles during the Russian summer offensive between the Pripyat and Bug Rivers, 22 June 1944–10 August 1944, including evacuation of Brest-Litovsk, 28 July 1944

IV. SS-Pz.Korps:

Counterattack in the area of Stanislavov and Radzymin, 28 July–12 August 1944

9. Armee (*General der Panzertruppe* Nikolaus von Vormann, *Gen.d.Pz.Tr.* Smilo Freiherr von Lüttwitz) 6 August–25 November 1944

Battles along the Vistula River in the Warsaw area, 27 July 1944–16 September 1944, including suppression of the Warsaw Uprising, 1 August 1944–2 October 1944

Positional warfare along the Vistula River and the bridgehead of Warka, 17 September 1944–12 January 1945

***IV. SS-Pz.Korps*:**

1st defensive battle for Warsaw (east of Radzymin), 13–30 August 1944
2nd defensive battle for Warsaw (at Zegrce), 31 August–9 October 1944
3rd defensive battle for Warsaw (at Nieporet-Serock), 10–28 October 1944
Defensive battles east of Modlin, 29 October–25 November 1944

2. Armee (*Generaloberst* Walter Weiss) 25 November–24 December 1944

***IV. SS-Pz.Korps*:**

Defensive battles east of Modlin, 25 November–24 December 1944

6. Armee (*General der Panzertruppe* Hermann Balck) 31 December 1944–8 May 1945

Battles between the Plattensee (Lake Balaton) and Danube River, 19 December 1944–5 March 1945, including defence of Budapest, 24 December 1944–12 February 1945

Tank battle on the Hungarian Plain at Stuhlweissenberg (Székesfehérvár), 6 March 1945–23 March 1945

Defensive and Withdrawal Battles south of the Danube to the eastern Alps 24 March–8 May 1945

***VI. SS-Pz.Korps*:**

1st relief attack of Budapests (Biseke and Pilis Mountains), 1–13 January 1945

Movement to Vesprem area and 2nd relief attack of Budapest, 14–27 January 1945 (advance to the Danube)

Withdrawal battles south of Stuhlweissenburg, 28 January–22 February 1945

Battle of Stuhlweissenburg, 23 February–15 March 1945

Withdrawal battles towards the *Reichsschutzstellung* and south of Fürstenfeld, 16–21 March 1945

Capitulation of the *Wehrmacht*, 8 May 1945

APPENDIX C

Selected Orders of Battle

10 September 1944: Second defensive battle of Warsaw

Divisions

3. SS-Panzer-Division Totenkopf
5. SS-Panzer-Division Wiking
Gren.Rgt. 1145
SS-Jäg.Btl. 500
Gren.Btl.z.b.V. 560
Fest.Inf.Btl. 1405
73. Infanterie-Division
2./Pz.Zerst.Btl. 475
Kgl. 1. ungarische Kavallerie-Division

Corps/Army TroopsT

Sturmbataillon AOK 9
Pz.Jag.Abt. 745
Pz.Zerst.Btl. 475
Fest.Pak-Kp. 2/VI
Fest.-Pak Kp. 4./II
Fest.M.G.Btl. 23
Fest.Pio.Btl. 9
Fest.Pio.Btl. 421
2./ and *4./Fest.Pio.Btl. 737*
2./Fest.Pio.Ausb.Btl. 5
Eisenbahn Panzerzug-Rgt. 1
Einsatz-Bttr./Beob.Abt. 1
schw.Art.Abt. (mot.) 154
II./ and *IV. Abt., Stellungs-Werfer-Rgt. 102*
5./II, 1./VI, 2./VI. and *4./II. Fest.Flak-Kp*

10 October 1944: Third defensive battle of Warsaw

Divisions

19. Panzer-Division
Fallschimr-Panzer-Division Hermann Göring
3. SS-Panzer-Division Totenkopf
5. SS-Panzer-Division Wiking
Kgl. 1. ungarische Kavallerie-Division

Corps/Army Troops

Beobachtungs-Abteilung 21
schwere-Heeres-Artillerie Abteilung 154
schwere-Heeres-Artillerie Abteilung 732
schwere-Heeres-Artillerie Abteilung 767
IV.Abt./Stellungs-Werfer Regiment 102
SS-Werfer-Abteilung 104
SS-Korps-Nachrichten-Abteilung 104
SS-Sanitäts-Abteilung 104
Kraftfahrzeug-Kompanie 104
Bekleidung-Instandsetzungs-Zug 504
SS-Feldpostamt 104

6 November 1944

Divisions

5. SS-Panzer-Division Wiking
3. SS-Panzer-Division Totenkopf

Corps Troops

Korps-Nachrichten-Abteilung 104
Korps-Kartenstelle 104
Feldgendarmerie-Trupp 104
Korps-Nachschubtruppen 104

Army Troops

SS-ARKO 504
Beobachtungs-Abteilung 21
schwere Artillerie-Abteilung 154
Stab und I./Stellungs-Werfer-Regiment 103
IV./Stellungs-Werfer-Regiment 102
SS-Werfer-Abteilung 504

Infanterie-Bataillon z.b.V. 560
Feldstrafgefangenen-Abteilung 1
Bau-Pionier-Bataillon 9
Pionier-Horchzug 5
Bau-Kompanie 901 (Ls)
Bau-Kompanie 902 (Ls)
Bau-Kompanie 903 (Ls)
Sicherungs-Bataillon 350
Panzerzug 30 (einsatzmäßig AOK 9 unterstellt)
Panzerzug (Lehr) 5 (Einsatzmäßig AOK 9 unterstellt)

APPENDIX D

German Army, *Waffen-SS* and U.S. Army Rank Equivalents

Wehrmacht-Heer	*Waffen-SS*	Abbreviation	U.S. Equivalent
Generalfeldmarschall	N/A	*G.F.M.*	General of the Army
Generaloberst	*SS-Obergruppenführer und Generaloberst der Waffen-SS*	*Gen.O./Obstgruf.*	General
General der Infantrie, Kavalerie, etc.	*SS-Obergruppenführer und General der Waffen-SS*	*Gen.d.Inf./Ogruf.*	Lieutenant General
Generalleutnant	*SS-Gruppenführer und Generalleutnant der Waffen-SS*	*Gen.Lt./Gruf.*	Major General
Generalmajor	*SS-Brigadeführer und Generalmajor der Waffen-SS*	*Gen.Maj./Brig. Fhr.*	Brigadier General
Oberst	*SS-Oberführer*	None/*Obf.*	Senior Colonel
Oberst	*SS-Standartenführer*	*O./Staf.*	Colonel
Oberstleutnant	*SS-Obersturmbann-führer*	*Oberstlt./Ostubaf.*	Lieutenant Colonel
Major	*SS-Sturmbannführer*	*Maj./Stubaf.*	Major
Hauptmann or *Rittmeister*	*SS-Hauptsturmführer*	*Hptm./Hstuf.*	Captain

Oberleutnant	*SS-Obersturmführer*	*Oberlt./Ostuf.*	First Lieutenant
Leutnant	*SS-Untersturmführer*	*Lt./Ustuf.*	Second Lieutenant
Stabsfeldwebel	*SS-Sturmscharführer*	*Stabs Fw.*/none	Sergeant Major
Oberfeldwebel	*SS-Hauptscharführer*	*Ofw./Hscha.*	Master Sergeant
Feldwebel	*SS-Oberscharführer*	*Fw./Oscha.*	Sergeant First Class
Unteroffizier	*SS-Unterscharführer*	*Uffz./Uscha.*	Staff Sergeant
Obergefreiter	*SS-Rottenführer*	*Ogefr./Rttf.*	Coporal/Specialist
Gefreiter	*SS-Sturmann*	*Gef./Strm.*	Private First Class
Obergrenadier, Oberkannonier, etc.	*SS-Obergrenadier,* etc.	none	Private Second Class
Grenadier, Kanonier, Funker, etc.	*SS-Grenadier,* etc.	none	Private

APPENDIX E

German Corps Staff Positions and U.S. Army Equivalents

The following comparison of German World War II Corps staff positions and their equivalent U.S. Army staff positions has been included in order to compare and contrast how they paralleled one another in function and how they diverged from one another in certain cases.

German Staff Position	**U.S. Army Equivalent**
Chef des Generalstabes	Chief of Staff
Operations Section	
Ia (*1. Generalstabsoffizier* or 1st General Staff Officer)	G-3
O1 (*1. Ordonnanz Offizier*)	Deputy G-3
Ia F (*Fliegerverbindungsoffizier* or *Flivo*)	Assistant G-3 (Air)
Ia Korps Pionier-Führer (*Pi.Fhr*)	Corps Engineer
Ic (*3. Generalstabsoffizier*)	G-2
Ic AO (*Abwehroffizier*)	G-2 Counterintelligence
O3 (*3. Ordonnanzoffizier*/*Gehilfe des Ic*)	Assistant G-2
O4 (*4. Ordonnanzoffizier*/*Gehilfe des Ic*)	Assistant G-2
Supply and Administrative Section	
Ib or *Qu.1* (*2. Generalstabsoffizier* or *Quartiermeister*)	G-4
Qu 2 (*Korps-Nachschubführer*/*Offizier für Verkehrsregelung*)	Deputy G-4/Supply Services Administration

O2 (*3. Ordonnanzoffizier/Gehilfe des Ib*)	Assistant G-4
Wa-Mun (*Waffen und Munitions Offizier*)	Assistant G-4/Ammunition Supply Officer
IVa (*Korpsintendant*)	Corps Headquarters Supply and Services Officer/Deputy Adjutant General
IVb (*Korpsarzt*)	Corps Surgeon
IVb (*Korpszahnarzt*)	Corps Dental Section
IVc (*Korpsveterinär*)	Corps Veterinary Section
V (*Korps-Ingeneur/Technischer Führer für das Kraftfahrwesen or TFK*)	G-4 Maintenance Officer
Feldpostamt	G-1 Adjutant General Section

Adjutant Section

IIa (*Adjutant*)	G-1 (Officer Records)
IIb	Deputy G-1 (Enlisted Records)
III (*Korpsrichter*)	Judge Advocate
Kommando des Hauptquartier (*Kdo d. HQu.*)	Headquarters Commandant

APPENDIX F

Glossary

Abteilung (*Abt.*): Literally, detachment. A German unit of company size or greater, though normally of battalion size. Traditionally used to designate artillery, armor, or reconnaissance battalions.

Abteilungsartzt: Unit physician or medical doctor.

Armeekorps (*AK*): German Infantry Corps consisting of two or more divisions.

Armee-Oberkommando (*AOK*): Army Headquarters, under which several *Armeekorps* or division might operate.

Auffrischung: Reconstitution, a weeks-long process wherein a unit that has been destroyed or in combat for a prolonged period of time needs to be pulled out of the line and rebuilt in a rest area behind the front lines, including the absorbtion of replacement personnel, weapons, and equipment.

Aufklärungsabteilung (*Aufkl.Abt.*): Reconnaissance Battalion.

Ausbildung: Training, including individual and unit level. Normally carried out when not in combat.

Ausführung (*Ausf.*): Model, or type. Used to designate a particular version of a vehicle or weapon.

Befehlshaber: Army or army group commander.

Befehlspanzer: Command tank, equipped with necessary radio equipment to command and control armored formations and to communicate with adjacent and higher units.

Bergepanther: Tank recovery vehicle build on the chassis of *Pz. V* Panther

Berichtszeit: Reporting time stated for morning, midday, and daily reports.

Bewährungsbataillon: A probationary unit, consisting of soldiers convicted of non-capital offenses and reduced in rank that have been given an opportunity to "redeem" their honor by serving as a front-line infantryman. Considered to be "*wehrwürdig*" (worthy of bearing arms) and not to be confused with *Straf* (Penal) units.

Einsatzbereit: Operational, especially in regards to armor vehicles, meaning that the vehicle is fully capable of shooting, driving, and communicating.

Ersatzheer: The Replacement, or Home Army, responsible for training replacements and sustaining the forces of the Field Army (*Feldheer*) fighting on the various fronts.

Fahrer: Vehicle driver; implies that the soldier also maintains the vehicle.

Fahrzeug und Motorenbau GmbH (*FAMO*): German automobile and truck manufacturer famous for their production of the enormous half-track prime mover, the 18-ton *Sd.Kfz. 9*.

Fallschirmjäger: Paratrooper.

Fallschirm-Panzerkorps Parachute *Panzer* Corps.

Feldausbildungs: Designation of a training unit located in close proximity to the front lines established to provide advanced individual training or reclassification training for soldiers from other branches of the *Wehrmacht* being transferred to ground combat branches, such as the infantry.

Feldgendarmerie: Field police. Normally tasked with traffic regulation, also serve a disciplinary role or assisting a division's intelligence staff with counterespionage work.

Feldlazarett: Field hospital.

Fernschreiben: Message sent via *Hellschreiber* or teletype.

Flakvierling: four-barreled 20mm *Flak*

Fliegerabwehrkanonone (*FlaK*): Any kind of German antiaircraft gun.

Fliegerverbindungsoffizier (*Flivo*): *Luftwaffe* officer, usually a qualified pilot, assigned or attached to a ground unit to coordinate the employment of air assets in support of combat operations.

Freiwilligen: Volunteer; pertains especially to the *Waffen-SS* or foreign units serving under the German banner.

Frontleitstelle: Office set up near railroad stations or in populated areas to greet, receive, and forward troops to their units in the *Kampfraum*.

Frontschwein: Literally "front-line pig." Slang for veterans who had survived serving in the front lines.

Führungsabteilung: The operations and intelligence staff of a German brigade-level unit or higher, usually consisting of the *Ia* (Operations) and *Ic* (Intelligence) officers and their assistants.

Gefechtstand: Command post, usually located closer to the front than a *Hauptquartier*.

Gefechtsvorposten: Screen line, or forward line of troops who serve as an early warning to spot or delay an approaching enemy. Usually designates a thin line of troops who are required to fall back into the main defense line upon contact with the enemy.

Gruppe: Group; in an infantry company, usually denotes a rifle squad.

Hauptquartier: Headquarters; may denote the headquarters company of a divison, corps, or field army.

Heer: German Army.

Heeresgruppe (*H.Gr.*): Army Group.

Heeres-Drückvorschrift: Army regulation published and disseminated throughout the *Wehrmacht-Heer* and *Waffen-SS*.

Heeresrüstungsamt: The ordnance department of the German Army that was responsible for managing the provision of weapons and equipment, including armored vehicles, for the field forces.

Infanterie-Division (*Inf.Div.*, or *I.D.*): German Army infantry division.

Jagdpanzer: Special tank destroying mounting a large caliber antitank gun built on a tank chassis, such as the Czech 38t or *Pz. IV.*

Jäger: *Luftwaffe* designation of their ground combat infantry.

Kampfgruppe (*K.Gr.*): A temporary ad hoc organization, which may be anything from a company to an army group in size plus attached troops, normally identified by its commander's name.

Kampfraum: Opertional area, combat area, or combat zone.

Kampfstärke: Combat strength, used as a means to measure the combat power of an infantry, mechanized, or armored division, focusing on the number of ground troops serving in the front line, specifically infantry, combat engineer, and reconnaissance troops.

Karabiner: Carbine.

Kommandeur: Unit commander, designated by official orders confirming an officer in that position, as opposed to being in an acting command capacity.

Kraftfahrzeug (*Kfz.*): Any German motor vehicle, except armor.

Kraftrad (*Krad*): Motorcycle.

Kriegsberichter (*KB*): War correspondent.

Kriegsmarine: German Navy.

Kriegsstärkenachweisung (*K.St.N.*): War Strength Inventory Directive, a document similar to the modern U.S. Army's table of organization that describes an organization's structure and lists the total number of personnel and major end items authorized.

Kübelwagen: Literally "bucket car."Slang term for Volkswagen equivalent of U.S. Jeep.

Landeschützen-Bataillon (*Ldsch.Btl.*): German local defense battalion, formed from older reservist.Often used for local security duties in the occupied regions or during emergencies as front-line infantry.

Landser: German slang for infantryman.

Luftflotte: Air Fleet, *Luftwaffe* administrative headquarters similar in function to an army headquarters, or *Armee-Oberkommando* (AOK).

Luftwaffe: German Air Force.

Mannschaften: Enlisted men.

Marder: Self-propelled antitank gun, usually mounted on an obsolete tank chassis such as a *Pz. II* or Czech 38t.

MP-40: *Maschinepistole 40*; German automatic 9mm machine pistol designed for use by assault troops.

MP-44: *Maschinepistole 44*; German 7.92mm assault rifle capable of semiautomatic and full automatic fire; also known as the *Sutrmgewehr* (assault rifle) Stg. 1944.

Nebelwerfer: "Smoke launcher" or mobile rocket launcher firing high-explosive projectiles ranging in size from 15cm to 32cm; had a distinctive moaning sound when fired, giving rise to the nickname "moaning minnies."

Ordnungspolizei: Order Police; paramilitary police force, frequently organized into battalions and regiments operating under the auspices of the SS, frequently used for rear-area security duties as well as for combatting partisans.

Pakfront: German term for an integrated Red Army antitank gun defense, usually consisting of multiple antitank gun units, employing everything up to and including the 8.5cm gun.

Panzer Korps (*Pz.Korps*): German tank corps headquarters, capable of controlling two to four tank, armored infantry, or infantry divisions as well as various corps troops, such as artillery, engineer, antiaircraft, and antitank battalions or regiments.

Panzerfaust: A recoilless antitank grenade launcher designed to be used against armor at ranges from 25–100 meters.It consisted of a steel launching tube, which contained a percussion-fired propellant charge, and a hollow-charge antitank grenade mounted at the end. Could penetrate up to 152mm of rolled steel plate.

Panzergrenadier (*Pz.Gren.*): Armored or mechanized infantryman.

Panzergruppe (*Pz.Gr.*): Armored group, could range in size from battalion to field army.

Panzerkampfwagen (*Pz.Kfw.*): Armored battle vehicle, or tank, called *Panzer* for short.

Panzerabwehrkanone (*PaK*): Antitank gun.

Panzerjäger: Antitank troops.

Panzerkorps (*Pz.Korps*): Armored corps, controlling two or more divisions of various types, though primarily trained and equipped to control armored divisions or *Panzergrenadier* divisions.

Rollbahn: "Trunk road" or main supply route for divisions and higher.

Raketenpanzerbüchse: A rocket-propelled antitank launcher, better known as the *Panzerschreck* ("Tank Terror"). Its 8.8cm rocket was extremely effective against all types of Allied armor.

Ritterkreuz: Knight's Cross of the Iron Cross. The highest class of the Iron Cross and the most prized of the German World War II military decorations.

Sanitäter: Medic or corpsman.

Schützenpanzerwagen (*SPW*): Armored Personnel Carrier of the *Sd.Kfz.* 250 or 251 type.

Schwere Panzerabteilung (*s.Pz.Abt.*): Heavy tank battalion, usually equipped with *Pz. VI* Tiger tanks.

Schwerpunkt: German term of the military art that designates where the point of main effort is for any given operation, whether offensive or defensive.

Schwimmwagen: Amphibious version of the Volkswagen.

Sicherheitsdienst (*SD*): Security Service of the SS; charged with combating espionage.

Sicherungs-Regiment (*Sich.Rgt.*): Line of communications security regiment, often consisted of older *Landes-Schüzten* personnel. Often committed to front-line combat when situations dictated.

Sonderkraftfahrzeuge (*Sd.Kfz.*): Special purpose vehicle, such as tanks, half-tracks, or recovering vehicles.

Sperrverbände: Blocking formations, established for the purpose of barring or blocking important roads or highways to prevent breakthroughs by enemy mobile formations. Normally formed using *Bau-Pionier* (construction engineers) or *Pioniere* with explosives, barrier materials, and antitank weapons.

SS-Führungshauptamt (*SS-FHA*): The main leadership office of the SS, responsible for coordinating the manning, equipping, and training of SS units, including the *Waffen-SS*.

Stammlager (*Stalag*): Collection Camp; type of German prisoner of war camp.

Stielhandgranate: German designation of their stick grenade, the *Stielhandgranate* 24, which held ⅓lb of TNT.

Strafbataillon: Punishment battalion, usually consisting of men who have been charged with non-capital offenses and have been sent to one of these units to serve out their term of punishment, usually near the front lines and in conditions that are considered extremely hazardous. Survivors are usually restored to their previous ranks or may be posted to a *Bewährungsbataillon* (see above) for further rehabilitation.

Stuka: Short for *Sturzkampfflugzeug*, or dive-bomber. Generally refers to the Junkers Ju-87.

Sturmabteilungen (*SA*): Paramilitary arm of the Nazi Party which propelled Hitler to power. Its influence was severely reduced when it attempted to compete with the SS.

Sturmgeschütz (*StuG*): Armored assault gun specifically built to provide close-in infantry support using its 7.5cm or 10.5cm howitzer.Normally built on a *Pz. III* or *IV* chassis, they were at a disadvantage when fighting tanks in open terrain due to their lack of a rotating turret, but were formidable when employed in built-up areas or as a tank destroyer firing from hidden positions.

Totenköpfler: Informal term of endearment relating to the men of the *Totenkopf* Division.

Tross: The "Trains" where a unit's logistical and administrative units were located, from company to regimental level.

Volksgrenadier: Honorific title of an infantryman or the divisions formed during September 1944 under a new infantry division structure designed to economize on manpower by adding additional weaponry, such as more heavy weapons and the MP-44 *Sturmgewehr*.

Waffen-SS: Combat arm of Heinrich Himmler's SS.

Waffenwillig (*Wawis*): Term used to describe foreign "volunteers" who were willing to take up arms and fight alongside German forces.

Wehrkreis: Defense District, geographically designated areas in Germany and occupied areas of Europe that were designed to serve as the *Ersatzheer* (Home Army) base for the generation and constitution of forces for the *Feldheer* (Field Army), as well as to serve as the headquarters for controlling the various local security forces and POW camps in the zone of the interior.

Wehrmacht: The German Armed Forces, which included the *Heer*, *Luftwaffe*, and *Kriegsmarine*. Technically, the *Waffen-SS* was not a part of the *Wehrmacht*.

Wehrmachtbefehlshaber: Commander of the German Armed Forces in a geographic area; technically, had control over all three branches of the *Wehrmacht* but not the *Waffen-SS*.

Zeltbahn: German triangular-shaped camouflaged poncho, used as a rain cape, personal camouflage covering, or (when buttoned together with three others) a tent.

Zugführer: Platoon leader, usually a senior NCO.

Zugkraftwagen (*ZgKw*): Artillery prime mover.

Endnotes

Foreword

1 Three *Waffen-SS* officers were allowed to "observe" one of the *Kriegsakademie*'s general staff courses in 1940, though they did not formally complete training and were not awarded the title of *Generalstab* or General Staff Officer.
2 Order, dated 5 January 1945, issued by the *Kriegsarchiv* of the *Waffen-SS*.

Chapter 1: Activation of *IV. SS-Pz.Korps*

1 SS-Führungshauptamt, Amt V, Ha/Az. 21c 12.7.1943/Sa/W, Geheim, Tagesbefehl Nr II/5.745/43 von 3. August, mit Stand vom 31.7.1943.
2 Hausser's *SS Panzerkorps* would be renamed *II. SS-Panzerkorps* in June 1943 (Tessin, Vol. 2, p. 97).
3 Franz Husemann. *Die guten Glaubens waren*, Band II. (Osnabrück: Munin Verlag GmbH, 1977), pp. 207–08.
4 Hans Stöber. *Die lettischen Divisionen im VI. SS-Armeekorps*. (Osnabrück: Munin Verlag GmbH, 1981), p. 235.
5 *Oberkommando der Wehrmacht, Kriegsstärkenachweisung (Heer) Nr. 15: Generalkommmando (mot.)*, 1 March 1942.
6 In the late fall of 1944, a Corps Veterinarian, *SS-Staf.* Heinrich Wich, was finally assigned because so many attached *Heerestruppen* by that point of the war were horse-drawn.
7 *SS-Führungshauptamt, Org.Tgb.Nr. 1051/43 g.Kdos. Betr.: Aufstellung des Gen.Kdo.IV.SS-Pz.Korps mit 2 Anlagen, 5. Aug. 1943.*
8 Roger James Bender and Hugh Page Taylor. *Uniforms, Organization and History of the Waffen-SS*, Vol. 2. (San Jose: Bender Publishing, Inc. 1971), p. 40.
9 Wolfgang Vopersal. *Soldaten, Kampfer, Kameraden. Marsch und Kämpfe der SS-Totenkopf Division*, Vol. Va (Bielefeld, Germany: Selbstverlag der Truppenkameradschaft der 3. SS-Pz.Div. e.V., 1991), p. 116.
10 *SS-Führungshauptamt, Amt II/Org.Abt. 1E/IV(1), Tgb.Nr. 696/44 gKdos. 15 März 1944 Betr.: Monatliche Ist-Stärkemeldung an den Reichsfuehrer-SS.*
11 Shortly after being renamed and activated, *10. SS-Pz.Div.* was administratively transferred from *IV. SS-Pz.Korps* to *VII. SS-Pz.Korps*, since the former headquarters had been stripped of most of its staff in mid-October.
12 Vopersal, p. 116.
13 Taylor and Bender, p. 41.
14 John P. Moore. *Führerliste der Waffen-SS: Personalakten*, Vol. 3. (Portland: Self-published, 2003), Matthias Kleinheisterkamp file.
15 *Anlage zu Kdo.Stb. Reichsführer-SS, Tgb.Nr. Ia II 236/44 Betr. Personelle Lage, Gen.Kdo. IV.SS-Pz. Korps, 1. Juli 1944.*

16 Moore, Vol. 3, Nicolaus Heilmann file.

17 *Anlage 1 zu SS-FHA/Id(III) Nr. 2319/44 g.Kdos. vom 1 Aug. 1944 Betr: Generalstabsstellenbesesetzung in der Waffen-SS and Hans-Georg Model, Der deutsche Generalstabsoffizier* (Frankfurt: Bernard & Graefe Verlag für Wehrwesen, 1968), p. 253.

18 *SS-FHA Amt II Org.Abt.Ia/II g.Kdos. vom 30 Juni 1944, Betr.: Gen.Kdos. IV. und VII. SS-Pz.Korps.*

19 Vopersal, Vol. Va, pp. 118–19.

20 Eventually, an SS field army was activated on 24 September 1944. This army, first designated *6. Panzer Armee* or *PzAOK 6*, was redesignated as *6. SS-Panzer Armee* in April 1945. Commanded by *SS-Obergruppenführer* Sepp Dietrich, it controlled a number of SS and *Heer* corps and divisions until the capitulation in May 1945.

21 *Anlage zu Kdo.Stb. Reichsführer-SS, Tgb.Nr. Ia II 236/44 Betr. Personelle Lage, SS-Flak-Kompanie 104, 1. Juli 1944.*

22 They were *SS-Ostubaf.* Dr. Schneevogt, *SS-Stubaf.* Erich May, *SS-Ostuf.* Werner Hartmann, *SS-Stubaf.* Willi Baumann, and *SS-Stubaf.* Paul Barnekow. (Letter, Erich May to Wolfgang Vopersal, Wilke Archive, 25 January 1981).

23 Vopersal, Vol. Va, pp. 118–19.

24 Karl Ulrich. *Like a Cliff in the Ocean: The History of the 3. SS-Panzer-Division "Totenkopf"* (Winnipeg, Canada: J. J. Fedorowicz Publishing, Inc., 2002), p. 242.

25 *Armeeoberkommando 2, Ia Kriegstagebuch, Morgenmeldung* (morning reports) 22–24 July 1944.

Chapter 2: Organization and Duties of the *Panzer* Corps Headquarters and Staff

1 Helmuth Reinhardt. Military Study P-139: *Size and Composition of Divisional and Higher Staffs in the German Army* (Karlsruhe, Germany: Historical Division, Headquarters, U.S. Army Europe, 1954), pp. 24–27.

2 The *Waffen-SS* training and replacement system was maintained separately from that of the *Heer*, though it took in volunteers or draftees through the same home *Wehrkreise* (defense district) induction centers. Despite this duplication of effort, the SS maintained its own personnel system until the end of the war.

3 Author's interview with former *SS-Ustuf.* Günther Lange at his private residence in Handeloh, Germany, on 28 September 2017. Lange served as Gille's only O5 for the last 12 months of the war.

4 Reinhardt, p. 23A, Chart 4.

5 *Heeres-Dienstvorschrift H. Dv. g 92, Handbuch für den Generalstabsdienst im Kriege, Teil I und II* (Berlin: Reichsdrückerei, 1 August 1939), pp. 14–18.

6 Siegfried Westphal. *German General Staff Training and Development of German General Staff Officers.* MS P-031b, Project # 6, Vol. XXI. (Heidelberg: Historical Division, U.S. European Command, August 1948), pp. 57–58.

7 *Kriegsstärkenachweisung (Heer) Nr. 15, Generalkommando Pz.Korps*, 1 March 1942.

8 Reinhardt, p. 3, and H.Dv. G92, pp. 26, 28 and Table 2, 47.

9 Reinhardt, pp. 3, 13.

10 *Ibid*, p. 26.

11 *Ibid*, p. 8.

12 Reinhardt, p. 11. This practice of operating the *Hauptquartier* in a split fashion was also confirmed by Herbert Gille's aide-de-camp, former *SS-Ustuf.* Günther Lange in an interview with the author on 28 September 2017, as well as official records submitted by the corps which depicted both operating in different locations.

13 The names of corps commanders killed in action is detailed throughout Colonel French McLean's excellent *Quiet Flows the Rhein: German General Officer Casualties in World War II* (Winnipeg, Canada: J. J. Fedorowicz Publishing, Inc., 1996). By the beginning of June 1944, even before the great Soviet summer offensive began, 65 German general officers, including division and corps commanders, had already been killed in action.

14 *9. Armee Ia Kriegstagebuch, Ia Nr. 2168/44*, Radio Message from *H.Gr. Mitte*, 24 July 1944.

15 H. Dv. g. 92, 38.

16 *Ibid*, p. 38.

17 *Ibid*, p. 39.

18 *AOK 9, Ia Nr. 1772/44, Geschäftsordnung des Armeeoberkommando 9, Stand* 10 October 1944.

19 *Ibid*, p. 37.

20 A typical daily reporting standard operating procedure is found in the *AOK 9 Ia* message number 3690/44, *Meldungserstattung*, dated 3 August 1944. It includes formats, reporting times, reporting requirements, etc. for its subordinate corps and divisions.

21 Westphal, p. 61.

22 *Ibid*, p. 61.

23 The Great General Staff was an institution that dated back to the time of Prussian Generals Scharnhorst, Gneisenau, and Clausewitz, the founders of the Berlin *Kriegsakademie*. These men had decided in the aftermath of the Napoleonic Wars that never again would Prussia find itself as intellectually unprepared for war as it had been in October 1806, when Frederick the Great's legendary Prussian Army was resoundingly defeated by the smaller, better-led, and much more agile *Grande Armee* in the twin battles of Jena and Auerstädt.

24 Gerald Reitlinger. *The SS: Alibi of a Nation 1922–1945* (New York: The Viking Press, 1957), p. 84.

25 Richard Schulze-Kossens. *Militärischer Führernachwuchs der Waffen-SS* (Osnabrück: Munin Verlag, 1982), p. 97.

26 This was to be short-lived; the war was clearly going to last beyond anyone's initial rosy estimate, so the *OKH* ordered that the *Kriegsakademie* resume instruction on 15 January 1940 with an eight-week course, the first of 17 wartime general staff officer *Lehrgänge* (courses). Model, p. 114.

27 It moved back to Berlin in 1942, to Hirschberg in Silesia in October 1943, to Bad Kissingen in January 1945, and finally in March 1945 to Lengries in Bavaria, where it was still conducting classes when the war ended.

28 The Hubertus Hunt, traditionally conducted on 3 November in honor of St. Hubertus (655–727 AD), the patron saint of hunting.

29 Westphal, p. 5.

30 The *SS-Pz.Korps*, later renumbered as *II. SS-Pz.Korps*, began forming in Germany on 9 July 1942 under the leadership of *SS-Ogruf.* Paul Hausser.

31 Schulze-Kossens, p. 98

32 Generally, this equated to four to six months prior service as an O1 or battalion/regimental *Adjutant*, a month of preliminary instruction and practical experience on a corps or division staff, four months attending the *Kreigsakademie*, a month at a weapons school after graduation, and six to nine months in probationary status while serving in an actual general staff officer position (Ia, Ib, or Ic) at the division or corps level.

33 Schulze-Kossens, p. 99.

34 Hans-Georg Model. *Der deutsche Generalstabsoffizier: Seine Auswahl und Ausbildung in Reichswehr, Wehrmacht und Bundeswehr* (Frankfurt: Bernard & Graefe Verlag für Wehrwesen, 1968), pp. 117–19, 126.

35 By way of comparison, by the end of the war, approximately 350 *Heer* general staff officers had been killed or wounded, a number roughly equal to the entire general staff immediately prior to the start of World War II. This does not include those captured, which would account for the remaining 1,000 or so. (source: Westphal, p. 58)

36 Westphal, p. 57.

37 By 1945, the requirement for qualified general staff officers by the *Heer* alone amounted to approximately 1,100 men. (Westphal, p. 83)

38 The *SS-Ahnenerbe* was an institute in Nazi Germany sponsored by the SS established to research the archaeological and cultural history of the Aryan race. Founded on 1 July 1935 by Heinrich Himmler and two other crack-pot SS racial theorists, the *SS-Ahnenerbe* later conducted experiments on dead (and living) concentration camp inmates and launched overseas expeditions in an attempt to prove that mythological Nordic populations had once ruled the world. For more information, see Chapter 1 in Heather Pringle's *The Master Plan: Himmler's Scholars and the Holocaust* (NY: Hyperion, 2006).

Chapter 3: Organization of Corps and Army Troops

1 *SS-Führungshauptamt, Amt. II Org.Abt. Ia/II, Tagebuch Nr. 3465/44 g.Kdos.*, 4 October 1944. Subject: *Kriegsgliederungen der Gen.Kdos.SS-Pz.Korps.*

2 *Ibid.*

3 *Verzeichnis der gültigen KStN und KAN für Sondertruppen der Reichsführer-SS, Anlange zur Verfügung SS-FHA, Amt II, Org.Abt. ia/II Tgb. Nr. 4079/44 g. Kdos.*, issued 28 November 1944.

4 *SS-Führungshauptamt, Kdo.Amt d. Waffen-SS, Org. Tgb. 1051/43 g.Kdos.*, 5 August 1943, Subject: *Aufstellung des Gen.Kdos. IV. SS-Panz.Korps.*

5 The official justification for not activating the battalion was due to the overall shortage of both SS-men and tanks to flesh it out. Even *schw.SS-sPz.Abt. 503*, the designated heavy tank battalion for the *III. (germ.) SS-Pz.Korps*, never reached its authorized strength. The Totenkopf Division's Tiger-equipped *9. Kompanie* was supposed to be assigned to *schw.SS-Pz.Abt. 502* in May 1944, but Hitler personally intervened on two occasions on behalf of the division, directing that the Inspector of Panzer Troops on 10 and again on 11 May 1944 grant permission to the division that would allow it to keep the company as well as to be issued new tanks. Source: *Insp.d.Pz.Tr., Führer Vorträge*, 10 and 11 May 1944, NARA Records Group T-78, Roll 720.

6 *Anlage 1 z. Kdo. Stb. RF-SS, Tgb. Nr. II 236, 44 g.Kdos.* Report dated 1 July 1944.

7 *Ibid.* Memo, *Adjutant der Reichsführer-SS* (RFSS) to *Kommandostab*, RFSS, 7 September 1944. Subject: *Stärkemeldung der Waffen-SS*, as of 5 September 1944.

8 *Oberkommando des Heeres, Org.Amt., Kriegsstärkenachweisung Nr. 15*, 1 February 1943.

9 *Ibid.*

10 *Oberkommando der Wehrmacht, Heeresdienstvorschrift H.dV. g92, Handbuch für den Generalstabsdienst im Kriege*, 1 August 1939, 32.

11 Email from Günther Lange, 11 March 2016.

12 *K.St.N.* Nr. 2075 *Panzerkorps-Kartenstelle*, dated 1 April 1942.

13 The *Korpsnachrichtenabteilung* and its subunits were organized using no less than five separate *K.St.N.*s, including *K.St.N.* Nr. 805 *Stab einer Panzerkorpsnachrichten-Abteilung* dated 1 May 1944; Nr. 833 *Korpsfernsprech-betriebs-Kompanie* dated 1 January 1944; Nr. 843 *Feldfernkabel-Kompanie* dated 1 January 1944; Nr. 872 Versorgungs-staffel einer Korpsnachrichten-Abeilung dated 1 May 1944; and Nr. 973 Panzerkorps-*Funkkompanie* dated 1 January 1944. These *K.St.N.*s were continually updated throughout the war to reflect the introduction of newer equipment, changes in doctrine, and lessons learned from the field, as well as other factors.

14 The nomenclature, description, and capabilities of all German radio and communication equipment employed by the *Wehrmacht* can be found in the U.S. War Department Technical Manual TME 11-227, *German Armed Forces Signal Communication Equipment Directory*, published June 1944.

15 *Ibid*, 10.

16 *Ibid*, 11.

17 *Ibid*, 4.

18 *K.St.N.* Nr. 973, *Panzer-Korps Funkkompanie*, dated 1 January 1944, 3.

19 Frank Dörenberg, "The Feld-Hellschreiber," 26 September 2017. This 26-page online article provides a concise description of the technical characteristics of this unique device as well as how it was used in the field by the *Wehrmacht* during World War II (https://www.nonstopsystems.com/radio/hellschreiber-the-feld-hell.htm).

20 *K.St.N.* Nr. 198, *Fliegerabwehr-Kompanie* (3.7cm *Flak mot.Z.*) dated 1 April 1944.

21 U.S. Army Technical Manual TM-E 30-451, Handbook on German Military Forces (Washington, D.C.: War Department, 15 March 1945), VII-39–VII-40.

22 *SS-Führungshauptamt/Amt II Org.Abt. Ia/II Tgb.Nr. 2202/45 g.Kdos. v. 26.3.1945. Betr.: Bezeichnung der Feldeinheiten der Waffen-SS, Stand 1.3.1945.*

23 The *Begleitkompanie* was composed of six separate elements, each with its own *K.St.N.*, including Nr. 1121 *Führer Schwere-Kompanie (mot.)*; Nr. 1153 *Kradschützen-Zug*; Nr. 1123 *Infanterie-Geschutz-Zug*; and Nr. 1380 *Schützen-Zug*, all dated 1 November 1941; *K.St.N.* Nr. 1148a Panzerjüger-Zug dated 1 December 1942; and Nr. 162 *schwere-Maschinegewehr-Zug* dated 1 February 1941.

24 The appropriate *K.St.N.*s included Nr. 1207 *Kommandeur der Panzerkorps-Nachschubtruppen*; Nr. 1217a *Kraftfahrkompanie 90 tonnen*; Nr. 1225 *kleine Kraftwagenkolonne 30 Tonnen*; and Nr. 1231 *grosse Kraftwagenkolonne 60 Tonnen*, all dated 1 November 1943; Nr. 1051 *Kraftfahrzeug-Instandsetzungs-Zug (mot.)* dated 1 February 1944; and Nr. 1232 *grosse Kraftwagenkolonne für Betriebsstoff 50 cbm.* dated 1 October 1937.

25 *AOK 9 Ia KTB, Anlage, Nr. 3710/44 gen.Kdos. von 3.5.44; 5. SS-Pz.Div. "Wiking" Zustandbericht*, 1 September 1944, Werturteil.

26 *Anlage 2* to *SS-Führungshauptamt, Amt. II Org.Abt. Ia/II, Tagebuch Nr. 3465/44 g.Kdos.*, 4 October 1944. Subject: *Kriegsgliederungen der Gen.Kdos. SS-Pz.Korps.*

27 *SS-Führungshauptamt, Org.Tgb.Nr. 3080/42 geheim,* Subject: *Aufstellung einer SS-Bekleindungs-Instandsetzungs-Kp. (mot.) für die SS-Div. "Wiking,"* 26 May 1942.

28 *SS-K.St.N. für SS-Bekleidungs-Instandsetzungs-Kompanie*, dated 21 December 1942.

29 *Abschrift, Anlage zu Org.Abt.Nr. I/20 901/44 g. Kdos.* dated 28 November 1944, Subject: *Verzeichnis der gültigen K.St.N. and K.A.N. für Sondertruppen der Reichsführung SS.*

30 *K.St.N. Nr. 2251 Feldpostamt (mot.)* dated 1 April 1935.

31 *Aufstellung des Gen.Kdo.IV.SS-Pz.Korps, SS-Führungshauptamt, Kommandoamt der Waffen-SS, Berlin-Wilmersdorf*, 5 August 1943, *Anlage* 2, 1.

32 *SS-Standarte "Kurt Eggers," Lagebericht 44/1* (Berlin-Zehlendorf, 1 January 1944).

33 *SS-Standarte "Kurt Eggers," Befehl zur Neugliederung der Feldeinheiten der SS-Standarte "Kurt Eggers"* (Berlin-Zehlendorf, 1 May 1944).

34 *Ibid.*

35 *Kriegsgliederung der Gen.Kdos.SS-Pz.Korps, SS-Führungshauptamt, Amt II Organizations-Abteilung Ia/II*, Berlin-Wilmersdorf, 4 October 1944, p. 4. At its peak, *"Kurt Eggers"* had grown to 1,750 officers and men, organized into 27 units in the field and with members from 15 different European countries, according to Ingo Seidel in *Kampfpropaganda: Die SS-Standarte Kurt Eggers* (Norderstedt, Germany: Books on Demand GmbH, 2012), p. 32.

36 *Führerstellenbesetzungsliste SS-Standarte "Kurt Eggers,"* dated 1 July 1944, and *SS-Stammkarte* (personnel file) and *Personalkartei-Fragebogen* (personal information questionnaire) dated 4 September 1944 and 24 June 1944 for Dibowski and Zarp, respectively.

37 Message from *Kampfpropaganda-Zug Ungarn* to *SS-Standarte "Kurt Eggers,"* 10 January 1945, signed by *SS-Ustuf.* Erich Kernmayr, and *Dance of Death* by Erich Kern (London: Collins, 1951), p. 224.
38 Reinhardt, pp. 3, 13.
39 *K.St.N.* Nr.24 dated 9 May 1940, updated 1 January 1945.
40 The role and duties of the ARKO are described concisely and accurately by former *SS-Obergruppenführer* Walter Staudinger, ARKO of *6. SS-Panzerarmee*, in Foreign Military Study FMS # B-347, *The Artillery Command of the Sixth Panzer Army during the Ardennes Offensive, 1944–1945* (Konigstein, Germany: U.S. Army Europe Historical Division, 12 January 1951), pp. 4–6.
41 Anonymous, "SS-Werfer-Abteilung 504, Solche Kerle!" in *Der Freiwilliger*, Vol. 9/65 (Osnabrück: HIAG/Munin Verlag, 1965), pp. 9–11.
42 Handbook on German Military Forces, VII-89 to VII-91.
43 *Artillerie-Einsatz im Bereich der Heeresgruppe Mitte* (diagram), 19 November 1944.
44 Handbook on German Military Forces, VII-25 to VII-30.
45 *SS-Führungshauptamt, Amt II, Org.Abt. Ia/II, Tgb.Nr. 1633/43 g.Kdos*, Berlin, dated 26 October 1943, Subject: *Umgliederung der 9.SS-Panz.Gren.Div. "Hohenstaufen"* in *9.SS-Panz.Div. "Hohenstaufen."*
46 *SS-FHA, Amt II, Org.Abt. Ia/II, Tgb.Nr. II/2568/45 geh.* Teletype dated 6 February 1945, Subject: Transfer of *s.SS-Art.Abt. 504* and *SS-Beob.Bttr. 504* to *IV. SS-Pz.Korps.*
47 *Oberkommando der Heeresgruppe Mitte, Stabsoffizier für Artillerie (Stoart) Nr. 39/44 g.Kdos. Chefs.* Subject: *Gliederung der Artillerie im Bereich der Heeresgruppe Mitte* (diagram), 1 November 1944.
48 For a detailed listing of the individual elements *of Pz.Korps Santitäts-Abteilung 104*, refer to Anlage 2, p. 2, SS-Führungshauptamt Kdo.Amt. d.Waffen-SS, Org.Tgb.Nr. 1051/43 g.Kdos., Subject: *Aufstellung des Gen.Kdo. IV.SS-Panz.Korps*, dated 5 August 1943.
49 Medical operations doctrine in the corps area are described in pages 62–68 in Volume I of *Heeresdienst-vorschrift H.Dv. 90-1, Versorgung des Feldheeres*, published in 1942.
50 Tessin, *Verbände und Truppen der deutschen Wehrmacht und Waffen-SS*, Vol. 1 (Osnabrück: Biblio-Verlag, 1973), p. 284.
51 The destruction of the *73. Inf.Div.* will be discussed in a following chapter.
52 *Oberkommando des Heeres, Chef der Heeresrüstung und Befehlshaber des Ersatzheeres, AHA/Ic Nr. 8320/44 g.Kdos. geheim*; Subject: *Umbennenungen Nachstehende Einheiten*, dated 25 October 1944, p. 1.
53 *Ibid*, p. 9.
54 A useful description of German medical units and their capabilities can be found in "German Medical Services" in *Tactical and Technical Trends* Vol. 35, 1943 (Washington, D.C.: War Department, 7 October 1943), pp. 40–44.
55 *K.St.N.* 1365 *Krankenkraftwagen-Zug* dated 1 November 1941.
56 Special SS *K.St.N. Krankenkraftwagen-Zug* dated 1 December 1942.
57 Special SS *K.St.N. verst.Zug Krankentransport-Kompanie* dated 1 December1942.
58 Special SS *K.St.N. Stab SS-Korps Santitäts-Abteilung (mot.) Generalkommando (Panzer)*, dated 1 December1942.
59 These will be mentioned when appropriate in the succeeding chapters.

Chapter 4: The Leaders and Divisions

1 Franz W. Seidler, in *Die SS: Elite unter dem Totenkopf–30 Lebensläufe* by Ronald Smelser and Enrico Syring (Eds) (Munich: Ferdinand Schoningh, 2000), p. 173.
2 Seidler, p. 173.
3 Seidler, p. 174.
4 Seidler, pp. 174–75.

5 The *Verfügungstruppe* was the paramilitary arm of the SS, formed, trained and equipped as an infantry formation, augmented shortly thereafter by supporting arms, such as artillery, engineer, signal, and antitank units.

6 Seidler, p. 176.

7 Unless otherwise noted, the portion detailing Gille's military career as an officer of the *Waffen-SS* comes from his official file kept by the SS Personnel Office, now maintained by the Berlin Document Center. File reproduced by John P. Moore in his *Führerliste der Waffen-SS*, Part 2 (Portland, OR: J. P. Moore Publishing, 2003).

8 C.S.D.I.C. (U.K.) Special Recording Report # 1219, conversation between Prisoners of War *SS-Standartenführer* Hans Lingner, former Commanding Officer, *17. SS-Pz.Gren.Div. "Gotz von Berlichingen,"* and *Hauptmann* "Y" of the *276. Volks-Grenadier Division*, recorded 17 February 2017.

9 Legend holds that the *Wiking* Division was predominantly composed of "Nordic" volunteers, but that was never the case. While the division did indeed adopt a Nordic persona, highlighted by a clever propaganda campaign, the bulk of the division from beginning to end consisted overwhelmingly of native Germans and towards the latter half of the war, increasing numbers of ethnic Germans (*Volksdeutsche*) from southeast Europe. As of 22 June 1941, the division included 631 Dutch nationals, 294 Norwegians, 216 Danes, 421 Finns, one Swede, one Swiss and an unknown number of Flemish-speaking Belgians. In all, the division included 1,143 Germanic volunteers. Three months later, the division counted 1,416 of these men, less than 10 percent of the total number of men assigned to the division, which marched into the Soviet Union that summer with over 18,000 men. Source: *European Volunteers: 5 SS Panzer Division Wiking* by Peter Strassner (Winnipeg, Canada: J. J. Fedorowicz Publishing, 1988), p. 9.

10 Until recently, the *Wiking* Division had enjoyed a reputation of being a "clean" unit that had committed relatively few atrocities during the early stages of Operation *Barbarossa*. These assertions were thoroughly debunked in a 2019 study by Dr. Lars Westerlund of the National Archives of Finland, who discovered that the division, under Felix Steiner's command, had participated in or abetted a number of atrocities between July 1941 and early 1943, including the summary execution of hundreds of Soviet POWs, reprisal killings of Soviet civilians, and the murder of thousands of innocent Jews, often in cooperation with *SS Einsatzgruppen*. Source: Lars Westerlund, *The Finnish SS-Volunteers and Atrocities, 1941–1943* (Helsinki: The National Archives of Finland, 2019).

11 The *Wiking* Division was initially assigned as part of *Heeresgruppe Süd*'s armored reserve.

12 Biography of Max Wünsche's career being prepared by Ms. Carol Byrne, Dublin, Ireland, 2018.

13 Michael L. Hadley. *Count not the dead: the popular image of the German submarine* (Montreal, Canada: McGill-Queen's Press, 17 March 1995), p. 170.

14 Letter from Ernst Fick to Karl Wolf, 27 January 1942, *Reichsführer-SS* (RFSS) Microfilm 38.

15 Seidler, p. 179.

16 Fritz Hahl. *Mit "Westland im Osten* (Osnabrueck: Munin Verlag, 2000), pp. 121–22, and Fritz Hahl and Franz Hack, *Panzergrenadier der Panzerdivision "Wiking"im Bild*. (Osnabrück: Munin Verlag, 1984), pp. 195–96.

17 Hack, p. 199.

18 Von dem Bach suffered periodically from impacted bowels and hemorrhoids, a condition that required surgery in 1942. During periods of stress, his condition would occasionally flare up, rendering him nearly incapable of exercising command effectively. Upon evacuation from Kowel, he then flew privately to Karlsbad, where he was admitted to the Höhenvilla private clinic on 18 March 1944, an event that led Himmler to seek his whereabouts. After a search by the chief medical doctor of the SS, *Reichsartz SS und Polizei* Ernst-Robert Grawitz, he was located a week later. Apparently, Himmler forgave him for this infraction, for von dem Bach was assigned the prestigious mission of suppressing the Warsaw Uprising four months later, a task that was to earn him the award of the *Ritterkreuz* (Source: "Personalakte von dem Bach," *Führerliste der Waffen-SS*, Part I by John P. Moore, 2003).

19 The *Totenkopf* Division was reorganized as a *Panzer* division on 21 October 1943, the *Wiking* Division the following day. (Source: Georg Tessin, *Verbände und Truppen der deutschen Wehrmacht und Waffen-SS, 1939–1945, Die Landstreitkräfte*, Vol. 2, pp. 213, 321.

20 *OKH: Generalinspektorat der Panzertruppen, Gen.StdH. Organization-Abteilung Nr. 18 400/44 g.Kdos. vom 3.* August 1944 "*Panzer*-Division 44."

21 United States War Department Technical Manual TM-E 30-451, Handbook on German Military Forces, 15 March 1945, pp. II-26 and II-28.

22 Originally, in April 1944 the *Totenkopf* Division's *Panzer* regiment was supposed to transfer its *9. Kompanie* with all of its personnel and any remaining *Pz. VI* Tigers to the newly forming *schw. SS-Pz.Abt. 102*, a corps troops unit of the *II. SS-Pz.Korps*. During discussions between Hitler and Guderian, head of the General Inspectorate of *Panzer* Troops, that took place on 10 and 11 May 1944, Hitler directed that the *Totenkopf* Division be allowed to keep its *9. Kompanie* on its establishment, which it did until the end of the war. Source: NARA OKH Records Group T-78, Roll 720: OKH *Panzer* Production Reports 1943-45, *Führer Vorträge*, 10 and 11 May 1944, courtesy of Ian Michael Wood.

23 *5. SS-Pz.Div. Wiking, Ia, Tagebuch Nr. 77/44 gem/g.Kdos., Meldung vom* 1 August 1944 (Monthly Readiness Report).

24 *Ibid.*

25 *9. Armee, Ia Kriegstagebuch Anlage, Panzer- und Panzerabwehrwaffen*, reports dated 30 July and 21 August 1944.

26 Roger James Bender and Hugh Page Taylor, *Uniforms and History of the Waffen-SS*, Vol. 2. (Mountain View, California: R. James Bender Publishing, 1971), p. 100.

27 An excellent, well-researched and written reference detailing the early days of the *SS-Totenkopf* is Charles W. Sydnor Junior's *Soldiers of Destruction: The SS Death's Head Division, 1933–1945* (Princeton: Princeton University Press, 1977).

28 Sydnor, p. 93.

29 On 27 May 1940 alone, the *SS-Totenkopf* suffered 691 casualties, including 155 killed in action—a very high number of casualties for one day's fighting against a retreating enemy. A large proportion of these were suffered by *I./SS-TK Inf.Rgt. 1* at Les Paradis. Amazingly, two men survived the massacre and after being treated for their wounds by the *251. Inf.Div.* of the *Heer*, they testified after the war against Knöchlein at his murder trial. Found guilty, he was hanged by the British on 21 January 1949. (Sydnor, pp. 106–07.)

30 After Le Paradis, there were a number of massacres of civilians that occurred around the same time frame. The atrocity at Le Paradis was not an isolated event, but part of the divisional culture. The division's three infantry regiments had also been used during the invasion of Poland on "security and pacification" operations, that in several instances involved shooting Jews, "suspect" civilians and Polish army stragglers, clergy, intellectuals, and other proscribed groups. This pattern of behavior established so early in the war set the *Totenkopf* apart from other units within the nascent *Waffen-SS*, a reflection of their origins in the KZ system. (Source: http://www.webmatters.net/txtpat/?id=270 , thanks to Tom Albright.)

31 Sydnor, p. 108.

32 *Ibid.*

33 *Ibid*, p. 191.

34 *Ibid*, pp. 197, 222.

35 Tessin, Vol. 14, p. 241.

36 Ullrich, *Like a Cliff in the Sea*, p. 172.

37 *SS-Führungshauptamt, Org.Tgb.Nr. 102/42 g.Kdos., Berlin Wilmersdorf, Betreff: Gliederung der SS-Divisionen*, 25 March 1942.

38 *Ibid.*

39 Syndnor, pp. 255–56.
40 Remy Spezzano and George Nipe, *Blood, Steel and Myth: The II. SS-Panzer-Korps and the Road to Procharowka, July 1943* (Southbury, CT: RZM Publishing, 2011), p. 34.
41 Kamen Nevenkin, *Fire Brigades: The Panzer Divisions 1943–1945* (Winnipeg, Canada: J. J. Fedorowicz Publishing, 2008), p. 825.
42 Spezzano and Nipe, p. 37.
43 Monthly readiness report, dated 1 August 1943.
44 Nevenkin, p. 829.
45 Monthly readiness report, dated 1 July 1944.
46 Adolf Hitler, Daily Situation Brief for 31 August 1944.
47 Christopher Dillon. *Dachau and the SS: A Schooling in Violence* (London: Oxford University Press, 2015), p. 76.

Chapter 5: The Tank Battle of Praga

1 *Fernspruch* (radio message) *des AOK 2, Ia Tgb.Nr. 1615/44 g.Kdos. von 28. Juli 1944, 8 p.m.* Hereafter referred to as 8 p.m. radio message from *2. Armee Headquarters*, 28 July 1944.
2 David M. Glantz. "The Red Army's Lublin-Brest Offensive and Advance on Warsaw (18 July–30 September 1944): an Overview and Documentary Survey" in *Journal of Slavic Military Studies*, Vol. 19, 2006 (London: Taylor & Francis Group LLC, 2006), pp. 404, 407.
3 Rolf Hinze. *East Front Drama–1944* (Winnipeg, Canada: J. J. Fedorowicz Publishing, 1996), pp. 290–91. This is a translation of an earlier work published by Motorbuch Verlag in 1988.
4 *Tagesmeldung, 2. Armee*, 29 July 1944 11:10 p.m.
5 Glantz, in *Journal of Slavic Studies*, p. 408.
6 In fact, *VIII. Armeekorps* was forced to the north, where it was incorporated into Weiss's *2. Armee* order of battle.
7 *Führungsabteilung Ia Kriegstagebuch Nr. 11, AOK 9*, entry 25 July 1944. Note: The *9. Armee*, the *2. Armee*'s neighbor to the south, was anticipating the attachment of *IV. SS-Pz.Korps* during the following week in order to carry out the army's anticipated counteroffensive, and was therefore monitoring the status of Gille's corps very closely.
8 Vopersal, Vol. Va, p. 173.
9 8 p.m. radio message from *2. Armee Headquarters*, 28 July 1944.
10 Peter Strassner. *European Volunteers: 5. SS-Panzer-Division Wiking* (Winnipeg, Canada: J. J. Fedorowicz Publishing, 1988), p. 173.
11 *Ibid.*
12 Interestingly, *IV. SS-Pz.Korps* had two *Chef des Stabes* at the same time—one in charge of the actual corps headquarters and the other with the acting staff consisting of *Wiking* officers—a situation that would exist for the next several days, though only the staff accompanying Gille could actually fulfill that role.
13 Vopersal, Vol. Va, p. 192.
14 Moore, Vol. 6, Richard Pauly file, and Kurt Mehner, *Die deutsche Wehrmacht 1939–1945: Führung und Truppe*. (Norderstedt: Militaer-Verlag Klaus D. Patzwall, 1993), p. 195. Pauly, a junior major by this point, had already completed certain portions of required general staff officer training. He had previously served as a company commander and regimental adjutant in the *Totenkopf* Division from 1939–42. Immediately prior to his assignment to *IV. SS-Pz.Korps*, Pauly had served for nearly two years as a tactics instructor and student group leader at the *SS-Junkerschule* in Braunschweig.
15 Vopersal, Vol. Va, p. 213.

16 *SS-Pz.Rgt. 5* reported that its *Panzer IVs* had been experiencing an usual failure rate of tank engines that had sidelined 10 tanks, roughly half of the number on-hand *with I.Abt./SS-Pz.Rgt. 5*. Since all of these tanks were relatively new, sabotage at the factory was suspected.

17 *2. Armee Tagesmeldung*, 29 August 11:10 p.m., p. 3.

18 Vopersal, Vol. Va, p. 179.

19 The *HGr. Mitte* instructions are detailed in the *9. Armee Ia KTB*, 26 July 1944, p. 8. Biała Podlaska, incidentally, could not be held beyond the evacuation of Brest-Litovsk; the order was subsequently modified several days later to indicate that the *2. Armee* line was to be held between Siedlce and Minsk Mazowiecki.

20 These units were *Sich.Btls. 315* and *945*, *Landesschutz Btl. 898*, and *II.Btl./Gren.Rgt. 170* of the *73. Inf.Div.* (Source: *2. Armee Ia KTB*, 3 August 1944, Subject: Security Troops).

21 From "War Correspondent, Gösta Borg" by Martin Månsson, extract from Norbert Bacyk's *Warsaw II: The Tank Battle at Praga July–September 1944, The 4th SS Panzer Corps vs. the First Belorussian Front* (Stockholm: Leandor & Ekholm Publishing, 2009), pp. 197–98.

22 On 29 July 1944, the *Totenkopf* Division had 2,950 infantrymen and combat engineers operating under its banner, including several hundred men that were attached from three security battalions and the battalion from the *73. Inf.Div.* (source: Übersicht über Kampfstärken und Kampfstärken je kilometer. Headquarters, 2. Armee, dated as of 3 August 1944).

23 Vopersal, Vol. Va, p. 190.

24 *Ibid*, p. 187.

25 Klapdor, pp. 317–18.

26 2. *Armee Ia Kriegstagebuch, Tagesmeldung*, p. 2, 2 August 1944, 10:30 p.m.

27 *Kavallerie-Korps Harteneck* was named after its commander, *General der Kavallerie* Gustav Harteneck.

28 *9. Armee Ia Kreigstagebuch, Anlage VIII, Panzer und Panzerabwehrwaffen*, dated 30 July 1944.

29 Bacyk, p. 59. The numbers quoted in an official Soviet source in Bacyk's book conflict with those mentioned in Glantz's study, which states that the number of tanks available for the battle was 300, but this may include only the units directly involved in the battle of Praga, whereas the official source quoted by Bacyk most likely includes every unit in the 2nd Tank Army. Glantz, *Journal of Slavic Studies*, p. 413. The number is based on Glantz's review of official Red Army records from the period.

30 Frieser, *et al*, Vol. 8, *Germany and the Second World War*, pp. 579–80.

31 *2. Armee Ia Kriegstagebuch, Tagesmeldung*, 31 July 1944, 11 p.m.

32 *2. Armee Ia Kreigstagenbuch, Morgenmeldung*, 1 August 1944, 5:50 a.m.

33 *2. Armee Ia Kreigstagebuch, Tagesmeldung*, 1 August 1944, 11 p.m.

34 Kistemaker, quoted in *Standartenführer Johannes Mühlenkamp und seine Manner*, Part 2, by Paul Oosterling, Ron Erlings, and Hans Fischer (Erpe, The Netherlands: Uitgeverij De Krijger, 2003), p. 339.

35 *Ferngespräche* (message log), *2.Armee Ia Kriegstagebuch, Anlage*, 1 August 1944.

36 *2. Armee, Ia KTB, Anglagen, Fernschreiben*, 11:50 a.m. 1 August 1944. In addition to 10 motors for *Pz. IVs*, the division also requested five motors for *Pz. V* Panthers and a number of return rollers, track assemblies, road wheels, and final drive assemblies for both types of tanks. Incidentally, Thomale replaced Heinz Guderian, who had been chosen by Hitler to be the new chief of staff of the German Army.

37 *Ibid*, telephone conversation between Krebs and Model, 8:10 p.m., 1 August 1944.

38 Shortly after 31 July 1944, the *174. Res.Div.* was incorporated entirely into the reconstituting *26. Inf.Div.* and then disbanded.

39 *2. Armee Ia KTB*, Order issued for 1 August 1944, 8:50 p.m.

40 *2. Armee Ia KTB, Anlagen,* Telephone Conversation log, 6:20 p.m., 1 August 1944.
41 Joachim Neumann. *Die 4. Panzer-Division 1943–1945, Bericht und Betrachtung zu den zwei letzten Kriegsjahren im Osten* (Bonn: Selbstverlag Neumann, 1989), pp. 440–41.
42 *2. Armee Ia KTB, Anglagen,* Telephone Conversation log, 2:45 p.m., 2 August 1944.
43 Radio Message Log, Headquarters *IV. SS-Pz.Korps* to *AOK 2,* 6:40 p.m., 2 August 1944.
44 *2. Armee Ia KTB,* Radio Message, 9:15 p.m., 2 August 1944.
45 *IV. SS-Pz.Korps Ia Tagesmeldung,* 3 August 1944.
46 9. *Armee Ia KTB, Tagesmeldung,* 3 August 1944, p. 26.
47 Michael Wood. *Tigers of the Death's Head: SS Totenkopf Division's Tiger Company* (Mechanicsburg, PA: Stackpole Books, 2013), p. 156. When the *9.Kp./SS-Pz.Rgt. 3's* Tigers attempted to traverse Warsaw's Marszalkowska Street on 1 August on its way to join the rest of the division near Sokolow, it was set upon by a number of Polish insurgents who used Molotov cocktails and a captured *Panzerfaust* in an attempt to knock them out. One was set on fire and abandoned by its crew, while another was later destroyed in the fighting. A provisional tank company, named *Panzerkompanie Totenkopf,* commanded by *SS-Ostubaf.* Wolf, was formed using replacement tanks, including at least two Tigers, and apparently this company was involved in suppressing the uprising until the end of August. The bulk of *9. Kompanie* was able to join the rest of the division in the field by 3 August, though at least six tanks were left at the Stauffer barracks in Warsaw until they could be repaired.
48 *2. Armee Ib (O.Qu.) KTB,* Radio message, 3 August 1944.
49 Radio Message, *IIb 2. Armee* to *IIb Heeresgruppe Mitte,* 2 August, and *Ia 2. Armee, Übersicht über die infanteristisches Kampfstärke der Divisionen und Brigaden, Stand vom 3 August 1944.*
50 *Oberkommando, Heeresgruppe Mitte Ia KTB, Tagesmeldung,* 8 August 1944.
51 *2. Armee Ia KTB, Tagesmeldung,* 4 August 1944.
52 Telephone Conversation Log, *2. Armee Ia KTB,* 4 August 1944, 5:15 a.m. to 2:50 p.m.
53 This link up and the subsequent capture of Krubki was reported by a radio message from *IV. SS-Pz.Korps* that was received by *2. Armee Ia* at 7:20 a.m. Evidently, no one read it or reported it, since it was not mentioned in the telephone conversation at 8 a.m. between Model and Weiss.
54 *IV. SS-Pz.Korps Ia Zwischenmeldung,* 4 August 1944.
55 Radio Message, *AOK 9, Tagesbefehl,* 1:45 p.m., 4 August 1944.
56 *KTB, I. Abt./SS-Pz.Abt. 5,* 2:05 p.m., 4 August 1944.
57 *2. Armee Ia KTB, Anlage,* Radio Message from Chief of Staff, *2. Armee* to *SS-Staf.* Mühlenkamp, 2:50 p.m., 4 August 1944.
58 *2. Armee Ia KTB, Anlage,* Radio message to *Frontleitstellen 3, 24* and *34,* 4 August 1944. Subject: *Sammelstellen für Urlauber und Versprengte.*
59 Rokossovsky, *A Soldier's Duty,* p. 255, as quoted on p. 618 in *Absolute War: Soviet Russia in the Second World War* by Chris Bellamy (New York: Vintage Books, 2007).
60 Frieser, *et al,* p. 581.
61 Neumann, p. 447.
62 Werner Haupt. *Army Group Center 1941–1945* (Atglen, PA: Schiffer Publishing, 1997), p. 209.
63 Norbert Bacyk. *Warsaw II: The Tank Battle at Praga July–September 1944—The 4th SS Panzer Corps vs. the First Belorussian Front* (Stockholm: Leandoer & Ekholm Publishing, 2009), p. 84.
64 Frieser, *et al,* Vol. 8, *Germany and the Second World War,* p. 581.
65 Bacyk, p. 92.
66 Ibor Nabolsin, *Stalin's Favorite: The Combat History of the 2nd Guards Tank Army from Kursk to Berlin, Volume 2: July 1944–May 1945* (Solihull, U. K.: Helion & Company Limited, 2016), p. 99.
67 Glantz, *Journal of Slavic Military Studies,* p. 417–18.
68 *Ibid,* p. 418.

Chapter 6: Operational Interlude: *Unternehmen Brückenschlag*

1 *KTB HGr. Mitte, Ia Nr. T 4046/44 geheim, Tagesmeldung 5.8.1944, 1. Hauptquartier HGr. Mitte,* 1:00 a.m., 6 August 1944, 1.

2 *Ibid*, 4.

3 *KTB AOK 9, Ia Tagesmeldung*, 5 August 1944, 30–31.

4 *KTB AOK 9, Ia Anlage, Nr. 5348/44 geheim*/Radio Message dated 5 August 1944.

5 *KTB AOK 9, Ia Anlage, Panzer und Panzerabwehrwaffen*, 7 August 1944.

6 As of 12 August, there were 22 armored fighting vehicles from the *Totenkopf* Division still attached to *SS-Einsatzgruppe Reinefarth*, which was tasked with eliminating the Polish Home Army in Warsaw by the *SS-HSSPF*. Included in this number were 8 *Pz. IV*, 1 *Pz. V*, 6 *Pz. VI* and 7 self-propelled 15cm infantry howitzers (Grille). Source: *KTB AOK 9, Anlage*, Radio Message addressed to *Wehrmachtskommandantur* Warsaw at 4:20 a.m., 12 August. Additionally, two batteries from *SS-Flak-Abt. 5 "Wiking"* were still attached to the *Luftwaffe*'s *Flak-Brig. 10* in Warsaw, a unit attached to *Gruppe von dem Bach* that were used to defend key bridges within the city from air attack. They would not return to the *Wiking* Division until late September 1944.

7 Glantz, p. 418. Gusev's army, consisting of 25,000 men, small even by Soviet standards, had been undergoing reconstitution since late July after suffering heavy casualties during the battle for Brest-Litovsk.

8 *KTB AOK 9 Tagesmeldung, Ia Nr. T12876/44 geheim*, 8 August 1944, 10:30 p.m.

9 During the course of this spoiling attack, *4. Pz.Div*'s tank regiment claimed the destruction of 23 Soviet tanks. (Neumann, p. 447).

10 *KTB AOK 9, Tagesmeldung, Ia Nr. T 12891/44 geheim*, 9 August 1944, 10:30 p.m.

11 The *Auflockerung, Räumung, Lähmung und Zerstörung* orders, known as *ARLZ-Massnahmen* (scorched earth measures), were first offically institued on the Eastern Front on 14 February 1943 after an order was issued by Hitler's Headquarters directing units, during certain withdrawal operations, to destroy everything of value that could not be used or taken away.

12 *KTB AOK 9, Ia Anlage, Kampfstärken* dated 13 August 1944, 2.

13 *Ibid.*

14 *AOK 9 Ia KTB, Anlage, Nr. 3710/44 gen.Kdos. von 3.5.44; 5. SS-Pz.Div. "Wiking" Zustandbericht*, 1 September 1944, Werturteil. The operational element of *Einsatz-Brigade Speer* may have been *9.–11.* And the *13. Kompanie* from *NSKK-Kraftwagen* Transport Regiment 9 (Speer), a unit formed during August 1944 in Eastern Poland/Galicia.

15 *KTB AOK 9, Ia Anlage, Panzer und Panzerabwehrwaffen*, 13 August 1944.

16 *Oberkommando der Heeresgruppe Mitte, StoArt Nr. 36/44, gKdosGliederung der Artillerie im Bereich der Heeresgruppe Mitte*, 1 September 1944.

17 Hellschreiber message from *9. Armee* to *IV. SS-Pz.Korps*, 4 p.m., 13 August 1944. *Bewährungs* units were composed of soldiers found guilty of minor criminal charges though still deemed *Wehrwürdig* or worthy to bear arms. A notch above the 999-series penal battalions, soldiers in *Bewährungs* units could regain their rank and military honor if they followed orders and behaved creditably in combat. *Inf.Btl.z.b.V. 560*, commanded by *Maj.* Friedrich-Karl Ritter, served under the command of *IV. SS-Pz.Korps* sporadically between July and November 1944. It would normally suffer heavy casualties, be pulled out of the line, rebuilt with more "probationary" soldiers, and sent back into the line again, normally during a critical point in the fighting, where it would once again suffer heavy casualties that would necessitate its reconstitution.

18 *Oberbefehlshaber der I. Armee, Betr: Munitionseinsatz, Ia/OQu. Nr. 683/44 g.Kdos.*, 10 August 1944.

19 Fritz Hahl, "Westland im Osten: Erinnerung eines hochausgezeichneten Frontoffiziers des SS-Regiments "Westland," in *der europäischen SS-Panzerdivision "Wiking"* (Osnabrück, Germany: Munin-Verlag GmbH, 2000), p. 143, 146.

20 Message from *9. Armee* to *IV. SS-Pz.Korps*, 10:30 p.m., 12 August 1944.

21 There is a report dated 4 March 1945 submitted to Berlin that shows that *IV. SS-Pz.Korps* had one *Panzergrenadier* battalion from the *Totenkopf* Division serving as its corps reserve, but there are no other mentions.

22 This reflects the date when Gille was officially appointed the commander of the *IV. SS-Pz.Korps*, which did not actually become operational until 28 July, eight days later.

23 Strassner, Appendix 35, pp. 269–70.

Chapter 7: The First Defensive Battle of Warsaw

1 *Germany and the Second World War*, Vol. VIII, p. 605.

2 On 8 August, the 2nd Tank Army and its subordinate units began moving to the Kowel area for reconstitution and as part of this movement, Popov's VIII Guards Tank Corps was detached from the army in mid-August. All of the still-serviceable tanks from the III Tank Corps were handed over to VIII Guards Tank Corps before it departed for Kowel and Popov's corps was placed under the operational control of 47th Army. (Source: Igor Nebolsin, *Stalin's Favorite: The Combat History of the 2nd Guards Tank Army from Kursk to Berlin. Vol. 2, July 1944–May 1945* [Solihull, U. K.: Helion & Company Limited, 2016], p. 99.)

3 Nebolsin, p. 87.

4 *AOK 9 Ia KTB No. 4142/44 g.Kdos. an Obkdo. HGr. Mitte*, 17 August 1944: *Lagebericht der 9. Armee vom 17.8.1944.*

5 *IV. SS-Pz.Korps Morgenmeldung*, 5:15 a.m., 18 August 1944, and Klapdor, p. 328.

6 Strassner, p. 174, and Ullrich, p. 244.

7 David M. Glantz, *Atlas of the Lublin-Brest Operation and the Advance on Warsaw from 18 July to 30 September 1944* (Carlisle, PA: Privately published, 2005), p. 117, and *Germany and the Second World War*, Vol. VIII, p. 606.

8 According to the VIII Guards Tank Corps war diary, it had the following numbers of operational tanks available for the offensive on 18 August 1944: 11 JS-IIs, 34 T-34s, 69 M4A2 Shermans, 12 SU-85 assault guns, 12 SU-76 assault guns, and 3 SU-57 assault guns. It had an unknown number of tanks undergoing repair. This number does not include tanks belonging to independent tank regiments assigned to the field armies. Translation of VIII Guards Tank Corps records by Mr. A. Artyom, to whom the author is indebted.

9 Ulrich, p. 244.

10 Vopersal, Vol. Va, p. 301.

11 Strassner, p. 174.

12 *Namentliche Verlustmeldung 4/44* and *10/44, II.Btl./SS-Pz.Gren.Rgt. 9 "Germania,"* August 1944.

13 *AOK 9 Ia KTB Anlage, Einheitliche Kampfstärke des IV. SS-Panzerkorps*, dated 17 August 1944.

14 Adolf Reinicke. *Die 5. Jäger-Division* (Eggolsheim, Germany: Dörfler Zeitgeschichte, 1989), pp. 329–30.

15 *AOK 9 Ia KTB Vororientierung*, 6:05 p.m., 18 August 1944.

16 *AOK 9 Ia KTB Tagesmeldung, Ia Nr. T12914/44 geheim* dated 11:30 p.m., 18 August 1944, 1.

17 *I.Abt./SS-Pz.Rgt. 5 KTB*, entry dated 9:15 p.m., 18 August 1944, 44.

18 *AOK 9 KTB der Führungsabteilung Textband Nr. 11*, entry dated 18 August 1944, 59–60.

19 Klapdor, p. 340.

20 Klapdor, p. 341.

21 *AOK 9 Ia KTB, Morgenmeldung IV. SS-Pz.Korps*, 7:40 a.m., 19 August 1944.

22 Vopersal, Vol. V.a., p. 336.

23 Ian Michael Wood. *Tigers of the Death's Head: SS Totenkopf Division's Tiger Company.* (Mechanicsburg, PA: Stackpole Books, 2013), pp. 150–51.

24 Vopersal, p. 338.
25 Klapdor, p. 342.
26 *Ibid*, p. 339.
27 *AOK 9 KTB der Führungsabteilung Textband Nr. 11*, entry dated 19 August 1944, 61.
28 Vopersal, Vol. Va., p. 339.
29 *AOK 9 Ia KTB Vororientierung*, 5:50 p.m., 19 August 1944.
30 Vopersal, Vol. Va., p. 339.
31 Vopersal, Vol. Va., p. 339, and *AOK 9 KTB der Führungsabteilung Textband Nr. 11*, entry dated 19 August 1944, 61.
32 *AOK 9 KTB der Führungsabteilung Textband Nr. 11*, entry dated 19 August 1944, 62.
33 *AOK 9 Ia KTB, Morgenmeldung IV. SS-Pz.Korps*, 7:10 a.m., 20 August 1944.
34 Klapdor, pp. 344–45. In recognition of the decisive and effective leadership he displayed that day, Senghas was later awarded the Knight's Cross on 11 September 1944.
35 Wood, p. 151.
36 Franz Hack. Panzergrenadiere der Panzerdivision "Wiking", in *Bild*, pp. 203–04
37 *SS-Pz.Rgt. 5 KTB*, entry dated 20 August 1944, 45.
38 *AOK 9 Ia KTB, Tagesmeldung*, dated 11:55 p.m., 21 August 1944, 2.
39 *AOK 9 KTB der Führungsabteilung Textband Nr. 11*, entry dated 20 August 1944, 66.
40 *AOK 9 Ia KTB Anlage, Kampfstärke* on 20 August 1944, dated 21 August, 2–3.
41 This exchange between Gille and von Vormann is documented in von Vormann's evening journal, *AOK 9 KTB der Führungsabteilung Textband Nr. 11*, entry dated 20 August 1944, p. 66. Incidentally, both SS divisions' replacement units still had not arrived at the front.
42 *AOK 9 Ia KTB Anlage, Nachmeldung, Stand der einsatzbereiten Panzer und Panzerabwehrwaffen am 19 August 1944, Pz.Div. "Wiking."*
43 Tessin, Vol. 13, p. 300, and *AOK 9 KTB Ia Anlage, Kampfstärke* on 17 and 21 August 1944.
44 Vopersal, Vol. Vb, p. 344.
45 *AOK 9 KTB der Führungsabteilung Textband Nr. 11*, entry dated 21 August 1944, 69.
46 *SS-Pz.Rgt. 5 KTB*, entry dated 21 August 1944, 46.
47 Vopersal, Vol. Vb, p. 344.
48 *AOK 9 KTB der Führungsabteilung Textband Nr. 11*, entry dated 21 August 1944, 69.
49 *IV. SS-Pz.Korps, Morgenmeldung*, 6:55 a.m., 22 August 1944.
50 *AOK 9 Ia KTB Anlage, Kampfstärke* on 20 August 1944, dated 21 August, 2–3.
51 Gille, quoted in Vopersal, Vol. Vb, p. 346.
52 *AOK 9 Ia KTB, Vororientierung*, 6 p.m., 23 August 1944.
53 *AOK 9 KTB der Führungsabteilung Textband Nr. 11*, entry dated 23 August 1944, 76.
54 *AOK 9 KTB der Führungsabteilung Textband Nr. 11*, entry dated 23 August 1944, p. 77, and *AOK 9 Ic Zwischenmeldung*, 23 August 1944.
55 *AOK 9 Ia KTB Tagesmeldung*, 10:20 p.m., 23 August 1944.
56 *AOK 9 Ia KTB Anlage, Nachmeldung, Stand der einsatzbereiten Panzer und Panzerabwehrwaffen am 24 August 1944, Pz.Div. "Wiking."*
57 *SS-Pz.Rgt. 5 KTB*, entry dated 24 August 1944, 47.
58 *AOK 9 Fernschreiben an Gen.Kdo. IV. SS-Pz.Korps*, 9:35 a.m., 24 August 1944.
59 War Diary, First Belorussian Front, 1–31 August 1944, pp. 280–83. Available at https://pamyat-naroda.ru/documents/view/?id=211326093.
60 *AOK 9 Ia KTB Vororientierung*, 5:45 p.m., 25 August 1944.
61 *IV.SS-Pz.Korps Morgenmeldung*, 6:47 a.m., 26 August 1944.
62 *AOK 9 Ia KTB Tagesmeldung*, 11:45 p.m., 26 August 1944, 1–2.
63 *Ibid*, 1.
64 *Ibid*, 2.

65 Klapdor, p. 349.
66 *Ibid*, p. 350.
67 Klapdor, p. 350, and *KTB, I.Abt./SS-Pz.Rgt. 5*, entry dated 26 August 1944, 44–45.
68 Klapdor, pp. 350–51.
69 *Ibid*, p. 353.
70 *Ibid.*
71 According to the battalion's war diary, there were still three operational *Pz. IV*s and two *StuG IV*s, not counting those under repair, which came to six additional vehicles (one *Pz. IV* and five *StuG IV*s). These vehicles had been committed elsewhere or had been evacuated previously, and were not among those trapped in the Ślężany bridgehead. *I. Abt./SS-Pz.Rgt. 5 KTB*, 27 August 1944.
72 *AOK 9 Ia Tagesmeldung*, 26 August 1944, 1.
73 These could have been misidentified, since that type of tank was no longer in front-line service; more than likely, they had destroyed KV-85 or JS-II tanks, which used the same hull but were equipped with larger-caliber cannon.
74 *IV. SS-Pz.Korps Morgenmeldung*, 7 a.m., 27 August 1944.
75 *AOK 9 Ia KTB Vororientierung*, 6:05 p.m., 27 August 1944.
76 *AOK 9 Ia KTB Tagesmeldung*, 11:30 p.m., 27 August 1944, 1–2.
77 *Ibid*, 2.
78 *AOK 9 Ia KTB Anlage, Einheitliche Kampfstärke des IV. SS-Panzerkorps*, dated 27 August 1944, and *Stand der einsatzbereiten Panzer und Panzerabwehrwaffen am* 27 August 1944.
79 *Ibid.*
80 Glantz, p. 421, and *Germany and the Second World War*, Vol. VIII, p. 606.
81 *AOK 9 Ia Morgenmeldung*, 6:35 a.m., 28 August 1944.
82 *AOK 9 Ia Vororientierung*, 5:50 p.m., 28 August 1944, and Vopersal, Vol. Vb, p. 367.
83 *AOK 9 Ia Morgenmeldung*, 6:55 a.m., 29 August 1944, and Vopersal, Vol. Vb, p. 364.
84 *AOK 9 Ia Tagesmeldung*, 11:05 p.m., 29 August 1944, 1–2.
85 *Ibid*, p. 2.
86 *Ibid*, p. 1.
87 Martin Steiger, quoted in Willy Fey, *Armor Battles of the Waffen-SS, 1943–45* (Mechanicsburg, PA: Stackpole Books, 2003), . 84.
88 *IV. SS-Pz.Korps Morgenmeldung*, 6:45 a.m., 30 August 1944.
89 Vopersal, Vol. Vb, p. 364.
90 *AOK 9 Ia Tagesmeldung*, 11 p.m., 30 August 1944, 1–2. *SS-Arko 104*, supporting Gille's corps, submitted a report that estimated that a total of 83 Soviet batteries were engaged against them, or roughly 400–500 guns (Vopersal, Vol. Vb, p. 370).
91 *AOK 9 Ia Tagesmeldung*, 11 p.m., 30 August 1944, 1.
92 *AOK 9 Ia Anlage Kampfstärke am* 28 August 1944, 3.
93 *5. SS-Pz.Div. Wiking Ia Tgb.Nr. 94/44 g.Kdos, Zustandbericht und Kriegsgliederung nach dem Stand vom 1.* September 1944.
94 Ibid, Wehrurteil, 2.
95 *3. SS-Pz.Div. Totenkopf Ia Tgb.Nr. 1030/44 g.Kdos, Zustandbericht und Kriegsgliederung nach dem Stand vom 1.* September 1944.
96 *Ibid*, Wehrurteil, 2.
97 19. *Pz.Div., Ia Meldung Zustandbericht, Kriegsgliederung und Wehrurteil nach dem Stand vom 1.* September 1944. However, the division's tank regiment would not join *the IV. SS-Pz.Korps*' order of battle until later.
98 *AOK 9 IIa/b, Vortragsnotiz, Verluste-Ersatz* August 1944 (*nur deutsche Verbände*), dated 6 September 1944.
99 Glantz, p. 429.

100 *Ibid*, p. 418.
101 War Diary, First Belorussian Front, 1–31 August 1944, pp. 281–82.

Chapter 8: The Second Defensive Battle of Warsaw Part I

1 *Verlustmeldungen, Band Nr. Ws 664, Hqu. Kdo. IV. SS-Pz.Korps* and *Band Nr. Ws 666, SS-Nachr. Abt. 104*, July–August 1944. These documents are stored in the Berlin Document Center, currently being incorporated into the *Bundesarchiv* along with records from the *Deutsche Dienststelle*. Research courtesy of Mr Geir Brendan.
2 Vopersal, Vol. 5b, p. 383.
3 *AOK 9 KTB der Führungsabteilung Textband Nr. 11*, entry dated 31 August 1944, 97.
4 Vopersal, Vol. 5a, pp. 161–62.
5 A detailed message was issued on 25 August that detailed the concerns voiced by the *9. Armee* commander that described the measures that its subordinate corps and other major subordinate commander were to implement should any Hungarian units under their command display any signs of wavering or going over to the enemy camp. One of these measures, as mentioned, was the need to anticipate the collapse of Hungarians divisions in combat and to have a ready reserve force to plug the gap until a larger reserve force could be inserted into the line. Fernschreiben, *Kommandeur, AOK 9*, 3 a.m., 25 August 1944.
6 *Magyar Királyi Honvédség*, or the Royal Hungarian Army.
7 *AOK 9 Ia KTB, Anlage, Bericht Nr. 5, Deutscher Verbindungs-Kommando 22 bei Kgl.Ung. II. Res.-Korps, Ia Nr. 2273/44* dated 22 September 1944. This periodic report by *Oberstleutnant* von Walterstorff, the liaison officer attached to the Hungarian Corps providing rear area security in the *9. Armee Kommando Rückwärtiger-Gebiet* (army rear area command), outlines the attitudes of the Hungarians towards the Poles and provides an objective assessment of the Hungarian Army units to date, including praise in certain instances where Hungarian troops, in particular the *1. Ung.Kav.Div.* and the *5. Res.Inf.Div.*, distinguished themselves.
8 *AOK 9 Ia KTB, Morgenmeldung*, 7 a.m. 31 August 1944.
9 *AOK 9 Ia KTB, Vororientierung*, 6:05 p.m., 31 August 1944, and Vopersal, Vol Vb, p. 378.
10 *AOK 9 Ia KTB, Tagesmeldung*, 22:45 p.m., 31 August 1944, and Vopersal, Vol. Vb, p. 378.
11 *Wehrmachtsbericht* dated 2 September 1944.
12 *AOK 9 Ia KTB, Tagesmeldung*, 22:45 p.m., 31 August 1944.
13 *Ibid* and his SS Service Record in John P. Moore's *Führerliste der Waffen-SS*, Disc 4.
14 *Morgenmeldung, IV. SS-Pz.Korps*, 4:55 a.m., 1 September 1944, submitted by *SS-Oscha.* Schlemmer.
15 This account and those that describe the day's events are found in the *AOK Ia KTB Morgenmeldung, Zwischenmeldung* and *Tagesmeldung* for 1 September 1944, as well as the morning reports sent in to *9. Armee* from the corps themselves. Additionally, Vopersal's Vol. Vb gives a detailed description of the fighting that day on pp. 381–83.
16 *AOK 9 Ia KTB Anlage, Funkspruch*, received at 2:40 p.m., 1 September 1944.
17 *AOK 9 Ia KTB, Tagesmeldung*, 11:15 p.m., 1 September 1944.
18 The movement of the *542. Gren.Div.* had actually progressed to the point when one of its battalions, *I. Btl./Gren.Rgt. 1076*, had actually arrived in the corps rear area of the *IV. SS-Pz.Korps* behind the *kgl. 1. ung.Kav.Div.* on 1 September before it was recalled several days later. Although it was technically attached to Gille's corps, it was never shown as contributing to its *Kampfstärke* and never moved into the front lines to begin relieving the Hungarian division. (Source: *AOK 9 Ia Kampfstärken Stand 3*, September 1944.)
19 *AOK 9 KTB der Führungsabteilung Textband Nr. 11*, entry dated 1 September 1944, 99.

20 Fernschreiben, *AOK 9* to *IV. SS-Pz.Korps* and *Gruppe von dem Bach*, dated 12 p.m., 1 September 1944.

21 Fernschreiben, *AOK 9* to *IV. SS-Pz.Korps*, dated 12 p.m., 31 August, and 1:30 a.m., 1 September 1944.

22 Martin Månsson, "War Correspondent Gösta Borg," in Bacyk, *Warsaw II*, pp. 197–98.

23 *AOK 9 KTB der Führungsabteilung Textband Nr. 11*, entry dated 1 September 1944, 99.

24 In addition to the reference mentioned here, Tessin Vol. 10 only states that it was transferred to the Warsaw area in September 1944 and reported as having been officially disbanded the following month.

25 A Red Army tank corps, based on its 1944 table of organization, was authorized a maximum strength of 10,500 men, 189 tanks, 24 assault guns, 36 antitank guns, a motorized infantry regiment, an artillery regiment, and supporting troops, making it roughly equal in strength on paper to a German *panzer* division. The biggest difference between the two was that while the Red Army could replace destroyed tanks quickly, the *Wehrmacht* could not. (Source: Vopersal, Vol. Vb, p. 386).

26 *AOK 9 Ia KTB, Fernschreiben an IV. SS-Pz.Korps*, 7 p.m. 4 September 1944.

27 Its actual commander, *SS-Hstuf.* Heinz Murr, had been seriously wounded in action on 13 August near Okuniew and would not return to resume command of his battalion until the end of September 1944.

28 *AOK 9, Ia KTB, Fernschreiben an Gren.Brig. 1131*, 7 p.m. 5 September 1944.

29 Klapdor, p. 360.

30 *Ibid*, pp. 360–61.

31 *AOK 9 1a KTB, Korps-Morgenmeldungen*, 5:35 a.m., 6 September 1944.

32 *AOK 9 KTB der Führungsabteilung Textband Nr. 11*, entry dated 6 Septemer 1944, 110.

33 War Diary, VIII Guards Tank Corps, 18 August to 5 September 1944. During this period, it records that its losses were as follows: 8 T-34, 49 M4A2 Shermans, 8 Valentine tanks, 8 JS-II, 6 SU-85, and 6 SU-76 destroyed, with 36 more of all types damaged but repairable, for a total number of 121 destroyed or put out of action. The corps also lost 1,800 men killed, wounded, and missing. (Translation of VIII Guards Tank Corps war diary courtesy of Mr Artyom Astafiev of Moscow, Russia.)

34 Ullrich, p. 246.

35 *AOK 9 Ia KTB Anlagen, Fernschreiben an den Kommandierenden General des IV. SS-Pz.Korps, Herrn SS-Gruppenführer Gille*, 9 September 1944.

36 This number is an estimate, based on strength reports from 1 September from the *Totenkopf* and *Wiking* Divisions (13,868 and 14,528, respectively) as well as the estimated numbers of the nearly full-strength *73. Inf.Div.* (12,000) and 1st Hungarian Cavalry Division (16,896), plus corps troops (1,520), and attachments.

Chapter 9: The Second Defensive Battle of Warsaw Part II

1 *AOK 9 Ia KTB, Tagesmeldung, Ia Nr. T13003/44 geheim*, 11:10 p.m., 10 September 1944, 1.

2 *AOK 9 Ia KTB, Anlagen, Fernschreiben an IV. SS-Pz.Korps*, 1:30 pm., 21 August 1944.

3 Ziemke, *Stalingrad to Berlin: The German Defeat in the East*, p. 344.

4 *AOK 9 Ia KTB, Anlage, Bewegungsübersicht*, 8 September 1944, 2.

5 *Befehle des Generalstabs des Heeres, I/ 7425/44 geh. v. 13.7.1944 und I/ 8260/9 geh. vom 20.7.1944, "Durch OKL sind 40,000 Uffz. und Mannschaften zum Heer versetzt, davon 26,000 beschleunigt zur Waffen-SS."* In the course of the following month another order was issued by Himmler on 2 August 1944 that declared, in his capacity as Commander of the *Ersatzheer*, that for assignment

purposes, personnel from the *Wehrmacht, Waffen-SS* and *Polizei* were deemed interchangeable. These orders had been precipitated by a *Führerbefehl* issued on 8 July 1944, wherein Hitler stated that there were too many excess *Luftwaffe* airmen and not enough airplanes, so they should be transferred to fight on land.

6 A good account of the service rendered by the Ukrainian volunteers during the battles of Warsaw can be found in Michael O. Logusz's *Galicia Division: The Waffen-SS 14th Grenadier Division 1943–1945* (Atglen, PA: Schiffer Military History, 1997), pp. 285–86.

7 *Ibid*, pp. 284–89.

8 *AOK 9 Ia KTB, Anlagen, Fernschreiben an Gruppe Sikenius und Sturm-Btl. AWS*, 9 p.m., 9 September 1944.

9 Glantz, in *Journal of Slavic Military Studies*, p. 407.

10 Ibid, p. 428.

11 Bacyk, pp. 118–19.

12 Glantz, p. 423.

13 Glantz, p. 423. Glantz quotes from the official Red Army account of the fighting, as described in the First Belorussian Front's War Experience Section.

14 *AOK 9 Ia KTB Tagesmeldung, Ia Nr. T13003/44 geheim*, 10 September 1944 at 11:10 p.m., 1, and *AOK 9 KTB der Führungsabteilung, Textband Nr. 11*, entry dated 10 September 1944, 121. Despite assertions to the contrary, Hähling was relieved of command due to his wounds, not his performance, which up to this point had been satisfactory. After recovering from his wounds, he was appointed acting commander of the *87. Inf.Div.*, followed by assignment as the commander of the *126. Inf.Div.* He was captured in Kurland in May 1945 and was released from Soviet captivity in 1951. He died on 20 May 1983 in Finsterwalde.

15 *AOK 9 Ia KTB Anlage, Fernschreiben an 19. Pz.Div.*, dated 10 September 1944, at 10:30 p.m.

16 A comparison of *Kampfstärke* between 9 and 10 September provides an illustration of the scale of the fighting and the number of casualties suffered by each of the divisions during one day of fighting alone. According to unit strength returns of 9 and 10 September 1944, the *73. Inf.Div.* lost 645 men killed, wounded, and missing, while the 1st Hungarian Cavalry Division lost 411, the *Totenkopf* Division 610, and the *Wiking* Division (with attached units) 406.

17 *AOK 9 Ia KTB Anlage, Tagesmeldung Gruppe von dem Bach*, 10 September 1944, 8:30 p.m.

18 *AOK 9 Ia KTB Anlage, Vororientierung an HGr. Mitte*, 11 September 1944, 4:05 p.m.

19 *AOK 9 Ia KTB Anlage, Meldungen und Befehle, Fernschreiben an Gen.Kdo. IV. SS-Pz.Korps Nr. 4903/44 geh.* 12 September 1944, 10:30 a.m.

20 *AOK 9 Führungsabteilung KTB*, entry dated 12 September 1944, p. 126.

21 *Korps-Gefecthstand, IV. SS-Pz.Korps*, German Cross in Gold awards submission document for *SS-Oberführer* Kurt Brasack, Addendum dated 3 October 1944.

22 *AOK 9 Ia KTB Anlage, Stand der Einsatzbereiten Panzer und Panzerabwehrwaffen am* 12 September 1944 *Abends*, 2.

23 *AOK 9 Führungsabteilung KTB*, entry dated 12 September 1944, 128.

24 Navenkin, pp. 553–54.

25 By 10 September, the combined effective strength of the two battalions from Major Nähring's *Pz.Gren.Rgt. 73* had been reduced to 177 combat troops, less than 16 percent of what was authorized. (Source: *AOK 9 Ia KTB, Anlage, Kampfstärken vom* 10 September 1944, 3.)

26 *AOK 9 Ia KTB Anlage, Meldungen und Befehle, Fernschreiben an dem Herrn Kommandeur, Kgl. ung. 1. Kav. Div.*, 14 September 1944, 9:30 p.m.

27 *AOK 9 Ia KTB Anlage, Meldungen und Befehle, Fernschreiben an Gen.Kdo. IV. SS-Pz.Korps Nr. 4877/44 geh.* 12 September 1944, 9:30 p.m.

28 *AOK 9 Ia KTB Anlage, Stand der Einsatzbereiten Panzer und Panzerabwehrwaffen am* 13 September 1944 *Abends*, 2.

29 *AOK 9 Ia KTB Anlage, Meldungen und Befehle, Fernschreiben an Gen.Kdo. IV. SS-Pz.Korps Nr. 4934/44 geh.* 13 September 1944, 5:30 p.m.
30 *Ibid.*
31 *AOK 9 KTB der Führungsabteilung,* Textband Nr. 11, entry dated 13 September 1944, 131.
32 *Ibid,* 130.
33 *AOK 9 Ia KTB, Anlage, Kampfstärken vom* 10 September 1944, p. 1. Adding in the Tross and other non-combat elements of the regiment, as well as men in the regimental antitank and infantry howitzer companies, the combined actual strength, or *Iststärke,* of the regiment was probably between 1,800 and 2,000 men.
34 *IV. SS-Pz.Korps Morgenmeldung,* 6:15 a.m. 14 September 1944, and *Guppe von dem Bach, Morgenmeldung,* 14 September 1944.
35 *IV. SS-Pz.Korps Tagesmeldung,* 9:45 p.m., 14 September 1944, 2.
36 *Tagesmeldung, IV. SS-Pz.Korps,* 14 September, 7:22 p.m. One officer from the *25. Pz.Div.* later reported that the division and its attached elements that day suffered as many as 300 casualties and that after one day of fighting, many of its troops were exhausted. (Source: Norman Davies, *Rising '44: The Battle for Warsaw* [New York: Viking Press, 2003], p. 367.)
37 Knobelsdorff, p. 275, and *AOK 9 Ia KTB Tagesmeldung,* 10:21 p.m., 16 September 1944.
38 Wood, p. 153.
39 Vopersal, p. 415, and *AOK 9 Ia KTB Tagesmeldung,* 16 September 1944.
40 In eight days between 7 and 15 September, the Hungarians had suffered over 1,115 casualties in its fighting units alone, nearly 30 percent of its total *Kampfstärke.* The losses suffered on 16 September, though unrecorded, must have been high, as Gille described the division as being "*stark mitgenommen*" (badly shaken). (Source: *IV. SS-Pz.Korps, Abendmeldung,* 16 September 1944, and *AOK 9 Ia KTB Anlage, Kampfstärken zwischen 7 und 15* September 1944.)
41 *Tagesmeldung, IV. SS-Pz.Korps,* 16 September 1944.
42 *AOK 9 KTB der Führungsabteilung,* Textband Nr. 11, entry dated 16 September 1944, 137–39.
43 Bacyk, p. 143.
44 *AOK 9 Ia KTB, Morgenmeldung der Korps,* 6:02 a.m., 17 September 1944.
45 Bacyk, p. 131.
46 Figures are drawn from *AOK 9 Ia KTB Anlage,* including *Kampfstärken* from 10 and 17 September 1944.
47 *AOK 9 Ia KTB, Anlage, Stand der einsatzbereiten Panzer und Panzerabwehrwaffen am* 17 September 1944, *Abends.*
48 *AOK 9 KTB der Führungsabteilung,* Textband Nr. 11, entry dated 17 September 1944, 140–41.
49 *Heeresgruppe Mitte, Ia KTB,* entry dated 17 September 1944, 130.
50 These tanks had been reported earlier that day by *Luftwaffe* reconnaissance as moving south–southeast, away from the *IV. SS-Pz.Korps.* Both Gille and von Vormann interpreted this movement to be part of a general repositioning of Soviet armor for the next phase of the offensive, but in this case both men were mistaken.
51 *AOK 9 KTB der Führungsabteilung,* Textband Nr. 11, entry dated 17 September 1944, 130.
52 This point is clearly conveyed in the opening paragraph of the *HGr. Mitte Kriegstagebuch,* which summarizes the overall situation at the close of the day. *Generaloberst* Reinhardt is clearly more concerned about the situation in the *3. Pz.Armee* area of operations than that obtaining in his other three armies. Given what was at stake, i.e., the separation of *HGr. Mitte* from *HGr. Nord,* it is hard to disagree with his observation.
53 Ullrich, p. 294.
54 On that day, *SS-Pz.Rgt. 5* had 23 *Pz.Kfw. V* Panthers operational, 3 *Pz.Kfw. IV* and an undetermined number of *Sturmgeschütze.* (Source: *AOK 9 Ia KTB, Anlage, Stand der einsatzbereiten Panzer und Panzerabwehrwaffen am* 18 September 1944, *Abends.*)

55 *IV. SS-Pz.Korps Tagesmeldung*, 18 September 1944, 2.

56 Davies, pp. 377–78, 379.

57 Incidentally, Gille nominated Ritter for the Knight's Cross in recognition of his and his battalion's performance while attached to the *IV. SS-Pz.Korps*. The award was approved on 2 October 1944.

58 Bacyk, p. 137. Tank and personnel losses were tallied from the VIII Guards Tank Corps War Diary, 10–20 September 1944, and pp. 48–54.

59 With the return of von Lüttwitz's corps, *Gruppe von dem Bach* was relieved for any responsibility of defending along the river and instead was tasked solely with suppressing the uprising. (Source: *AOK 9 KTB der Führungsabteilung*, Textband Nr. 11, entry dated 18 September 1944, 144.)

60 The depleted condition of the division was laid out in explicit terms in a special report completed by the division's Ia dated 21 September 1944.

61 *Oberkommando des Heeres, Chef der Heeresrüstung und Befehlshaber des Ersatzheeres, AHA/Ic Nr. 8320/44, Betr: Umbennenung*, 25 October 1944, p. 9, "*Bezug: OKH/Gen.StdH./Org.Abt. Nr. II/46851/44* of 6 October 1944."

62 This and following conversations that took place throughout the day are recorded in the *HGr. Mitte Ia KTB* for 18 September 1944, pp. 135–36.

63 *AOK 9 Ia KTB Anlage, Fernschreiben Ia Nr. 5081/44*, issued 9 a.m., 19 September 1944.

64 *IV. SS-Pz.Korps, Tagesmeldung*, 8:20 p.m., 19 September 1944.

65 *Ibid.*

66 Bacyk, p. 144.

67 *AOK 9 KTB der Führungsabteilung*, Textband Nr. 11, entry dated 19 September 1944, 147, and Courts Martial Directive, 19 September 1944. (Source: *AOK 9 Ia Anlage Ia Nr. 5082/44, Fernschreiben an den Kommandeur der 19. Pz.Div.*, 11:05 a.m., 19 September 1944.)

68 *Heeresgruppe Mitte, Ia KTB*, entry dated 19 September 1944, 144–45.

69 *Ibid*, 146.

70 *Ibid*, 144.

71 Bacyk, p. 138.

72 *IV. SS-Pz.Korps, Tagesmeldung*, 8:00 p.m., 20 September 1944.

73 *Heeresgruppe Mitte, Ia KTB*, entry dated 20 September 1944, 152, and Bacyk, p. 138.

74 Initially, Reinhardt wanted *Gen.d.Pz.Tr.* Maximilian Freiherr von Edelsheim to serve as the corps commander, but on 21 September he was selected instead to command the *XLVIII. Pz.Korps*, clearing the way for Fries to assume command instead. (Source: *Heeresgruppe Mitte, Ia KTB*, entry dated 20 September 1944, 152.)

75 *AOK 9 Ia KTB Anlage, Meldungen und Befehle, Fernschreiben Nr. 5133/44*, issued 8:05 p.m., 20 September 1944, 1–2.

76 Wolf Keilig, *Das Deutsche Heer, 1939–1945*: Volume 211, *Die Generalität des Heeres im 2. Weltkrieg* (Bad Nauheim: Podzun-Verlag, 1956), p. 353.

77 The final tally of Polish dead and wounded was shocking. During the several crossing attempts made between 17–20 September, the 1st Polish Army lost 1,987 dead or missing and 289 wounded, while only 627 men were successfully evacuated after the landings were called off. Most of their weapons and equipment were lost as well. Afterwards, Polish reports indicated that the crossings had failed due to poor communication, the lack of cooperation by General Bór and the *Armia Krajowa*, and insufficient training in river crossing operations by the units concerned. In his view, Rokossovsky felt that the crossing had been rushed and suffered from "overzealousness." One result of the failed attempt was the transfer of the 1st Polish Army's commander, General Berling, to the position of Deputy Commander of the Soviet-sponsored Polish Army. He was temporarily replaced by his second in command, Colonel General Karol W. Świerczewski. (Source: Bacyk, pp. 144–45.)

78 *AOK 9 KTB der Führungsabteilung*, Textband Nr. 11, entry dated 22 September 1944, 151–52.
79 *Heeresgruppe Mitte, Ia KTB*, entry dated 22 September 1944, 161–62.

Chapter 10: An Unexpected Lull in the Action

1 Rokossovsky, p. 264.
2 According to the *HGr. Mitte KTB* on 25 September 1944, 2,400 replacements were either on their way to join the *IV. SS-Pz.Korps*' combat units in the field or were already undergoing training in the field replacement or field training battalions of both divisions. (Source: *HGr. Mitte Ia KTB*, entry dated 25 September 1944, 173.)
3 *Kampfgruppe Braune* was led by the commander of the *Wiking* Division's combat engineer battalion, *SS-Ostubaf.* Fritz Braune. Braune was elevated to the position instead of Flügel due to his seniority and depth of experience, but he only held the position until 1 October, when he departed to become the new corps' *Pionierführer*, replacing *SS-Ostubaf.* Erich May. The following day, his *Kampfgruppe* was disbanded when it was replaced by the *Germania* Regiment. May himself was transferred to become the corps *Pionierfuehrer* of the newly activated *XI. SS-Armeekorps*.
4 During its 31-day period of service as part of the *IV. SS-Pz.Korps*, the *Kgl. ung. 1. Kav.Div.* had suffered the loss of 181 killed, 1,191 wounded, and 66 missing in action, for a total of 1,438 men. (Source: *AOK 0 Ia KTB, Anlagen, Bericht, Verbindungsstab 22, Verluste Kgl.Ung. 1. Kav.Div. und 5. Res.Div., Ia Nr. 2273/44*, dated 22 September 1944.)
5 Detailed instructions for the construction of field fortifications, including diagrams for each type of position to be built, had been issued earlier by the *9. Armee* staff engineer officer. (Source: *AOK 9 Ia KTB, Anlage, Ausbauleitung für die Weichsel-Ostpreussenstellung: Anweisungen fuer den Stellungsbau, Ia Nr. 3342/44*, dated 18 July 1944.)
6 The commander of the *Totenkopf Alarmbataillon* was *SS-Hstuf.* Erich Dümmer, acting commander of the staff company, *SS-Pz.Gren.Rgt. 6*, while that of the *Wiking*'s was *SS-Stubaf.* Joachim Stoige, commander of *SS-Flak-Btl. 5*. (Source: Vopersal, p. 430.)
7 *AOK 9 Ia KTB, Chefsachen, Betr: Unternehmen "Sternschnuppe," Abt. Ia Nr. 5199/44*, dated 22 September 1944, 9:00 p.m., and *AOK 9 Ia KTB Anlage, Stand der einsatzbereiten Panzer und Panzerabwehrwaffen*, 27 September 1944.
8 *AOK 9 Führungsabteilung KTB*, entries dated 29 and 30 September 1944, 161–63.
9 Bernau, p. 134.
10 Rokossovksy, p. 265.
11 In his memoirs, Rokossovsky states that with regard to preparing a defense against any future large-scale German offensives, "we had learned our lesson" (Rokossovsky, p. 266).
12 The *2. Armee Oberquartiermeister*'s armored vehicle status report for October 1944 revealed that the units under *XX. Armeekorps* taking part in *Sonnenblume* lost a total of 87 tanks, assault guns, and tank destroyers between 1 and 31 October. Of these, 19 were recovered and repaired or sent back to Germany for long-term rebuild. (Source: *AOK 2 O.Qu./V KTB, Anlage: Ausfälle an gep. Kfz. In Monat Oktober 1944 auf Grund der täglichen Panzermeldungen*, dated 12 November 1944.)
13 *AOK 9 Führungsabteilung KTB*, entries dated 8 October 1944, 180.
14 *AOK 9 Ia KTB, Anlage, Beabsichige Kräfteverteilung und Gliederung der 9. Armee, AOK 9 Abt. Ia Nr. 5257/44*, dated 24 September 1944, 1.
15 *Stärkemeldung des B.d.Waffen-SS Böhmen und Mähren, Abt. Ia, Az. 12d Hu./Sch., Tagebuch Nr. 2960/44* of 12 September 1944, and *AOK 9 Ia KTB, Anlage, Bewegungsbericht*, 23 September 1944, 1.

16 In recognition of their service while assigned to the *Wiking* Division, on 4 November 1944, *Staf.* Ullrich issued a special order thanking and commending them for their performance. Of the 1,000 Ukrainians who served with the *Wiking* Division during September and October 1944, approximately 750 returned to their original division. (Source, courtesy of Mike Melnyk: *SS-Pz. Div. Wiking, Kdo.Div.Gef.St.* 4 November 1944, *Betr: Divisions-Sonderbefehl anl. Der Verabschiedung der gal. Waffen-Willigen am* 3 November 1944.)

17 *OKH/Gen.St.d.H./Org.Abt.Nr. I/10705/44, Betr: Personelle Auffrischung der SS-Pz.Div. Wiking und Totenkopf,* dated 16 September 1944.

18 Alfred Vogt, "*Erlebnisbericht*" in *der Freiwillige,* 1/1989 (Osnabrück: Munin Verlag GmbH, 1989), p. 10.

19 *SS-FHA, Abt. IIa, Stärkemeldungen,* Status as of 5, 10, and 20 September 1944.

20 Copy of Willy Kirschmeier's *SS Soldbuch* and *Wehrpass* in author's collection.

21 *SS-Führungshauptamt, Amt II Org.Abt.Ia/II, Tgb.Nr. 3465/44, Betr: Kriegsgliederungen der Gen. Kdos. SS-Pz.Korps,* dated 4 October 1944.

22 Roland Pfeiffer, undated manuscript, "*SS-Werfer-Abteilung 504*", and Anonymous, "*SS-Werfer-Abteilung 504*" in *Der Freiwillige,* Vol. 9, 1965 (Osnabrück, Germany: Munin Verlag GmbH, 1965), pp. 9–11.

23 *AOK 9, Ia KTB Anlage, Stärkemeldungen,* August–October 1944.

24 *Gen.Kdo. IV. SS-Panzerkorps, Adjutantur IIa: Verleihungsliste Nr.1,Korps-Gefechtsstand,* 9 October 1944.

25 *3. SS-Pz.Div. "Totenkopf," Ia Tgb.Nr. 1140/44, Betr: Zustandbericht nach dem Stand vom 1.10.44,* dated 4 October 1944, 5 pages.

26 *5. SS-Pz.Div. "Wiking," Ia Tgb.Nr. 104/44, Betr: Zustandbericht nach dem Stand vom 1.10.44,* dated 5 October 1944, 4 pages.

27 Nevenkin, pp. 715–17.

28 Roger James Bender and George A. Petersen, *Hermann Göring: from Regiment to Fallschirmpanzerkorps* (San Jose: R. James Bender Publishing, 1975), pp. 46–48.

29 *Fs.Pz.Div. 1 "Hermann Göring," Ia Tgb.Nr. 117/44, Betr: Zustandbericht,* 4 November 1944.

30 *19. Pz.Div, Ia Tagebuch Betr: Zustandbericht nach dem Stand vom 1.10.44,* dated 1 October 1944.

31 *AOK 9 Ia KTB, Tagesmeldung,* entry dated 5 October 1944 at 10 p.m.

32 *IV. SS-Pz.Korps Ia KTB, Tagesmeldungen* entries dated 24–29 September 1944.

33 Koruck 532, *Ia KTB, Brief an dem A.O.K. 9 O.Qu,* 6 October 1944, and Letter, *der Amtskommisar des Amtsbezirks Modlin,* and *den Herrn Kreisbauernführer,* in Betr Plöhnen *Erfassungswesen im Amtsbezirks Modlin,* dated 3 October 1944.

34 Letter, *der Oberbefehlshaber der 9. Armee an dem Kommandierenden General des IV. SS-Pz.Korps, O.Qu.Nr. 8203/44,* dated 8 October 1944.

35 *Vorschlag für die Verleihung des Deutschen Kreuzes in Silber an SS-Ostubaf. Hans Scharff, Korps Gefechtsstand, der Kommandierende General des IV. SS-Panzerkorps,* dated 1 January 1945.

36 Yerger, *Waffen-SS Commanders,* Vol. II (Krüger–Zimmermann), pp. 302, 305–06, and Schneider, p. 392.

37 *Personalakte,* Franz Kleffner. (Source: John Moore, *Führerliste der Waffen-SS, Personalakte,* 2003, Disk 3.)

38 Strassner, p. 179, and Bernau, p. 134.

39 *SS-Pz.Rgt. 5 Wiking KTB,* entry dated 10 October 1944 at 12:30 p.m.

40 *I. Abt./SS-Pz.Rgt. 5 Wiking KTB,* entry dated 23 October 1944 at 7:30 p.m.

41 Oosterling, Erlings, and Fischer, pp. 399–400, 406. How or where he received the wound is not noted. Perhaps it had been due to an air attack on Berlin or incurred while he was out in the field visiting *panzer* units.

Chapter 11: The Third Defensive Battle of Warsaw

1 Rokossovsky, p. 264.

2 Bacyk, pp. 154–55.

3 Frieser, Schmider, Schonherr, Schreiber, Wegner, *et al*, Vol. VIII, p. 609.

4 Shortly after the German invasion of the Soviet Union on 22 June 1941, the STAVKA halved the size of the Red Army's infantry division to speed up wartime mobilization. The resulting division structure was authorized only 9,000 men. After the war, the Red Army settled on a standard size for its rifle divisions of 11,000 men. (Source: Department of the Army Pamphlet No. 30-2, *The Soviet Army* [Washington, D. C: Department of the Army, July 1949], p. 49.)

5 These numbers do not equate to front-line strength or *Kampfstärke* of either side. Factoring in that aspect, considering that the Red Army had far fewer men in its logistics units at the division level as compared to their *Wehrmacht* counterparts, the strength ratios most likely approached three or four to one in actuality in favor of the Soviets and even greater at the point of main effort.

6 Strassner, p. 181, Vopersal, p. 443, and Glantz, *Atlas of the Lublin-Brest Operation and the Advance on Warsaw*, p. 156.

7 Strassner, p. 181.

8 Klapdor, p. 367. This marked an increase from the previous number of 165 batteries identified as recently as 30 September. (Source: Strassner, p. 180.)

9 *Ibid*, p. 181.

10 *Ibid*, p. 182.

11 *IV. SS-Pz.Korps Ia KTB, Tagesmeldung* dated 8 October 1944.

12 According to the *9. Armee* war diary, von Lüttwitz was mainly expecting the offensive to spring forth from the Magnuszew bridgehead against *VIII. Armeekorps* at any time after 8 October, not against Gille's corps. Though the *9. Armee* operations branch did admit the possibility of another attack against *IV. SS-Pz.Korps*, this course of action was seen as the least likely of three possible threats. (Source: *AOK 9 Ia KTB, Tagesmeldung, Ia Nr. 13116/44*, 10:40 p.m. dated 8 October 1944.) In the *9. Armee* war diary on 2 October, von Lüttwitz discusses his preliminary plans for conducting an attack against the Magnuszew bridgehead, using two *panzer* divisions (including perhaps the *Fs.Pz. Div. "HG"*) and a number of *Heerestruppen*. Clearly, he was thinking much about Gille's situation. (Source: *AOK 9 Führungsabteilung KTB*, entry dated 2 October 1944, 169.)

13 *IV. SS-Pz.Korps Ia KTB, Tagesmeldung* dated 6 October 1944.

14 Vopersal, p. 442.

15 Strassner, pp. 181–82.

16 *IV. SS-Pz.Korps Ia KTB, Tagesmeldung* dated 9 October 1944 at 8:15 p.m., as well as Bernau, pp. 134–35, and Strassner, p. 182. Brasack describes in detail this "preventive barrage" technique in a post-war interview conducted by the U.S. Army. (Source: MS # D-228, "Russian Artillery in the Battle for Modlin and German Countermeasures," Department of the Army, Office of the Chief of Military History, Washington, D.C., undated.)

17 *AOK 2, Ib KTB, Ib Tagesmeldung für Gen.Kdo. IV. SS-Pz.Korps*, 10 October 1944, and Bernau, p. 134.

18 Vopersal, p. 445.

19 Rokossovsky, pp. 264–65.

20 Bernau, p. 135.

21 *Kampfgruppe Braune* had been disestablished and replaced by the *Germania* Regiment after 2 October 1944. (Source: *AOK 9 Ia KTB, Anlage, Bewegungsbericht*, 1 October 1944, 1.)

22 *AOK 9 Ia KTB, Besprechungspunkte für Aussprache Oberbefehlshaber Heeresgruppe Mitte mit Oberbefehlshaber AOK 9*, dated 10 October 1944, 1.
23 *AOK 2, Ib KTB, Ib Morgenmeldung für Gen.Kdo. IV. SS-Pz.Korps*, 10 October 1944.
24 Glantz, *Atlas of the Lublin-Brest Operation and the Advance on Warsaw*, p. 156, and *AOK 9 Ia KTB* Situation Map, 9 October 1944.
25 *IV. SS-Pz.Korps, Ia KTB, Tagesmeldung*, 10 October 1944.
26 Bacyk, p. 156.
27 *AOK 9, Ia KTB, Vororientierung*, 10 October 1944 at 5:55 p.m.
28 Von Knobelsdorff, p. 276, and *IV. SS-Pz.Korps, Ia KTB, Tagesmeldung*, 10 October 1944.
29 Wood, p. 154. During this counterattack, one Tiger was damaged by an antitank gun with three of its crewmembers reported as being killed in action, including *SS-Oscha.* Wendt. The tank was later recovered.
30 Vopersal, p. 449.
31 Ullrich, p. 247, and Schneider, p. 35.
32 *AOK 9, Ia KTB, Vororientierung*, 10 October 1944.
33 *SS-Pz.Rgt. 5, Ia KTB*, entry dated 10 October 1944, 70.
34 Ullrich, pp. 249–50, and Vopersal, p. 451.
35 *AOK 9, Ia KTB Anlage, Nachmeldung zur Tagesmeldung vom* 10 October 1944.
36 *AOK 2, Ib KTB, Ib Tagesmeldung für Gen.Kdo. IV. SS-Pz.Korps*, 11 October 1944.
37 *IV. SS-Pz.Korps, Ia KTB, Tagesmeldung*, 10 October 1944.
38 *AOK 9 Führungsabteilung KTB*, entry dated 10 October 1944, 181–82.
39 *AOK 2 Ib KTB, Ib IV. SS-Pz.Korps Tagesmeldung* for 10 October 1944.
40 *AOK 9 Ia KTB, Morgenmeldung*, 6:35 a.m., 11 October 1944.
41 Vopersal, p. 453.
42 Wood, p. 154, and Vopersal, p. 453.
43 Vopersal, p. 453.
44 Vopersal, p. 453, and *IV. SS-Pz.Korps Ia Tagesmeldung*, 11 October 1944 at 7:00 p.m.
45 Vopersal, pp. 453–54.
46 Klapdor, p. 371.
47 Vopersal, p. 455, and *Ia KTB, SS-Pz.Rgt. 5*, dated 11 October 1944, 72.
48 *IV. SS-Pz.Korps, Ia KTB Tagesmeldung*, 11 October 1944.
49 *AOK 2 Ib KTB, Ib IV. SS-Pz.Korps Tagesmeldung* for 11 October 1944.
50 *AOK 9 Ia KTB, Anlage, Stand der einsatzbereiten Panzer und Panzerabwehrwaffen*, 11 October 1944.
51 *AOK 9 Führungsabteilung KTB*, entry dated 11 October 1944, 183–84.
52 *Ibid.*
53 Klapdor, p. 372.
54 Strassner, pp. 183–84.
55 *Ibid*, p. 184.
56 Anonymous, "SS-Werfer Abteilung 504" in *Der Freiwillige*, Vol. 9, 1965 (Osnabruck: Munin Verlag, 1965), pp. 10–11.
57 Klapdor, p. 372.
58 Strassner, p. 184.
59 *IV. SS-Pz.Korps, Ia Tagesmeldung*, 12 October 1944, 8:58 p.m.
60 On 12 October alone, *IV. SS-Pz.Korps*, excluding *19. Pz.Div.*, had fired 425 tons of explosives at the enemy, an average of 20,000 shells of all types. (Source: *AOK 2 Ib KTB, Ib IV. SS-Pz.Korps Tagesmeldung* for 12 October 1944.)
61 *AOK 9 Ia KTB, Anlage, Stand der einsatzbereiten Panzer und Panzerabwehrwaffen*, 12 October 1944.

62 *IV. SS-Pz.Korps, Ia Tagesmeldung*, 12 October 1944, 8:58 p.m.
63 *AOK 9 Führungsabteilung KTB*, entry dated 12 October 1944, 185–86.
64 Vopersal, p. 461.
65 *IV SS-Pz.Korps Ia KTB, Tagesmeldung* for 13 October 1944.
66 Klapdor, pp. 372–73.
67 *Ibid*, pp. 373–74.
68 *AOK 2 Ib KTB, Ib IV. SS-Pz.Korps, Tagesmeldung* for 13 October 1944.
69 *IV SS-Pz.Korps Ia KTB, Tagesmeldung* for 13 October 1944.
70 *AOK 9 Führungsabteilung KTB*, entry dated 13 October 1944, 186–188.
71 Vopersal, p. 463.
72 *Ibid.*
73 *AOK 9, Ia Morgenmeldung*, 14 October 1944.
74 *IV SS-Pz.Korps Ia KTB, Tagesmeldung* for 14 October 1944.
75 *AOK 9 Ia KTB, Anlage, Stand der einsatzbereiten Panzer und Panzerabwehrwaffen*, 14 October 1944.
76 *AOK 9 Führungsabteilung KTB*, entry dated 14 October 1944, 189–90.
77 Wood, p. 154, and Vopersal, p. 467.
78 Vopersal, p. 466.
79 Klapdor, p. 374.
80 Klapdor, p. 374, Strassner, pp. 186–87, and *AOK 2 Ib KTB, Ib IV. SS-Pz.Korps Tagesmeldung* for 15 October 1944.
81 *IV SS-Pz.Korps Ia KTB, Tagesmeldung* for 15 October 1944.
82 *AOK 9 Führungsabteilung KTB*, entry dated 15 October 1944, 191–93.
83 According to one source, this was indeed part of a clever Soviet deception plan carried out by Chuikov's 8th Guards Army, devised by Rokossovsky to mislead the German high command. If it was, it proved to be very effective. (Source: Bacyk, p. 157.)
84 *AOK 9 Chefsachen, Notiz zum Besuch des Herrn Oberbefehlshabers der Heeresgruppe Mitte*, 15 October 1944.
85 *AOK 9 Chefsachen, Notiz zum Besprechung beim Oberbefehlshabers der Heeresgruppe Mitte*, 15 October 1944.
86 The *9. Armee* commander mulled these points over in his nightly narrative to *HGr. Mitte* on 15 October.
87 *AOK 2 Ib KTB, Ib IV. SS-Pz.Korps Tagesmeldung* for the period 9–16 October 1944.
88 *IV SS-Pz.Korps Ia KTB, Tagesmeldung* for 16 October 1944.
89 *AOK 9 Führungsabteilung KTB*, entry dated 16 October 1944, 194–95.
90 Strassner, p. 187.
91 *IV SS-Pz.Korps Ia KTB, Tagesmeldung* for 17 October 1944.
92 These figures and statistics are derived from *AOK 2 Ib KTB, Ib IV. SS-Pz.Korps Tagesmeldung* for 10–16 October 1944, the *AOK 9 Ia KTB Anlage, Stand der einsatzbereiten Panzer und Panzerabwehrwaffen* dated 16 October 1944, and the *AOK 9 Ia KTB Anlage, Kampfstärken der Divisionen*, 16 October 1944. *SS-Jäg.Btl. 501* had absorbed over 100 replacements since its arrival in Modlin.
93 *AOK 9 Führungsabteilung KTB*, entry dated 17 October 1944, 196–97.
94 *IV SS-Pz.Korps Ia KTB, Tagesmeldung* for 17 October 1944, sent at 7:40 p.m., and 18 October at 7:55 p.m.
95 *AOK 9 Ia KTB, Anlage, Bewegungsbericht*, 19 October 1944.
96 *AOK 9 Führungsabteilung KTB*, entry dated 18 October 1944, 198–99.
97 Klapdor, p. 375.
98 *IV. SS-Pz.Korps Ia KTB, Tagesmeldung* for 19 October 1944.
99 *AOK 9 Führungsabteilung KTB*, entry dated 19 October 1944, 200–02.

100 Klapdor, p. 376.
101 Schneider, p. 335, and Strassner, pp. 188–89.
102 Knobelsdorff, p. 277.
103 *IV. SS-Pz.Korps Ia KTB, Tagesmeldung* for 20 October 1944.
104 *I. Abt./SS-Pz.Rgt. 5 KTB*, entry dated 21 October 1944, 57.
105 *SS-Pz.Rgt. 5 KTB*, entry dated 21 October 1944, 78.
106 *IV. SS-Pz.Korps Ia KTB, Tagesmeldung* for 21 October 1944.
107 *AOK 9 Ia KTB Anlage, Stand der einsatzbereiten Panzer und Panzerabwehrwaffen* dated 22 October 1944.
108 *AOK 2 Ia KTB Anlage*, Situation map dated 23 October 1944.
109 *I. Abt./SS-Pz.Rgt. 5 KTB*, entry dated 22 October 1944, 58, and *SS-Pz.Rgt. 5 KTB*, entry dated 22 October 1944, 79.
110 *IV. SS-Pz.Korps Ia KTB, Tagesmeldung* for 22 October 1944.
111 *AOK 9 Führungsabteilung KTB*, entry dated 22 October 1944, 209–11.
112 *AOK 2 Ib KTB, Ib IV. SS-Pz.Korps Tagesmeldung* for the period 21–24 October 1944.
113 *AOK 9, Ia KTB, Tagesmeldung der 9. Armee*, 22 October 1944, 11:00 p.m.
114 According to the U.S. Army's field manual of military terms, the term "active defense" is defined as "The employment of limited offensive action and counterattacks to deny a contested area or position to the enemy." (Source: DoD Dictionary of Military and Associated Terms [Washington, D.C.: U.S. Department of Defense, May 2019], p. 7.)
115 *I. Abt./SS-Pz.Rgt. 5 KTB*, entry dated 23 October 1944, 58.
116 *IV. SS-Pz.Korps Ia KTB, Tagesmeldung* for 23 October 1944.
117 *AOK 9 Führungsabteilung KTB*, entry dated 23 October 1944, 211–13.
118 *SS-Pz.Rgt. 5 KTB*, entry dated 22 October 1944, 80.
119 *I. Abt./SS-Pz.Rgt. 5 KTB*, entry dated 23 October 1944, 59.
120 *AOK 9 Ia KTB Anlage, Stand der einsatzbereiten Panzer und Panzerabwehrwaffen* dated 24 October 1944.
121 *IV. SS-Pz.Korps Ia KTB, Tagesmeldung* for 24 October 1944.
122 *AOK 9 Führungsabteilung KTB*, entry dated 24 October 1944, 213–15.
123 *I. Abt./SS-Pz.Rgt. 5 KTB*, entry dated 25 October 1944, 59.
124 *IV. SS-Pz.Korps Ia KTB, Tagesmeldung* for 25 October 1944.
125 *AOK 9 Führungsabteilung KTB*, entry dated 25 October 1944, 216–17.
126 *IV. SS-Pz.Korps Ia KTB, Tagesmeldung* for 26 October 1944.
127 *AOK 9 Führungsabteilung KTB*, entry dated 26 October 1944, 218–19.
128 *SS-Pz.Rgt. 5 KTB*, entry dated 27 October 1944, 82, and *I. Abt./SS-Pz.Rgt. 5 KTB*, entry dated 27 October 1944, 60.
129 *IV. SS-Pz.Korps Ia KTB, Tagesmeldung* for 27 October 1944.
130 *AOK 9 Führungsabteilung KTB*, entry dated 27 October 1944, 220.
131 Rokossovsky, pp. 264–65.
132 *IV. SS-Pz.Korps Ia KTB, Tagesmeldung* for 28 October 1944.
133 *AOK 9 Führungsabteilung KTB*, entry dated 28 October 1944, 221–23.
134 War Diary, First Belorussian Front, p. 248, and Frieser, *et al*, p. 609.
135 Glantz, *The Red Army's Lublin-Brest Offensive and Advance on Warsaw*, p. 407
136 War Diary, First Belorussian Front, period including 1 August to 31 October 1944.
137 This number was derived from a tally of the daily reported number of Soviet tanks contained in the daily armor strength reports sent to *9. Armee*. (Source: *AOK 9 Ia KTB Anlage, Stand der einsatzbereiten Panzer und Panzerabwehrwaffen* from 10–28 October 1944.)
138 Ullrich, p. 250.

139 Rokossovsky, p. 264.

140 Bacyk, p. 159. This is based on the summary of an *OKW* report for the period of 1 August to 15 September. (Source: *OKH, GenStdH, Org. Abt. Nr. 1/154212/44, Aufschlüsselung der unwiederbringlichen Verluste Juni–November 1944 nach Kriegsschauplätzen, 2.12.44, H 1/450m* file.)

141 Monthly *Zustandsberichte* for the *Wiking* and *Totenkopf* Divisions for October, dated 4 November 1944.

Chapter 12: The Battle of Modlin 29 October–25 November 1944

1 The only other official records for that period are the war diaries of the *SS-Pz.Rgt. 5* headquarters and *I. Abt./SS-Pz.Rgt. 5*. Both of these, however, end on 30 November 1944. No other war diaries for the division are known to exist beyond that point, though there is a rumor that a portion of the *Wiking* Division's *KTB* from the end of the war is in the hands of a private collector in France.

2 To piece together the events those followed and determine where they fit in the greater historical narrative, the writer had to resort to the daily corps situation reports sent to the *9. Armee* operations department, as well as the *9. Armee* daily reports describing what was occurring in the rest of the army's as well as the neighboring *2. Armee* area of operations. The war diaries of the *Wiking* Division's *panzer* regiment, as well as Vopersal's history of the *Totenkopf* Division, also helps to fill in the gaps.

3 *SS-Pz.Rgt. 5, Ia KTB*, entry dated 9 November 1944, 83, and *I. Abt./SS-Pz.Rgt. 5 Ia KTB*, entries dated 29–31 October 1944, 60–61.

4 These figures are derived from the *Verlustmeldungen* (casualty reports) from *Gen.Kdo. IV-SS Pz.Korps*, Vol. Nr. Wa-664 to Wa-666, covering the period August 1944, and *SS-Werfer Abt. 504*, Wa-703, covering the period September to November 1944. The casualty lists for the *Waffen-SS* are stored in Berlin at the former Berlin Document Center, now accessed as part of the *Bundesarchiv-Militärarchiv*. The equipment losses were found in the *2. Army Ib KTB*, daily corps reports from the Ib, *SS-Pz.Korps*, 10–28 October 1944.

5 *AOK 9 Ia KTB, Anlage, Notiz: Luftwaffen-Ersatz für IV. SS-Pz.Korps*, 26 October 1944. This document lists how many *Luftwaffe* replacements were received by the *IV. SS-Pz.Korps* and their current disposition as of that date. It was prepared at the behest of the *9. Armee* commander who wanted a report detailing what Gille had done with so many new replacements.

6 *3. SS-Pz.Div. 3 Totenkopf, Ia Tgb.Nr. 1245/44 an Gen.Insp.d.Pz.truppen, Abt. Feldheer: Zustandbericht nach dem Stand vom* 4 November 1944.

7 *5. SS-Pz.Div. 5 Wiking, Ia Tgb.Nr. 120/44 an Gen.Insp.d.Pz.truppen, Abt. Feldheer: Zustandbericht nach dem Stand vom* 4 November 1944.

8 In his memoirs, Heinz Guderian does not make this point clear (Guderian, pp. 300–304). However, during a mid-day situation briefing to Hitler that took place on 6 November 1944 at his headquarters in Rastenburg, Hitler asked *Gruf.* Hermann Fegelein, Himmler's representative at *OKW* headquarters, whether the *Wiking* Division could be pulled out to become an armored reserve. Fegelein and *Gen.Lt.* Walter Wenck, the *OKH*'s operations officer, both told him it would be good to do so. After mulling it over briefly, Hitler said "I don't want to tear apart the [*IV. SS-Panzer*] corps; that is very clear." After that, the matter was dropped, either because of inertia or because while it would be possible to withdraw one of Gille's divisions, it would not be possible to do so with both. Most likely because no one wanted to contradict Hitler, it was not brought up again. (Source: Heiber and Glantz, *Hitler and His Generals: Military Conferences 1942–1945* [New York: Enigma Books, 2003], 511.)

9 *5. SS-Pz.Rgt., Ia KTB*, entry dated 29 October 1944, 82.

10 From the printed program distributed for the ceremony held in the archives of Günter Lange, Handeloh, Germany.

11 Following the war, the new Polish Communist government ripped up all the German grave markers so that the German soldiers' cemetery in Modlin was difficult to find without a knowledgeable guide. In 1993, Germany and Poland finally concluded an agreement for the restoration of the cemetery, which is maintained outside of the old Modlin fortress by the *Volksbund Deutsche Kriegsgräberfürversorge* (German War Graves Commission). (Sources: Report by Reiner Melsbach, former member of *8. Kp./Pz.Rgt. 5, "Erlebnis Bericht Rund um Warschau im July 1996," Wiking Ruf*, Vol. 2, 1996 [Hamburg: Truppenkameradschaft Wiking, 1996], 122–24.) Currently, records of the *Volksbund Deutsche Kriegsgräberfürsorge e. V.* indicate that 2,679 German soldiers from World War II are buried there in the 1.3-hHectare (3.2-acre) site located at Deutsches Kriegsgräberfeld auf dem Festungsfriedhof in Modlin, ul. Gen. Bema 1 Nowy Dwór Mazowiecki 5 05–160 Modlin.

12 *AOK 2, Ib KTB, Tagesmeldung Ib, SS-Pz.Korps*, 6 November 1944.

13 Ullrich, . 250.

14 *AOK 9, Ib KTB, Tagesmeldung Ib, SS-Pz.Korps*, 9 November 1944.

15 *AOK 9, Ia KTB Anlage, Notiz: Id Besprechung bei Heeresgruppe Mitte am* 6 November 1944.

16 *AOK 9, Ia KTB Anlage, Notiz: Geworbene polinische Freiwillige*, 27 November 1944.

17 Rokossovsky, pp. 267–68.

18 Wood, p. 155.

19 This was a play on Heinrich Himmler's title of *Reichsführer-SS* and their rank of *Rottenführer* (corporal). Since they felt that they were just as valuable to Germany as Himmler, especially as soldiers, they jokingly felt that they should have a title commensurate with this vaunted status.

Bibliography

Books and Journal Articles

Anonymous. "SS-Werfer-Abteilung 504–Solche Kerle!" *Der Freiwillige*, Vol. 9, 1965 (Osnabrück, Germany: Verlag der Freiwillige GmbH, 1965).

Bacyk, Norbert. *Warsaw II The Tank Battle at Praga July–September 1944: The 4th SS Panzer Corps vs. the 1st Belorussian Front* (Stockholm: Leandoer & Eckholm Publishing, 2006).

Balck, Hermann. *Order in Chaos: The Memoirs of General of Panzer Troops Hermann Balck* (Lexington, KY: The University Press of Kentucky, 2015).

Batov, Pavel I. *Campaigns and Battles* (Moscow: Progress Publishing, 1965).

Bender, Roger J., and Taylor, Hugh-Page. *Uniforms, Organization and History of the Waffen-SS* Vol. 2 (San Jose: R. James Bender Publishing, 1971).

Bernau, Gunter. *SS-Panzer Artillerie-Regiment 5 in der Panzer-Division Wiking* (Wuppertal, Germany: Eigenverlag Kameradschaft ehem. Pz.Art.Rgt. 5, 1990).

Condell, Bruce, and Zabecki, David T. (eds). *On the German Art of War: Truppenführung: German Army Manual for Unit Command in World War II* (Mechanicsburg, PA: Stackpole Books, 2008).

Davies, Norman. *Rising '44: The Battle for Warsaw* (New York: Viking Press, 2003).

Erlings, Ron, Fischer, Hans, and Oosterling, Paul. *Standartenführer Johannes Mühlenkamp und seine Männer* (Erpe, The Netherlands: Uitgeverij De Krijger, 2003).

Fey, Willi. *Armor Battles of the Waffen-SS, 1943–45* (Winnipeg, Canada: J. J. Fedorowicz, 1990).

Fraschka, Günter. *Mit Schwerten und Brillanten: Die Träger der höchsten deutschen Tapferkeitsauszeichnung* (Munich: Limes Verlag Niedermayer & Schlüter GmbH, 1977).

Frieser, Karl-Heinz (editor and contributing author), Schmider, Klaus, Schönherr, Klaus, Schreiber, Gerhard, Ungvary, Krisztian, and Wegner, Bernd. *Germany and the Second World War, Vol. VIII: The Eastern Front 1943–1944—The War in the East and on Neighboring Fronts* (Oxford: Clarendon Press, 2017).

Glantz, David M. "The Red Army's Lublin–Brest Offensive and Advance on Warsaw (18 July–30 September 1944): An Overview and Documentary Survey" In *Journal of Slavic Military Studies*, 19: 401–441 (London: Taylor & Francis Group, LLC, 2006).

Glantz, David M. *Atlas of the Lublin–Brest Operation and the Advance on Warsaw* (Carlisle, PA: Privately published, 2005).

Guderian, Heinz. *Panzer Leader* (New York: Ballantyne Books, 1957).

Hack, Franz. "Kämpfe in Ungarn" in *Unsere Wiking Ruf*, 7/2002 (Ziegenhain, Germany: Truppenkameradschaft 5. SS-Panzer Division Wiking, Geschichtlicher Verein Treysa, 2002).

Hahl, Fritz. *Mit "Westland" im Osten* (Osnabrück, Germany: Munin Verlag, 2000).

Haupt, Werner. *Army Group Center: The Wehrmacht in Russia 1941–1945* (Atglen, PA: Schiffer Military History, 1997).

Haupt, Werner: *Die Schlachten der Heeresgruppe Mitte aus der Sicht der Divisionen* (Friedberg, Germany: Podzun-Pallas Verlag, 1983).

Heder, Eberhard. "Der Kampf des IV. SS-Panzerkorps um Budapest" in *Unsere Wiking Ruf*, 7/2002 (Ziegenhain, Germany: Truppenkameradschaft 5. SS-Panzer Division Wiking, Geschichtlicher Verein Treysa, 2002).

Heiber, Helmut, and Glantz, David M. (eds). *Hitler and His Generals: Military Conferences 1942–1945* (New York: Enigma Books, 2003).

Hinze, Rolf. *East Front Drama—1944* (Winnipeg, Canada: J. J. Fedorowicz Publishing, Inc., 1996).

Husemann, Franz. *Die guten Glaubens waren*, Band II (Osnabrück: Munin Verlag GmbH, 1977).

Jauss, Karl. *Glück Allein Kann Es Nicht Gewesen Sein* (Göppingen, Germany: Privately published, 1984).

Isaev, Aleksei and Kolomiets, Maksim. *Tomb of the Panzerwaffe: The Defeat of the Sixth SS Panzer Army in Hungary 1945* (Solihull, U.K.: Helion & Company Ltd., 2014).

Klapdor, Erich. *Mit dem Panzeregiment 5 Wiking im Osten* (Siek, Germany: Privately published, 1981).

Knobelsdorff, Otto von. *Geschichte der niedersächsichen 19. Panzer-Division 1939–1945* (Friedberg, Germany: Podzun-Pallas Verlag GmbH, 1985).

Kurowski, Franz. *Panzer Aces II: Battle Stories of German Tank Commanders of WWII* (Mechanicsburg, PA: Stackpole Books, 2004).

Kursietis, Andris J. *The Hungarian Army and its Military Leadership in World War II* (New York: Axis Europa Books & Magazines, 1999).

Lange, Günther (ed.). *Unser Wiking Ruf*, Nr. 8/2003 (Ziegenhain, Germany: Truppenkameradschaft 5. SS-Panzer Division Wiking, Geschichtlicher Verein Treysa, 2003).

Maier, Georg. *Drama Zwischen Budapest und Wien: Der 6. Panzerarmee, 1945* (Osnabrück: Munin Verlag, 1985).

Mehner, Kurt. *Die Deutsche Wehrmacht 1939–1945: Führung und Truppe* (Norderstedt, Germany: Militair-Verlag Klaus D. Patzwall, 1993).

Model, Hans-Georg. *Der deutsche Generalstabsoffizier* (Frankfurt am Main: Bernard Graefe Verlag für Wehrwesen, 1968).

Moore, John P. *Führerliste der Waffen-SS: Personalakten*, Vols 1–6 (Portland: Self-published, 2003).

Munoz, Antonio J. *Forgotten Legions: Obscure Combat Formations of the Waffen-SS* (New York: Axis Europa Book, 1991).

Munoz, Antonio J. "Teutonic Magyars: Hungarian Volunteers in the Waffen-SS 1944–1945" in Kursietis, Andris J. *The Hungarian Army and its Military Leadership in World War II* (New York: Axis Europa Books, 1999).

Nebolsin, Igor. *Stalin's Favorite: The Combat History of the 2nd Guards Tank Army from Kursk to Berlin* (Solihull, U.K.: Helion & Company, 2016).

Nevenkin, Kamen. *Fire Brigades: The Panzer Divisions 1943–1945* (Winnipeg, Canada: J. J. Fedorowicz, 2008).

Pierek, Perry. *Hungary 1944–1945: The Forgotten Tragedy* (Nieuwegein, The Netherlands: Aspekt Publishing, 1996).

Regiments-Kameradschaft des ehemaligen SS-Panzergrenadier Regiment 10 "Westland," *Panzergrenadiere der Panzerdivision "Wiking" im Bild* (Osnabrück, Germany: Munin Verlag GmBH, 1984).

Regiments-Kameradschaft Panzerregiment 5 "Wiking." *Verweht sind die Spuren: Bilddokumentation 5. SS-Panzerregiment "Wiking"* (Osnabrück, Germany: Munin Verlag GmBH, 1979).

Reitlinger, Gerald. *The SS: Alibi of a Nation 1922–1945* (New York: The Viking Press, 1957).

Rikmenspoel, Marc. *Soldiers of the Waffen-SS: Many Nations, One Motto* (Winnipeg, Canada: J. J. Fedorowicz Publishing, Inc., 1999).

Rokossovsky, Konstantin. *A Soldier's Duty* (Moscow: Progress Publishers, 1985).

Schneider, Jost W. *Their Honor Was Loyalty! An Illustrated and Documentary History of the Knight's Cross Holders of the Waffen-SS and Police 1940–1945* (San Jose: R. James Bender Publishing, 1977).

Schulze-Kossens, Richard. *Militärischer Führernachwuchs der Waffen-SS* (Osnabrück: Munin Verlag, 1982).

Smelser, Ronald, and Syring, Enrico. *Die SS: Elite unter dem Totenkopf–30 Lebensläufe* (Paderborn, Germany: Ferdinand Schöningh, 2000).

Stein, George H. *The Waffen SS: Hitler's Elite Guard at War, 1939–45* (NY: Cornell University Press, 1984).

Stöber, Hans. *Die lettischen Divisionen im VI. SS-Armeekorps* (Osnabrück: Munin Verlag GmbH, 1981).

Stoves, Rolf O. G. *1. Panzer-Division 1935–1945: Chronik einer der drei Stamm-Divisionen der deutschen Panzerwaffe* (Bad Nauheim: Verlag Hans-Henning Podzun, 1961).

Strassner, Peter. *European Volunteers: 5 SS Panzer Division Wiking* (Winnipeg, Canada: J. J. Fedorowicz Publishing, 1988).

Számvéber, Norbert. *The Sword Behind the Shield: a Combat History of the German Efforts to Relieve Budapest 1945—Operation "Konrad" I, II, III* (Solihull, U.K.: Helion & Company Ltd, 2015).

Trevor-Roper, H.R. *Hitler's Secret Conversations, 1941–1944* (New York: Farrar, Straus and Young, Inc., 1953).

Ulrich, Karl. *Wie ein Fels im Meer: 3. SS-Panzerdivision "Totenkopf,"* Vol. 2 (Osnabrück: Munin-Verlag, 1984).

Ungváry, Krisztián. *The Siege of Budapest: 100 Days in World War II* (New Haven: Yale University Press, 2002).

Vopersal, Wolfgang. *Soldaten, Kämpfer, Kameraden, Marsch und Kämpfe der SS-Totenkopf Division* Vols. Va and Vb (Bielefeld, Germany: Selbstverlag der Truppenkameradschaft der 3. SS-Pz.Div. e.V., 1991)

Vuksic, Velimir. *SS Armor on the Eastern Front 1943–1945* (Winnipeg, Canada: J. J. Fedorowicz Publishing, Inc., 2005).

Wegner, Bernd. *The Waffen-SS: Organization, Ideology and Function* (Oxford: Basil Blackwell Ltd, 1990).

Westerlund, Lars. *The Finnish SS-Volunteers and Atrocities, 1941–1943* (Helsinki: The National Archives of Finland, 2019).

Wood, Ian M. *Tigers of the Death's Head: SS Totenkopf Division's Tiger Company* (Mechanicsburg, VA: Stackpole Books, 2013).

Yerger, Mark. *German Cross in Gold Holders of the SS and Police*, Vols 8 & 9 (CA: R. James Bender Publishing, 2015.)

Yerger, Mark. *Waffen-SS Commanders: The Army, Corps and Divisional Leaders of a Legend*, Vols I and II (Atglen, PA: Schiffer Military History, 1997).

Ziemke, Earl F. *Stalingrad to Berlin: The German Defeat in the East* (Washington, D. C: U.S. Army Center of Military History, 2002).

Published Official Government Records, Manuals and Internal Publications

Foreign Military Studies

Berlin, Wilhelm. *Comments on the Study "Russian Artillery in the Battle for Modlin and German Countermeasures,"* MS C-030, undated manuscript (Heidelberg: Historical Division, U.S. European Command).

Brasack, Kurt. *Russian Artillery in the Battle for Modlin and German Countermeasures*, MS D-228 (Heidelberg: Historical Division, U.S. European Command, 29 July 1952).

Dörffler-Schuband, Werner. *Officer Procurement in the Waffen-SS: Reception, Processing and Training*, Military Study D-178 (Heidelberg: Office of the Chief Historian, Headquarters, U.S. European Command, Ref. Draft published 13 July 1945).

Förtsch, Hermann. *Training and Development of German General Staff Officers*, MS P-031b, Project # 6, Vol. VIII (Heidelberg: Historical Division, U.S. European Command, 22 June 1951).

Gille, Herbert Otto, *The 4th SS Panzer Corps May 1945*, Military Study #B-166 (Heidelberg: History Division, U.S. Army Europe, 27 April 1946).

Krause, Walther. *Fighting in West Hungary and East Steiermark in the Area of the Sixth Army from March 25 to May 8, 1945*, MS B-139 (Heidelberg: Historical Division, U.S. Army Europe, 13 June 1952).

Reinhardt, Helmuth. *Size and Composition of Divisional and Higher Staffs in the German Army*, Military Study P-139 (Karlsruhe, Germany: Historical Division, Headquarters, U.S. Army Europe, 1954).

Rendulic, Lothar Dr. *Report of the Commander: Stabilization of Eastern Front*, MS #B-328 (Frankfurt: U.S. Army Europe Historical Division, 1 April 1947).

Reuther, Karl, and Ulms, Ulrich. *XII SS Corps: Reflections and Experiences* (Heidelberg: Historical Division, U.S. European Command, 8 December 1947).

Westphal, Siegfried. *German General Staff Training and Development of German General Staff Officers*, MS P-031b, Project # 6, Vol. XXI (Heidelberg: Historical Division, U.S. European Command, August 1948).

Contemporary German Operational and Doctrinal Sources

Armeeoberkommando 9, Ia Nr. 1772/44, 10 April 1944, *Geschäftsordnung des Armeeoberkommando 9.*

Kriegsstärkenachweisung (Heer) Nr. 15 Generalkommando (mot.), mit Anmerkungen und Ergänzungen, 1 August 1942.

Kriegsstärkenachweisung (Heer) Nr. 25 Stab eines Artilleriekommando (mot.), mit Anmerkungen und Ergänzungen, 1 January 1945.

Kriegsstärkenachweisung (Heer) Nr. 805 Korpsnachrichten Abteilung (mot.), mit Anmerkungen und Ergänzungen, 1 May 1944.

Kriegsstärkenachweisung (Heer) Nr. 1207 Kommandeur der Korps-Nachschubtruppen z.b.V., mit Anmerkungen und Ergänzungen, 1 November 1943.

Kriegsstärkenachweisung (Heer) Nr. 1302 Stab einer Heeressanitäts-Abteilung (mot.), mit Anmerkungen und Ergänzungen, 1 April 1944.

Kriegsstärkenachweisung (Heer) Nr. 1342 Feldlazarett (mot.), 1 October 1937.

Kriegsstärkenachweisung (Heer) Nr. 2075 Korps Kartenstelle (mot.), 1 October 1938.

Kriegsstärkenachweisung (SS) Nr. 1361 Krankentransport-Kompanie, 1 October 1937.

Kriegsstärkenachweisung (SS) SS-Kriegsberichter Zug (mot.), 1 January 1943.

Kriegsstärkenachweisung (SS) SS-Bekleindungs-Instandsetzungs-Kompanie, 1 June 1942.

Kriegstagebuch (Ia), SS-Pz.Rgt. 5, 26 March–30 November 1944.

Kriegstagebuch (Ia), I. Abteilung, SS-Pz.Rgt. 5, 9 February–30 November 1944.

Kriegstagebuch (Ia) und Anlagen, XXIII. Armee-Korps, 15–31 July 1944.

Kriegstagebuch (Ia) und Anlagen, Armeeoberkommando (AOK) 2, 25 July–6 August 1944. (This includes morning, midday, evening, and daily reports, as well as armor and infantry strengths, radio and/or telephone message transcripts, reports from subordinate units, commanders' daily summaries, rail and highway movement status, and orders/instructions from higher headquarters, including *Heeresgruppe Mitte*.)

Kriegstagebuch (Ib) und Anlagen, Armeeoberkommando (AOK) 2, 1 October–31 December 1944. (This includes daily reports, including ammunition, fuel, and food expenditures, tank and other armored vehicles losses, and daily supply status for the *IV. SS-Pz.Korps* compiled by the *Quartiermeister*.)

Kreigstagebuch (Ia) Anlagen, Armeegruppe Balck/Armeeoberkommando 6 (AOK) 6, 1 January–3 February 1945. (This includes orders, armor, and infantry strengths, transcripts of radio and/or telephone message traffic, reports from subordinate units, rail and highway movement status, and orders/instructions from higher headquarters, including *Heeresgruppe Süd*.)

Kreigstagebuch (Ia) und Anlagen, Armeeoberkommando (AOK) 9, 1 August–31 December 1944. (This includes morning, midday, evening, and daily reports, as well as armor and infantry strengths, radio and/or telephone message transcripts, reports from subordinate units, commanders' daily summaries, rail and highway movement status, and orders/instructions from higher headquarters, including *Heeresgruppe Mitte*.)

Kriegstagebuch (Ia), Heeresgruppe Mitte, 18 July–6 August 1944 and 16–30 September 1944.

Oberkommando des Heeres. Heeres-Drückvorschrift (H.Dv.) g 90, Versorgung des Feldheeres, Teil I und II (Berlin: Reichsdrückerei, 1 June 1938 and 1 June 1942).

Oberkommando des Heeres. Heeres-Drückvorschrift (H.Dv.) g 92, Handbuch für den Generalstabsdienst im Kriege, Teil I und II (Berlin: Reichsdruckerei, 1 August 1939).

Oberkommando des Heeres. Heeres-Drückvorschrift (H.Dv.) 300/1, Truppenführung, Teil I (Berlin: Reichsdruckerei, 17 October 1933).

Oberkommando des Heeres, Kriegswissenschafft Abt. Gen.St. des Heeres, Nr. 1500/40. Bestimmungen für die Führung von Kriegstagebüchern und Tätigkeitsberichen (Berlin: Reichsdrückerei, 23 April 1940).

Personnel and Materiel Strength Reports, including monthly *Kriegsgliederung*, for *19. Pz.Div.* August–November 1944.

Personnel and Materiel Strength Reports, including monthly *Kriegsgliederung*, for *Fs.Pz.Div.* Hermann Goering August–November 1944.

Personnel and Materiel Strength Reports, including monthly *Kriegsgliederung*, for *3. SS-Pz.Div. Totenkopf* July 1944–March 1945.

Personnel and Materiel Strength Reports, including monthly *Kriegsgliederung*, for *5. SS-Pz.Div. Wiking* July 1944–March 1945.

SS-Führungshauptamt, Amt II, Org. Abt. Ia/II SS-Führungshauptampt. Kriegsgliederungen der Panzer Divisionen der Waffen-SS (Berlin: SS-Führungshauptampt, 24 October 1944).

Contemporary Red Army Operational and Doctrinal Sources

War Diary, First Belorussian Front, 1 August–30 November 1944. TsAMO, Fund: 233, Inventory: 2356, Case: 329. Authors: Lieutenant General I. Boykov and Colonel Kramar. Documents found at https://pamyat-naroda.ru/documents/view/?id=211326088.

War Diary, VIII Guards Tank Corps, 17 July–30 November 1944, TsAMO, Fund: 3407, Inventory: 1, Case: 130. Authors: Major General of Tank Troops G. V. Koshelev and Lieutenant Colonel Sekutorov. Documents found at https://pamyat-naroda.ru/documents/view/?id=133726762.

Interviews

Interview with *Oberstleutnant* (Ret.) Günther Lange, Handeloh, Germany, 7 October 2017.

Index

Aleksandrów 200, 217–220, 247, 291, 304, 310, 315, 322, 327, 358, 364, 375
Allgemeine-SS 4, 66, 80, 90, 349, 443
Anin 259, 266
Annopol 284, 289, 291, 292, 297, 303, 310, 314, 326, 336, 348, 417
Arciechów 228–229, 282
ARKO 104 (SS) 19, 58, 148, 212, 243, 310, 327, 340, 383, 426, 455, 459, 466, 471, 481
Armia Krajowa 119, 239, 244, 245, 253, 264, 276, 283, 288, 301, 3126, 323, 325, 334, 438
Audörsch, *Oberst* Oskar 277, 285, 289, 293, 301, 306, 309, 451
Augustowka 400

Bach, *Ogruf.* Erich von dem 72, 126, 356
Bachmann, *Hstuf.* Christian 388
Bad Tölz 37, 39, 40, 375
Balck, *Gen.d.Pz.Tr.* Hermann 209, 483
Baranow 466, 471
Bärwind, *Ustuf.* Horst 376
Batov, Col.Gen. Pavel I. 331–333, 387, 395, 396, 399, 403, 405, 406
Bauer, *Ustuf.* Helmut 234, 237, 348, 365, 408
Becker, *Oberstlt.* Otto 111
Benjaminów 119, 200, 210, 214, 215, 219, 222, 227
Berling, Lt.Gen. Zygmunt 157, 158, 255, 257
Bernhard, *Gen.Lt.* Friedrich 328, 348
Betzel, *Gen.Maj.* Clemens 122, 132, 143
Biała Podlaska 107
Białobrzegi 435, 452
Białoleka 294, 295, 298, 304, 310, 363
Bialystok 10, 73, 74, 78, 89, 95, 108, 111, 139, 140, 144, 145, 148, 176, 222
Bielany 277
Biermeier, *Stubaf.* Fritz 363–364
Bogdanov, Col. Gen. Semyon I. 96
Bolesławowo 424, 458
Borg, *Ustuf.* Gösta 107, 221, 222
Borki 200, 201, 214, 219, 222, 224, 226, 227, 228, 232, 239, 258, 260, 264, 268, 278
Bór, General (Codename) 134
Borchert, *Hstuf.* Otto 264
Böhme, *Gen.Maj.* Hermann 245, 336
Brasack, *Brig.Fhr.* Kurt 58, 91, 212, 243, 273, 274, 327, 356, 357, 369, 374, 378, 383, 449, 459
Braune, *Stubaf.* Friz 116, 327, 331
Braunschweig 38, 66, 349
Brockdorff-Ahlefeldt, *Gen.d.Inf.* Walter von 82
Bródnowski Cemetery 288, 359, 412, 413, 419, 420, 423, 439
Brückenschlag 137–155
Bug River 11, 74, 78, 96, 97, 103, 105, 109, 117, 133, 174, 175, 192, 201, 207, 222, 227, 228, 233, 252, 314, 424
Bugmünde (NowyDwór) 340, 440
Bünning, *Ostubaf.* Hans 103, 239, 278, 282, 446

Cegielnia 215, 217, 218, 450
Choszczówka 388, 426
Chotomów 383, 433, 435, 440, 451, 458, 460, 464, 466, 473
Chuikov, Col.Gen. Vasily I. 96, 116, 119, 126, 183, 414, 429
Ciemne 216
Cisie 192
Cummerow, *Brig.Fhr* Hermann 30, 31, 32
Czarnów 192–193
Czeremcha 93, 97, 103, 105, 107, 108, 109, 113
Czerniakow 296

Dabrowa 190, 211, 220, 227, 228, 229, 233, 362
Dabrówka 177, 184, 186, 189, 194
Dachsstellung 406, 421, 422, 423, 424, 426
D'Alquen, *Staf.* Günther 56
Darges, *Ostubaf.* Fritz 121, 124, 130, 151, 152, 177, 179, 220, 226, 243, 304, 350, 385, 404, 412, 420, 442, 451, 473
Debe 381, 420, 421, 423, 424, 427, 439, 456, 461, 464, 469
Debiča 73, 78, 197, 202, 365
Debinki 241, 249, 332
Demblin 111
Demyansk 82–84, 90, 350
Derlacz 440, 449, 457, 470, 471
Dibowski, *St.Oberjunker* Otto 57
Dluga Kościelna 129
Dluga River 143
Dobczyn 122, 183, 189, 191
Drewnica 238, 270
Dręszew 189
Drewnica Forest 238, 270
Dubovoi, Maj.Gen. Ivan V. 113
Duczki 217
Duza 247
Dworzec 146
Dybów 119, 122, 196, 198, 199
Dzbanice 234
Dzierzenin 232, 234, 236, 237, 240

Eberhard, *Ostuf.* Adolf 9, 51, 91, 231, 376, 418
Ehrath, *Ostubaf.* Fritz 103, 215, 264
Elsnerów 273, 278, 287
Ersatzheer 14, 38, 60, 61, 181, 184, 346

Fabianów 179
Fallschirmjäger 132
Feldlazarett 60–62, 212, 455, 458
Felzmann, *Gen.d.Art.* Maximilian 95, 117, 119, 120, 122, 400, 401, 429, 474
Fingerspitzengefühl 26, 112
Flatow, Uscha. 295
Flesch, Uscha. 182–183
Flügel, *Hstuf.* Hans 152, 160, 166, 169, 170, 213, 238, 241, 245, 247, 249, 252, 261, 265, 268, 278, 304, 311, 327, 331, 332, 365, 376, 380, 381, 394, 416, 420, 431, 442, 449, 450
Förster, Uscha. 169–170
Franek, Fritz von *Gen.Lt.* 111, 153
Fuchsstellung 285, 301, 392, 399, 400, 402, 403, 410–414, 421, 424, 427, 430, 432, 433, 435, 436, 439, 448, 449, 450

Galicians 314
Garwolin 111, 153
Gasiorowo 240–241, 245–246, 248–249, 261, 331–332
German Units
Army Groups
H.Gr. A 68, 450, 471–473
H.Gr. Mitte 8, 74, 78, 88–89, 95, 97, 103, 105, 110, 118–119, 125, 128–249, 268–425
H.Gr. Nord 82, 97, 138, 209
H.Gr. Nordukrain 73, 96–97, 110, 209
H.Gr. Süd 68, 71, 85, 87, 297, 394
H.Gr. Südukrain 187, 209, 216
Armies
2. Armee 11, 74, 78, 84, 93–475
3. Pz.Armee 138–146, 155, 209
4. Armee 107, 209, 229, 336, 471
4. Pz.Armee 72, 74, 87, 96–97, 107, 209, 297, 400, 450, 452, 460, 466, 471
6. Armee 209
8. Armee 87, 187, 209, 247
9. Armee 28, 79, 89, 104–476
Corps
IV. SS-Pz.Korps 1–11, 13–483
VIII. A.K. 110
XX. A.K. 95, 98, 110, 116, 119, 140, 160–194, 214, 227, 230–249, 305, 311, 331, 332, 353, 399, 406–422, 461, 463
XXIII. A.K. 98
XXXIX. Pz.Korps 110, 111, 117–130, 137, 138, 140
XL. Pz.Korps 474–475
XCVI. Pz.Korps 162, 191, 196, 217, 288, 304
LVI. Pz.Korps 77, 96, 110, 183, 186, 190, 209, 211, 227, 240, 247, 248, 249, 255, 258, 262, 278, 292, 296, 298, 302, 306, 311–336, 392–400, 429, 450, 452, 460, 471–474
Korps Harteneck 111, 115, 116, 139

Gruppe v. d. Bach 158, 178, 183–186, 193, 203–239, 243–438

Brigades

Gren.Brig. 1131 132, 144, 146, 147, 152, 180–248, 342, 453

Gren.Brig. 1132 26y2

Dirlewanger Brigade 288, 326, 373

Kaminski Brigade 126, 288, 335

Infantry Divisions

5. Jäg.Div. 143–146, 152, 162–214, 230

6. Inf.Div. 110

7. Inf.Div. 74, 167

17. Inf.Div. 110, 119, 240, 450

26. Inf.Div. 110

35. Inf.Div. 230–237, 244, 331

73. Inf.Div. 61–474

211. Inf.Div. 230

541. Gren.Div. 126, 230

542. Gren.Div. 220–244, 331, 332, 406, 412, 425, 463

Korps-Abt. E 96, 117, 119

Panzer Divisions

3. SS-Pz.Div. 8, 10, 40, 75, 76, 87, 89, 93, 120, 155, 475

4. Pz.Div. 73, 78, 95, 107–146, 244, 247

5. SS-Pz.Div. 8, 10, 39, 75, 93, 120, 155, 275, 375, 405

6. Pz.Div. 210, 321

19. Pz.Div. 111–459

25. Pz.Div. 276–467

Fs.Pz.Div. Hermann Göring 75, 93, 104–476

Security Divisions 95

203. Sich.Div. 95

391. Sich.Div. 247, 328

Infantry Regiments

Pz.Gren.Rgt. HG 1 86

Gren.Rgt. 4 197, 341

SS-Pz.Gren.Rgt. 5 86, 91, 104, 118, 215, 227, 457

SS-Pz.Gren.Rgt. 6 86, 90, 91, 103, 303, 349, 350, 363

SS-Pz.Gren.Rgt. 9 39, 73, 123, 160

SS-Pz.Gren.Rgt. 10 70, 79, 147, 149, 264, 336

Gren.Rgt. 62 167

Gren.Rgt 70 259, 267, 271, 272, 330, 474

Gren.Rgt. 170 105, 314, 316, 322

Gren.Rgt. 186 245, 266, 271, 278, 281, 286, 440

Pz.Gren.Rgt. 73 192, 196, 199, 200, 201, 214–249, 265–363, 417, 433

Pz.Gren.Rgt. 74 201, 271, 279–281, 294, 301, 363, 382, 400, 409, 417

Pz.Gren.Rgt. 146

Gren.Rgt. 1077 201, 271, 279–281, 294, 307, 363, 382, 400, 403, 409, 417

Gren.Rgt. 1145 197, 201, 204, 214, 222, 226, 228, 229, 239, 242, 268, 327, 336

Artillery Regiments

SS-Pz.Art.Rgt. 3 315, 366, 419, 423, 440

SS-Pz.Rgt. 3 88–116, 131, 145, 147, 163, 173, 177, 182, 195, 200, 220, 235, 241, 259, 288, 294, 303, 363, 370, 377, 388, 411, 416, 440, 457, 469

SS-Pz.Art.Rgt. 5 203, 239, 241, 260, 278, 282, 288, 295, 311, 322, 332, 344, 357, 416, 433, 446, 474

SS-Pz.Rgt. 5 14, 73, 109, 116–457

Pz.Art.Rgt. 19 224, 265, 294, 418, 433

Art.Rgt. 173 273

Werfer-Rgt. 102 473

Werfer-Rgt. 103 473

Panzer Regiments

SS-Pz.Rgt. 3 88–116, 131, 145, 147, 163, 173, 177, 182, 195, 200, 220, 235, 241, 259, 288, 294–295, 303, 363, 370, 377, 388, 411, 416, 440, 457, 469

SS-Pz.Rgt. 5 14, 73, 109, 116–457

Pz.Rgt. 9 289

Pz.Rgt. 27 197, 201, 265–295, 303, 333, 363, 372–431

Pz.Rgt. 35 122, 132, 143

Fs.Pz.Rgt. HG 345

Police and SS Regiments

SS-Pol.Rgt. 17 264, 429

Pol.Schtz.Rgt. 34 264, 328, 329

Battalions

SS-Pz.Aufkl.Abt. 3 214, 222, 388

SS-Pz.Aufkl.Abt. 5 79, 147, 197, 203, 215, 226, 329, 344, 358, 365, 371, 375, 380, 389, 439, 445, 464, 474

SS-Pio.Btl. 3 267, 295

SS-Pio.Btl. 5 176, 226, 233, 234

SS-Flak Abt. 3 311, 388

SS-Flak Abt. 5 163, 203, 220, 376, 405

SS-Pz.Jäg.Abt. 3 171, 219, 294. 388

SS-Pz.Jäg.Abt. 5 123, 148, 181, 186, 228, 232, 402, 408, 412

Sturm-Btl. AOK 9 259, 294, 388, 415, 418, 429, 433
Beob.Abt. 21 292, 455
Pz.Aufkl.Abt. 25 289
Pz.Pio.Btl. 87 289
Pz.Jäg.Abt. 173 271
Flak-Art.Abt. 272 417
SS-Gren.Btl. 500 174
Gren.Btl. z.b.V. 560 201, 204, 214, 222, 224, 226, 228, 248, 268, 306, 309, 318, 327, 335, 336, 347, 370, 373, 398, 415, 424, 457, 464, 466, 471
Pz.Jäg.Abt. 743 225, 252, 259, 268, 272, 281, 300, 304, 319, 342
Fest.Inf.Btl. 1405 204, 220, 226, 233, 241, 242, 311, 327, 336
Gille, *Gruf.* Herbert Otto 10, 13, 65, 91, 39
Glinki 259, 261
Gocław 279
Gocławska 279
Göring, *Reichsmarschall* Hermann 75, 93, 104, 107–138, 154, 168, 183, 247, 254, 258, 270, 279, 285, 286, 293, 297–366, 445, 476
Grabie Stare 163, 167, 168, 170, 171, 188, 191, 195
Grabina 303, 359, 426
Grabner, *Hstuf.* Heinrich 405, 425
Grafenwöhr 5, 89
Grebkow 116, 121
Grodno 10, 88, 89, 101, 104–107, 111, 315
Grodzisk 133
Grossrock, *SS-Ostuf.* Alfred 117, 169, 186
Grund, *Hstuf.* Paul 366
Grzybowa 147
Guderian, *Gen.Oberst* Hans 286, 301, 308, 314, 317, 403, 448, 460
Gusev, Lt.Gen. Nikolai 116, 118, 125, 127, 135, 142, 144, 157, 210, 268, 357, 387, 391, 409, 434, 456
Guzowatka 189, 200

Hack, *Stubaf.* Franz 32, 226, 264
Halinow 129, 131, 132
Harteneck, *Gen.d.Kav.* Gustav 111, 115, 116, 139
Harwik, *Ustuf* 166, 173
Hausser, *SS-Ogruf.* Paul 1, 14, 77, 84
Häusser, *Hstuf.* Alfred 54
Hähling, Kurt *Gen.Maj.* 111, 142, 144, 154, 162, 197, 215, 223, 245, 252, 253, 258, 259, 261, 318
Heder, *Hstuf.* Eberhard 376, 380, 381, 385, 390, 397
Heidelager training area 79, 111
Heilmann, *Oberführer* Nikolaus 2, 5, 7, 10, 11, 38, 79, 98, 101, 102, 133, 152
Henryków 289, 304, 360, 363, 377
Himmler, *Reichsführer-SS* Heinrich 1–6, 22, 30–43, 53, 55, 60, 61, 67, 69, 70, 79, 81, 84, 128, 181, 254, 337, 338
Hitler, *Reichskanzler* Adolf 1, 5, 6, 30, 31, 32, 33, 37, 41, 42, 56, 60, 68, 72, 73, 76, 80, 84–90, 95, 96, 112, 154, 165, 255, 286, 301, 308, 309, 314, 317, 320, 334, 350, 403, 447, 454, 455, 463
Honsell, *Ostubaf.* Wilhelm 52
Hüppe, *Stubaf.* Hubert 48

Ibrányi, *Gen.Maj.* Mihály 176, 252, 258, 266, 267, 271, 278, 281, 285, 288, 293, 296, 300, 303, 308, 311, 327, 436
Izbica 413, 417, 419, 420, 423–427, 450

Jablonna 176, 254, 263, 265, 300, 303, 304, 307, 316, 336, 350, 359, 363–473
Jablonna-Legjonowo 176, 254, 263, 300, 303–306, 316, 350, 359, 363–467
Jackowo 192–195, 214
Jadow 140, 146, 170
Jadwinin 165–166
Jasienica 160, 166, 168
Jósefów 363–426
Jüttner, *Ogruf.* Ernst 1, 6, 31, 34, 36, 44, 53, 61

Källner, *Gen. Maj.* Hans 122, 204, 255, 262, 265–436
Kałuszyn 104, 109, 120, 133, 413, 440, 457, 468
Kampfgruppe 73, 77, 78, 83, 96, 103, 109–471
Kampfraum 8, 58, 78, 144, 270, 386
Kampinos Forest 328–330, 3532, 425, 428, 432, 433, 435, 452
Karniewek 230–257
Kąty-Borucza 130
Kawęczyn 271–272

Kazuń-Niemiecki 442
Kałuszyn 104, 109, 120, 133, 413, 457, 468
Kepa 279, 429, 440
Kernmayr, *Ostuf.* Erich 57
Kielpinska 429, 440, 461
Kirschmeier, *SS-Oscha.* Willy 340, 341
Kistemaker, *Uscha.* Henk 117
Kleffner, *Ostubaf.* Franz 350
Klein Kazun 284, 297, 300, 330, 386, 392
Klein, *Oberst* Gerhard 328
Kleine, *Maj.* Otto 39, 79, 152
Kleinheisterkamp, *Gruf.* Matthias 6–10, 33, 40, 52, 61, 79, 101, 479
Klembów 163–195
Kleszczele 93–110
Klose, *Stubaf.* Wilhelm 39
Klusek 240, 241, 248
Kobylka 238, 266
Kochwolo-Lasków 178
Kolpakchi, Lt.Gen. Vladimir Y. 110
Komorowski, General Tadeuz "Bór" 134
Konev, Army General Ivan 97, 209
Korück 532 297, 328, 348, 457
Kossmann, *Oberst* Karl-Richard 405–417
Kowel 66, 71–242
Kozłowska 167, 169–178
Kozły 172–173
Kościelna 129
Kraft, *Sturmmann* Gerd 214
Kraszew 199
Krebs, *Gen.Lt.* Hans 118, 131, 133
Kriegsakademie 14, 17, 30–40, 45, 69, 79, 80, 91, 152
Krolewski 359, 364
Krubin 420, 440
Krubki 131
Kruger, *Stubaf.* Karl 6, 9, 48
Krusze 171–180
Kuligów 192–259
Kurochkin, Gen. Pavel 82

Ladzyn 120
Łajsk 359, 376, 380, 383, 404, 413, 415–416, 418–420
Lassen, *Oberst* Ernst-August 124–125, 129
Latowicz 153
Laziska 120
Leibstandarte Adolf Hitler 30, 32, 41, 80, 84–86, 90
Lejanów 369, 388, 401
Lemkuhl, *Sturm.* Erich 177
Letniska Forest 378, 380, 384, 389–390, 394, 403, 408, 412–413
Lewicpol 288
Lichte, *Ostuf.* Karl-Heinz 172, 375
Litevski 95
Litovsk 10, 74, 78, 88–89, 95, 98, 148, 238
Litzmannstadt (Łódź) 194, 442,
Liw 102–103, 108, 118, 121
Łomża 107
Losice 96
Lotze, *Ostuf.* Gerhard 375
Łozy 101
Luchinsky, Lt.Gen. Alexander 210
Ludwinów 129, 461
Ludwinowo 461
Luftflotte 329, 494
Lüttwitz, *Gen.d.Pz.Tr.* Smilo von 247, 255, 292, 302, 312, 314, 316–318, 320, 323, 325, 329, 335, 348–349, 351, 354–356, 358, 367–368, 372–373, 378, 382, 386–387, 391–396, 398–400, 403, 406–407, 410, 414–415, 417–418, 421–422, 425, 428–429, 431–432, 435, 450–452

Magnuszew 116, 119, 126, 130, 132, 134, 138–139, 146, 148, 158, 168, 176, 183, 190–191, 195, 197, 207, 211, 231, 236, 240, 244, 255–256, 262, 265, 269, 276
Małe 240–241, 247
Małopole 184, 186, 189–192, 194
Manstein, *G.F.M.* Erich von 71–72, 85, 112
Marcelin 369, 379, 388, 407, 415
Marki 238, 281, 285, 287, 436, 448
Marjanów 219, 221,
Marymont 303
Marynino 238
Masarie, *Stubaf.* Arzelino 104, 153
Maskirovka 251, 391, 403, 452, 468
May, *Ostubaf.* Erich 233, 251
Metzger, *Ostuf.* Eberhad 231, 233–237, 241, 249
Michałów 116–118, 120, 124, 127, 129, 131, 303, 310, 315, 322, 359, 366, 370, 372, 376, 381, 384, 396, 401, 404, 412, 416, 426
Michałów Estate 366, 372, 376, 381, 384, 396, 401, 404, 416

Mińsk Mazowiecki 112
Mittelbacher, *Ostuf.* Leopold 365
Młociny 242, 276–277, 284, 287, 298, 316, 360, 362, 368, 386, 417
Model, *G.F.M.* Walter 27, 112, 154, 403
Modlin 105, 112, 133, 140, 144, 151, 157, 166, 176, 194, 210, 222, 231, 233, 248–249, 253–254, 257, 260–261, 276, 284–285, 287, 292, 297–298, 301, 303–304, 324–427
Mokobody 140
Mokotów 126, 207, 245, 253, 316–317, 323–324, 326, 333
Mordy 104
Mostówka 181
Mościska 175
Mörchingen 6, 7, 8
Mühlenkamp, *Staf.* Johannes 32, 73, 78–79, 98, 103, 117–118, 121, 124, 127, 131, 133, 151–152, 155, 164, 174, 177–178, 182, 185–186, 190, 193, 199, 202–203, 214, 220, 246, 252, 268, 278, 282, 288, 291, 295, 322, 336, 344, 350–351, 364, 376, 381, 385, 405, 416, 436,
Murowanka 241
Młociny 242, 276–277, 284, 287, 298, 316, 360, 362, 368, 386, 417
Mürr, *Hstuf.* Heinz 173, 223, 286, 302

Nachtwey, *Maj.d.Schutzpolizei* 328–329
Nadma 219, 221, 223, 238
Nähring, Maj. Alfred 214, 224, 226, 232, 236, 239, 249, 265, 307, 363
Narew River 74, 78, 107, 137, 140, 146, 158, 180, 195, 197, 205, 207, 211, 220, 228–230, 244, 262, 284, 352, 359, 411–412
Nedderhof, *Stubaf.* Alfred 336, 364–365, 375
Neff, *Ustuf.* Helmut 172, 230, 236, 294, 321, 415, 431
Nicolussi-Leck, *Ostuf.* Karl 73, 173, 442
Niemiecki 440, 442, 457
Nieporet 210–211, 288, 291–292, 295, 304, 315, 336, 351, 356, 358–359, 363–365, 369, 371, 374, 377–378, 381-382, 384, 390, 391–392, 394–397, 406, 482
Novo Dobre 145
Nowy Dwór 298, 340, 418, 420, 439–442, 457, 460–461

Oberkommando des Heeres (OKH) 15
Oeck, *Stubaf.* Herbert 111, 123, 232, 408, 446
Okuniew 112–143
Okunin 340, 440
Olin, *Ustuf.* Ola 234
Operation *Bagration* 74, 78, 88, 93, 104, 105, 110, 209
Opole Stare 104
Ordnungspolizei 2, 18, 32, 335
Orzechowo 431
Ossów 196, 215, 221, 223, 270
Ostrołęka 230
Ostrow 133, 229
Otwock 111, 258

Panzerabwehrkanone 154
Panzerfaust 108, 187, 222, 301, 375, 453
Panzerschreck 154, 187, 222, 323
Pauly, *Stubaf.* Richard 37, 38–152
Pilawa 295
Pittschellis, *Stubaf.* Adolf 171
Pleiner, *Hstuf.* Franz 365, 371, 397
Płudy 304, 360, 370, 377, 379, 388
Poddebe 420, 439
Pogorzelec 237–241
Polish Army (Soviet)
Armies
  1st Polish 93, 126, 134, 157, 158, 162, 174, 198, 211, 218, 255–474
Divisions
  1st Rifle 406, 409, 412
  2nd Rifle 473
Polish Exile Government 134
Pólko 131, 218
PolkowKopratyny 131
Poniatowski 280, 312, 420, 423
Poniatów 280, 312, 420, 423, 448, 457, 460, 468
Popov, Maj.Gen. Alexei F. 85, 113, 125, 127, 162, 194, 262, 270, 306, 357, 358, 386–457
Popov, Col.Gen. Vasily 142, 210, 404
Praga 11, 93–476
Priess 86, 88, 89, 90
Puławy 96, 105, 110, 113, 116, 138, 139, 146, 148, 158, 185, 207–451
Pułtusk 225–432
Płudy 304–388

Radzievsky, Lt.Gen. Alexei 96, 101, 105, 111–157
Radzymin 112–470
Radzyminska 210, 215, 227, 235–236, 252, 258, 281, 282, 287
Rajszew 439–440
Rausch, *Stubaf.* Friedrich 40
Red Army Units (see Soviet Units) 119, 127
Reinhardt, *Gen.Oberst.* Georg-Hans 13, 154–475
Rejentówka 260, 268, 282
Rembelsz 294, 298, 300–370
Rembertów 11, 97, 145, 188, 221, 259–271
Rentrop, *Stubaf.* Fritz 39, 40
Rhein 65, 69, 447
Ritter, *Maj.* Friedrich-Karl 68–72, 148, 201, 214, 222, 226, 228, 232, 239, 242, 268, 306, 335, 342, 347, 370, 398, 415, 425, 433, 457, 463, 364, 466
Rogów 101–102
Rokossovsky 93–158, 168, 178–465
Roman, *Gen.d.Art.* Rudolf von 93–104, 153, 175, 331, 406, 407
Rożopole 248, 303, 327, 360, 363–426
Rózan 230, 244, 256, 257, 314, 324, 406, 407, 436
Rshev 2
Rundstedt, *G.F.M.* Gerd von 1
Rynia 252, 260, 268, 282, 327, 348, 3539, 365, 371, 405, 406, 412
Rzadza River 122, 195, 16, 198, 260
Rzonza River 167

Sandomierz 209
Saska Kapa 280
Saucken, *Gen.Lt.* Dietrich von 110, 117, 121–145
Säumenicht, *Hstuf.* Rudolf 166, 192–195
Scharff, *Ostubaf.* Hans 40, 52, 80, 118, 128, 213, 322, 348, 349, 458
Schlemmer, *Oscha.* 378
Schlieper, *Oberst* Franz 262, 266, 271, 274, 308, 318, 429, 436
Schmalz, *Gen.Maj.* Wilhelm 118, 122, 127, 301, 307–309, 312, 345
Schmidt, *Hstuf.* Walter 166, 173, 178, 379, 380, 389, 401
Schnaubelt, *Oscha.* Alois 405
Schönfelder, *Ostubaf.* Manfred 33, 36, 38, 39, 69, 74, 79, 100, 152, 263, 355, 377, 378
Schicker, *Ustuf.* Otto 169
Schramm, *Ostuf.* Erich 172, 259, 272, 303
Schumacher, *Hstuf.* Helmut 226
Schumacher, *Ostuf.* Kurt 166, 173
Schweiss, *Oscha.* 390, 404
Senghas, *Ostuf.* Paul 177, 193, 194
Serock 105, 112, 134, 140, 157, 180, 193, 194, 196, 210, 214, 215, 220, 227, 230–449
Sieckenius, *Gen.Maj.* Rudolf 247, 255, 276, 279, 285, 293, 296, 298, 306, 312–316, 323
Siedlce 89, 93, 95, 98, 100–152, 203
Sielce 207, 277, 290
Siemiatycze 109
Sitne 167, 173, 174
Sixt, *Gen.Lt.* Friedrich 175
Skierdy 440
Skrzeszew 359, 406, 412, 416, 431, 449, 450, 470
Skubianka 411, 413
Ślężany 190, 192, 193, 213
Słopsk 180, 182, 184–189, 194, 195
Słupno 215, 218, 222, 224, 227, 258, 260, 266–304
Sochaczew 128
Sokólow 101, 103, 110, 118, 126
Solki 145
Sonnenblume 328–333, 369, 399, 417, 436
Söth, *Oberst* Wilhelm 144
Soviet Units
Fronts
- First Belorussian 74–473
- First Ukrainian 97, 209
- Second Belorussian 387, 465
- Southwest 82–471

Armies
- 2nd Tank Army 74, 93, 96, 97, 101, 105, 108, 109, 111, 113, 115–162, 187, 197, 207, 216, 262, 437
- 8th Guards Army 96, 116, 119, 126, 276, 391, 402, 414, 422, 428
- 28th Army 162, 175, 185, 210, 211, 248, 255, 409, 410
- 47th Army 95–473
- 65th Army 126, 230, 245, 331, 332, 333, 353, 387, 395–458

69th Army 110, 209
70th Army 142, 144, 157, 162, 179, 185, 210, 262, 268, 272, 278, 292, 356, 358, 359, 378–457
Corps
I Guards Tank 111–435
II Guards Cavalry 93, 107, 116, 120, 123, 135, 256
III Tank 101–306
III Guards Rifle 162, 230
VIII Guards Tank 111–435
XI Tank 83, 107
XVI Tank 111–153
XX Rifle 331
LXXVII Rifle 143, 162, 271, 287, 295
XCVI Rifle 162, 191, 196, 217, 288, 304
CXIV Rifle 162, 182, 189, 192, 195, 199, 241, 267, 364
CXXV Rifle 188, 196, 172, 281, 287
CXXVIII Rifle 162, 230
CXXIX Rifle 123, 162, 221, 223, 260
Divisions
1st Rifle 406, 409, 412, 451
20th Rifle 192
38th Guards Rifle 219, 322, 358, 364, 389, 412
54th Guards Rifle 409
55th Guards Rifle 228
60th Rifle 164, 166, 171, 195, 311, 365, 370, 371, 449
76th Rifle 224, 280, 358, 388, 390, 470
76th Guards Rifle 200, 217, 224, 374
132nd Rifle 266, 291, 466
152nd Rifle 184
143rd Rifle 217, 218, 281, 304
160th Rifle 164, 166, 195, 311, 365, 371
165th Rifle 179
175th Rifle 218, 258, 259, 266, 270, 279, 304
185th Rifle 217, 470
234th Rifle 221, 246, 362
260th Rifle 171M 370
328th Rifle 188, 303, 348, 358, 416
413th Rifle 199, 219, 224, 358
Brigades
15th Motorized Rifle 116
50th Tank 123
51st Tank 123
57th Motorized Rifle 123
60th Guards Tank 359
103rd Tank 123
SS-Führungshauptamt 227, 338
Staedke, *Gen.Maj.* Helmut 318, 452, 472
Steiger, *Oscha.* Martin
Stalin, Josef 68, 84, 87, 96, 108, 171, 209, 222, 256–57, 302, 356, 381, 409, 416, 434, 437–438, 448, 452, 465, 468
Stanisławów 104, 107, 109, 116, 121, 124, 127, 129, 130, 131, 139, 140, 143–145, 160, 248, 260, 282, 291, 294, 423
Stanisławówo 450
STAVKA 154, 210, 229, 256, 257, 261, 332, 368, 438
Steiner, *Ogruf.* Felix 4, 6–7, 32, 68, 70, 505
Steinmetz, *Ostuf.* Christian 52
Sternschnuppe 297, 317–318, 328–329, 331, 334, 336, 396
Struga 260, 268, 278, 282
Sulejów 147, 165–167
Swientek, *Ostubaf.* Josef 91, 419
Szadki 91, 419
Szamocin 303–304
Szybalin 449, 460
Słopsk 180, 182, 184–186, 188–189, 194–195
Słupno 215, 218, 222, 224, 227, 258, 260, 262, 266–267, 272, 278, 281–282, 288–289, 304
Stoige, *Stubaf.* Joachim 220

Tarchomin 362, 377, 415, 417, 420, 427
Targowek 280–281
Thoma, *Ostuf.* Aloys 118
Thomale, *Gen.Lt.* Wolfgang 118
Tiemann, Gen.d.Pz.Tr. Otto 11, 98
Titschkus, *Uscha.* Afred 389
Tłuszcz 140, 145, 146–147, 149, 164–166, 169, 173
Tomaszów 291–293, 295, 304, 310, 358–359, 363, 367, 369–370
Toruń 145, 287, 442
Trojany 173, 175, 179,182, 184
Trzepowo 234, 237
Trzianna 222
Tłuszcz 140, 145–147, 149, 164–166, 169, 173

Ullrich, *Staf.* Karl 79, 91,103, 151, 227, 349–351, 364, 416, 420–423, 435–436, 439, 443, 445–447, 457, 460, 466, 468–469
Ultrata 271
Utrata 280

Vedeneev, Nikolai D. Maj.Gen. 112, 113, 122
Velde, *Hstuf.* Johann-Friedrich 40
Vengel, *Sturmann* Hans 370
Viktor, *Ostuf.* Ludwig 55

Wagner, *Hstuf.* Heinz 264
Warka 293–294, 300, 373, 395–396, 400, 403, 405–406, 429, 432, 435, 456
Wawer 258–259, 266
Weerts, *Ostuf.* Hans 364–365
Wegierskie 379, 388, 399, 401, 407, 411, 417
Wegrow 103, 105, 108, 109, 115, 135, 144
Weirzbica 234
Weiss, *Gen.Oberst* Walter 74, 78, 93, 95–96, 98,105, 109, 113, 118–120, 125, 130–133, 158, 180, 195, 209, 230, 415, 474
Wesola 252, 267, 270
Westphal, Hstuf. Werner 29, 37, 39, 72, 102, 152
Wierzbno 119, 123
Wieś 167–169, 171, 173–174
Wiethüchter, *Ostuf.* Rolf 214–215
Wilga 111, 153
Wiśniewo 363, 369
Woła 185, 191, 194–195, 363, 388, 401, 419, 423, 461
Woła-Aleksandra 375
Wołomin 117, 122–123, 126–127, 129, 131–132, 145, 176, 196, 200, 210, 215, 217–219, 221, 223, 225, 227, 231–232, 235, 238–239, 244, 248, 251–252, 261
Wólka-Radzyminska 166–167, 169–170, 173–174, 178–210, 215, 227, 235, 252, 258, 281–282, 287
Wünnenberg, *Ogruf.* Alfred 2
Wymysły 166
Wyszków 175, 230–231, 397
Włochy 286, 309, 311

Zabki 266, 271–273, 278–279
Zabrodzie 175, 177–181
Zacisze 281, 287
Zagościniec 188
Zagroby 299, 365, 371, 375–376, 380–381, 384, 389, 394, 396, 399, 401, 404, 406–408, 411, 416, 426–427
Zährl, *Uscha.* 370
Zakret 129, 143, 188
Załubice 199, 211, 214, 217, 227–228, 239, 266, 278, 371
Zarp, *Ustuf.* Kristian 57
Zastów 258–259
Zawady 196
Załubice 199, 211, 214, 217, 227–228, 239, 266, 278, 371
Zegrze 105, 112, 115, 117, 122, 123, 134, 144, 157, 177, 197, 2121, 214, 232, 235, 248, 257, 261, 276, 284, 287, 289, 292, 293, 297, 298, 304, 326, 327, 336, 348, 356, 359, 365, 371, 374, 378, 382, 383, 389, 392, 393, 405, 409, 410, 456
Zeran 327, 358, 360, 363, 382
Zerzeń 259
Zielona 163
Zielonka 177, 252, 270–278, 285, 288
Zjawisko 199
Zoliborz 126, 207, 243, 253, 277, 285, 289, 290, 292, 293, 296, 301–346
Zorawka 129
Zugehör, *Oberst* Günter 418–433
Zybtki 215
Żyrardów 285, 330–331